Decision Making Through Operations Research

SECOND EDITION

The Wiley Series in

MANAGEMENT AND ADMINISTRATION

ELWOOD S. BUFFA, Advisory Editor
University of California, Los Angeles

PRINCIPLES OF MANAGEMENT: A MODERN APPROACH: FOURTH EDITION
  Henry H. Albers
OPERATIONS MANAGEMENT: PROBLEMS AND MODELS, THIRD EDITION
  Elwood S. Buffa
PROBABILITY FOR MANAGEMENT DECISIONS
  William R. King
MODERN PRODUCTION MANAGEMENT, FOURTH EDITION
  Elwood S. Buffa
CASES IN OPERATIONS MANAGEMENT: A SYSTEMS APPROACH
  James L. McKenney and Richard S. Rosenbloom
ORGANIZATIONS: STRUCTURE AND BEHAVIOR, VOLUME I, SECOND EDITION
  Joseph A. Litterer
ORGANIZATIONS: SYSTEMS, CONTROL AND ADAPTATION, VOLUME II
  Joseph A. Litterer
MANAGEMENT AND ORGANIZATIONAL BEHAVIOR:
A MULTIDIMENSIONAL APPROACH
  Billy J. Hodge and Herbert J. Johnson
MATHEMATICAL PROGRAMMING: AN INTRODUCTION TO THE
DESIGN AND APPLICATION OF OPTIMAL DECISION MACHINES, 2nd Edition
  Claude McMillan
DECISION MAKING THROUGH OPERATIONS RESEARCH, 2nd Edition
  Robert J. Thierauf and Robert C. Klekamp
QUALITY CONTROL FOR MANAGERS & ENGINEERS
  Elwood G. Kirkpatrick
PRODUCTION SYSTEMS: PLANNING, ANALYSIS AND CONTROL
  James L. Riggs
SIMULATION MODELING: A GUIDE TO USING SIMSCRIPT
  Forrest P. Wyman
BASIC STATISTICS FOR BUSINESS AND ECONOMICS
  Paul G. Hoel and Raymond J. Jessen
BUSINESS AND ADMINISTRATION POLICY
  Richard H. Buskirk
INTRODUCTION TO ELECTRONIC COMPUTING: A MANAGEMENT
APPROACH
  Rodney L. Boyes, Robert W. Shields and Larry G. Greenwell
COMPUTER SIMULATION OF HUMAN BEHAVIOR
  John M. Dutton and William H. Starbuck
INTRODUCTION TO GAMING: MANAGEMENT DECISION SIMULATIONS
  John G. H. Carlson and Michael J. Misshauk
PRINCIPLES OF MANAGEMENT AND ORGANIZATIONAL BEHAVIOR
  Burt K. Scanlan
COMMUNICATION IN MODERN ORGANIZATIONS
  George T. and Patricia B. Vardaman
THE ANALYSIS OF ORGANIZATIONS, SECOND EDITION
  Joseph A. Litterer
COMPLEX MANAGERIAL DECISIONS INVOLVING MULTIPLE OBJECTIVES
  Allan Easton
MANAGEMENT SYSTEMS, SECOND EDITION
  Peter P. Schoderbek

Decision Making Through Operations Research

SECOND EDITION

Robert J. Thierauf
Professor of Management
Xavier University

Robert C. Klekamp
Associate Professor of Management
Xavier University

John Wiley & Sons, Inc.
New York London Sydney Toronto

Copyright © 1970, 1975, by John Wiley & Sons, Inc.

All rights reserved. No part of this book may be reproduced by any means, nor transmitted, nor translated into a machine language without the written permission of the publisher.

Library of Congress Cataloging in Publication Data

Thierauf, Robert J
  Decision making through operations research.

(Wiley series in management and administration)
Includes bibliographies and index.
1. Operations research. 2. Decision-making—
Mathematical models. I. Klekamp, Robert C., 1931-
joint author. II. Title.
HD20.5.T56   1975   658.4′03   74-19473
ISBN 0-471-85861-7

Printed in the United States of America

10 9 8 7 6 5 4

Preface

The primary purpose of the second edition, like the first, is to present the **current** techniques of operations research in such a way that they can be readily comprehended by the average business student taking an introductory course in operations research.

The structure of the new edition is strengthened because it follows a more logical sequence for presenting a comprehensive treatment of standard operations research techniques. It focuses initially on an overview of opertions research, followed by a presentation of standard OR models that employ probability and statistics, matrix algebra, calculus, simulation techniques, and advanced topics in their solution. A brief look into the future of operations research concludes the book. A fictional but typical-type manufacturing firm, the American Products Corporation, is used as the central example at the end of each chapter.

The book can be used for any convenient time period—one quarter, one semester, or the entire year. Chapters can be omitted without destroying the unity of a course since each chapter has been written to stand on its own. This allows for a wide variability of emphasis for each major topic covered.

The problems at the end of each chapter are designed to challenge the reader's understanding of the subject matter. Answers to the problems can be checked by referring to the last Appendix. Experience using the first edition indicates that an individual's comprehension of the various quantitative methods is improved immeasurably by working through and understanding the solutions to the problems. Also, several of the problems can be solved by the computer, either in a batch-processing or a time-sharing mode.

I am indebted to various people who helped in this endeavor, particularly the many users of the first edition. I am deeply grateful to Professors A. Eugene Abrassart, Oregon State University; Myron K. Cox, Wright State University; Adolf Diegel, University of South Alabama; Weechet Ganjanaket, Texas Southern University; James Hershauer, Arizona State University; Arthur Kraft, Ohio University; Ross Lanser, San Jose State University; Wesley D. Ratcliff, Texas Southern University, and Bernard Shapiro, Lowell Technological Institute, for their helpful suggestions. In addition, I thank my former professor, Professor James A. Black, of The Ohio State University (currently at Miami University) who was instrumental in formulating my ideas for the first and second editions. I congratulate Professors Virgil Carter (Cincinnati Bengals), Vincent Caruso, Michael Dreskin, Albert Klee, William Lewis, and J. Michael Thierauf at Xavier University for their constructive criticism. I am eternally indebted to Professor Robert C. Klekamp for his helpful suggestions and contributions in the revised edition. For his herculean efforts, he is welcomed as a coauthor, replacing Professor Richard A. Grosse who passed away in 1970. Finally, I thank the following graduate students for their contributions to the revised manuscript: James Blaser, Kerry Buck, David Colson, John Commons, Harold Fogg, Robert Harrison, David Huiett, John Iannone, Eugene Koehl, William Laib, Samuel Leary, Thomas Maxwell, Jerell McCullough, Robert McCall, Patrick McGuire, Daniel Milne, William Murphy, Elmo Rose, Andrew Rucker, Woody Scoutten, Floyd Soule, Michael Taggert, Arthur Thornton, and Gerald Witt. These students represent many disciplines found in business, resulting in an interdisciplinary-reading and problem-solving committee.

Robert J. Thierauf
December, 1974

Contents

PART I OVERVIEW OF OPERATIONS RESEARCH   1

1 Operations Research—An Introduction   3
History of Scientific Management
History of Operations Research
Relationship to Computer
Essential Operations Research Characteristics
Operations Research Defined
Model Defined
Types of Models
Types of Mathematical Models
Essential Aspects of the Model
Quantitative Models To Be Covered
Summary

2 Operations Research in the Firm   33
Guidelines for Success in Operations Research
Problem Areas of Operations Research
Organizing for Operations Research
Successful Operations Research Areas
American Products Corporation
Summary

PART II OPERATIONS RESEARCH MODELS—PROBABILITY AND STATISTICS   56

3 Decision Theory   57
Probability Terms
Statistical Independence
Statistical Dependence
Relationship Between Independence and Dependence

Probability Problem
Revision of Probabilities
Selection of Best Criterion
Decision Trees
Decision Tree Application—American Product Corporation
Summary

4 Decision Making with Uncertain Demand   58
Discrete Probability Distribution
Continuous Probability Distribution
Uncertain Demand Application—American Products Corporation
Summary

5 PERT/Time, PERT/Cost, and PERT/LOB   120
PERT/Time
Computer PERT Packages
Advantages and Disadvantages of PERT
PERT/Cost
PERT/LOB
PERT/LOB/Cost
Various Applications of PERT
Probability of Finishing a PERT Project
PERT Application—American Products Corporation
Summary

PART III OPERATIONS RESEARCH MODELS—MATRIX ALGEBRA   156

6 Linear Programming   157
Basic Requirements for a Linear Programming Problem
Graphic Method of Linear Programming
Algebraic Method of Linear Programming
Simplex Method of Linear Programming
Maximization Problem
Minimization Problem
Duality of Linear Programming Problem
Advantages of Linear Programming Methods
Cautions of Linear Programming Methods
Applications of Linear Programming
Linear Programming Application—American Products Corporation
Summary

7 Transportation Methods   213
Methods for Solving the Transportation Problem
Vogel's Approximating Method
Stepping-Stone Method—Using the Northwest Corner Rule and Inspection

Modified Distribution Method (MODI)
Simplex Method of Linear Programming (Digital Computer)
Placement of Orders on Machines
Other Problems Utilizing the Transportation Model
Distribution, A Part of the Total Company Model
Transportation Application—American Products Corporation
Summary

8 Games and Strategies   253
Two-Person, Zero-Sum Games
Mixed Strategies and Game Values (2×2 games)
Mixed Strategies and Game Values (3×3 and larger games)
Basic Limitations of Game Theory
Game Theory Application—American Products Corporation
Summary

9 Markov Analysis   282
Procedure 1—Develop Matrix of Transition Probabilities
First-Order and Higher-Order Markov Analysis
Procedure 2—Calculate Future Probable Market Shares
Possible Market Shares (Higher Order)
Procedure 3—Determine Equilibrium Conditions
Management Uses of Markov Analysis
Other Uses of Markov Analysis
Markov Analysis Application—American Products Corporation
Summary

PART IV OPERATIONS RESEARCH MODELS—CALCULUS   310

10 Classical Optimization Techniques   311
Differentiation
Integration
Partial Derivatives
Lagrange Multipliers
Calculus Application—American Products Corporation
Summary

11 Inventory Control Models   343
Functions Performed by Inventories
Basic Inventory Decisions
Inventory Costs
Concept of Average Inventory
Economic Ordering Quantity
Quantity Discounts
Reorder Point and Safety (Buffer) Stock
Inventory and Uncertainty
EOQ Applied to Production
Future Inventory Methods

Inventory Application—American Products Corporation
Summary

12 Integer and Nonlinear Programming — 383
Specialized Types of Integer and Nonlinear Programming Problems
Integer Linear Programming
Nonlinear Objective Function and Linear Constraint
Nonlinear Objective Function and Nonlinear Constraint
Quadratic Programming
Nonlinear Programming Application—American Products Corporation
Summary

PART V OPERATIONS RESEARCH MODELS—SIMULATION TECHNIQUES — 411

13 Queuing Models — 413
Use of Arrival Rates and Service Rates
Queuing Applications
Uniform Arrival and Service Times
Single-Channel Queuing Theory
Multichannel Queuing Theory
Monte Carlo Approach to Queuing
Queuing (Servicing) Application—American Products Corporation
Summary

14 Simulation — 449
Simulation Defined
Operational Gaming Method
Monte Carlo Method
System Simulation Method
Advantages and Limitations of Simulation Techniques
Systematic Computer Approach to Simulation
General Simulation Languages
Random Number Generator
Simulation in the Firm
Simulation Application—American Products Corporation
Summary

PART VI OPERATIONS RESEARCH MODELS—ADVANCED TOPICS — 493

15 Dynamic Programming — 495
Characteristics of Dynamic Programming
Structure of Dynamic Programming
Production Smoothing Problem
Distribution of Salesman for Various Marketing Areas
Purchasing Under Uncertainty

Comparison of Dynamic and Linear Programming
Dynamic Programming Application—American Products Corporation
Summary

16 Heuristic Programming — 520
Definition of Heuristic Programming
Characteristics of Heuristic Programming
Locating Warehouses
Traveling Salesman Problem
Project Scheduling
Other Heuristic Applications
Advantages and Limitations of Heuristic Programming
Heuristic Programming Application—American Products Corporation
Summary

17 Behavioral Models — 540
Definition of Behavioral Models
Underlying Theory of Many Behavioral Models
Designing Behavioral Models
Marketing Behavioral Models
Employee Behavioral Models
Personnel Behavioral Application—American Products Corporation
Summary

PART VII FUTURE OF OPERATIONS RESEARCH — 568

18 Operations Research—Present and Future — 569
Current Quantitative Marketing Models
Current Quantitative Physical Distribution Models
Current Quantitative Manufacturing Models
Current Quantitative Finance Models
Current Quantitative Accounting Models
Current Quantitative Corporate Planning Models
Operations Research—An Overview
Conclusion

APPENDIXES — 601

A Vectors, Matrices, and Determinants
B Differentiation and Integration
C Areas Under the Curve
D Values of the Exponential Function
E Random Numbers Table
F Answers to Problems

INDEX — 645

1
Overview of Operations Research

Chapter ONE
Operations Research– An Introduction

Today, management operates in a dynamic business environment that is subject to a bewildering number of changes. Many of these changes can be initiated by the manager, but usually they are not. They are dictated by shortened product life cycles and technological advances. Similarly, governmental and social environments are important change factors since the firm is strongly affected by an awareness of social consequences in its pursuit of profits. In view of these facts, today's efficient firm must rely heavily on quantitative methods and computers to handle its many routine and complex well-structured problems. This releases management to deal with the increasing load of poorly structured (nonprogrammable) problems that confront it. Thus management needs considerable computer assistance when employing mathematical business models to cope with the greatly increased complexity of its job.

Management has at its disposal several approaches in interpreting, analyzing, and solving business problems. Generally, the complexity of the problem indicates the appropriate method of analysis. The conventional approach follows past techniques and solutions. This method, being so static, offers little or nothing to the advancement of management since it is in opposition to the dynamics of business. A second approach, the observational approach, is the method of watching and learning from other managers in similar situations. It, too, is poor but improvements can be applied on occasion to improve a particular technique. Another approach to the solution of business problems is the systematic approach. This utilizes the concept of theoretical systems which may be somewhat different from the actual problem under study. Systematic approximation can be useful in obtaining a final solution since it utilizes a combination of approaches, in particular, the scientific method. Even though scientific management was aimed initially at manufacturing activities, its basic methodology can be applied to most current and future business problems.

History of Scientific Management

The exact origin of the scienctic method is not known. Individual cases that have used the fundamentals of the scientific method have been found in writings thousands of years old. Moses' father-in-law, Jethro, is given credit for a treatise on organization principles in the Old Testament. Of more recent origin is the nineteenth-century work of Charles Babbage, *On the Economy of Machinery and Manufactures*.

Frederick Winslow Taylor, an American engineer, has been bestowed the title "Father of Scientific Management." His process of investigation was essentially based upon an analysis of the duties and tasks of shop foremen. His scientific management was concerned with first line managers who should know the jobs of their men and then follow through to see that the jobs are performed in the best and most economical way. Taylor was concerned with the efficiency of the shop. He directed his attention to finding out how much one man could produce in one day through experimentation and not just subjective evaluation. As a result, he discovered some men were capable of doing an efficient job while others were not. He found some of the inefficient ones were more efficient in other jobs. Thus the idea of worker selection and training was defined. He established standards for workers and utilized specialization in manufacturing. In effect, Taylor applied scientific analysis to manufacturing problems; his techniques could be classified as an early form of operations research. His recommendations for scientic management can be set forth as follows:

1. Management must use the scientific rather than the rule-of-thumb approach.
2. Harmonious organization is obtained by assigning the appropriate man to each set of operations.
3. Cooperation between labor and management personnel must be achieved.
4. The best means of economical production has to be chosen.
5. Specialization of workers has to be obtained with the aim of increasing efficiency in production.
6. A striving for enterprise and individual prosperity must be accomplished.[1]

Henry L. Gantt, an associate of Taylor in the early scientific management era, is best known for his work in production scheduling. Prior to his time, bottlenecks were somewhat ignored. Gantt mapped each job from machine to machine in order to allow for and minimize every production delay. If machine loadings were planned months in advance by using the Gantt procedure, it was possible to quote delivery dates much more accurately. In addition, he contributed greatly to the scientific approach by considering the human aspect of management's attitude toward labor. The personnel department was recommended by Gantt as an integral part of Taylor's scientific approach.

The studies made by Taylor and Gantt were further advanced by the contributions of Frank B. and Lillian E. Gilbreth in the 1910s. Motion study, as a scientific approach, came into being. This consisted of dividing work into the most fundamental elements possible, studying these elements separately and in a relationship to one another, and using these studied ele-

---

[1] F. W. Taylor, *Principles of Scientific Management*, New York: Harper & Bros., 1910, p. 140.

[2] F. B. Gilbreth and L. E. Gilbreth, *Applied Motion Study*, New York: The Macmillan Company, 1917.

ments for building methods of least waste.[2] While Frank Gilbreth's studies were mostly related to production, Lillian Gilbreth's studies were concerned with the psychological point of view. The Gilbreths' contribution to scientific management complemented Taylor's time study.

Summarizing the 1910s in the United States, Taylor was interested in finding the one best way to accomplish a single task in a manufacturing process. The Gilbreths directed their efforts toward eliminating the wastefulness from unnecessary and inefficient motion in a particular task while Gantt looked at the manufacturing process from an overall point of view. Around the same time in Europe, a French engineer by the name of Henry Joseph Fayol published a book, *Administration Industrielle et Générale*, which dealt with the principles of general management. Fayol primarily studied the upper echelons of the firm from the higher levels to the lower levels. This is in contrast with Taylor who was concerned with studying the lower levels of the organization. Fayol's work is considered to complement Taylor's studies; that is, not only did they study opposite levels of the organization, but they also applied the scientific approach to the analysis of business problems. Taylor, Gantt, the Gilbreths, and Fayol all made significant contributions to scientific management by utilizing the scientific method for determining what should be accomplished under the existing conditions.

History of Operations Research

It is difficult to mark the official beginning of operations research. Many early pioneers, like those just mentioned, were performing work that today would be considered operations research. As early as 1914, F. W. Lanchester, in England, published papers on the theoretical relationships between victory and superiority in manpower and firepower. In the United States, Thomas Edison, as early as World War I, was given the task of finding the maneuvers of merchant ships that would be most effective in minimizing shipping losses to enemy submarines. Instead of risking ships in actual war conditions, he made use of a "tactical game board" for a solution. Around the same time (late 1910s), a Danish engineer, A. K. Erlang of the Copenhagen Telephone Company, was performing experiments involving the fluctuation of demand for telephone facilities upon automatic dialing equipment. His work is the foundation for many mathematical models used in waiting line theory today.

In the 1930s, Horace C. Levenson applied sophisticated mathematical models to large amounts of data which would otherwise have been totally unmanageable. One of his most interesting and best known studies involved customers refusing to accept C.O.D. packages from a relatively small order house. The rejection rate was about 30 percent of gross sales. Two causes of rejection were isolated: first, more expensive orders were more frequently refused; and second, merchandise shipped later than five days after the order was placed. On the average, orders older than five days were not profitable. With such data available, it was relatively easy for the mail order firm to compare the cost of rejection with the higher cost of fast shipping and thereby determine the optimum shipping effort.

Starting in 1937, British scientists were increasingly asked to help the military learn how to use the newly developed radar in locating enemy aircraft. The scientists, working on different aspects of this problem, were brought together in September, 1939, at H.Q. Fighter Command (RAF). This group, considered to be the nucleus of the first operations research group, steadily extended its scope of activities beyond its original problem of radar and its integration with ground observers.

Not long after the formation of this group, the Anti-Aircraft Command Research Group was brought together to study anti-aircraft aiming problems (September, 1940). The distinguished British physicist P. M. S. Blackett headed the group. They were to study the performance of gun control equipment in the field, especially during its actual use by the troops against the enemy. The first two members of the group were physiologists, the next two were mathematical physicists, then an astrophysicist, an Army officer, and a former surveyor. The team was later completed with a third physiologist, a general physicist, and two mathematicians. They became known as "Blackett's Circus."[3] A broad spectrum of disciplines in this group of 11 scientists is apparent. The group expanded and split into an Army and a Navy group, resulting in all of Britain's military forces having an operational research group engaged in military research early in the war (1941). This type of scientific activity came to be known in Britain as "Operational Research" since the first studies were devoted to the operational use of radar and were carried out by scientists expert in radar research.

Sir Robert Watson-Watt, who claims to have launched the first two OR studies in 1937, recommended that operations research be introduced into the departments of the Secretary of War and the Secretary of the Navy in the United States. By April, 1942, the decision to introduce operational research at a high level had been made and implemented. The initial problems included radar and the development of merchant marine convoys designed to minimize losses from enemy submarines. In the U.S. Air Force, it became known as "Operational Analysis" and in the U.S. Army and Navy as "Operations Research and Operations Evaluation."[4] This type of activity grew not only in Britain and the United States but also in Canada and France during World War II.

When World War II terminated, new types of management problems, created by the nationalization of industry and the need to rebuild large segments of the nation's industrial facilities, called for a new approach in Britain. This call was answered by the operational research workers who had moved in to work on government and industrial problems. Management consulting, which never had been popular in Britain, caught on because British managers were willing to try a new approach to raise productivity and profits—operational research.

---

[3] J. G. Crowther and R. Whiddington, *Science at War*, London: Her Majesty's Stationery Office, 1947, p. 96.

[4] Sir R. Watson-Watt, *Three Steps to Victory*, London: Odhams Press, 1959, p. 204.

For some years after the war, most British industries where operational research was carried out had only a few men in the field. However, during the latter half of the 1950s, the germinating seed burst into full bloom. Existing OR groups expanded to cope with the greatly increased demand from within their own firms. Other firms went quickly into OR activity. British operational research is characterized by a number of large OR groups. The United Steel Companies group has over 100 people, the National Coal Board about 100. The British Iron and Steel Research Associates, British Petroleum, and Richard Thomas & Baldwin all have more than 50 OR personnel. Many medium sized firms have several performing OR work. It is difficult to conceive any single type of industry where OR is not used.[5] In Britain, operational research has gained a strong foothold in business and government for solving difficult and complex problems.

In the United States, "Operations Research" (first coined in this country by McCloskey and Trefethen in 1940) took on a somewhat different direction. Military research increased at the end of the war, resulting in OR men being retained by the military. In fact, many more were added. Industry and government were subjected to the same stimulation as their counterpart in Britain. Initially, industry and government were somewhat indifferent to operations research. It was not until 1950 that OR began to be taken seriously by American industry.

The United States began to enter a second industrial revolution of automation as electronic computers began to make their appearance in government and industry (the first industrial revolution had replaced men with machines). In the 1950s the computer brought with it a host of new system problems for which no past experience was wholly adequate. Its capabilities were staggering to the present crop of managers. OR personnel, who had spent a decade in military operations research, were quick to seize the opportunities opened to them. Operations research scientists quickly adopted the computer as an essential tool. As increasingly significant ways of utilizing the computer were developed, the spread of OR accelerated. The advent of the computer along with the development of OR methods, then, brought the industrial executive and OR worker together in an activity that is still growing at a very fast rate.

During this period (1950s), linear programming gave industrial operations research a major boost. This technique, basically the application of linear algebra to resource allocation, had applications in many industries. It gave OR personnel a foot in the door of many industrial firms. Many techniques known only to operations researchers, such as PERT and simulation, are used widely today. Probability and statistics, basic to any work in operations research, introduced the notions of confidence limits and probability of occurrence in place of simple averages. The various techniques associated with OR are treated later in this chapter. These form the basis for the subject matter of the entire book.

---

[5] R. L. Ackoff and R. Rivett, *A Manager's Guide to Operations Research*, New York: John Wiley & Sons, 1963, p. 8.

Even though there was a large movement of OR personnel to industry, operations research was still evident in the military through its contracts. The Department of Defense gradually shifted to the weapons-system, management concept and imposed contractual requirements for defense industries to undertake operation research. Defense research and development money spurred the growth of "think factories" and "advanced study programs," creating an enlarged demand for operations research and systems analysis. Thus operations research became a key tool in battles for budgets and contracts.

The first operations research conference in the United States for industry, held at the Case Institute of Technology in Cleveland (1951), relied on military studies since it was almost imposssible to find industrial studies for presentation. Today, most of *Fortune's* 500 largest corporations are benefiting from operations research. Several societies have been formed here and abroad to bring OR professionals together. These include the British Operational Research Society (founded in 1950), the Operations Research Society of America (1952), The Institute of Management Science (1953), and the American Institute of Decision Sciences (1969). In the United States, the number of persons engaged in operations research has increased from a handful in the early 1940s to well over 20,000 today. Academic institutions offering courses and degrees on the subject are no longer unusual. Educational institutions in the United States and the United Kingdom have adopted operations research as part of higher learning curriculums. Today, operations research is practiced and taught extensively not only in the United States and United Kingdom, but also in Europe, Australia, India, Japan, and Israel.

Relationship to Computers

It is appropriate to conclude this historical overview of operations research with a brief discussion of its close relationship to computer methodology. Earlier it was stated that the computer was a primary factor in the growth of operations research. Partly this was because most of the operations research techniques would be completely impractical for any real problem without the modern computer to produce the final results. Most large scale applications of operations research techniques which require only minutes on a computer could take weeks, months, and sometimes years to produce results manually. But even more significantly, computers have ready access to certain kinds of management information without which many OR projects would be meaningless. OR professionals would be hard pressed to enumerate applications not dependent critically on the computer for implementation.

It is certainly unquestioned that the computer is an indispensable tool and integral part of operations research, and that computer methodology and OR methodology are developing in parallel. Today, most OR personnel are knowledgeable about computers right up to the point of software development. It seems likely that in the next decade the dividing line between operations research and computer methodology will disappear and leave the two areas combined in the form of a more general and comprehensive management science.

Essential Operations Research Characteristics

From the foregoing evolution and development of operations research, the essential characteristics of OR are:

1. Examine functional relationships from a systems overview.
2. Utilize the interdisciplinary or mixed-team approach.
3. Adopt the planned approach (updated scientific method).
4. Uncover new problems for study.

1. Examine Functional Relationships from a Systems Overview

The first characteristic of operations research means that the activity of any function or part of a firm has some effect on the activity of every other function or part. In order to evaluate any decision or action in an organization, it is necessary to identify all the important interactions and to determine their impact on the whole organization versus the function originally involved. Initially, the functional relationships in a project are deliberately expanded so that all the significantly interacting functions and their related components are contained in a statement of the problem. Thus, when dealing with an OR problem, the functions and their related components must be examined and selected in light of the significance and the measurability of their interactions. To state it another way, a systems overview consists of surveying the entire area under the manager's control instead of one specialized area. This approach provides a basis for initiating inquiries into problems that seem to be affecting performance at a higher or lower level or at the same level.

Many problems that look relatively easy to solve on the surface actually resemble an iceberg. For example, inventory, which may not seem complicated at first inspection is extraordinarily complex. The manufacturing department is looking for long, uninterrupted runs to reduce set-up costs and clean-up costs. To solve the problem with this viewpoint in mind may not be complex. However, these long runs may result in large inventories of raw materials, work in process, and finished goods in relatively few product lines. This can result in bitter conflicts with the marketing department, not to mention the finance and personnel departments. Inventory, as a manufacturing function, cannot be isolated from the functions of marketing, finance, and personnel. Marketing, wanting to give immediate delivery for a wide variety of product (product lines), desires a diverse and large inventory. Similarly, it would like a flexible manufacturing department that can fill special orders on short notice. Finance wants to keep inventory at a low dollar value in order to optimize capital investments that tie up assets for indeterminate periods. Finally, personnel wants to reduce labor turnover by smoothing out manufacturing runs so as to keep all temporary layoffs to a minimum. With the guaranteed annual wage becoming prevalent, there is a great need to stabilize production since workers are basically paid whether there is work or not. The optimum inventory policy then affects the operations of many functional areas.

In view of the preceding difficulties, the OR group should analyze the problem with painstaking care, examining all elements in each department affected. These elements might include: the cost of material procurement; manufacturing, set-up, and clean-up costs; competitive forces and prices; and the costs of holding inventories and stockout costs. When all factors affecting the system are known, a mathematical model can be started. The solution to this model, having properly related the functions (marketing, manufacturing, finance, and personnel) and their component parts, should result in optimizing profits for the firm as a whole, often referred to as "optimization." "Suboptimization" generally refers to the condition where specific profit objectives for the firm's various functions are maximized individually. In the inventory problem, long manufacturing runs may produce the lowest costs for the manufacturing department, but if the merchandise cannot be sold, what good is the merchandise? Thus, the best solution for this inventory problem is one that leads to optimization for the whole firm, but not necessarily to optimization for the various functions (departments) of the firm. It is necessary to modify the action for each level so as to effect balance in the various functions and subfunctions. This approach brings about the simultaneous attainment of the objectives for the firm and its parts.

Suboptimization can also be applied to the entire firm rather than its component parts. When this is the case, a suboptimum solution is usually the result of unclear objectives or objectives that conflict with or contradict each other within a firm. Suboptimization similarly results when an optimum solution for the short run is adopted without consideration of the long run. The failure to take into account the intangible and nonquantifiable factors can result in suboptimization. Other cases of suboptimization result from the failure to examine all alternatives available or to take into consideration all relevant information.

The opposite of suboptimization is "overoptimization." This condition results from optimizing to an extreme degree, that is, the costs of applying very exacting OR models are far greater than the expected savings. In the preceding inventory example, an elaborate OR model could be constructed that results in several decimal place accuracy. Actually, this enlarged approach to optimizing inventory levels is unwarranted since the additional costs of such accuracy far outweigh the potential of the model during its expected life.

2. Utilize the Interdisciplinary or Mixed-Team Approach

During the early years of operations research, there was a great shortage of scientists (mathematicians, physicists, chemists, engineers, and statisticians). The military operations research groups had to build up their staffs, not by selection but by acquisition. Out of this forced approach to operations research came a recognition that the interdisciplinary team was valuable. They found that one can speak of physical problems, chemical problems, biological problems, psychological problems, social problems, and economic problems as though these are categorized in nature. Actually, the various disciplines describe different ways of studying the same problem.

When a scientist is confronted with a new problem, he tries to abstract the essence of the problem and determine if this same type problem has been undertaken previously. If he finds a similar problem in his own field, he can determine whether or not certain methods used before can be adapted to the problem at hand. In this way, the various members with their respective backgrounds can bring to the problem approaches that otherwise might not be considered. Thus, operations research makes use of this simple principle: people from different disciplines can produce more unique solutions, with a greater probability of success, than could be expected from the same number of people from any one discipline. This principle is illustrated in the foregoing inventory example.

A mathematician, looking at an inventory problem, would formulate some type of mathematical relationships between the manufacturing department and final shipment. These relationships might be directly or indirectly tied in with quantity and time factors. A chemical engineer might look at the same problem and formulate it in terms of flow theory since he has methods at his disposal for solutions using this approach. A cost accountant conceives this inventory problem in terms of its component costs (direct material, direct labor, and overhead) and how costs can be controlled and reduced. Several other disciplines could be brought to bear on the problem. Which of the alternative methods from the various disciplines is most beneficial depends upon the existing circumstances. The inventory problem is quite complex when it cuts across the entire firm; thus it is necessary to look at the problem in many different ways in order to determine which one (or which combination) of the various discipline approaches is the best.

One of the main reasons for the existence of operations research groups is that they bring the latest scientific know-how to bear on the problem. Just as important is their ability to develop new methods, procedures, and systems which are more effective in approaching the problem than any that are presently available. This makes sense since no one person has the time available to acquire all the useful scientific information from all disciplines to have at his immediate disposal. The interdiscipline approach has this added advantage—it recognizes that most business problems have accounting, biological, economic, engineering, mathematical, physical, psychological, sociological, and statistical aspects. It stands to reason that the individual phases of a problem can best be understood and analyzed by those trained in the appropriate fields.

3. Adopt the Planned Approach (Updated Scientific Method)

Operations research, like most other disciplines, makes use of the scientific method which has been updated to reflect technological advances, such as the computer. Most scientific research, for example, chemistry and physics, lends itself extremely well to laboratory study. Controlled experiments under prescribed conditions can be performed without too much interference from the outside world. However, this is not the case with business problems or systems under study by the OR team. Furthermore, OR problems are generally different and sometimes impossible to manipulate and control in their own environment for purposes of experimentation. For example, it would be very difficult to use different prices in the various market regions of a firm without causing some type of ill will if customers found out about this preferential price treatment. Other experiments could be too costly or time consuming. Thus it appears that operations research has insurmountable handicaps to overcome.

Upon closer examination of other disciplines, the same restriction on the use of the experimental method is present. In astronomy, for example, the astronomer is in the same position as an OR worker, that is, he cannot manipulate the system he studies. Both build a mathematical model which is a representation of the actual problem or system under study. A model, representing the structure of the actual system in quantitative terms, can be manipulated and analyzed. This allows for all types of experimentation, the basic limitation set forth previously. The operations researcher can change certain variables while holding others constant in an effort to find out how the system would be affected. Hence it is possible to simulate the real world and experiment with it in abstract terms.

The mathematical models may be very difficult to construct and may turn out to be complex mathematical expressions. Business models, ultimately, take the form of a system of equations. Underlying these mathematical relationships (simple or complex) is an equation which has a relatively simple structure. Some term (desired solution or performance) is equated to some relationship(s) between a group of controlled variables and uncontrolled variables. The controlled variables might include the following: selling prices, number of products manufactured, cost aspects, number of salesmen, and budget constraints. The values for each controlled variable is set forth by management. However, uncontrolled variables are not subject to management's control. These might include: prices of competitors, cost of raw materials, labor costs, demand of customers, and location of customers. The solution to a mathematical model or equation can be thought of as a function of controlled and uncontrolled variables, related in some precise mathematical manner.

The objective equation developed (utilizing controlled and uncontrolled variables) may have to be supplemented by a set of restrictive statements on the possible values of the controlled variables. For example, in theoretical mathematics, it is possible to deal with minus values. However, this is not possible in business problems since you either produce the item or you do not. Similarly, you either spend the money or you do not. Another example is the amount allocated to departments in terms of a budget which cannot be exceeded. These constraints are expressed as a set of supplementary equations or inequalities where the greater-than, less-than conditions are used. This is quite apparent in linear programming.

In many problems, it may be difficult to reflect the relative importance of and conflict among the multiplicity of objectives involved in a decision, like inventory. Basically, the objectives of OR models are of two types: the minimizing of costs in terms of inputs; and the maximizing of outputs or sales income to the firm. One might think of the first class of objectives as those which involve retaining things of value already acquired, whereas the second involves obtaining things of value which are not presently possessed. The minimization of costs and the maximization of sales income lead to optimization of profits for the firm.

As stated previously, the basic approach of the operations research is the scientific method. Its basic steps are: observation, definition of the real problem, development of alternative solutions, selection of optimum solution using experimentation, and verification of optimum solution through implementation. These are the traditional steps in the scientific method. An updated version of this method includes mathematical modeling (described briefly earlier), use of the standard techniques of operations research, establishing proper controls, and the utilization of computer capabilities. Each phase of the updated scientific method or the planned approach will be discussed in Chapter 2.

4. Uncover New Problems for Study

A fourth characteristic of operations research, which is often overlooked, is that in the solution of an OR problem new problems are uncovered. All interrelated problems uncovered by the OR approach do not have to be solved at the same time. However, each must be solved with consideration for other problems if maximum benefits are to be obtained. It can be said that operations research is not effectively used if it is restricted to one-shot projects. Greatest benefits can be obtained through continuity of research. Application of research findings need not wait until all the interrelated problems are solved.

Consulting firms, called in to solve a particular problem, find that they have "a tiger by the tail." What originally appears to be a simple and isolated problem frequently turns out to be interconnected with many other operating problems of the firm. With an initial expansion of the problem, the solutions to the parts should be interrelated to assure best overall performance. This approach avoids the problem of optimization in one area (department or function) at the expense of suboptimization for the entire firm.

For example, consider a warehouse stock control study for a certain paint manufacturer that ended up as an analysis of the paint blending mills. The operations researchers found that warehouse inventory levels were at the mercy of plant production output. This depended on the amount of paint blended in the roller mill each day. An extensive effort was needed to determine why the mill output varied so greatly. When the production problems were identified, several changes in engineering and raw material specifications were made. Thus, the warehouse inventories were brought under control, the physical inventory was reduced, and production costs were lowered.

Based on the interrelationships within a problem, the project may appear to be endless. However, the project can end where the limits of the control exercised by the manager (to whom operations research personnel report) stops. It also can end when more fruitful areas of research compete for the researcher's time or when the added income does not justify added costs. It should be observed that the dynamics of business today necessitates going back and reviewing projects undertaken some time ago, say two to three years. Subsequent findings may require adjusting previous solutions through the use of revised mathematical models, new input data, and like items. What is best for the firm today may not be best tomorrow.

Operations Research Defined

Now that a brief history of operations research and its essential characteristics have been set forth, a definition of operations research can be developed logically. Several definitions have been presented by many authors; some are too general or just plain misleading. One of the earlier definitions by Morse and Kimball states: "Operations research is a scientific method of providing executive departments with a quantitative basis for decisions regarding the operations under their control."[6] The deficiency of this definition should be apparent. Instead of using operations research in the definition, replace it with another business discipline, such as cost accounting, and see what happens. The definition applies to cost accounting as well as other disciplines. Thus this definition is deficient since it does not distinguish operations research from a number of other disciplines.

The best known OR textbook of the 1950s defined operations research in this manner: "OR in the most general sense can be characterized as the application of scientific methods, techniques, and tools to problems involving the operations of systems so as to provide those in control of the operations with optimum solutions to the problems."[7] This definition does not include all of the essential characteristics of OR set forth in the previous section. For example, the use of an interdisciplinary approach is not indicated. (The use of an interdisciplinary approach in this book means utilizing at least two people who have somewhat different educational and experience backgrounds.) This definition is certainly an improvement over the first definition, but it is still not perfect.

Miller and Starr, like the preceding authors, view operations research as being applied to executive type problems. They define operations research as follows: "OR is applied decision theory. Operations research uses any scientific, mathematical, or logical means to attempt to cope with the problems that confront the executive when he tries to achieve a thoroughgoing

---

[6] P. M. Morse and G. E. Kimball, *Methods of Operations Research*, New York: John Wiley & Sons, 1951, p. 1.

[7] G. W. Churchman, R. L. Ackoff, and E. L. Arnoff, *Introduction to Operations Research*, New York: John Wiley & Sons, 1957, pp. 8-9.

rationality in dealing with his decision problems."[8] More recently, Harvey M. Wagner stated: "For convenience, and with reasonable accuracy, you can simply define operations research as a scientific approach to problem-solving for executive management."[9] It appears that both definitions are much too general and suffer from much the same shortcomings as the others.

Other authors have defined operations research as a listing of the various techniques that have come to be associated with it. Still others have defined OR in terms of what practitioners do. The Operations Research Society of America came up with the following definition: "Operations research is an experimental and applied science devoted to observing, understanding, and predicting the behavior of purposeful man-machine systems; and operations-research workers are actively engaged in applying this knowledge to practical problems in business, government, and society."[10]

Upon examination of the foregoing definitions, certain common ideas seem to emerge: the use of the scientific method; study of complex relationships; and provision of a basis for decision making. These attributes relate to the essential characteristics of operations research discussed previously. Operations research, then, can best be defined in terms of its basic characteristics as follows: "Operations Research utilizes the planned approach (updated scientific method) and an interdisciplinary team in order to represent complex functional relationships as mathematical models for the purpose of providing a quantitative basis for decision making and uncovering new problems for quantitative analysis." In essence, the four characteristics of operations research have been incorporated in the definition. The inclusion of a quantitative basis for decision making was necessary since the results of operations research should be applied to the problem at hand.

One last comment is needed regarding the use of the output from OR methods. In some cases, the answers supplied by mathematical models through a computer system may need to be modified to reflect future business conditions. In other cases, the output is a guide for the manager to follow without the need for changes. Yet in some instances, OR techniques provide a range of feasible solutions for management. Operations research, then, includes more than just developing models for specific problems. Its important contribution is the application of its output for decision making at the lower, middle, and top management levels. The manager's experience, upcoming business conditions, and the output from a mathematical model form the best combination for planning, organizing, directing, and controlling the firm's activities.

---

[8] D. W. Miller and M. K. Starr, *Executive Decisions and Operations Research*, Englewood Cliffs, N.J.: Prentice Hall, 1960, p. 104.

[9] H. M. Wagner, *Principles of Operations Research, With Applications to Managerial Decisions*, Englewood Cliffs, N.J.: Prentice-Hall, 1969, p. 4.

[10] "Appendix I, The Nature of Operations Research," *Operations Research*, September, 1971, p. 1138.

Model Defined

The definition of operations research, given in the previous section, makes use of the term "mathematical models." Generally, a model is defined as a representation or abstraction of an actual object or situation. It shows the relationships (direct and indirect) and the interrelationships of action and reaction in terms of cause and effect. Since a model is an abstraction of reality, it may appear to be less complex than reality itself. The model, to be complete, must be representative of those aspects of reality that are being investigated.

One of the basic reasons for developing models is to discover which variables are the important or pertinent ones. The discovery of the pertinent variables is closely associated with the investigation of the relationships that exist among the variables. Quantitative techniques such as statistics and simulation are utilized to investigate the relationships that exist among the many variables in a model. Many models presented throughout this book will depict explicit relationships and interrelationships among the variables.

Types of Models

Different classifications of models provide an added insight into their essentials since they can be described in many ways. Models can be categorized by their types, dimensionality, function, purpose, subject, or degree of abstraction. The most common basis is *types* of models. The basic types include: iconic (physical), analogue (diagrammatic), and symbolic (mathematical).

Iconic (Physical) Models

An iconic model is a physical representation of some item either in an idealized form or on a different scale. To state it another way, a representation is an iconic model to the extent that its properties are the same as those possessed by what it represents. Iconic models are well suited for describing events at a specific moment of time. A photograph, for example, could be an iconic model of a manufacturing department, whereas the actual operations of this department constructed in terms of a small working model (another iconic model) may be too costly to build and to modify in order to study possible improvements. Another characteristic of an iconic model is its dimensions, that is, two dimensions (photo, blueprint, and map) or three dimensions (globe, automobile, and airplane). When a model surpasses the third dimension, as is the case in many operations research problems, it is no longer possible to construct it physically. It belongs to another category of models called symbolic or mathematical.

Analogue (Diagrammatic) Models

Analogue models can represent dynamic situations and are used more than iconic models since they can depict (i.e., "are analogous to") the characteristics of the event under study. Demand curves, frequency distribution curves in statistics, and flow charts are examples of analogue models. An analogue model often is well suited for representing quantitative relationships between properties of different classes of things. By transforming properties into analogous properties, we can frequently increase our ability to make changes. Another advantage of an analogue over an iconic model is that the analogue can usually be made to represent many different processes of the same type. This is apparent in the analogue of the work-in-process and finished goods flow in a factory. In another example, an iconic model could not be used effectively to study the effect of certain changes in quality control. A flow chart, being the analogue, is simple and effective in such a situation.

Symbolic (Mathematical) Models

Our main interest is symbolic models, which are representations of reality. They take the form of figures, symbols, and mathematics. They start as abstract models which we form in our minds and then are set forth as symbolic models. A type of symbolic or mathematical model most commonly used in operations research is an equation. An equation is concise, precise, and easily understood. Its symbols are not only much easier to manipulate than words, but they are grasped more quickly.

An equation is, in a sense, the universal language of operations research. Since it is a "language," it employs a symbolic logic. The most formidable deterrent to understanding the concepts contained in this book does not lie in the complexity of the concepts. It lies in the frustration that results when one attempts to understand a new language without understanding its symbols. The authors have made every attempt to simplify the subject matter for ease of understanding. However, as with any language, usage is the key to fluency and understanding.

Symbolic models are used in this book in a broad sense. Not only are equations examples of symbolic models, but common business models include such items as an income statement and a firm's organization chart. It should be kept in mind that problems can and do arise for which analogies are more efficient than symbolic models. For example, a system may be so complex that the amount of work required to construct a symbolic model is too expensive when related to the potential gains. Often, it is difficult to assign a model to only one class. This is particularly true of simulation models, which are analogue models and are described by means of mathematical symbols.

Types of Mathematical Models

Since mathematical models are our main concern, they are separated into categories. This gives us a logical basis for classifying the basic models used in operations research literature. The listing on the following pages is by no means complete, but the accompanying discussion of those listed will provide an understanding of essential differences in OR models.

Quantitative Versus Qualitative

Most thinking about business problems starts with qualitative models and gradually develops to a point where quantitative models can be used. The qualitative model treats only the qualities or properties of the OR problem's components while the development of a quantitative model requires numerical definition of the problem. A mathematical equation is a quantitative model because it represents a relationship or condition between constants and variables. Formulas, matrices, diagrams, or series of values, obtained by algebraic processes, are common examples of mathematical models. In fact, a set of equations or inequalities often describes many OR models.

Operations research deals with systematizing qualitative models and developing them to the point where they can be quantified. This does not mean that OR methodology can quantify all qualitative situations. Many problems cannot be accurately quantified due to one or more of the following: the techniques for measurement are too inadequate, too many variables are involved, certain variables are unknown, particular relationships are unknown, and relationships whose pecularities and exceptions are too complex to be stated quantitatively. However, by use of logical analysis, classification systems, methods of ranking, set theory, dimensional analysis, and decision theory, operations research can bring certain useful techniques to bear on such problems.

Standard Versus Custom Made

Standard models are used to describe those techniques that have become associated with operations research. To use these techniques, insert the proper numbers from a specific business problem into the standard model for an answer. On the other hand, a custom-made model results from using the basics of various disciplines, particularly mathematics, to build a model that fits the particular problem. This will be apparent in the last chapter. Many times OR personnel read through the various publications of operations research only to find that no standard model applies to the problem under study. In such cases, it is necessary to construct a custom-built model which may extend the time and cost to solve the problem.

Probabilistic Versus Deterministic

Models can be separated into two categories: those that are probabilistic and those that are deterministic. Models based on probability and statistics and concerned with future uncertainties are called probabilistic models. In effect, we are dealing basically with decision making under uncertainty. Those quantitative models that do not contain probabilistic considerations are termed deterministic models. Examples of these found in this book are: inventory, linear programming, and PERT. For these models, attention is focused on those situations in which the critical factors, taken into account, are assumed to be determinate or exact quantities. Even though both of these models are concerned with present and future events, precise and determinate values are used in deterministic models while in probabilistic models this is not necessarily the case. Rather, there is a review of past experience for estimating the probabilities of occurrences for the relevant present and future conditions in decision making under uncertainty.

Descriptive Versus Optimizing
In some situations, a model is built simply to be a mathematical description of a real world condition. These are called descriptive models and have been used in the past for enabling one to learn more about the problem. In addition, such a model can be used to display the situation more vividly, to show how it can be rearranged, and to determine the values about the situation which are implied by the extenuating circumstances, but which are not clearly observable to the viewer. If there are choices, the model will display these choices and can help the observer to evaluate the results of one choice over another. The descriptive model has the capability of being solved. However, no attempt is made in the model to select the best among the alternatives.

When comparison is made with an optimizing model, a concerted attempt is made to reach an optimum solution when presented with alternatives. Previously we noted that it is possible not to reach an optimum solution when a narrow approach is used in the scope of an operations research problem. When an optimization model is properly solved, it yields the best alternative according to the input criteria. An optimization model, then, is concerned with an optimum answer, whereas the descriptive model does not attempt to select the best alternative, but only to describe the choices that are present.

Static Versus Dynamic
Static models are concerned with determining an answer for a particular set of fixed conditions that will probably not change significantly in the short run. A good example of this type of model is linear programming, where the constraints are fixed in terms of individual product time requirements and hours available per shift in the short run. A static model will result in the best solution based on this static condition. However, production capacity and product time requirements can and do change eventually due to internal and external conditions.

A dynamic model is subject to the time factor, which plays an essential role in the sequence of decisions. Regardless of what the prior decisions have been, the dynamic model enables one to find the optimal decisions for the periods that still lie ahead. For example, incorrect decisions could have been made regarding inventory by the manufacturing department. Based upon a dynamic model that considers future period-by-period requirements, an optimal production schedule can be devised. The distinction between static and dynamic models will become apparent in the chapter on dynamic programming.

Simulation Versus Nonsimulation
The advent of computers has made a lasting impression on the various areas of operations research, in particular, simulation models. Simulation

is a method involving step-by-step sequential calculations where the workings of large-scale problems or systems can be reproduced. In many cases, where complex relationships of both predictable and random natures occur, it is easier to set up and run through a simulated situation on a computer than it is to develop and use a mathematical model representing the entire process under study. Still, in other cases, where there is no analytic solution available, a search on a computer for an ever-improving answer through sequential solution of alternatives is made until an optimal solution is approximated. The input data in a simulation model may be real or generated data. While some problems lend themselves to use of random numbers and empirical data for simulation models, many other problems lend themselves to nonsimulation models, such as optimization models. These, which may or may not utilize the computer, have techniques tailor-made for their respective solutions. A custom-built model for a specific solution is generally the better approach when simulation is not compatible with the operations research problem under study.

Essential Aspects of the Model

Having separated the preceding models into various classes, we can now set forth a general OR model which will be representative of a system under study. The OR model takes the form

$$E = f(X_1, X_2, \ldots X_n; Y_1, Y_2, \ldots Y_n)$$

where

E = objective measure of the system's effectiveness (objective function)
$X_1, X_2, \ldots X_n$ = system variables that are subject to control (controllable variables)
$Y_1, Y_2, \ldots Y_n$ = system variables that are not subject to control (uncontrollable variables)

The restriction on values of the variables may be expressed in a supplementary set of equations and inequalities. The extraction of a solution from such a model consists of determining the values of the control variables X_i for which the measure of effectiveness is maximized. In some cases, the measure of effectiveness might consist of minimization. Thus, certain questions must be answered about the foregoing factors before a mathematical model can be constructed that solves the problem understudy (Figure 1-1).

To illustrate the foregoing generalized model, consider the flow of vehicular traffic at a toll bridge during rush hours. E stands for the average delay experienced by motorists at the toll booths during peak periods. The X's which are controllable variables refer to the manned toll booths, that is, X_1 represents the number of these booths, X_2 the number of automatic collection machines, and so forth. On the other hand, the Y's are those variables that are not subject to managerial control. Y_1 is the average number of cars arriving at the toll booths during the peak hours; Y_2 is the mix of

1. What is the objective measure of effectiveness? That is, how will we express the solution to the problem (in dollars saved, units sold, items produced, etc.)?
2. What are the factors under our control (the controllable variables)? That is, what aspects of the problem can we do something about?
3. What are the factors not under our control (the uncontrollable variables)? That is, what aspects of the problem do we have to accept as given?
4. What is the relationship between these factors and the objective(s)? That is, can this relationship be expressed in the form of mathematical relationships that will constitute a model of the problem?

Figure 1-1 Four questions that must be answered about a problem before a mathematical model can be constructed.

cars, trucks, and buses, and the like. Based on these factors, the problem is to minimize the average delay by motorists subject to the availability of booths, capabilities of these booths, personnel on duty, and funds available to service the toll bridge. Thus, the best solution is sought within the framework of the problem's constraints.

Constructing the Model
The best way to start constructing a model is to itemize all the components that will contribute to the effectiveness of the system's operation. Once the list of component elements is complete, the next step is to determine whether or not each of these components should be used. This is difficult to do, since it is almost impossible to control the behavior of a single variable due to its functional relationship with others. On occasion a variable that is dropped because it was believed to be insignificant later may be found to be important for a good solution. It is recommended that all available data be tested experimentally or by some statistical method to overcome the difficulty. This extra step of experimenting before selecting the critical elements increases the probability of having a successful model.

Once the important elements have been selected, it may be convenient to combine or divide the elements. For example, receiving costs are combined with raw material purchase and freight cost. When each element has been finalized, it is necessary to determine whether it is fixed or variable (uncontrollable or controllable). Following this breakdown, the next step is to assign a symbol to each element where at least one symbol represents the measure of effectiveness or ineffectiveness. We can construct a single equation or a set of equations to express the effectiveness of the process or system. The resulting formula(s) is (are) a symbolic or mathematical model of the elements under consideration, which allows us to evaluate the results by varying certain elements within the constraints.

Role of the Model
The development of the first model (Model 1) is actually only a part of a larger process. This is apparent in Figure 1-2. The evolution of a successful

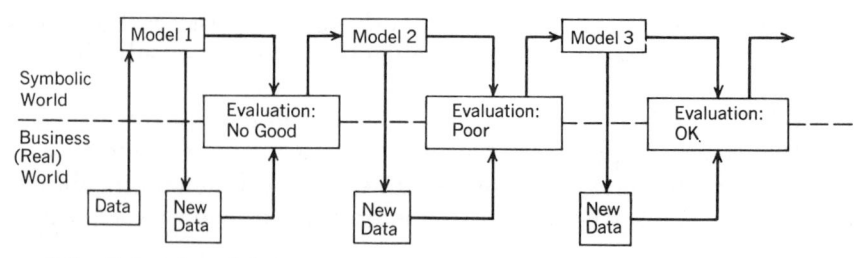

Figure 1-2 Role of models in an operations research project.

model generally follows this long drawn-out process. The first model is often very wide of the target. In fact, it can be so far off that operations personnel may feel like giving up the entire project in utter disgust. However, a fresh look by other OR people; further study, analysis, and serious thinking; and introduction of more statistically controlled data can change the evaluation from "no good" to "poor." Model 2, which is a major or a minor revision of Model 1 plus more representative data found by using statistical techniques, gives a major boost to the OR project. Model 3, a revision to Model 2 plus more refinement of the data, may bring about the desired result. This process can certainly be extended beyond Model 3 if needed. In effect, these successive stages allow the OR group to "zero in" on an optimum solution for the project.

Although Figure 1-2 gives the impression that there is an end to the sequence in building the final model (Model 3), there is actually no end to the process. Even after a model has years of successful usage to a firm, changing conditions may occur which necessitate reworking of the model to maximize revenue and profits and, at the same time, minimize costs. The process starts all over again and a new model must then be developed. Generally, the model will be easier to develop because the OR team has had previous exposure and experience with it. In effect, any OR model should be reviewed periodically to determine if any changes are desirable. It should be strongly emphasized that attitudes—indicating the ultimate has been obtained—can be misleading and a barrier to progress.

Since changing conditions make it necessary to revise the model, we can say that a model is neither true nor false but is one of relevance to the problem at hand. The model may be correct for one firm yet fail dismally for another. Alternatively, it may have been an effective model based upon existing market conditions, but later becomes inefficient under changed conditions. The criterion from the standpoint of the model's effectiveness is: Does it fit the existing conditions of today and the near future? Referring to Figure 1-2, Model 3 is effective for the firm while Models 1 and 2 do not fit current demands of the firm.

Evaluation of the Model

From the preceding discussion, we can conclude that a model which fails to predict what will happen in the real world must give way to a revised model that correctly reflects reality. Only in this manner can a proper evaluation be made. Otherwise, the relative advantages would certainly be overshadowed by its disadvantages. Given that standard or custom-built OR models are being properly utilized by the firm, their relative advantages are many. An important advantage of model building is that it provides a frame of reference for consideration of the problem, that is, the model may indicate gaps which are not apparent immediately. Upon testing the model, the character of the failure might give a clue to the model's deficiencies. Some of the greatest advances in science have resulted from the failure of a particular model.

From a cost standpoint, a complex problem can be expressed in a mathematical model that will allow one to change parameters in an effort to see the results without undertaking actual construction of the project. For example, a placement of plants and warehouses which does not best meet the present and future needs of customers can reduce profits. The time factor is also involved since the results (favorable and unfavorable) can be obtained within a relatively short time as opposed to waiting a much longer time for the completion of the project and actual day-to-day operations. With the constant squeeze on profits, the cost and time savings of operations research models make them worthy of managerial adoption as a decision tool.

Once a problem is expressed in mathematical notation and equation form, there is the advantage of the manipulative facility of mathematics. We can insert different values into the mathematical model and study the behavior of the system. If properly undertaken, statements about the sensitivity of the system to a change in any of the variables can be made. Also, the symbolic language offers advantages in communication since it allows a precise statement of the problem as opposed to a verbal description. The use of mathematical forms makes for better description and comprehension of the facts. It brings to light factors and uncovers relationships that were neglected in verbal description.

Models, which allow one to predict based upon past or present information, can be utilized for training purposes. These allow the trainee to see the results of his decision without having to make the actual decision. By using a model, a wrong decision on his part will not affect the firm's actual position. Models enable the trainee to distinguish between the controllable and noncontrollable variables as well as to determine the relative importance of each variable. Moreover, they allow him to examine cause and effect relationships that may not be readily apparent.

Mathematical models have the ability to expose the abstraction in a problem. In considering a complex world, the individual is made to select those attributes and concepts that are applicable. The mathematical model indicates what data should be collected to deal with the problem quantitatively. It makes it possible to deal with the problem in its entirety and allows a consideration of all the major variables of the problem simultaneously. A computer can be used to manipulate the major variables and factors of a model, which facilitates an understanding of the effect each has on the other.

Stating routine problems mathematically so that their solutions can be obtained by mathematical procedures has another advantage. If a satisfactory solution can be obtained through OR methods, managers can relegate these type problems to the computer and concentrate their efforts on identifying the sufficient factors of important problems that do not lend themselves to OR analysis. Many business problems require intuition and judgment for their solution. Hence, OR can release managerial time for poorly structured problems and their solutions, thereby increasing overall efficiency of the firm's resources.

Mathematical models have their drawbacks, one of which is the usual problem dealing with abstraction. This means that the model may require gross oversimplification and thus may inaccurately reflect the real world. Another problem of abstraction is failing to take into account all the exceptions. This can be an error of omission or commission. Also, it is difficult to define all the elements of a model in mathematical terms and set them down on paper. At the end of the initial process of abstraction, the model is so complex that it becomes very difficult to document the elements properly. This means changes are extremely difficult to make correctly.

There is a danger that an operations research worker may become so attached to his model that he will insist it represents the real world when it does not. If the same model were applied to the problem for another firm, it might be representative. What was said previously about a model applies here (it is neither true nor false, but one of relevance to the problem at hand). A model, being the creation of man, is only as good as the originator. If the person who builds the model does not know what he is doing, the output of the resulting model will reflect it. The GIGO[11] principle of data processing is applicable. This type of situation can be remedied by a competent staff, well trained in the concepts of model building.

Models can sometimes be very expensive to originate compared to the expected return from their use. Not only is there a question of marginal income and marginal cost, but of communications with management personnel who do not understand the models and hence have a difficult time accepting the results. Often it is more efficient to use direct methods than involved mathematical models. Many management people have a tendency to interpret the results rigidly instead of using them as decision making tools. The output of the model, tempered with the experience of management involved and consideration for present and future conditions (external and internal), is the best way to reap the benefits of operations research.

Quantitative Models to be Covered

Many OR models have been developed and applied to business problems. They can be grouped into several basic types which form the basis for the book's structure. No attempt will be made at this point to explain the vari-

---

[11] Garbage In, Garbage Out.

ous methods and models of operations research. Rather, an overview is set forth for the following:

Decision theory
Sequencing models
Allocation models
Assignment models
Competition models
Classical optimization techniques
Replacement models
Inventory models
Queuing models
Simulation techniques
Dynamic programming models
Routing models
Heuristic methods
Behavioral models
Combined OR methods

Decision Theory
The essential characteristics of decision theory is that the consequences of courses of action are generally not known. In these instances, probabilities are associated with the various states of nature. Depending on how much we know about the states of nature, we can refer to decision making under certainty, risk, and uncertainty. Most business problems deal with the last condition. Another way of predicting the future even though only a minimum amount of information is available is through Bayesian statistics. In addition to covering these elements of decision theory, Chapters 3 and 4 will treat discrete and continuous probability plus general stochastic (ability —but not with absolute certainty—in knowing what will take place) models. Thus, it will be shown that decision theory is useful in the reduction of uncertainty facing the manager.

Sequencing Models
Sequencing models involve determining an optimal sequence for a set of jobs or events or the best sequence for servicing customers in order to minimize total time and costs. In Chapter 5, the procedures for a network analysis of PERT (Program Evaluation Review Technique)/Time, PERT/Cost, and PERT/LOB are presented. These techniques are currently being applied to research and development, construction, new product planning, and similar areas. Other sequencing problems such as machine scheduling are solved by using simulation and heuristic techniques.

Allocation Models
When there are a number of activities to be performed, alternative ways of doing them, and limited resources or facilities for performing each activity in the most effective way, there is an allocation problem of these scarce

resources. The problem is to combine activities and resources in an optimal manner so that overall efficiency is maximized, that is, profit is maximized and cost is minimized. This is known as "mathematical programming." When the constraints are expressed as linear equations, this is known as "linear programming" (Chapter 6). If any of the constraints are nonlinear, this is called "nonlinear programming" (Chapter 12). The duality theory of linear programming that establishes a relationship between two different formulations of the same problem is presented in the chapter on linear programming. In addition to linear and nonlinear programming, there are other types of programming—integer, quadratic, convex, stochastic, decision, parametric, and dynamic. They differ in the kinds of data they can handle and the kind of assumptions that are made. Some of these latter types are covered in the nonlinear programming chapter.

Assignment Models
The simplest type of allocation model involves the assignment of a number of jobs to the same number of resources(men). This is called an "assignment problem." This problem type becomes more complex if some of the jobs require more than one resource and if the resources can be used for more than one job. An example of this is the "transportation problem." Both problem types—assignment and transportation—will utilize the MODI method and the stepping-stone method (Chapter 7) in their solution.

Competition Models
The theory of games (Chapter 8) provides a conceptual framework within which most competitive problems can be formulated. It has been used effectively by business to develop advertising strategies, pricing policies, and timing for the introduction of new products. Statistical decision theory and simulation have been used successfully in games. The use of gaming theory has brought educational benefits to the training of military and industrial personnel. In Chapter 9, Markov analysis will be discussed. The Markov process is a method of predicting competitive changes over time if customer brand loyalties and present market shares are known.

Classical Optimization Techniques
Classical or traditional optimization techniques are associated with the maxima and minima procedures of calculus. Briefly, when a characteristic can be represented by an equation in one variable that plots as a smooth continuous curve, the maximum or minimum values of the curve can be found by setting the first derivative equal to zero for locating horizontal or flat spots on the curve. Then, the mathematical signs of the second derivative at these points is examined for proving the problem. Where two parameters are involved such that x and y determine variable z, maxima and minima can be found by using partial derivatives in a process similar to that employed for a one-variable case. In Chapter 10, commonly applied areas of calculus are covered—differentiation, integration, partial derivatives, and the Lagrange multiplier. These mathematical techniques which are applied

to optimization problems are capable of directly selecting the best choice without going through many iterative steps.

Replacement Models
Replacement problems are generally of two types: those involving items that degenerate over a period of time and those that fail after a certain amount of time. The first group refers to a firm's fixed assets—machines, trucks, and equipment—which are high cost items. Those in the second type are relatively inexpensive—vacuum tubes, tires, tubes, and like items. Solutions to the first type are obtained by use of calculus in Chapter 10 and by dynamic programming. The model for the second type considers replacing items as they fail, replacing all items at specified intervals, or combinations of these. Statistical sampling and probability theory can be used for their solution.

Inventory Models
Inventory models (economic order quantity equations), the subject matter for Chapter 11, are concerned with two decisions: how much to order at one time and when to order this quantity in order to minimize total cost. Carrying costs, ordering costs of inventory, and shortage costs are determined so that a cost effectiveness relationship (model) can be used by management to select an appropriate balance between cost and shortages. Lowest-cost decision rule for inventory management can also be obtained by calculus, probability theory, dynamic programming, and computer simulation. Since these different methods provide additional approaches to inventory problems, other chapters will discuss the alternative approaches.

Queuing Models
Queuing, sometimes referred to as waiting line theory, is concerned with uniform or random arrivals at a servicing or processing facility of limited capacity. The objective of this model is to allow one to determine the optimum number of personnel or facilities necessary to service customers when considering the cost of service and the cost of waiting or congestion (Chapter 13). An inventory problem can be viewed as a queuing problem. Items in stock can be considered as an idle service facility waiting for customers. The demand for stock is an arrival for service and the outage of stock can be looked upon as a queue of customers. Theory of queues makes use of probability theory and calculus.

Simulation Techniques
Simulation is covered briefly in Chapter 13 as a part of queuing theory while a more complete treatment is given in Chapter 14. Random numbers are used to simulate arrivals and service times. Simulation, which lends itself to a computer, generates factors like potental sales or delayed shipments by inspecting random number tables that are integral to the program. The computer output shows the results that could have been obtained if the decision criteria had been used.

Dynamic Programming Models

Dynamic programming, an outgrowth of mathematical programming, is explored in Chapter 15. It will be seen that dynamic programming models are extremely useful for processes that extend over a number of time periods or events. Instead of optimizing each decision as it occurs, dynamic programming takes into account the effects of decisions today on future time periods. Most dynamic programming problems require the use of a computer to manipulate the myriad of data.

Routing Models

One of the most prominent routing problems is the "traveling salesman problem." The need is to select a route that starts at his own city, goes through each city only once, and returns to his home city in the shortest distance in terms of time or cost. This will be discussed in Chapter 16. The routing model has been applied to production where the number of models or items produced is analogous to cities. Changeover production costs correspond to the costs of travel between cities.

Heuristic Methods

Heuristic methods denotes learning or self-adopting systems. The heuristic model uses rules of thumb and educated guesses to explore the most likely paths in coming to a conclusion. This replaces checking all the alternatives (too many for another quantitative approach) to find the best one. This technique, covered in Chapter 16, appears to be very promising for the future of operations research.

Behavioral Models

Behavioral models represent a new and exciting direction for operations researchers. However, they are relatively unexplored at this time. Initially, it is expected that behavioral phenomena will be incorporated into modified standard OR methods. Next, problems with strong behavioral aspects, such as marketing problems, will be explored. Considerable behavioral research is necessary before behavioral models become operational. A discussion of this new direction and solution to typical behavioral problems is found in Chapter 17.

Combined or Methods

An important thrust in operations research now and in the future is combining OR methods for some type of master model. Several of the preceding models can be brought together to produce a new group of OR tools for managers. A production control problem, for example, usually includes some combination of inventory allocation and waiting line models. While the usual procedure for solving combined processes consists of solving them one at a time in some logical sequence, operations research must combine the models initially, where there are interrelationships, for an optimum solution. This approach will be quite evident in Chapter 18.

The foregoing classifications do not cover all operations research problems. However, they do include a great many that have been encountered up to this time. Even though the list is incomplete, it does enable the manager to perceive what is common to all problems and reminds him that quantitative methods are available for solving problems. The reader should not be too influenced by the name of the model, but rather keep an open mind so as to make analogies to comparable business situations. For example, inventory models are readily applicable to the problems of working capital, personnel, and cash. Waiting line models are readily applicable to inventory. Thus imagination can be an important key to the advancement of OR techniques.

Summary

Operations research, although originally not so titled, is of ancient lineage. Its main roots have arisen more recently for two reasons. The first is the need for scientific study of managerial problems (those involving the interrelationships of functional units of the firm) and the second relates to the opportunity for scientists to attack new problems of the military during World War II. These two motivating forces combined to produce operations research as it is known today. Operations research is defined as the utilization of a planned approach and an interdisciplinary team in order to represent complex functional relationships as mathematical models for the purpose of providing a quantitative basis for decision making and uncovering new problems for quantitative analysis.

Operations research is an aid or guide to supplement business judgment—not supplant it. OR is a managerial tool designed to increase the effectiveness of managerial decisions as an objective supplement to the subjective feelings of the manager. In brief, operations research attempts to supply meaningfully analyzed information on those "how," "when," and "what if" questions that were traditionally left to hunch, intuition, judgment, and hopeful guesses. It is an approach to operational analysis which enables the manager to improve his decision making ability.

Operations research may suggest alternative courses of action when a problem is analyzed and a solution is attempted. The study of complex problems by OR techniques is useful only when a choice between two or more courses of action is possible. Those problems which have one or very few solutions under limiting conditions will show no significant improvement in their solution when utilizing quantitative methods. In the final analysis, quantitative models of operations research are additional tools that enable the decision maker to be objective in choosing a course of action among many alternatives.

The list of theories, techniques, methods, and models that has become associated with operations research has grown over the years. By no means is this list complete. There is a definite tendency today to combine several of the OR techniques into more advanced models. It is natural that operations research should be headed in this direction since many of the basic functions of the firm have some affect on the other functions. To evaluate any decision or action in the firm from the standpoint of maximizing income or minimizing cost, all significant interactions need to be identified and their combined impact on the firm as a whole needs to be evaluated. This analytical approach calls for more sophisticated models. In the next chapter, additional material on operations research will be presented before going on to a detailed discussion of the various quantitative models of operations research.

Questions

1. Distinguish among the following: optimization, suboptimization, and over-optimization.
2. What are the essential characteristics of operations research? Explain.
3. What contributions has operations research made to business and government in the United States and in Britain?
4. How can models be classified? Which is the best classification in terms of learning and understanding the fundamentals of operations research?
5. Name and briefly describe the basic types of mathematical models.
6. (a) What are the basic steps in constructing a model?
   (b) What is its relationship to the real world?
   (c) How can one decide whether a model should optimize profits, sales, costs, or some other factor?
7. What are the advantages and disadvantages of models?
8. What areas of operations research have made a significant impact on the firm?
9. Why is it important to keep an open mind in utilizing OR techniques?

Bibliography

R. L. Ackoff and P. Rivett, *A Manager's Guide to Operations Research*, New York: John Wiley & Sons, 1963.

R. L. Ackoff and M. W. Sasieni, *Fundamentals of Operations Research*, New York: John Wiley & Sons, 1968.

P. G. Carlson, *Quantitative Methods for Managers*, New York: Harper & Row, Publishers, 1967.

C. W. Churchman, *The Systems Approach*, New York: Dell Publishing Company, 1968.

C. W. Churchman, R. L. Ackoff, and E. L. Arnoff, *Introduction to Operations Research*, New York: John Wiley & Sons, 1957.

P. E. Green and R. E. Frank, *A Manager's Guide to Marketing Research*, New York: John Wiley & Sons, 1967.

D. W. Miller and M. K. Starr, *Executive Decisions and Operations Research*, Englewood Cliffs, N.J.: Prentice-Hall, 1969.

C. M. Paik, *Quantitative Methods for Managerial Decisions*, New York: McGraw-Hill Book Company, 1973.
S. B. Richmond, *Operations Research for Management Decisions*, New York: The Ronald Press Company, 1968.
G. M. F. di Roccaferrera, *Operations Research Models for Business and Industry,* Cincinnati, O.: South-Western Publishing Company, 1964.
H. M. Wagner, *Principles of Operations Research, With Applications to Managerial Decisions,* Englewood Cliffs, N.J.: Prentice-Hall, 1969.

Chapter TWO

Operations Research in the Firm

Several terms used in the definition of operations research given in Chapter 1 are examined in more detail within this chapter. The guidelines for success in operations research, including the planned approach (updated scientific method), and the related problem areas are explored. More will be said about the use of the interdisciplinary approach in getting an OR group started within the firm. A list of problems that have been solved successfully by operations research will serve as a guide for newly formed units in getting started on OR projects. Also, the American Products Corporation (a typical manufacturing firm) is presented, thereby providing a background for applying OR models at the end of each forthcoming chapter.

Guidelines for Success in Operations Research

The experience of many firms indicates that the effectiveness of operations research has resulted from observing certain guidelines. These guidelines for success in operations research may reveal nothing new to the reader, but they will be helpful in planning, organizing, directing, and controlling OR activities within the firm. It should be somewhat obvious that the use of the planned approach is a requirement of successful operations research. The major phase of any OR project is the planned approach, the first guideline for discussion.

Utilization of the Planned Approach (Updated Scientific Method)

The planned approach that deals with problems such as conflicting objectives, policies, and alternatives has as its primary goal the development and application of quantitative models to specific problems. Its basic approach consists of the following steps: (1) observation, (2) definition of the real problem, (3) development of alternative solutions (models), (4) selection of optimum solution (model) using experimentation, and (5) verification of optimum solution (model) through implementation. This traditional method has been updated to include model development in conjunction with the current tools of operations research and the utilization of the computer. This will be apparent in the discussion of each step of the planned approach. The planned approach has one more step than the scientific method, namely, (6) the establishment of proper controls.

Step 1. Observation

The traditional approach to the scientific method starts with the observation of the phenomena surrounding the problem, that is, observing the facts, opinions, and symptoms concerning the problem. Observation may be a casual glance or a concentrated, detailed, and lengthy one based upon the

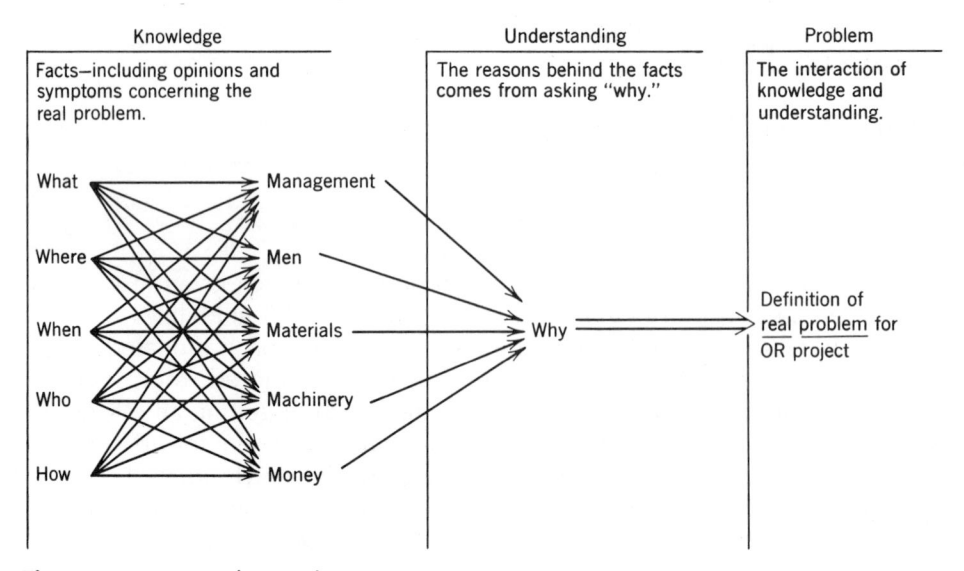

Figure 2-1 An *understanding* of the pertinent *knowledge* within the OR project leads to a definition of the *real problem*.

requirements of the problem under study. Observation is used to identify problems. The capable manager is always alert and sensitive to the presence of problems. He must be certain that he has identified the basic or real problem and not just a symptom of it.

After recognizing a problem, the manager should call upon the operations research team (located within or outside the firm) to begin work. The operations researchers must be alert during this initial step. They will probably hear such words as "too much," "poor," and "insufficient," which reflect the lack of clarity of established facts as to the nature and extent of the problem. Thus, the operations research group must be observant concerning the conditions surrounding the problem, asking questions of what, where, when, who, and how regarding the firm's resources—management, men, materials, machinery, and money. Basically, understanding the reasons behind the facts comes from asking "why," as illustrated in Figure 2-1. Not only does the gathering of facts help to develop a network of knowledge and understanding about the problem, but also assists ultimately in determining the real problem as well as arriving at a sound and worthwhile solution.

Step 2. Definition of the Real Problem
In the second step, the effective interaction of knowledge (facts) with understanding (reasons behind the facts) leads to the definition of the real problem (Figure 2-1). The OR team determines those factors affecting the problem, in particular, the variables, constraints, and assumptions. The variable factors are those for which decisions have to be made. They might include the level of inventory or the amount of advertising. The constraints restrict the solution of the problem. Examples include stockouts allowed

once every six months, productive capacity of a given manufacturing department, and minimum cash requirements. Assumptions necessary to the solution of the real problem must be set forth. These might include a uniform rate of growth for the firm and its products and a constant product mix or price. Thus, every effort should be made to quantify those factors affecting the problem. A thorough examination of these factors must be undertaken to insure that the real problem will be solved upon conclusion of the study.

Step 3. Development of Alternative Solutions (Models)

The next important step in this problem-solving approach is to develop alternative courses of action or tentative solutions to the real problem. To state it another way, several hypotheses are formulated based upon the "Principle of Multiple Hypotheses" set forth by Ralph C. Davis in his book, *The Fundamentals of Top Management*. A hypothesis is nothing more than a tentative solution to a problem. Most of the time in an OR study, the alternative courses of action or hypotheses take the form of mathematical models. Mathematical models can be developed by the appropriate tools of the trade or can be custom-built to accommodate the real world problem. They are generally computer oriented for a final solution.

Each of the mathematical models developed entails three stages, which are:

- Data analysis.
- Model development.
- Model validation.

The first stage (data analysis) is concerned with defining the assumptions, constraints, events, relationships, variables, and other factors deemed important to the mathematical modeling process. Basically, this data is a synthesis of the above step (Step 2 in the planned approach).

In the second stage (model development), the OR model is structured according to the parameters set forth in the data analysis phase. Whenever possible, information relating to the model's behavior, caused by varying input parameters, should be obtained. Such an analysis is commonly referred to as *sensitivity analysis* and is especially needed when the parameters cannot to be determined accurately. Whether the parameters are actual values, estimates, or both, the model will normally consist of mathematical relationships expressed as equations and functions. In addition, this stage should incorporate features in the model's structure that will facilitate its validation —the next stage.

Since most OR models are computer oriented, the third stage (model validation) focuses on the programming and debugging of the model. It is concerned with the soundness of the programmed logic so that the model's structured components can be verified before experimentation with the model is undertaken per the step below (Step 4 in the planned approach). In cases where OR packages are available from computer manufacturers, testing of these programmed packages are generally not necessary.

It has been noted in this third step of the planned approach that several models may be developed if several approaches initially look promising in terms of a final solution to the problem. As each model is developed, its respective deficiencies become apparent, that is, the model's behavior is inconsistent with that of the modeled problem. Thus certain models which looked promising at the outset may have to be discarded. Instead of a half dozen models, the choice might be narrowed to one, two, or three candidates.

Many times clearly stated objectives are neglected in this step. The OR study tries to take into account as broad a scope of objectives as possible. The problem is to determine which alternative model (course of action) is most effective relative to the set of pertinent objectives. Consequently, in formulating the problem, a measure of effectiveness must be specified in terms of specific objectives. This is helpful in reducing the number of tentative models.

Step 4. Selection of Optimum Solution (Model) Using Experimentation
Once the number of alternative models or solutions has been narrowed, those remaining are evaluated in order to select the optimum one. If the resulting model fits one of the well-known OR techniques (subject matter of this book), then a solution may be obtained by it. On the other hand if the mathematical relationships of the model are too complex for the standard OR techniques, a custom-made model is required. Thus, the selection of the appropriate model is dependent on the nature and complexity of the problem under investigation.

There are essentially two procedures for deriving an optimum solution from a model: analytic and numerical. Briefly, analytic procedures consist of employing mathematical deduction, such as algebra and calculus. Numerical procedures which make use of computers are concerned with trying various values for the control variables in the model, comparing the results obtained, and selecting those control variables that yield an optimum solution. These procedures vary from simple trial-and-error to complex iterative processes. The optimum solution found by experimentation must take into account achieving the objective(s) set forth in the study.

Step 5. Verification of Optimum Solution (Model) through Implementation
In the final phase of the scientific method, the OR group verifies experimentally the chosen model. While experimentation is often on a limited basis, verification involves most or all of the target population (as defined in statistics). This step is necessary because the reaction of competitors, consumer buying traits, and comparable factors observed in the limited sample tested experimentally may not hold true for the target population. In order to verify the optimum model or solution, it must be translated into a set of operating procedures capable of being understood and applied by the personnel who will be responsible for their use. Major or minor changes must be specified and implemented. Dual operations, sometimes called parallel operations, are needed to test the efficiency of the new method compared to the old method. Initially one phase or section is converted in order to highlight any shortcomings of the model (solution). This can be a very trying process since a variable which was initially determined to be

insignificant (was ignored) may be found to be a critical factor (variable). The dynamics of the business world can cause this to happen overnight. The resistance of operating personnel to changes can cause additional problems to OR teams.

Step 6. Establishment of Proper Controls
Once the results have been interpreted and action has been recommended and implemented through the fifth and final phase of the scientific method, the planned approach goes one step further. It establishes controls. A solution derived from a model remains an optimum one as long as the variables retain their original relationships. The solution goes out of control when the variables and/or one or more of the relationships between the variables have changed significantly. The significance of the change depends on the cost of changing the present model versus the deviation under the changed conditions from the true optimum solution. To establish control over the model (solution), it is necessary to establish an information system that will permit feedback to the particular management level(s) responsible and accountable. Continuous monitoring of the system through feedback provides a means for modifying the system as external-internal conditions and demands change over time. If changes are necessary, the study should be reviewed, starting again with the first phase of the planned approach. It is obvious that OR projects are continuous since the firm is operating in a dynamic as opposed to a static economy.

The six steps are seldom, if ever, conducted in a particular order since there is usually a constant interplay between the steps of operations research. For example, an exact and precise formulation of the problem is not completed until the project is about completed. However, these six steps provide a helpful conceptual framework when dealing with a complex problem. The methodology certainly gives direction to one's thinking as some other general method would not. In Figure 2-2, the problem-solving steps to be followed by the operations research team are recapped. The first five steps are basically the scientific method with the additions of the sixth step, model development, techniques (tools) of the trade, and computer for an updated scientific method or planned approach to OR problems. Also, the feedback loop links the final step back to the beginning one.

Solve Problem Rather Than Apply Techniques
Successful operations research from a management viewpoint is one of an approach to problem solving rather than an associated collection of quantitative methods. Basically, operations research is an extension of managerial tools for decision making. One of the best ways to prevent an OR study from going overboard in application of techniques is to state initially the objective, scope of the study, and the general approach to be used. If a standard OR technique is best suited for the problem under study, it should be used. If, on the other hand, a standard technique is not rightfully applicable, the "cookbook approach" should be discarded in favor of a "tailor-made" technique. This makes sense since the main objective of the OR

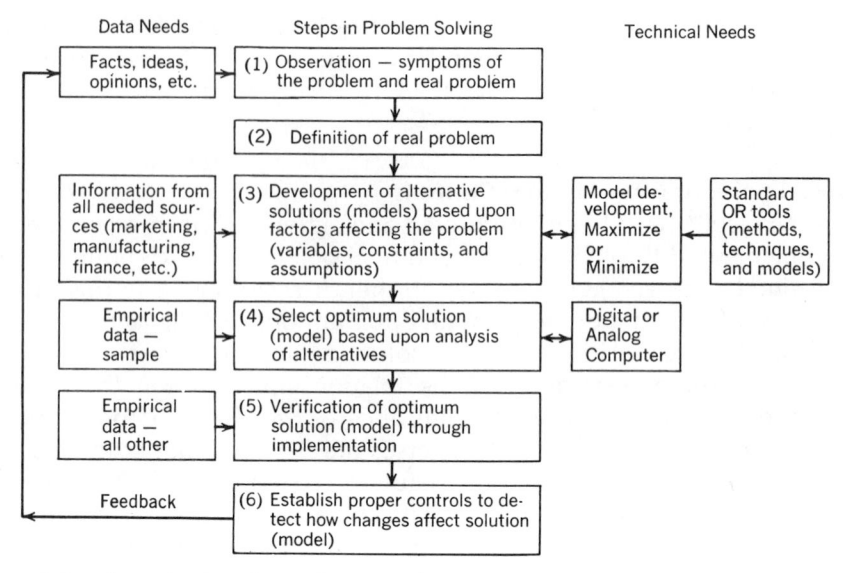

Figure 2-2. Steps in the planned approach.

study is to solve the problem and not just apply techniques. The methods or techniques are secondary.

Select Projects Carefully
Whether an OR project is undertaken by a well established internal group or an outside consulting firm, the effectiveness of operations research depends greatly on the proper selection of projects. Top management and operating management should play a part in selecting the projects because many of the benefits from operations research come from studies that cross functional and departmental boundaries. Furthermore, management can be helpful in estimating the degree of success as well as the potential benefits from such a study. The proper selection of OR projects is critical to a newly formed OR team since the eyes and ears of the firm are focused on them. Selection of projects with a high probability of being successful and with immediate payoffs is an intelligent way of gaining the confidence of management and operational personnel. To further guarantee success for a new group, the guidance of an outside consulting firm or an experienced group leader should be utilized during this critical period.

In firms where an OR team is well established in the eyes of management and operating personnel, projects that encompass the whole firm or ones that cut across many of the firm's functions should not be undertaken until the intermediate phases have been analyzed and solved. The firm can benefit from a thorough analysis of the component parts before taking on a large project that can become a nightmare due to the myriad of details and complexities involved. It is better for the OR group to go forward step by step rather than forward three steps and back six steps. An analysis of the intermediate phases of a larger problem should take into account the larger overall objective. A thorough analysis and solution of the important intermediate phases certainly makes a larger OR project much easier to solve.

Like computers, operations research is relatively expensive. This means that OR should not be employed on all problems but only on those in which foreseeable gains over costs make it a logical choice. OR techniques can be applied efficiently to problems which are recurring in nature, rather than a one time situation, and where there is an opportunity to choose among alternatives. The OR projects selected should include problems where a real opportunity exists for quantitative study and measurement with a large number of controlled variables and a small number of relevant, uncontrolled variables. Other candidates for OR study are problems which are large and complex as well as those which are current and pressing where operations research solutions would be more accurate and less expensive than any other methods of analysis. Problems that do not exhibit one or more of the preceding characteristics may not be suitable OR projects. A listing of common operations research areas appears later in the chapter and should be helpful in selecting appropriate projects for any OR group.

Organization for Problem Solving

Even though an operations research team makes use of the planned approach, solves problems rather than applies techniques, and selects its projects carefully, there still is no guarantee of success. Its success depends to a great degree on the organization of OR activity and the staffing of the OR group. If a team is to solve problems within the firm, it must have personnel competent in developing mathematical models and communicating recommendations to the various levels of management and their subordinates. To develop a model and state that it speaks for itself is violating a fundamental principle of communication.

In order to bring all details and exceptions to light, it is particularly important to draw on the experience of management and operating personnel alike. One effective way to make sure that all details, including exceptions, have been given to the OR team is "selling" operating personnel on the merits of the new approach. If these individuals can be shown the major benefits of the new system—time to plan the activities of their departments and time to train operating personnel versus the present pressure-filled situation of trying to meet crises as they arise—most rational operating managers will volunteer information in order to get their areas back under control again.

Not only must the OR staff be competent and supplied with all the necessary details, it must have access to, and cooperation from, a sufficiently high enough level of management to insure implementation of results. This does not necessarily mean that the operations research manager should report directly to a director or a vice president of a firm, but the line of access must be there. If the OR group does not have the backing of top management, it will have an impossible task in implementing larger projects that cut across several or all functions of the firm. When all is said and done, the OR group must have access to and support of top management and ready access to all company information. It matters little in what particular department the OR group is formally located.

Compiling Quality Input Data

Compiling quality input data can represent a major part of the time and cost of an OR study. If this is the case, an early analysis of the solution's sensitivity to input data should be undertaken in order to prevent gathering unnecessary data on the problem. Further, this initial analysis may indicate certain areas where accurate measurement and control of data are extremely important. Too often, data needed on an OR problem is not available in the format desired.

In a typical OR study, the operations researchers need to observe the problem under study, see what data is available, and collect as well as test the quality of preliminary values before starting on models and measures of effectiveness. When referring to the quality of data, one measure is *accuracy* which measures the difference between the data and the true value of whatever the data represents. Generally, the accuracy of data can be enhanced by improving the methods by which the data is gathered. Another measure of data quality is *precision*, that is, a measure of the repeatability of data. If the same measurement were taken on the same subject on two different occasions, would the same data result? Hence, data should contain these qualitative factors for true input to the OR modeling process.

Data collection may be as simple as gathering accounting and inventory computer printouts for the past several years. Frequently, however, quality of data is lacking. Data is not in a meaningful form and a carefully designed data gathering program must be developed. Thus, operations researchers must answer several questions before gathering the data, such as what do we want to learn from the data? What final decision(s) will be made based on the data or what conclusion(s) will be drawn? In essence, will the data collected be appropriate for the final use intended?

One final comment on compiling input data is worth noting. Careful analysis of needed data early in the problem can save many weeks and months of lost time later in the project. It is quite frustrating to learn halfway through the project that certain data which could have been supplied initially is now needed. It is better to compile too much than too little data, especially when such data is the output of a computer run. Frequently, in using computers, the additional data costs little since the output of a computer system is limited by its slowest unit, such as an on-line printer.

Problem Areas of Operations Research

The guidelines for success in operations research have undoubtedly helped many firms to undertake and complete many difficult projects. Despite the success of many firms using these guides, they have not met with universal approval. Any representative sample of companies would reveal a large number of disillusioned rather than enthusiastic management personnel. Discontinued rather than flourishing projects would be found. Why the success in one company and not in another? In this section, we will focus on some of the problem areas of operations research. These are not presented to discourage operations research activities but rather are offered as constructive criticism to enlighten management on the possible dangers that may impede the completion of OR projects. If management can be made aware of potential problem areas and recognize problems as they occur, corrections can be made on the spot rather than at some later time when the whole OR project has soured or gone beyond the point of repair. The reader will notice a relationship with the guidelines for success in operations research.

Computer Groping
Some OR projects have failed due to the substitution of high-speed, brute-force computer groping in place of sound analysis. This happens when a computer is utilized as a "toy," that is, a computer is available and the operations researchers must impress everyone with their need for it by solving complex problems. Computer time is used for many inconsequential runs, resulting in excessive computer costs on a project. Instead of using the planned approach where a computer becomes an integral part of the fourth step (select optimum solution), computer groping is used throughout the analysis. A logical and orderly approach is replaced by a haphazard one. It may seem strange to the reader that OR people, schooled in the rigorous and logical methods of mathematics, would pursue such an approach. This situation is generally applicable to untrained OR people who feel they must show immediate results. If they stood back and took an overall objective view, they would find that they could avoid many painful setbacks by utilizing the planned approach.

Overemphasis on Technique
An examination of the numerous techniques and available computer time may, in itself, be a problem. The OR group might direct all their efforts to the mechanics of the technique and how it should be programmed rather than directing them to the end product, which is to solve a particular problem. As a result, operations researchers have taken up insignificant problems merely because a technique is known and a computer is available. Other OR personnel have warped the problem to fit an available model rather than take the time to construct a specialized model. Still others have been concerned with the elegance of a method which can lead to an elaborate and correct answer but which may be too complex or too late to be useful. This approach also leads to "overoptimization," that is, attempting to obtain the last few points of improvement by a detailed and costly analysis. In this case, the cost of the marginal gain far exceeds the gain itself. Many times a less complicated model will yield the bulk of the potential gain at a greatly reduced cost with a higher likelihood of success.

As can be seen from the foregoing discussion, too often techniques dominate the problem. Instead of being used as a means toward an end (solving the problem), they turn out to be an end in themselves. However, they are pivotal in this field and are essential for the continued progress of operations research. Thus quantitative methods should be placed in their proper perspective—both good and bad aspects should be considered—when solving an OR problem.

Lack of Organization

Operations research programs fail to gain acceptance and implementation due to lack of proper organization. This occurs when the OR group members fail to draw upon the experience and judgment of line managers and their subordinates. By not getting company people to participate in the project from the very start, the OR team may not learn the technical aspects of the operations or may define unrealistic objectives. In essence, this important knowledge of the facts, which should be incorporated into the constraints, assumptions, and the model itself, is cast aside. Success in any type of OR study depends upon the ability to use the experience of certain individuals and to apply this information along with other pertinent data within or outside the firm. Any person who claims he is an expert in operations research and does not make use of the experience and judgment of line managers and their subordinates is either a fraud or a genius. (The authors are inclined to feel that the former is more likely true.)

Inadequate participation of management, particularly the managerial level that must act on the recommendations, is another aspect of poor organization. Too often OR groups feel their responsibility ends with the completion of the mathematical model. The effectiveness of operations research depends on obtaining the cooperation and participation of the various management levels who have the final word concerning the functions under study or who are affected by the final recommendations. Similarly, it is necessary to have the participation of operating management and their subordinates since these people must be convinced of the usefulness and validity of the project. It is essential that at least operating management be in favor of implementing the solution set forth by the operations researchers. Any noticeable resistance at any level of management, coupled with the resistance of their subordinates, substantially reduces the chances for a successful OR project. Some items that can cause resistance to the acceptance of an OR solution are: managers do not understand the model, prejudice against quantitative techniques in general, reluctance to change the status quo, managers' unwillingness to use computers as aids in decision making since they feel their own experience is the best guide, and suspicion of monitoring being done by the home office to check on them. The list could become quite long since the natural tendency of people is to fear the unknown and resist any sort of change in the status quo.

Ineffective Communication

Closely related to the preceding problem areas of operations research is one of communication. Even though the model may be 100 percent correct, the

OR team must effectively communicate the results of its study to all involved in the study. This includes all levels of management (top, middle, and lower) and their subordinates, line and staff. It is frequently difficult for people (OR and non-OR personnel) to come away from a meeting with the same message or understanding of the problem under study. The operations research group is certain to encounter communication difficulties if the presentation is too highly technical or does not specify the assumptions and limitations of the project. Since operations researchers tend to operate in a world somewhat different from that of operating managers, the OR team must be willing to expend considerable effort so that its presentations are understood. Unless this is done, ineffective communication will greatly reduce the chances of a successful OR project.

Failure to Establish Controls

In some cases OR projects which were thought to be progressing on schedule in terms of results have run into serious trouble at the very end of the project due to a failure to test the model and solution adequately before implementation. The OR group has failed to establish proper controls in terms of feedback to itself and management. Here the group has not set up a system of dual operations where the new can be compared to the old or, if this was done, no feedback of good, bad, or indifferent results was reported to anyone. Thus the model, thought to be a true representation of reality, turns out to be invalid and perhaps more costly to the firm. This could have been avoided by monitoring and evaluating the results of the model once it was placed into operation on a test basis. Establishing controls also applies to periodic reviews of successfully implemented projects as set forth under the guidelines for successful operations research.

Organizing for Operations Research

The initiation of OR activity in a firm can be approached in four ways: internally training people from the organization, hiring experienced OR specialists, hiring an external consulting group, and using a combination of company personnel and outside consultants. The cost involved in setting up an operations research department is high, which precludes its use by small firms. This is where outside consulting firms can be extremely useful to small business. Today most firms with internal OR groups have annual sales of $40 million and over where cost savings can be substantial.

Internal Operations Research Group

Starting with internal personnel for an operations research group in a medium sized firm, there are a number of important factors that should be considered. The first is that at least two men should be selected in order to provide a fruitful interaction and exchange of ideas. This is in line with the interdisciplinary approach to operations research. They should complement one another not only in background, but also in temperament. One of the two individuals should know the interworkings of the firm and the key people in each of the major functions and subfunctions of the firm. This is extremely helpful for problems that cut across many of the firm's major functions. Since operations research makes great use of mathematical modeling, each person should have at least a degree in mathematics, engineering, or science. Advanced degrees are helpful, but more important is a knowledge of probability, statistics, and mathematics as well as an understanding of the standard OR techniques. In addition, the individuals should enjoy working on real world problems that are simple or complex and should be interested in solving problems rather than just applying techniques. The task of operations research is to build models for existing real world problems rather than to search for problems to fit existing techniques. The two men should be able to communicate with all levels in the firm—management and operating personnel alike. These two men should be familiar with operations research literature and spend some time initially visiting well established OR groups. It is also extremely valuable for the team to be responsible to one man at the top. Often, they are assigned a project, for example, by a planning group. Unless one of this group is designated as the "pro-team" contact, the OR team will find themselves bogged down in justifying their existence rather than getting on with the job to be done.

The most effective and efficient way of initiating OR projects is to use the outside services of a consulting firm that has the capability of working with the internal group of two men described previously. Outside guidance may be needed for a period of approximately two years. However, even after this initial period, it is advantageous to continue the use of outside consultants to insure objectivity, breadth of scope, and direction in the firm's OR undertakings. During the initial two-year period, arrangements must be made for the two operations researchers to attend classes and seminars in operations research under the guidance of an experienced OR specialist. Reading current literature is a must for the OR team. Generally speaking, after two years, operations research personnel should be able to deal with most of the OR projects with which they are faced. If OR personnel are not capable of doing this, the firm needs to take a second look at its group.

Initial Operations Research Problems

As might be suspected, the importance of the first problem which an operations research team undertakes cannot be overestimated. This initial encounter can make or break the team. Many of the firm's personnel, including management, know the department exists but will have no real idea of what they are doing or what they are trying to accomplish. Since this will be a "showpiece" for the OR group, it is wise to tackle a problem that has a good chance of success with a reasonable rate of cost savings associated with it. This will probably be in the area of manufacturing since production managers are accustomed to looking at their problems in a quantitative manner and in having someone advise them on their operations. The particular problem could be waiting lines at tool cribs, out of stock conditions for raw materials at critical times, erratic swings in manufacturing of parts, or poor scheduling of production orders. In essence, the operations research team must learn to crawl before it walks.

As in most cases, experience is an excellent teacher. The second project always seems to go more smoothly because the team builds knowldge from the lessons learned in its first encounter. Success in initial projects will further management's confidence in the OR group undertaking problems of greater complexity. As time goes on, the OR group will be able to direct the attention of management to important future problems. Not only is the OR team solving problems for management—the team also is assisting management in identifying possible future crises which are, many times, wide in scope and of a long-range nature. This can be a major contribution of operations research.

An OR study can raise more questions than it can answer. This can lead to a more penetrating inquiry into the operations of the system and what it is intended to do. The final result is a greater insight and overview of the system with far-reaching benefits and improvements to the firm.

On the other hand, the glowing benefits just set forth can be lost forever if the initial projects are too broad in scope, too complex, too slow, or nonexistent in results. Too often OR groups make glib promises of large savings for a small cost. These optimists can be spotted by a simple test. It will take two good, experienced men several months to get familiar with the problem, collect existing data, and perform the necessary steps (except implementation) of the planned approach on the simplest procedures, forms, people, machines, and working out the inevitable "bugs" that are part of the real world in the implementation phase. These changes can take from three months to two years or more, depending on the problem. During this period, the OR team needs to answer a host of questions, ranging from the absurd to frankly embarrassing questions (for example, a question about something that was overlooked). The important point is that operations research is basically "research," which takes time to do properly. No one can ask realistically that a project be completed in a few weeks, nor can anyone in operations research promise this.

Mixture of Operations Research Team
As the OR group grows in members, new disciplines are brought to bear on problems. The participants of the team should be chosen according to the kinds of problems that must be analyzed. For example, military problems may benefit more from certain disciplines than those of private industry. The firm's team might include personnel trained in mathematics, (especially, applied mathematics as used in operations research), statistics, a physical science, engineering, economics, sociology, and psychology. Generally, a well balanced OR group would be roughly one-third mathematicians and statisticians, one-third physical scientists and engineers, and one-third economists and behavioral scientists. Courses for the team may be organized within the firm with participation and supervision by operations research consultants.

An industrial OR problem seldom requires more than six men to work on it. It is reasonable to plan on an average of three men to a project and not less than two. Each member of the group generally works on several projects at a time, but each has the responsibility for one project. This type of work load is somewhat similar to that undertaken by personnel working for a consulting firm.

Location of Operations Research Team
The question of where to locate an OR team within the firm has received a great deal of attention. Naturally, there is no one preferred position for all firms. Successful groups have reported to the president, executive vice president, the vice president in charge of management information systems, the vice president in charge of finance, vice president in charge of manufacturing, vice president in charge of research and development, and the controller. The advantage of reporting to top management is that it gives operations research a firm basis of operations. The group is forced into the front line of decision making where its work will have an immediate usefulness to management. In addition, by having the backing of top management and prestige within the firm, the group will be able to cut across departmental lines.

Generally, the internal operations research team is associated with the computer department. One reason is that accessibility to a computer has become a mainstay of OR activity. A less obvious reason is the fact that operations research has not always been successful over the years within the firm. By locating the OR group within the computer department—in particular, with systems analysis personnel—the group has been given greater stability because computers are here to stay. Many firms have a group within the computer area who are capable of operations research and systems analysis work. This merger with the computer function should bring benefits to operations research since electronic data processing cuts across most of the firm's functions. Just as operations research recognizes that any action in one part of the system has some effect on every other part, this OR characteristic (functional relationship in a system) is likewise understood and practiced by computer personnel. Thus the two groups complement one another to the benefit of all concerned, especially in terms of the firm's objectives.

For most operations research projects, it is recommended that the OR Task Force consist of the following:

1. One or more management scientists (operations researchers)—persons with skills and experience in applying operations research techniques to real management decision problems.
2. One or more computer scientists—individuals whose primary orientation is toward the use of computing power to manipulate data and develop information. (In some cases, the computer scientists and management scientists may be the same persons.)
3. One or more well-rounded, nontechnical personnel—employees who know the organization better than the computer scientists or management scientists, know where to obtain information, facilitate

the cooperation of operating personnel, and finally are better equipped to help the Task Force "sell" the project solution(s) than anyone else.
4. One or more representatives from the problem area—personnel who are concerned with the operating functions being studied and who perhaps know the detailed exceptions and problems better than anyone else.

The foregoing composition will vary in size based on the complexity of the problem and the time factor involved in the project.

The OR Task Force is responsible to a Management Steering Committee composed of those executives whose functions (departments) are affected by the study. The purpose of this "interparticipative" project effort is to allow management the opportunity of providing judgmental inputs and participating in the discussion of difficult problem areas. The Steering Committee, in turn, reports to top management on the project's progress. This apparently unwieldly procedure of committees is beneficial in the sense that it serves to filter the research and help prevent errors. It helps pinpoint all the relationships between processes and departments that must enter into a successful model. The committees also prepare the way for OR personnel, in the sense that they enlist the cooperation of operating personnel and boost their chance of acceptance.

Successful Operations Research Areas

In the first chapter, it was shown that many management problems can be reduced to a listing of basic forms for which quantitative techniques have been developed. Unfortunately, most managers normally do not think of problems in terms of basic forms or underlying structures, but more in terms of their content—the area of business in which these problems arise. Thus the wide range of problems where operations research has been successfully applied in business and industry will be better understood by discussing problems in terms of their content (functional areas of the firm). The listings given below for the functional areas of a firm are a sample of the many problems that have been explored and successfully solved by operations research personnel. Some of these functional OR projects may well involve the business as a whole.

Marketing and Physical Distribution
Operations research is being applied increasingly to marketing. It has been used to determine how much of the total marketing budget should be spent on personal selling, advertising, and sales promotion. In terms of personal selling, OR studies have determined the number of salesmen, number of accounts to be assigned for each salesman, and how often they should call on a particular purchasing agent. Similarly, operations research has been used to determine the optimum size of sales territories, the number and

distribution of sales offices, and the allocation of sales effort to the different territories. Advertising has been approached in terms of optimizing the frequency of exposures and messages to the particular market segment at the lowest cost. The effect of promotional activity over the firm's many accounts has been studied.

Operations research has helped in the development and introduction of many new products. It has helped in product selection, timing of new products, demand forecasting, and in forecasting the competitive actions of other firms. OR has determined what package sizes, models, colors, and shapes the final product should have in order to be successful in the marketplace. It has determined the guarantee policy and period as well as the service that should be provided.

In regard to physical distribution, OR models have been developed to locate and determine the size of warehouses, distribution centers, and retail outlets. Decisions for internal space allocation for display and stock accessibility have been forthcoming from operations research. Decisions also have been made on company-owned outlets versus franchises. Multilevel inventory control systems and transportation policies have been undertaken.

Purchasing

When purchasing raw materials, operations research has been used to develop rules where prices are stable or highly erratic over a certain time period. A correct purchasing approach must take into account the quantity to buy and the source of supply. Some other important purchasing considerations for an OR model are: holding costs of inventory, purchasing costs, perishability of the item, cost of transportation, available storage, location of supplies, and ability to substitute another raw material in its place.

Bidding policies and probabilities of winning bids have been explored by operations research. This, in turn, has been related to the predictions of competitive behavior. Operations research has undertaken many studies directed at determining whether to purchase assembled parts or to manufacture the items. Factors to be considered are: how often the item is purchased, purchasing prices, fixed and variable costs of manufacturing, present plant loading, and delivery time. This is basically a breakeven problem.

OR studies are concerned also with the optimum purchasing of fixed assets in terms of machine models and specific manufacturers. Models have been developed for optimum replacement of equipment after so many years. Studies have been made to determine when new or used equipment should be purchased or whether equipment should be rented.

Manufacturing

Operations research has gained a strong foothold in the area of manufacturing. It has been used to allocate production orders to the firm's various plants on the basis of production and transportation costs. Production and employment in OR studies have been stabilized through consideration of hiring costs, training, layoffs, and firings. Operations research has been used in the selection of plant sites and sizes (and related warehouses), the optimum manufacturing mixes, and the type and amount of equipment that should be installed. When there is a multiplant operation, OR models have been developed to determine what plants should be shut down, under what circumstances, and how the work load of the closed plants should be reallocated to the remaining operating plants.

Manufacturing operating policies, in many cases, can best be optimized by utilizing operations research. Studies have included production planning and production scheduling where decisions on product mixes, sequencing, overtime, and additional (second and third) shifts must be made. Quality control systems have been studied by developing a criterion of acceptance for products based upon balancing quality with cost factors.

Maintenance in terms of prevention and correction is another fertile area for operations research. Quantitative methods have determined maintenance crew requirements as well as how these requirements relate to the timing of equipment replacement. The effects of maintenance policies on the smoothness of manufacturing facilities and labor utilization have been determined. Material handling and traffic (internal and external) problems have been resolved. The problem of how many machines (varying types) has been solved in terms of a single operator to produce the best balance of material flow and operating costs. Operations research, to a certain degree, has helped in the planning and scheduling of job shop operations. It has been a great help in balancing the overall costs of employee waiting time against attendant's cost at the tool and supply cribs.

This sample of manufacturing problem areas that have been successfully solved by operations research should give a better understanding of why the manufacturing department is a logical starting point for a newly formed operations research group.

Accounting and Finance
Operations research studies have been employed in developing automated data processing and accounting procedures that minimize office costs and, at the same time, are conducive to good internal control. Such studies have been used in the development of computer sampling techniques in order to provide greater audit reliability. Sampling has also been used in providing optimal procedures for dealing with claims and complaints. Pilferage problems have been examined and solved.

Cash flow analysis, long-range capital requirements, alternative investments, sources of capital, and dividend policies are common finance problems solved. Operations research has been applied to the design of portfolios (stocks and bonds) in order to maintain their value under changing conditions. Credit policies, credit risks, and delinquent account procedures have been studied with promising results.

Personnel
The impact of automation and the feasibility of accelerating automation to reduce manufacturing costs without causing hardships to factory employ-

ees is a problem for OR study and solution. Past studies have determined what mixture of age and skills is best under certain conditions. Causes of accidents, problems of labor turnover, and absenteeism are examined so they can be minimized for the firm. The methods of operations research have been utilized to recruit personnel, effectively classify them, and assign them jobs where they will have the highest performance. Evaluation of incentive pay, in terms of increasing production, has also been explored and solved in the area of personnel.

Research and Development
Budgets for R & D and the proper allocation to basic or applied research have been solved. The amount for each project, the size of the R & D facility, and related staff have been determined in previous OR studies. The effectiveness and organization of research activities have also been carefully scrutinized.

Operations research has been used in determining areas where R & D should be concentrated, based upon assumed or actual results; in developing guidelines for evaluating different designs; and in determining the life expectancy and reliability that should be designed into a product. With the pressure on profits these days, it is being used more and more to schedule and control the development of R & D projects in order to reduce their time and cost requirements.

Planning
Numerous overall planning projects—the redefinition of the firm's objectives, a new organization structure, overall optimal company policies, programs for fully developing the firm's resources—have been undertaken where the operations research group has played a key role in their solution. Long-range plans for enlarging the firm through product diversification and mergers are common problems handled by more established OR groups.

In many extremely complex situations, such as R & D projects, construction of a new plant, and launching of a new product, the total effort can be broken down into a large number of activities. Some of the activities must wait for others to be completed before they can be started, whereas others can be carried out in parallel. Once the sequence of activities has been logically defined, the critical activities can be determined to spotlight future bottlenecks. Planning methods (PERT) have been devised to control and reduce the time and related costs where possible.

The foregoing problem areas that have been examined and solved by operations researchers working closely with operating personnel attests to the dynamic nature of this discipline. Computer systems, especially those that are capable of real-time responses, have provided the needed thrust for greater application of OR models. In essence, real-time systems that have the ability to feed back information in sufficient time to control their environment have made it possible to bring decision makers and operations researchers into a much more intimate contact for timely decisions.

American Products Corporation

In the coming chapters of this book, the OR technique developed within each chapter will be highlighted further by application to the American Products Corporation. The purpose of this approach is to demonstrate typical OR applications within a manufacturing environment. Although the problems have been simplified, this does not detract from the types of problems that have been successfully solved by the firm's operations research group.

The American Products Corporation is a medium-size firm that engages in the manufacture of home products. The firm's sales are currently $100 million per annum and are projected to increase annually by 5 percent during the next several years. Its product line consists of over 100 products which can be categorized into 10 basic product groups. Variations of these basic products are for specific customers whose requirements differ due to the markets they serve. For large orders, products are shipped directly to retailers from the firm's four manufacturing plants. All other orders are shipped from the firm's 15 warehouses to the many retailers that the firm serves.

Corporate headquarters are located in Chicago, next to one of the manufacturing plants. The other three manufacturing plants are found in Buffalo, Cincinnati, and Cleveland. Wherever a manufacturing plant is located, a warehouse is attached. The remaining 11 warehouses are geographically dispersed throughout the United States. The present employment level for the firm's entire operation is approximately 7000 employees.

The firm is organized around the major functions found in a typical manufacturing firm. These include marketing, research and development, engineering, manufacturing, purchasing, physical distribution, accounting and finance, and personnel. Also, the firm has recently installed a real-time management information system. Vice presidents for each of these major functions report to the executive vice president who reports to the president. In a similar manner, various corporate headquarter managers, plant managers, and warehouse managers report directly to their respective vice presidents.

The operations research group is located at corporate headquarters and is an integral part of the management information system staff (Figure 2-3). Specifically, the operations researchers are on the same level as the systems

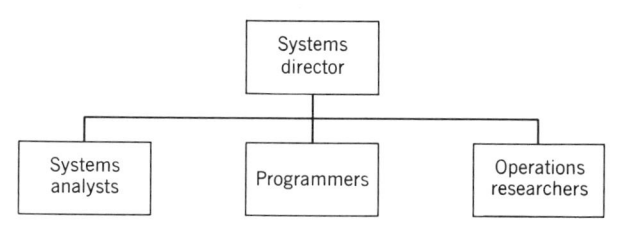

```
                    Systems
                    director
        ┌──────────────┼──────────────┐
    Systems       Programmers      Operations
    analysts                       researchers
```

Figure 2-3 The organization of the operations research group at corporate headquarters—the American Products Corporation. The systems director reports directly to vice president in charge of the management information system.

analysts and programmers. Also, they are located physically next to these two groups. This arrangement is beneficial since there is a constant interchange of ideas and information among these groups. The heads of the three groups report to the systems director who reports to the vice president in charge of the management information system. Although not shown in Figure 2-3, other directors in charge of daily data processing operations report directly to the same vice president.

This brief background on the American Products Corporation will be sufficient to visualize the applications of OR techniques throughout the coming chapters.

Summary

The planned approach to operations research was set forth in this chapter with emphasis on the model itself. Guidelines for success in operations research as well as its related problems were presented to give a balanced perspective. It should be obvious that OR studies can benefit every firm, the only difference being one of size and not of substance. Many OR projects raise more questions than they answer, which forms the basis for more detailed and penetrating inquiries into the operations of the firm. These investigations, if channeled properly, result in a greater insight regarding the inner workings of the firm. The ultimate result should have even more far-reaching benefits and improvements in terms of the firm's decision making process.

The task of the OR specialist is to provide management with appropriate quantitative methods necessary in decision making. He (she) must be prepared to discuss and defend his (her) conclusions based on the facts as given. In those cases where some of the important factors affecting business decisions are intangible or qualitative, he must be flexible enough to permit the output from his quantitative decision model to be modified by these factors. Quantitative methods of operations research are not aimed at replacing or reducing the manager's role in the decision. Rather, they are adding a new dimension to management's decision making process by improving the quality or correctness of the decision. Based on these facts, management must gradually become more of an applied science.

As more managers become capable of using computer output based on quantitative decision models, they will start asking for and demanding more solutions to present problems on this basis. This type of environment undoubtedly will be receptive to OR teams, who will move on to problems of even greater complexity than those of today. The marriage of management and operations research, then, will provide more effective control of firms where complexity is the norm rather than the exception.

Questions

1. What is the planned approach? How does it differ from the scientific method?
2. (a) What are the basic guidelines for success in operations research?
   (b) What are the basic problem areas of operations research?
3. How does one go about organizing for effective operations research? Explain.
4. What is the biggest contribution of operations research to the business world today? Explain.
5. Does operations research deal with all the problems faced by all levels of management? Explain.
6. Under what conditions would operations research have a difficult time in arriving at an optimum answer? Explain.
7. Operations research has been characterized as a "tool designed to increase the effectiveness of managerial decisions as an objective supplement to the subjective feelings of the decision maker." Explain what is meant by this statement.

Bibliography

R. L. Ackoff and R. Rivett, *A Manager's Guide to Operations Research*, New York: John Wiley & Sons, 1963.

R. L. Ackoff and M. W. Sasieni, *Fundamentals of Operations Research*, New York: John Wiley & Sons, 1968.

N. L. Enrick, *Management Operations Research*, New York: Holt, Rinehart and Winston, 1965.

J. H. Huysmans, *The Implementation of Operations Research*, New York: John Wiley & Sons, 1970.

D. W. Miller and M. K. Starr, *Executive Decisions and Operations Research*, Englewood Cliffs, N.J.: Prentice-Hall, 1969.

P. Rivett, *Principles of Model-Building, The Construction of Models for Decision Analysis*, New York: John Wiley & Sons, 1973.

C. H. Springer, R. E. Herlihy, and R. I. Beggs, *Advanced Methods and Models*, Homewood, Ill.: Richard D. Irwin, 1965.

2
Operations Research Models – Probability and Statistics

Chapter THREE
Decision Theory

Decision theory in business today plays an important role in helping managers make decisions. Since we live in a world where the course of future events cannot be predicted with absolute certainty, the best we can do is to reach approximate solutions based upon the likelihood of possible future events. We assign a certain value to probability, which can range from 0 to 1, zero being completely pessimistic and one being completely optimistic about the occurrence of a particular event under certain conditions. When individuals are involved in assigning a probability factor to a particular event, we have come to accept this assigned probability as being valid. Probability also can be based on historical data, the manager's feelings about an event, or some other basis. Thus the manager, having some knowledge about the possible outcomes of his many decisions, can reach better decisions in the long run by organizing his information and structuring it within the framework of probability theory.

In this chapter, probability theory under statistical independence and statistical dependence with particular emphasis on Bayes' theorem will be set forth with appropriate examples. The various criteria for solving business problems under uncertainty will be discussed. The utilization of probability and decision trees will help clarify all the possible outcomes of events based upon existing conditions. Even though probability can be useful in maximizing profits for a single undertaking, this chapter will stress probability on a continuing basis.

Probability Terms

Before discussing the six basic types of probability under statistical independence and dependence, the probability terms to be used throughout this chapter are explained. An understanding of these terms allows us to pursue a logical framework for probability models. The utilization of probability trees is also helpful for an understanding of the subject.

Subjective and Objective Probabilities

Upon examination of a business problem that can be solved at least in part by probability, the question arises: What kind of probabilities should be used? First, probabilities can be subjective or objective. Subjective probabilities are educated guesses, whereas objective probabilities are based upon historical data and common experience to support the assignment of probabilities. Frequently, historical data is not available, which means the decision maker must rely on his own estimation of the various possible outcomes. It should be recognized that one has to guess only in part for subjective probability since much is known from experience and intuition. Of the two approaches, objective probability is preferred to subjective probability. However, there may be a need to reconsider the distribution of probability factors. The past is not a complete predictor of the future. The objective probabilities may have to be tempered based upon the judgment and intuition of the decision maker. Thus in certain cases subjective and objective probabilities may have to be combined. The attendant circumstances must be surveyed to determine what type of probability should be employed within the problem.

An example of subjective probability deals with the purchase of a new seasonal item by a retail store. The outside salesman and the retailer, working together, can determine the optimum quantity to stock. The retailer, knowing the local market in depth, and the outside salesman, having been through this type of experience many times, will generally assign about the same probability of success for the various possible quantities to stock. Based upon agreement on these subjective probabilities, the salesman and retailer could determine the optimum level for this seasonal product. Methods for solving such problems will be found in this chapter and the next.

Consider the tossing of a fair coin (with a head on one side and a tail on the other). If it is tossed, both heads and tails are equally likely to occur. The probability of .5 that the coin will come up heads on any toss is called objective probability because it is empirically evident. Half the time in an infinite number of tosses the result will be heads, and half the time it will be tails. Translating this objective probability into probability terms, we have a .5 or 50 percent probability that heads will occur on any toss and a .5 or 50 percent probability that tails will occur on any toss. This is written as follows: $P(H) = .5$ and $P(T) = .5$ where their probabilities total 1.0.

Unconditional (Marginal) Probability

The probabilities associated with tossing a coin (or any comparable events) are called unconditional or marginal probabilities because the outcome of any toss is in no way conditioned or affected by the preceding toss. In effect, each toss of the coin stands on its own. For example, if we toss a fair coin five times and get tails on all five tosses, what is the probability of a head on the next toss? Since the coin is not biased, we know that any toss is not conditioned by a prior toss. We can assign a probability of .5 to heads and .5 to tails on the sixth toss or any other toss. It should be noted that the sum of these two unconditional probabilities is 1.0. This is important in probability theory since the probabilities of all possible outcomes for a given action must add up to 1.0 even though no two of the possible outcomes occur at the same time.

The probability of any given outcome for a given action must be between zero and one inclusively. The sum of all these probabilities must be one. If a biased coin is used where $P(H) = .9$ and the $P(T) = .1$, the sum of these probabilities still is 1.0. If we assign a probability of zero to an occurrence, we are stating that the occurrence will never take place. On the other hand, if we assign a probability of one to an occurrence, we are expressing wtih complete certainty that the event will take place. Most business problems have probabilities that range somewhere between zero and one. Any probability between 0 and 1 inclusive is written as $0 \leq P \leq 1$. This means that the probability of an outcome must be greater than or equal to 0 and less than or equal to 1.

Mutually Exclusive Events
Returning to the example of the fair coin, there are two possible outcomes, heads and tails. On any one toss, either heads or tails can come up, but not both at the same time. Events are said to be mutually exclusive if one and only one outcome can occur at a time. The important point in determining whether events are mutually exclusive is: Can two or more events occur at one time? If the answer to this question is yes, the events are not mutually exclusive.

The probabilities of events that are mutually exclusive can be added. Their total must sum to 1.0 since the list includes all possible outcomes. For example, the list of all the possible outcomes for two tosses of a coin is as follows:

Events	Probability
$H_1 H_2$	.25
$H_1 T_2$	.25
$T_1 H_2$	.25
$T_1 T_2$	.25
	1.00

These events add up to 1.0 since there are only four possible outcomes and each event (two tosses of a coin) is equally likely to occur. Mutually exclusive events are those where only one outcome can take place at a time and whose list of all possible outcomes totals 1.0.

Collectively Exhaustive Events
In the fair coin example, there are two possible outcomes—heads and tails. The list of these outcomes is collectively exhaustive since the results of any toss must be either heads or tails. To state it another way, a list which contains all of the possible outcomes for a given action is said to be collectively exhaustive. In the case of two tosses in a row, there are four possible outcomes and no others. The list of four outcomes is collectively exhaustive.

A list of events, then, may be not only mutually exclusive but also collectively exhaustive. The toss of a coin is mutually exclusive if only one outcome is possible at a time while the listing for a coin is collectively exhaustive since no other outcome is possible. Also, the sum of the probabilities must be one for mutually exclusive and collectively exhaustive events.

DECISION THEORY 59

Statistical Independence

Events in probability theory may be either statistically independent or dependent. If two events are independent, the occurrence of the one event does not affect the probability of the occurrence of the second event. Under statistical independence (as well as statistical dependence), there are three probability types: marginal, joint, and conditional.

Marginal Probabilities

The simplest of all probabilities is marginal probability under statistical independence. It is defined as the probability of the occurrence of an event. Each event stands alone and is in no way connected with the preceding or succeeding event(s). This is found, for example, in each toss of a coin no matter how many tosses may precede it and succeed it or what their respective outcomes may be. In effect, each toss of a coin is a statistically independent event and stands on its own.

The formula for marginal probability under statistical independence is

$$P(A) = P(A) \qquad \text{(Equation 3-1)}$$

This is read as: the probability of event A occurring is the probability of event A. In the fair coin example, the probability of getting heads (event A) equals .5 and the probability of tails (event A) equals .5. Using a biased coin, the $P(H) = .9$ and $P(T) = .1$ because the outcome of each toss is completely unrelated to the outcomes of other tosses. It does not matter whether the coin is fair or biased in order to have marginal probability under statistical independence.

Joint Probabilities

When two or more events are independent, the probability of these events occurring together or in succession is equal to the product of the probabilities of the individual events. Stated mathematically, the equation for joint probability is

$$P(AB) = P(A) \times P(B) \qquad \text{(Equation 3-2)}$$

where

$P(A)$ = probability of event A occurring
$P(B)$ = probability of event B occurring
$P(AB)$ = probability of events A and B occurring together or in succession

Referring again to our fair coin, the probability of heads in two successive tosses is the probability of heads on the first toss (.5) times the probability of heads on the second toss (.5). Using Equation 3-2, the probability of two heads in a row is

$$P(H_1 H_2) = P(H_1) \times P(H_2) \quad \text{or} \quad P(HH) = .5 \times .5 = .25$$

Using the same equation, the probability of three heads in three successive tosses is

$$P(H_1H_2H_3) = .5 \times .5 \times .5 = .125$$

In like manner, the probability of four heads on four successive tosses is

$$P(H_1H_2H_3H_4) = .5 \times .5 \times .5 \times .5 = .0625$$

If an unfair coin is used, where $P(H) = .9$ and $P(T) = .1$, the probability of four heads on four successive tosses is

$$P(H_1H_2H_3H_4) = .9 \times .9 \times .9 \times .9 = .6561$$

while the probability of getting four tails on four successive tosses is

$$P(T_1T_2T_3T_4) = .1 \times .1 \times .1 \times .1 = .0001$$

From the foregoing illustration, it should be apparent that joint probability deals with mutually exclusive events and collectively exhaustive events. The construction of a probability tree, showing all possible outcomes for three tosses of a fair coin, is shown in Figure 3-1. The starting point for the probability tree is the first toss. The first toss is connected to the second toss and the third toss is linked in a similar manner. Notice that the sum of all the possible outcomes for each toss is one, which is a requisite for mutually exclusive and collectively exhaustive events. It should be noted that the same type of probability tree can be constructed for an unfair coin. The resulting probability tree would be like the one in Figure 3-1, except that the probability factors and circled figures would be changed.

Based upon the outcomes of a probability tree, a tabular list of outcomes can be constructed as shown in Table 3-1. This table shows the results for a fair coin where $P(H) = .5$ and $P(T) = .5$ and a biased coin where

TABLE 3-1
List of All Possible Outcomes for Three Tosses of a Fair Coin and a Biased Coin

	First Toss			Second Toss			Third Toss	
	Probability			Probability			Probability	
Possible Outcomes	Fair Coin	Biased Coin	Possible Outcomes	Fair Coin	Biased Coin	Possible Outcomes	Fair Coin	Biased Coin
H_1	.5	.9	H_1H_2	.25	.81	$H_1H_2H_3$	.125	.729
T_1	.5	.1	H_1T_2	.25	.09	$H_1H_2T_3$	.125	.081
	1.0	1.0	T_1H_2	.25	.09	$H_1T_2H_3$	.125	.081
			T_1T_2	.25	.01	$H_1T_2T_3$	.125	.009
				1.00	1.00	$T_1H_2H_3$	.125	.081
						$T_1H_2T_3$	.125	.009
						$T_1T_2H_3$	.125	.009
						$T_1T_2T_3$	.125	.001
							1.000	1.000

DECISION THEORY 61

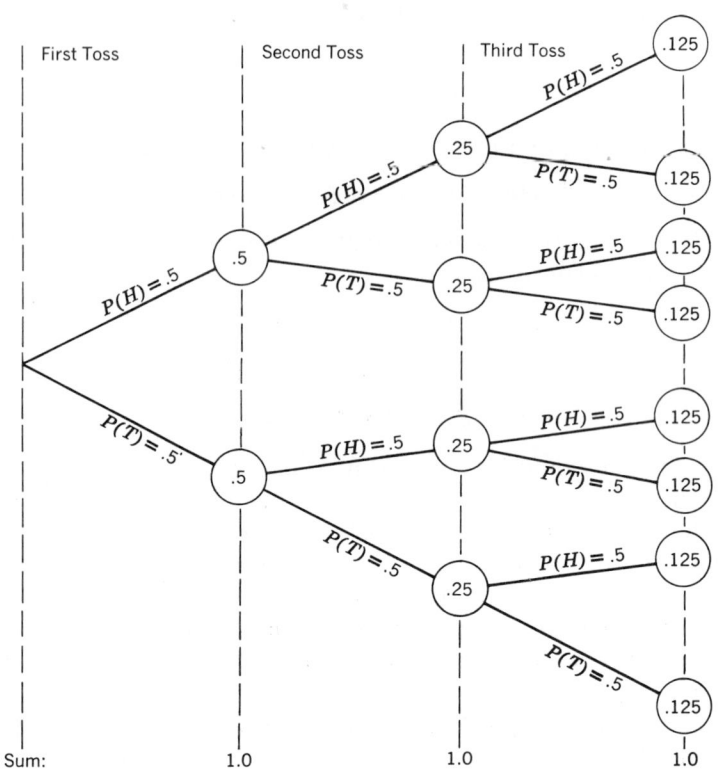

Figure 3-1 Probability tree for three tosses of a fair coin.

$P(H)=.9$ and $P(T)=.1$. The values in Table 3-1 are for three tosses of a coin, which means it is possible to get three heads or three tails in a row initially. However, over a long series of tosses, results will reflect the equal chance or bias condition.

Conditional Probabilities

Having considered marginal and joint probabilities, the remaining probability under statistical independence is conditional probability. Conditional probability is written $P(A|B)$: the probability of event A, given that event B has occurred. Thus, conditional probability is given as $P(A|B)=P(A)$ where the term to the right of the equal sign is the same as Equation 3-1. Its meaning can be clarified by recalling that independent events are those whose probabilities are in no way affected by the occurrence of any other event—preceding, following, or occurring at the same time.

To illustrate the meaning of conditional probability, a question can be raised: What is the probability that the second toss of a fair coin will be heads, given that heads resulted from the initial toss? This can be written as: $P(H_2|H_1)$. It should be remembered that the result of the initial toss has no effect on the result of the second toss since the events are independent of one another. The probability of heads on the second toss is .5 for this fair coin. Thus we can say that $P(H_2|H_1)=P(H)=.5$.

62 OPERATIONS RESEARCH MODELS—PROBABILITY AND STATISTICS

Statistical Dependence

Statistical dependence is present if the probability of some event is affected by or dependent upon the happening of some other event. Dependence adds a new dimension to probability theory from that set forth in the previous sections. The types of probabilities associated with dependence are the same as for independence.

Marginal Probabilities

The marginal probability of a statistically dependent event is the same as that for a statistically independent event or $P(A)$ in Equation 3-1. Why is this so? "Marginal" means one and only one probability is considered. Even if two dependent events are involved, marginal probability under statistical dependence applies to only one of them by definition.

In order to illustrate the idea of dependence, in place of the fair coin, three urns containing colored balls will be used. The urns which contain the balls are as follows:

Urn 1	3 red and 6 white
Urn 2	5 blue and 4 green
Urn 3	7 yellow and 2 orange

If a red ball is drawn from urn 1, we draw a ball from urn 2. If a white ball is drawn from urn 1, we draw a ball from urn 3. This arrangement can be diagrammed as follows:

```
                    | 3 Red   |
                    | 6 White |   Urn 1

          If Red↓              ↓If White

 Urn 2   | 5 Blue  |           | 7 Yellow |   Urn 3
         | 4 Green |           | 2 Orange |
```

It is logical to ask whether the probability of drawing a blue ball is affected by the color of the ball we draw from urn 1. It certainly is, since only urn 2 has blue balls. The only way to draw from urn 2 is to draw initially one of the red balls from urn 1. In effect, the two events—the drawing from urn 1 and the drawing from urn 2—are statistically dependent.

When applying marginal probability under statistical dependence to the above example, the probability of drawing a red ball $P(R)$ from urn 1 is three red balls out of nine balls or a .333 probability. Similarly, the probability of drawing a white ball $P(W)$ from urn 1 is .667 probability. The values for this first draw are shown in Figure 3-2. Thus, Equation 3-1 or $P(A)$ is used.

Conditional Probabilities

The conditional probability of a statistically dependent event is more com-

DECISION THEORY 63

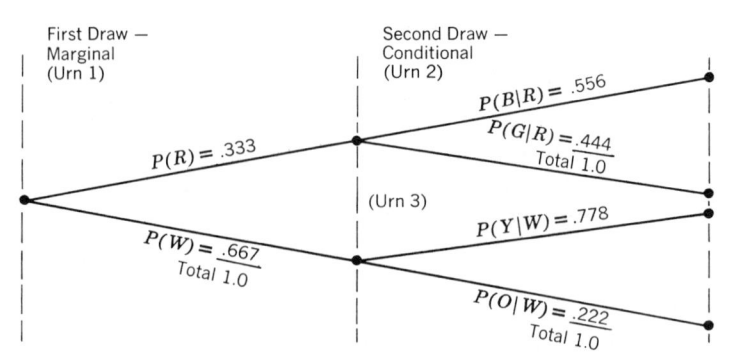

```
First Draw —                Second Draw —
Marginal                    Conditional
(Urn 1)                     (Urn 2)
                                         P(B|R) = .556
                                         P(G|R) = .444
            P(R) = .333                  Total 1.0

                            (Urn 3)
                                         P(Y|W) = .778
            P(W) = .667
            Total 1.0
                                         P(O|W) = .222
                                         Total 1.0
```

Figure 3-2 Probability tree for first draw from urn 1 and second draw from urns 2 and 3.

plex than that of a statistically independent event. The formula for conditional probability (basically Bayes' formula) is

$$P(A|B) = \frac{P(AB)}{P(B)}$$ (Equation 3-3)

The equation is read: the probability of event A, given event B has occurred, is the probability of events A and B occurring together or in succession divided by the probability of event B. Conditional probability can be understood by continuing the illustration of the three urns and the colored balls.

If someone draws a ball from urn 1 and it is red, what is the probability of drawing a blue ball from urn 2? Stating the problem in terms of probability, what is the conditional probability that the second ball is blue, given that the first ball is red or $P(B|R)$? The question can be expressed in a form of a probability tree as in Figure 3-2. From the original statement of the data, we know there are three red and six white balls in the first urn and five blue and four green balls in the second urn. The problem, first, is to find the simple probabilities of the red and white balls in the first urn. This can be done by dividing the number of balls in each category by the total number of balls in urn 1. This is done as follows:

$$P(R) = 3/9 = .333$$
$$P(W) = 6/9 = .667$$
$$\overline{1.000}$$

Of the nine balls in urn 1, .333 are red and .667 are white, as shown in Figure 3-2. Similarly, calculating the probability of a blue ball in urn 2, given that the first ball in urn 1 is red, as in Figure 3-2, the total of blue balls (five) is divided by the total of all the balls (nine) in urn 2. The $P(B|R)$ is .556 and $P(G|R)$ is .444. The same type of calculation is made for urn 3 where $P(Y|W)$ is .778 and $P(O|W)$ is .222.

We can assure ourselves that these events are dependent in Figure 3-2 by observing that the color of the ball from urn 1 determines the color of the ball from the other two urns. Since color of urn 1 directly affects the color for urn 2 or urn 3, these two events are said to be dependent. Before illustrating Equation 3-3 for conditional probability under statistical dependence in our example, we shall first examine joint probability under statistical dependence, which is actually a restatement of Equation 3-3.

Joint Probabilities

Having solved for conditional probability under conditions of dependence, or $P(A|B) = P(AB)/P(B)$, we can solve this equation for $P(AB)$. This can be done by cross-multiplication, resulting in the equation for joint probability under statistical dependence:

$$P(AB) = P(A|B) \times P(B) \qquad \text{(Equation 3-4)}$$

The equation reads: the joint probability of events A and B equals the probability of event A, given that event B has occurred, times the probability of event B.

Returning to our example, the question can now be asked, what is the probability of drawing one red ball and one blue ball in a row? This is joint probability under statistical dependence which can be solved by using Equation 3-4 as follows:

$$P(BR) = P(B|R) \times P(R)$$
$$= .556 \times .333$$
$$= .185$$

Referring to the probability tree in Figure 3-2, the joint probabilities at the end of the second draw, after initially drawing from urn 1, are the following:

Event	Marginal P(B)	×	Conditional P(A|B)	=	Joint P(AB)
BR	$P(R) = .333$		$P(B\|R) = .556$		$P(BR) = .185$
GR	$P(R) = .333$		$P(G\|R) = .444$		$P(GR) = .148$
YW	$P(W) = .667$		$P(Y\|W) = .778$		$P(YW) = .519$
OW	$P(W) = .667$		$P(O\|W) = .222$		$P(OW) = .148$
					1.000

Notice the sum of the joint probabilities is one since the events are mutually exclusive and collectively exhaustive. The four figures above normally would be shown at the end of the four legs in the probability tree in Figure 3-2 and would be termed joint probability. The formula for joint probability is marginal probability times conditional probability, all of which are under dependence.

Based upon the preceding data, a joint probability table can be constructed as in Table 3-2. The intersections of the rows and columns are joint probabilities. The column to the extreme right gives the marginal probabilities of the outcome for the first draw while the bottom row gives the marginal probabilities of the outcomes of the second draw. Basically, Table 3-2 summarizes the data for our example of the three urns and the colored balls.

DECISION THEORY   65

TABLE 3-2
Joint Probability Table for Three Urns

First Draw ↓	Second Draw →	B or Y	G or O	Marginal Probability of Outcome on First Draw
R		P(BR) .185	P(GR) .148	.333
W		P(YW) .519	P(OW) .148	.667
Marginal Probability of Outcome on Second Draw		.704	.296	1.000

Having developed data for marginal, conditional, and joint probabilities under statistical dependence in our illustration, we can return to demonstrating that $P(B|R) = .556$ and $P(G|R) = .444$. The lack of values for joint probabilities necessitated this delay. Using Equation 3-3, the calculations are

$$P(B|R) = \frac{P(BR)}{P(R)} = \frac{.185}{.333} = .556$$

$$P(G|R) = \frac{P(GR)}{P(R)} = \frac{.148}{.333} = .444$$
$$\overline{1.000}$$

Comparable calculations for $P(Y|W)$ and $P(O|W)$ are

$$P(Y|W) = \frac{P(YW)}{P(W)} = \frac{.519}{.667} = .778$$

$$P(O|W) = \frac{P(OW)}{P(W)} = \frac{.148}{.667} = .222$$
$$\overline{1.000}$$

Relationship between Independence and Dependence

The formulas developed for probability under statistical independence and dependence in the preceding sections are summarized in Table 3-3. In this

TABLE 3-3
Formulas Under Statistical Independence and Dependence

Probability Type	Symbol	Formula Under Statistical Independence	Formula Under Statistical Dependence
Marginal	$P(A)$	$P(A)$ (Equation 3-1)	$P(A)$ (Equation 3-1)
Joint	$P(AB)$	$P(A) \times P(B)$ (Equation 3-2)	$P(A|B) \times P(B)$ (Equation 3-4)
Conditional	$P(A|B)$	$P(A)$ (Equation 3-1)	$P(AB)/P(B)$ (Equation 3-3)

section, relationships between independence and dependence are examined. First, mathematical relationships are explored for conditional probability under statistical dependence, leading to the development of Bayes' theorem. Next, a sample business problem which initially is statistically independent become dependent when the original investment is changed.

Mathematical Relationships
The conditional probability under statistical dependence—Equation 3-3—is $P(A|B) = P(AB)/P(B)$. Under independence, Equation 3-2 for joint probability is $P(AB) = P(A) \times P(B)$. By substituting $P(A) \times P(B)$ for $P(AB)$ in Equation 3-3, the revised equation for conditional probability is

$$P(A|B) = \frac{P(A) \times P(B)}{P(B)} \qquad \text{(Equation 3-5)}$$

Since $P(B)$ is in both the numerator and denominator on the right side of the equation and cancels out, then $P(A|B)$ equals $P(A)$. The resulting equation is known as the mathematical definition of statistical independence.

This mathematical manipulation can be illustrated by the following example. What is the probability of heads on the third toss of a fair coin, given that tails has occurred on the first two tosses. Using Equation 3-3 for conditional probability under dependence, the following equation results:

$$P(H_3|T_1T_2) = \frac{P(H_3) \times P(T_1) \times P(T_2)}{P(T_1) \times P(T_2)} = \frac{.5 \times .5 \times .5}{.5 \times .5} = .5$$

Moreover, the problem can be written using Equation 3-5,

$$P(H_3|T_1T_2) = \frac{P(H_3) \times P(T_1) \times P(T_2)}{P(T_1) \times P(T_2)} = \frac{.5 \times .5 \times .5}{.5 \times .5} = .5$$

Notice that when using Equations 3-3 and 3-5 the terms are the same. By expanding either equation, we have shown that $P(H_3|T_1T_2) = P(H_3)$.

Bayes' theorem, which is

$$P(A_i|B) = \frac{P(A_i) \times P(B|A_i)}{P(A_1) \times P(B|A_1) + \cdots + P(A_m) \times P(B|A_m)} \text{(Equation 3-6)}$$

is derived initially by using Equation 3-3 (conditional probability under statistical dependence). Equation 3-3 is then restated in terms of Equation 3-4 (revised for convenience) as follows:

$$P(A|B) = \frac{P(AB)}{P(B)} \qquad \text{(Equation 3-3)}$$

$$P(A_iB) = P(B) \times P(A_i|B) \qquad \text{(Equation 3-4)}$$

where A_i is the unknown probability or similarly

$$P(A_iB) = P(A_i) \times P(B|A_i)$$

Since the left sides of these last two equations are the same, the right sides must equal each other. Thus the new equation is

$$P(B) \times P(A_i|B) = P(A_i) \times P(B|A_i)$$

DECISION THEORY 67

Dividing both sides by $P(B)$, the resulting equation is

$$P(A_i|B) = \frac{P(A_i) \times P(B|A_i)}{P(B)}$$

In the foregoing equation, $P(B)$ can be written as $P(A_1B) + \cdots + P(A_mB)$ since these two (or more) probabilities are mutually exclusive events. Also, it should be pointed out that $P(A_1B) + \cdots + P(A_mB)$ are collectively exhaustive events and, therefore, must total 1.0. Thus, the new equation is

$$P(A_i|B) = \frac{P(A_i) \times P(B|A_i)}{P(A_1B) + \cdots + P(A_mB)}$$

Having seen that $P(A_iB) = P(A_i) \times P(B|A_i)$ or $P(A_1B) = P(A_1) \times P(B|A_1)$, then, we can write $P(A_mB) = P(A_m) \times P(B|A_m)$. Substituting these new expressions for $P(A_1B)$ and $P(A_mB)$ in the above equation, the resulting equation is Bayes' theorem:

$$P(A_i|B) = \frac{P(A_i) \times P(B|A_i)}{P(A_1) \times P(B|A_1) + \cdots + P(A_m) \times P(B|A_m)}$$

(Equation 3-6)

It should be remembered that we wish to know the probability of event A_i (one possible outcome), given that event B has occurred. The other possible mutually exclusive outcomes are $A_1, A_2, \ldots, A_{i-1}, A_{i+1}, \ldots, A_m$.

Probability Problem

Relationships between probability formulas under statistical independence and dependence can be shown within a business problem where the original investment value is altered. For example, consider a firm which has excess cash funds of $50,000 only for investing in two projects during this month and next month. The firm can invest in the first project which is equally likely to result in a profit of $7000 or a loss of $3000 on an investment of $40,000. Assuming that the investment plus the profit or minus the loss is available one month hence, the second project is equally likely to result in a profit of $8000 or a loss of $3500 within one month on an investment of $38,500. It is further assumed in the problem that the firm is offered the opportunity of investing in projects of this kind periodically. Also, the return on excess cash funds is to be ignored within the problem.

Using the information set forth above, what should the firm do? Should it invest in the first project only, the second project only, both projects, or do nothing (the return is negative, zero, or below the established rate of return for the firm)? In addition, suppose that the excess cash funds available are $40,000 and not $50,000 as initially, what should the firm do?

To answer the first question above, a logical starting point is determining if sufficient funds will be available to undertake the second project since there are more than ample funds for undertaking the first project. If there is a profit on the first project, the firm should have $57,000 ($50,000 cash funds + $7000 profit) available for the second project. If there is a loss,

$47,000 ($50,000 cash funds – $3000 loss) will be available to undertake the second project. In both cases, there is sufficient capital to undertake the second investment of $38,500. Thus, we can say that the first and second projects are statistically independent, that is, whether we gain or lose on the first project, there is sufficient capital to undertake the second project.

Based on the original investment, the calculations for *expected payoff* or *expected profits*—profits that can be expected over a series of the same investment opportunities—are set forth in Table 3-4. Although all values are calculated under statistical independence, marginal probability (Equation 3-1) is employed for the first project only and the second project only while joint probability is utilized for the combined projects. It should be noted that the combined projects could have been solved by marginal probability under statistical independence, that is, the first project (expected profit of $2,000) and the second project (expected profit of $2250) could be summed for the highest expected profit of $4250.

Having solved the initial investment problem, we can now solve for the condition where only $40,000 of excess cash funds is available initially. This amount is just equal to the first investment requirement. If the firm experiences a gain of $7000 on the first project, there is sufficient money available for the second project—$47,000 ($40,000 investment + $7000 profit) is greater than the $38,500 required for the second project. On the other hand, if the firm loses on the first project, there is insufficient capital for the second project—$37,000 ($40,000 investment – $3000 loss) is less than $38,500. Thus, statistical dependence has been determined within the problem.

Calculated values in the restatement of the problem are given in Table 3-5. The calculations and the type of probability for both projects alone remain the same. However, the value for the combined projects are differ-

TABLE 3-4
Expected Profits Based On Original Investment of $50,000

First Project Only (marginal probability under statistical independence)		Combined Projects (joint probability under statistical independence)	
$ 7000 × .5	= $3500	$7000 + $8000 =	
– 3000 × .5	= –1500	$15,000 × .25	= $3750
1.0		$7000 + (– $3500) =	
Total expected profits	$2000	$3500 × .25	= 875
		– $3000 + $8000 =	
Second Project Only		$5000 × .25	= 1250
(marginal probability under statistical independence)		– $3000 + (– $3500) =	
$ 8000 × .5	= $4000	– $6500 × $\frac{.25}{1.0}$	= –1625
– 3500 × $\frac{.5}{1.0}$	= –1750	Total expected profits	$4250
Total expected profits	$2250		

TABLE 3-5
Expected Profits Based On Revised Investment of $40,000

First Project Only (marginal probability under statistical independence)			Combined Projects (joint probability under statistical dependence)		
$ 7000 × .5	=	$3500	$7000 + $8000 = $15,000 × .25	=	$3750
−3000 × $\frac{.5}{1.0}$	=	−1500	$7000 + (−$3500) = $3500 × .25	=	875
Total expected profits		$2000	−$3000[a] × $\frac{.50}{1.0}$	=	−1500
Second Project Only (marginal probability under statistical independence)			Total expected profits		$3125
$ 8000 × .5	=	$4000			
−3500 × $\frac{.5}{1.0}$	=	−1750			
Total expected profits		$2250			

[a] Undertaking the second project is impossible.

ent as well as the type of probability. As illustrated, the highest expected profit is $3125 based on joint probability under statistical dependence.

Revision of Probabilities

Prior estimates of probabilities can be revised as more knowledge is gained about the event(s). These altered probabilities are called revised probabilities and can be of great help in decision making under uncertainty. For example, consider a manufacturer who has several semi-automatic machines in his plant which produce very low cost parts. The firm has found from past experience that if the machine is properly set up, it will produce 90 percent acceptable parts, whereas if it is incorrectly set up, it will produce 30 percent acceptable parts. The firm has also learned from previous experience that 75 percent of the setups have been correctly made. Given the first part is good on the first machine, what is the revised probability that the setup has been correctly made?

The first step in answering the question for this first semi-automatic machine is to prepare a table that contains the given information (Table 3-6). An examination of Table 3-6 reveals that the sum of the probabilities for correct and incorrect setups is 1.0 since two types of setups constitute a mutually exclusive and collectively exhaustive list. However, the sum of figures .9 and .3 does not equal 1.0 since they represent conditional probabilities of getting one good part, given a correct setup or an incorrect setup, respectively. The last column is the joint probability of one good part and a correct setup occurring together, or .75 × .9 = .675. Likewise, the joint probability of one good part and incorrect setup occurring together is .075 or

70   OPERATIONS RESEARCH MODELS—PROBABILITY AND STATISTICS

TABLE 3-6
Probability Table Given One Good Part for the Event

Event	P(B) Marginal P (event)		P(A|B) Conditional P (1 good part|event)		P(AB) Joint P (1 good part, event)
Correct setup	.75	×	.90	=	.675
Incorrect setup	.25	×	.30	=	.075
	1.00				.750

$.25 \times .3$. The total of these joint probabilities, .75, is the marginal probability (see previous section—Bayes' theorem where joint probabilities were totaled for marginal probability) of getting one good part. To determine the revised probability that the setup has been correctly performed, the formula for conditional probability under statistical dependence is used as follows:

$$P(A|B) = \frac{P(AB)}{P(B)} \qquad \text{(Equation 3-3)}$$

$$P(\text{correct setup}|1 \text{ good part}) = \frac{P(\text{correct setup, 1 good part})}{P(1 \text{ good part})}$$

$$= \frac{.675}{.75} = .9$$

The probability of a correct setup, given one good part, is .9, which is compared to the previous experience of .75. Based upon this comparison, the operator should continue to operate the machine. However, due to the low value of each item, two more parts might then be run. Suppose the next two parts were also found to be good. What is the revised probability that the setup has been correctly made? The calculated values are found in Table 3-7.

TABLE 3-7
Probability Table Given Three Good Parts for the Event

Event	P(B) Marginal P(event)	P(A|B) Conditional P(3 good parts|event)	P(AB) Joint P(3 good parts, event)
Correct setup	.75	.9×.9×.9 = .729	.5468
Incorrect setup	.25	.3.×3.×3 = .027	.0068
	1.00		.5536

Now that we have computed the necessary probabilities, we can again revert to Equation 3-3 for an answer. Thus the calculations are

$$P(\text{correct setup}|3 \text{ good parts}) = \frac{P(\text{correct setup, 3 good parts})}{P(3 \text{ good parts})}$$

$$= \frac{.5468}{.5536} = .988$$

TABLE 3-8
Probability Table Given One Bad Part for the Event

Event	P(B) Marginal P(event)	P(A|B) Conditional P(1 bad part|event)	P(AB) Joint P(1 bad part, event)
Correct setup	.75	.1 (1.0 − .9)	.075
Incorrect setup	.25	.7 (1.0 − .3)	.175
	1.00		.250

The revised probability that the machine is correctly set up is 98.8 percent. In effect, we have revised our original probability (.75) of a correct setup to a much higher figure (.988) based upon three good parts produced initially.

Suppose in this problem, instead of getting one good part initially, we got one bad part. What is the probability that the machine is set up correctly? Data in Table 3-6 would have to be revised as shown in Table 3-8. The conditional probabilities for one bad part would be the complement of conditional probabilities for one good part. These are entered in Table 3-8 as well as new figures for the joint probabilities. Using the general formula $P(A|B) = P(AB)/P(B)$, the calculations are

$$P(\text{correct setup} | 1 \text{ bad part}) = \frac{P(\text{correct setup}, 1 \text{ bad part})}{P(1 \text{ bad part})}$$

$$= \frac{.075}{.250} = .3$$

The probability that the machine is correctly set up is .3 versus .75. This revised probability indicates that the machine is not correctly set up and adjustment is deemed necessary.

In the illustration, it would have been possible to have combinations of acceptable and unacceptable parts. Upon running the first few parts, the first five machine parts were tested to be: bad, good, bad, good, and good. Based upon these operating conditions, should the operator continue? The probabilities for these conditions appear in Table 3-9. The revised proba-

TABLE 3-9
Probability Table Given Three Good and Two Bad Parts for the Event

Event	P(B) Marginal P(event)	P(A|B) Conditional P(GP|event)	P(BP|event)	P(3GP,2BP|event)	P(AB) Joint P(3GP,2BP,event)
Correct setup	.75	.9	.1	.1×.9×.1×.9×.9 = .00729	.0054675
Incorrect setup	.25	.3	.7	.7×.3×.7×.3×.3 = .01323	.0033075
	1.00				.0087750

bility that the machine is correctly set up again utilizes the formula for conditional probability under dependence. The calculations are

$P(\text{correct setup}|BP, GP, BP, GP, GP)$

$= \dfrac{P(\text{correct setup}, BP, GP, BP, GP, GP)}{P(BP, GP, BP, GP, GP)}$

$= \dfrac{.0054675}{.0087750}$

$= .623$ (do not continue manufacturing, but check machine setup)

The origin of the preceding examples of revised probabilities goes back to Thomas Bayes in the eighteenth century. The basic formula for conditional probability under statistical dependence is attributed to him and is the starting point for his more elaborate theorem (given in a preceding section). Basically, his theorem states how probabilities, or opinions about how likely an event is to occur, ought to be appraised in the light of new information. In effect, Bayes and decision theorists recognize that while man can rationally reach conclusions different from an original set of circumstances, he tends to cling stubbornly to the past even if contradicted by subsequent evidence.

Selection of Best Criterion

With this brief background on some of the essentials of probability theory, we are now in a position to discuss the selection of a best decision criterion that centers on the utilization of probability factors. Depending on how much we know about the states of nature or the business environment, we can refer to decision making under

1. Certainty.
2. Risk.
3. Uncertainty.
4. Competitive conditions.

Even though four decision criteria have important distinctions in their decision making processes, they all utilize a payoff matrix. A matrix is a two-dimensional array of figures arranged in rows and columns where each row stands for an available strategy while each column represents the state of nature. The entry at the intersection of each row and column is the payoff or the measure of the utility of the specific outcome that occurs for a particular strategy and a given state of nature. In essence, the payoff matrix contains all of the possible outcomes in a business problem. The problem is to determine which strategy is best in light of the existing or possible states of nature.

Decision Criterion under Certainty
Decision making under certainty occurs when the decision maker has avail-

able to him the state of nature that will occur with complete certainty, that is, a probability of 1.0 can be assigned to a specific state of nature. In a payoff matrix, there is only one column that applies. The strategy (row) which has the largest payoff should be selected since there is no logical reason for doing otherwise. For example, consider the following payoff matrix, which has the profits shown from undertaking a certain project. The decision maker, knowing with certainty that N_2 state of nature (N_2 might be

		States of Nature		
		N_1	N_2	N_3
	S_1	$22,000	$15,000	$ 8,000
Strategies	S_2	25,000	17,000	10,000
	S_3	28,000	19,000	11,000

a period of no change in GNP while N_1 is a period of 2-5% increase in GNP and N_3 is a period of 2-5% decrease in GNP) will occur, will select strategy S_3 since it offers the highest return. The decision criterion for certainty is to select that strategy which has the largest payoff based upon a given state of nature.

In some cases, the payoff matrix cannot be written down since the number of strategies is enormous. This can best be illustrated by an example in a manufacturing plant where there are several machines of differing designs and for different purposes. Each machine requires various amounts of total time for each customer contract. The resulting cost difference makes one machine suited for a particular contract. To set forth all possible rows and columns would not be economically feasible. However, this problem may be solvable by other operations research methods.

Decision Criterion under Risk

Decision making under risk refers to the condition in which there are a number of states of nature, and the decision maker knows the probability of occurrence for each of these states of nature. In certain business problems, the probabilities of the respective states of nature are known since they are based upon past experience or objective probabilities. An inventory decision problem for optimum stocking of machinery replacement parts is an example of decision making under risk since historical data on parts replaced can be compiled for a certain period of time. Another example is life insurance where insurance rates are based on life expectancy factors. A common example is a food processor which grows its own crops. Based on the firm's past experience with planting three types of crops in a particular area of the country, the following payoff matrix has resulted over the past years for the three states of nature (N_1 = good weather, N_2 = variable weather, and N_3 = bad weather):

This problem leads to the question: What strategy is best? The logical decision maker, as in the case for decision making under certainty, will

		States of Nature		
		N_1	N_2	N_3
Probability		.25	.50	.25
Strategies	S_1	$40,000	$60,000	$10,000
	S_2	50,000	40,000	15,000
	S_3	60,000	20,000	12,000

select that strategy which has the largest payoff. The equations for computing expected payoffs for the strategies (ES) are as follows:

$$ES_1 = P_{11}p_1 + P_{12}p_2 + \cdots + P_{1j}p_j$$
$$ES_2 = P_{21}p_1 + P_{22}p_2 + \cdots + P_{2j}p_j$$
$$\cdots\cdots\cdots\cdots$$
$$ES_i = P_{i1}p_1 + P_{i2}p_2 + \cdots + P_{ij}p_j$$

(Equation 3-7)

where
$$p_1 + p_2 + p_3 + \cdots + p_j = 1$$

In the first equation, the notation for payoff P_{11} stands for the first row and first column, the second P_{12} stands for the first row and second column, and so forth, while $p_1, p_2, \ldots, p_j$ are the associated probabilities. Using past or objective probabilities of .25, .50, and .25 for N_1, N_2, and N_3 states of nature, respectively, in Equation 3-7, we can calculate the expected payoff for each of the three strategies ($i = 1, 2,$ and 3):

$$ES_1 = \$40,000\,(.25) + \$60,000\,(.50) + \$10,000\,(.25) = \$42,500$$
$$ES_2 = \$50,000\,(.25) + \$40,000\,(.50) + \$15,000\,(.25) = \$36,250$$
$$ES_3 = \$60,000\,(.25) + \$20,000\,(.50) + \$12,000\,(.25) = \$28,000$$

Since the expected payoff is greatest for the first strategy, that is the strategy to select.

Suppose the probabilities in our problem are different; say they are .50, .25, and .25, respectively, for the three states of nature. The new expected payoffs would then be:

$$ES_1 = \$40,000\,(.50) + \$60,000\,(.25) + \$10,000\,(.25) = \$37,500$$
$$ES_2 = \$50,000\,(.50) + \$40,000\,(.25) + \$15,000\,(.25) = \$38,750$$
$$ES_3 = \$60,000\,(.50) + \$20,000\,(.25) + \$12,000\,(.25) = \$38,000$$

The largest expected payoff is the second strategy and not the first strategy. It should be obvious by now that revised probabilities for the various states of nature, particularly a very high probability factor for N_1, would result in selecting the third strategy. Thus the critical factors are the probabilities assigned within the problem.

In revising the payoff matrix of the preceding problem, the payoffs for the strategies remain the same except that there is one change in the $S_1 - N_3$ payoff from $10,000 to zero. The firm, if it selects the first strategy and has bad weather, does not have any payoff for this condition. However, if the firm selects strategy two or three, it never risks having a zero return. So this question arises: Should a decision maker forgo a small amount of expected payoff in order to avoid the possibility of no return at all? On the surface, this appears to be a valid objection to the rule stated earlier that the strategies with the largest expected payoff should be selected. A logical decision maker might reject the first strategy since his utility for dollars cannot be measured by the dollar amounts. In essence, the payoffs are incorrect from his viewpoint. Nevertheless, if payoffs are to be measured in terms of the decision maker's utility or satisfaction, he has no other rational decision criterion than to select that strategy with the highest expected payoff.

Decision Criteria under Uncertainty

The third type of decision criteria deals with decision making under uncertainty. This means that the probabilities of occurrence for the various states of nature are not known. Business problems of this type arise where there is no past experience for determining the probabilities of occurrence for the various states of nature. Problems associated with a new product, increasing plant capacity, and floating a new stock issue are examples of decision making under uncertainty. The approach to this type of decision making is much more complex than with decision making under certainty and risk.

The four basic approaches to decision making under uncertainty can best be illustrated by the following example. A firm is contemplating an introduction of a revolutionary new product with all new packaging to replace an existing product at a much higher price (S_1), or a moderate change in the ingredients of the existing product with new packaging at a small increase in price (S_2), or a small change in the ingredients of the existing product and the only change in packaging is to include the word "new" with a negligible increase in price (S_3). The three possible states of nature are: expansion of the economy (N_1), no expansion or contraction of the economy (N_2), and contraction of the economy (N_3). The market research department has calculated the expected payoffs in terms of yearly net profits before federal income taxes to be as follows:

		States of Nature		
		N_1	N_2	N_3
Strategies	S_1	$500,000	$100,000	($ 50,000)
	S_2	300,000	250,000	0
	S_3	100,000	100,000	100,000

Based upon this data, there is one basic difference between this case and the previous example for decision making under risk. There are no probability factors for the various states of nature. The decision maker has no way to calculate an expected payoff for the three strategies. In theory, then, there is no best criterion for selecting a strategy for the firm. Instead of one criterion, there are several different criteria. Each of these criteria has its own rationale to justify its utilization. The choice of a specific criterion is determined by the size of the firm, the firm's objectives and policies, the feelings of a decision maker, or some other logical basis. As one might suspect, varying conditions can affect the selection of different strategies. This is somewhat analogous to the situation with changing probability factors for decision making under risk. Four criteria for decision making under certainty are discussed below within this framework.

The Hurwicz Decision Criterion. The Hurwicz decision criterion is one of optimism based upon the idea that we do get some favorable or lucky breaks. Since nature can be good to us, the decision maker should select that state of nature which will yield him the highest payoff for the strategy selected. The procedure in our example is to look at the various payoffs for each strategy and select the highest amount for each strategy. The figures would be as follows:

Strategy	Largest Payoff
1	$500,000
2	300,000
3	100,000

Since the firm feels that nature will be favorable to it, the largest payoff of $500,000 would be chosen. This payoff is often referred to as a *maximax* (maximum maximum), which is the largest of the maxima for each strategy.

Hurwicz did not suggest that the decision maker be completely or 100 percent optimistic in all cases. This would be like living in a utopian state, which of course does not exist in the real world. To overcome this complete optimism, he introduced the concept—*coefficient of optimism.* This means that the decision maker takes into consideration both the largest and smallest payoffs and weighs their importance according to some probability factors (values range from zero where the decision maker is completely pessimistic to one where the individual is completely optimistic). The probabilities assigned to largest and smallest payoffs (which must total 1.0) are based upon how the decision maker feels about optimistic conditions. If the firm in our example has a coefficient of optimism of .667, it would be satisfied to receive a maximum payoff which has a probability of occurrence of 2/3 in a lottery and a minimum payoff which has a probability of occurrence of 1/3. In order to select the highest payoff among all these strategies, it is necessary to make the following calculations:

Strategy	Maximum Payoff	Minimum Payoff	Expected Payoff
1	$500,000	($ 50,000)	$500,000(.667) + ($ 50,000)(.333) = $316,667
2	$300,000	$0	$300,000(.667) + $0 (.333) = $200,000
3	$100,000	$100,000	$100,000(.667) + $100,000 (.333) = $100,000

Using the Hurwicz criterion, the firm should select strategy one—the introduction of a revolutionary new product with all new packaging to sell at a higher price.

If a small firm utilizes this approach, it is possible that nature would not be favorable to it, resulting in a loss of $50,000 if strategy one is selected. A small firm must take a second look before pursuing the Hurwicz criterion since such an approach could result in severe financial setbacks and possible bankruptcy for the firm. On the other hand, a medium sized firm and a large firm might consider this approach since a loss of this amount could be written off against its other profitable operations. However, full utilization of this approach for all projects by medium and large firms could result in substantial overall losses, as in the case of small firms. This approach, then, is readily applicable to all sized business firms, but it must be used with good judgment.

The Wald Decision Criterion. The decision criterion of Wald is the opposite of that of Hurwicz. Wald suggested that the decision maker should always be pessimistic or conservative, resulting in a *maximin* criterion. This maximin payoff approach means that the decision maker should base his decision on the constant malevolence of nature. Under these continually adverse circumstances, the individual should select the strategy that will give him as large a minimum payoff as possible. In our example, the worst state of nature would be a contraction or a recession in the economy (N_3). If strategy one or strategy two were selected, the payoff would be a loss of $50,000 or zero profits, respectively. If strategy three were selected, the payoff would be $100,000 for N_3 as well as for the other two states of nature. In essence, the worst state of nature that could happen would give a payoff of $100,000, shown as follows:

Strategy	Minimum Payoff
1	($ 50,000)
2	0
3	100,000

Wald's criterion dictates that strategy three be selected as the largest of the minimum payoffs—the maximum minimum (maximin).

The small businessman, due to the very size of his business, must adopt this conservative approach. Since he has all or most of his assets invested in one location, he must be careful not to lose them. A safe and certain return allows the small business firm to survive while one wrong move (such as undertaking a project at the wrong time) can be detrimental to it. This approach must also be practiced by medium sized and large firms to a certain degree if they are to survive. A completely optimistic approach must be tempered by a conservative approach to provide a cushion for projects that may go bad due to unforeseen problems. Just as the first criterion of Hurwicz is applicable to the business world, so is the Wald decision criterion.

The Savage Decision Criterion. A somewhat different criterion is that of Savage. He points out that a decision maker might experience regret after the decision has been made and the state of nature has occurred. The individual may have wished he had selected a completely different strategy. The Savage decision criterion attempts to minimize the regret before actually selecting a particular strategy. Savage does this by initially constructing a regret matrix. Referring to N_1 state of nature, Savage suggests that the amount of regret can be measured by the difference between the payoff he actually may receive and the payoff he could have received. The highest payoff for the N_1 column is $500,000. If N_1 occurred and strategy one was selected, the decision maker would have experienced no regret. Hence a value of zero is assigned in the regret matrix. Suppose the decision maker had selected strategy two and N_1 had occurred; he would have experienced a regret of $200,000 ($500,000−$300,000). In a similar manner, if the individual had selected strategy three and expansion of the economy (N_1) had come about, he would have experienced a regret of $400,000 ($500,000−$100,000). The remaining values are calculated in a similar fashion for the following regret matrix:

		States of Nature		
		N_1	N_2	N_3
	S_1	$0	$150,000	$150,000
Strategies	S_2	200,000	0	100,000
	S_3	400,000	150,000	0

The decision maker can insure himself against experiencing extreme regrets by selecting the strategy that has the minimum of such maximum, the *minimax*. To state it another way, the decision maker will first select the highest regret value from each possible strategy based upon the above regret matrix and construct a new table which appears as follows:

Strategy	Maximum Regret
1	$150,000 (appear twice)
2	200,000
3	400,000

In order to assure a minimum of regret, the decision maker would then select that strategy which would give him a minimum of regret or strategy one based upon the preceding data. The minimax regret is $150,000 which is the maximum regret the decision maker need experience. It should be remembered that he may experience less regret than this, but by using strategy one, this is the most regret he should experience.

An individual (or firm) taking this approach to decision making under uncertainty might be called a bad loser. Depending upon the values con-

DECISION THEORY 79

tained in a payoff matrix, the strategy selected will tend toward the optimistic criterion or pessimistic criterion. In our example, this criterion of regret tended toward optimism. As far as small, medium, or large firms go, it has less application than the prior two criteria. Great use can be made by applying this criterion to individual projects in the long run so as to minimize regrets on the average for each project.

The Laplace Decision Criterion. The preceding criteria have been of relatively recent origin compared to the Laplace decision criterion, which dates back over 2500 years. This approach assumes that the various states of nature all have an equal chance of occurring or every state of nature is as likely to occur as another. For each payoff, the expected amount is calculated and the strategy with the highest expected payoff is selected. Thus, this criterion is one of rationality and is based on the principle of insufficient reason—one state of nature is as likely to occur as another. The principle of insufficient reason, when used with probabilities, is related to the name of Bayes. His famous hypothesis states that if we know of no reason for probabilities to be different, we should consider them to be equal.

One of the better known arguments for the principle of insufficient reason was given during the Middle Ages. In the fourteenth century, Jean Buridan invented an imaginary ass, known today as Buridan's Ass, which was supposed to be placed in the middle (exactly) of two identical bales of hay. He stated that since the ass had no good reason to go to one bale versus the other bale, it would starve to death. Another interesting application of this principle is the toss of a fair coin. How do we know that a fair coin has a probability of .5 showing heads and a probability of .5 showing tails? One answer is the principle of insufficient reason. Since there is no logical reason for a coin coming up one way versus another, the probabilities must be equal, or .5, for there are only two possibilities. This principle is as applicable to business problems as any other principle if used properly within its limits.

Application of the rationality criterion is not too complex. Since we have three separate states of nature in our illustration and each has an equal chance of occurring or .333 probability, the calculations for each strategy are given below:

Strategy	Expected Payoff
1	$1/3 \times \$500,000 + 1/3 \times \$100,000 + 1/3 \times (\$50,000) = \$183,333$
2	$1/3 \times \$300,000 + 1/3 \times \$250,000 + 1/3 \times \$0 = \$183,333$
3	$1/3 \times \$100,000 + 1/3 \times \$100,000 + 1/3 \times \$100,000 = \$100,000$

The largest expected payoffs apply to strategies one and two. Generally only one strategy will be selected since there is only one value that is the largest.

The question can again be asked: How can rationality be utilized by the various sized firms in the real world? In many cases, the states of nature may be fairly well known in advance. For example, a recession generally follows a war that has operated under a combination guns and butter economy. Periods of contraction or dips in economic activity are followed by periods of expansion. An extensive examination of the economy for our illustration may favor one of the three states of nature. In reality, each state of nature, for the most part, does not have an equal chance of occurring. An examination of historical data might disclose that the economy expands more than it contracts. If the states of the economy do not have an equal chance of happening, the various sized firms should recognize this factor in their selection of an appropriate strategy. The small firm is forced to take a conservative approach since economic conditions can change quickly. Again, such a firm must pursue a cautious strategy. The medium and larger firms can better utilize this approach if the economic outlook (or states of nature) could go any way. Thus the Laplace decision criterion is better applied to firms that are not small.

The foregoing examination of the four criteria under uncertainty indicates that every strategy was selected one or more times. Strategy one was selected for two of the decision criteria—Hurwicz and Savage. Strategy three was selected by the Wald criterion. Strategy one and two, having the same value, were selected for the Laplace criterion. Obviously, there appears to be no best criterion. Therefore the choice of criterion must be left up to the decision maker, who is guided by his firm's size, company objectives and policies, his feelings, or some other rational criterion. To state it another way, an individual is free to select that criterion which reflects the value system to which he adheres. The difference between these four approaches and those which are less structured and "intuitive" is that the former consciously applies a value system while the latter simply subconsciously limits the alternatives. Nevertheless, the material in this book will assume a criterion of rationality unless otherwise stated. The Laplace criterion is the only one that expresses no attitude except the desire to be rational.

No matter what criteria under uncertainty is employed, *sensitivity analysis* is an important element in reaching a final answer for decision-theory problems. The decision maker, having made a preliminary test of estimates, makes variations in these estimates. If the variations do not change the answer, he need go no further. However, if the answer is sensitive to these changes, he may redefine his preliminary estimates before finalizing his decision.

Decision Criterion under Competitive Conditions
The last decision criterion occurs when the strategies and the states of nature are determined, at least to some extent, by the actions of a firm's competitor(s). Under these competitive conditions, the field of decision theory expands into what is known as game theory, the subject matter for Chapter 8. The works of Von Neumann and Morgenstern, in particular, have shown game theory to be helpful and effective under competitive conditions.

Decision Trees

Having had a brief look at probability theory and methods for selecting the best decision criterion, we will now focus on decision trees, which are basically graphic representations of probability logic applied to decision alternatives. A decision tree is so named because it looks like a tree, although for convenience it is a horizontal one. The base of the tree is the beginning decision point. Its branches begin at the first chance event. Each chance event produces two or more possible effects, some of which lead to other chance events and subsequent decision points. Figures on which the tree's values are based come from careful research. This provides probabilities for certain chance events and predicted payout or cash flow estimates of each possible outcome as influenced by various possible chance events.

Suppose your firm wants to decide whether to continue regional distribution of a product or expand to national distribution. This represents a decision point for the firm. The chance events affecting the national distribution decision are whether there will be a large national demand for the product, an average national demand, or a limited national demand. If there is a large demand, you can expect to make $4 million while $2 million and $0.5 million can be expected in profits for average and limited national demand, respectively. The probability factors are .5, .25, and .25, respectively. Three more payouts can be predicted if the firm continues with regional distribution. If regional demand is large, the firm can realize $2 million. On the one hand, if regional demand is average, an estimated profit of $1.8 million will result. On the other hand, if the regional demand is limited, an estimated profit of $1.5 million will result. This is shown in Figure 3-3. The addition of the expected profits (conditional profits × mar-

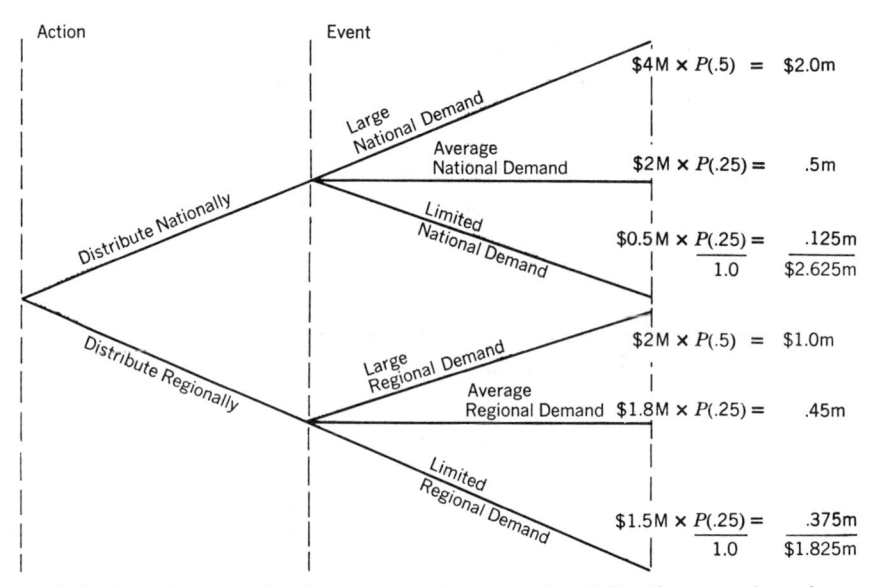

Figure 3-3 Decision tree for firm contemplating national distribution of products.

82   OPERATIONS RESEARCH MODELS—PROBABILITY AND STATISTICS

ginal probabilities) reveals that it would be better for the firm to distribute nationally.

Capital Investment Using a Decision Tree
The preceding problem illustrates the basic concept of what decision trees are. The following example will be more indicative of the real world problems confronting the manager. Consider a firm which is a manufacturer of component parts in a growing industry. Presently, five automatic machines are operating at full capacity for one of its products. Sales demand has been rising for this product. The problem now confronting management is whether to install another automatic machine or to place its employees on overtime. After a careful analysis of market conditions, the consensus was there is a .667 probability that sales would increase 25 percent for this one product within a year. There is a .333 probability that sales might drop by as much as 5 percent.

Presently, the firm, due to its growth, has strained its working capital, resulting in a difficult cash position. It was decided to state all figures in terms of net cash flow to the firm. A careful analysis of the data showed that a 25 percent increase in sales would result in a $350,000 cash flow for the new equipment versus a $325,000 cash flow for overtime. Similar analysis showed a 5 percent sales drop would generate a $200,000 cash flow for new equipment versus $280,000 for the overtime alternative. It is obvious that if sales rose, the decision to go with new equipment would be the best. However, with a sales decrease, it would be more painful to the firm than the elimination of overtime. The solution to the problem is to construct a decision tree and multiply each event's values by the probability for that event (Figure 3-4). The better choice is to utilize overtime for the next year.

Management need not stop here with a one-year basis but may look several years ahead. In this problem, we shall limit ourselves to one more

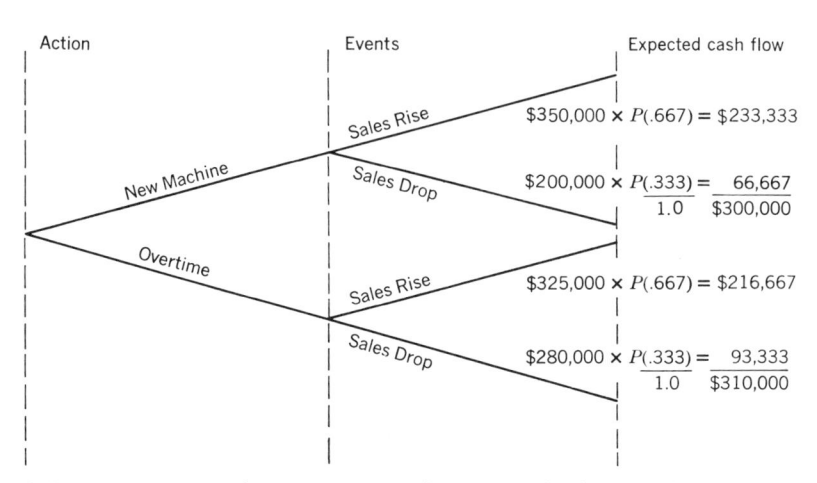

Figure 3-4 Decision tree for one year to determine the best path— new machine or overtime.

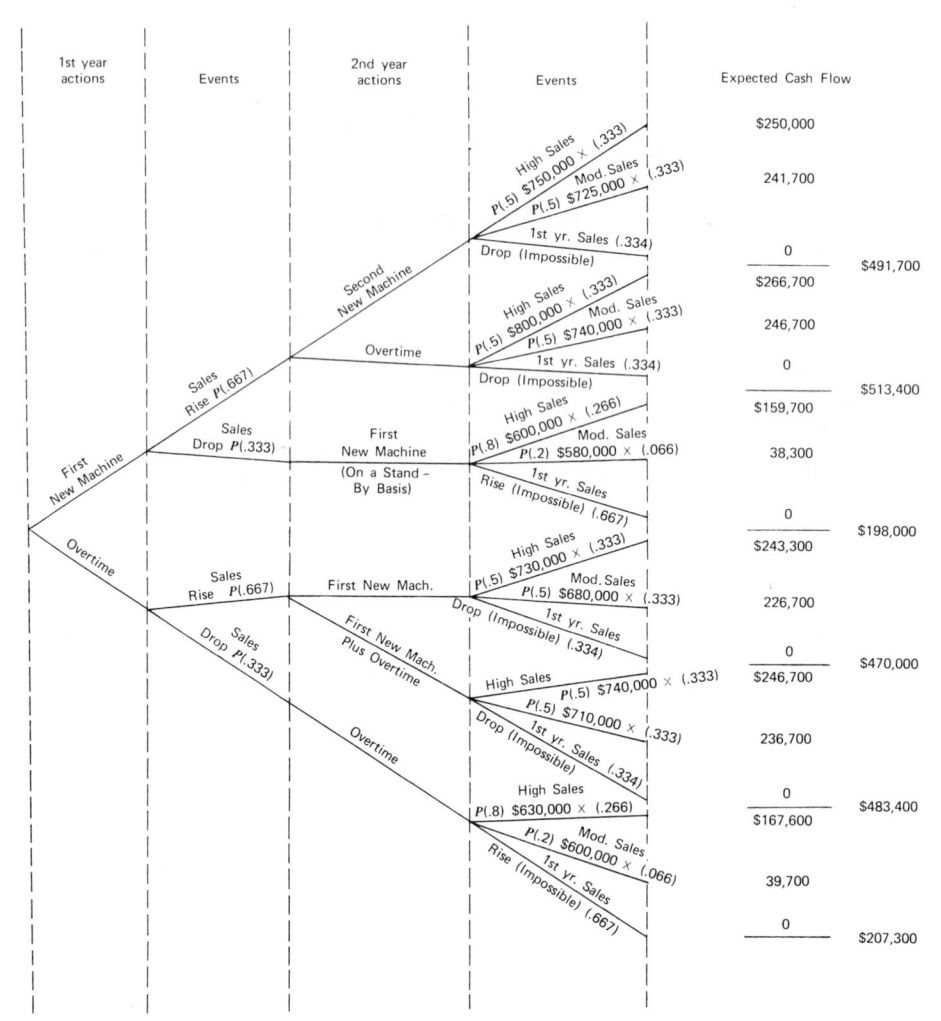

Figure 3-5 Decision tree for two years to determine the best path—new machine(s) or overtime.

year, the second year. After management conferred on the prospects of sales, it concluded that even if sales dropped by 5 percent in the first year, the probability was .8 that sales would increase by 25 percent in the second year. There was also a probability factor of .2 that sales would increase by 12.5 percent in the second year even if the first year had a sales decrease. Management agreed that if sales rose by 25 percent in the first year, there was a 50-50 chance that they would increase further in the second year by either 25 or 12.5 percent. The data, including the calculated expected cash flows or payouts for the second year, is presented in Figure 3-5. It is apparent that a new automatic machine in the first year and overtime in the second year is the best solution on a two-year basis.

84 OPERATIONS RESEARCH MODELS—PROBABILITY AND STATISTICS

Pricing using a Decision Tree

Several progressive firms are using Bayesian decision theory as a marketing tool for the likely response of customers and competitors to a contemplated company price modification decision. One interesting application relates to a firm that had been selling a certain industrial product for several years, capturing 40 percent of the market. Its current price is $1 per pound. Management wanted to penetrate a new market with its product since it would be a good substitute for a product that is currently produced by six firms. The new pricing structure was—maintain the current price or cut the price to $0.93, $0.85, and $0.80, respectively. A problem of this type generates myriads of considerations for the decision maker, such as the questions which follow. How would the six firms react to this substitute product in terms of price reduction? How much penetration in the new segment would take place without a price reduction? If this market segment were not penetrated, what would be the probability that competition would start price reductions soon?

The phase of gathering data consisted of getting realistic subjective probabilities from marketing personnel regarding the possible states of the uncertainties in the problem. Next, it was necessary to estimate the payoffs of the various courses of action. A decision tree analysis reveals that there were over 400 possible outcomes. Due to the large number of possible outcomes, the estimates of expected payoffs were processed on a computer. The solution to this problem indicated that, in all cases, a price reduction had a higher expected payoff than maintaining the current price. Of the three lower prices, the lowest price of $0.80 had the highest expected payoff. Last, to check the sensitivity of the results to the original assumptions, the results were recomputed for alternative assumptions on the rate of market growth and the appropriate cost of capital. Again, the ranking in terms of the expected payoff was not affected by the change in the assumptions.

Decision Trees Versus Probability Trees

Decision trees are basically an extension of probability trees. However, there are several basic differences, the first being that the decision tree utilizes the concept of "rollback" to solve a problem. This means starting at the right-hand terminus with the highest expected value of the tree and working back to the current or beginning decision point to determine the decision or decisions that should be made. Most decisions require trees with numerous branches and more than one decision point. It is the multiplicity of decision points that make the rollback process necessary. A comparison of Figures 3-1 and 3-5 reveals that the former contains only events while the latter contains both actions and events. Another difference is that the probability tree is primarily concerned with calculating the correct probabilities, whereas the decision tree utilizes probability factors as a means in arriving at a final answer.

A most important feature of the decision tree, not found in probability trees, is that it takes time differences of future earnings into account. This can be substantial. At any stage of the decision tree, it may be necessary to weigh differences in immediate cost or revenue against differences in value at the next stage. Even though not stated, discounting cash flow was utilized in the capital investment versus overtime problem since the time factor was two years.

There are several useful techniques for pruning bushy decision trees. One is the use of common sense, that is, eliminating possible actions which are not initially promising. For example, the firm can do nothing about prices or raise prices slightly, moderately, or greatly. The raising of prices to a great degree would probably welcome new competition, who would ultimately have a depressing effect upon this firm. Another method for thinning a tree would be to reduce the number of branches, say from six to two or three more promising ones. With careful analysis of the data, it is possible to trim a decision tree down to its principal branches before presenting it to management for review.

Decision Tree Application—American Products Corporation

The American Products Corporation is currently facing a production problem on a large packaging machine in one of its plants. Regarding the specific operating problem, there are 48 hours of manufacturing time to go before a scheduled shutdown for major repairs. One of the machine's major parts has developed some visible defects which have not yet had any effect on production. However, it may suddenly fail at any time in the next 48 hours of production and, therefore, force an emergency shutdown.

Based on these conditions, the production foreman can take one of two paths. He can repair the machine now on a planned basis which will take four hours since servicemen are available or run the risk of a sudden breakdown which will require eight hours due to the need to call in mechanics, make the repairs, and restart the machine. In both cases, production time is evaluated to be worth $100 per hour. Any lost time can be measured by this hourly rate.

Years of experience with this packaging machine indicates that there are 8 chances in 10 in making it through the 48 hours without a breakdown. The probability of running for this time period without failure, then, is .8. On the other hand, there is a .99 probability of the major part holding up during the 48 hours after a shutdown for repairs now.

The problem can be diagrammed as a decision tree. As illustrated in Figure 3-6, the basic decision is whether to continue manufacturing or to shutdown for repairs now. If the decision is to keep on running the machine, the best possible outcome for this 48 hour period is $4800 ($100/hour × 48 hours). Introducing the probability factor of .8 results in a calculated value of $3840. In a similar manner, if the machine's major part fails during the next 48 hours, the best possible outcome is $4000 [$4800 − ($100/hour × 8 hours)] since eight hours are lost making emergency repairs. The resultant calculated value is $800 or $4000 times the probability factor of .2 (1.0 − .8).

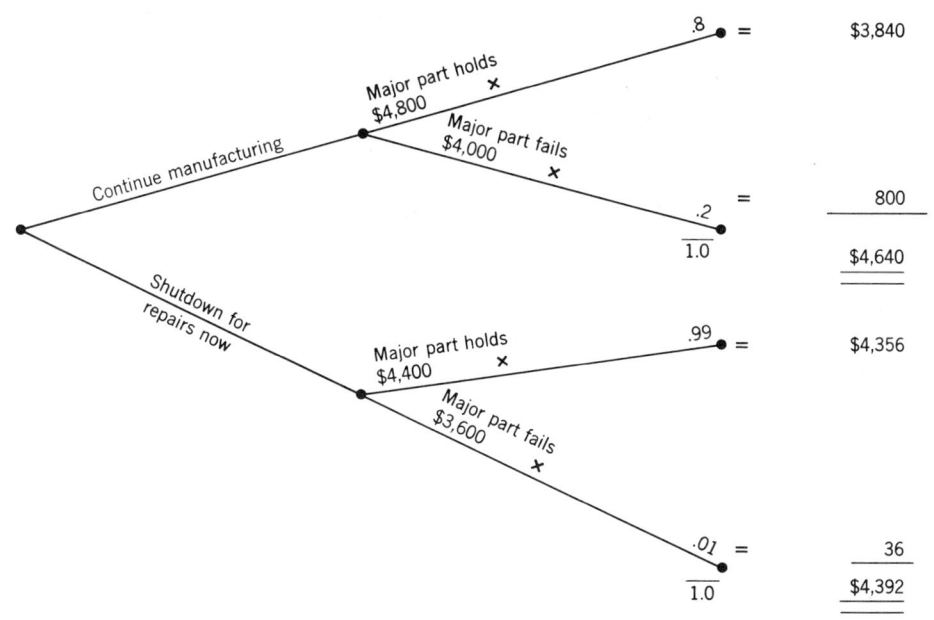

Figure 3-6 Decision tree to determine best decision in terms of highest expected value—American Products Corporation.

The summation of these values ($3840+$800) or $4640 is the expected value, that is, an average value which the firm would receive going through the same set of operating conditions many times.

Referring again to Figure 3-6, the decision to shutdown for repairs now has a similar analysis to that above. The highest possible outcome of continuous manufacturing after shuting down for repairs now is $4400 or $4800 less $400—four hours for downtime ($100/hour×4 hours). This value multiplied by the .99 probability factor is $4356. The last value to be calculated is the possibility of two shutdowns for repairs during the 48-hour period which has a .01 probability of occurrence. Under these conditions, the calculated value of $36 is $3600—based on 36 hours of operations [48 hours−(4 hours+8 hours)] times the probability factor of .01 (1.00−.99). The total expected value when shuting down now for repairs is $4392.

An analysis of the foregoing data (summarized in Figure 3-6) indicates that the production foreman is better off to continue manufacturing than shuting down for repairs now. In addition, other questions can be asked about the problem, such as, what range of probability values would allow the production foreman to continue manufacturing?

Summary

Decision theory, as set forth in this chapter, is part of the required background needed by anyone contemplating work in the area of operations research. Since the analysis given here of each area is brief, textbooks on this subject should be consulted for advanced work.

It must be stressed that the terms expected payoff, profit, or cash flow in probability theory do not refer to a single event or project. The expected value is an average of what would happen if such occurrences were repeated over and over again. The expected value for the outcome of a biased die might be 3.5. We know that it is impossible to get a 3.5 on a single toss. The 3.5 indicates the average value that is expected to occur in the long run. This same type of rationale applies to the selection of the highest expected payoff from the various possible alternatives, not on a one time basis, but continually over the years to maximize a firm's return on its total assets.

The application of probability theory to various quantitative methods will be evident throughout the forthcoming chapters. The current state of the Bayesian model is one of development. Several applications have been reported for pricing, new product introduction, and marketing research. In a similar manner, decision trees seem to have made substantial inroads, as is evidenced by the outpouring of literature on the subject. Decisions trees that are large lend themselves to a computer for a fast and accurate answer under varying conditions that are characteristic of the real world. Decision theory, then, is an important tool for operations researchers.

Questions

1. How do probability formulas differ under statistical independence and dependence?
2. What important contribution has Bayes made to probability theory?
3. Explain and evaluate the four criteria under uncertainty.
4. What are the essential differences between a probability tree and a decision tree?

Problems

3-1 (a) Using a fair coin, what is the probability of flipping two heads and two tails in a row? What is the probability of flipping four heads in a row?
 (b) What is the probability of getting at least one head on four tosses of a fair coin?
 (c) Using an unfair coin where $P(H) = .8$ and $P(T) = .2$, answer (a) and (b) above.
 (d) What type of probability is represented in (a), (b), and (c) above?

3-2 A box contains the following balls:
 3 yellow and red stripes
 2 yellow and red dots
 3 yellow

6 orange and red stripes
4 orange and red dots
2 orange

(a) What is the probability that the ball is orange, given that it has red stripes?
(b) What is the probability that the ball has red dots, given that it is yellow?
(c) What type of probability is represented in this problem?

3-3 Three boxes which are green, blue, and gray contain balls that are black and white.
The number of black and white balls in the three boxes are:

Box	No. of Black Balls	No. of White Balls	Total
Green	8	6	14
Blue	4	2	6
Gray	2	8	10

The initial draw can be made from any box where three balls are to be drawn. After each draw, the balls are to be replaced. When a black ball is drawn, the next draw must be made from the gray box; if a white ball is drawn, the next draw must be made from the green box.

(a) What is the probability of drawing black, white, and white balls in that order if the first draw is made from the green box?
(b) What is the probability of drawing black, white, and black balls in that order if the first draw is made from the blue box?
(c) If the first draw is made from the blue box, what is the probability that the third draw will be made from the gray box?
(d) What type of probability is represented in this problem?

3-4 The Ranco Manufacturing Company has sufficient capital on hand to invest in new machinery and equipment that can be used in the production of one new product only. Since the firm has three proposed products—X, Y, and Z—under consideration, only one of these products can be placed into production. In view of the capital constraint, the firm's marketing managers have been asked to estimate sales and their probability of occurrence. They are as follows:

Proposed Product	Estimated Annual Sales	Probability of Occurrence
X	$600,000	.6
	400,000	.3
	200,000	.1
Y	$600,000	.4
	300,000	.4
	200,000	.2
Z	$700,000	.1
	500,000	.3
	400,000	.6

DECISION THEORY 89

Estimated fixed and variable costs for these products were obtained from the engineering and cost accounting departments. For all practical purposes, their costs are identical. Thus, the expected sales become the focal point in deciding which product should be placed into production.

Based on the foregoing data, what product can be expected to produce the highest expected profits for the firm? Assume in the problem that the firm utilizes this approach periodically in determining which new products they should market.

3-5 The Ritter Machine Company can purchase a certain small casting from three different vendors. The casting is an integral part of the firm's best selling product. Currently, the prices being paid for the rough castings are:

Vendor	Price/Unit
A	$.50
B	.55
C	.60

Total machining costs by the firm's lathe department is $0.90 per casting. Based on buying in 1000 lots from three vendors over the last several months, the firm has compiled scrappage probability data (on the 1000 lots) which is:

Vendor	Scrappage Probability
A	.15
B	.07
C	.05

These values are considered representative of future scrappage probabilities. Given the foregoing data, what vendor should be selected to supply the rough castings in order to minimize the firm's future expected costs?

3-6 The controller of the Regis Corporation has asked you to determine the expected sales level based on the marketing department's projections for the coming year. The firm is typified by a small number of relatively large sales projects versus a product line reflecting many small dollar sales. The following data represents the sales projects as submitted to the controller.

Sales Project	Amount (000)
A	$362
B	447
C	443
D	540
E	319
F	180
G	1343
	$3,634 Total Sales Forecast

90 OPERATIONS RESEARCH MODELS—PROBABILITY AND STATISTICS

The following additional data was supplied by the marketing department.

Project	Probability of Project Being Let During Coming Fiscal Year	Probability of Regis Being Awarded the Project If Let
A	.7	.5
B	.9	.6
C	.8	.8
D	.6	.7
E	.9	.7
F	1.0	1.0
G	1.0	1.0

(a) What sales level can the Regis Corporation expect for the coming fiscal year?
(b) What type of probability is illustrated in the problem?

3-7 Mr. Johnson has total cash of $100,000 for investing in various projects and cannot raise any additional capital during this month or next month. He is offered the opportunity of participating immediately in the first of the two separate projects A and B. Project A is equally likely to result in a profit of $12,000 or a loss of $5,000 on an investment of $50,000. Assuming that the principal plus the profit or minus the loss is available one month hence, project B is equally likely to result in a profit of $18,000 or a loss of $12,000 on an investment of $48,000. Ignore the computations for return on excess cash funds for the entire problem. It should be remembered that Mr. Johnson is offered the opportunity of investing in projects of this kind periodically. What is the greatest expected profit for Mr. Johnson?

For the same information as above, the total cash available is now $50,000. What should Mr. Johnson do under this changed condition? Contrast the type of probability used in determining your answer with that used to find your original answer.

3-8 The Jamson Company has total excess cash funds of $60,000 for investing during this month and next month in various projects. The cash flow statement, prepared by the accounting department, indicates this. The firm has been offered the following investment opportunities. It can participate immediately (start of this month) in a project by investing $60,000, which is equally likely to result in a net profit of $20,000 or a loss of $10,000 within this month. In effect, the company will have its principal along with a profit or loss back by the end of this month. At the same time, the firm is informed that one month hence, it will be given the opportunity of investing $55,000 in another investment which is equally likely to result in a net profit of $15,000 or a net loss of $5,000. The assumption in this problem is that the Jamson Company, every two months, examines its cash position to determine the feasibility of investing excess cash.
(a) What should the firm do regarding the four alternatives?
(b) What type of probability is found in the answer to (a)?

Suppose the firm is informed one month hence that the second investment will

DECISION THEORY 91

require only $45,000 rather than the $55,000 as originally stated. Answer (a) and (b) above.

3-9 The Hartwood Manufacturing Company has $100,000 available to invest in machinery and equipment. If business conditions continue as they are, the investment will return 15 percent, but if there is a mild recession, it will return only 3 percent. The money can also be invested in certificates of deposit for a certain return of 5 percent. What probability must the firm assign to a recession to make the two investments have the same expected monetary value?

3-10 The Cincinnati Chemical Company has found from experience that 20 percent of its setups for combining chemicals have been unacceptable. It has also found that the chemical process will produce 95 percent acceptable chemical batches if it is correctly set up and 10 percent acceptable chemical batches will be produced if errors have been made in the setup. The setup is made for combining chemicals and the first four batches are tested for acceptability. The batches were found to be acceptable, acceptable, unacceptable, and acceptable.
(a) Should the line personnel continue manufacturing?
(b) Suppose the batches were found to be unacceptable, acceptable, unacceptable, and unacceptable. Should manufacturing continue?

3-11 The Gulf Machinery Co. has a group of six semiautomatic machines used in the production of part No. 1250. The firm has decided to develop a table that can be used by its machine operators to determine the advisability of rechecking the setup. It has compiled from past experience the following data. The probability that a machine is correctly set up is .9; if correctly set up, the probability of a good part is .95. On the other hand, if the machine is not correctly set up, the probability of a good part is .2.
(a) Develop a table that can be read by the machine operators for testing four parts.
(b) What type of probabilities are used in developing this table?

3-12 The New Products Group of the Henderson Manufacturing Company is about to present the profit feasibility of a new product to management. The firm has experienced problems in determining long-range profitability and the manager of this group knows this will be one of the main interests of management in the presentation. Sales estimates that three separate volumes can be maintained depending on the amount of discount allowed. The following table has been developed by marketing to show sales volumes at each price level as well as the probability of selling these units.

Selling Price	Units	Prob.	Units	Prob.	Units	Prob.
$9	100,000	1.0	150,000	.75	200,000	.50
8	—	—	50,000	.25	100,000	.25
7	—	—	—	—	100,000	.25
Cumulative Probability		1.0		1.00		1.00
Volume Plans	100,000		200,000		400,000	

92 OPERATIONS RESEARCH MODELS—PROBABILITY AND STATISTICS

Presently, material costs are $5 per unit. However, engineering personnel are working on future modifications to reduce costs which will be incorporated in the presentation. Reduction in material costs are expected to be $0.25 per unit. Variable manufacturing costs, in addition to materials, are $1.75 per unit. Yearly fixed costs, which is primarily necessary equipment investment needed at the three levels, are $125,000, $150,000, and $240,000 respectively. Marketing, general, and administrative costs are estimated to be $1.50 per unit at the 100,000 unit level, $1.25 per unit at the 200,000 unit level, and $1.00 per unit at the 400,000 unit level.
(a) On a profit per unit basis, what sales volume should the manager recommend?
(b) Does this volume provide the highest profits?

3-13 The Texas Company has received a request to bid on 250,000 special transistors. It should be noted that the firm receives many bids of this nature throughout the year for its various products—standard and special. The firm estimates the following machinery is necessary to take on this order:

Manufacturing Method	Total Cost of Machinery	Variable Cost per Unit
A	$100,000	$1.55
B	175,000	1.40
C	200,000	1.25

Since this may be the first and last contract of this kind, the entire amount of machinery costs should be allocated to this bid. Manufacturers of this equipment have agreed to accept cancellation of the machinery if the Texas Company fails to get the contract since all machinery will be shipped from their present stock Great importance is placed on prices, which are as follows:

Price/Unit	Probability of Getting Contract
Bid $2.50	1/3
Bid $2.30	2/3
Bid $2.20	3/4

Of the several alternatives available to the Texas Company, what price should the firm quote and what method of manufacture should be used? This is an example of what type probability?

3-14 The North America Corporation is submitting a proposal to the United States Navy for the development of an advanced carrier-based reconnaissance aircraft. It has asked three electronic manufacturers to submit bids on two phases of development (described by specification) for a new airborne navigational computer. The bids are as follows:

	Phase I	Phase II
DCA	$1,100,000	$1,000,000
Rollins	1,250,000	950,000
Central Electric	1,200,000	1,000,000

Since the Navy is very sensitive to cost overruns, it has asked that the proposed price include probable cost overruns, if any. The following information was supplied regarding cost overruns:

	Phase I Amount of Overrun	Phase I Probability of Overrun	Phase II Amount of Overrun	Phase II Probability of Overrun
DCA	$150,000	.15	$150,000	.5
	85,000	.35	100,000	.4
	0	.50	0	.1
Rollins	$100,000	.25	$200,000	.25
	50,000	.25	100,000	.25
	25,000	.25	50,000	.25
	0	.25	0	.25
Central Electric	$100,000	.25	$200,000	.333
	50,000	.50	100,000	.333
	0	.25	0	.333

Given the foregoing data, which proposal should be accepted for lowest development cost? Assume in the problem that the North America Corporation conducts bidding of large contracts on this basis regularly.

3-15 You are the executive vice president of Cutler Relays, Inc., which manufactures electrical relays. The government is letting a contract for 5 million relay units within the next month. Possible bids and resulting probabilities of winning the contract are as follows:

Price per Unit	Probability of Getting the Contract
Bid $4.50	25%
Bid $4.40	50%
Bid $4.30	75%

A second major government contract is anticipated in the latter part of the year. Production facilities are adequate to take on both contracts. The probability of getting the second contract is much higher depending on the firm's investment in special test equipment available later this year. The cost of the test equipment must be written off over the life of the second contract. In order to get timely delivery of the special test equipment, it must be ordered before bidding on the second contract. Probabilities associated with the test equipment are shown as follows:

Investment in Special Test Equipment	Increased Probability of Getting the Contract
$2.0 million	20%
2.4 million	40
2.6 million	60
3.0 million	80

Present costs per unit are $3.80. These costs will remain the same if the company allows the union to go out on a presently pending strike. If the strike occurs, a cost of $300,000 will be incurred by the company plus the company will be unable to bid on the first contract. In order to avoid the strike, the company can give into the union demands but this will mean a cost per unit of $4.00 each.

The anticipated net profit for the second contract is $3.5 million if the cost per unit is $4.00 and $4.5 million if the cost per unit is $3.80, excluding the investment in special test equipment. An immediate decision on the strike is required.

(a) Since you are the executive vice president of Cutler Relays, Inc., how many alternatives are available to you?
(b) Which is the best alternative in view of the fact that the firm undertakes contracts of this type throughout the year?

3-16 Mr. Goodwin is the president of the Goodwin Manufacturing Company and is 65 years old and a widower. A substantial portion of his personal estate is invested in the stock of this closely held company, which manufactures a product in a highly competitive field. Mr. Goodwin has been able to maintain his company's position in a declining industry purely by his aggressiveness and by his relentless driving of himself and of all those who work for him.

He has a married daughter and a married son who has been with him in the business for many years, never having worked any other place. The son's personality is completely different from that of his father. He has never been allowed an opportunity to demonstrate his competence. His father is from the old school, believing that there is one right way to operate a business—his way. Consequently, he has doubts about his son's ability.

In his business there is neither depth nor breadth in management. Mr. Goodwin has not only played all the positions on the management team but also has been the cheerleader. Even though his health has been good, it is beginning to fail due to age and he is aware of this. He realizes that if he is going to find an answer to his problem, he must find it soon since each year sees him faltering more and more in the making of decisions.

Recently, he has been worrying about what will happen to his estate. He wants to be fair to both of his children, but he doesn't know what to do with the business. Several years ago, he was approached by a prospective purchaser. At first, he considered the idea of selling, but later rejected the offer without giving any good reason.

Using a decision tree, plot his available alternatives. What should Mr. Goodwin do based upon the given information?

Bibliography

H. Bierman, C. P. Bonini, and W. H. Hausman, *Quantitative Analysis for Business Decisions*, Homewood, Ill.: Richard D. Irwin, 1973.

G. J. Brabb, *Introduction to Quantitative Management*, New York: Holt, Rinehart and Winston, 1968.

G. Hadley, *Introduction to Probability and Statistical Decision Theory*, San Francisco: Holden-Day, 1967.

F. S. Hillier and G. J. Lieberman, *Introduction to Operations Research*, San Francisco: Holden-Day, 1967.

C. M. Paik, *Quantitative Methods for Managerial Decisions*, New York: McGraw-Hill Book Company, 1973.

W. S. Peters and G. W. Summers, *Statistical Analysis for Business Decisions*, Englewood Cliffs, N.J.: Prentice-Hall, 1968.

R. Schlaifer, *Analysis of Decisions Under Uncertainty*, New York: McGraw-Hill Book Company, 1969.

C. H. Springer, R. E. Herlihy, R. T. Mall, and R. I. Beggs, *Probabilistic Models*, Homewood, Ill.: Richard D. Irwin, 1968.

Chapter FOUR

Decision Making With Uncertain Demand

In the real world, management of a firm cannot know in advance what the exact demand for its products will be. Nor can it be expected to know precisely what its costs and profits will be, based upon an uncertain demand. Under these circumstances, management must develop the best forecasts for sales and costs, thereby making a decision based on these estimates. The situation is not as hopeless as it might seem, particularly in the area of potential demand, if probability is utilized in the original forecasts. This approach looks to past demand for a product in order to assign probabilities to future sales. The assumption in this method is that the future will follow past sales patterns. This is especially true of products that are purchased frequently, such as consumer products.

The various ways of determining an optimum number of products to stock will be considered in this chapter. The first part will explore a problem with a limited demand. Expected profit and loss tables will be developed for conditions under uncertainty. Marginal analysis will also be used to solve the proper stocking of inventory for a discrete distribution. The last part of the chapter will handle decision making under uncertainty where there is a continuous probability distribution. In effect, appropriate quantitative methods will be discussed for the proper stocking of inventory when past demand is considered representative of future demand.

Discrete Probability Distribution

In order to understand the subject matter in this section, a problem dealing with a discrete probability distribution under uncertainty is presented. Consider a small doughnut shop which buys its doughnuts from a local bakery. Doughnuts sell for $0.80 per dozen and cost $0.50 per dozen delivered to the shop. Doughnuts left at the end of the day are sold at $0.40 per dozen. Demand for doughnuts is relatively constant over time, but varies from day to day. The results of recent daily demand is given on the top of the next page for the small shop. The problem now facing the doughnut shop is: What is the optimum quantity to stock in order to maximize expected profits? It should be noted that the shop buys only on a dozen basis from the bakery.

An inspection of the data used in compiling demand indicates that a random variable is present. A random variable can be defined as a value that changes, occurrence (or event) after occurrence (or event), in no predictable sequence. In the problem, this means we have no definite way of predicting tomorrow's sales of doughnuts. However, we do know the value of the random variable ranges from 40 dozens to 47 dozens daily. Not only is the data a random distribution of past sales with an increment of one unit,

No. Days Sold	Daily Demand (dozens)	Relative Frequency (probability)
5	40	.05
10	41	.10
10	42	.10
20	43	.20
20	44	.20
15	45	.15
15	46	.15
5	47	.05
100 days		1.00

but also the information is a discrete distribution since the sales volume can take on only a limited number of values. Thus the distribution for the doughnut shop is discrete and random. There are only eight possible values in the example for sales volume and there is no way of knowing which one quantity customers will buy on a certain day.

Method 1—Conditional Profits

The term conditional profit means the amount that will result based upon a certain combination of supply and demand quantities. To state it another way, the firm can anticipate profits based upon the condition of selling so many units and stocking so many units. One way of attacking the doughnut sales problem is to construct a conditional profits table which shows the results of all combinations of possible sales and inventories. Profits can be either positive or negative and are conditioned upon a combination of a specific stocking action and a specific sales demand. Table 4-1 is a conditional profits table for the problem under study.

An examination of the first column in Table 4-1 reveals that the stock-

TABLE 4-1
Conditional Profits Table

Possible Sales Demand (dozens)	Possible Inventory Action (dozens)							
	40	41	42	43	44	45	46	47
40	$12.00	$11.90	$11.80	$11.70	$11.60	$11.50	$11.40	$11.30
41	12.00	12.30	12.20	12.10	12.00	11.90	11.80	11.70
42	12.00	12.30	12.60	12.50	12.40	12.30	12.20	12.10
43	12.00	12.30	12.60	12.90	12.80	12.70	12.60	12.50
44	12.00	12.30	12.60	12.90	13.20	13.10	13.00	12.90
45	12.00	12.30	12.60	12.90	13.20	13.50	13.40	13.30
46	12.00	12.30	12.60	12.90	13.20	13.50	13.80	13.70
47	12.00	12.30	12.60	12.90	13.20	13.50	13.80	14.10

ing of 40 dozens each day will always result in a profit of $12.00 or 40 dozens stocked times $0.30 per dozen ($0.80 selling price per dozen minus $0.50 cost per dozen). Even though customers might want 41 through 47 dozens on different days, the doughnut shop can sell only those items it has in stock, 40 dozens. Moving over to the next column, the stocking of 41 dozens and selling of 41 dozens results in a profit of $12.30 ($0.30 times 41 dozens). The profits below this equal combination of stocking and demand is also $12.30. The same rationale applies: you can sell only those items in stock. The figures to the left of the diagonal in Table 4-1 are computed in like manner and the same reasoning applies.

Moving to the right of the diagonal in Table 4-1, consideration must now be given to the salvage value of the unsold items. Conditional profit for stocking 41 units when the demand is 40 units can be computed in two ways:

Profit on the 40 dozens		Profit on the 40 dozens	
(40 × $0.30 per dozen)	$12.00	(40 × $0.30 per dozen)	$12.00
Less cost of the 1 dozen		Less cost on 1 dozen	
unsold	(0.50)	unsold ($0.50 cost less	
	$11.50	$0.40 salvage value)	(0.10)
Plus salvage value of			
1 dozen unsold	0.40		
Conditional Profit	$11.90	Conditional Profit	$11.90

Referring to the last column where 47 dozens are stocked, the calculation for a sales demand of 41 dozens is as follows:

Profit on the 41 dozens	
(41 × $0.30 per dozen)	$12.30
Less: Loss on 6 dozens	
unsold ($0.10 × 6)	(0.60)
Conditional Profit	$11.70

The remaining calculations to the right of the diagonal in Table 4-1 are made in a similar fashion.

No conditional profit table can tell management how many items to stock each and every day in order to have the highest possible profits. It only shows what kind of profit or loss is available to the firm if a certain number of items are stocked and a specific number of items are sold. With an uncertain demand which represents many of the situations in the real world, the manager must decide the number of items to stock before demand is known. Only under conditions of certainty, which rarely exist in inventory, does the conditional profit table show the largest profit for stocking a certain number of units.

Expected Profits under Uncertainty

Having determined the conditional profits table (Table 4-1) for the doughnut shop problem, the next step is to determine the optimum number of dozens to buy daily. This can be done by assigning probabilities to the

TABLE 4-2
Expected Profit from Stocking Forty-three and Forty-five Dozens

Sales Demand (dozens)	Conditional Profit— Stock 43 dozens	Prob.	Expected Profit 43 doz.	Sales Demand (dozens)	Conditional Profit— Stock 45 dozens	Prob.	Expected Profit 45 doz.
40	$11.70 ×	.05 =	$0.585	40	$11.50 ×	.05 =	$0.575
41	12.10 ×	.10 =	1.210	41	11.90 ×	.10 =	1.190
42	12.50 ×	.10 =	1.250	42	12.30 ×	.10 =	1.230
43	12.90 ×	.20 =	2.580	43	12.70 ×	.20 =	2.540
44	12.90 ×	.20 =	2.580	44	13.10 ×	.20 =	2.620
45	12.90 ×	.15 =	1.935	45	13.50 ×	.15 =	2.025
46	12.90 ×	.15 =	1.935	46	13.50 ×	.15 =	2.025
47	12.90 ×	.05 =	0.645	47	13.50 ×	.05 =	0.675
		1.00	$12.720			1.00	$12.880

possible outcomes or conditional profits. These probability factors and conditional profits are brought together to compute the expected monetary profit for any possible inventory action. The expected monetary profit is defined as the highest profit the firm can expect to make over a long period of time, assuming the probabilities of demand remain the same for specific inventory quantities. In Table 4-2, the expected profits from stocking 43 and 45 dozens are calculated.

A summary of all possible inventory stockings is given in Table 4-3. The optimum stock action is 45 dozens since it results in the greatest expected profit. This action will result in the highest daily profits and maximum total profits over a period of time. It is important to remember that we have not removed uncertainty from the problem, but have called upon past experience to determine the best possible inventory action. Also, we still do not know exactly how many dozens will be requested on any specific

TABLE 4-3
Expected Profits for All Possible Inventory Quantities

Possible Inventory Quantities (dozens)	Expected Profit
40	$12.00
41	12.28
42	12.52
43	12.72
44	12.84
45	12.88
46	12.86
47	12.78

day. In fact, we are not sure of making exactly $12.88 from the stocking of 45 dozens the day after this study has been completed; but we will average profits of that amount over a period of time if past sales demand is representative of future demand.

Method 2—Conditional Losses

An alternative method to any problem that makes use of a conditional profits table is a conditional losses table, shown in Table 4-4. Notice that no profits or losses exist on the diagonal since these levels represent the best possible conditional profits available to the firm. For example, if 44 dozens are stocked and demanded, supply equals demand for the greatest conditional profits with no losses occurring. The figures to the left of the diagonal represent *opportunity* losses or those sales lost by being out of inventory when demand is present. On the other hand, the figure to the right of the diagonal represent *obsolescence* losses. These losses are caused by having too much inventory.

As stated above, the values to the left of the zeros are opportunity losses resulting from demands that cannot be met. If only 40 dozens are stocked while 41 dozens are demanded by customers, there is a loss of $0.30 ($0.80 selling price less $0.50 cost) as shown in the first column to the left. The subsequent figures below increase by an increment of $0.30 since the possible demand which cannot be met by the available supply of 40 dozens increases by one dozen each time. The obsolescence losses to the right of the zeros in Table 4-4 are calculated in a slightly different manner. The cost per dozen, $0.50, is reduced by the salvage value of $0.40 for a net obsolescence loss of $0.10 per dozen. The stocking of 41 dozens when demand is only 40 dozens results in an obsolescence loss of $0.10 on the 41st dozen.

The next step in the conditional loss method is to assign probabilities to the demand factors, ranging from 40 to 47 dozens. By applying the probabilities to the conditional losses, the expected losses can then be

TABLE 4-4
Conditional Losses Table

Possible Sales Demand (dozens)	\multicolumn{7}{c}{Possible Inventory Action (dozens)}
	40	41	42	43	44	45	46	47
40	$0.00	$0.10	$0.20	$0.30	$0.40	$0.50	$0.60	$0.70
41	0.30	0.00	0.10	0.20	0.30	0.40	0.50	0.60
42	0.60	0.30	0.00	0.10	0.20	0.30	0.40	0.50
43	0.90	0.60	0.30	0.00	0.10	0.20	0.30	0.40
44	1.20	0.90	0.60	0.30	0.00	0.10	0.20	0.30
45	1.50	1.20	0.90	0.60	0.30	0.00	0.10	0.20
46	1.80	1.50	1.20	0.90	0.60	0.30	0.00	0.10
47	2.10	1.80	1.50	1.20	0.90	0.60	0.30	0.00

TABLE 4-5
Expected Losses from Stocking Forty-three and Forty-five Dozens

Sales Demand (dozens)	Conditional Loss—Stock 43 dozens		Prob.		Expected Loss 43 doz.	Sales Demand (dozens)	Conditional Loss—Stock 45 dozens		Prob.		Expected Loss 45 doz.
40	$0.30	×	.05	=	$0.015	40	$0.50	×	.05	=	$0.025
41	0.20	×	.10	=	0.020	41	0.40	×	.10	=	0.040
42	0.10	×	.10	=	0.010	42	0.30	×	.10	=	0.030
43	0.00	×	.20	=	0.000	43	0.20	×	.20	=	0.040
44	0.30	×	.20	=	0.060	44	0.10	×	.20	=	0.020
45	0.60	×	.15	=	0.090	45	0.00	×	.15	=	0.000
46	0.90	×	.15	=	0.135	46	0.30	×	.15	=	0.045
47	1.20	×	.05	=	0.060	47	0.60	×	.05	=	0.030
			1.00		$0.390				1.00		$0.230

calculated. This is shown in Table 4-5 for stocking 43 and 45 dozens. The remaining expected losses are determined for the other six possible inventory actions as shown in Table 4-6.

Again, the stocking of 45 dozens produces the lowest expected loss just as it produced the highest expected profit. The optimum stock level, then, is the one which minimizes the expected loss. This is obvious upon inspection of Table 4-7. Notice that all expected gains and losses total the same amount. The rationale is that the same conditional profit and loss tables plus assigned probabilities are used throughout the problem.

Expected Profits with Perfect Information

Completely reliable information about the future, referred to as perfect information, removes all uncertainty from the problem. This condition

TABLE 4-6
Expected Losses for All Possible Inventory Quantities

Possible Inventory Quantities (dozens)	Expected Losses
40	$1.11
41	0.83
42	0.59
43	0.39
44	0.27
45	0.23
46	0.25
47	0.33

TABLE 4-7
Expected Profits and Losses under Uncertainty

	Possible Inventory Action (dozens)							
	40	41	42	43	44	45	46	47
Expected profits (per Table 4-3)	$12.00	$12.28	$12.52	$12.72	$12.84	$12.88	$12.86	$12.78
Expected losses (per Table 4-6)	1.11	0.83	0.59	0.39	0.27	0.23	0.25	0.33
Totals	$13.11	$13.11	$13.11	$13.11	$13.11	$13.11	$13.11	$13.11

allows demand to vary from day to day, yet the individual knows in advance how many units are going to be sought out by the various buyers or customers. In essence, he has the proper level of stock on hand at all times. Under these idealistic conditions, the conditional profits on the diagonal in Table 4-1, multiplied by their respective probabilities, produce the greatest expected profits shown in Table 4-8. The maximum expected profit for the illustrative problem is $13.11. If the corresponding conditional loss table is used, all zeros on the diagonal times their respective probabilities are zero. This makes sense because the total $13.11 agrees with the totals for the various levels of inventory in Table 4-7.

Assuming that the manager of the doughnut shop could get his hands on perfect information regarding the future, what would the value of such data be? It would be necessary for him to compare the cost of obtaining this data with the additional profits he would realize as a result of perfect information. In the illustration, the maximum average daily profit is $13.11 with perfect information, whereas the best expected daily profit under uncertainty is $12.88. The difference of $0.23 (Table 4-7) is the highest amount the manager would be willing to pay per day for a perfect forecast of daily demand. This difference is referred to as the EVPI—expected value of perfect information. To pay more than $0.23 for the perfect forecast would lower the daily expected profits.

TABLE 4-8
Expected Profit under Certainty

Sales Demand (dozens)	Conditional Profit	Prob.	Expected Profit
40	$12.00	.05	$ 0.600
41	12.30	.10	1.230
42	12.60	.10	1.260
43	12.90	.20	2.580
44	13.20	.20	2.640
45	13.50	.15	2.025
46	13.80	.15	2.070
47	14.10	.05	0.705
		1.00	$13.110

Method 3—Marginal Analysis

The previous sections gave two methods for solving problems with uncertain demand—conditional profits and conditional losses tables which determine the highest expected profit for a discrete distribution of inventory quantities. There are two alternative methods that utilize marginal analysis in solving this type of problem.

In the preceding illustrative problem, the use of conditional and expected profits and losses tables could have become unwieldy if the distribution of demand had ranged over a large number of values rather than just 40 through 47 dozens. The number of calculations would have been too numerous with a high chance of error and a high time requirement. Besides, the wide range of demand could represent but one of many hundreds and thousands of products which would require similar computations. The marginal approach avoids the problems of excessive calculations.

The starting point for marginal analysis is to remember that the sum of the probabilities of two events must be one, that is, the probability of selling an additional unit (last unit added) is a specific figure (say .7) and the probability of not selling an additional unit (last unit added) is the complement of this figure (say .3). If we let p be the probability of selling one additional item, the probability of not selling it is $1-p$. If the last unit added can be sold, an increase in the conditional profit can be made with a resulting increase in expected profits. This is called marginal profit, MP. In the problem, the marginal profit from the sale of an additional unit is $0.80 (selling price) minus $0.50 (cost) or $0.30 per dozen. The construction of the conditional profits table (Table 4-1) made use of this marginal approach. On the other hand, the effect of stocking an additional unit and not selling it reduces conditional profits, as was demonstrated in Table 4-1. The amount of reduction in profits from stocking an item that is not sold is referred to as marginal loss, ML. The calculation for ML is the cost of the unsold unit less the salvage value if applicable. In the problem, the cost of $0.50 is reduced by a salvage value of $0.40 for a net marginal loss of $0.10.

The basic rule to follow regarding the addition of the last unit is: the expected MP must be greater than the expected ML from stocking that unit. The reason we are using "greater than" rather than "equal to" is that an equal condition results in an even exchange of dollars for the last unit and does not maximize the firm's return on its total assets (which include inventory). Hence the general rule is that additional units should be stocked so long as the probability of selling the additional unit is greater than the calculated p. An exception to the rule, where the equality condition would be rightfully applicable, is a department store that is trying to maximize profits as well as the customer's satisfaction—knowing items are available in the store when requested. If too many items in the various departments are not available when a customer wants them, he will shop elsewhere. This ultimately will have a direct effect on the firm's return on total assets.

In an equation for the marginal approach, the left side of the equation is the expected marginal profit from stocking and selling an additional unit. This can be written as $p(MP)$ or the probability that the unit will be sold times the marginal profit of the unit. The right side of the equation is

$(1-p)$ (ML), the expected marginal loss from stocking an additional unsold unit. To state it another way, it is the probability that the unit will not be sold $(1-p)$ times the marginal loss incurred if the unit is unsold (ML). The equation for maximizing profit on the optimum quantity to stock is:

$$p(MP) = (1-p)(ML) \qquad \text{(Equation 4-1)}$$
$$p(MP) = ML - p(ML)$$
$$p(MP) + p(ML) = ML$$
$$p(MP + ML) = ML$$
$$p = \frac{ML}{MP + ML} \qquad \text{(Equation 4-2)}$$

In Equation 4-2, p stands for the minimum probability of selling an additional inventory item in order to justify the stocking of that additional inventory item. Using the rule set forth above, we should stock additional inventory items as long as the probability of selling these additional items is greater than the calculated p.

The proper handling of Equation 4-2 can best be shown by referring to the illustration. First, a value for p must be determined. The marginal profit per dozen is $0.30 (selling price less cost) and the marginal loss per dozen is $0.10 (cost less salvage value). A value for p is calculated as follows:

$$p = \frac{ML}{MP + ML} = \frac{\$0.10}{\$0.30 + \$0.10} = \frac{\$0.10}{\$0.40} = .25$$

Next, a cumulative probability distribution schedule of sales needs to be constructed, as in Table 4-9. The cumulative probabilities in the last column are the probabilities that sales will reach or exceed each of the eight sales levels. For example, the cumulative probability value of .35 assigned to sales of 45 dozens or more can be calculated in the following manner:

    Probability of selling 45 dozens   .15
    Probability of selling 46 dozens   .15
    Probability of selling 47 dozens   .05
                                             .35 probability of selling
                                                  45 dozens or more

TABLE 4-9
Cumulative Probabilities of Sales

Sales (dozens)	Probability of Sales Level	Cumulative Probability for Sales Will Be at this Level or Greater
40	.05	1.00
41	.10	.95
42	.10	.85
43	.20	.75
44	.20	.55
45	.15	.35
46	.15	.20
47	.05	.05
	1.00	

Having determined a value for p of .25 and a cumulative probability of sales schedule, we can apply the marginal analysis rule for stocking an additional unit. Additional dozens should be stocked so long as the probability of selling at least an additional dozen is greater than p. In our illustration, the cumulative probability for stocking 45 dozens is .35, which is greater than p (.25). This comparison satisfies our rule. To insure that no better answer exists, comparison is now made for the next higher level of sales, 46 dozens. The cumulative probability of stocking and selling 46 dozens is .20, which is less than .25. Thus the answer must be 45 dozens and not 46 dozens according to our rule. Suppose the cumulative probability of selling 46 dozens was .25. Here we would have an equality in our comparison. The rule states that the cumulative probability must be greater than p. Therefore we would stock 45 and not 46 dozens. The marginal analysis method gives the same answer as the previous methods.

Method 4—Alternative Marginal Analysis

An alternative method to marginal analysis is comparing the expected marginal profit [cum p (MP)] and the expected marginal loss [(1 − cum p) (ML)] where cum is the cumulative probability for sales will be at this level or greater. The rule for this fourth method is: the expected marginal profit from stocking a unit must be greater than the expected marginal loss from stocking it. The values for the various expected marginal profits and marginal losses are given in Table 4-10. Again, the quantity to be stocked is 45 dozens since the expected marginal profit ($0.105) is greater than the expected marginal loss ($0.065). The reader will observe that this greater than condition applies to selling 40 through 45 dozens. However, the rule (starting with a maximum stock condition) is concerned with the first greater than condition after passing a less than or equal to condition. This assumption is in agreement with the foregoing rule since we are interested in the first time the expected marginal profit from selling an additional unit is greater than the expected marginal loss of not selling that additional unit.

Of the foregoing four methods (summarized in Figure 4-1), only the first

TABLE 4-10
Expected Marginal Profits and Expected Marginal Losses

Sales (dozens)	cum p(MP)	(1 − cum p)(ML)
40	$.300	$.000
41	.285	.005
42	.255	.015
43	.225	.025
44	.165	.045
45	.105	.065
46	.060	.080
47	.015	.095

Method 1—Conditional Profits

Construct a conditional profits table showing the possible sales and inventory actions. For each level of inventory, multiply the conditional profits times the probability factors and sum these values for total expected profits. Select the inventory level that gives the highest expected profit.

Method 2—Conditional Losses

Construct a conditional losses table showing the possible sales and inventory actions. For each level of inventory, multiply the conditional losses times the probability factors and sum these values for total expected losses. Select the inventory level that gives the lowest expected loss.

Method 3—Marginal Analysis[1]

Calculate minimum probability of selling an additional unit (units) or p per the following equation:

$$p = \frac{ML}{MP + ML} \qquad \text{(Equation 4-2)}$$

Next, compare the cumulative probability for sales to calculated p. The optimum quantity to stock is that point where the first cumulative probability for sales is still greater than the calculated p. This cutoff point is based on the rule that additional units should be stocked so long as the probability of selling the additional units is greater than the calculated p. It should be noted that this method does not provide for calculating the expected profits.

[1] An alternative approach is to restate Equation 4-2 as:

$$p = \frac{MP}{ML + MP}$$

and reverse the foregoing procedures.

Method 4—Alternative Marginal Analysis

Calculate the expected marginal profits and expected marginal losses for each level of stock, as follows:

Expected Profit	Expected Loss
cum p (MP)	(1 − cum p) (ML)

The highest stock level where the expected profit is still greater than the expected loss is the desired inventory level. As with Method 3, this approach does not provde a means for calculating expected profits.

Figure 4-1 Available methods for solving a discrete probability distribution problem with an uncertain demand.

method allows for calculating expected profits given a discrete probability distribution problem. However, each method has a different way of viewing the same problem. For example, in Method 4 above, the difference of $0.12 between the expected marginal profit of $0.165 and the expected marginal loss of $0.045 at the 44th level per Table 4-10 is the same increase appearing in total expected profits Table 4-3 (Method 1) from the 43rd inventory level of $12.72 to the 44th level of $12.84. Also, the $0.12 increase is the cause of falling expected losses in Table 4-6 (Method 2) from the 43rd inventory level of −$0.39 to the 44th level of −$0.27. Likewise, the $0.04 difference between the expected profit of $0.105 and the expected loss of

$0.065 in Table 4-10 is the same difference appearing in Tables 4-3 and 4-6 when going from the 44th inventory level to the 45th level. All other values, then, in Tables 4-3, 4-6, and 4-10 can be related in a similar manner for Methods 1, 2, and 4.

Continuous Probability Distribution

Four different methods for dealing with problems of a discrete probability distribution of sales (limited values) have now been presented. However, in many inventory problems, the distribution of sales is not limited to a few values and the increment of item values is not constant. When a distribution of this kind occurs, it is called a *continuous distribution*. The use of the previous methods is neither feasible nor practical. Another method is necessary at this point in conjunction with the use of p in Equation 4-2. This method incorporates *standard deviation*.

Step 1. Calculate the Arithmetic Mean

The continuous probability distribution method will be illustrated by enlarging upon the data (selling price = $0.80 per dozen, cost = $0.50 per dozen, salvage value = $0.40 per dozen, and $p = .25$) given in the preceding example. The data for the problem is found in Table 4-11, which represents data for 50 days. This data can, in turn, be approximately graphed as shown in Figure 4-2 in the form of a bell-shaped curve after drawing a line through the points. The average sales or arithmetic mean ($\bar{X}$) is 48.4 dozens per day, based upon the following equation:

$$\bar{X} = \frac{\Sigma X}{N}$$

$$= \frac{2420}{50} = 48.4 \text{ dozens}$$

(Equation 4-3)

where X represents each data value and N is the number of entries.

TABLE 4-11
Sales in Dozens for 50 Days

47	67	49	55	40	50	48	49	49	49
48	46	43	51	51	62	41	50	62	45
50	55	48	33	41	45	46	45	60	39
49	32	49	47	47	48	60	51	43	51
50	47	43	50	48	65	48	46	49	55

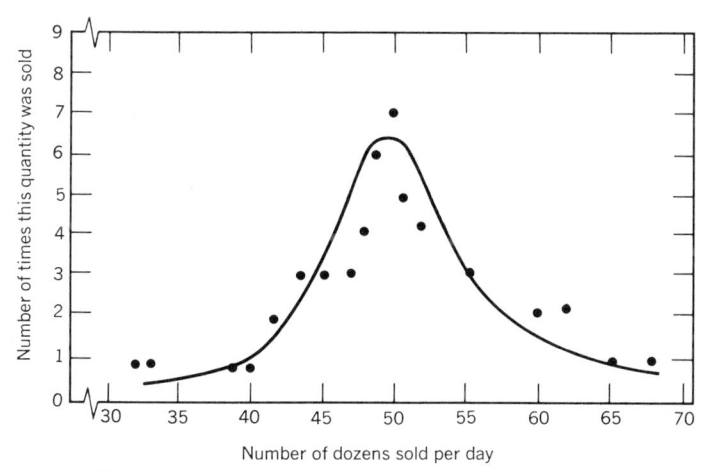

Figure 4-2 The bell-shaped curve—continuous probability distribution of past sales for 50 days.

Step 2. Compute the Standard Deviation

An examination of the bell-shaped curve in Figure 4-2 reveals that most of the values tend to cluster around the average. Intuitively, this is as one would expect; the instances of days with very high sales or very low sales are few. In the field of statistics, a measure of the tendency for the data to disperse in a regular manner around the average is termed "standard deviation." The approach for calculating the standard deviation which will be of help in making inferences about our past data in Table 4-11 consists of the following procedures. The first is to subtract the arithmetic mean ($\bar{X}=48.4$) from each of the values (X ranges from 32 to 67) and square each of these differences. Consideration must be given to the frequency (f) for each X value. The squared differences are totaled. Finally, it is necessary to calculate the square root of the answer found by dividing the sum of the squared differences ($\Sigma fd^2 = 2358$) by the number of entries ($N=50$). The calculations for standard deviation are found in Table 4-12. The standard deviation, denoted by σ (sigma), is 6.87 dozens.

Now that the standard deviation of 6.87 dozens has been determined by Equation 4-4, what can be done with this standard deviation value? Of what value is it to us? Standard deviation, being a unit of measurement for dispersion just as an inch is a unit of measurement of length, has been statistically proven that in a perfect bell-shaped curve, approximately 68.27 percent of all values fall within plus or minus one standard deviation from the arithmetic mean. Similarly, it has been found that approximately 95.45 per cent of all values lie within two standard deviations plus or minus from the average while over 99.73 percent of all the values are within three standard deviations plus or minus from the arithmetic mean. Applying these facts to the problem, where the arithmetic mean for past sales is 48.4 dozens, approximately 68 percent of future demand will be between 55.27

TABLE 4-12
Computations for Standard Deviation

Values of X		Arith. Mean $\overline{X}$		Square Each of the Differences (d²)		Frequency f		Squared Differences (fd²)
32	−	48.4	=	(−16.4)²	×	1	=	269
33	−	48.4	=	(−15.4)²	×	1	=	237
39	−	48.4	=	(− 9.4)²	×	1	=	88
40	−	48.4	=	(− 8.4)²	×	1	=	71
41	−	48.4	=	(− 7.4)²	×	2	=	110
43	−	48.4	=	(− 5.4)²	×	3	=	87
45	−	48.4	=	(− 3.4)²	×	3	=	35
46	−	48.4	=	(− 2.4)²	×	3	=	17
47	−	48.4	=	(− 1.4)²	×	4	=	8
48	−	48.4	=	(− 0.4)²	×	6	=	1
49	−	48.4	=	(0.6)²	×	7	=	3
50	−	48.4	=	(1.6)²	×	5	=	13
51	−	48.4	=	(2.6)²	×	4	=	27
55	−	48.4	=	(6.6)²	×	3	=	131
60	−	48.4	=	(11.6)²	×	2	=	269
62	−	48.4	=	(13.6)²	×	2	=	370
65	−	48.4	=	(16.6)²	×	1	=	276
67	−	48.4	=	(18.6)²	×	1	=	346
						50		2,358

$$\sigma = \sqrt{\frac{\Sigma fd^2}{N}} = \sqrt{\frac{2358}{50}} = \sqrt{47.2} = 6.87 \qquad \text{(Equation 4-4)}$$

dozens (48.4+6.87) and 41.53 dozens (48.4−6.87) if the curve is perfectly bell shaped as in Figure 4-2. In a similar manner, about 95 percent of future sales will be between 62.14 dozens (48.4+6.87×2) and 34.66 dozens (48.4−6.87×2). If one desires to determine the future sales for approximately 99 percent of the time, they will range between 69.01 dozens (48.4+6.87×3) and 27.79 dozens (48.4−6.87×3). To solve this type problem more easily, tables are available that show the expected positions of all values in a distribution and the number of points contained at any value of the standard deviations (σ) from the average.

Step 3. Determine a Value for p

Having answered the first question regarding what can be done with the calculated standard deviation value, we will answer shortly the second question—its value to us. Previously, the value for p was calculated to be .25, which means that additional dozens should be stocked as long as the probability of selling the additional unit is greater than p. The value for p can also be represented as .25 of the area under the normal distribution curve

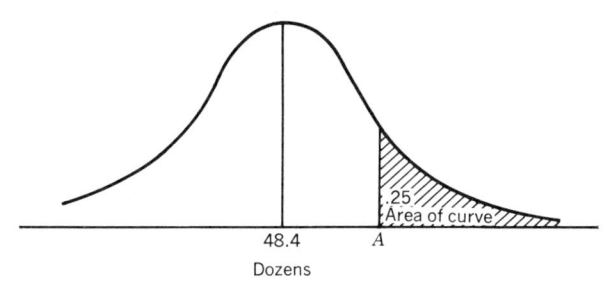

Figure 4-3 Continuous probability distribution curve where $p = .25$.

which is shown in Figure 4-3. The vertical line going through the center of the bell shaped curve is the arithmetic mean of 48.4 dozens. As we move to the right of this vertical line representing the arithmetic mean, the probability that a certain quantity can be sold decreases. Thus we will stock additional dozens until just before we reach point A. To stock a quantity up to the point represented by point A would represent an equal to condition. However, we will use point A in determining the answer, then adjust for a greater than condition.

Step 4. Calculate Standard Deviation from the Arithmetic Mean

In order to locate point A, refer to Appendix C for areas under the curve. This table indicates how many standard deviations it takes to include any part of the area under the curve, starting from the left-hand end of the curve and going to the right. In our problem, the open area must be .75 (1.00 − .25) of the total area under the curve since the shaded area is .25. Even though .75 does not appear per se in the table, the closest value is .74857 for a standard deviation value of .67. This means that the .75 area under the curve is located between the left-hand end of the bell-shaped curve and a point .67 standard deviation to the right of the arithmetic mean. Point A, then, is .67 standard deviation to the right of the arithmetic mean of 48.4 dozens.

Step 5. Determine the Inventory Level

Having previously calculated one standard deviation to be 6.87 to the right (or left) of the arithmetic mean (Table 4-12), the value of .67 times 6.87 equals 4.6 dozens. Point A is located 4.6 dozens to the right of the arithmetic mean of 48.4. The value at point A is 53 dozens (48.4 + 4.6). This brings us to the vertical line for point A for an equal to condition, that is, additional quantities should be stocked as long as the probability of selling that unit is equal to p. To change the answer in our problem to a greater than condition, the value at point A should be changed from 53 to 52 dozens so as to move out of the shaded area into the open area. This is

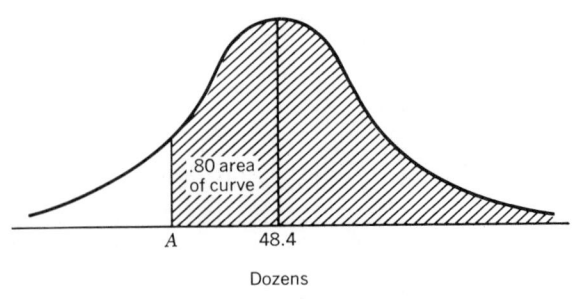

Figure 4-4 Continuous proability distribution curve where $p=.80$.

basically the same approach utilized in the marginal analysis method for a greater than condition.

Suppose the value of p in our problem was not .25 but some other value, say .80. Again, this revised problem can be illustrated by using a normal distribution curve. This time we shall start from the right-hand end of the curve as shown in Figure 4-4. Now point A lies to the left of the arithmetic mean, whereas in the preceding problem it was to the right of the average. The procedure for reading the area under the curve from the appendix is simplified in the revised problem. When the optimum inventory level is smaller than the arithmetic mean, the distance between point A and the arithmetic mean can be taken directly from the appendix. Looking for .8 in the table, the closest value is .79955, which is interpreted as .84 for the distance being measured in terms of standard deviation from the arithmetic mean. Thus, the .84 represents the area under the curve between the right-hand end of the curve and point A.

Having determined values for p and the distance between point A and the arithmetic mean (.84), we can now solve for point A in terms of an equal to condition initially:

$$.84 \times \text{standard deviation} = .84 \times 6.87 = 5.77 \text{ dozens}$$
$$\text{Point } A = 48.4 \text{ dozens} - 5.77 \text{ dozens}$$
$$= 42.63 \text{ dozens (equal condition)}$$

The optimum inventory position (must be in whole dozens) would not be rounded to 43 dozens. Going into the shaded area of the bell-shaped curve results in a less than condition for p. Thus the optimum inventory level is 42 dozens.

The foregoing steps involved in solving a problem with a continuous probability distribution are found in Figure 4-5. For fast and accurate results, these steps can be easily computerized, operating effectively in a real-time or batch processing mode.

What was stated previously for discrete distribution of demand also holds true for continuous distribution. Although probability cannot assure that the best decision will be made each and every day, it does allow for the optimum profits in the long run for decision making with uncertain demand and random day by day demand fluctuations. A word of caution is necessary: since business data may not be distributed in a bell-shaped

Step 1—Calculate the Arithmetic Mean
Calculate the arithmetic mean ($\overline{X}$) per the formula:

$$\overline{X} = \frac{\Sigma X}{N} \qquad \text{(Equation 4-3)}$$

Step 2—Compute the Standard Deviation
Subtract the arithmetic mean from values within the problem and square their differences. Next, multiply these differences (d^2) times their frequencies (f), resulting in fd^2 values. The sum of these values (Σfd^2) and the number (N) of frequency values are entered in the following equation for determining standard deviation:

$$\sigma = \sqrt{\frac{\Sigma fd^2}{N}} \qquad \text{(Equation 4-4)}$$

Step 3—Determine a Value for p
Determine the p value (minimum probability of selling an additional unit or units in order to justify the stocking of that additional unit or units) per the equation:

$$p = \frac{ML}{MP + ML} \qquad \text{(Equation 4-2)}$$

Step 4—Calculate Standard Deviation from the Arithmetic Mean
Calculate the standard deviation from the arithmetic mean. If calculated p (per Step 3) is less than .5, subtract from 1.0 to obtain the complimentary value; otherwise, leave calculated p as is. In either case, refer to Appendix C—Areas Under the Curve, interpolating as necessary to find the standard deviation value from the arithmetic mean. If calculated p is less than .5, the standard deviation will lie to the right of the arithmetic mean. On the other hand, if calculated p is greater than .5, the standard deviation will lie to the left of the arithmetic mean.

Step 5—Determine the Inventory Level
Calculate the number of units to the right (p is less than .5) or left (p is greater than .5) of the arithmetic mean. Thus, multiply the standard deviation value from the arithmetic mean (per Step 4) by the standard deviation (per Step 2). Where p is less than .5, add this calculated unit value to the arithmetic mean; where p is greater than .5, subtract this new unit value from the arithmetic mean. In either case, round the value down to stay out of the shaded area (for a greater than condition).

Figure 4-5 Steps involved in solving a continuous probability distribution problem with an uncertain demand.

(normal) manner, other quantitative methods may be required for an optimum solution.

Uncertain Demand Application—American Products Corporation

The American Products Corporation recently held a meeting of the firm's marketing managers and OR personnel. The outcome of this meeting was that overall company profits could be improved if a more scientific basis was employed in determining the proper manufacturing runs for all of the firm's seasonal products. This group decided that only the large sales volume seasonal products, should be handled on this basis for the next selling season. Also, they calculated seasonal demand and probabilities for these products, one of which is reproduced below for Product 15:

Seasonal Demand	Probability of Seasonal Demand
50,000	.30
55,000	.25
60,000	.20
65,000	.15
70,000	.10
	1.00

During the course of this meeting, the marketing managers set the selling prices for these products after evaluating the cost factors, supplied by the firm's accounting department. For the product under study, the wholesale selling price was set at $7.95. The estimated fixed and variable costs total $6.45. All unsold items of Product 15 can be sold at the end of the selling season for a price of $4.95 to discount stores, resulting in a $1.50 loss on each item.

Based on the foregoing data, OR personnel calculated a value for p to determine the minimum probability of selling additional units as follows:

$$p = \frac{ML}{MP + ML} = \frac{\$1.50}{\$1.50 + \$1.50} = .5$$

Next, they constructed Table 4-13 for the cumulative probabilities of seasonal demand. With a value for p and the cumulative probability per a seasonal demand table, they applied the rule for marginal analysis (Method 3), that is, additional 5000 units should be manufactured so long as the prob-

Table 4-13
Cumulative Probabilities of Seasonal Demand for Product 15—American Products Corporation

Seasonal Demand	Probability of Seasonal Demand	Cumulative Probability for Seasonal Demand Will Be at This Level or Greater
50,000	.30	1.00
55,000	.25	.70
60,000	.20	.45
65,000	.15	.25
70,000	.10	.10
	1.00	

TABLE 4-14
Expected Profits from Manufacturing 55,000 Units—American Products Corporation

Seasonal Demand	Conditional Profits—Manufacture 55,000 Units	×	Probability	=	Expected Profits—Manufacture 55,000 Units
50,000	$67,500		.30		$20,250
55,000	82,500		.25		20,625
60,000	82,500		.20		16,500
65,000	82,500		.15		12,375
70,000	82,500		.10		8,250
			1.00		$78,000

ability of selling these additional 5000 units is greater than p. Thus, the cumulative probability value for manufacturing 55,000 units is .70 which is greater than p (.5).

Having established the manufacturing level (based on seasonal demand), the expected profits under uncertainty for the next selling season are determined. Rather than calculate conditional profits for all manufacturing levels, expected profits for the 55,000 level only are set forth in Table 4-14. Total expected profits based on an uncertain seasonal demand sum to be $78,000 for Product 15.

Summary

The methods presented in this chapter for decision making with uncertain demand apply to conditions where demand is discrete or continuous. The calculations involved are not particularly complex, but can be time consuming. When such a condition arises, a computer should be employed to minimize the laborious task of analyzing past sales data and producing a solution which is usable. In this manner, these decision-making methods can be tools for long-run analysis.

Decision making with uncertain demand is not restricted to inventory problems. Problems dealing with uncertainty are rightfully applicable to new products and new markets. In fact, individuals and firms can handle their decision problems as if they are problems dealing with uncertainty. An understanding of the fundamentals of probability theory for the states of nature or uncertainty about the future should be of help to decision makers in that it makes them quantify the problem. Instead of operating in the dark, the assignment of probability factors, based upon subjective and/or objective probabilities and tempered with expected changes, can only help improve the quality of the manager's decisions. The manager must remember that if his competitor(s) resorts to the proper utilization of decision theory and he does not, he may be jeopardizing the firm's future.

Questions

1. Distinguish among the following: conditional profits, expected profits, short run profits, and net profits.
2. Of the several methods for solving a problem that has a discrete distribution with an uncertain demand, which one results in the least amount of computations?
3. When solving a problem that has a continuous distribution with an uncertain demand, how can the concept of standard deviation help in the problem's solution?

Problems

4-1 Given is the following distribution of unit sales and relative probability factors:

Units Sold	Probability of Selling these Units
50	.10
51	.35
52	.40
53	.15
	1.00

Cost per unit is $10.00 and sales price is $15.00 per unit.
(a) Prepare a conditional profits table and a conditional losses table.
(b) Prepare expected profits and losses tables under uncertainty.
(c) Determine the expected value of perfect information.

4-2 The French Baking Company operates many retail outlets. It has decided to apply probability in order to determine whether or not profits can be improved by first looking at white bread. White bread is baked in units of 20. The following data was compiled for white bread from the load sheets of the firm's delivery trucks.

Delivery Truck Daily Demand	Relative Frequency
1,060	.055
1,080	.100
1,100	.100
1,120	.150
1,140	.200
1,160	.175
1,180	.125
1,200	.075
1,220	.020
	1.000

White bread sells for $0.25 a loaf on an average and costs (fixed and variable) $0.19 per loaf delivered to its retail outlets. Bread left over at the end of the day is returned to the baking plant and is sold for $0.10 per loaf to institutions.

(a) Determine the optimum quantity to bake in terms of the firm's delivery trucks.
(b) What is the maximum expected profits under uncertainty?
(c) What would be the maximum expected profits under certainty if this were possible?

4-3 Bohr Bros., Inc., operates a small floral shop adjoining one of its eight large greenhouses. It specializes in the raising of mums, which are sold to other florists. However, it stocks mums for sale in its small floral shop for customers in its immediate market area. Mums are sold for $3.00 per dozen and cost $2.00 per dozen to grow and cut. Unsold mums left at the end of the second day after cutting are sold at $0.75 per dozen to other flower shops in the lower income markets. Demand for mums during the winter months is relatively constant over a period of time but varies from day to day. Given is the following tabulation of recent demand:

Daily Demand	Relative Frequency
20	.05
22	.10
24	.25
26	.30
28	.20
30	.10
	1.00

(a) What is the optimum quantity to stock?
(b) What is the maximum expected profit under uncertainty based upon the given schedule for demand?

4-4 Novelty, Inc., must decide whether to manufacture and market a new seasonal novelty which has just been developed to sell at $1.75 per unit. If the firm decides to manufacture it, special machinery must be purchased and scrapped after the season is over. A machine costing $1100 will result in a variable cost of manufacturing of $0.90 per unit. A machine costing $3000 will produce a variable cost of $0.60 per unit. Fortunately, the firm will be able to manufacture in small batches as sales occur. Thus there is no problem of unsold merchandise at the end of the season. The firm's probability distribution for sales in units is:

Sales in Units	Probability
2,000	.20
4,000	.40
8,000	.40
	1.00

Based upon the calculations for expected profits, what should the firm do?

4-5 The Jones Company buys a certain non-perishable item which sells for $16 and costs $12. A tabulation of recent demand for the product appears as follows:

Quantities Sold	Number of Days
80	14
81	36
82	70
83	30
84	20
85	10

Future demand for this product during the next 30 days should be comparable to past demand.
(a) What is the expected marginal profit and marginal loss from stocking the eighty-third unit?
(b) Should the eighty-third unit be stocked? If not, what level of inventory in units should be carried daily?

4-6 The Adam Shoe Company specializes in the manufacture of men's shoes. Its lowest price shoe which sells for $10.00 per pair and cost $8.00 per pair (total fixed and variable costs) is an important sales volume leader. All unsold shoes at the end of each season for this lowest price shoe are sold to discount houses at $6.00 per pair. The estimated demand and their probabilities for the coming season are as follows:

Seasonal Demand (pairs)	Probability
100,000	.10
90,000	.15
80,000	.25
70,000	.25
60,000	.15
50,000	.10
	1.00

(a) What quantity should the company manufacture for the coming season?
(b) What is the maximum expected profit based on the uncertain demand for the coming season?

4-7 Cosmetics, Inc., has under consideration the production of a new hair shampoo for women. The proposed selling price is $1.25 per bottle. The projected variable cost is $0.90 per bottle. An investment of $80,000 in fixed costs is necessary to undertake this project. The new product is expected to have a product life of five years. The market research group has estimated yearly demand to be as follows:

Yearly Demand	Probability
25,000	.05
50,000	.10
75,000	.20
100,000	.30
110,000	.35

118 OPERATIONS RESEARCH MODELS—PROBABILITY AND STATISTICS

(a) Based upon the facts given in the problem, should the new product be placed into production?

(b) What additional factors, not given in the problem, should have been considered before making a final decision?

4-8 The main product of the Orlando Manufacturing Company sells for $20 each and costs $16. Analysis of past sales data indicates that sales average 40 units per day with a standard deviation of 10 units. What level of inventory should the firm carry?

4-9 Byrnes Sales, Inc., is contemplating the use of quantitative methods to determine the optimum level of inventory for its principal product. They have come to you with the following facts. The product sells for $22 and costs $12 from the wholesaler plus $6 for fixed and variable costs for the firm itself. A tabulation of recent demand which should be typical of future demand is as follows:

34	36	26
26	18	38
26	18	36
20	20	20
26	34	34
16	40	26
14	38	44
20	10	18
16	36	14
26	34	34

What optimum level of inventory would you recommend to management?

Bibliography

H. Bierman, C. P. Bonini, and W. H. Hausman, *Quantitative Analysis for Business Decisions*, Homewood, Ill.: Richard D. Irwin, 1973.

G. J. Brabb, *Introduction to Quantitative Management*, New York: Holt, Rinehart and Winston, 1968.

G. Hadley, *Introduction to Probability and Statistical Decision Theory*, San Francisco: Holden-Day, 1967.

F. S. Hillier and G. J. Lieberman, *Introduction to Operations Research*, San Francisco: Holden-Day, 1967.

R. I. Levin and C. A. Kirkpatrick, *Quantitative Approaches to Management*, New York: McGraw-Hill Book Company, 1971.

C. M. Paik, *Quantitative Methods for Managerial Decisions*, New York: McGraw-Hill Book Company 1973.

W. S. Peters and G. W. Summers, *Statistical Analysis for Business Decisions*, Englewood Cliffs, N.J.: Prentice-Hall, 1968.

S. B. Richmond, *Operations Research for Management Decisions*, New York: The Ronald Press Company, 1968.

R. Schlaifer, *Analysis of Decisions Under Uncertainty*, New York: McGraw-Hill Book Company, 1969.

Chapter FIVE
PERT/Time, PERT/Cost, and PERT/LOB

Program Evaluation and Review Technique—PERT—had its beginnings in the Gantt chart. It was developed for the Polaris project in 1958 by the Navy Special Projects Office and Lockheed Aircraft Corporation in cooperation with Booz, Allen & Hamilton, a management consulting firm. This chapter will concentrate not only on a PERT network system developed by this group, but also on PERT/Cost and PERT/LOB, further refinements of PERT. PERT's advantages and disadvantages will be enumerated to demonstrate its applicability to certain business and industrial projects.

PERT/Time

The PERT technique is a method of minimizing trouble spots—production bottlenecks, delays, and interruptions—by determining critical activities before they occur so various parts of an overall job can be coordinated. It is basically a planning and control technique that utilizes a network to complete a predetermined project or schedule. A technique of this type helps to facilitate the communications function in the firm by reporting favorable as well as unfavorable developments before they happen. In effect, PERT tries to keep managers appraised of all critical factors and considerations that bear on their decisions. From this standpoint, it can be a valuable managerial tool in decision making.

Gantt Chart—Background of PERT

The Gantt milestone chart, a forerunner of PERT, is a chart depicting the work to be done. It has a time scale across the bottom of the chart that depicts the specific tasks relative to the entire project. The Gantt chart shows the relationships among the milestones within the same task, but not the relationships among the milestones contained in different tasks. This can best be illustrated by Figure 5-1. Each of the circles (milestones) represents the accomplishment of a specific phase of the total undertaking and each rectangle represents a task.

Modification of Gantt's milestone chart to show the interrelationships among all milestones in a project is achieved in three steps. The first is removal of the rectangles. These are replaced by arrows connecting the milestones (Figure 5-2).

The second step involves adding the relationships among the milestones for the various tasks (Figure 5-3). Here several milestones must precede other milestones. For example, milestone 5 cannot be started before

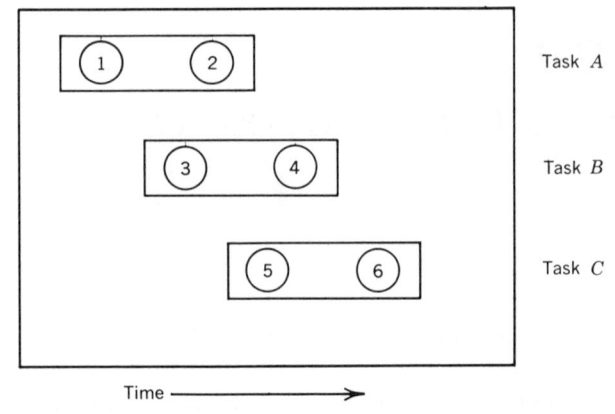

Figure 5-1 Gantt milestone chart.

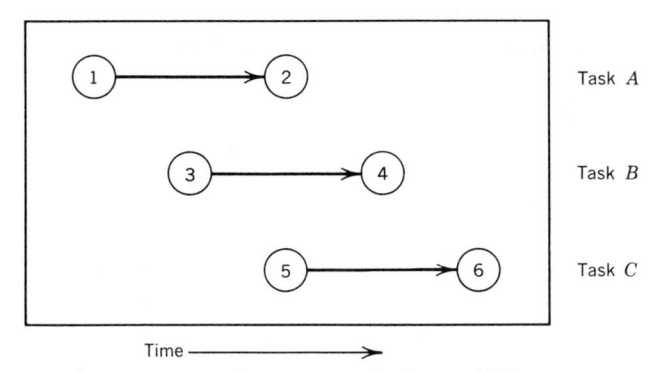

Figure 5-2 Gantt chart—remove rectangles, replace with arrows.

milestones 1 and 3 are completed. This type of relationship is true for all other cases in the illustration. It should be noted that milestone 1 is the starting point while milestone 6 is the ending point of the project.

In the final step (Figure 5-4) the term "task" is dropped since all the relationships, irrespective of the task involved, are shown by arrows. Further, the horizontal time scale of the Gantt chart is dropped and replaced by individual time on each of the arrows. The transformation from the

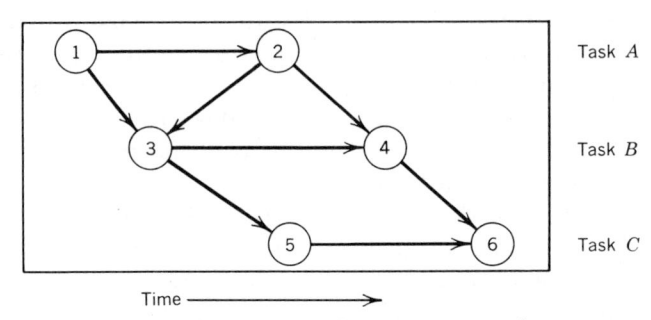

Figure 5-3 Gantt chart partially transferred to PERT network.

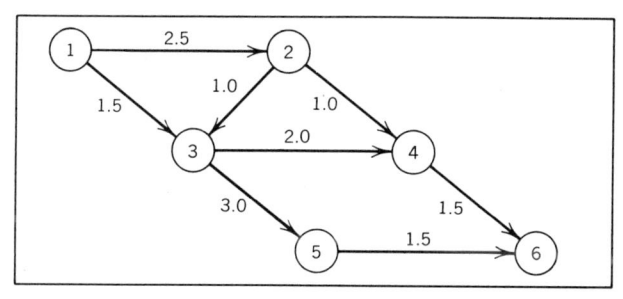

Figure 5-4 Complete transformation of Gantt chart to PERT network.

Gantt chart to a PERT network is now complete. The major advantage of this change should be evident. We now have all the interrelationships among the milestones. The project is viewed as an integrated whole (not a number of tasks) and each leg of the network has its own time value. In addition, this transformation permits the use of a network for large and complicated projects and utilizes statistics for determining estimated completion dates.

Methodology of PERT/Time
The six steps utilized in a PERT/Time project for planning and control are developed below. Throughout, basic terms are defined as they are needed. A sample problem is illustrated in the discussion so as to highlight the methodology of PERT/Time. A summary of the important steps involved in solving a PERT/Time problem concludes the section.

Step 1. Prepare PERT Network

A PERT network (Figure 5-5) has some differences from that of the Gantt chart. The first to be considered is terminology. A PERT network is concerned with developing a logical sequence of the activities which are undertaken to carry out the project and the interrelationships of these activities

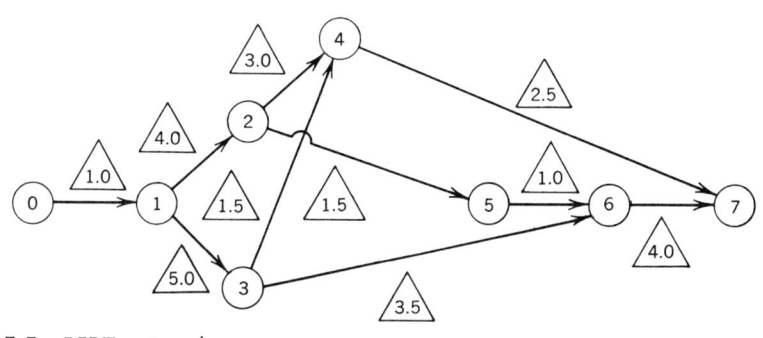

Figure 5-5 PERT network.

over time. The term "activity" (job) is defined as one work step in the total project and is represented by an arrow. The tail of the arrow represents the beginning of the activity and the head represents its completion. The length, shape, or position of the arrow is unimportant. The important thing is the way the activities, represented by arrows, are linked together in a time sequence for an operational network.

In constructing an arrow diagram, the planner should think through the activities required and their respective time relationships. This can be accomplished by writing out a list of the activities in the project. In a very complex project, it may not seem possible to list all the activities initially. However, additional activities will come to light as the arrow diagram is developed. Next, the planner should determine the logical order of the activities, that is, how does this activity fit in with other activities? Does this particular activity precede or follow, or is it concurrent with another activity? Finally, it is necessary to draw the arrow diagram to show how the activities are interrelated in time. The planner should watch for activities that are too large or too small. It is possible that a large activity can be treated as more than one activity or many small activities can be combined into a single activity.

The starting and ending points of activities, shown in Figure 5-5 as circled numbers, are called "events (nodes)." Events are points in time as contrasted with activities which have a time length or duration. Events are numbered serially from start to finish of a project. The general rule for numbering is that no event can be numbered until all preceding events have been numbered. Referring to Figure 5-5, this means that no event can be numbered until we have first numbered the tail of each arrow whose head points to the next event. The number at the head of an arrow is always larger than that at its tail.

The term "network" relates to the activities and events that are combined together, resulting in a diagram such as Figure 5-5. Within this network, we can see that event 0 is the network beginning event while event 7 is the network ending event. Upon inspection of event 6, we notice that activities 3–6 and 5–6 lead to it, which means that event 6 is the ending event for these two activities. In a similar manner, event 2 begins two activities, 2–4 and 2–5, which indicates that event 2 is the beginning event for two activities. The same type of reasoning is applicable to the other activities and events in the PERT network.

The preceding PERT network shows simple relationships in time sequence. Often the relationships are more complex. In some cases, these require the use of nonactivity arrows inserted to clarify the activity pattern. These are called "dummy arrows." They are represented by dotted line arrows. Figure 5-6 gives an example of a dummy arrow. C is dependent only on A being completed while D is dependent on both A and B being completed. Thus, A and B, being concurrent activities, as are C and D, indicate that C is dependent only on A being completed, not on B being completed. A dummy arrow in any situation does not represent an activity and thus has no time duration. It can be used effectively in those situations where activities can be overlapped to accelerate a project.

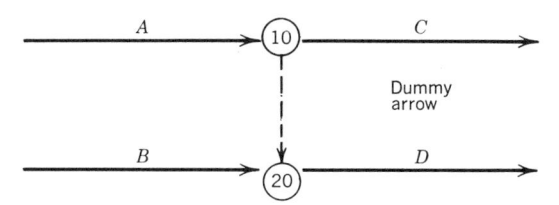

Figure 5-6 Example of a dummy arrow.

Step 2. Calculate Expected Times

Assigning time to individual activities is essential in order to complete a PERT network. Should this be done on the basis of the lowest possible cost, irrespective of the time required; the shortest possible time, regardless of costs; some compromise between the two; or some other basis? To answer, it is necessary to utilize statistics, in particular, the bell-shaped curve and the beta distribution. As you will recall from statistics, most groups of data tend to form a bell shape when plotted (Figure 5-7). However, some variables are not normally distributed and do not form a bell shape. Instead, the variables are unsymmetrical in one direction, as shown in Figure 5-7.

Since data from the business world reflects basically one of the three curves in Figure 5-7, the designers of PERT were faced with finding a particular kind of distribution that would satisfy the conditions of the shortest (optimistic), longest (pessimistic), and most likely times. We do not have the space to relate all the complicated statistics and algebra necessary to prove the validity of the weighted average used in the final formula for PERT. It should be somewhat obvious that the most likely time (m) should be weighted much heavier than the most optimistic (a) and the most pessimistic (b). There is certainly more of a chance that the project will be completed closer to the most likely time than the other two extreme times. The approximation formula developed for the expected time of an activity (t_e) is

$$t_e = \frac{a + 4m + b}{6} \quad \text{(Equation 5-1)}$$

When using this formula for a normal bell-shaped curve, the calcu-

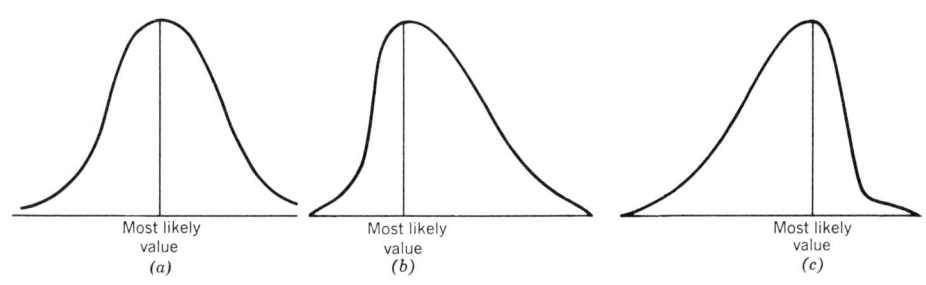

Figure 5-7 Bell-shaped curve and beta distribution curves. (a) Normal bell-shaped curve, (b) and (c) Beta distribution, unsymmetrical in one direction.

$a = 4$ $m = 6$ $t_e = 7.2$ $b = 15$

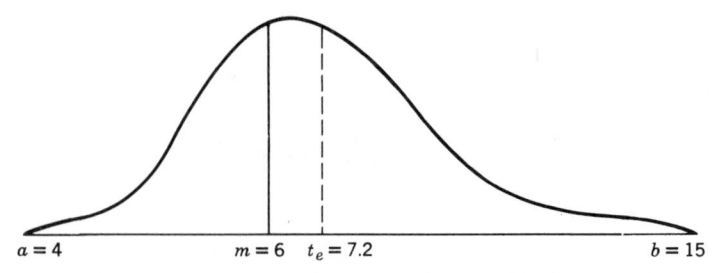

Figure 5-8 Beta distribution—t_e to the right of most likely time due to the time factor m.

lated value for t_e represents the midvalue of the bell-shaped curve, which is what we desire for this type curve. Let us take a look at two examples for curves that are unsymmetrical and plot them for a beta distribution. The first time estimates for a beta distribution showing expected time (in weeks) lying to the right of the most likely time are: $a=4$ (most optimistic), $m=6$ (most likely), and $b=15$ (most pessimistic). Using Equation 5-1, the value for t_e equals 7.2 weeks. The values for this example are plotted in Figure 5-8. The 15 weeks pessimistic estimate pulled the expected time t_e farther to the right on the distribution.

In our second example of a beta distribution, it is unsymmetrical in the other direction. This time t_e lies to the left of the most likely time. The three time estimates are: $a=4$, $m=12$, and $b=15$. This results in an elapsed time of 11.2 weeks as shown in Figure 5-9. This example indicates that the estimator is a bit optimistic since t_e lies to the left of the most likely time.

The expected time t_e represents the particular time value (hours, days, weeks, or some other basis). If we erect a perpendicular line for the value t_e (as shown in Figures 5-8 and 5-9), about half of the area under the curve will be to either side of this line. In a normal bell-shaped curve as stated previously, the most likely time is the average or expected time. However, in the beta distribution, skewed to the right or left, the expected time will lie to the right or left of the most likely value depending upon the three time figures. Studies have been made regarding the accuracy of t_e in a beta distribution. They all seem to indicate the error in calculating the expected

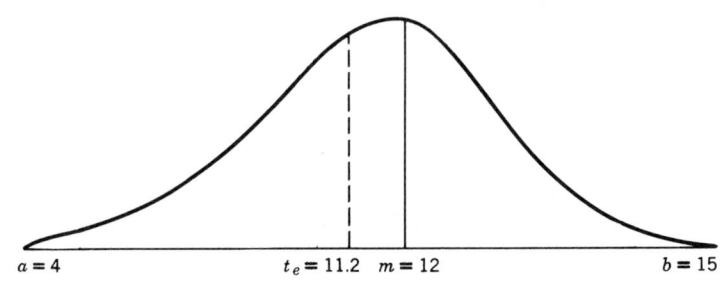

$a = 4$ $t_e = 11.2$ $m = 12$ $b = 15$

Figure 5-9 Beta distribution—t_e to the left of most likely time due to the time factor m.

time was too small to have any material effect in most business and industrial applications.

Step 3. Determine Earliest Expected and Latest Allowable Times

Before determination can be made of the critical path, we must know more about the event time, that is, the aggregate time required to reach a certain event in a project. An event can have one or more values depending on activity-time relationships. Many events have a range of possible event times. In order to determine the event time, we need to know the earliest expected time as measured from the start of the project and a latest allowable time as measured from the finish of the project. Or to put it another way, it is necessary to know the earliest time at which the activities originating from an event can be started. This is the earliest expected time. Similarly, it is necessary to know the latest time at which activities terminating at an event can be completed and still permit the entire project to be finished on schedule. This is called the latest allowable time.

The "earliest expected time" (T_E) can be illustrated by using Figure 5-5 as revised in Figure 5-10 for insertion of earliest expected times (shown in squares). The earliest expected time for event 0 is zero since no activity time has preceded it. The zero event time becomes the base time to which all subsequent times are added. The earliest expected time for event 1 is the sum of the base time 0 and the duration of the activity 0–1 (1 week) or zero plus one equals one week. The earliest expected time for event 2 is the sum of the earliest expected time for event 1 (1 week) plus the duration of activity 1–2 (4 weeks), which is 5 weeks. Up to this point, the procedure is a simple summation.

When an event has two or more activities flowing into it, the earliest expected time for this particular event requires a choice. In our illustration, the earliest expected time for event 4 requires a choice: either the sum of the earliest expected time for event 2 (5 weeks) plus the duration of the activity 2–4 (3 weeks) equals 8 weeks or the earliest expected time for event 3 (6 weeks) plus the duration of activity 3–4 (1.5 weeks) equals 7.5 weeks.

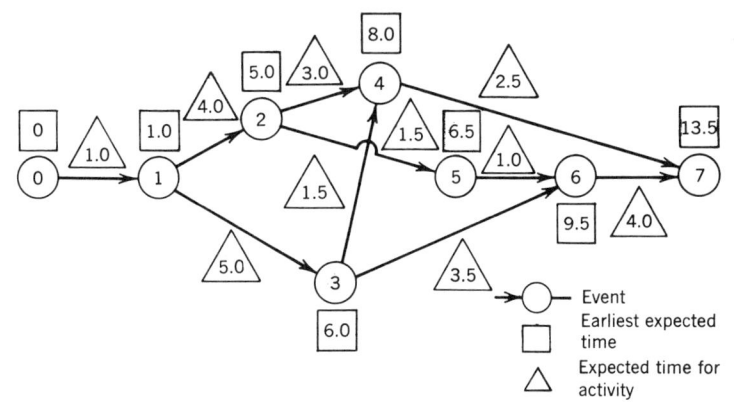

Figure 5-10 PERT network—earliest expected time T_E.

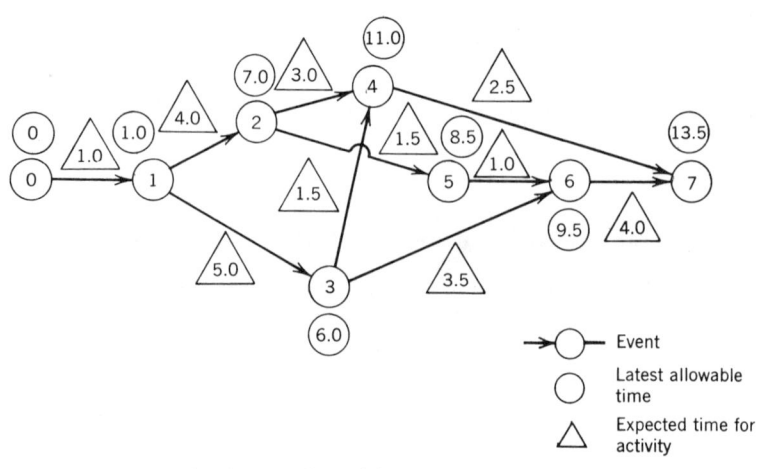

Figure 5-11 PERT network—latest allowable time T_L.

Since activity 4–7 cannot begin until both activities 2–4 and 3–4 are completed, it is necessary to select the maximum time of 8 weeks as the earliest expected time for event 4. The rule to follow for determining earliest expected times is: when there is a choice of event times, take the maximum time.

The "latest allowable time" (T_L), as previously stated, is the latest time at which each activity can be completed and still permit the entire project to be completed on time. In computing latest allowable times (shown in circles), we begin at the end of the project with a latest expected time of 13.5 weeks for event 7 as in Figure 5-11. The latest allowable time for event 4 is the difference between the latest allowable time for event 7 (13.5 weeks) and the duration of activity 4–7 (2.5 weeks) or 13.5 minus 2.5 equals 11 weeks. The latest allowable time for event 3 is the latest allowable time for event 4 (11 weeks) minus the duration of activity 3–4 (1.5 weeks) or 9.5 weeks. Likewise, the latest allowable time for event 3 is also the latest allowable time for event 6 (9.5 weeks) minus the duration of activity 3–6 (3.5 weeks) or 6 weeks. We now have to make a choice between the two latest allowable times (9.5 weeks and 6 weeks). The choice must be 6 weeks since the latest allowable time is the latest time at which activities terminating in that event may be completed. This allows activities following the event to terminate with the earliest project completion date of 13.5 weeks. The rule to remember here for determining latest allowable times is: when there is a choice of event times, take the minimum time.

Step 4. Locate Critical Path(s)

Having determined earliest expected and latest allowable times, these now can be brought together in a single network as shown in Figure 5-12. The critical path in the network is the longest time path throughout the network or 0–1–3–6–7. Observe that for each of the events on the critical path, its earliest event time T_E is equal to its latest event time T_L. This means that the latest allowable time in which each event can be completed is equal to

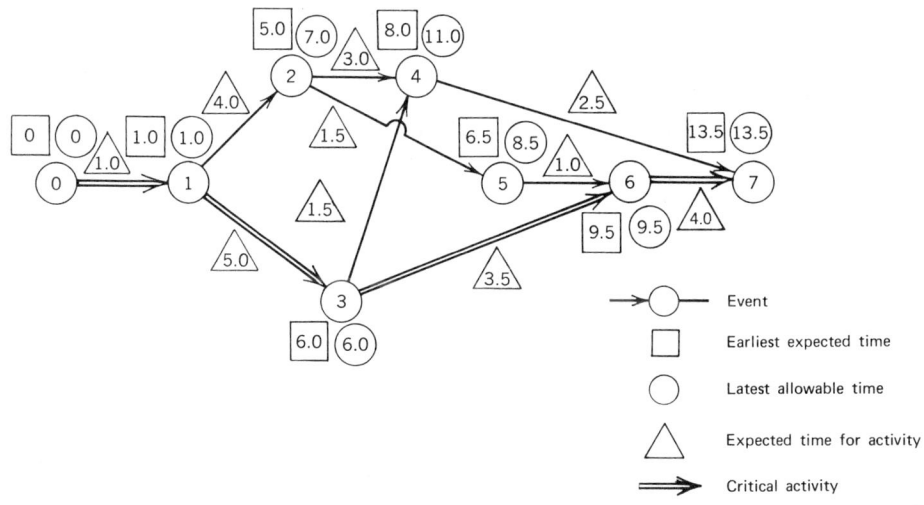

Figure 5-12 PERT network—earliest expected and latest allowable times, T_E and T_L, respectively.

the earliest date on which we can expect each event to be completed. Thus there is no spare (slack) time and the events must be completed exactly as scheduled to meet our completion time of 13.5 weeks. Although not illustrated in this example, it is possible to have more than one critical path.

Step 5. Calculate Slack

Observing events 2 and 4 which are not on the critical path, we could fall behind on activity 1–2 as much as 2 weeks and on activity 2–4 as much as 3 weeks and still not jeopardize finishing the network in 13.5 weeks. Thus, the network enables one to see where time can or must be saved and where the schedule can slide for a while if it is advantageous.

The time to spare in a PERT network, commonly referred to as slack, can be defined in two ways. *Total slack* is the length of time an activity may be delayed from its earliest start without affecting the completion time of the entire project. *Free slack* of an activity is the amount of time an activity may be delayed from its earliest start without affecting the earliest start of succeeding activities. It is possible that an activity may have total slack, but no free slack.

The formula for slack S (total) is the difference between the latest allowable time T_L and the earliest expected time T_E, defined as:

$$S = T_L - T_E \qquad \text{(Equation 5-2)}$$

In addition to slack at events 2 and 4 in Figure 5-12, there is slack at event 5 in the amount of 2 weeks. Knowing the amount of slack related to the different events, it may be possible to switch resources—men, machinery, and materials—to the critical path in order to shorten the total project time. This is one of the basic reasons for using PERT.

So far, slack has been discussed in terms of *positive slack*. It is possible

TABLE 5-1
Summary of Expected Time (t_e), Latest Allowable Time (T_L), Earliest Expected Time (T_E), and Slack (T_L-T_E) for the PERT/Time Project

Preceding Event	Event	t_e	T_L	T_E	Slack T_L-T_E
—	0	0	0	0	0
0	1	1.0	1.0	1.0	0
1	2	4.0	7.0	5.0	2.0
1	3	5.0	6.0	6.0	0
2	4	3.0	11.0	8.0	3.0
2	5	1.5	8.5	6.5	2.0
3	4	1.5	11.0	8.0	3.0
3	6	3.5	9.5	9.5	0
4	7	2.5	13.5	13.5	0
5	6	1.0	9.5	9.5	0
6	7	4.0	13.5	13.5	0

to talk in terms of *negative slack*. This means that some of the events on the critical path(s) and noncritical path(s) are behind schedule.

The events and related times that appear in Figure 5-12 can be scheduled in terms of events and amount of slack time. This is done on the basis of event numbering as in Table 5-1. Note that there is a zero slack for the events on the critical path.

Step 6. Evaluate PERT Network

Once the network has been drawn, all time values calculated (t_e, T_L, T_E, and slack), and the critical path(s) determined, the real job of PERT has actually just begun. This is where *sensitivity analysis* plays an important role. Activities whose times have been estimated may have no effect on the critical path even if they fall behind schedule. However, other estimated timed activities may be on the critical path or may be critical at a later date. The effect of these initial path activities must be assessed. Hence, adjustments and revisions to the original plans may be necessary to assure that the PERT network is completed within a scheduled end date.

If overall times are unsatisfactory, several methods of adjustment are available to the planner, one being the interchanging of men, machines, and materials (if they are comparable) from the noncritical path(s) to the critical path(s). Another network adjustment is reducing the technical specifications of the project. An example is the reduction in the amount of testing required on the project. If activities can be rearranged, it may be possible to speed up the completion of a project. The overlapping of concurrent activities may be available to the planner. Moreover, the use of overtime provides additional flexibility for network replanning and adjustment. Thus, the planner has several alternatives available for adjusting the critical path(s) in order to improve completion dates throughout the project.

The foregoing steps for developing a final PERT project are summarized in Figure 5-13. As indicated above in the final step, the user has the capability of redoing the PERT network if need be to meet a specified completion date. Generally, any "trading off" of resources, revision in standards, and/or specifications will necessitate a recomputation of times—expected, earliest expected, latest allowable, slack, and critical path(s).

Step 1—Prepare PERT Network
Prepare the PERT/Time network without considering activity times or completion dates. Connect the succession of inter-relationships through the use of event symbols (circled numbers) and activity flows (arrows).

Step 2—Calculate Expected Times
Calculate the expected time (t_e) for each activity by inserting three time estimates—optimistic (a), most likely (m), and pessimistic (b)— in the following equation:

$$t_e = \frac{a + 4m + b}{6} \qquad \text{(Equation 5-1)}$$

As each t_e is calculated, it is entered on the network (shown in a triangle below the appropriate activity arrow).

Step 3—Determine Earliest Expected and Latest Allowable Times
Determine earliest expected times (T_E—shown in squares above the appropriate events) by adding the expected times, starting with the first event and going from left to right. However, when an event has two or more activities flowing into it, take the maximum time.

Determine latest allowable times (T_L—shown in circles above the appropriate events) by subtracting the expected times, starting with the last event and going from right to left. However, when an event has two or more activities flowing out of it, take the minimum time.

Step 4—Locate Critical Path(s)
Locate the critical path(s) by determining the longest time path(s) throughout the network. This is accomplished by observing the events on the critical path—their earliest expected times are equal to their latest allowable times.

Step 5—Calculate Slack
Calculate the amount of slack for each activity by taking the time difference between the latest allowable time (T_L) and the earliest expected time (T_E) for the same event, utilizing the following equation:

$$S = T_L - T_E \qquad \text{(Equation 5-2)}$$

Step 6—Evaluate PERT Network
Evaluate the PERT network from an overview standpoint. If total time is unsatisfactory, realign resources, add personnel from noncritical activities, utilize overtime, and comparable schemes to improve completion dates throughout the project. Redo the PERT network employing the preceding steps. Any "trading off" of foregoing items will generally necessitate a recomputation of network times.

Figure 5-13 Steps employed in developing a final PERT project.

Computer PERT Packages

When a network consists of very few activities and events or when one person has knowledge regarding the whole project, decisions regarding the initial network's critical path(s), rearrangement, and rescheduling should not be too difficult. However, in the development of complex networks where many men, machines, and materials are involved, the use of a computer becomes a necessity. A computer, employing a PERT packaged routine, provides a method of checking actual progress against the schedule. It can determine the slack time in the network as of a certain time, say this week. This allows the manager to shift resources if possible, rearrange subnetworks and like items, in an attempt to complete the project in the shortest feasible time. Also, it can print an event report (starting from the first event to the last), latest allowable time report, and departmental reports for events.

What is the cutoff point for a manual versus a computer approach to a PERT network? Obviously, a network of 1000 activities could not be handled properly using manual methods since one error could mean the wrong critical path was selected. Approximately 100 activities is a lower limit for a computer application with a weekly updating of changes to produce a new critical path and related reports. Since many firms have a computer available, the problem of accuracy with a manual approach can be solved by a computer approach. Furthermore, most projects do not follow original plans and revisions must take place each time an activity exceeds its planned time or is completed in less than its planned time. These constant revisions can play havoc with manual methods. The computer has the ability to produce orderly reports faster and more accurately for those involved, especially those who want their reports yesterday. Complexity, accuracy, length of the project, number of events, and the frequency of output desired are determinants of whether a computer should be used.

Advantages and Disadvantages of PERT

Some of the advantages of PERT should be evident from earlier sections of this chapter. From a management point of view, PERT specifies how planning is to be done. It provides management with an approach for keeping planning up to date as the various events are accomplished and as conditions change. PERT permits management to foresee quickly the impact of deviations from the plan and thus to take corrective action in anticipation of potential trouble spots rather than after the fact. A rough rule of experience is that only 10 percent of the activities in a project will be critical at any one time. Probably PERT's principal value is in helping management achieve an objective or complete a project with minimum time and cost expenditures.

Under the PERT approach, every manager of an activity knows the precise starting time for his work. He knows he has a coordinating responsibility with other managers of activities and is aware of the results expected.

Management responsibilities are precisely and empirically designated. PERT helps remove vagueness from the assignment of responsibility. It assists in eliminating one of the major blocks in relating planning to day-to-day operations. Although thus far we have dealt basically with the planning values of PERT, operating values are similarly applicable. Many managers have reported improved management control, identification of problem areas, improved communications, improved management of resources, improved decision making, improved progress reporting, and savings of time.

Regarding the last operating value—savings of time—several studies have indicated that PERT time savings for most firms have ranged from 5 to 20 percent which can be translated directly into dollar savings even though the savings might not be on a one for one basis. Aside from the direct savings to the firm, there are other benefits, such as earlier generation of revenue and the introduction of a new product or process ahead of competition. It is conceivable that these indirect PERT savings could outweigh those that are directly apparent.

In addition to the benefits available to management, PERT provides a way of thinking through all the steps and interrelationships for a project in a methodical manner to reduce oversight of certain activities and events. Another important advantage of PERT is that it provides a number of checks and safeguards against going astray in developing a plan; that is, in making the network, the arrow diagram must show exactly which activities immediately precede and follow each one of the component activities in the project. Even though this quantitative technique has its origin in higher mathematics, its execution requires only simple arithmetic. This is in sharp contrast with some of the other mathematical techniques presented in this book. Another valuable characteristic is its flexibility, which allows varying degrees of refinement necessary and the use of costing procedures depending on the needs of the project. PERT can be useful as a simulation device. It allows the formulation and evaluation of alternative plans before actual implementation.

Despite the glowing advantages just set forth, there are some shortcomings to the PERT network. Surveys made by several reputable firms have pinpointed some noteworthy problems, the first dealing with securing realistic time and cost estimates. This is particularly true when a new and different type project is undertaken and little previous experience exists. Securing both operating and management acceptance is termed a serious problem. This stems from the natural reluctance of people to accept and effect changes. Training of personnel is also a major problem. This comes from the resistance to change and the time requirement necessary to learn PERT effectively. Developing a clear, logical network is a troublesome area. There appears to be no way to assure that the network accurately reflects the best thinking of those planning the work. This difficulty comes from the fact that PERT is no better than the persons who provide the input. One of the most mentioned trouble areas of PERT is determining the correct level of network detail. This is actually a matter of judgment and experience. Many companies tend to vary the detail of the networks, depending upon the management level and the usage to which they are put.

There are certain kinds of projects in which PERT may not be useful; for example, projects which are too nebulous or changeable to allow any kind of methodical planning and simple, even though large, projects involving only an uncomplicated succession of end-to-end activities. Integrating network techniques with existing budgeting and cost accounting procedures, and padding of original estimates by personnel who know that times and costs will be reviewed closely are other difficulties. There may be a problem of juggling resources to accommodate several programs at once. There can be the further difficulty of integrating "PERTed" and "non-PERTed" projects.

The variety of conditions present in firms makes it difficult to come to a precise conclusion on what it may cost to apply PERT. A few firms regard its costs too high, whereas others consider it moderate or minimal. When dealing in terms of PERT/Time networks, cost has ranged from 0.5 to 2 percent of total project costs. For PERT/Cost networks, costs are 1 to 5 percent of project costs. The general consensus of firms using PERT indicates that its costs are not a major deterrent to its use. This is understandable since there are direct and indirect cost savings from using this technique, as was pointed out earlier. Since there are planning costs associated with other non-PERTing techniques, one should consider only the extra costs for using PERT over some other planning technique. The marginal cost for using PERT should be compared to its marginal savings. Such an analysis generally favors the implementation of PERT. This is readily understandable since savings of workers' time, the major cost for most projects, means large cost savings.

PERT/Cost

PERT/Cost, developed in 1962 as an expansion of PERT/Time, integrates time data with cost data. It incorporates both time and cost into a network so that their trade-offs can be calculated. This technique shifts the focus from volume, such as cost per piece produced, to cost for each activity. It cuts across the traditional accounting boundaries of departments and accounting periods. PERT/Cost requires a high degree of coordination of engineering, estimating, control, and accounting activities.

Time-Cost Relationship

To explain the nature of PERT/Cost, it is essential to understand certain terms. Two time and cost estimates are indicated for each activity in the network. They are a normal estimate and a crash estimate. The *normal estimate* of time is analogous to the expected time estimate. Normal cost is the cost associated with finishing the project in the normal time. The *crash time estimate* is the time that would be required if no costs were spared in trying to reduce the project time. The project manager would do whatever was necessary to speed up the work. Crash cost is the cost associated with doing the job on a crash basis in order to minimize completion time.

Time-cost relationships can take on many forms, as pictured in Figure 5-14. Case *A* is a time-cost relationship in which a reduction of time can be

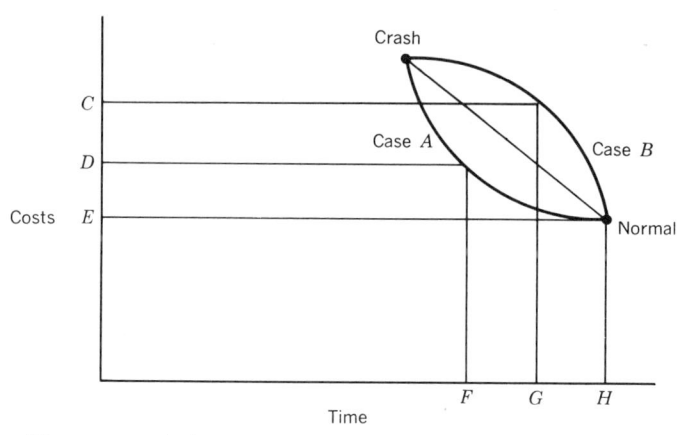

Figure 5-14 Time-cost relationships.

effected with a modest increase in cost. On the other hand, case B is a time-cost relationship in which a reduction in time can be effected with a large increase in cost. The more usual kind of cost-time relationship is the straight line drawn between case A and case B, which is a reasonably accurate linear approximation of the true relationship. To demonstrate a modest increase in cost for case A and a large increase in cost for case B, several lines have been drawn in Figure 5-14. Lines D, E, F, and H are applicable to case A, while lines, C, E, G, and H are related to case B.

The principal reason for using linear approximations in place of the true time-cost curves is to determine quickly the cost of expediting any one of the activities in a network without getting bogged down in complicated accounting concepts, such as the reallocation of costs on some accounting basis. However, the true time-cost curve can be determined and employed as illustrated in the master problem for the chapter. Experience with this scheduling technique has shown that the extra expenditure to determine what these precise relationships are is not warranted. Since we have noted the rationale for treating a time-cost as a straight line, each unit reduction in time produces an equal increase in cost. The incremental cost I_c is the crash cost C_c minus normal cost N_c divided by the normal time N_T minus crash time C_T. This is shown as:

$$I_c = \frac{C_c - N_c}{N_T - C_T} = \frac{\triangle \text{Cost}}{\triangle \text{Time}} \qquad \text{(Equation 5-3)}$$

PERT/Cost Problem

We are now in a position to demonstrate how the incremental costs for each activity can be used to reduce the total project time at the least additional cost. Table 5-2 shows time and cost for each activity on a normal basis and a crash basis. Incremental costs for each activity also are shown, calculated by Equation 5-3. The PERT network on a normal time-cost basis

TABLE 5-2
Normal and Crash Time-Cost Values Plus Incremental Costs

Activity	Normal Time (N_T)	Crash Time (C_T)	Normal Direct Cost (N_c)	Crash Direct Cost (C_c)	Weekly Incremental Cost (I_c)
0–1	1	1	$ 5,000	$ 5,000	Not applicable
1–2	3	2	5,000	12,000	$7,000
1–3	7	4	11,000	17,000	2,000
2–3	5	3	10,000	12,000	1,000
2–4	8	6	8,500	12,500	2,000
3–4	4	2	8,500	16,500	4,000
4–5	1	1	5,000	5,000	Not applicable
			$53,000	$80,000	

in Figure 5-15 is based upon this table. It can be seen that the normal time for the illustration is 14 weeks at a cost of $53,000. When the same problem is crashed in terms of time and cost, the time is 10 weeks at a cost of $80,000. However, we should consider whether it is necessary to crash every activity in order to meet the time requirements of 10 weeks. The answer to this question will become apparent at the end of the problem.

The network found in Figure 5-15 is the starting point for crashing the program down to 10 weeks. The first and last activities cannot be crashed since an incremental cost cannot be computed. The starting point in our compression process is to determine the critical path which is 0–1–2–3–4–5. In order to shorten the time factor by 1 to 13 weeks, it is clear that one of the activities (on the critical path) must be shortened since they determine the total project time. Reviewing the incremental costs for the critical activities in Figure 5-15, activity 2–3 has the lowest incremental cost, or $1000. This is our selection to reduce the project time at the least additional cost. The revised PERT network is found in Figure 5-16.

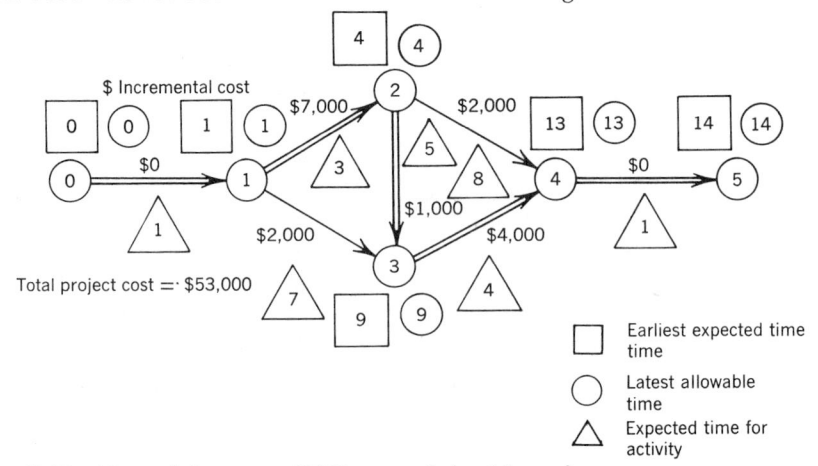

Figure 5-15 Normal time-cost PERT network for 14 weeks.

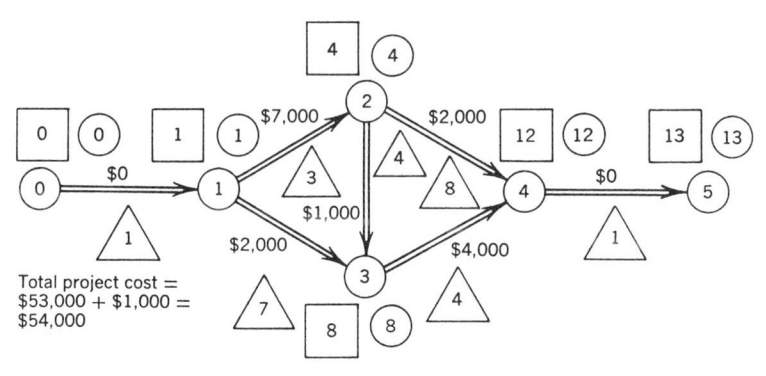

Figure 5-16 Time-cost PERT network for 13 weeks.

Inspection of Figure 5-16 reveals there are three critical paths (0–1–2–3–4–5, 0–1–2–4–5, and 0–1–3–4–5). In effect, all the activities have now become critical. It is now necessary to shorten certain critical activities in order to reduce total project time to 12 weeks. There are three combinations of two activities to choose from: 1–2 and 1–3 with a total increment cost of $9000; 1–2 and 3–4 with a combined incremental cost of $11,000; and 2–4 and 3–4 with a total increment cost of $6000. The last provides the lowest cost of the three combinations of two activities. There is another possibility, the combination of three activities. Here 1–3, 2–3, and 2–4 total a combined $5000, a figure that clearly is preferable. The revised PERT network for 12 weeks is shown in Figure 5-17.

Based upon the crash time initially given, it is evident that activity 2–3 has reached its limiting crash point in terms of time (3 weeks) and cannot be shortened further. The combination of three activities cannot be used again in reducing the project completion time from 12 weeks. We now are forced to use the combinations of two activities which were set forth earlier. With all activities still being critical, the least costly combination is the 2–4 and 3–4 activities for a total cost of $6000. This change is effected in Figure 5-18.

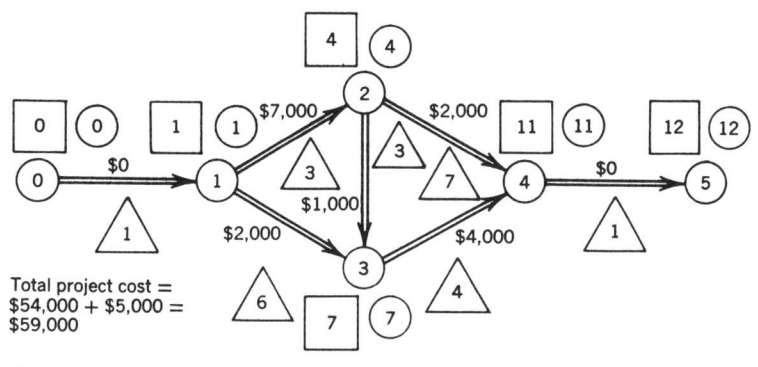

Figure 5-17 Time-cost PERT network for 12 weeks.

PERT/TIME, PERT/COST, AND PERT/LOB   137

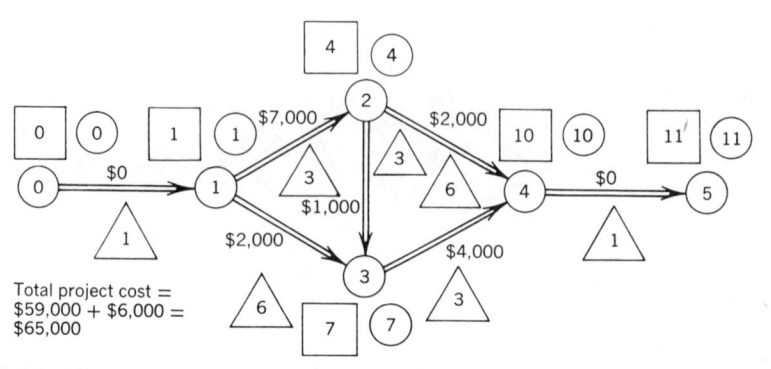

Figure 5-18 Time-cost PERT network for 11 weeks.

It was noted earlier that activity 2-3 had reached its limiting crash duration. The same now holds true for activity 2–4. Again we are confronted with all activities being critical and the combinations of two activities, either 1–2 and 1–3 or 1–2 and 3–4. The least cost combination is $9000 for the first combination, which is reflected in Figure 5-19.

Now that activities 1–2, 2–3, and 2–4 have reached their crash time, and all activities are still critical, we have crashed the project as far as possible. The reduction process is complete except for the question raised regarding the necessity to crash every activity in the project. Table 5-3 will serve as a basis for answering this question.

The project cost of $74,000 for a crash time of 10 weeks is called a "modified crash program." Since the expenditure of an additional $6000 does not further reduce the project completion time, there would be no logical reason for spending the entire $80,000. Instead of crashing every activity, we need crash only the critical activities. An examination of the original data reveals that it was not necessary to crash the following activities:

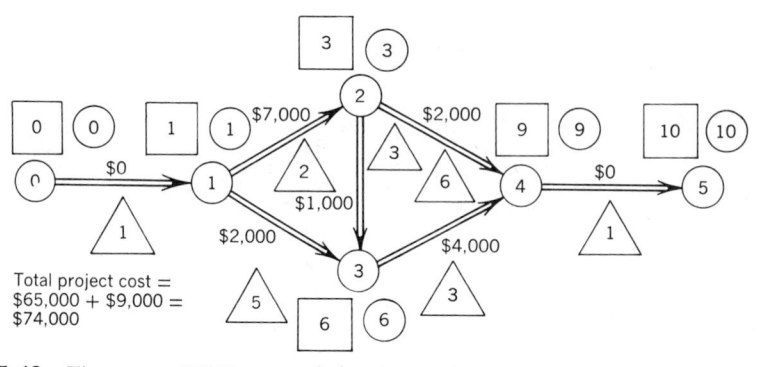

Figure 5-19 Time-cost PERT network for 10 weeks.

138   OPERATIONS RESEARCH MODELS—PROBABILITY AND STATISTICS

Activity	Week	Cost
1–3	1 (from 5 to 4)	$2,000
3–4	1 (from 3 to 2)	4,000
		$6,000

TABLE 5-3
Comparison of Normal and Crash Time-Cost Values

Project Time	Least Additional Cost	Project Cost
14 weeks (normal) (Figure 5-15)	—	$53,000
13 weeks (Figure 5-16)	$1,000	54,000
12 weeks (Figure 5-17)	5,000	59,000
11 weeks (Figure 5-18)	6,000	65,000
10 weeks (modified crash—Figure 5-19)	9,000	74,000
10 weeks (crash)	6,000	80,000

PERT/Cost Comments

The PERT/Cost illustration is intended to demonstrate the principles and procedures followed in reducing a project. Even in this relatively simple example, there were some complexities in searching the various combinations of activities which result in the least additional cost to the project when compression is used. Obviously, to approach a PERT/Cost problem manually is difficult and generally requires the use of a computer program. The original statement regarding the size of a PERT/Time network (approximately 100 activities) for using a computer needs to be revised substantially lower for a PERT/Cost network. Searching all the possible combinations can prove to be a tedious and time-consuming task, not to mention the possibility of errors. For these reasons, a computer PERT/Cost program should be used in a network of approximately 25 or more activities which are closely interconnected.

The benefits and limitations attributable to PERT/Time are readily applicable to PERT/Cost. Several limitations, extensions of those previously mentioned, need to be explained here. No manager wants to encounter cost overruns which would reflect adversely on his performance. As a result, he is tempted to pad the cost estimates initially to compensate for any possible error in the time estimates for a fixed cost contract. On the other hand, for cost-plus contracts, particularly those of the government, there may be little or no penalty for underestimation of costs. Contractors tend to understate costs in order to win the contract and then make little effort to control cost. Revisions partially absolve the individual(s) responsible for the original estimates since the final costs are really for a new contract, not for the one whose cost estimate was originally formulated. Even if costs are overstated or understated based upon the type of contract, it is difficult to extrapolate from past cost patterns reliable future project costs, certainly a limitation on the effectiveness of this technique. There is a further problem of cost allocation since it is generally difficult, if not impossible, to assign departmental expenses accurately among projects. Whatever reason for misallocation of costs, there is always a danger that these misleading figures will be used as a basis for estimating costs of comparable projects.

Like other control techniques, PERT/Cost is no panacea since its usefulness is directly dependent upon the data fed into the system. This, in turn, depends upon the efficiency of the operating personnel. If unreliable data is fed into the PERT/Cost program, then the same type of information will be its output. However, efforts have been under way to improve the PERT/Cost system in order to alleviate the difficulties in the areas of cost. Perhaps more attention should be devoted to increasing the capabilities of the operating personnel who are responsible for the day to day functions of the PERT/Cost system.

PERT/LOB

The first generation of PERT is called PERT/Time while the second generation is referred to as PERT/Cost. A third generation, called PERT/LOB (Line of Balance), is useful for the many activities between the research and development phase and the quantity production phase. The LOB technique itself has been a tool in the control of production activities for some 30 years. Many firms have employed PERT in the development phase of large projects while utilizing LOB in the production phase. The problem with this approach is that there is no effective managerial tool to employ during the transition from development to prototype and add-on production. The transition phase can prove to be crucial due to such reasons as commitments to customers and best utilization of factory facilities. PERT/LOB is designed not only to control through the critical transition phase, but also to monitor the normal production stages of a project. Management can plan, organize, direct, and control the entire development, using this third generation of PERT. The firm can bid more realistically and can estimate costs more accurately on a life-cycle basis, especially when dealing with government contracts.

Essentials of LOB

Basically, LOB is a charting technique for collecting, measuring, and presenting information relating to time and work done during production. The progress of the interrelated activities is compared with actual versus planned performance. The feedback to management is concerned with timely information about these critical areas—where the project now stands, where it is behind schedule, and where it is ahead of schedule. Line of balance is concerned with a means of integrating and checking on the production flow so as to meet customer delivery requirements.

An examination of the four LOB phases reveals the first to be the objective or the required delivery date. The delivery information can be broken down into the planned schedule and the actual schedule. Once the objective is determined, the next phase is to define the program, that is, make use of a graphic flow chart plotted against the lead time required before shipment. The progress of the project is monitored at certain control points (key plant operations or assembly points). The lead time scale represents the number of working periods (hours, days, or weeks), counting backwards from total completion, that are needed to complete each major milestone in the entire project. The third task is to construct a program progress chart (bar chart) which depicts the cumulative quantities of materials, parts, and subassemblies processed at the control points as of a given time. The last phase of LOB depicts the cumulative parts or components in terms of end items (set for each control point) which must have been completed as of the progress review date. The end result is the characteristic step-down contour of a line balance. At this point, LOB can be compared with the actual performance of each item in terms of a graphical portrayal for the project.

PERT/LOB Method
Having briefly described what LOB is, attention is now focused on the PERT/LOB technique, which integrates the planning elements of PERT with the production control elements of LOB. This integrated technique broadens the scope of PERT by allowing inclusion of repetitive activities in the network. In addition to highlighting critical activities and problem areas (present and future), it takes into account the present status of repetitive activities. It helps to predict schedule requirements at any point in time and to relate their current efforts to future schedules. As with PERT, PERT/LOB utilizes a time-oriented network with activities. All the steps occurring in both the planning and control phases of PERT apply also to this technique.

The initial step for this technique involves stating the objectives of the project. These objectives are subdivided with ever-greater detail so that the lowest breakdown items (end items) can be subdivided into work packages Time estimates then must be established for the various activities. However, for the repetitive activities, a time estimate should be made for each batch or lot size. It should be remembered that the size of the batch may range from a single unit to the entire production quantity. The time estimate should reflect this. Therefore one batch time is the activity time. The batch size quantity takes into consideration the required number of items, inventory data, processing times, line balancing, resource availability, and other pertinent factors. In repetitive activities, it may be possible to start production on the second batch before the first batch is completed.

The preceding work breakdown structure provides a basis for the construction of a network with any desired level of detail, in particular, one-time activities and repetitive activities. A repetitive activity is represented in the network by an open box and activity arrow while a repetitive event is shown by an X in a circle. The repetitive events of the network become the LOB control points. An example of the PERT/LOB system is found in Figure 5-20 where only three levels of activities and events are shown. For top management, this example is a one-time activity, whereas for the next levels

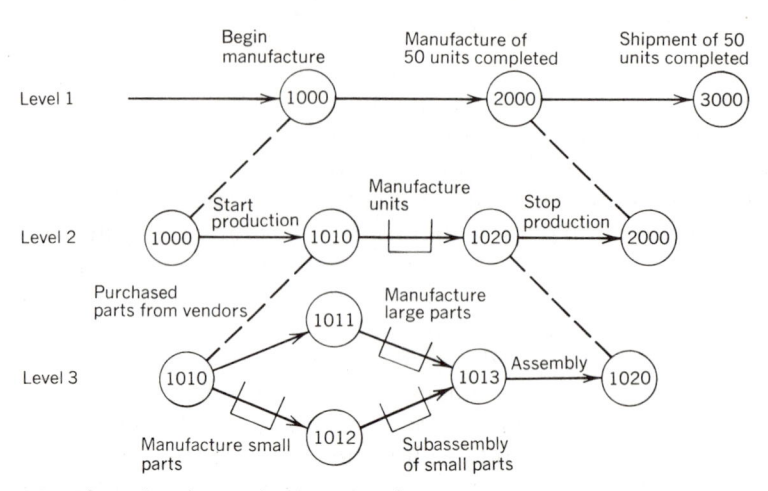

Figure 5-20 Three-level PERT/LOB network.

of management (level 2 and level 3) it is a repetitive activity. The dashed lines indicate the additional detail for an event or activity on each level. Additional levels are applicable to Figure 5-20 but are not shown.

Basically, calculations are similar to those found in a PERT system. The only notable difference is that repetitive activities have multiple contact points rather than a single point. As a result, the earliest expected time, the latest allowable time, and slack time are calculated for each batch of repetitive activities. Generally, a computer is needed for these calculations.

The basic computer reports are the milestone report, the production status report, and the activity report. The first report deals with the events (milestones); it is designed to show top management whether or not work on the milestone jobs is on schedule. The production status report is concerned with essential production information at each of the control points on the PERT/LOB network and shows the projected completion dates for the control point activities. The last report, the activity report, shows how different jobs stand in relation to the schedule.

The PERT/LOB technique is usable for any situation in which PERT or LOB has application. While PERT is better where no repetitive activities are present, LOB is better where there are no one time activities present. However, in most actual situations, there is some midpoint between PERT and LOB. It is for these conditions that PERT/LOB was developed.

PERT/LOB/Cost

The integration of cost into the basic PERT/LOB technique requires only the addition of the cost planning and control aspects utilized by PERT/Cost. The cost module portion of the PERT/Cost technique can be added to the PERT/LOB technique at any time it is considered desirable. The cost planning and control structure for PERT/LOB/Cost, as in PERT/Cost, is the work breakdown structure. Additional actions required to attain a PERT/LOB/Cost technique (also required with PERT/Cost) include the following:

1. Coding.
2. Establishment of cost categories.
3. Cost and resource estimating.

It should be noted that the PERT/LOB/Cost technique requires no change in commonly used production costing systems.

Various Applications of PERT

The first application of PERT, the Polaris project, has been extended to many different ones. PERT has been successfully used in the construction industry, particularly in the building of large structures. The scheduling of government and commercial aircraft; the design, development, and testing of new machines; first production runs; installing fixed assets; and plant layout are a few examples of how it can be applied to the manufacturing function of the firm. PERT techniques also have been used in the administrative function of the firm. These include streamlining paperwork systems, making major administrative systems revisions, planning acquisitions of firms, R & D program planning, and corporate profit plan development. Computer installation and conversion in which there are a large number of varied and dependent activities is a logical candidate.

By no means has the marketing function been neglected. Controlling the developments and launching of new products may well be the most important use of PERT (construction and R & D have been the most extensive areas of PERT use in the past). New products that have short life cycles call for a high degree of coordination of men, materials, machines, and money. This plus the importance of timing points to the need for an effective quantitative technique. It is surprising that marketing was not one of PERT's first applications.

These are some of the basic areas where PERT/Time, PERT/Cost, and PERT/LOB has been applied. No matter what the application is, costs for the appropriate PERT technique include the salaries and fringe benefits of those engaged in "PERTing" (full time or part time), computer time (if applicable), overhead (prorated), and an amount for supplies. These costs versus the costs of traditional methods is the incremental cost of using PERT. However, as was pointed out earlier in this chapter, there are direct and indirect savings to offset the incremental costs. Management should recognize the deficiencies of older methods and instead of asking the cost of such a system, should ask: Can we afford not to use PERT now that it is available?

Probability of Finishing a PERT Project

The preceding PERT approaches can be augmented by determining the probability of finishing a project which necessitates calculating the standard deviation for an activity. By way of review, standard deviation is a measure of the relative dispersion of a probability distribution about its mean. Since three time estimates (a, m, and b) have been determined, the distance between the a time and the b time represents the distance from the extreme left-hand end to the extreme right-hand end of a distribution of possible activity times. This distance can be represented by approximately ±3 standard deviations (σ) which can be expressed mathematically as:

$$6\sigma = b - a$$
$$\sigma = \frac{b-a}{6}$$ (Equation 5-4)

Thus, one standard deviation for an activity equals $(b-a)/6$.

In order to determine the probability of finishing a PERT network, the first step is to calculate the activity and expected times per Figure 5-21. For this simple PERT network, the individual standard deviations which represent dispersion of activities around their most likely times must also be calculated (Figure 5-21). The next step is to calculate the earliest expected time (T_E) for the network-ending event on the critical path(s). In the illustration, T_E is calculated to be 17.0 weeks (5.0+6.0+6.0) for the final event 40 on the critical path.

Now that T_E has been calculated for event 40, the standard deviation for this event must be determined, which is the square root of the sum of standard deviations squared for each activity. The formula is given as:

$$\sigma_E \text{ (network ending event)} = \sqrt{\Sigma \sigma_1^2 + \sigma_2^2 + \ldots \sigma_n^2}$$
(Equation 5-5)

In the example, the standard deviation for the ending event on the critical path calculates to be 1.5 weeks as follows:

$$\begin{aligned}\sigma_E \text{ (event 40)} &= \sqrt{(1.0)^2 + (1.0)^2 + (.5)^2} \\ &= \sqrt{1 + 1 + .25} \\ &= \sqrt{2.25} \\ &= 1.5 \text{ weeks}\end{aligned}$$

	Activity Time (weeks)			Expected Time (weeks)	Standard Deviation of Activity (weeks)
Activity	a	m	b	t_e	$\frac{b-a}{6}$
10–20[a]	2.0	5.0	8.0	5.0	1.0
10–40	9.0	15.0	21.0	15.0	2.0
20–30[a]	3.0	6.0	9.0	6.0	1.0
30–40[a]	4.5	6.0	7.5	6.0	.5

[a] Critical path.

Figure 5-21 Calculation of expected (t_e) and standard deviation (σ) for activities in a simple PERT network.

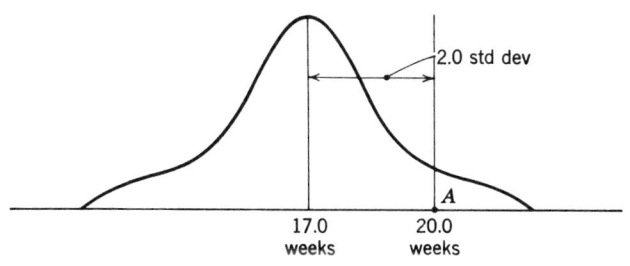

Figure 5-22 Normal distribution curve for illustrative PERT problem.

At this point, two important measures of this PERT network have been determined; (1) $T_E = 17.0$ weeks and (2) $\sigma_E = 1.5$ weeks.

If the times are assumed to be distributed symmetrically around 17.0 weeks in Figure 5-22, half of the time we can expect to finish the PERT project before 17.0 weeks, and half of the time we can expect to finish the project later than 17.0 weeks. A question can be raised: What are the chances of finishing the project some time after 17 weeks, say within 20 weeks (point A, Figure 5-22)? It would be necessary to calculate the number of standard deviations from the mean to point A which is:

$$\frac{20.0 - 17.0}{1.5} = 2.0 \text{ std. dev.}$$

Referring to Appendix C for areas under the curve 2.0 standard deviations to the right of the mean, we locate the value .97725. This means that we have better than a 97 percent chance of completing the PERT project within 20 weeks.

PERT Application—American Products Corporation

The American Products Corporation has just started developing a new product for the home market. The marketing department realizes that the first firm to market this new product will benefit greatly during its introductory phase. In fact, a survey of its marketing staff indicates that high profits will be made during the first weeks of sale. For this reason, two other firms are currently developing a similar product. Trade sources reveal that the American Products Corporation and these two competitors will introduce the product on almost the same date, that is, approximately six months hence (refer to time scale in Figure 5-23).

Further discussion with the marketing staff indicates that additional profits are available to the firm during the first six weeks if it is able to market the product ahead of its competition. Specifically, the extra profits for this period are attributed to a higher selling price and is estimated to be $45,000. Based on this fact, the operations research section was given the data found in Figure 5-23 and Table 5-4.

Utilizing the procedures set forth for PERT/Cost in the chapter, it is

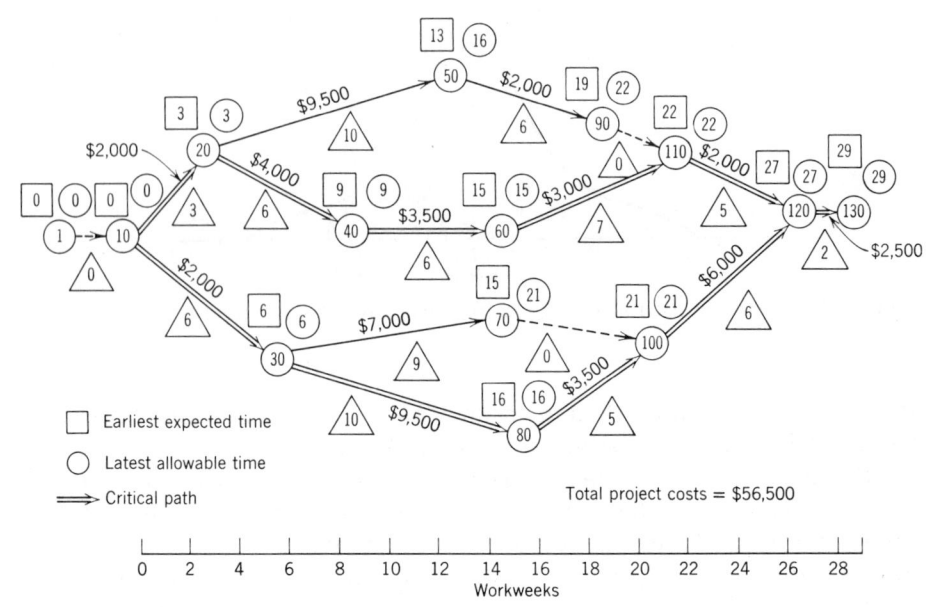

Figure 5-23 PERT network illustrating the expected times, earliest expected times, latest allowable times, normal costs, and critical paths—American Products Corporation.

necessary to shorten the activities along the critical path per Figure 5-23. This can be undertaken by examining the data found in Table 5-4. It should be noted that incremental weekly costs are nonlinear in many cases. For example, crash costs for activity 20-50 are nonlinear for the seventh week while linear for weeks eight and nine. Also, activities cannot be crashed to their lowest time level (one week), except for activity 120-130. Thus, time and cost constraints must be considered when developing a final solution.

Since the foregoing data was immediately available to the operations researcher, it was possible to develop an answer the same day. A computer PERT/Cost program package was utilized to develop the modified crash cost program, the results of which are shown in Table 5-5. Based upon the estimated additional profit of $45,000 for the first six weeks and crash costs of $23,000, the recommendation should be to crash the project by six weeks.

Summary

Now that the planning and operating values of PERT are fairly well known, the technique will undoubtedly be extended to many new areas. PERT has been used extensively by governmental agencies. Many of their contractors are required to utilize this technique in submitting bids as well as in the performance of work. However, firms required to use it as a condition of getting and maintaining contracts should recognize the benefits of such a technique and not approach this requirement with a negative attitude.

TABLE 5-4
Time Estimates, Activity Times, Total Activity Costs, and Incremental Weekly Crash Costs—American Products Corporation

Activity	Time Estimates a	m	b	Activity Time in Weeks Normal (t_e)	Crash	Total Activity Costs Normal	Crash	Incremental Weekly Crash Costs
1–10[a]								
10–20	2	3	4	3		$2000		
					2		$4500	$2500
10–30	4	5	12	6		2000		
					5		5000	3000
					4		9000	4000
20–40	5	6	7	6		4000		
					5		9000	5000
20–50	7	9	17	10		9500		
					8		12000	1250
					7		15000	3000
30–70	6	9	12	9		7000		
					8		8000	1000
					7		10500	2500
30–80	7	10	13	10		9500		
					8		12000	1250
					7		15000	3000
40–60	3	6	9	6		3500		
					5		4000	500
50–90	5	6	7	6		2000		
					4		4000	1000
					3		7000	3000
60–110	5	6	13	7		3000		
					6		4000	1000
					5		8000	4000
70–100[a]								
80–100	2	5	8	5		3500		
					4		4000	500
					2		8000	2000
90–110[a]								
100–120	4	6	8	6		6000		
					3		10000	1333
110–120	4	5	6	5		2000		
					4		4000	2000
120–130	1	2	3	2		2500		
					1		4000	1500
						$56,500		

[a] Dummy activity.

TABLE 5-5
Normal Project Cost Versus Modified Crash Cost—American Products Corporation

Project Time	Least Additional Cost	Project Cost
29 weeks (normal—Figure 5-23)		$56,500
28 weeks	$ 500 + $ 500	57,500
27 weeks	1000 + 1250	59,750
26 weeks	2500 + 1333	63,583
25 weeks	2000 + 1333	66,916
24 weeks	4000 + 1334	72,250
23 weeks (modified crash)	1000 + 5000 + 1250	79,500

Discussion of PERT in this chapter has included the methods of constructing networks using time and cost figures, the benefits of the technique, the problems involved, and the requirements for their effective usage. Increased experience by business and government has demonstrated its high management value. The technique has been applied to a variety of situations around the world with relatively beneficial results. The problem areas associated with its application are not inherent in the technique itself—they will be resolved as more experience is gained. PERT, then, has proven to be an effective management tool that can be utilized by most companies in almost every industry.

Questions

1. Discuss the similarities and differences between the Gantt chart and PERT/Cost.
2. Distinguish among a normal time plan, a crash plan, and a modified crash plan.
3. What are the principal difficulties with PERT? How can they be overcome?
4. How does PERT/Cost differ from PERT/LOB?

Problems

5-1 Mr. Ralph Meeker is currently evaluating five different types of franchises that have varying levels of risk. Since the value of a franchise is determined by future income which the franchise will generate, the projected income statement is used as the starting point which, in turn, is adjusted for cash flow under optimistic, most likely, and pessimistic conditions. After cash flow projections have been determined for a stated number of years into the future, their present values are ascertained by discounting back to the current time for optimistic, most likely, and pessimistic conditions. The discount rate employed considers the risk level for each type of franchise. Once the present values of each potential franchise are ascertained, they are grouped, shown as follows:

Franchise Opportunity	Optimistic Net Present Value	Most Likely Net Present Value	Pessimistic Net Present Value
1	$30,000	$12,000	($50,000)
2	100,000	25,000	(5,000)
3	25,000	12,000	(10,000)
4	70,000	40,000	(100,000)
5	25,000	(10,000)	(80,000)

Based on the foregoing facts, rank the five proposals according to their "expected value" estimates.

5-2 A new computer system for the Lawrence Company has to be installed now that the order for an IBM 370 (Model 135) has been finalized. Management wants to know how long it would take to install the new computer system, keeping in mind that the present system employs an IBM 360 (Model 30) computer. Since a change of this type can cause many personnel problems if it is not handled properly, it was decided to use PERT in order to insure a smooth installation of the computer equipment. You have been appointed to develop the PERT network of events and activities as well as the most critical path. In order to determine the most critical path, the events have been given a serial number and shown in terms of sequence, that is, event 6 can be completed only after event 5 is completed. You have been asked to make recommendations based upon the results of your PERT network. The time for each event is in weeks.

Event	Preceding Event	Optimistic Time a	Most Likely Time m	Pessimistic Time b
1	0	0.1	1.0	2.0
2	1	1.0	3.0	4.0
3	2	4.0	6.0	12.0
4	2	0.1	2.0	4.0
5	4	1.0	1.5	3.0
6	5	1.0	4.0	8.0
7	5	1.0	3.0	4.0
8	7	1.0	2.0	4.0
9	6	0.1	1.0	4.0
9	7	0.1	2.0	3.0
10	6	0.1	1.0	3.0
10	7	0.1	1.0	2.0
11	2	0.1	1.0	2.0
12	11	6.0	13.0	30.0
13	12	10.0	12.0	40.0
14	9	0	0	0
14	10	0	0	0
14	11	0	0	0
14	13	0	0	0
14	3	0	0	0
14	8	0	0	0

5-3 Cosmetics, Inc., has decided to market a revolutionary new product for the consumer market. The problems of how to plan and control the various phases of this project—sales promotion, training of salesmen, pricing, packaging, advertising, and manufacturing—are obvious to management. They have asked you to guide them through this difficult situation using PERT/Time since time is of the essence. The first firm to market this type of product will reap very high profits as well as having its image enhanced by marketing such a revolutionary product. A list of the activities with the expected times is given below in terms of weeks:

Activities—Manufacturing	Activity Description	Expected Time t_e
1–2	Study equipment requirement	0.5
2–3	Select supplier of equipment	0.5
3–4	Determine manufacturing procedures	2.0
4–13	Determine quality control procedures	2.0
3–5	Determine optimum purchasing and inventory procedures	2.0
3–12	Equipment received and installed in plant	7.0
5–6	Place order for raw materials	1.0
6–13	Manufacture and receipt of raw materials for test and first production runs	3.0
10–13	Receipt of containers and packaging supplies	0.5
12–13	Personnel available for first production run (some of the men on the first shift will be moved to second shift)	0
13–14	Manufacture test run	2.0
14–16	First production run (enough goods to distribution channels for product introduction)	6.0

Activities—Marketing		
3–7	Pricing of product (using optimization)	1.0
7–8	Rough out art work and finalize	3.0
8–9	Send out advertising material and packaging to suppliers	0.5
9–10	Time to produce advertising material and its receipt	4.0
14–15	Sales meeting	0.5
15–16	Sales training	1.0

Activities—Accounting		
3–11	Determine costs of new product	1.0
11–13	Financing of inventories for new product	2.0

Based upon the above activities, determine the critical path. Give recommendations that might speed up the project.

5-4   The President of Ricardo Manufacturing Company has an opportunity to participate in a project that has a sales price of $90,000 but must be completed within 8 weeks. This letter of intent was received Friday afternoon. Late the same afternoon, both the superintendent of production and the cost accountant completed the appropriate time and costs for you based upon past jobs. Since the president needs an answer at 8:30 A.M. on Monday (start of the 8 weeks), you have been requested to work Saturday and determine the profitability of the project on an 8-week basis. An answer at 8:30 A.M. Monday allows the firm to start the production order at 10:00 A.M. in order to stay within the 8 weeks requested by the customer. The time and cost under normal conditions without crashing the project are based upon an 11-week basis. What answer should the President give the customer on Monday morning? A table of times and costs is listed below.

Event	Preceding Event	Normal t_e (wks.)	Normal Cost	Crash Weeks	Crash Cost
4	1	2	$ 8,000	1	$13,000
2	1	3	7,000	1	19,000
3	1	6	11,000	5	13,500
4	2	4	6,000	3	10,000
3	2	2	9,000	1	10,000
5	2	7	8,500	6	11,500
5	4	4	10,500	3	16,000
5	3	3	5,000	2	7,000

5-5   Several departmental managers of Ryan Aircraft, Inc., have been given the task of determining the times and costs of a new component that the firm may manufacture. Top management wants accurate time and cost estimates since this will be a fixed fee contract with no provision for renegotiating in case of modifications. Rather than give the departmental managers the time requirements of the customer and amount per component, top management feels more accurate answers will be forthcoming if this information is kept secret. You, one of the departmental managers, have been given one week to supply answers regarding the following: the critical path initially, modified crash plan in terms of time and cost for the various weeks, and total crash cost. After three days of analysis, the following time (in weeks) and costs were developed:

Activity	Activity Description	Optimistic Time a	Most Likely Time m	Pessimistic Time b	Normal Cost N_c	Time to Crash Activity C_T	Crash Cost C_C
1–2	Special component study	3.0	3.5	4.5	$ 8,000	2.6	$10,000
1–3	Layouts	4.0	5.0	6.0	15,000	3.0	20,000
1–4	Subsystem design	3.5	4.5	6.0	25,000	3.6	32,500
2–5	Vendor evaluation	2.0	2.2	3.5	4,000	1.4	6,000
3–5	Subcontract specs.	3.0	3.5	4.5	6,000	2.6	7,500
4–6	Subsystem tests	8.0	9.0	12.5	45,000	8.4	60,000
5–7	Subcontract work	7.5	8.5	11.5	35,000	6.8	50,000
3–6	Final drawings	6.0	7.5	12.0	30,000	6.0	40,000
6–7	Fabrication	7.5	9.0	12.5	35,000	7.33	42,500

5-6 The Arcose Machinery Company has been offered a contract to build and deliver nine extruding presses to the Homestead Bottling Company. The contract price is contingent on meeting a specified delivery time, a bonus being given for early delivery. The marketing department has established the following cost and time information.

Activity	Normal Time (weeks) a	b	m(t_e)	Cost	Crash Time (weeks)	Cost
1–2	1	5	3	$ 5,000	1	$ 9,000
2–3	1	7	4	8,000	3	14,000
2–4	1	5	3	4,000	2	6,000
2–5	5	11	8	5,000	7	6,000
3–6	2	6	4	3,000	2	5,000
4–6	5	7	6	2,000	4	3,600
5–7	4	6	5	10,000	4	14,000
6–7	1	5	3	7,000	1	10,600

The normal delivery time is 16 weeks for a contract price of $62,000.

(a) Based on the calculated profitability for each specified delivery time below, recommend the delivery schedule that the Arcose Machine Company should follow.

Contract Delivery Time (Weeks)	Contract Amount
15	$62,500
14	65,000
13	70,000
12	72,500

(b) Based on the foregoing data, what are the chances of completing the contract sometime after the normal delivery time, say one week later?

Bibliography

R. L. Ackoff. and M. W. Sasieni, *Fundamentals of Operations Research,* New York: John Wiley & Sons, 1968.

R. D. Archibald and R. L. Villoria, *Network-Based Management Systems,* New York: John Wiley & Sons, 1967.

B. Baker and R. L. Eris, *An Introduction to PERT/CPM,* Homewood, Ill.: Richard D. Irwin, 1964.

N. Enrick, *Management Operations Research,* New York, Holt, Rinehart and Winston, 1965.

H. Evarts, *Introduction to PERT,* Boston: Allyn and Bacon, 1964.

F. S. Hillier and G. J. Lieberman, *Introduction to Operations Research,* San Francisco: Holden-Day, 1967.

A. Iannone, *Management Program Planning and Control with PERT, MOST & LOB,* Englewood Cliffs, N.J.: Prentice-Hall, 1971.

R. Levin and C. Kirkpatrick, *Planning and Control with PERT/CPM,* New York: McGraw-Hill Book Company, 1966.

K. G. Lockyer, *An Introduction to Critical Path Analysis,* New York: Pitman Publishing Company, 1964.

R. Miller, *Schedule, Cost, and Profit Control with PERT: A Comprehensive Guide for Program Management,* New York: McGraw-Hill Book Company, 1963.

J. J. Moder and C. R. Phillips, *Project Management with CPM and PERT,* New York: Reinhold Publishing Corporation, 1964.

New Uses and Management Implications of PERT, Booz, Allen & Hamilton, 1964.

J. J. O'Brien, *Scheduling Handbook,* New York: McGraw-Hill Book Company, 1969.

L. R. Shaffer, J. B. Ritter and W. L. Meyer, *Critical Path Method,* New York: McGraw-Hill Book Company, 1965.

J. W. Wiest and F. Levy, *A Management Guide to PERT/CPM,* Englewood Cliffs, N.J.: Prentice-Hall, 1969.

3
Operations Research Models – Matrix Algebra

Chapter SIX

Linear Programming

Linear programming had its beginnings in the input-output method of analysis developed by the economist W. W. Leontief. The present-day version is of more recent origin. Hitchcock first interpreted a "transportation type problem" in 1941, while Koopmans studied the same topic in 1947. In 1945, Stigler studied the "diet problem" (concerned with separate entities that can be selected and used in diversified quantities by choosing, combining, or mixing them with the purpose of obtaining an expected result). The current state of the art is attributed to Dr. George D. Dantzig, a mathematician who introduced his "simplex method" as a systematic procedure for solving a linear programming problem.

During 1947, George Dantzig (with Marshall Wood and their associates) was involved in a project for the United States Air Force which resulted in the search for a technique capable of solving military planning problems. The essence of the research lay in viewing interrelations between activities of a large organization as a linear programming model and determining the optimizing program by minimizing a linear objective function. Dantzig indicated that this new approach could be widely applied to business problems, as is evident today.

Basic Requirements for a Linear Programming Problem

Before discussing the necessary requirements for a linear programming problem, a definition of linear programming is needed. Management has at its disposal money, men, machines, and materials which are in limited supply. If these resources were unlimited, there would be no need for management tools like linear programming. Having limited resources, the firm should seek the best allocation of its resources in order to maximize profits. However, there are innumerable problems involved in allocating scarce resources. One approach that has demonstrated potential in this area is linear programming.

Perhaps the best way of defining "linear programming" is to examine the meaning of the words. The adjective "linear" is used to describe a relationship among two or more variables which are directly and precisely proportional. For example, if we say $x = f(y)$ where f is a linear function, then any change in x results in a constant proportional change in y. If this were graphed, the relationship would be expressed by a straight line—hence, linear. The term "programming" makes use of certain mathematical techniques to arrive at the best solution utilizing the firm's limited resources. Another word for programming could be computing, since it stands for calculating some unknown from a set of equations and/or inequalities under certain conditions expressed mathematically. This chapter will demonstrate the mathematics for the graphic, algebraic, and simplex methods.

By gathering together the underlying concepts for both words, linear programming can be defined as a mathematical technique for determining the best allocation of a firm's limited resources. A mathematician might be more technical in defining linear programming by stating that it is a method of solving problems in which an objective function must be maximized or minimized when considering certain constraints. An economist might define linear programming as a method for allocating limited resources in a manner that satisfies the laws of supply and demand for the firm's products. A businessman might look upon linear programming as one of management's tools for solving problems that are in conformity with the firm's clearly defined objectives. Regardless of the way one defines linear programming, certain basic requirements (five) are necessary before this technique can be employed in business problems.

1. Well-Defined Objective Function

A well-defined objective must be stated; this objective may serve to maximize contribution by utilizing the available resources, or it may produce the lowest possible cost by using a limited amount of productive factors, or it may determine the best distribution of the productive factors within a certain time period. It should be remembered that sales volume is linearly related not to profits but to total contribution (selling price minus variable cost per unit times the number of units sold). This requirement, then, is that an objective function be clearly defined mathematically.

2. Alternative Courses of Action

Second, there must be alternative courses of action. For example, it may be possible to make a selection between various combinations of manpower and automatic machinery. Or it may be possible to allocate manufacturing capacity in a certain ratio for the manufacture of a firm's products.

3. Objective Function and Constraints Must Be Expressed Mathematically

Another requirement is that equations and inequalities must describe the problem in linear form. Linearity in linear programming is a mathematical term used to describe systems of simultaneous equations of the first degree which satisfy the objective function and constraints. Constraints (restraints) are expressed mathematically by equations or inequalities. In essence this requirement dictates that the firm's objective and its constraints be expressed mathematically as linear equations or inequalities.

4. Variables Must Be Interrelated

Another necessary condition is that it be possible to formulate mathematical relationships among the variables describing the problem. To state it another way, the requirement is that variables in the problem must be interrelated.

5. Resources Must Be In Limited Supply

The resources must be finite and economically quantifiable. For example, each plant has a limited number of hours available—labor hours are finite. Since the cost of direct labor has an impact on profit, it is also economic. The allocation of this resource will be demonstrated in the next sections.

Graphic Method of Linear Programming

The graphic method of linear programming focuses on the intersection of lines for a two-dimensional approach. The intersection of planes in three dimensions or the use of one dimension, which is trivial, are not treated here. It should be noted that the four steps of the graphic method can be used only where no more than three variables are involved since we cannot draw in more than three dimensions.

In order to relate the fundamentals of linear programming throughout this chapter, the following example will be used. The Revco Corporation has one small plant located on the outskirts of a large city. Its production is limited to two industrial products, Alpha (A) and Beta (B). The unit contributions (unit selling price minus unit variable costs) for each product have been computed by the firm's accounting department as $10 for product Alpha and $12 for product Beta. Each product passes through three departments of the plant. The time requirements for each product and total time available in each department are as follows:

Department	Hours Required Product Alpha	Hours Required Product Beta	Available Hours this Month
1	2.0	3.0	1,500
2	3.0	2.0	1,500
3	1.0	1.0	600

Stating these requirements in mathematical terms, Revco wishes to maximize the objective function:

$$Z \text{ (total contribution)} = \$10A + \$12B$$

subject to the following contraints:

$$2A + 3B \leq 1500 \quad \text{Department 1}$$
$$3A + 2B \leq 1500 \quad \text{Department 2}$$
$$A + B \leq 600 \quad \text{Department 3}$$

where

A = the number of units for product Alpha
B = the number of units for product Beta

LINEAR PROGRAMMING

The first equation above, dealing with total contribution, is an equality. However, the next three equations are inequalities where the sign $\leq$ means "is equal to or less than." In all three equations, the firm can produce any combination of products that will be equal to or less than the available stated hours in each department. In this sense, an inequality is less restrictive than a corresponding equality. Inequalities can also have a sign $\geq$ which means "is equal to or greater than." Most constraints in a linear programming problem are expressed as inequalities which set upper and lower limits but do not express exact equalities. The equal to condition is not required in the expression of inequalities. The step-by-step procedures for solving the foregoing system equality and the three inequalities are given below.

Step 1. Define the Problem Mathematically

The first step in the graphic method is stating the collected information in mathematical form, as shown above. The objective function ($Z=\$10A+\$12B$) shows the relationship of output to contribution. (Z for a two-product problem refers to the third dimension for plotting contribution.) The three inequalities refer to the time used making one unit of products Alpha and Beta on the left-hand side of the inequality and the total time available in the departments on the right-hand side. The hours needed to make one unit of product Alpha times the number of units produced for Alpha plus the hours required to make one unit of product Beta times the number of units produced for Beta must be equal to or less than the time available in each department. It should be noted that all three inequalities represent capacity restrictions regarding output and not contribution.

The values calculated for products Alpha and Beta must be positive since one either produces a unit of a product or does not. Thus, all elements in the solution of a linear programming problem must be greater than or equal to zero ($A \geq 0$ and $B \geq 0$). These two additional constraints mean the solution must lie in the positive quadrant of the graph (X and Y are positive). Summarizing the first step in terms of equations and inequalities, the sample problem stated mathematically is:

$$\text{Maximize } Z = \$10A + \$12B$$

Subject to these constraints:

$$2A + 3B \leq 1500$$
$$3A + 2B \leq 1500$$
$$A + B \leq 600$$
$$A \geq 0$$
$$B \geq 0$$

Step 2. Graph the Constraint Inequalities

Next the constraint inequalities are graphed. In the problem, product Alpha is shown on the X axis and product Beta on the Y axis. Any of the three inequalities can be drawn on the graph by locating their two terminal points and joining these points by a straight line. Referring to the first inequality ($2A+3B \leq 1500$), the two terminal points can be found in the following manner. If all the time in department 1 is used in making product Alpha and if no units of product Beta are made, then 750 units of product Alpha can be made. This is calculated as follows:

$$2A + 3(0) \leq 1500$$
$$2A \leq 1500$$
$$A \leq 750 \quad \text{(maximum number of Alpha units)}$$

The first point (750 units of product Alpha and zero units of product Beta) is graphed in Figure 6-1. The second point is computed in the same manner, only this time all the hours available are used in making the maximum units (500) of product Beta and zero units of product Alpha. The calculations are as follows:

$$2(0) + 3B \leq 1500$$
$$3B \leq 1500$$
$$B \leq 500 \quad \text{(maximum number of Beta units)}$$

The second point (zero units of product Alpha and 500 units of product Beta) is graphed in Figure 6-1.

After locating the two terminal points, a straight line can be drawn (Figure 6-1). The same procedure is used for the other two inequalities which are plotted in Figure 6-2. In order to complete products Alpha and Beta, all three departments must be utilized. This means that the feasible solution area is the striped area in Figure 6-2. It contains all possible combinations of products satisfying the original inequalities.

What happens when a combination of output for products Alpha and Beta results in a solution outside the striped area? This means that we

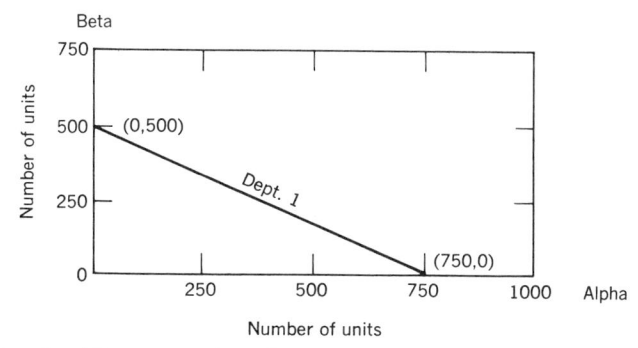

Figure 6-1 Graph of Equation $2A + 3B = 1500$.

have violated one or more of the given constraints. For example, if management decided to make 100 units of product Alpha and 550 units of product Beta with a total contribution of $7600 (100×$10+550×$12) as shown by point K in Figure 6-2, the time required to make these units falls within the time available in department 2, but exceeds the time available in departments 1 and 3. Based upon the existing constraints, the solution is not feasible.

Step 3. Plot the Objective Function

The third step is to plot the objective function, which is given as $Z = \$10A + \$12B$. This can be done by first letting total contribution equal some minimum dollar amount, say $1200, an amount easily attainable per the given constraints. The objective function can be rewritten as $1200 = $10A + $12B. In order to plot this equation (Figure 6-3), two terminal points must be located and joined with a straight line. The calculations are:

When $A = 0$:
$$\$1200 = \$10(0) + \$12B$$
$$B = 100 \text{ units (of product Beta)}$$

When $B = 0$
$$\$1200 = \$10A + \$12(0)$$
$$A = 120 \text{ units (of product Alpha)}$$

The area of feasible solutions (D, E, F, and G) has been taken from Figure 6-2 and is shown with the contribution equation $1200 = $10A + $12B in Figure 6-3. A parallel line can now be drawn from the original objective

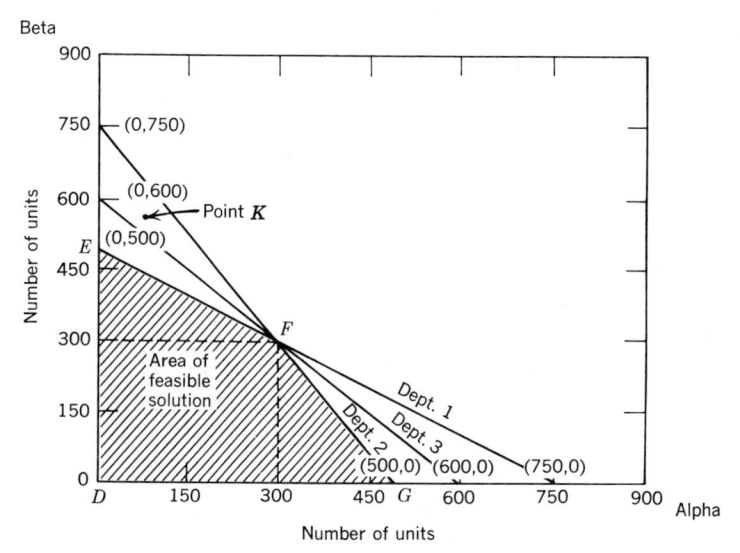

Figure 6-2 Graph of problem constraints (Step 2).

162 OPERATIONS RESEARCH MODELS—MATRIX ALGEBRA

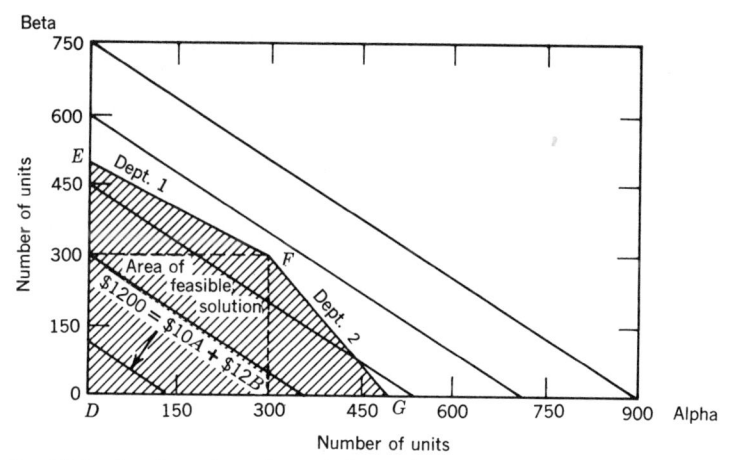

Figure 6-3 Objective function plotted (Step 3).

function line to the farthest point in the area of feasible solution. Another method for reaching the farthest point in the feasible solution area is to use higher amounts for contribution and calculate new values for products Alpha and Beta. In effect, a series of objective function lines can be drawn to determine the farthest point from the origin, as shown in Figure 6-3. The contribution line which can be located farthest from the origin (point D) contains all the combinations of products—Alpha and Beta—that will generate the greatest possible contribution. As long as at least one point on this maximum contribution line is still within the feasible solution area, that point represents the most profitable combination of products. In our problem, point F is the farthest point in the area of feasible solutions and represents the most profitable combination of products. Dotted lines indicate this best combination, namely 300 units of product Alpha and 300 units of product Beta.

Step 4. Solve Using Simultaneous Equations

The final step is to solve simultaneously the equations of the two lines which intersect at point F in Figure 6-3. The two equations for departments 1 and 2 are common to point F. As noted in Step 3, the numerical values for both products were read off the graph. However, in most cases, there is difficulty in reading a precise answer for real world problems. The equations for departments 1 and 2 are solved simultaneously as follows:

$$2A + 3B = 1500 \text{ (dept. 1)} \quad 2A + 3B = 1500$$
$$3A + 2B = 1500 \text{ (dept. 2)} \quad \underline{-2A - \tfrac{4}{3}B = -1000}$$
$$B = 300$$

Substituting 300 for B into the equation for department 2, the value for A equals 300 (3A + 600 = 1500). Using the total contribution equation, Z = $10A + $12B, the total contribution is $6600 ($10 × 300 + $12 × 300).

LINEAR PROGRAMMING 163

Step 1—Define the Problem Mathematically

Determine the *objective function* (an equality) and the *constraints* (inequalities) in the problem. It should be noted that the values calculated for products to be manufactured must be positive. Thus, all values found in the solution of a linear programming problem must be greater than (if they are to be manufactured) or equal to zero (if they are not to be manufactured).

Step 2—Graph the Constraint Inequalities

Draw a constraint line for each of the constraint inequalities (say departments) by locating its two terminal points and joining these points by a straight line. Each of the two terminal points is determined by dividing the total time (say hours) available by the time necessary (say hours) to manufacture a unit of one product only. For example, if all the time within a department is used in making the first product only versus a second product, then so many units of the first product can be made, resulting in the determination of one of the two terminal points. The same type of calculation is made for the second product, thereby establishing the other terminal point.

Step 3—Plot the Objective Function

Determine two terminal points that represent physical quantities whose total contribution is easily attainable. Next, join these terminal points with a straight line which represents an initial objective function line. Draw one or more parallel lines from the original objective function line to the farthest point out in the feasible solution area. That point (could be a series of points) on the maximum objective function line which still lies within the feasible solution area represents the most profitable combination of products.

Step 4—Solve Using Simultaneous Equations

Solve the problem for quantities to be manufactured by solving simultaneously the equations of the two lines for the farthest point (or points) determined in step (3) above. Also, place these resulting quantities to be manufactured in the contribution equation for determining total contribution.

Figure 6-4 Steps employed in the two-dimensional graphic method of linear programming.

The foregoing steps used in the graphic method of linear programming are set forth in Figure 6-4 for a two-dimensional approach. For three-product analysis, the same procedures can be employed.

Another approach to the graphic method of linear programming is testing the corners. For the sample problem, this means to test the four points (D, E, F, and G) of Figure 6-3 that delineate the striped area to determine which yields the highest contribution. Basically, this is the comparison of the heights of the contribution lines at the corners in the two-product problem. (Had we been working a problem with three or more products, we could not graph the additional dimension for contribution.) A graphing of contribution for points D through G in Figure 6-3 would indicate that point F has the highest contribution (Z) in three-dimensional space based on the following data:

$$\text{Point } D \ (0,0) = \$10(0) + \$12(0) = 0$$
$$\text{Point } E \ (0,500) = \$10(0) + \$12(500) = \$6000$$
$$\text{Point } F \ (300,300) = \$10(300) + \$12(300) = \$6600$$
$$\text{Point } G \ (500,0) = \$10(500) + \$12(0) = \$5000$$

This approach can replace Steps 3 and 4 of the traditional graphical method. However, more simultaneous equations are used in order to determine the proper quantities for each product.

Algebraic Method of Linear Programming

The preceding example will be used to demonstrate the algebraic method of linear programming. The problem, stated algebraically, is

$$\text{Maximize } Z = \$10A + \$12B$$

Subject to:

$$2A + 3B \leq 1500 \quad \text{(department 1)}$$
$$3A + 2B \leq 1500 \quad \text{(department 2)}$$
$$A + B \leq 600 \quad \text{(department 3)}$$
$$A \geq 0, \ B \geq 0$$

In order to use the algebraic method, it is necessary first to convert the three inequalities into equations for the departments. This can be performed by adding a slack variable for each department, that is, add to each inequality a variable that will take up the slack or time not used in a department. The following slack variables (in hours) will be used:

$$S_1 = \text{unused time in department 1}$$
$$S_2 = \text{unused time in department 2}$$
$$S_3 = \text{unused time in department 3}$$

It should be noted that the foregoing slack variables are positive, caused by the departmental constraints being equal to or less than ($\leq$). However, if the department constraints were greater than or equal to ($\geq$), *surplus variables* would have been introduced, sometimes referred to as negative slack variables. An example of the surplus variable is found in the American Products Corporation at the end of the chapter (where the contract assures a certain supplier of an order for at least 2600 units per month).

The slack variable S_1 is equal to the total amount of time available in department 1 or 1500 hours minus any hours used in processing products Alpha and Beta. The same type of reasoning is applicable to S_2 and S_3. The original inequalities for the three departments now can be expressed by writing equations for the slack variables as follows:

$$S_1 = 1500 - 2A - 3B \quad \text{(Equation 6-1)}$$
$$S_2 = 1500 - 3A - 2B \quad \text{(Equation 6-2)}$$
$$S_3 = 600 - A - B \quad \text{(Equation 6-3)}$$

The value of these equations is that they show the relationship among the variables in the first solution (S_1, S_2, and S_3 or unused time) and the other variables. This is why they are called relationship equations. The *first solution* is as follows:

$A = 0$ units of product Alpha
$B = 0$ units of product Beta
$S_1 = 1500 - 2(0) - 3(0) = 1500$ unused hours in dept. 1
$S_2 = 1500 - 3(0) - 2(0) = 1500$ unused hours in dept. 2
$S_3 = 600 - 1(0) - 1(0) = 600$ unused hours in dept. 3

Since these slack variables (S_1, S_2, and S_3) have no value in that no profit or loss is charged against idle time in a department, the objective function can be written to include the slack variables with zero profit contributions:

$$\text{Contribution} = \$10A + \$12B + \$0S_1 + \$0S_2 + \$0S_3 \qquad \text{(Equation 6-4)}$$

In the initial solution, we are actually at the point of origin (0,0), shown as point D in Figure 6-3. This point (0,0) reflects only unused capacity. Substituting the quantities for A, B, S_1, S_2, and S_3 in the contribution equation, the first solution is

$$\begin{aligned}\text{Contribution} &= \$10A + \$12B + \$0S_1 + \$0S_2 + \$0S_3 \\ &= \$10(0) + \$12(0) + \$0(1500) + \$0(1500) + \$0(600) \\ &= \$0\end{aligned}$$

The initial solution for contribution is algebraically possible but not financially attractive to the firm.

After converting the inequalities into equations in order to obtain an initial solution (first step), the second step is to examine the contribution equation to see if further improvement in profits is possible. It is obvious that further improvement is possible by manufacturing some units of products Alpha and Beta in exchange for all of the unused time in the three departments (which has no value at this point). The most logical starting basis is to manufacture that product which produces the highest contribution per unit. This is product Beta with $12 per unit. How many units of product Beta should be produced? This can be determined in the following manner:

Department 1:
$$\frac{1500 \text{ hours available}}{3 \text{ hours per unit of product Beta}} = 500 \text{ units of product Beta}$$
Department 2:
$$\frac{1500 \text{ hours available}}{2 \text{ hours per unit of product Beta}} = 750 \text{ units of product Beta}$$
Department 3:
$$\frac{600 \text{ hours available}}{1 \text{ hour per unit of product Beta}} = 600 \text{ units of product Beta}$$

The time required to process one unit of product Beta in department 1 where there are 1500 available hours is 3 hours. The number of units that can be made must be 500 units (as computed above). The same analysis is applicable to departments 2 and 3. Of the three values calculated, department 1 is our limiting department since it limits production to only 500 units of product Beta. We would like to produce 750 units (could be accomplished in department 2), but departments 1 and 3 do not permit it. Substituting the values $A=0$ and $B=500$ in Equations 6-1 to 6-3, the resulting values for unused time in the three departments are

$$S_1 = 1500 - 2(0) - 3(500) = 0$$
$$S_2 = 1500 - 3(0) - 2(500) = 500$$
$$S_3 = 600 - 1(0) - 1(500) = 100$$

The *second solution* is as follows:

$A = 0$ units for product Alpha
$B = 500$ units of product Beta
$S_1 = 0$ unused hours in department 1
$S_2 = 500$ unused hours in department 2
$S_3 = 100$ unused hours in department 3

$$\text{Contribution} = \$10A + \$12B + \$0S_1 + \$0S_2 + \$0S_3$$
$$= \$10(0) + \$12(500) + \$0(0) + \$0(500) + \$0(100)$$
$$= \$6000$$

Having calculated the contribution to be $6000, we next ask whether further improvement in contribution is possible. Before this question can be answered, several changes must be effected. Since we are producing 500 units of product Beta, the unused time in department 1 is now zero. Equations 6-1 to 6-3 must be changed to reflect this fact. First, it is necessary to solve for product Beta or to change Equation 6-1. This equation is used since the slack time in department 1 is zero.

$$S_1 = 1500 - 2A - 3B \qquad \text{(Equation 6-1)}$$
$$3B = 1500 - 2A - S_1$$
$$B = 500 - \frac{2}{3}A - \frac{1}{3}S_1 \qquad \text{(Equation 6-5)}$$

Putting the value for B into Equations 6-2 and 6-3, the new equations for S_2 and S_3 are

$$S_2 = 1500 - 3A - 2B \qquad \text{(Equation 6-2)}$$
$$S_2 = 1500 - 3A - 2\left(500 - \frac{2}{3}A - \frac{1}{3}S_1\right)$$
$$S_2 = 1500 - 3A - 1000 + \frac{4}{3}A + \frac{2}{3}S_1$$
$$S_2 = 500 - \frac{5}{3}A + \frac{2}{3}S_1 \qquad \text{(Equation 6-6)}$$
$$S_3 = 600 - A - B \qquad \text{(Equation 6-3)}$$
$$S_3 = 600 - A - \left(500 - \frac{2}{3}A - \frac{1}{3}S_1\right)$$
$$S_3 = 600 - A - 500 + \frac{2}{3}A + \frac{1}{3}S_1$$
$$S_3 = 100 - \frac{1}{3}A + \frac{1}{3}S_1 \qquad \text{(Equation 6-7)}$$

Notice what has happened in Equations 6-5, 6-6, and 6-7. The quantities for our second solution appear to the right of the equal sign. In other words, we have subtracted the making of 500 units of product Beta from all of the available time in departments 2 and 3. Another way of viewing the mathematical procedures is to realize that equations must be developed for those variables that have some quantity related to them. In the example, equations must be developed for B, S_2, and S_3 in the second solution. On the other hand, there is no need to develop equations for those items which have zero values, such as A and S_1 in the second solution. This makes sense for if we tried to take quantities away from zero values (A and S_1), we would end up with minus figures. As stated previously, we can deal only with plus figures for quantities produced and unused time.

Returning to the question—Is further improvement possible?—the answer can be determined by placing the second solution Equations 6-5, 6-6, and 6-7 for B, S_2 and S_3 into the objective function:

$$\text{Contribution} = \$10A + \$12\left(500 - \frac{2}{3}A - \frac{1}{3}S_1\right) + \$0(0)$$

$$+ \$0\left(500 - \frac{5}{3}A + \frac{2}{3}S_1\right) + \$0\left(100 - \frac{1}{3}A + \frac{1}{3}S_1\right)$$

$$= \$10A + \$6000 - \$8A - \$4S_1$$
$$= \$6000 + \$2A - \$4S_1 \hspace{2cm} \text{(Equation 6-8)}$$

This expression for contribution, Equation 6-8, indicates that $6000 can be made along with additional profits since the plus sign indicates an additional profit of $2 for each unit of product Alpha that can be produced. This may appear to be contradictory since the contribution for product Alpha is $10 and not $2. However, it must be remembered that product Alpha cannot be made except by sacrificing some units of product Beta. Product Alpha requires 2 hours in department 1 while product Beta requires 3 hours in the same department. In order to bring a unit of product Alpha into the solution, it is necessary to forgo the manufacture of ⅔ unit of product Beta. Thus we lose ⅔ of $12 because we make ⅔ less of product Beta, but gain $10 for each unit of product Alpha we produce. The loss of $8 and a gain of $10 results in a net gain of $2 as shown in Equation 6-8: contribution = $6000 + $2A − $4S_1$. The $-\$4S_1$ in this equation means that if we take away 1 hour in department 1 for some other product, this will cost us $4. To prove this, we have decided in the second solution (not the final one) to produce 500 units of product Beta. Each of the 500 units (product Beta) requires 3 hours in department 1. To take away one hour from department 1 gives up ⅓ unit of product Beta or ⅓ times $12 or $4. The revised contribution equation indicates the favorable and unfavorable implications of the two courses of action. The question now is, how many units of product Alpha should be produced?

Returning to Equations 6-5 to 6-7, a simplified way of answering this question is to use the first two terms to the right of the equal sign (divide first quantity by second quantity):

Department 1

$$\frac{500 \text{ units of Beta now being manufactured}}{\text{⅔ units of Beta given up for each unit of Alpha}} = 750 \text{ units of Alpha}$$

Department 2

$$\frac{500 \text{ hours available in department 2}}{5/3 \text{ net hours required by each unit of Alpha}} = 300 \text{ units of Alpha}$$

Department 3

$$\frac{100 \text{ hours available in department 3}}{1/3 \text{ net hours required by each unit of Alpha}} = 300 \text{ units of Alpha}$$

A way of explaining how 750 units of Alpha were derived in department 1 is to remember that for 2 units of product Beta which are given up in this department, we can manufacture 3 units of product Alpha. If we gave up all 500 units of product Beta in department 1, we could make 750 units of product Alpha. However, units of product Alpha must pass through departments 2 and 3. When production of product Beta is lowered by 2/3 in department 1 (figure shown above), one result is to free 2/3 of the 2 hours for a unit of product Beta that it must have in department 2. The time freed is 4/3 hour (2/3 × 2 hours) for every 2/3 product Beta given up. On the other hand, product Alpha that replaces 2/3 of product Beta requires 3 hours in department 2. The 3 hours required for each unit of product Alpha minus the 4/3 hours released with reducing production by 2/3 of product Beta equals a net requirement of 5/3 hours for product Alpha in department 2 (figure shown above). The same type of logic is applicable to department 3.

Of the three values calculated above, departments 2 and 3 are the limiting departments since both limit production to only 300 units. Thus we have decided to manufacture 300 units of product Alpha in the third solution. Substituting 300 for A and zero for S_1 in Equations 6-5 to 6-7, the resulting values (products and unused time) are:

$$B = 500 - \frac{2}{3}(300) - \frac{1}{3}(0) \qquad \text{(Equation 6-5)}$$

$$B = 500 - 200$$
$$B = 300 \text{ units}$$

$$S_2 = 500 - \frac{5}{3}(300) + \frac{2}{3}(0) \qquad \text{(Equation 6-6)}$$

$$S_2 = 500 - 500$$
$$S_2 = 0$$

$$S_3 = 100 - \frac{1}{3}(300) + \frac{1}{3}(0) \qquad \text{(Equation 6-7)}$$

$$S_3 = 100 - 100$$
$$S_3 = 0$$

The *third solution* is:

$A = 300$ units of product Alpha
$B = 300$ units of product Beta
$S_1 = 0$ unused hours in department 1
$S_2 = 0$ unused hours in department 2
$S_3 = 0$ unused hours in department 3

$$\text{Contribution} = \$10A + \$12B + \$0S_1 + \$0S_2 + \$0S_3$$
$$= \$10(300) + \$12(300) + \$0(0) + \$0(0) + \$0(0)$$
$$= \$6600$$

At this point all unused time in departments 1, 2, and 3 have been utilized with the production of 300 units for both products Alpha and Beta. The contribution is $6600. The question is asked again, is this the optimum amount for the firm? Before this can be answered, it is necessary to solve for those variables (A and B) that have a value in the third solution. Solving for A using Equations 6-6 and 6-7 is as follows:

$$S_2 = 500 - \frac{5}{3}A + \frac{2}{3}S_1 \qquad \text{or} \qquad S_3 = 100 - \frac{1}{3}A + \frac{1}{3}S_1$$

$$\frac{5}{3}A = 500 + \frac{2}{3}S_1 - S_2 \qquad\qquad \frac{1}{3}A = 100 + \frac{1}{3}S_1 - S_3$$

$$A = 300 + \frac{2}{5}S_1 - \frac{3}{5}S_2 \qquad\qquad A = 300 + S_1 - 3S_3$$

(Equation 6-9)

Previously, having solved for B in Equation 6-5, we can substitute either equation above for A in Equation 6-5. The last equation (Equation 6-9) has been selected to be substituted for term A in Equation 6-5, as follows:

$$B = 500 - \frac{2}{3}A - \frac{1}{3}S_1 \qquad \text{(Equation 6-5)}$$

$$B = 500 - \frac{2}{3}(300 + S_1 - 3S_3) - \frac{1}{3}S_1$$

$$B = 500 - 200 - \frac{2}{3}S_1 + 2S_3 - \frac{1}{3}S_1$$

$$B = 300 - S_1 + 2S_3 \qquad \text{(Equation 6-10)}$$

The two equations for the third solution are repeated below for convenience. Basically, these are the equations for departments 1 and 3 restated:

$$A = 300 + S_1 - 3S_3 \qquad \text{(Equation 6-9)}$$
$$B = 300 - S_1 + 2S_3 \qquad \text{(Equation 6-10)}$$

A value can be calculated for department 2 from Equation 6-6 which utilizes Equation 6-9 for term A:

$$S_2 = 500 - \frac{5}{3}A + \frac{2}{3}S_1 \qquad \text{(Equation 6-6)}$$

$$S_2 = 500 - \frac{5}{3}(300 + S_1 - 3S_3) + \frac{2}{3}S_1$$

$$S_2 = 500 - 500 - \frac{5}{3}S_1 + 5S_3 + \frac{2}{3}S_1$$

$$S_2 = -S_1 + 5S_3 \qquad \text{(Equation 6-11)}$$

Now that the necessary equations have been developed, based upon our third solution, calculations for the contribution equation are:

Contribution $= \$10(300 + S_1 - 3S_3) + \$12(300 - S_1 + 2S_3)$
$\qquad + \$0(0) + \$0(0) + \$0(0)$
$\qquad = \$3000 + \$10S_1 - \$30S_3 + \$3600 - \$12S_1 + \$24S_3$
$\qquad = \$6600 - \$2S_1 - \$6S_3$ \hfill (Equation 6-12)

Examination of the coefficients for the two variables S_1 and S_3 indicates no further improvement in contribution is possible. Adding any units for S_1 and S_3 would not add to profits but decrease profits due to the negative signs. The final solution (300 units each of products Alpha and Beta) has been reached with an optimum contribution of $6600. This is and must be the same solution found when using the graphic method.

One last check should be made to insure that the constraints of the problem have not been violated. The original equations, given at the beginning of this section, are:

$$2A + 3B \leq 1500$$
$$3A + 2B \leq 1500$$
$$A + B \leq 600$$

Substituting the appropriate values for A and B in the preceding equations, the results show that we are within the constraints of the problem:

$$2(300) + 3(300) \leq 1500$$
$$600 + 900 \leq 1500$$
$$1500 = 1500$$
$$3(300) + 2(300) \leq 1500$$
$$900 + 600 \leq 1500$$
$$1500 = 1500$$
$$(300) + (300) \leq 600$$
$$600 = 600$$

In many cases, there may be unused time in a problem. The time used for production plus unused time must equal the original constraints or an error has been made.

When comparison is made between the graphic and the algebraic methods, a distinct advantage is found with the latter method since it allows for the solution of a problem where there are more than three possible products. The graphic method is limited to three products (dimensions). However, when a comparison is made between the algebraic and the simplex methods, the simplex method takes preference since it lends itself best to digital computers. Similarities between the algebraic and simplex methods will be indicated in the next section.

Simplex Method of Linear Programming

Most production mix problems reach a complexity, say a dozen products and the same number of departments, which makes the algebraic solution impractical. A procedure to solve an enlarged problem is called the simplex method of linear programming. The computational procedure used is an iterative process, sometimes referred to as an *algorithm*, that is, the same basic computational routine is used over and over again. This results in a series of successively improved solutions until the best one is found. A basic characteristic of the simplex method is that the last solution yields a contribution as large as or larger than the previous solution in a maximization problem. In a minimization problem, the simplex method determines a cost that is the same or lower than the previous one. This feature assures that the optimal answer can finally be reached.

The simplex method, consisting of four steps, utilizes matrix algebra which will be found in the Appendix A of this book. Also found in this Appendix is background material on vectors and determinants which will be useful for this chapter and succeeding chapters. A reader who is unfamiliar with these subjects should read this Appendix before proceeding any further in this chapter. In the simplex method, we will be forming an inverse of a matrix to solve a set of simultaneous equations. The formation of the inverse will not be accomplished in the same manner as that found in Appendix A; however, it is still an inverse. Briefly, the preceding material of this chapter has solved a set of relationship equations by simultaneous equations while the next sections for the simplex method of linear programming utilize matrix algebra.

Maximization Problem

The maximization problem set forth previously will be used again. Stated in an acceptable format for the simplex algorithm, it is:

$$\text{Maximize } Z = \$10A + \$12B + \$0S_1 + \$0S_2 + \$0S_3 \quad \text{(Equation 6-4)}$$

Subject to:

$$1500 \text{ hours} = 2A + 3B + S_1 + 0S_2 + 0S_3 \quad \text{(Equation 6-13)}$$
$$1500 \text{ hours} = 3A + 2B + 0S_1 + S_2 + 0S_3 \quad \text{(Equation 6-14)}$$
$$600 \text{ hours} = A + B + 0S_1 + 0S_2 + S_3 \quad \text{(Equation 6-15)}$$

As in the algebraic method, it is necessary to convert the inequalities into equations by adding slack variables. In addition, the simplex method requires that any unknown which appears in one equation must appear in all equations. However, the unknowns that do not affect an equation are written with a zero coefficient. In the sample problem, the equation for department 1 shows zero coefficients for slack time in departments 2 and 3.

In order to simplify handling the equations in the problem, they can be placed in a tabular form, known as a tableau—refer to Tableau I. Appendix A shows how a system of equations can be solved by working only with the coefficients; thus, the variables need not be written.

Starting with the left-hand column in Tableau I, the C_j column contains the contribution per unit for the slack variables S_1, S_2, and S_3. The zero indicates that the contribution per unit is zero. The rationale is that profits are not made on unused time in a department, but on time used. The

TABLEAU I
Linear Programming Maximization Problem

C_j	Product Mix	Quantity	$10 A	$12 B	$0 S_1	$0 S_2	$0 S_3	Contribution per Unit Variables
$0	S_1	1,500	2	3	1	0	0	⎫
$0	S_2	1,500	3	2	0	1	0	⎬ Coefficients
$0	S_3	600	1	1	0	0	1	⎭
			Body Matrix		Identity Matrix			
	Z_j	$0	$0	$0	$0	$0	$0	Contribution lost per unit
	$C_j - Z_j$		$10	$12	$0	$0	$0	Net contribution per unit

second column, product mix, contains the variables in the solution which are used to determine total contribution. In the initial solution, no products are being made. The values for S_1, S_2, and S_3 must contain all of the unused time in the problem, which is found in the third column—quantity. The starting solution will be zero contribution since no units of products Alpha and Beta are being manufactured. This is represented by $0 ($0×1500+ $0×1500+$0×600) in the Z_j row for the third column. Since no units of Alpha and Beta are being manufactured, the first solution, as with the algebraic method, is:

$$A = 0$$
$$B = 0$$
$$S_1 = 1500$$
$$S_2 = 1500$$
$$S_3 = 600$$

This is essentially represented by the first three columns of Tableau I.

The *body matrix* consists of the coefficients for the real product variables in the first tableau. Referring to the first row and A column, the coefficient 2 means that if we wanted to bring one unit of product Alpha into the solution, we would have to give up 2 hours of S_1 in department 1. To state it another way, it takes 2 hours to make product Alpha in department 1. Likewise, the element 3 in the B column, first row, indicates that production of one unit of product Beta would require us to give up 3 hours in department 1. In reality, what we have in the coefficients of the body matrix is the rate of substitution.

The *identity matrix* in the first simplex tableau represents the coefficients of the slack variables that have been added to the original inequalities to make them equations. As stated previously, any unknown that occurs in one equation must appear in all equations but with a zero coefficient so as not to affect the equation.

Referring to the element in the S_1 column, first row, the 1 indicates that in order to make 1 hour of S_1 available, it would be necessary to give up one of the 1500 hours in the initial solution. The zero in the S_2 column, first row, indicates that making one hour in department 2 available for other purposes has no effect on S_1 (slack time of department 1). The logic used for S_2 is also applicable to the S_3 column, first row.

The same type of rationale is applicable to the next two rows (S_2 and S_3) in Tableau I. Basically, we are dealing with substitution rates, that is, the addition of products Alpha and Beta into the solution and the withdrawal of time from the three departments' slack time S_1, S_2, and S_3.

The last two rows of the first simplex tableau are used to determine whether or not the solution can be improved. Evaluation of the last row or the C_j-Z_j row is the first step in the simplex method and, therefore, will not be treated in this section. However, the second last row or the Z_j row is explained here. The Z_j row value under the quantity column indicates an initial solution of zero contribution for the firm. The other five values of $0 are the amounts by which contribution would be reduced if one unit of the variables (A, B, S_1, S_2, and S_3) was added to the mix. Another way of defining the Z_j row for the five variables is the contribution lost per unit. For example, if we desire to make one unit of product Alpha, the coefficients $\begin{pmatrix} 2 \\ 3 \\ 1 \end{pmatrix}$ in the body matrix tell us we must give up 2 hours of S_1 (department 1) unused time, 3 hours of S_2 (department 2) unused time, and 1 hour of S_3 (department 3) unused time. Since slack time is worth $0 per hour, there can be no reduction in contribution. The calculation for how much contribution is lost by adding one unit of product Alpha to production is:

$$\begin{array}{lr} \text{Number of hours of } S_1 \text{ given up} & 2 \\ \times \text{Contribution per unit of } S_1 \times \$0 = \$0 \\ \text{Number of hours of } S_2 \text{ given up} & 3 \\ \times \text{Contribution per unit of } S_2 \times \$0 = \$0 \\ \text{Number of hours of } S_3 \text{ given up} & 1 \\ \times \text{Contribution per unit of } S_3 \times \$0 = \$0 \\ \hline \text{Total contribution given up} & \$0 \end{array}$$

Tableau I to Tableau II

In order to understand the interworkings of Tableau I and all subsequent tableaus, the four steps employed in the simplex method are treated in detail. Also, the relationships of the algebraic and simplex methods are demonstrated periodically throughout the iterative procedures. In this section, only the steps involved in going from Tableau I to Tableau II are discussed.

Step 1. Select the Column with the Highest Plus Value

Evaluation of the last row in the initial tableau represents the first step in our computational procedure for the sample maximization problem. The

TABLEAU II
Linear Programming Maximization Problem

C_j	Product Mix	Quantity	$10 A	$12 B	$0 S_1	$0 S_2	$0 S_3
$12	B	500	2/3	1	1/3	0	0 replacing row
$0	S_2	500	1 2/3	0	−2/3	1	0 remaining row with new values
$0	S_3	100	1/3	0	−1/3	0	1 remaining row with new values
	Z_j	$6000	$8	$12	$4	$0	$0
	$C_j - Z_j$		$2	$0	−$4	$0	$0

final row is the net contribution that results from adding one unit of a variable (product) to production. As shown in Tableau I, if one unit of product Alpha is added to the solution, the contribution to the solution is $10. The contribution is $12 for one unit of product Beta and $0 for S_1, S_2, and S_3. An examination of the figures in the $C_j - Z_j$ row reveals that the largest positive value is $12. A plus value indicates that a greater contribution can be made by the firm. A negative value would indicate the amount by which contribution would decrease if one unit of the variable for that column were brought into the solution. The largest positive amount in the last row is selected as the optimum column or $12 per unit for product *Beta* since we want to maximize total contribution. When no more positive values remain in the $C_j - Z_j$ row and values are zero or minus in a maximization problem, total contribution is at its greatest value.

Before exploring additional computational procedures for going from Tableau I to Tableau II, a comparison is made between the algebraic method and the simplex method (first tableau). Equations 6-1, 6-2, and 6-3 are reproduced below for the algebraic method:

$$S_1 = 1500 - 2A - 3B \qquad \text{(Equation 6-1)}$$
$$S_2 = 1500 - 3A - 2B \qquad \text{(Equation 6-2)}$$
$$S_3 = 600 - A - B \qquad \text{(Equation 6-3)}$$

These equations can be expressed in terms of unused time as:

$$1500 = 2A + 3B + S_1$$
$$1500 = 3A + 2B + S_2$$
$$600 = A + B + S_3$$

By adding zero coefficients for S_1, S_2, and S_3 where needed, the results are the same as those found in Equations 6-13 to 6-15. These equations are, as explained previously, the basis for Tableau I of the simplex method. Equation 6-4 for the objective function is the same for both methods.

Step 2. Determine the Replaced (old) Row

Once the initial simplex tableau has been constructed and the variable (optimum column) has been selected (first step) which contributes the most per unit ($12 per one unit of product Beta), the second step is to determine which variable should be replaced. To state it another way, inspection of the optimum column ($12 for product Beta) indicates that the variable B should be added to the product mix, replacing row S_1, S_2, or S_3. To determine which variable will be replaced, divide the value in the quantity column by the corresponding coefficient in the optimum column. Select the row with the smallest positive quantity as the row to be replaced. As in the previous method, the firm would like to produce the largest quantity, but consideration must be given to the constraints in the problem. The possible units are computed as follows:

S_1 row $\quad \dfrac{1500 \text{ hours—unused time}}{3 \text{ hours required per unit of product Beta}}$
$$= 500 \text{ units of product Beta}$$

S_2 row $\quad \dfrac{1500 \text{ hours—unused time}}{2 \text{ hours required per unit of product Beta}}$
$$= 750 \text{ units of product Beta}$$

S_3 row $\quad \dfrac{600 \text{ hours—unused time}}{1 \text{ hour required per unit of product Beta}}$
$$= 600 \text{ units of product Beta}$$

Based on these calculations for product Beta, row S_1 will be replaced in the second tableau by 500 units of product Beta; it is called the replaced row. The elements common to the optimum column and three rows $\begin{pmatrix} 3 \\ 2 \\ 1 \end{pmatrix}$ are called intersectional elements. Having picked the optimum column and the replaced row, we are now ready to work on an improved solution, found in Tableau II.

Step 3. Compute Values for the Replacing (new) Row

In the third step, the first row to determine in the second tableau is the new B row (replacing row) for the S_1 row (replaced row). The B row is computed by dividing each value in the replaced row (S_1) by the intersectional element (3) of the replaced row. The results for the new B row are: $1500/3 = 500$ (quantity column), $2/3 = 2/3$ (A column), $3/3 = 1$ (B column), $1/3 = 1/3$ (S_1 column), $0/3 = 0$ (S_2 column), and $0/3 = 0$ (S_3 column). These become the values for the first row (B) in Tableau II.

Step 4. Calculate New Values for Remaining Rows

The fourth and final step in our computational procedures is to calculate all new values for the remaining rows (S_2 and S_3). The formula for calculating these new rows is

$$\begin{pmatrix} \text{Former ele-} \\ \text{ment in the} \\ \text{remaining} \\ \text{row} \end{pmatrix} - \left[\begin{pmatrix} \text{Former in-} \\ \text{tersectional} \\ \text{element of} \\ \text{remaining} \\ \text{row} \end{pmatrix} \times \begin{pmatrix} \text{New corre-} \\ \text{sponding} \\ \text{element in} \\ \text{replacing} \\ \text{row} \end{pmatrix} \right] = \begin{pmatrix} \text{New value} \\ \text{for remain-} \\ \text{ing row} \end{pmatrix}$$

Based upon this formula, the values in Tableau II for the new S_2 and S_3 rows are:

Row S_2:

$$1500 - (2 \times 500) = 500$$
$$3 - \left(2 \times \frac{2}{3}\right) = 1\frac{2}{3}$$
$$2 - (2 \times 1) = 0$$
$$0 - \left(2 \times \frac{1}{3}\right) = -\frac{2}{3}$$
$$1 - (2 \times 0) = 1$$
$$0 - (2 \times 0) = 0$$

Row S_3:

$$600 - (1 \times 500) = 100$$
$$1 - \left(1 \times \frac{2}{3}\right) = \frac{1}{3}$$
$$1 - (1 \times 1) = 0$$
$$0 - \left(1 \times \frac{1}{3}\right) = -\frac{1}{3}$$
$$0 - (1 \times 0) = 0$$
$$1 - (1 \times 0) = 1$$

The procedure for calculating the last two rows in Tableau II has been explained previously. The computations for the Z_j row are:

Z_j (total contribution) $= \$12(500) + \$0(500) + \$0(100) = \$6000$
Z_j for $A = \$12\left(\frac{2}{3}\right) + \$0\left(1\frac{2}{3}\right) + \$0\left(\frac{1}{3}\right) = \$8$
Z_j for $B = \$12(1) + \$0(0) + \$0(0) = \$12$
Z_j for $S_1 = \$12\left(\frac{1}{3}\right) + \$0\left(-\frac{2}{3}\right) + \$0\left(-\frac{1}{3}\right) = \$4$
Z_j for $S_2 = \$12(0) + \$0(1) + \$0(0) = \$0$
Z_j for $S_3 = \$12(0) + \$0(0) + \$0(1) = \$0$

The calculations for the $C_j - Z_j$ row are:

A (variable), $\$10$ C_j (contr./unit) $- \$8$ Z_j (contr. lost/unit)
$$= \$2 \; C_j - Z_j \text{ (net contr./unit)}$$

LINEAR PROGRAMMING

$$
\begin{array}{ll}
B, & \$12-\$12=\$0 \\
S_1 & \$0-\$4=-\$4 \\
S_2 & \$0-\$0=\$0 \\
S_3 & \$0-\$0=\$0
\end{array}
$$

These steps complete the second tableau. The total contribution is now $6000 versus $0 in the first tableau. The presence of a positive $2 in the last row of the A column denotes a better overall contribution is available to the firm; thus it is necessary to complete a third tableau.

Before doing so, a comparison of the algebraic (second solution) and simplex methods (second tableau) might help clarify our thinking on the two methods. The algebraic equations developed in relationship to the second solution are reproduced below:

$$B = 500 - \frac{2}{3}A - \frac{1}{3}S_1 \qquad \text{(Equation 6-5)}$$

$$S_2 = 500 - \frac{5}{3}A + \frac{2}{3}S_1 \qquad \text{(Equation 6-6)}$$

$$S_3 = 100 - \frac{1}{3}A + \frac{1}{3}S_1 \qquad \text{(Equation 6-7)}$$

To restate these equations in terms of units of products and unused time, they are

$$500 = \frac{2}{3}A + B + \frac{1}{3}S_1$$

$$500 = \frac{5}{3}A - \frac{2}{3}S_1 + S_2$$

$$100 = \frac{1}{3}A - \frac{1}{3}S_1 + S_3$$

Adding zero coefficients for the variables B, S_2, and S_3, the results are the same as those of Tableau II. Equation 6-8 under the algebraic method is the same as the last row ($C_j - Z_j$) in Tableau II, except for the variables with zero coefficients.

It might be helpful at this point to examine the coefficients of the variables in Tableau II, particularly in row B and row S_2, to understand what they mean. The logic applicable to row S_2 will be also applicable to row S_3. The value (2/3) in the A column, row B means that for every unit of product Alpha processed in department 1, 2/3 unit of product Beta must be given up to provide the required 2 hours. The 1 in the B column, row B indicates that we have a one for one substitution or each unit of product Beta added to production replaces one unit of product Beta in the solution. The third item (1/3) in the B row requires that for every hour of S_1 added to the solution reduces the production of product Beta by 1/3 unit. The coefficients of zero for S_2 and S_3 in the B row indicate that adding one unit of S_2 or S_3 has no effect (0) on product Beta. Returning to the quantity column, the value of 500 means 500 units of product Beta should be produced.

Dropping down to the next row (S_2), the value in column A indicates that adding one unit of product Alpha replaces 1⅔ hours of S_2. The next column (B) with a zero value has this meaning: adding one unit of B has no effect on S_2. The same is true for column S_3 in this row. The coefficient (−⅔) in the S_1 column can be explained by the following:

Units of B now in the solution	500
If 1 unit of S_1 is added to the solution, B is reduced by	−⅓
New quantity of B	499⅔
2 hours per unit of B required in department 2	×2
Total hours required to make 499⅔ units of B in department 2	999⅓
Total hours required to make 500 units of B (2×500)	1000
Total hours freed by adding 1 unit of S_1	−⅔

The 1 in the S_2 column of the S_2 row indicates if we add 1 hour of S_2, we must subtract 1 hour of S_2 in order not to exceed 1500 hours. The value of 500 in the quantity column for this row indicates the number of unused hours for department 2.

Tableau II to Tableau III

Returning to the computational procedures used in the simplex method, the first step is to determine the optimum column. This is the A column of Tableau II. Units of product Alpha will be added to the solution, replacing one of the variables B, S_2, or S_3, since an additional contribution of $2 per unit is available. The replaced row is found as the second step in the simplex method. Again, the values in the quantity column are divided by the corresponding intersectional elements in the optimum column as follows:

B row:
$$\frac{500}{2/3} = 750$$

S_2 row:
$$\frac{500}{1\,2/3} = 300$$

S_3 row:
$$\frac{100}{1/3} = 300$$

Based on the foregoing calculations, a condition of *degeneracy* exists since there is a tie between the S_2 and S_3 rows, that is, the quantity (300) is common to both. In this problem, the simplex method will give the correct answer if we choose either of the two rows in Tableau III. Hence, the S_3 row will be arbitrarily designated as the replaced row.

For larger problems, the simplex algorithm will generally give the correct answer if any of the two (or more) tied rows is chosen. However, the remaining tied row (or rows) may have to be selected if the first choice does not produce a solution. Thus, the general rule for degeneracy is: if the selected row does not lead to a solution, that is, the simplex tableaus begin to repeat themselves, then choose the other tied row (or one of the other tied rows) at the point where the degeneracy was discovered.

In addition to the foregoing degeneracy condition, a tie can also occur in the $C_j - Z_j$ row. However, such a condition is not called degeneracy since either of the tied variables can be chosen to enter the next tableau. The variable selected may affect the number of tableaus required in the problem but never the final outcome.

Returning to the third step in the simplex method, a new replacing row is computed in Tableau III. The replacing row is calculated by dividing each

TABLEAU III
Linear Programming Maximization Problem

C_j	Product Mix	Quantity	$10 A	$12 B	$0 S_1	$0 S_2	$0 S_3
$12	B	300	0	1	1	0	−2 remaining row with new values
$ 0	S_2	0	0	0	1	1	−5 remaining row with new values
$10	A	300	1	0	−1	0	3 replacing row
	Z_j	$6,600	$10	$12	$2	$0	$6
	$C_j - Z_j$		$0	$0	−$2	$0	−$6

number in the replaced row by the intersectional element of the replaced row, which is

$$\frac{100}{1/3} = 300; \quad \frac{1/3}{1/3} = 1; \quad \frac{0}{1/3} = 0; \quad \frac{-1/3}{1/3} = -1; \quad \frac{0}{1/3} = 0; \quad \frac{1}{1/3} = 3$$

The replacing row (A) has the following values: 300, 1, 0, −1, 0, and 3.

The last step is concerned with calculating new values for row B (300, 0, 1, 1, 0, and −2) and row S_2 (0, 0, 0, 1, 1, and −5). These have been entered in the third tableau (see earlier procedure and formula). The last two rows are determined in the manner set forth previously. The total contribution in the third tableau is $6600 versus $6000 in Tableau II. The completed third tableau indicates no further improvements in contributon can be made. The optimum is the same as for the two previous methods, 300 units each of products Alpha and Beta should be produced with no unused time remaining.

Tableau III for the simplex method shows a definite link to the third (and final) solution utilizing the algebraic method. The three remaining equations for the algebraic method are

$$A = 300 + S_1 - 3S_3 \qquad \text{(Equation 6-9)}$$

$$B = 300 - S_1 + 2S_3 \qquad \text{(Equation 6-10)}$$

$$S_2 = -S_1 + 5S_3 \qquad \text{(Equation 6-11)}$$

Rewriting these equations in terms of quantities to produce, the new equations are

$$300 = A - S_1 + 3S_3$$
$$300 = B + S_1 - 2S_3$$
$$0 = S_1 + S_2 - 5S_3$$

By adding zero coefficients for the variables A, B, and S_2, the resulting equations are the same as those found in tabular form in the last tableau. Equation 6-12, or $\$6600 - \$2S_1 - \$6S_3$, is the same as the $C_j - Z_j$ row in Tableau III, except for variables with zero coefficients. The relationship of the two methods should be clear by now.

It is suggested that the calculated values derived in the problem be placed back in the original constraint inequalities for the three departments to test whether or not the values are within the constraints. This was done at the end of the section on the algebraic approach and will not be repeated here.

An important feature of the simplex method involves the inversion of the original body matrix. Many times an optimum solution utilizing the simplex method will be reached before a complete inversion of the body matrix (2×2, 3×3, . . .). The inversion of the original body matrix is part of the computational procedures for the simplex method. In the sample problem, a complete inversion was not possible since we did not have a square matrix in the beginning. Notice the location of 0s and 1s in the body matrix of Tableau III.

The foregoing iterative steps of a maximization problem are set forth in Figure 6-5 for the simplex method. They lend themselves to computer processing. The computer algorithm can be illustrated by a flowchart per Figure 6-6. (Reference can be made to procedures used in developing Tableaus I to III.)

Minimization Problem

The preceding material (graphic, algebraic, and simplex methods) has been concerned exclusively with a maximization problem. The computational procedure for the simplex method is readily applicable to a minimization problem whose main objective is to minimize costs. This can be illustrated by the following problem.

The Toms River Chemical Corporation must produce 1000 pounds of a special mixture for a customer which consists of ingredients 01X, 02X, and 03X. Ingredient 01X costs $5 per pound, 02X costs $6 per pound, and 03X costs $7 per pound. No more than 300 pounds of 01X can be used and at least 150 pounds of 02X must be used. In addition, at least 200 pounds of 03X is required. Since the firm desires to minimize costs, the problem is determining what amount of each ingredient the firm should include in the mixture.

Step 1—Select the Column With the Highest Plus Value
Calculate the values for the final row in the simplex tableau, that is, the C_j-Z_j row and select that column which has the largest positive value for C_j-Z_j. If no more positive values remain in the C_j-Z_j row, that is, only zero or minus values remain, total contribution is at its greatest. The iterative steps are complete.

Step 2—Determine the Replaced (old) Row
Determine the replaced (old) row by dividing the values in the quantity column of the simplex tableau for each row by the intersectional elements in the optimum column (selected per Step 1 above). Select the row with the smallest positive quantity as the row to be replaced.

Step 3—Compute Values for the Replacing (new) Row
Compute values for the replacing (new) row in the next tableau—takes the place of the replaced (old) row in the prior tableau. New values for the replacing row are calculated by dividing each value in the replaced (old) row by the intersectional element of the replaced row. Also, the variable in the product mix column for the new row must be changed to that found in the optimum column per Step 1 above.

Step 4—Calculate New Values for Remaining Rows
Calculate new values for all remaining rows in the tableau started in Step 3 above. The formula for calculating these new row values, other than the Z_j and C_j-Z_j rows, is:

$$\begin{pmatrix} \text{Former} \\ \text{element} \\ \text{in the} \\ \text{remaining} \\ \text{row} \end{pmatrix} - \left[\begin{pmatrix} \text{Former} \\ \text{intersectional} \\ \text{element of} \\ \text{remaining} \\ \text{row} \end{pmatrix} \times \begin{pmatrix} \text{New} \\ \text{corresponding} \\ \text{element in} \\ \text{replacing} \\ \text{row} \end{pmatrix} \right] = \begin{pmatrix} \text{New value} \\ \text{for} \\ \text{remaining} \\ \text{row} \end{pmatrix}$$

while the variables in the product mix column remain unchanged. The last two rows (Z_j and C_j-Z_j) are calculated. The iterative procedure loops back to Step 1 above in order to determine if there is need for developing another tableau.

Figure 6-5 Iterative steps employed in a maximization problem for the simplex method of linear programming.

The problem first must be stated in mathematical form. Based on data given, the equality and inequalities are:

$$\text{Minimize cost} = \$5X_1 + \$6X_2 + \$7X_3$$

Subject to:

$$X_1 + X_2 + X_3 = 1000 \text{ pounds}$$
$$X_1 \leq 300 \text{ pounds}$$
$$X_2 \geq 150 \text{ pounds}$$
$$X_3 \geq 200 \text{ pounds}$$

where

X_1 = number of pounds for ingredient 01X
X_2 = number of pounds for ingredient 02X
X_3 = number of pounds for ingredient 03X

The statement that no more than 300 pounds of X_1 can be used means that we can use any amount up to and including 300 pounds. This can be

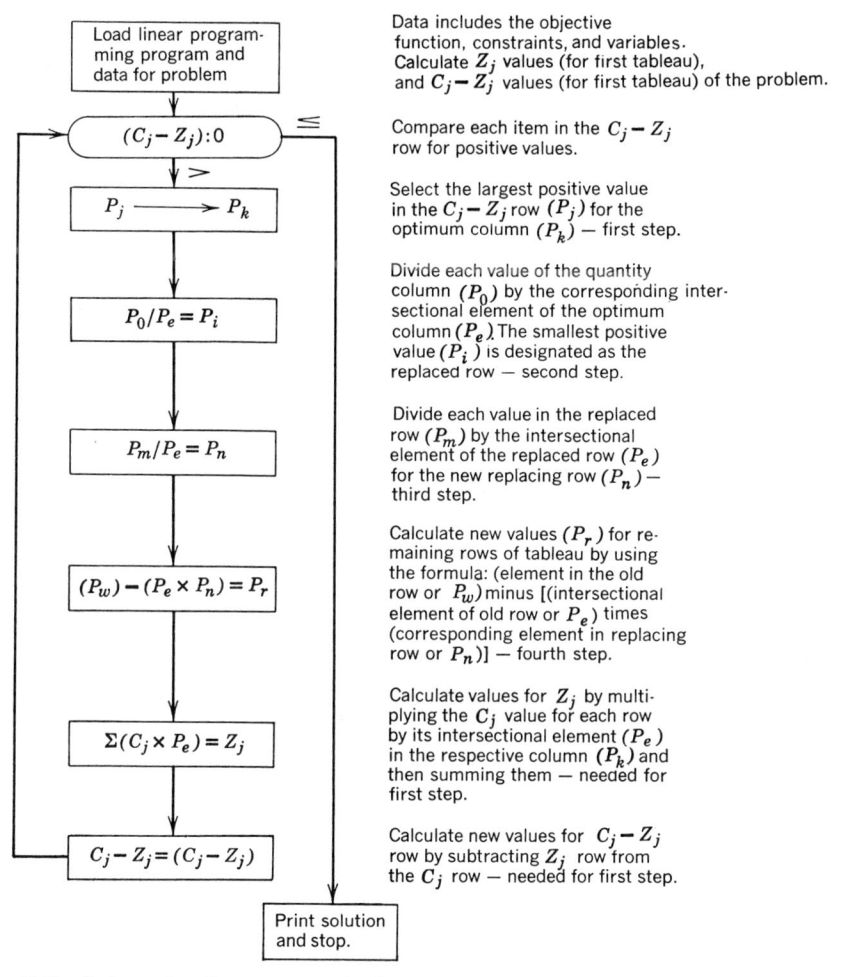

```
┌─────────────────────────┐     Data includes the objective
│ Load linear program-    │     function, constraints, and variables.
│ ming program and        │     Calculate $Z_j$ values (for first tableau),
│ data for problem        │     and $C_j - Z_j$ values (for first tableau) of the problem.
└───────────┬─────────────┘
            ▼
      ┌──────────────┐  ≤      Compare each item in the $C_j - Z_j$
   ──▶│ $(C_j-Z_j):0$├────▶    row for positive values.
      └──────┬───────┘
             │ >
             ▼                  Select the largest positive value
      ┌──────────────┐          in the $C_j - Z_j$ row $(P_j)$ for the
      │ $P_j ⟶ P_k$  │          optimum column $(P_k)$ — first step.
      └──────┬───────┘
             ▼                  Divide each value of the quantity
      ┌──────────────┐          column $(P_0)$ by the corresponding inter-
      │ $P_0/P_e=P_i$│          sectional element of the optimum
      └──────┬───────┘          column $(P_e)$. The smallest positive
                                value $(P_i)$ is designated as the
                                replaced row — second step.
             ▼                  Divide each value in the replaced
      ┌──────────────┐          row $(P_m)$ by the intersectional
      │ $P_m/P_e=P_n$│          element of the replaced row $(P_e)$
      └──────┬───────┘          for the new replacing row $(P_n)$ —
                                third step.

             ▼                  Calculate new values $(P_r)$ for re-
                                maining rows of tableau by using
      ┌───────────────────┐     the formula: (element in the old
      │$(P_w)-(P_e×P_n)=P_r$│   row or $P_w$) minus [(intersectional
      └──────┬────────────┘     element of old row or $P_e$) times
                                (corresponding element in replacing
                                row or $P_n$)] — fourth step.

             ▼                  Calculate values for $Z_j$ by multi-
                                plying the $C_j$ value for each row
      ┌──────────────────┐      by its intersectional element $(P_e)$
      │ $Σ(C_j × P_e)=Z_j$│     in the respective column $(P_k)$ and
      └──────┬───────────┘      then summing them — needed for
                                first step.

             ▼                  Calculate new values for $C_j - Z_j$
      ┌────────────────────┐    row by subtracting $Z_j$ row from
   ──│ $C_j-Z_j=(C_j-Z_j)$ │    the $C_j$ row — needed for first step.
      └────────────────────┘
             ▼
      ┌──────────────┐
      │Print solution│
      │and stop.     │
      └──────────────┘
```

Figure 6-6 Subroutine for a computer linear programming program.

written as $X_1 ≤ 300$ pounds. The second (and third) restriction above means that we may use more than 150 (200) pounds, but not less than 150 (200) pounds since $X_2 ≥ 150$ ($X_3 ≥ 200$) pounds.

Just as a starting point was necessary in the maximization problem, the same holds true for a minimization problem. The initial solution for the previous problem resulted in no profit, which is actually an unrealistic solution. However, it did furnish us with a basis for getting started and moving toward a better solution. Again, we need a mathematical starting point. However, this time the cost will be very high, which will permit us to search for a lower cost mixture.

The second constraint in the problem is $X_1 ≤ 300$ pounds. For this restriction, a slack variable (S_1) is added since X_1 in the optimum solution might be less than 300. The S_1 slack variable represents the difference between the possible 300 pounds of X_1 and the actual number of pounds of X_1. This inequality now can be written as an equation: $X_1 + S_1 = 300$ pounds.

LINEAR PROGRAMMING   183

In the first solution X_1, X_2, and X_3 can equal zero in the first constraint equation. But instead of using a slack variable, an artificial variable (A_1) which represents a new ingredient with a very high cost M (say $100 a pound) will be utilized. The resulting equation is $X_1+X_2+X_3+A_1=1000$. Having a very high cost assures us that it will not be present in the final solution. The first tableau will show a quantity of 1000 pounds for the A_1 artificial variable. The artificial *variable* is a computational device. It is used for an "equality" constraint (such as the first constraint in this problem) and for "greater-than-or-equal-to constraints (such as the third and fourth constraints in this problem). However, it is not needed for "less-than-or-equal-to" constraints.

The third and fourth constraints must be converted into equations by adding negative slack variables. The resulting equations are:

$$X_2 - S_2 = 150 \text{ pounds}$$
$$X_3 - S_3 = 200 \text{ pounds}$$

The slack variable, S_2, represents the amount by which X_2 will exceed 150 pounds in the final solution. (The same type of rationale applies to S_3 and 200 pounds.) For example, if X_2 is 500 pounds in the last tableau, then S_2 must be 350 pounds for the equation to be valid $(500-350=150)$. However, it is possible that X_2 equals 150 pounds in an optimum solution, which means the value of S_2 would be zero $(150-0=150)$.

Going one step further, we must ask what happens if X_2 equals zero in the initial solution. The first solution would be $0-150= -150$ or $S_2= -150$ pounds. This cannot be, since -150 pounds makes no more sense than -300 units of product Alpha or Beta. Thus we must prevent S_2 from appearing in the initial solution. This can be done by letting S_2 equal zero. If both X_2 and S_2 are zero in the initial solution, then we must introduce a new ingredient that will be an acceptable substitute for X_2 in the first solution. This new ingredient can be thought of as a very expensive substance, say $100 ($M$) per pound or the artificial variable mentioned earlier for a greater-than-or-equal-to condition. The high price of A_2 reassures us that it will never appear in the final solution. The third and fourth constraint equations above can be written to include these artificial variables as follows:

$$X_2 - S_2 + A_2 = 150 \text{ pounds}$$
$$X_3 - S_3 + A_3 = 200 \text{ pounds}$$

Although the artificial variable was not demonstrated for a maximization problem, it can be used. A maximization problem may require minimum sales requirements to be produced. Hence, both artificial and slack variables must be introduced. For example, if the minimum sales requirements for Product X_{20} is 500 units, the equation to express this condition is: $X_{20} - S_{20} + A_{20}$ where the subscript 20 refers to the appropriate variable for Product 20. The C_j value for these variables are: current contribution for Product 20, zero, and $-M$, respectively.

In order to insert the proper values in the first minimization tableau, it is necessary to state the cost function and constraint equations. For the cost function, a zero cost must be shown for the slack variables (S_1, S_2 and S_3) and M cost for the artificial variables (A_1, A_2, and A_3). For the constraint equations, it will be recalled that any unknown in one constraint equation must appear in all equations. The appropriate variable must be inserted with zero coefficients. The final cost function and constraint equations, applicable to the first tableau, are:

Minimize cost = $\$5X_1 + \$6X_2 + \$7X_3 + \$MA_1$
  $+ \$0S_1 + \$0S_2 + \$MA_2 + \$0S_3 + \$MA_3$ (Equation 6-16)

Subject to:

$X_1 + X_2 + X_3 + A_1 + 0S_1 + 0S_2 + 0A_2 + 0S_3 + 0A_3 = 1000$ (Equation 6-17)

$X_1 + 0X_2 + 0X_3 + 0A_1 + S_1 + 0S_2 + 0A_2 + 0S_3 + 0A_3 = 300$ (Equation 6-18)

$0X_1 + X_2 + 0X_3 + 0A_1 + 0S_1 - S_2 + A_2 + 0S_3 + 0A_3 = 150$ (Equation 6-19)

$0X_1 + 0X_2 + X_3 + 0A_1 + 0S_1 + 0S_2 + 0A_2 - S_3 + A_3 = 200$ (Equation 6-20)

Upon inspection of the foregoing equations and Tableau IV, it should be apparent why A_1, S_1, A_2, and A_3 were selected as the beginning product mix. The artificial variables (A_1, A_2, and A_3) enable us to keep the starting equations in balance. The same can also be said for the slack variable S_1. The artificial variables, by having a very high cost, assure us that they will not appear in the final solution. The computational procedures for a minimization problem are identical to those used for the previous maximization problem, except for modifying Step 1.

Since the optimum solution is concerned with minimizing costs, the optimum column is found by choosing the one that has the largest negative value in the C_j-Z_j row and not the largest plus value as in a maximization problem. The most negative column is selected because this value will decrease costs the most. Upon inspection of Tableau IV, the most negative value (assuming that M equals $100) is $6-2M$; thus X_2 is the optimum column (first step). Note the relatively high cost of the solution, $1350M$.

Calculations for the last two rows in Tableau IV that were needed in this first step are:

Z_j row

Z Total = $\$M(1000) + \$0(300) + \$M(150) + \$M(200) = \$1350M$
$ZX_1 = \$M(1) + \$0(1) + \$M(0) + \$M(0) = \$M$
$ZX_2 = \$M(1) + \$0(0) + \$M(1) + \$M(0) = \$2M$
$ZX_3 = \$M(1) + \$0(0) + \$M(0) + \$M(1) = \$2M$
$ZA_1 = \$M(1) + \$0(0) + \$M(0) + \$M(0) = \$M$
$ZS_1 = \$M(0) + \$0(1) + \$M(0) + \$M(0) = \$0$
$ZS_2 = \$M(0) + \$0(0) + \$M(-1) + \$M(0) = -\$M$
$ZA_2 = \$M(0) + \$0(0) + \$M(1) + \$M(0) = \$M$
$ZS_3 = \$M(0) + \$0(0) + \$M(0) + \$M(-1) = -\$M$
$ZA_3 = \$M(0) + \$0(0) + \$M(0) + \$M(1) = \$M$

TABLEAU IV
Linear Programming Minimization Problem

C_j	Product Mix	Quantity	$5 X_1	$6 X_2	$7 X_3	$M A_1	$0 S_1	$0 S_2	$M A_2	$0 S_3	$M A_3
$M	A_1	1,000	1	1	1	1	0	0	0	0	0
$0	S_1	300	1	0	0	0	1	0	0	0	0
$M	A_2	150	0	1	0	0	0	−1	1	0	0
$M	A_3	200	0	0	1	0	0	0	0	−1	1
	Z_j	$1,350M	$M	$2M	$2M	$M	$0	−$M	$M	−$M	$M
	$C_j − Z_j$		$5 − M	$6 − 2M	$7 − 2M	$0	$0	$M	$0	$M	$0

Replaced row

$C_j - Z_j$ row

$C_{x_1} - Z_{x_1} = \$5 - \$M = \$5 - \$M$
$C_{x_2} - Z_{x_2} = \$6 - \$2M = \$6 - \$2M$
$C_{x_3} - Z_{x_3} = \$7 - \$2M = \$7 - \$2M$
$C_{A_1} - Z_{A_1} = \$M - \$M = \$0$
$C_{S_1} - Z_{S_1} = \$0 - \$0 = \$0$
$C_{S_2} - Z_{S_2} = \$0 - (-\$M) = \$M$
$C_{A_2} - Z_{A_2} = \$M - \$M = \$0$
$C_{S_3} - Z_{S_3} = \$0 - (-\$M) = \$M$
$C_{A_3} - Z_{A_3} = \$M - \$M = \$0$

In the second step, the replaced row is found by dividing the values in the quantity column by their corresponding intersectional elements in the optimum column and selecting the row with the smallest number of units. These values are calculated as follows:

A_1 row $= \dfrac{1000}{1} = 1000$

S_1 row $= \dfrac{300}{0} =$ Not defined; therefore it is ignored

A_2 row $= \dfrac{150}{1} = 150$

A_3 row $= \dfrac{200}{0} =$ Not defined; therefore it is ignored

The A_2 row, the smaller value of the two, is designated as the replaced row.

For the third step, the replacing row (X_2) is determined by dividing each value in the replaced row (A_2) by the intersectional element of the replaced row (A_2). Since the intersectional element is one, the values remain the same. Only the variable A_2 needs to be changed to X_2.

In the fourth and final step, new values for the A_1, S_1, and A_3 rows must be calculated for Tableau V. The formula is

Former element in the remaining row − (Former intersectional element of remaining row × New corresponding element in replacing row) =
New value for remaining row

The calculations for the new rows are:

A_1 Row	S_1 Row	A_3 Row
$1{,}000 - (1 \times 150) = 850$	$300 - (0 \times 150) = 300$	$200 - (0 \times 150) = 200$
$1 - (1 \times 0) = 1$	$1 - (0 \times 0) = 1$	$0 - (0 \times 0) = 0$
$1 - (1 \times 1) = 0$	$0 - (0 \times 1) = 0$	$0 - (0 \times 1) = 0$
$1 - (1 \times 0) = 1$	$0 - (0 \times 0) = 0$	$1 - (0 \times 0) = 1$
$1 - (1 \times 0) = 1$	$0 - (0 \times 0) = 0$	$0 - (0 \times 0) = 0$
$0 - (1 \times 0) = 0$	$1 - (0 \times 0) = 1$	$0 - (0 \times 0) = 0$
$0 - (1 \times -1) = 1$	$0 - (0 \times -1) = 0$	$0 - (0 \times -1) = 0$
$0 - (1 \times 1) = -1$	$0 - (0 \times 1) = 0$	$0 - (0 \times 1) = 0$
$0 - (1 \times 0) = 0$	$0 - (0 \times 0) = 0$	$-1 - (0 \times 0) = -1$
$0 - (1 \times 0) = 0$	$0 - (0 \times 0) = 0$	$1 - (0 \times 0) = 1$

TABLEAU V
Linear Programming Minimization Problem

	C_j	Product Mix	Quantity	$5 X_1	$6 X_2	$7 X_3	$M A_1	$0 S_1	$0 S_2	$M A_2	$0 S_3	$M A_3
	$M	A_1	850	1	0	1	1	0	1	−1	0	0
	$0	S_1	300	1	0	0	0	1	0	0	0	0
	$6	X_2	150	0	1	0	0	0	−1	1	0	0
Replaced row	$M	A_3	200	0	0	1	0	0	0	0	−1	1
		Z_j	$1,050M+$900	$M	$6	$2M	$M	$0	$M−6	−$M+6	−$M	$M
		$C_j − Z_j$		$5−$M	$0	$7−2M	$0	$0	−$M+6	$2M−6	$M	$0

188 OPERATIONS RESEARCH MODELS—MATRIX ALGEBRA

When the intersectional element is zero, such as for the S_1 row and the A_3 row, the values of the new row are the same as the old row. This condition is true of all succeeding tableaus in which an intersectional element of a row is zero.

Inspection of Tableau V reveals the optimum column to be X_3. The replaced row is A_3 and the replacing row is X_3 in the next tableau. Notice that the total cost has decreased from $1350M to $1050M + $900 between the first two tableaus. The optimum column in Tableau VI is X_1 and the replaced row is S_1. These changes are reflected in Tableau VII, the fourth tableau in the problem. Again the cost has decreased from the preceding tableaus.

In Tableau VII, there is presently $350M in the total cost function. Nevertheless, total cost is still declining. The optimum column is S_2. When the calculation is made for the replaced row, the value for the X_2 row is -150 $[150/(-1)]$. This is not a feasible solution since we cannot have a minus quantity in the final solution. Therefore it is discarded as a possibility for the replaced row. The only positive quantity for the replaced row is $A_1(350)$. Again, new rows are determined, as in Tableau VIII. (pg. 191)

Inspection of the $C_j - Z_j$ row reveals that no negative values remain. The optimum solution has been reached. Moreover, the total cost solution no longer contains an artificial variable (M). In addition, it is necessary to make certain that the values for the variables X_1, X_2, X_3, and S_2 in the tableau satisfy the original restrictions. Reviewing the original constraint equations, they are:

$$X_1 + X_2 + X_3 + A_1 = 1000 \qquad \text{(Equation 6-17)}$$

$$X_1 + S_1 = 300 \qquad \text{(Equation 6-18)}$$

$$X_2 - S_2 + A_2 = 150 \qquad \text{Equation 6-19)}$$

$$X_3 - S_3 + A_3 = 200 \qquad \text{(Equation 6-20)}$$

Substituting the values into the equations, it will be seen that we still are within the constraints of the problem when $X_1 = 300$, $X_2 = 500$, $X_3 = 200$, and $S_2 = 350$. All other variables have a value of zero.

$$300 + 500 + 200 = 1000 \qquad \text{(Equation 6-17)}$$
$$1000 = 1000$$

$$300 + 0 = 300 \qquad \text{(Equation 6-18)}$$
$$300 = 300$$

$$500 - 350 + 0 = 150 \qquad \text{(Equation 6-19)}$$
$$150 = 150$$

$$200 - 0 + 0 = 200 \qquad \text{(Equation 6-20)}$$
$$200 = 200$$

TABLEAU VI
Linear Programming Minimization Problem

	C_j	Product Mix	Quantity	$5 X_1	$6 X_2	$7 X_3	$M A_1	$0 S_1	$0 S_2	$M A_2	$0 S_3	$M A_3
	$M	A_1	650	1	0	0	1	0	1	−1	1	−1
Replaced row	$0	S_1	300	1	0	0	0	1	0	0	0	0
	$6	X_2	150	0	1	0	0	0	−1	1	0	0
	$7	X_3	200	0	0	1	0	0	0	0	−1	1
		Z_j	$650M+$2,300	$M	$6	$7	$M	$0	$M−6	−$M+6	$M−7	−$M+7
		$C_j − Z_j$		−$M+5	$0	$0	$0	$0	−$M+6	$2M−6	−$M+7	$2M−7

TABLEAU VII
Linear Programming Minimization Problem

	C_j	Product Mix	Quantity	$5 X_1	$6 X_2	$7 X_3	$M A_1	$0 S_1	$0 S_2	$M A_2	$0 S_3	$M A_3
	$M	A_1	350	0	0	0	1	−1	1	−1	1	−1
Replaced row	$5	X_1	300	1	0	0	0	1	0	0	0	0
	$6	X_2	150	0	1	0	0	0	−1	1	0	0
	$7	X_3	200	0	0	1	0	0	0	0	−1	1
		Z_j	$350M+$3,800	$5	$6	$7	$M	−$M+5	$M−6	−$M+6	$M−7	−$M+7
		$C_j − Z_j$		$0	$0	$0	$0	$M−5	−$M+6	$2M−6	−$M+7	$2M−7

TABLEAU VIII
Linear Programming Minimization Problem

C_j	Product Mix	Quantity	$5 X_1	$6 X_2	$7 X_3	$M A_1	$0 S_1	$0 S_2	$M A_2	$0 S_3	$M A_3
$0	S_2	350	0	0	0	1	−1	1	−1	1	−1
$5	X_1	300	1	0	0	0	1	0	0	0	0
$6	X_2	500	0	1	0	1	−1	0	0	1	−1
$7	X_3	200	0	0	1	0	0	0	0	−1	1
	Z_j	$5,900	$5	$6	$7	$6	−$1	$0	$0	−$1	$1
	$C_j − Z_j$		$0	$0	$0	$M−6	$1	$0	$M	$1	$M−1

Duality of Linear Programming Problems

For every maximization (or minimization) problem, there is a related unique problem of minimization (or maximization) involving the same data which also describes the original problem. The initial problem is called the *primal* problem and the related problem is called the *dual* problem. However, two paired problems are defined as dual problems due to the fact that both are formed from the same set of data. As one might suspect, the data is arranged differently in their mathematical presentation. When one is considered to be primal, the other is the dual.

The question can be raised, what is the value of the dual if the optimal solution is found with the primal problem? First, the solution of a linear programming problem may be easier to obtain through the dual than through the primal problem. Consider a primal problem involving three products with seven departments or seven rows (slack variables). The first simplex tableau for this problem will have seven rows while the dual of the same problem will have only three rows. This causes a reduction in the number of tableaus required for a final answer. In addition, the calculation of the dual allows us to check on the accuracy of the primal solution.

In order to demonstrate the duality of a problem, the maximization problem presented in this chapter will be utilized. The original equations are reproduced here for the primal problem:

$$\text{Maximize } Z = \$10A + \$12B + \$0S_1 + \$0S_2 + \$0S_3 \quad \text{(Equation 6-4)}$$

Subject to:

$$2A + 3B + S_1 + 0S_2 + 0S_3 = 1500 \quad \text{(Equation 6-13)}$$

$$3A + 2B + 0S_1 + S_2 + 0S_3 = 1500 \quad \text{(Equation 6-14)}$$

$$A + B + 0S_1 + 0S_2 + S_3 = 600 \quad \text{(Equation 6-15)}$$

$$A \geq 0, \quad B \geq 0$$

Although some problems are symmetrical in that the number of constraints (rows) equals the number of variables (columns), the problem we are studying, however, is unsymmetric since the rows and columns are not equal, that is, there are two products and three departments. The unsymmetric dual becomes:

$$\text{Minimize} = 1500y_1 + 1500y_2 + 600y_3$$

Subject to:

$$2y_1 + 3y_2 + y_3 \geq 10$$
$$3y_1 + 2y_2 + y_3 \geq 12$$

The initial step is to eliminate the inequalities. This can be done by adding a slack variable (minus) and an artificial variable (plus). As stated in the preceding section on a minimization problem, the artificial variable is used for the greater than or equal to condition. The minimization function and inequalities become:

$$\text{Minimize} = 1500y_1 + 1500y_2 + 600y_3 + 0y_4 + My_5 + 0y_6 + My_7$$

(Equation 6-21)

Subject to:

$$2y_1 + 3y_2 + y_3 - y_4 + y_5 = 10 \qquad \text{(Equation 6-22)}$$

$$3y_1 + 2y_2 + y_3 - y_6 + y_7 = 12 \qquad \text{(Equation 6-23)}$$

An optimal solution, using the primal, was obtained in Tableaus I to III. The same problem, using the dual, will be completed in the same number of tableaus since the number of iterations required by the simplex method is dependent upon the number of replaced rows in the tableau. Tableau IX is the first of this unsymmetric dual; here M equals 1000. Based upon

TABLEAU IX
Unsymmetric Dual Problem

Quantity	Product Mix	Contribution per Unit	1,500 y_1	1,500 y_2	600 y_3	0 y_4	M y_5	0 y_6	M y_7
M	y_5	$10	2	3	1	−1	1	0	0
M	y_7	$12	3	2	1	0	0	−1	1
	Z_j	$22M	5M	5M	2M	−M	M	−M	M
	$C_j - Z_j$		1,500 −5M	1,500 −5M	600 −2M	M	0	M	0

Tableau IX, the optimum column is y_1 or y_2. Column y_1 will be used first. The replaced row is y_7.

In Tableau X, the optimum column is y_2 since it has the largest negative amount. The replaced row is the y_5 row. This leads to the last tableau (Tableau XI).

Since there are no minus figures in the last row, the solution has been reached. The $C_j - Z_j$ in the final tableau contains the solution values of the primal, that is, the slack columns of y_4 and y_6 represent the 300 units of products Alpha and Beta, respectively. Also, the total contribution is the same as that found in Tableau III, the final tableau for the primal.

By now, what actually happened should be apparent. There has been a transpose of the matrix (of the structural coefficients) in the primal problem into the matrix (of the structural coefficients) in the dual. If there are n structural variables and m slack variables in the primal problem, there will be m structural variables and n slack variables in its dual. A graphical presentation of the dual is found in Figure 6-7 and will help clarify this transpose. Contrast this presentation with Figure 6-2 (or 6-3) for the primal. The striped area in Figure 6-7 is complementary to the striped area of Figure 6-2.

Sensitivity Analysis

After a linear programming problem has been solved, it is recommended that the effect of discrete changes in the problem's parameters on the current optimal solution be studied. Hence, it is usually advisable to perform *sensitivity analysis* or *postoptimality analysis*. If the objective function solu-

TABLEAU X
Unsymmetric Dual Problem

Quantity	Product Mix	Contribution per Unit	1,500 y_1	1,500 y_2	600 y_3	0 y_4	M y_5	0 y_6	M y_7
M	y_5	$2	0	1⅔	⅓	−1	1	⅔	−⅔
1,500	y_1	$4	1	⅔	⅓	0	0	−⅓	⅓
	Z_j	$2M	1,500	1,000	500	−M	M	−500	500
		+$6,000		+1⅔M	+⅓M			+⅔M	−⅔M
	$C_j − Z_j$		0	500	100	M	0	500	−500
				−1⅔M	−⅓M			−⅔M	+1⅔M

TABLEAU XI
Unsymmetric Dual Problem

Quantity	Product Mix	Contribution per Unit	1,500 y_1	1,500 y_2	600 y_3	0 y_4	M y_5	0 y_6	M y_7
1,500	y_2	$1.20	0	1	0.2	−0.6	0.6	0.4	−0.4
1,500	y_1	$3.20	1	0	0.2	0.4	−0.4	−0.6	0.6
	Z_j	$6,600.00	1,500	1,500	600	−300	300	−300	300
	$C_j − Z_j$		0	0	0	300	M−300	300	M−300

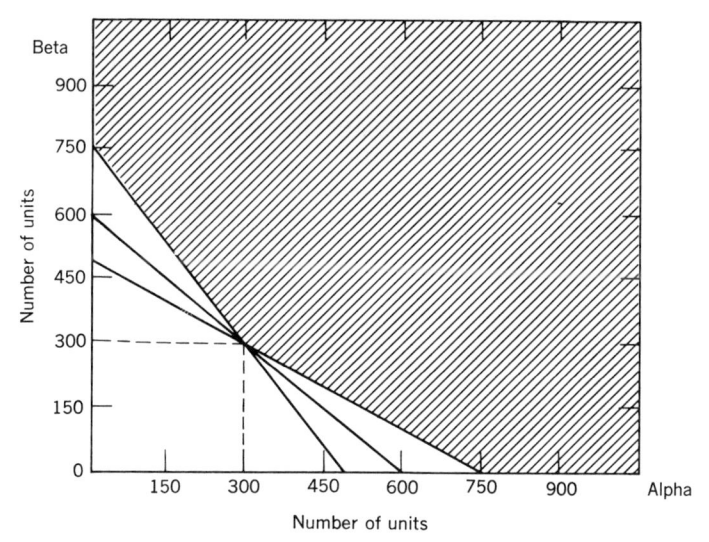

Figure 6-7 Graphic representation of the dual problem.

tion is relatively sensitive to changes in certain parameters, special attention must be given to these parameters such that the final solution gives consideration to most of their likely values. For such situations, it is not necessary to solve the problem from the very beginning each time a minor change is made. Using the previous optimal solution and the corresponding set of equations, it is usually possible to check whether or not the basis is optimal and, if not, to utilize it as a beginning point for solving the new optimal solution.

Advantages of Linear Programming Methods

Up to this point, the chapter has concentrated on the various methods for solving linear programming problems. By no means does this exhaust the various approaches that are available to solve this class of problems. A shortened version of the simplex method, making use of a pivot element (pivot row and pivot column), will be found in one or more books appearing in the bibliography of this chapter. The next several chapters will utilize the simplex method plus presenting additional techniques for solving mathematical programming problems.

The allocation of so much space within this book for linear programming implies that it has many advantages for the user. Several important advantages are self-evident. Among these is the optimum use of productive factors within the firm. Linear programming indicates how a manager can most effectively employ his productive factors by more efficiently selecting and distributing these elements. The more efficient use of manpower and machines can be obtained as a solution to a well-structured linear programming problem.

Another advantage is the improved quality of decisions. The manager becomes more objective (obtained by the process of linear programming) and less subjective (how I feel in light of the existing conditions). The individual who utilizes linear programming methods must analyze business problems as they actually are and collect only the data pertinent to the mathematical formulation. The manager, having a clear picture of the relationships within the basic equations and inequalities or constraints, can better understand the problem and its related solution.

Consideration must be given to the fact that linear programming gives possible and practical solutions since there might be other constraints operating outside of the problem which must be taken into account, for example, sales demands. Just because we can produce so many units does not mean that they can be sold. On the other hand, it might be necessary to restrict a certain amount of production volume for less profitable items which are necessary for a complete product line. Unless these less profitable items are made and included in the product line, customers will buy elsewhere. This latter situation can be handled easily by taking the time available initially and subtracting the time necessary for the minimum sales requirements (profitable and less profitable products) and solving for the mixture of products based upon the remaining time available in the various departments. The fact that the method of linear programming allows modification of its mathematical solution for the sake of convenience must, in itself, be considered an advantage.

The simplex method gives the user an opportunity to calculate *shadow prices*. The use of shadow prices provides relevant information for decisions concerning the acquisition of additional resources needed to meet some objective, such as maximizing contribution. The shadow price shows the additional contribution generated by relaxing a constraint and thus sets an upper limit on the cost to acquire one more unit of a constraining factor. To state it another way, the shadow price measures the value or worth of relaxing a constraint by acquiring an additional unit of that factor of production. The value of additional resources can be compared to the actual cost of acquiring these resources, thereby allowing decisions to be made on the basis of these comparisons.

Although the foregoing advantages are somewhat obvious, a frequently overlooked advantage (refutes the accountant's point of view in selecting those products with the highest contribution) is one relating to the identification of production bottlenecks. Consider the following problem where the marketable products A, B, C, and D of the Sawbrook Company, Inc., have a contribution of $4.00, $3.75, $3.60, and $3.00 respectively. The production requirements and time available are as follows:

	Time Required per Product (hours)				Time Available Next Week (hours)
	A	B	C	D	
Dept. 1	0.3	0.3	0.3	0.2	250
Dept. 2	0.7	0.6	0.7	0.8	1,000
Dept. 3	0.35	0.3	0.3	0.2	250
Dept. 4	0.2	0.25	0.25	0.22	250

A quick inspection of this problem indicates that the most profitable items should be promoted and the less profitable ones not promoted. The marketing, accounting, and production managers, using this premise, came up with the quantities to be produced and sold. The assumption in this problem is that the customer can be made to switch among the four products since all are identical type products. The rate of substitution of one product for another is unusually high.

Inasmuch as the firm's managers wanted to take full advantage of the highest contribution rate and the sales demands of customers, they decided to allocate production in this manner: 60 percent to product A, 25 to product B, 10 to product C, and 5 to product D. The minimum sales requirements needed for each product takes up 5 percent of total production. This is the reason for 5 percent of total weekly production time being allocated to product D. The calculations for allocated production time are depicted in Table 6-1.

Using the rationale set forth previously for linear programming, that is, selecting the lowest of the values calculated for the various products in each of the departments (circled figures), the production schedule (60 percent for product A, 25 for product B, 10 for product C, and 5 for product D) and contribution expected are as follows:

Product A: 429 units × $4.00 = $1,716.00
Product B: 208 units × $3.75 =   780.00
Product C: 83 units × $3.60 =   298.80
Product D: 57 units × $3.00 =   171.00
               Total contribution $2,965.80

When applying the simplex method to this problem, the initial production for minimum sales requirements must be calculated, as in Table 6-2. The minimum sales requirements (based on production) are:

Product A: 36 units × $4.00 = $144.00
Product B: 42 units × $3.75 = 157.50
Product C: 42 units × $3.60 = 151.20
Product D: 57 units × $3.00 = 171.00
         Total contribution for minimum sales requirements
                        (based on production) $623.70

Now that the minimum sales requirement and its related contributions have been computed, it is necessary to calculate the remaining time available for production of A, B, C, and D or some combination of these products. This is determined in Table 6-3.

The first tableau can be determined for this linear programming maximization problem now that the remaining time has been computed (Tableau XII).

The final tableau for this problem is Tableau XIII. The total contribution from the last tableau ($2930.60) plus the contribution based upon the minimum sales requirements ($623.70) is $3554.30. The original contribution

TABLE 6-1
Allocated Production Time

	Product A (60% of production)	Product B (25% of production)	Product C (10% of production)	Product D (5% of production)	Time Available Next Week (hours)
Dept. 1	$\frac{150 \text{ hr}}{0.3 \text{ hr/unit}} = 500$	$\frac{62.5 \text{ hr}}{0.3 \text{ hr/unit}} = \boxed{208}$	$\frac{25 \text{ hr}}{0.3 \text{ hr/unit}} = \boxed{83}$	$\frac{12.5 \text{hr}}{0.2 \text{ hr/unit}} = 63$	250
Dept. 2	$\frac{600}{0.7} = 857$	$\frac{250}{0.6} = 417$	$\frac{100}{0.7} = 143$	$\frac{50}{0.8} = 63$	1,000
Dept. 3	$\frac{150}{0.35} = \boxed{429}$	$\frac{62.5}{0.3} = \boxed{208}$	$\frac{25}{0.3} = \boxed{83}$	$\frac{12.5}{0.2} = 63$	250
Dept. 4	$\frac{150}{0.2} = 750$	$\frac{62.5}{0.25} = 250$	$\frac{25}{0.25} = 100$	$\frac{12.5}{0.22} = \boxed{57}$	250

TABLE 6-2
Production for Minimum Sales Requirements

	Product A (5% of production)	Product B (5% of production)	Product C (5% of production)	Product D (5% of production)	Time Required for Minimum Sales Requirements, (hours)
Dept. 1	$\dfrac{12.5 \text{ hr}}{0.3 \text{ hr/unit}} = 42$	$\dfrac{12.5 \text{ hr}}{0.3 \text{ hr/unit}} = \boxed{42}$	$\dfrac{12.5 \text{ hr}}{0.3 \text{ hr/unit}} = \boxed{42}$	$\dfrac{12.5 \text{ hr}}{0.2 \text{ hr/unit}} = 63$	50
Dept. 2	$\dfrac{50}{0.7} = 71$	$\dfrac{50}{0.6} = 83$	$\dfrac{50}{0.7} = 71$	$\dfrac{50}{0.8} = 63$	200
Dept. 3	$\dfrac{12.5}{0.35} = \boxed{36}$	$\dfrac{12.5}{0.3} = \boxed{42}$	$\dfrac{12.5}{0.3} = \boxed{42}$	$\dfrac{12.5}{0.2} = 63$	50
Dept. 4	$\dfrac{12.5}{0.2} = 63$	$\dfrac{12.5}{0.25} = 50$	$\dfrac{12.5}{0.25} = 50$	$\dfrac{12.5}{0.22} = \boxed{57}$	50

TABLE 6-3
Remaining Time Available for Production

	Available Time	Product A	Product B	Product C	Product D	Remaining Time
Dept. 1	250 hr	36 units × 0.3 = −10.8 hr	42 units × 0.3 = −12.6 hr	42 units × 0.3 = −12.6 hr	57 units × 0.2 = −11.4 hr	202.6 hr
Dept. 2	1,000 hr	36 units × 0.7 = −25.2 hr	42 units × 0.6 = −25.2 hr	42 units × 0.7 = −29.4 hr	57 units × 0.8 = −45.6 hr	874.6 hr
Dept. 3	250 hr	36 units × 0.35 = −12.6 hr	42 units × 0.3 = −12.6 hr	42 units × 0.3 = −12.6 hr	57 units × 0.2 = −11.4 hr	200.8 hr
Dept. 4	250 hr	36 units × 0.2 = − 7.2 hr	42 units × 0.25 = −10.5 hr	42 units × 0.25 = −10.5 hr	57 units × 0.22 = −12.5 hr	209.3 hr

LINEAR PROGRAMMING

TABLEAU XII
Linear Programming Maximization Problem (First Tableau)

C_j	Product Mix	Quantity	$4.00 A	$3.75 B	$3.60 C	$3.00 D	$0 S_1	$0 S_2	$0 S_3	$0 S_5
$0	S_1	202.6	0.3	0.3	0.3	0.2	1	0	0	0
$0	S_2	874.6	0.7	0.6	0.7	0.8	0	1	0	0
$0	S_3	200.8	0.35	0.3	0.3	0.2	0	0	1	0
$0	S_4	209.3	0.2	0.25	0.25	0.22	0	0	0	1
	Z_j		$0	$0	$0	$0	$0	$0	$0	$0
	$C_j - Z_j$		$4.00	$3.75	$3.60	$3.00	$0	$0	$0	$0

was $2965.80. The improved solution of linear programming represents an increase in weekly contribution of $588.50, a significant one.

In the example, product D, originally produced only to meet the minimum sales requirements (based on 5 percent of total production time), or 57 units, is the biggest volume product with 940 (883+57) units. A comparison of the original and improved solution is as follows:

	Original Solution		Improved Solution	
Product A	429 units × $4.00 =	$1,716.00	106.4 units × $4.00 =	$ 425.60
Product B	208 units × $3.75 =	780.00	42 units × $3.75 =	157.50
Product C	83 units × $3.60 =	298.80	42 units × $3.60 =	151.20
Product D	57 units × $3.00 =	171.00	940 units × $3.00 =	2,820.00
Total Contribution		$2,965.80		$3,554.30

Although product A did show a high unit contribution, it was a bottleneck in Department 3. Why is this department a bottleneck for product A? This question can be answered by examining Tableau XIII for unused department time. Variables S_1 and S_2, representing Departments 1 and 2, have remaining time. Since the variables S_3 and S_4 do not appear in this final tableau, time in Departments 3 and 4 must have been exhausted. Analysis of Tableau XIII clearly indicates that Department 2 is not a bottleneck department due to the 119.8 remaining hours. However, Department 1, which has 4.0 remaining hours has, for all practical purposes, no remaining time. Based on the foregoing evaluation of used time for Departments 1, 3, and 4, it is necessary to examine the first tableau (XII) for product A. Time to produce this product is .3, .35, and .2 in Departments 1, 3, and 4, respectively. Since there is zero time available in these departments, and the time factor to manufacture product A in Department 3 is the highest, Department 3 is the present bottleneck.

When bottlenecks occur, some machines cannot meet demand while other equipment stands idle part of the time. As a result, imbalance is an important cost factor which more than offsets the gains from high unit contribution. Thus a foremost advantage (perhaps the most significant to many companies) is the highlighting of bottlenecks in their present operations.

TABLEAU XIII
Linear Programming Maximization Problem (Final Tableau)

C_j	Product Mix	Quantity	$4.00 A	$3.75 B	$3.60 C	$3.00 D	$0 S_1	$0 S_2	$0 S_3	$0 S_4
$0	S_1	4.0	0	0.017	0.017	0	1	0	− 0.7	− 0.28
$0	S_2	119.8	0	− 0.3	− 0.2	0	0	1	0.15	− 3.77
$4	A	70.4	1	0.43	0.43	0	0	0	5.93	− 0.54
$3	D	883.0	0	0.755	0.755	1	0	0	− 5.38	9.43
	Z_j	$2,930.60	$4	$3.985	$3.985	$3	$0	$0	$7.58	$26.13
	$C_j − Z_j$		$0	−$0.235	−$0.385	$0	$0	$0	−$7.58	−$26.13

LINEAR PROGRAMMING 201

Ignoring bottlenecks can result in promoting the wrong product(s). Experience gained from periodic LP analysis will help management determine where new equipment should be installed for those departments limiting overall plant capacity.

Cautions of Linear Programming Methods

There are some cautions or difficulties associated with every mathematical method, no matter how glowing its merits. Linear programming is no exception. The operations research team must define the objective function and constraints which can change overnight due to internal as well as external factors. There is the necessity of keeping current reliable data so that it is available when needed. Obviously, the more rigidly the data adheres to the reality of the situation, the more reliable will be the solution.

Managers who contemplate using this technique must be sure that they have a practical application for the selected method of linear programming. Another way of stating it is that even though the problem is correctly stated and formulated mathematically, there may be some limiting factors from a practical point of view. For example, if not enough time has been allotted to the proper collecting of data, garbage-in, garbage-out will result. To cite another example, the computed program available cannot handle all the constraints. If used, constraints will have to be dropped which could render the output basically unusable.

Where the objective function and constraints are nonlinear, extreme caution must be used when applying linear programming. The misapplication of linear programming under nonlinear conditions usually results in an incorrect solution. The problem and related techniques dealing with this topic will be covered in Chapter 12.

The last limitation is the costs related to maintaining linear programming solutions. As stated previously, cost factors, constraints, and similar data are continually changing. By the time the initial data has been collected and properly formulated, it may be out of date. Thus we have a maintenance cost for the factors necessary in problems of this type. It may be questionable whether the cost of programming with new data is worth the change. When the results are worth the total expenses involved in reprocessing the current data, this apparent limitation no longer applies.

When comparison is made between the advantages and limitations of linear programming, its advantages clearly outweigh its problems. Again, it should be made clear that linear programming techniques, like other mathematical tools, assist the manager in the task of deciding the most appropriate solution to a business problem. They are not a substitute for the manager.

Applications of Linear Programming

Basic linear programming applications were presented in this chapter for maximization and minimization problems. A cross section of business and industrial applications that are solvable by linear programming are given below:

- *Advertising media evaluation.* Analyzes the effectiveness of advertising space and time based on the available advertising media.
- *Blast furnace operation.* Aids production management in scheduling blast furnaces far more accurately and efficiently than possible with other analytical methods.
- *Blending of raw materials.* Helps in blending the various ingredients of a particular mix in order to meet specified requirements and assists manufacturing management by proportioning raw materials subject to quality restrictions.
- *Inventory scheduling.* Allows for the arrangement of raw materials and semifinished goods to minimize the firm's capital investment while maximizing efficient production flow.
- *Manpower management planning.* Allows personnel management to analyze personnel policy combinations in terms of their appropriateness for maintaining a steady-state flow of people into, through, and out of the firm.
- *Physical distribution.* Determines the most economic and efficient manner of locating manufacturing plants and distribution centers for physical distribution management.
- *Production scheduling.* Determines for manufacturing management the most profitable combination of products to manufacture for facilities possessing a wide range of production capabilities and the most efficient method for machine loading.
- *Raw material allocation.* Optimizes for buyers potential raw material sources for production and minimizes transportation costs.
- *Site location.* Helps top management in deciding which location is best for new plants, warehouses, and branch offices and where to eliminate existing facilities.
- *Time standards determination.* Assists time study personnel in determining standard times for those type of jobs in which the discrete work elements are essentially the same but vary in number.
- *Vendor quotation analysis.* Aids buyers in analyzing vendor quotations in cases where a number of products are quoted by many vendors.

In addition to the foregoing applications, accounting systems have been structured on linear programming models. The petroleum industry is a good example. To get an idea of the problem involved, a certain refinery must produce a specified amount of gasoline and oil with certain quality specifications. To accomplish this, the refinery has at its disposal certain processing units and a number of raw materials. The problem is to select that combination of raw materials and processing sequences which minimizes the total cost of meeting the stipulated market requirements. In terms of size, a sample model contains approximately 125 equations with 300 variables and slightly less than 3000 nonzero elements.

The internal accounting system of the refinery is responsibility-oriented using standard costs. The refinery is structured by divisions, each having departments with individual responsibility centers. Total costs are segregated into variable and fixed components. For each refinery, the firm has a mathematical model which is used for varied economic analysis. Actual blended and product production quantities are inserted into the model and an adjusted "optimum" budget is determined—reflecting the standard cost of producing the end products actually processed during the quarter. Actual results and budgeted figures are then compared in an effort to review the particular quarter's performance. The quarterly accounting system, in effect, is merely a flexible budgeting arrangement in which actual cost incurred in the production of a set of end products is compared with the standard cost for that set of end products. The standard is determined by optimizing the linear programming model with these end product quantities. This accounting approach allows comparison of what the firm has accomplished with what it should have accomplished using linear programming standards in order to determine accounting variances.

Linear Programming Application—American Products Corporation

The utilization of linear programming has enabled the American Products Corporation to minimize monthly costs of purchased materials and parts from multiple suppliers, each with a limited capacity, where the monthly demand for individual materials and parts fluctuates. The purchasing problem is not concerned primarily with how much to order but from whom to order when certain suppliers can furnish only a portion of the total requirements. For example, since no one outside foundry is geared to supply all the monthly requirements for a specific casting, the purchasing agents must buy from several suppliers—each with a limited capacity. The order quantity each foundry receives from the American Products Corporation depends on the quantities of each casting required each month as well as the relationship of its cost to the total costs of a group of castings furnished by that particular foundry and others. As expected, the prices of the foundries vary for the castings they are able to supply.

To simplify the purchasing problem, the discussion will be limited to three suppliers—A, B, and C—for the next month. The costs of purchased castings from each supplier and the variables, representing the monthly quantity of each casting available, are set forth in Figure 6-8. In addition, certain supplier limitations must be considered. The constraint equations are illustrated next to their corresponding limitations in Figure 6-9. Finally,

Supplier	Casting #22	Casting #38	Casting #41
A	$6.45 ($X_1$)	$7.85 ($X_2$)	$8.45 ($X_3$)
B	6.50 (X_4)	7.65 (X_5)	8.80 (X_6)
C	6.85 (X_7)	7.30 (X_8)	8.95 (X_9)

Figure 6-8 Costs and monthly quantities (X_n) of purchased castings—American Products Corporation.

	Supplier Limitation	Constraint Equation
A	Capacity limitation for all three castings is 2400 units per month.	$X_1+X_2+X_3 \leq 2400$
B	Capacity limitation for all three castings is 3000 units per month.	$X_4+X_5+X_6 \leq 3000$
	Capacity limitation of Casting #41 is 400 units per month.	$X_6 \leq 400$
	Contract assures this supplier of an order for at least 2600 units per month.	$X_4+X_5+X_6 \geq 2600$
C	Capacity limitation for all three castings is 2500 units per month.	$X_7+X_8+X_9 \leq 2500$
	Capacity limitation of Casting #38 is 500 units per month.	$X_8 \leq 500$

Figure 6-9 Supplier limitations and constraint equations for next month—American Products Corporation.

it is necessary to specify the castings required for the next month, which are:

Casting #22 $X_1+X_4+X_7=2100$
Casting #38 $X_2+X_5+X_8=2700$
Casting #41 $X_3+X_6+X_9=2000$

The foregoing data can now be used to construct the first simplex tableau (minimization), found in Tableau XIV. Although this tableau can be solved manually for this simplified problem, a computer should be employed for the real world situation. Based on the final simplex tableau, the breakdown of purchased castings for next month is set forth in Figure 6-10. The minimum total cost of purchased castings is $51,325 for next month.

Supplier	Casting #22	Casting #38	Casting #41
A	$6.45 × 400 = $ 2,580	$7.85 × 0 = $ 0	$8.45 × 2,000 = $16,900
B	6.50 × 800 = 5,200	7.65 × 2,200 = 16,830	8.80 × 0 = 0
C	6.85 × 900 = 6,165	7.30 × 500 = 3,650	8.95 × 0 = 0
	2,100 $13,945	2,700 $20,480	2,000 $16,900

Figure 6-10 Minimum monthly cost of each casting by supplier per final simplex tableau (minimization)—American Products Corporation.

Summary

Linear programming, a method of relatively recent origin, has made an impressive impact on solving many recurring business problems. Problems once thought to be unsolvable can be formulated in terms of an objective

TABLEAU XIV
First Tableau (minimization) for Linear Programming Problem—American Products Corporation.

C_j	Product Mix	Quantity	$6.45 X_1	$7.85 X_2	$8.45 X_3	$6.50 X_4	$7.65 X_5	$8.80 X_6	$6.85 X_7	$7.30 X_8	$8.95 X_9	$0 S_1	$0 S_2	$0 S_3	$0 S_4	$M A_1	$0 S_5	$0 S_6	$M A_2	$M A_3	$M A_4
$0	S_1	2400	1	1	1	0	0	0	0	0	0	1	0	0	0	0	0	0	0	0	0
$0	S_2	3000	0	0	0	1	1	1	0	0	0	0	1	0	0	0	0	0	0	0	0
$0	S_3	400	0	0	0	0	0	0	1	1	1	0	0	1	0	0	0	0	0	0	0
$M	A_1	2600	0	0	0	1	1	1	1	1	1	0	0	0	−1	1	0	0	0	0	0
$0	S_5	2500	0	0	0	0	1	0	0	1	0	0	0	0	0	0	1	0	0	0	0
$0	S_6	500	0	0	0	0	0	0	0	0	1	0	0	0	0	0	0	1	0	0	0
$M	A_2	2100	1	0	0	①	0	0	1	0	0	0	0	0	0	0	0	0	1	0	0
$M	A_3	2700	0	1	0	0	1	0	0	1	0	0	0	0	0	0	0	0	0	1	0
$M	A_4	2000	0	0	1	0	0	1	0	0	1	0	0	0	0	0	0	0	0	0	1
	Z_j	$9400M	$M	$M	$M	$2M	$2M	$2M	$M	$M	$M	$0	$0	$0	−$M	$M	$0	$0	$M	$M	$M
	$C_j−Z_j$		$6.45 −M	$7.85 −M	$8.45 −M	$6.50 −2M	$7.65 −2M	$8.80 −2M	$6.85 −M	$7.30 −M	$8.95 −M	$0	$0	$0	$M	$0	$0	$0	$0	$0	$0

            ↑
          Optimum Column

206 OPERATIONS RESEARCH MODELS—MATRIX ALGEBRA

function and constraints. Many successes of operations research can be attributed to the simplex method.

Like other OR techniques, the methods of linear programming have not been finalized at this time. Just as mathematical programming resulted in such areas as linear programming, transportation method, integer programming, nonlinear programming, and dynamic programming, more modifications of the basic simplex method will result in extending it to other difficult business problems, especially those that have nonlinear functions and constraints. Also, the more rigorous use of computers will bring new developments to the forefront. Linear programming, then, is a management tool and an analytical process that offers many advantages to the user for solving the firm's never-ending problems.

Questions

1. (a) What is linear programming?
   (b) What are its essential requirements?
2. What are the advantages and disadvantages of linear programming?
3. Discuss the relationship of the algebraic approach to the simplex method of linear programming.
4. Discuss the similarities and differences between a maximization problem and a minimization problem using the simplex method of linear programming.
5. Suggest areas where linear programming can be applied, other than those set forth in this chapter.

Problems

6-1 The Dumont Company, a manufacturer of test equipment, has three major departments for its manufacture of S-1,000 Model and S-2000 Model. Manufacturing times and monthly capacities are given as follows:

	Per Unit Time Requirements (hours)		
	S-1000 Model	S-2000 Model	Hours Available This Month
Main frame dept.	4.0	2.0	1,600
Electrical wiring dept.	2.5	1.0	1,200
Assembly dept.	4.5	1.5	1,600

The contribution of the S-1000 Model is $40 each and the contribution of the S-2000 Model is $10 each. Assuming that the company can sell any quantity of either product due to favorable market conditions, determine the optimal output for both models, highest possible contribution for this month, and slack time in the three departments. Use the graphic or algebraic method.

6-2 The Kenmore Corporation, a progressive manufacturer of military and civilian devices, is currently manufacturing a line of civilian hardware with a present daily production of 30 units for Model Z-1200 and 120 units of Model Z-1500. The vice president of manufacturing wants to know if profits could be increased by changing the product mix between the two models. The following information was compiled on the hours required to build each model and the capacities of the departments in the plant.

	Man-Hours Required		Department Capacity
	Model Z-1200	Model Z-1500	(Hours per day)
Department 1	2	0	300
Department 2	0	3	540
Department 3	2	2	440
Department 4	1⅕	1½	300
Contribution/unit	$50	$40	

(a) Determine the optimum product mix assuming the quantities can be sold. Use the graphic method.
(b) By how much would the optimum mix increase the contribution to fixed costs and profit?
(c) Suppose the price of Model Z-1200 is reduced by $10; what will the optimum product mix be? Use the graphic method.

The firm is contemplating a third product, Model Z-1800, which will utilize the same facilities as the two models for the military market. The departmental capacities will remain the same. The requirements for Model Z-1800 are: Department 1, 0.1 hour; Department 2, 3.6 hours; Department 3, 2.2 hours; and Department 4, 1.2 hours. The contribution for the new model is $55 each (use the original contribution for the other two models).

(d) Assuming the firm can sell any combination of quantities that it can produce, what is the optimum product mix and the highest daily contribution? Use the simplex method.
(e) Is the answer to (d) unique? Prove your answer. (*Hint:* graph the problem.)

6-3 The sales manager of the Rose Manufacturing Company has budgeted $120,000 for an advertising program for one of the firm's products. The selected advertising program consists of running advertisements in two different magazines. The advertisement for Magazine 1 costs $2000 per run while the advertisement for Magazine 2 costs $5000 per run. Past experience has indicated that at least 20 runs in Magazine 1, and at least 10 runs in Magazine 2 are necessary to penetrate the market with any appreciable effect. Also, experience has indicated that there is no reason to make more than 50 runs in either of the two magazines. Based on the foregoing data, how many runs (X) should be made in Magazine 1, and how many runs should be made in Magazine 2 to satisfy the foregoing restrictions and still not exceed the $120,000 budget?

6-4 The Henderson Food Products Company has established a new products division to develop and test market new snack-food items. The manager of this division is considering three promising products: A, B, and C. He feels that linear programming (simplex method) offers the best means for determining an optimum production schedule that allows producing these products simultaneously. The firm has three basic manufacturing departments: mixing, frying, and packing. The time requirements for each product and total available monthly hours are:

		Department	
Product	Mixing	Frying	Packing
A	.1 hr	.2 hr	.1 hr
B	.2 hr	.4 hr	.1 hr
C	.4 hr	.2 hr	.1 hr
Available monthly hours	5000	5500	4500

It is estimated that the contribution for Product A is $0.30, Product B is $0.40, and Product C is $0.50.

Based on the monthly time available in each department and product contribution, what is the optimum quantity for each product and total contribution?

6-5 The Cincinnati Chemical Company must produce 10,000 pounds of a special mixture for a customer. The mix consists of ingredients X_1, X_2, and X_3. X_1 costs $8 per pound, X_2 costs $10 per pound, and X_3 costs $11 per pound. No more than 3000 pounds of X_1 can be used and at least 1500 pounds of X_2 must be used. Also, at least 2000 pounds of X_3 is required.
 (a) Calculate the number of pounds for each ingredient to use in order to minimize total costs for 10,000 pounds.
 (b) Calculate the lowest total possible cost.
 (c) Are there any slack pounds in the problem?

6-6 Gas Turbine Incorporated is starting production of a polymeric composite blade. The blade consists of three basic components: resin, fiber, and glass cloth. The maximum resin content is 40 percent by weight, the minimum fiber content is 40 percent by weight, and the minimum glass cloth content is 20 percent by weight. Resin cloth costs $20.00 per pound while fiber costs $80.00 per pound and glass cloth costs $40.00 per pound.
 (a) What is the optimum percent composition of materials for minimum production cost per pound of this polymeric composite blade?
 (b) What is the lowest cost composition per pound for producting this blade?

6-7 Of the many products manufactured by the Arco Manufacturing Company, only products C, D, E, and F pass through the following departments: planner (small), milling (vertical), drilling (small), and assembly (small parts). The requirements per unit of product in hours and contribution are as follows: (See pg. 210.)

LINEAR PROGRAMMING

	Department				
	Planner	Milling	Drilling	Assembly	Contr./Unit
Product C	0.5	2.0	0.5	3.0	$8
Product D	1.0	1.0	0.5	1.0	$9
Product E	1.0	1.0	1.0	2.0	$7
Product F	0.5	1.0	1.0	3.0	$6

The available capacities this month for products, C, D, E, and F and minimum sales requirements are:

	Capacities (hours)		Minimum Sales Requirements
Planner	1,800	Product C	100 units
Milling	2,800	Product D	600 units
Drilling	3,000	Product E	500 units
Assembly	6,000	Product F	400 units

(a) Determine the number of products C, D, E, and F to manufacture this month to maximize contribution.
(b) Determine the total maximum contribution for products C, D, E, and F this month.
(c) Determine the slack time in the four departments.

6-8 The Gray Manufacturing Company has consistently followed a policy of producing those products which contribute the highest amount to fixed costs and profit. However, consideration has always been given to producing the minimum weekly sales requirements which are as follows for products K, L, M, and N:

Product K	25 units
Product L	30 units
Product M	30 units
Product N	25 units

The production requirements and time available for next week are:

	Time Required per Product (hours)				Time Available Next Week (hours)
	K	L	M	N	
Department 1	0.25	0.2	0.15	0.25	400
Department 2	0.3	0.4	0.5	0.3	1,000
Department 3	0.25	0.3	0.25	0.3	500
Department 4	0.25	0.25	0.25	0.25	500
Contribution/unit	$10.50	$9.00	$8.00	$10.00	

Presently, the weekly production mix (considering the minimum sales requirements) is:

Product K	1,533
Product L	30
Product M	30
Product N	25

(a) Is the present product mix and contribution for the firm optimum? If not, what should it be?

(b) What recommendations concerning production facilities should be made to the firm based upon the answer to (a)?

6-9 The LaCross Manufacturing Company is considering manufacturing a new product line, consisting of four products. Each product can be made by two different and distinct methods, one of which has two processes and the other three processes. All products will be made on a second shift basis. The product's selling price and variable costs as well as the probable quantities that can be sold per the marketing research group are given as follows:

	Product			
	1	2	3	4
Selling price to wholesaler (40% discount)	$100	$150	$125	$140
Variable costs—method A	80	135	120	135
Variable costs—method B	110	150	100	110
Quantity that can be sold	1,000	3,000	4,000	6,000

The manufacturing section of the firm has determined the manufacturing times for each process as follows:

	Product			
	1	2	3	4
Method A				
Department 20	3.0	3.6	2.0	3.5
Department 21	9.0	10.0	8.0	9.0
Department 22	1.0	1.0	0.5	0.5
Method B				
Department 31	4.0	4.0	2.0	4.0
Department 32	5.0	8.0	4.0	3.0

Monthly hours available are:

Department 20	15,000
Department 21	50,000
Department 22	8,000
Department 31	10,000
Department 32	10,000

What should the firm do in light of the production times and possible production bottlenecks in order to maximize total monthly contribution?

Bibliography

R. L. Ackoff and M. W. Sasieni, *Fundamentals of Operations Research,* New York: John Wiley & Sons, 1968.

E. K. Bowen, *Mathematics, With Applications in Management and Economics* Homewood, Ill.: Richard D. Irwin, 1972.

A. Chaines and W. W. Cooper, *Management Models and Industrial Applications of Linear Programming,* New York: John Wiley & Sons, 1961.

N. J. Driebeek, *Applied Linear Programming,* Cambridge, Mass.: Addison-Wesley, 1969.

F. S. Hillier and G. J. Liberman, *Introduction to Operations Research,* San Francisco: Holden-Day, 1967.

N. K. Kwak, *Mathematical Programming with Business Applications,* New York: McGraw-Hill Book Company, 1973.

R. I. Levin and R. P. Lamone, *Linear Programming for Management Divisions,* Homewood, Ill.: Richard D. Irwin, 1969.

N. P. Loomba, *Linear Programming, An Introductory Analysis,* New York: McGraw-Hill Book Company, 1964.

M. Simmonnard, *Linear Programming,* Englewood Cliffs, N.J.: Prentice-Hill, 1966.

W. R. Smythe, Jr., and L. A. Johnson, *Introduction to Linear Programming, With Applications,* Englewood Cliffs, N.J.: Prentice-Hall, 1966.

W. A. Spivey, *Linear Programming, An Introduction,* New York: The MacMillan Company, 1966.

R. S. Stockton, *Introduction to Linear Programming,* Homewood, Ill.: Richard D. Irwin, 1971.

J. E. Strum, *Introduction to Linear Programming,* San Francisco: Holden-Day, 1972.

S. I. Zukhovitskiy and L. I. Avdeyeva, *Linear and Convex Programming,* Philadelphia, Penn.: W. B. Saunders Company, 1966.

Chapter SEVEN

Transportation Methods

The origin of transportation methods dates back to 1941 when F. L. Hitchcock presented a study entitled *The Distribution of a Product from Several Sources to Numerous Localities*. This presentation is considered to be the first important contribution to the solution of transportation problems. In 1947, T. C. Koopmans presented a study, not related to Hitchcock's, called *Optimum Utilization of the Transportation System*. These two contributions helped in the development of transportation methods which involve a number of shipping sources and a number of destinations. Within a given time period, each shipping source (factory) has a certain capacity and each destination (warehouse) has certain requirements with a given cost of shipping from the source to the destination. The objective function is to minimize total transportation costs and satisfy the warehouse requirements within the factory capacity constraints. Within the framework of the transportation problem, other problem types have been solved, such as the optimum placement of orders on machines—to be covered later in the chapter.

Methods for Solving the Transportation Problem

Various approaches have been developed for solving the transportation problem: Vogel's approximation method (not always an optimal method), the stepping-stone method, the modified distribution method (MODI), the simplex method of linear programming, and the key-value method. This chapter will concentrate on the stepping-stone method, the MODI method, and the simplex method for obtaining an optimal solution. Initially, Vogel's approximation method will be presented for solving a transportation problem.

Vogel's Approximation Method

Vogel's approximation method (VAM) was originally developed to produce a starting solution; however, it very often produces the optimal solution to the problem in just one pass. Although VAM does not guarantee an optimal solution, it invariably produces a very good solution with comparatively little effort.

In order to illustrate the various methods for the transportation problem, one illustration will be used throughout the chapter so that the methods can be compared.

The Arcose Manufacturing Company has three factories: R, S, and T. These three factories supply one product to seven warehouses: A, B, C, D, E, F, and G. There are some slight differences in manufacturing costs for each factory, but the important factor is the cost of shipping from each factory to a particular warehouse. Each warehouse has a certain sales requirement, which is comparable to each factory having a certain capacity. Table 7-1 shows the costs of shipping from each factory to each warehouse, monthly factory capacities, monthly warehouse or sales requirements, and slack. The amount in the slack column is defined as the difference between total factory capacity and total warehouse requirements.

The steps employed in determining a VAM solution are given below:

1. *Calculate the difference between the two lowest distribution costs for each row and each column.* For example, in column A per Table 7-1, the three transportation costs are $6, $10, and $9. The two lowest costs are $6 and $9, their difference being $3. Other column and row values are calculated in a similar manner.
2. *Select the row or column with the largest difference and circle this value. In case of a tie, select that row or column that allows the greatest movement of units.* In the example, the R row is selected since it is the largest difference for rows and columns.
3. *Assign the largest possible allocation within the restrictions of the rim requirements (rows and columns) to the lowest cost cell for the row or column selected.* As shown in Table 7-2, cell R slack is the lowest cost cell, hence, 1000 units are assigned to that cell.
4. *Cross out any row or column satisfied by the assignment made in the prior step.* In Table 7-2, the slack column requirements have been satisfied with the assignment of 1000 units to cell R slack. Thus, all other unfilled cells in that column can be crossed out since no future assignments can be made to the slack column. Also, the "difference" column value is crossed out.
5. *Recalculate the differences as in step (1), except for rows and columns that have been crossed out.* These values are shown in Table 7-2. Actually, they are the same values except for the R-row value, having changed from a 4 to a 1.

The foregoing steps (2) through (5) are repeated until all assignments have been made. The final solution, illustrated in Table 7-3, is based on the row and column assignments which occurred in the following order:

Column slack	1,000 units, cell R slack
Column F	3,500 units, cell SF
Column A	1,000 units, cell RA
Row S	500 units, cell SG
Column E	2,000 units, cell TE
Column C	4,500 units, cell TC
Column D	4,000 units, cell RD
Column B	2,000 units, cell TB
Column G	1,000 units, cell RG
Column G	1,500 units, cell TG
	21,000 units

TABLE 7-1
Vogel's Approximation Method for Solving Transportation Problem—Table of Per Unit Transportation Costs, Monthly Factory Capacities, Monthly Warehouse Requirements, and Difference Values

To Warehouse / From Factory		A	B	C	D	E	F	G	Slack	Factory Capacity
		3	0	1	1	1	3	2	0	
R	3	$6	$7	$5	$4	$8	$6	$5	$0	7,000
S	2	$10	$5	$4	$5	$4	$3	$2	$0	4,000
T	3	$9	$5	$3	$6	$5	$9	$4	$0	10,000
Warehouse or Sales Requirements		1,000	2,000	4,500	4,000	2,000	3,500	3,000	1,000	21,000

(4)

TABLE 7-2
First VAM Assignment Satisfies the Slack Column Requirement—Row and Column Differences Are Recalculated

	3	0	1	1	1	3	2	~~4~~	
To Warehouse / From Factory	A	B	C	D	E	F	G	Slack	Factory Capacity
R	$6	$7	$5	$4	$8	$6	$5	$0 ⓵,000	7,000
S	$10	$5	$4	$5	$4	$3	$2	$0 X	4,000
T	$9	$5	$3	$6	$5	$9	$4	$0 X	10,000
Warehouse or Sales Requirements	1,000	2,000	4,500	4,000	2,000	3,500	3,000	1,000	21,000

Slack differences: ~~4~~ 1, 2, 3

216 OPERATIONS RESEARCH MODELS—MATRIX ALGEBRA

TABLE 7-3
Final VAM Assignments Yield an Optimum Solution (Refer to Tables 7-12 for the Stepping-Stone Method and 7-17 for the Modified Distribution Method)

To Warehouse From	A	B	C	D	E	F	G	Slack	Factory Capacity
Factory R	$6 (1000)	$7 X	$5 X	$4 (4000)	$8 X	$6 X	$5 (1000)	$0 (1000)	7,000
S	$10 X	$5 X	$4 X	$5 X	$4 X	$3 (3500)	$2 (500)	$0 X	4,000
T	$9 X	$5 (2000)	$3 (4500)	$6 X	$5 (2000)	$9 X	$4 (1500)	$0 X	10,000
Warehouse or Sales Requirements	1000	2000	4500	4000	2000	3500	3000	1000	21,000

The above allocation happens to be optimal and is the same answer given by the stepping-stone method (Table 7-12) and the modified distribution method (Table 7-17) later in the chapter.

Stepping-Stone Method—Using the Northwest Corner Rule and Inspection

The stepping-stone method, in its initial solution, can make use of the Northwest Corner rule. This rule dictates that the quantities shipped from the factories to the warehouses must begin in the upper left-hand corner. When this route is fully used, that is, the factory capacity or warehouse (sales) requirements are totally utilized, depending on which number is lower, the remainder of either the factory capacity or warehouse requirement is then assigned to the new row(s) or column(s) until it is fully used. Using this procedure, the table is filled from the upper left cell down to the lower right cell, fully using the warehouse requirement, then factory capacity, etc. In Table 7-4, the first shipping route, RA satisfies the warehouse requirement of A for 1000 units, and the second shipping route, RB, satisfies the warehouse requirement of B for 2000 units. However, for route RC, 4000 of the 4500 units satisfies R's factory capacity of 7000 (1000+2000 +4000). This means 500 units (4500−4000) are available for route SC, which now takes care of C's warehouse requirements. This same procedure is followed until all rim requirements, the limiting values for the factory capacity columns and the warehouse storage requirements rows, are fully satisfied.

If the factory capacity is in excess of warehouse (sales) requirements, this is known as *slack* for the factories. No cost is assigned to slack since there is no transportation cost involved. It is either excess capacity of a factory (s) or excess inventory at a factory (s). The slack column allows for

TABLE 7-4
Stepping-Stone Method Using the Northwest Corner Rule in the Initial Solution

Warehouse:	A	B	C	D	E	F	G	Slack	Factory Capacity
Factory: R	$6 1000	$7 2000	$5 4000	$4 −$2	$8 +$3	$6 −$3	$5 +$1	$0 $0	7,000
S	$10 +$5	$5 −$1	$4 500	$5 3500	$4 $0	$3 −$5	$2 −$1	$0 +$1	4,000
T	$9 +$3	$5 −$2	$3 −$2	$6 500	$5 2000	$9 3500	$4 3000	$0 1000	10,000
Warehouse Requirements	1000	2000	4500	4000	2000	3500	3000	1000	21,000

Total transportation costs $116,000.

the rim requirements of the factories to equal the warehouse requirements or the rows to equal the columns.

A faster initial starting point for the stepping-stone method is to use inspection in conjunction with the Northwest Corner rule, illustrated in Table 7-5 (the initial table for the stepping-stone method). The inspection method means that the quantities to be shipped are positioned in cells according to the Northwest Corner rule in order to have many of the lowest transportation costs associated with the filled cells (quantities to be shipped). As can be seen from Table 7-5, this means moving the columns around. The same procedure can also be applied to the rows, but is not used in this problem. The total shipping costs of Table 7-4 are $116,000 versus $94,500 for Table 7-5. It should be apparent that other possibilities for an initial

TABLE 7-5
Stepping-Stone Method Using Northwest Corner Rule and Inspection (First Table)

Warehouse:	D	C	F	G	E	B	A	Slack	Factory Capacity
Factory: R	$4 4000	$5 3000	$6 +$2	$5 +$6	$8 +$8	$7 +$7	$6 +$2	$0 +$5	7,000
S	$5 +$2	$4 1500	$3 2500	$2 +$4	$4 +$5	$5 +$6	$10 +$7	$0 +$6	4,000
T	$6 −$3	$3 −$7	$9 1000	$4 3000	$5 2000	$5 2000	$9 1000	$0 1000	10,000
Warehouse Requirements	4000	4500	3500	3000	2000	2000	1000	1000	21,000

Total transportation costs $94,500.

218 OPERATIONS RESEARCH MODELS—MATRIX ALGEBRA

solution exist. The use of inspection in the initial table for the stepping-stone method reduces the number of tables required for the lowest cost transportation schedule.

Step 1. Test for Degeneracy

Once the initial table has been determined using the Northwest Corner rule and inspection or some other initial solution method, the first step is to check whether or not the solution (quantities to ship) is degenerate. *Degeneracy* is a condition where it is not possible to evaluate all empty (unused) cells due to a smaller number of cells used than the rim requirements (rows and columns) minus one. Also, degeneracy is caused by too-many filled cells. The formula (Equation 7-1) to test for degeneracy is $m+n-1$, where m is the rows and n is the columns. In the example, $3+8-1=10$. The number of filled cells is 10. Therefore the problem is not degenerate. The method for handling a degenerate condition is explained in a subsequent section.

Step 2. Evaluate all Unfilled Cells

The second step is to determine a better shipping schedule by evaluating the unfilled cells or those cells which do not have scheduled shipments. Each cell that is not used must be evaluated. This evaluation method shows the net total cost effect of adding one unit to the cell route. Unfilled cells *SD* and *TD* of Table 7-5 will be used to illustrate this procedure.

If one unit is added to cell *SD*, it will cost the firm $5. Since rim requirements (rows and columns) must be satisfied, if one unit is added to cell *SD*, a unit must be subtracted from *RD* in order that the *D* column cells still total 4000 units. The unit subtracted from *RD* saves the firm a shipping cost of $4. Likewise, as a unit is subtracted from *RD*, a unit must be added to *RC* in order that the shipments of factory *R* still equal 7000 units. This costs the firm $5. Now that column *C* has one too many units, one unit must be subtracted from *SC*, which saves the firm $4. This is shown in Table 7-6. In

TABLE 7-6

Warehouse:	D	C	All Other	Slack	Factory Capacity
Factory: R	$4 3,999 →	$5 →3,001			7,000
S	$5 ↑ 1←	$4 ↓ 1,499	2,500		4,000
T			9,000	1,000	10,000
Warehouse Requirements	4,000	4,500	11,500	1,000	21,000

TRANSPORTATION METHODS 219

effect, a unit has been added to *SD*, subtracted from *RD*, added to *RC*, and subtracted from *SC*, thereby satisfying the rim requirements. If this change would take place, the cost factor is of utmost importance since $5 has been added (*SD*), $4 has been subtracted (*RD*), $5 has been added (*RC*), and $4 has been subtracted (*SC*) for net cost of plus $2 per unit (+$5−$4+$5−$4=+$2) to the firm. This means that every unit added to route *SD* will cost the firm an additional $2 per unit. It would certainly not be worthwhile for the firm to use this route if this were the only choice available.

An evaluation of cell *TD* in Table 7-5 is longer than the previous example. Adding one unit to cell *TD* costs the firm $6. In order to satisfy the rim requirements, one unit must be subtracted from cell *RD* for savings of $4. Similarly, for warehouse *C*, one unit must be added to cell *RC* (cost of $5) and one unit must be subtracted from cell *SC* (savings of $4). For warehouse *F*, one unit must be added to cell *SF* (cost of $3) and one unit must be subtracted from cell *TF* (savings of $9). The net result is a savings of $3 per unit (+$6−$4+$5−$4+$3−$9=−$3). It would pay the firm to use this route, shown in Table 7-7.

The two examples show that it is necessary to have three filled cells to evaluate unfilled cell *SD* and five filled cells to evaluate unfilled cell *TD*. Why is this so? Because the rim (row and column) requirements would not be met. If, for example, we moved one unit from *RD* to *RC*, the row requirement of 7000 units would be met, but not the column requirements of 4000 for warehouse *D* and 4500 for warehouse *C*. Thus we have moved at right angles or at 90-degree angles in order to satisfy the rim requirements of the problem.

It should be apparent how this approach got the name stepping-stone method. Only filled cells or stepping-stones can be used in the evaluation of an unfilled cell. Later, it will be shown that an epsilon (ε) in a cell is considered a filled cell. It should be pointed out that it is allowable to jump over cells (filled or unfilled) when forming a closed route to evaluate an unfilled cell.

The computations for the unused cells in Table 7-5 are as follows:

TABLE 7-7

Warehouse:	D	C	F	All Other	Slack	Factory Capacity
Factory: R	$4 3,999	$5 →3,001				7,000
S	↑	$4 1,499 ↓ →2,501	$3			4,000
T	$6 1←		$9 ↓ 999	8,000	1,000	10,000
Warehouse Requirements	4,000	4,500	3,500	8,000	1,000	21,000

	Unfilled Cells		Cost	
			Penalty	Savings
$SD =$	$+ \; 5-4+5-4$ (per above)	$=$	$+2$	
$TD =$	$+ \; 6-4+5-4+3-9$ (per above)	$=$		-3
$TC =$	$+ \; 3-4+3-9$	$=$		-7
$RF =$	$+ \; 6-3+4-5$	$=$	$+2$	
$RG =$	$+ \; 5-4+9-3+4-5$	$=$	$+6$	
$SG =$	$+ \; 2-4+9-3$	$=$	$+4$	
$RE =$	$+ \; 8-5+9-3+4-5$	$=$	$+8$	
$SE =$	$+ \; 4-5+9-3$	$=$	$+5$	
$RB =$	$+ \; 7-5+9-3+4-5$	$=$	$+7$	
$SB =$	$+ \; 5-5+9-3$	$=$	$+6$	
$RA =$	$+ \; 6-9+9-3+4-5$	$=$	$+2$	
$SA =$	$+10-9+9-3$	$=$	$+7$	
R Slack $=$	$+ \; 0-0+9-3+4-5$	$=$	$+5$	
S Slack $=$	$+ \; 0-0+9-3$	$=$	$+6$	

Step 3. Select Unfilled Cell with Largest Negative Value

Now that the evaluation of the cost values are complete (a plus sign denotes a cost penalty or higher transportation costs, whereas a negative sign denotes additional cost savings or lower transportation costs), the third step is to select the highest negative figure. This will enable the firm to ship at lower costs. Based upon the values found in Table 7-5, cell *TC* offers the best opportunity to reduce transportation costs further. Thus, this cell with a negative value of 7 is selected.

Step 4. Move as Many Units as Possible into Selected Cell

The fourth and final step of the stepping-stone method is moving as large a quantity as possible into the selected unfilled cell. Based upon the quantities shown in Table 7-5, the largest quantity is 2500 in the three filled cells that were used to evaluate unfilled cell *TC*. The following example will demonstrate the feasibility or nonfeasibility of moving 2500 units:

	Before		After	
Warehouse:	C	F	C	F
Factory:				
S	1,500	2,500	−1,000	+5,000
T		1,000	+2,500	−1,500

Based on this analysis, it is not feasible to move 2500 units into cell *TC* since two negative figures would appear in the adjoining cells. This is not

TABLE 7-8
Stepping-Stone Method (Second Table)

Warehouse:	D	C	F	G	E	B	A	Slack	Factory Capacity
Factory: R	$4 4000	$5 3000	$6 +$2	$5 −$1	$8 +$1	$7 $0	$6 −$5	$0 −$2	7,000
S	$5 +$2	$4 1500 − 1000 500	$3 2500 +1000 3500	$2 −$3	$4 −$2	$5 −$1	$10 $0	$0 −$1	4,000
T	$6 +$4	$3 +1000 1000	$9 1000 − 1000 +$7	$4 3000	$5 2000	$5 2000	$9 1000	$0 1000	10,000
Warehouse Requirements	4000	4500	3500	3000	2000	2000	1000	1000	21,000

Total transportation costs $87,500.

possible in the real world since no firm can deal in minus units. The same condition results in trying to move the second largest quantity or 1500 units. Thus only 1000 units can be moved into cell TC and is reflected in Table 7-8 (second table).

Stepping-Stone Method—Optimum Solution

The first step in all subsequent tables is to test for degeneracy, that is, does $m+n-1$ (Equation 7-1) equal the number of filled cells? The number of filled cells, 10, equals $3+8-1$. Since degeneracy is not applicable, the next step is to re-evaluate all unfilled cells in the manner shown for Table 7-5. The results are shown in Table 7-8. If an unfilled cell can be evaluated by more than one set of routes, the highest minus or lowest plus amount is inserted. However, this was not the case in the first or second table. Selecting the highest minus value in all of the unfilled cells results in moving products to cell RA for lower transportation costs. Again, the largest quantity will be moved into the unfilled cell as in Table 7-9 (third table).

Again, the first step in succeeding tables is to test for degeneracy (not applicable) in Table 7-9. The unfilled cells are evaluated, resulting in cell SG with the largest minus value. The movement of units is shown in Table 7-10 (fourth table).

Following the same steps as for the previous tables results in allocating units to an unfilled cell, R slack, per Table 7-11 (fifth table). Inspection of this table indicates two minus amounts of the same value. Unfilled cell RG was randomly selected since either cell RF or RG could have been used.

TABLE 7-9
Stepping-Stone Method (Third Table)

Warehouse:	D	C	F	G	E	B	A	Slack	Factory Capacity
Factory: R	$4 4000	$5 3000− 1000 2000	$6 +$2	$5 −$1	$8 +$1	$7 $0	$6 +1000 1000	$0 −$2	7,000
S	$5 +$2	$4 500	$3 3500	$3 −$3	$4 −$2	$5 −$1	$10 +$5	$0 −$1	4,000
T	$6 +$4	$3 1000+ 1000 2000	$9 +$7	$4 3000	$5 2000	$5 2000	$9 1000− 1000 +$5	$0 1000	10,000
Warehouse Requirements	4000	4500	3500	3000	2000	2000	1000	1000	21,000

Total transportation costs $82,500.

TABLE 7-10
Stepping-Stone Method (Fourth Table)

Warehouse:	D	C	F	G	E	B	A	Slack	Factory Capacity
Factory: R	$4 4000	$5 2000	$6 −$1	$5 −$1	$8 +$1	$7 $0	$6 1000	$0 −$2	7,000
S	$5 +$5	$4 500− 500 +$3	$3 3500	$2 +500 500	$4 +$1	$5 +$2	$10 +$8	$0 +$2	4,000
T	$6 +$4	$3 2000 +500 2500	$9 +$4	$4 3000− 500 2500	$5 2000	$5 2000	$9 +$5	$0 1000	10,000
Warehouse Requirements	4000	4500	3500	3000	2000	2000	1000	1000	21,000

Total transportation costs $81,000.

TABLE 7-11
Stepping-Stone Method (Fifth Table)

Warehouse: Factory:	D	C	F	G	E	B	A	Slack	Factory Capacity
R	$4 4000	$5 2000 −1000 1000	$6 −$1	$5 −$1	$8 +$1	$7 $0	$6 1000	$0 +1000 1000	7,000
S	$5 +$5	$4 +$3	$3 3500	$2 500	$4 +$1	$5 +$2	$10 +$8	$0 +$4	4,000
T	$6 +$4	$3 2500+ 1000 3500	$9 +$4	$4 2500	$5 2000	$5 2000	$9 +$5	$0 1000− 1000 +$2	10,000
Warehouse Requirements	4000	4500	3500	3000	2000	2000	1000	1000	21,000

Total transportation costs $79,000.

TABLE 7-12
Stepping-Stone Method (Sixth Table)

Warehouse: Factory:	D	C	F	G	E	B	A	Slack	Factory Capacity
R	$4 4000	$5 1000 −1000 $+1	$6 $0	$5 +1000 1,000	$8 +$2	$7 +$1	$6 1000	$0 1000	7,000
S	$5 +$4	$4 +$3	$3 3500	$2 500	$4 +$1	$5 +$2	$10 +$7	$0 +$3	4,000
T	$6 +$3	$3 3500 +1000 4500	$9 +$4	$4 2500 −1000 1500	$5 2000	$5 2000	$9 +$4	$0 +$1	10,000
Warehouse Requirements	4000	4500	3500	3000	2000	2000	1000	1000	21,000

Total transportation costs $78,000.

The optimal solution is reached in Table 7-12 (sixth table) since there are no minus signs to denote further cost savings. The final shipping schedule is:

Route	No. of Units	Cost per Unit	Total Monthly Transportation Costs
RD	4,000	$4	$16,000
RG	1,000	5	5,000
RA	1,000	6	6,000
R Slack	1,000	0	—
SF	3,500	3	10,500
SG	500	2	1,000
TC	4,500	3	13,500
TG	1,500	4	6,000
TE	2,000	5	10,000
TB	2,000	5	10,000
	21,000		$78,000

The shipping schedule is not a unique solution since at least one zero appears in the final solution. A zero in an unfilled cell means another alternative is available with the same total cost. In Table 7-11 there was another unfilled cell, RF, with the same minus value that could have been used in place of the unfilled cell RG.

Degeneracy

One method for saving computation time is to start with the existing shipping schedule. When using this initial basis, there is a chance of degeneracy. When an attempt is made to evaluate the unfilled cells, some of the cells cannot be evaluated because the number of filled cells does not equal the answer per Equation 7-1 ($m+n-1$) for the rim requirements.

The problem of degeneracy is apparent when using Table 7-4 as the basis for a second table. Evaluation of the unfilled cells reveals that cell SF has the largest negative value, thereby resulting in the greatest unit cost savings. If units are moved into this cell, the following movement of units takes place:

Warehouse:	D	F
Factory:		
S	3,500 − 3,500 = 0	+3,500
T	500 + 3,500 = 4,000	3,500 − 3,500 = 0

An examination of the above indicates that what started out as three filled cells is now two filled cells. This movement of goods is reflected in Table 7-13.

TABLE 7-13
Stepping-Stone Method Utilizing the Northwest Corner Rule in First Table (Table 7-4)

Warehouse:	A	B	C	D	E	F	G	Slack	Factory Capacity
Factory: R	$6 / 1000	$7 / 2000	$5 / 4000	$4 / −$2	$8 / +$3	$6 / +$2	$5 / +$1	$0 / $0	7,000
S	$10 / +$5	$5 / −$1	$4 / 500	$5 / ε	$4 / $0	$3 / 3500	$2 / −$1	$0 / +$1	4,000
T	$9 / +$3	$5 / −$2	$3 / −$2	$6 / 4000	$5 / 2000	$9 / +$5	$4 / 3000	$0 / 1000	10,000
Warehouse Requirements	1000	2000	4500	4000	2000	3500	3000	1000	21,000

Total transportation costs $98,500.

The first step in Table 7-13 is to test for degeneracy. Using Equation 7-1, we find the solution is degenerate at this stage. For computation purposes in degeneracy, one unfilled cell is considered artificially used where necessary, that is, an ε (epsilon) is placed in the cell as though it represented a very small quantity to be shipped through that cell route. The value of ε is actually zero when used in the movement of units from one cell to another.

The next step in Table 7-13 is to evaluate all unfilled cells. Due to degeneracy, several unfilled cells cannot be evaluated. Hence, it is necessary to place ε in a low-cost empty cell that allows evaluation of the remaining cells. The rationale for the placement of epsilon in a low-cost cell is that units are generally moved into a low-cost cell as opposed to a high-cost cell. Thus, the placement of ε in cell SD allows us to evaluate all unused cells which was not possible previously.

It is possible to have more than one epsilon in a transportation problem at the same time. Generally, this is caused by long paths where several filled cells become empty cells when the movement of units takes place. This is an extension of the preceding example for factories S and T and warehouses D and F. Once the ε is inserted, it stays in the table until it is no longer needed. For example, if the addition of 50 units to a cell that has ε contained therein (50+ε), the resulting figure is 50 units. If one or more εs remain in the final solution, they are ignored.

Also, it is possible not only to have too few filled cells, but also too many filled cells when applying the formula $m+n−1$. In this case, a reduction in the number of used cell routes is necessary. This can be accomplished by finding four (six, eight, . . .) used cell routes which form a closed system in moving units. This is shown on the top of next page by shifting 25 units.

A shift is made of 25 units, starting with cell A2. The choice for the switch is based upon costs factors or on a random basis to obtain an acceptable solution.

From Four Filled Cells		
Warehouse:	1	2
Factory:		
A	100	25
B	50	200

To Three Filled Cells		
Warehouse:	1	2
Factory:		
A	125	0
B	25	225

If for some reason a cell route is not feasible, that is, a factory cannot make the product or management wishes to eliminate the possibility of its use, a very high cost of $M can be used for that cell. A cell with a value of $M means that it will never enter the final solution. Another way of handling this problem is to cross out the cell in question and never use or evaluate it.

One last comment on the stepping-stone method using the Northwest Corner rule, as in Tables 7-4 and 7-13, is that the shipping costs are $116,000 and $98,500, respectively. When these tables are compared to Table 7-5 for the same method using inspection, the total monthly transportation costs are $94,500. Hence the use of inspection in the initial solution reduces the number of tables needed for a final solution.

The iterative steps involved in the stepping-stone method after setting up the first table are set forth in Figure 7-1.

Step 1—Test for Degeneracy

Test for degeneracy focuses on Equation 7-1. The degeneracy test formula is $m+n-1$ (m is the rows and n is the columns) while the resultant value of this equation should equal the number of filled cells. If the equation fails the equality test, too few filled cells mean that one or more epsilons must be added in step (2) below. Too many filled cells mean that their number must be reduced.

Step 2—Evaluate All Unfilled Cells

Calculate the net total cost or saving of adding one unit to the unfilled cell. This means finding a closed route of filled cells that can be used to evaluate the unfilled cell and recognizing that the rim (row and column) requirements cannot be violated. Hence, evaluation of an unfilled cell means moving at right angles or making 90 degree turns at filled cells only to form a closed route. It is allowable to jump over cells when forming a closed route to evaluate an unfilled cell. In those cases where there are too few filled cells based on the test in step (1), one or more epsilons must be placed in the table in order to evaluate the unfilled cells. Similarly, too many filled cells require reducing the number of these cells.

Step 3—Select Unfilled Cell With Largest Negative Value

Select from the unfilled cells that one which has the largest negative value. In those cases where two minus values are equal, select that one which will result in moving as many units as possible into the selected unfilled cell. When all unfilled cell values are plus or zero, an optimal solution to the problem has been found.

Step 4—Move As Many Units As Possible Into Selected Cell

Move as many units as possible into the selected unfilled cell. One word of caution—no negative quantities are allowed in the problem. Thus, filled cells cannot have values deducted from them that exceed their quantities.

Figure 7-1 Iterative steps in the stepping-stone method.

Modified Distribution Method (MODI)

An alternative to the stepping-stone method is the modified distribution method, commonly referred to as the MODI method. The major difference between these two methods is the way in which the unfilled cells are evaluated. The MODI method selects the particular unfilled cell that will yield the most improvement by a set of index numbers calculated for the rows and columns. The movement of maximum units are then made for that unfilled cell. In a similar manner, revised index numbers indicate the next best unfilled cell. The MODI method, like the stepping-stone method, continues until there are no more minus values in the unfilled cells.

Using the same problem set forth for the stepping-stone method, we shall illustrate the steps for the MODI method. Before developing the iterative steps, it is necessary to construct the first table. The MODI method employs the same procedures for developing the first table. Table 7-14, same as Table 7-4 of the stepping-stone method, shows the initial table utilizing the Northwest Corner rule.

TABLE 7-14
First Table of the MODI Method Using the Northwest Corner Rule
(Arrows Indicate the Reassignment of Quantities in Next Table)

To Warehouse / From Factory	$K_A = -6$	$K_B = -7$	$K_C = -5$	$K_D = -6$	$K_E = -5$	$K_F = -9$	$K_G = -4$	$K_{slack} = 0$	Factory Capacity
$R_R = 0$	$6 ⟨1000⟩	$7 ⟨2000⟩	$5 ⟨4000⟩	$4 −2	$8 +3	$6 −3	$5 +1	$0 0	7,000
$R_S = +1$	$10 +5	$5 −1	$4 ⟨500⟩	$5 ⟨3500⟩	$4 0	$3 5	$2 −1	$0 +1	4,000
$R_T = 0$	$9 +3	$5 −2	$3 −2	$6 ↑ ⟨500⟩	$5 ⟨2000⟩	$9 ↓ ⟨3500⟩	$4 ⟨3000⟩	$0 ⟨1000⟩	10,000
Warehouse Requirements	1000	2000	4500	4000	2000	3500	3000	1000	21,000

Total transportation costs $116,000.

Step 1. Test for Degeneracy

The initial step in the MODI method is to test for degeneracy as was performed for the stepping-stone method. Again $m+n-1$ (Equation 7-1) calculation must be made. In the example, $3+8-1$ equals 10, the number of filled cells. Thus, the problem is not degenerate. If the problem were degenerate, the required epsilon(s) must be entered, and the same procedures are followed as for the stepping-stone method.

Step 2. Calculate R and K Index Values

The second step is to calculate the index numbers where R represents row index numbers and K stands for column index numbers. For example, R_S is the row number for row S and K_B is the column number for column B. These values, together with the costs (denoted by C) associated with each cell—such as C_{SA}—are used to evaluate the unfilled cells in the next step. Thus, subscripts are used to specify the particular row (R) and column (K) while double subscripts identify a particular cell (C).

In order to compute R and K values, it is necessary to utilize the following formula for *filled cells* only:

$$R + K + C = 0 \quad \text{(Equation 7-2)}$$

where R = row index number
K = column index number
C = cost of each cell

Solving for the row index number yields

$$R = -(K + C) \quad \text{(Equation 7-3)}$$

and solving for the column index number produces

$$K = -(R + C) \quad \text{(Equation 7-4)}$$

Assigning a value of zero arbitrarily to the first row, R_R, in order to get started on the problem (could have assigned a value of zero to any row or any column), we can now calculate the required index values illustrated in Table 7-14 per Equations 7-3 and 7-4. Since $R_R = 0$, we can calculate the column index number, K_A, at the first filled cell RA, which is

$$K_A = -R_R - C_{RA} = 0 - 6 = -6$$

Similarly, we can calculate K_B and K_C at the filled cells RB and RC respectively knowing that $R_R = 0$ which are

$$K_B = -R_R - C_{RB} = 0 - 7 = -7$$
$$K_C = -R_R - C_{RC} = 0 - 5 = -5$$

Knowing the value for K_C, we can calculate the row index value, R_S, at the filled cell SC at follows:

$$R_S = -K_C - C_{SC} = -(-5) - 4 = +1$$

Moving from one filled cell to another, the remaining index values can be calculated.

$$K_D = -R_S - C_{SD} = -(+1) - 5 = -6$$
$$R_T = -K_D - C_{TD} = -(-6) - 6 = 0$$
$$K_E = -R_T - C_{TE} = \quad 0 - 5 = -5$$
$$K_F = -R_T - C_{TF} = \quad 0 - 9 = -9$$
$$K_G = -R_T - C_{TG} = \quad 0 - 4 = -4$$
$$K_{\text{slack}} = -R_T - C_{T\text{ slack}} = \quad 0 - 0 = 0$$

Step 3. Evaluate All Unfilled Cells

In the third step, all unfilled cells are evaluated by adding algebraically the R, K, and C values associated with them. Using Equation 7-2, the calculated values for the unfilled cells in Table 7-14 are:

Unfilled Cell	Calculation (Equation 7-2)	Improvement
SA	$+1 + (-6) + 10 = +5$	No
TA	$0 + (-6) + 9 = +3$	No
SB	$+1 + (-7) + 5 = -1$	Yes
TB	$0 + (-7) + 5 = -2$	Yes
TC	$0 + (-5) + 3 = -2$	Yes
RD	$0 + (-6) + 4 = -2$	Yes
RE	$0 + (-5) + 8 = +3$	No
SE	$+1 + (-5) + 4 = 0$	No
RF	$0 + (-9) + 6 = -3$	Yes
SF	$+1 + (-9) + 3 = -5$	Yes
RG	$0 + (-4) + 5 = +1$	No
SG	$+1 + (-4) + 2 = -1$	Yes
R slack	$0 + (0) + 0 = 0$	No
S slack	$+1 + (0) + 0 = +1$	No

As with the stepping-stone method, a minus value indicates further improvement in lowering costs is available (a cost reduction for every unit assigned to that cell) while a plus value indicates just the reverse. These values are entered in Table 7-14 and are the same as per Table 7-4 for the stepping-stone method. If all calculated values are plus and/or zero for the unfilled cells, an optimal solution has been reached like in the stepping-stone method.

Step 4. Select Unfilled Cell with Largest Negative Value

The fourth step is selecting that unfilled cell which has the largest negative, as in the stepping-stone method. Inspection of Table 7-14 reveals that cell SF has the largest negative, that is, -5.

It is also necessary in this step to find a closed route for the selected unfilled cell. The selected route must satisfy the following requirements (same as for stepping-stone method):

(a) The route must start and end at the cell with the largest negative value.
(b) The route can change directions only at cells that have an assignment of units.
(c) Only right angle or 90-degree turns are permitted.
(d) The route may pass over any number of cells.
(e) There will usually be only one possible route through the table.

Based on these requirements, the closed route for evaluating cell SF is illustrated in Table 7-14. The optimal solution has been found when all unfilled cells contain plus and/or zero values.

Step 5. Move as Many Units as Possible into Selected Cell

The final (fifth) step for the MODI method, as in the stepping-stone method, is to move as large a quantity as possible into the selected cell. Inspection of Table 7-14 indicates that 3500 units can be moved into cell SF. This movement of units is reflected in Table 7-15 (second table).

Modi Optimal Solution

The iterative process of the MODI method reverts to step (1) above. Table 7-15 is degenerate since $m+n-1$ $(3+8-1)$ does not equal the number of

TABLE 7-15
Second Table of the MODI Method (Arrows Indicate the Reassignment of Quantities in Next Table)

To Warehouse From Factory	$K_A = -6$	$K_B = -7$	$K_C = -5$	$K_D = -6$	$K_E = -5$	$K_F = -4$	$K_G = -4$	$K_{slack} = 0$	Factory Capacity
$R_R = 0$	$6 (1000)	$7 (2000)	$5 (4000)	$4 −2	$8 +3	$6 +2	$5 +1	$0 0	7,000
$R_S = +1$	$10 +5	$5 −1	$4 (500)	$5 ε	$4 0	$3 (3500)	$2 −1	$0 +1	4,000
$R_T = 0$	$9 +3	$5 −2	$3 −2	$6 (4000)	$5 (2000)	$9 +5	$4 (3000)	$0 (1000)	10,000
Warehouse Requirements	1000	2000	4500	4000	2000	3500	3000	1000	21,000

Total transportation costs $98,500.

filled cells (9). Thus, an epsilon, as in a preceding section for the stepping-stone method, must be placed within the table. It is found in cell SD. The calculations for the second and third steps, that is, R and K index values and unfilled cell values, are shown in the second table. For the fourth step, the unfilled cell with the largest minus value is selected. Since there are three amounts of equal value, cell TC is picked. (Note that unfilled cell RD cannot be selected due to the placement of epsilon, that is, units cannot be subtracted from epsilon.) The final step of the MODI method focuses on moving the largest quantity possible into the unfilled cell TC. This movement of units is depicted in Table 7-16 (third table).

TABLE 7-16
Third Table of the MODI Method (Arrows Indicate the Reassignment of Quantities in Next Table)

To Warehouse From Factory	$K_A=$ -6	$K_B=$ -7	$K_C=$ -5	$K_D=$ -8	$K_E=$ -7	$K_F=$ -6	$K_G=$ -6	$K_{slack}=$ -2	Factory Capacity
$R_R=0$	$6 ⓵⓪⓪⓪	$7 ②⓪⓪⓪	$5 ④⓪⓪⓪ →4	$4 +1	$8 0	$6 −1	$5 −2	$0	7,000
$R_S=+3$	$10 +7	$5 +1	$4 +2 ↑	$5 ⑤⓪⓪	$4 0	$3 ③⑤⓪⓪	$2 −1	$0 −2	4,000
$R_T=+2$	$9 +5	$5 0	$3 ⑤⓪⓪ ↑	$6 ③⑤⓪⓪ ↓	$5 ②⓪⓪⓪	$9 +5	$4 ③⓪⓪⓪	$0 ①⓪⓪⓪	10,000
Warehouse Requirements	1000	2000	4500	4000	2000	3500	3000	1000	21,000

Total transportation costs $97,500.

Again, the five steps of the MODI method are repeated for Table 7-16 and subsequent tables. It should be noted that the epsilon drops out of the third table; hence Table 7-16 is no longer degenerate. The seventh and final table of the problem is set forth in Table 7-17. The modified distribution iterative process, summarized in Figure 7-2, is complete when all unfilled cell values are plus or zero. The shipping schedule, unfilled cell values, and the transportation costs are the same as that found in Table 7-12 for the stepping-stone method. Thus, both methods produce the same results although their computational procedures differ.

TABLE 7-17
Seventh (Final) Table of the MODI Method

To Warehouse From Factory	$K_A=$ -6	$K_B=$ -6	$K_C=$ -4	$K_D=$ -4	$K_E=$ -6	$K_F=$ -6	$K_G=$ -5	$K_{slack}=$ 0	Factory Capacity
$R_R=0$	$6 ⓵⓪⓪⓪	$7 +1	$5 +1	$4 ④⓪⓪⓪	$8 +2	$6 0	$5 ①⓪⓪⓪	$0 ①⓪⓪⓪	7,000
$R_S=+3$	$10 +7	$5 +2	$4 +3	$5 +4	$4 +1	$3 ③⑤⓪⓪	$2 ⑤⓪⓪	$0 +3	4,000
$R_T=+1$	$9 +4	$5 ②⓪⓪⓪	$3 ④⑤⓪⓪	$6 +3	$5 ②⓪⓪⓪	$9 +4	$4 ①⑤⓪⓪	$0 +1	10,000
Warehouse Requirements	1000	2000	4500	4000	2000	3500	3000	1000	21,000

Total transportation costs $78,000.

Step 1—Test for Degeneracy

Test for degeneracy utilizing Equation 7-1. The number of rows (m) plus the number of columns (n) minus one equals the number of filled cells for a non-degenerate solution. If the $m+n-1$ does not equal the number of filled cells, the solution is degenerate. The required epsilon(s) must be entered in the table. Correspondingly, too many filled cells mean that their number must be reduced.

Step 2—Calculate R and K Index Values

Determine row (R) index numbers and column (K) index numbers by utilizing Equation 7-3 [$R = -(K+C)$] and Equation 7-4 [$K = -(R+C)$] respectively. By arbitrarily assigning a zero to the first row index value (could be any row or column), the required row and column index numbers can be calculated by moving from one filled cell to another.

Step 3—Evaluate All Unfilled Cells

Evaluate all unfilled cells by utilizing Equation 7-2 ($R+K+C=0$), that is, adding algebraically the R, K, and C values associated with each cell. These calculated values are entered in the appropriate unfilled cells. A minus value indicates further improvement in lowering overall costs, a plus value increasing costs, and a zero value indicating the same cost.

Step 4—Select Unfilled Cell with Largest Negative Value

Select that unfilled cell (evaluated in the prior step) which has the largest negative value and determine its closed route (as in the stepping-stone method). If two or more values have the same minus value, select that one which will result in the greatest movement of units into the unfilled cell. On the other hand, if all unfilled cells are evaluated to be plus and/or zero values, the iterative process of the MODI method is complete.

Step 5—Move As Many Units As Possible into Selected Cell

Move as large a quantity as possible into the selected unfilled cell. As indicated in the prior step, this movement of goods must be part of a closed route. Just as in the stepping-stone method, units cannot be subtracted from a cell that contains epsilon only.

Figure 7-2 Iterative steps in the modified distribution method (MODI).

Simplex Method of Linear Programming (Digital Computer)

In Chapter 6 the minimization problem using the simplex method of linear programming was presented. The transportation problem is of the same type. Linear programming searches for the optimum quantities of units to ship from each factory to each warehouse for a least cost solution.

Returning to our original problem (Table 7-1), we shall let a series of Xs represent the quantities to be shipped from the factories to the warehouses as follows:

Let X_1 represent that quantity shipped from R to A
Let X_2 represent that quantity shipped from R to B
Let X_3 represent that quantity shipped from R to C
Let X_4 represent that quantity shipped from R to D
Let X_5 represent that quantity shipped from R to E
Let X_6 represent that quantity shipped from R to F
Let X_7 represent that quantity shipped from R to G

Let X_8 represent that quantity shipped from S to A
Let X_9 represent that quantity shipped from S to B
Let X_{10} represent that quantity shipped from S to C
Let X_{11} represent that quantity shipped from S to D
Let X_{12} represent that quantity shipped from S to E
Let X_{13} represent that quantity shipped from S to F
Let X_{14} represent that quantity shipped from S to G
Let X_{15} represent that quantity shipped from T to A
Let X_{16} represent that quantity shipped from T to B
Let X_{17} represent that quantity shipped from T to C
Let X_{18} represent that quantity shipped from T to D
Let X_{19} represent that quantity shipped from T to E
Let X_{20} represent that quantity shipped from T to F
Let X_{21} represent that quantity shipped from T to G
Let X_{22} represent slack for Factory R
Let X_{23} represent slack for Factory S
Let X_{24} represent slack for Factory T

The foregoing variables appear in Table 7-18. The series of Xs, representing the various shipping quantities, have been inserted. The optimum solution must satisfy the column requirements, which are an equal condition, and the row requirements, which are equal or less than conditions. With the addition of the slack variables (X_{22}, X_{23}, and X_{24}), we have an equal to condition for the rows. All that remains is to add artificial variables (X_{25}, X_{26}, X_{27}, X_{28}, X_{29}, X_{30}, and X_{31}) to the column equations in order to generate an initial solution.

The restrictions for the first tableau appear as follows

$$X_1 + 0X_2 + 0X_3 + 0X_4 + 0X_5 + 0X_6 + 0X_7 + X_8 + 0X_9$$
$$+ 0X_{10} + 0X_{11} + 0X_{12} + 0X_{13} + 0X_{14} + X_{15} + 0X_{16} + 0X_{17}$$
$$+ 0X_{18} + 0X_{19} + 0X_{20} + 0X_{21} + 0X_{22} + 0X_{23} + 0X_{24} + X_{25}$$
$$+ 0X_{26} + 0X_{27} + 0X_{28} + 0X_{29} + 0X_{30} + 0X_{31} = 1000$$

TABLE 7-18

Warehouse:	A	B	C	D	E	F	G	Slack	Factory Capacity
Factory:										
R	X_1	X_2	X_3	X_4	X_5	X_6	X_7	X_{22}	7,000
S	X_8	X_9	X_{10}	X_{11}	X_{12}	X_{13}	X_{14}	X_{23}	4,000
T	X_{15}	X_{16}	X_{17}	X_{18}	X_{19}	X_{20}	X_{21}	X_{24}	10,000
Warehouse Requirements	1000	2000	4500	4000	2000	3500	3000	1000	21,000

Note: Xs represent shipments from factories to warehouses (X_1 to X_{21}) and slack variables (X_{22} to X_{24}).

$$0X_1 + X_2 + 0X_3 + 0X_4 + 0X_5 + 0X_6 + 0X_7 + 0X_8 + X_9$$
$$+ 0X_{10} + 0X_{11} + 0X_{12} + 0X_{13} + 0X_{14} + 0X_{15} + X_{16} + 0X_{17}$$
$$+ 0X_{18} + 0X_{19} + 0X_{20} + 0X_{21} + 0X_{22} + 0X_{23} + 0X_{24} + 0X_{25}$$
$$+ X_{26} + 0X_{27} + 0X_{28} + 0X_{29} + 0X_{30} + 0X_{31} = 2000$$
$$\cdots + X_3 \cdots + X_{10} \cdots + X_{17} \cdots + X_{27} \cdots = 4500$$
$$\cdots + X_4 \cdots + X_{11} \cdots + X_{18} \cdots + X_{28} \cdots = 4000$$
$$\cdots + X_5 \cdots + X_{12} \cdots + X_{19} \cdots + X_{29} \cdots = 2000$$
$$\cdots + X_6 \cdots + X_{13} \cdots + X_{20} \cdots + X_{30} \cdots = 3500$$
$$\cdots + X_7 \cdots + X_{14} \cdots + X_{21} \cdots + X_{31} \cdots = 3000$$
$$X_1 + X_2 + X_3 + X_4 + X_5 + X_6 + X_7 + 0X_8 + 0X_9 + 0X_{10}$$
$$+ 0X_{11} + 0X_{12} + 0X_{13} + 0X_{14} + 0X_{15} + 0X_{16} + 0X_{17} + 0X_{18}$$
$$+ 0X_{19} + 0X_{20} + 0X_{21} + X_{22} + 0X_{23} + 0X_{24} + 0X_{25} + 0X_{26}$$
$$+ 0X_{27} + 0X_{28} + 0X_{29} + 0X_{30} + 0X_{31} = 7000$$
$$\cdots + X_8 + X_9 + X_{10} + X_{11} + X_{12} + X_{13} + X_{14} \cdots \quad + X_{23} \cdots = 4000$$

$$\cdots + X_{15} + X_{16} + X_{17} + X_{18} + X_{19} + X_{20} + X_{21} \cdots \quad + X_{24} \cdots = 10{,}000$$

The preceding equations are shown in the first simplex tableau, Table 7-19. By using the procedures described in Chapter 6, the optimum shipping schedule results in a least cost solution of $78,000, the same result that appears in Table 7-12 (last table) for the stepping-stone method and in Table 7-17 (last table) for the MODI method.

The simplex algorithm is useful for a wide range of factory and warehouse choices that are too numerous to handle by the stepping-stone or MODI methods. A digital computer can be used whether it be in a batch or a real time processing mode to arrive at a final solution. This is why the linear programming approach is widely used in industry today.

Linear Programming (Analog Computer)

The preceding method of applying linear programming to the transportation problem utilizes the digital computer for an exact solution. However, several firms have developed an interesting approach to the transportation problem by using an analog computer. The solution will not be 100 percent correct, but its other benefits, many times, overcome this limitation.

This approach can be visualized by starting with two mills which supply a single product to four sales areas, shown in Figure 7-3. The direct costs of production at Mill 1 are $200 a unit (ton) while the same costs of production at Mill 2 are $210 a unit (ton). Freight costs range from $10 to $30 a unit (ton). The problem is to set up a distribution pattern whereby the total cost of meeting the demand is a minimum.

The least cost solution for this simplified problem is relatively straightforward. However, for most real world situations, the answer is not obvious nor is it readily developed by conventional OR methods. The digital computer requires considerable time to iterate a solution, and exploration of changes in the system requires equally lengthy additional computer runs.

TABLE 7-19
First Simplex Tableau for Transportation Problem

C_j	Shipping Mix	Quantity	$6 X_1	$7 X_2	$5 X_3	$4 X_4	$8 X_5	$6 X_6	$5 X_7	$10 X_8	$5 X_9	$4 X_{10}	$5 X_{11}	$4 X_{12}	$3 X_{13}	$2 X_{14}	$9 X_{15}
$0	X_{22}	7,000	1	1	1	1	1	1	1	0	0	0	0	0	0	0	0
$0	X_{23}	4,000	0	0	0	0	0	0	0	1	1	1	1	1	1	1	0
$0	X_{24}	10,000	0	0	0	0	0	0	0	0	0	0	0	0	0	0	1
$M	X_{25}	1,000	1	0	0	0	0	0	0	1	0	0	0	0	0	0	1
$M	X_{26}	2,000	0	1	0	0	0	0	0	0	1	0	0	0	0	0	0
$M	X_{27}	4,500	0	0	1	0	0	0	0	0	0	1	0	0	0	0	0
$M	X_{28}	4,000	0	0	0	1	0	0	0	0	0	0	1	0	0	0	0
$M	X_{29}	2,000	0	0	0	0	1	0	0	0	0	0	0	1	0	0	0
$M	X_{30}	3,500	0	0	0	0	0	1	0	0	0	0	0	0	1	0	0
$M	X_{31}	3,000	0	0	0	0	0	0	1	0	0	0	0	0	0	1	0
	Z_j	$20,000M	$M	$M	$M	$M	$M	$M	$M	$M	$M	$M	$M	$M	$M	$M	$M
	$C_j - Z_j$		$6-M	$7-M	$5-M	$4-M	$8-M	$6-M	$5-M	$10-M	$5-M	$4-M	$5-M	$4-M	$3-M	$2-M	$9-M

TABLE 7-19 (continued)
First Simplex Tableau for Transportation Problem

C_j	Shipping Mix	Quantity	$5 X_{16}	$3 X_{17}	$6 X_{18}	$5 X_{19}	$9 X_{20}	$4 X_{21}	$0 X_{22}	$0 X_{23}	$0 X_{24}	$M X_{25}	$M X_{26}	$M X_{27}	$M X_{28}	$M X_{29}	$M X_{30}	$M X_{31}
$0	X_{22}	7,000	0	0	0	0	0	0	1	0	0	0	0	0	0	0	0	0
$0	X_{23}	4,000	0	0	0	0	0	0	0	1	0	0	0	0	0	0	0	0
$0	X_{24}	10,000	1	1	1	1	1	1	0	0	1	0	0	0	0	0	0	0
$M	X_{25}	1,000	0	0	0	0	0	0	0	0	0	1	0	0	0	0	0	0
$M	X_{26}	2,000	1	0	0	0	0	0	0	0	0	0	1	0	0	0	0	0
$M	X_{27}	4,500	0	1	0	0	0	0	0	0	0	0	0	1	0	0	0	0
$M	X_{28}	4,000	0	0	1	0	0	0	0	0	0	0	0	0	1	0	0	0
$M	X_{29}	2,000	0	0	0	1	0	0	0	0	0	0	0	0	0	1	0	0
$M	X_{30}	3,500	0	0	0	0	1	0	0	0	0	0	0	0	0	0	1	0
$M	X_{31}	3,000	0	0	0	0	0	1	0	0	0	0	0	0	0	0	0	1
	Z_j	$20,000M	$M	$M	$M	$M	$M	$M	$0	$0	$0	$M	$M	$M	$M	$M	$M	$M
	$C_j - Z_j$		$5-M	$3-M	$6-M	$5-M	$9-M	$4-M	$0	$0	$0	$0	$0	$0	$0	$0	$0	$0

TRANSPORTATION METHODS 237

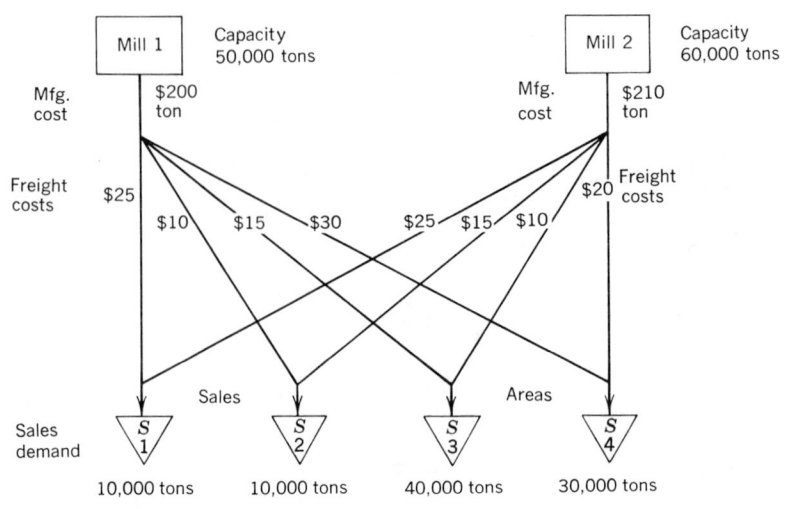

Figure 7-3 Two mills supplying one product to four areas.

These lengthy digital computer runs are overcome by utilizing an analog computer (Figure 7-4).

All the electrical currents in Figure 7-4 have their counterparts in the firm's physical distribution system in the form of plants, rail lines, sales areas, and like items. In the analog computer, an electrical current is used to simulate each paper mill, each sales demand, and all cost functions. Two

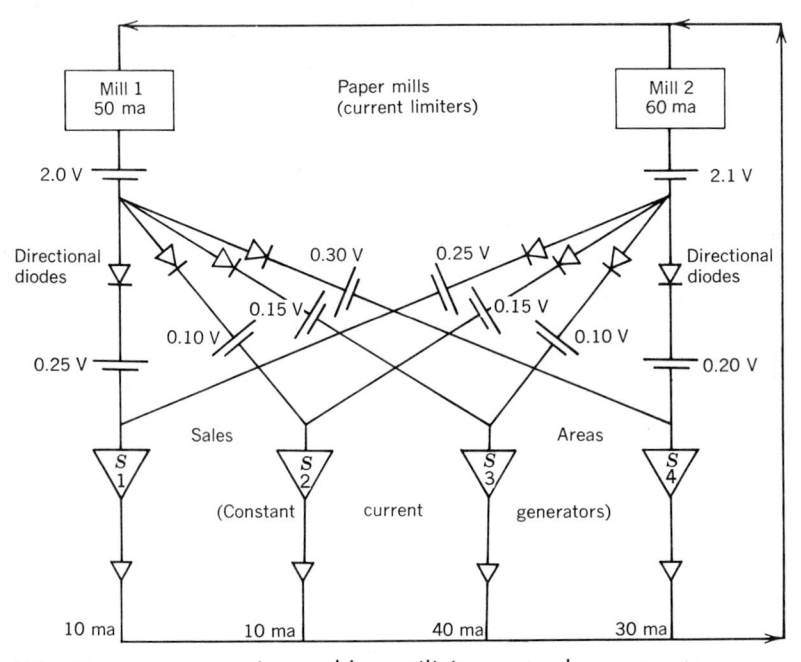

Figure 7-4 Linear programming problem utilizing on analog computer.

238 OPERATIONS RESEARCH MODELS—MATRIX ALGEBRA

types of current devices are used in the network to simulate paper mills and sales demand: (1) current limiter—allows the current to increase up to a maximum value but not to exceed this value (analogous to the paper mill capacity which cannot be exceeded); (2) constant current generator—maintains a constant current flow (simulates the sales demand).

Electrical elements have been inserted in Figure 7-4 to simulate the problem in Figure 7-3. A theorem by J. E. Maxwell states that the electrical current in any given network containing active or passive elements will divide in such a way that minimum power will be dissipated if resistance is negligible. This means that it is necessary only to set up electrical units proportional to the physical system values and then read the currents flowing in each link from manufacturing to customer. The current flowing is directly proportional to the amount of product which should be moved over this route to insure minimum total system cost. This procedure is followed in developing optimum production, distribution, and pulp movement patterns for every change in sales forecast and for every change in alignment of facilities for production and distribution.

This analog-computer approach allows for changes to be made in any of the factors without too much trouble. Contrast the changes to be made with a digital computer operating in a batch processing mode, that is, key punch new data cards for any minor changes, update present magnetic tape with current data, and iterate a solution with a computer. Since costs are continually increasing and sales patterns are changing, as are other internal and external factors, a constant updating process on the digital computer can be costly and time consuming. The difference between the 100 percent accuracy of the digital computer and the close to 100 percent accuracy of the analog computer more than offsets the higher costs of updating on the digital computer. Thus, many companies have resorted to simpler and more direct methods for solving complex problems in order to reduce overall costs.

Placement of Orders on Machines

Modified methods of the transportation problem are available to solve other recurring business problems. One method solves for the placement of orders on different machines. In the illustration, three machines are capable of producing four different products. An accurate survey of the machines' capabilities reveals that the machines differ in type and degree of automation. The time required to produce these four products also differ for each machine.

The total available times per month are: machine 1, 320 hours; machine 2, 390 hours; and machine 3, 375 hours. The products to be manufactured are: 1500 units of A, 1800 units of B, 2100 units of C, and 2250 units of D. Since some machines do not have the capability of producing some items due to their technical characteristics, Table 7-20 shows the number of units that can be produced in one hour by each machine.

The selling prices for each unit are: $2.45 for A, $2.40 for B, $2.25 for C, and $2.10 for D. The variable costs of production are: product A, $0.83, $0.91, and $0.87 for machines 1, 2, and 3, respectively; product B, $0.79, $0.93, and $0.91 for machines 1, 2, and 3, respectively; product C, $0.60 for machine 2; and product D, $0.81 and $0.82 for machines 2 and 3, respectively. The objective is to maximize the total contribution by scheduling and assigning the appropriate work load to the three machines. The contribution for each product is shown in Table 7-21.

The efficiency of the three machines must be considered. One must be selected in such a way that all machine time can be measured. Upon inspection of Table 7-20, machine 1 is unable to produce units of C and D and is slower in producing units A and B when compared to machine 2. The same reasoning can be applied to machine 3, which means machine 2 is best in terms of output. Machine 2 will be the common unit of production measurement. Since machine 2 is the basic unit of measurement, its efficiency will be established at 100 percent. Based on data in Table 7-20,

TABLE 7-20
Production Rate per Hour for Each Machine

Machine:	1	2	3
Unit:			
A	7.5	10.0	8.0
B	9.0	12.0	9.6
C		6.0	
D		9.0	7.2

the efficiency of machines 1 and 2 are 75 and 80 percent, respectively.

In order to set up a table that utilizes the stepping-stone method, the hours of machine 2 (standard) are used to find the other total standard hours for machines 1 and 3. The calculation for the standard machine hours is obtained by dividing the total number of units to be produced monthly by the number of units produced in 1 hour for machine 2. The results are:

Unit A:
$$\frac{1500 \text{ units}}{10 \text{ units produced per hour}}$$
= 150 standard hours needed to manufacture 1500 units of A

Unit B:
$$\frac{1800 \text{ units}}{12 \text{ units produced per hour}}$$
= 150 standard hours needed to manufacture 1800 units of B

Unit C:
$$\frac{2100 \text{ units}}{6 \text{ units produced per hour}}$$
= 350 standard hours needed to manufacture 2100 units of C

Unit D:

$$\frac{2250 \text{ units}}{9 \text{ units produced per hour}} = 250 \text{ standard hours needed to manufacture 2250 units of } D$$

Having determined the column totals for Table 7-22, it is necessary to calculate the productive capacity of each machine by the same unit of measure. The effective available capacity in hours is calculated by taking the available time each month and multiplying by the efficiency factor. The standard hours for the rows are:

Machine 1:

320 available hours × 75% efficiency = 240 standard hours

Machine 2:

390 available hours × 100% efficiency = 390 standard hours

Machine 3:

375 available hours × 80% efficiency = 300 standard hours

The total standard hours for the rows are 930 hours (machine capacities) while the total standard hours for the columns are 900 hours (requirements for units A, B, C, and D) in Table 7-22. This necessitates the need for column E of 30 hours, representing a hypothetical item with a zero contribution, analogous to slack in the transportation problem.

The last data necessary for the initial stepping-stone table is the contribution per standard machine hour. The values are obtained by multiplying the contribution per unit, shown in Table 7-21, by the production rates in pieces on an hourly basis for machine 2 (standard), as in Table 7-20. These calculations are found in Table 7-22 for the stepping-stone method.

In order to simplify the problem, inspection is used in the initial solution. Rows and columns are interchanged in order to reduce the number of tables needed to reach a solution. This is done by arranging the row contributions in descending order, starting from the left. This results in arranging the rows in this order: machine 1, machine 3, and machine 2. An alternative

TABLE 7-21
Contribution per Unit

Machine:	1	2	3
Unit:			
A	$2.45 − $0.83 = $1.62	$2.45 − $0.91 = $1.54	$2.45 − $0.87 = $1.58
B	$2.40 − $0.79 = $1.61	$2.40 − $0.93 = $1.47	$2.40 − $0.91 = $1.49
C		$2.25 − $0.60 = $1.65	
D		$2.10 − $0.81 = $1.29	$2.10 − $0.82 = $1.28

TRANSPORTATION METHODS

TABLE 7-22
Production Requirements and Contribution Table for the Stepping-Stone Method

Unit:		A	B	C	D	E	Capacity of Machines (std. hrs.)
Machine:	1	$16.20 ($1.62×10)	$19.32 ($1.61×12)			$0	240
	2	$15.40 ($1.54×10)	$17.64 ($1.47×12)	$9.90 ($1.65×6)	$11.61 ($1.29×9)	$0	390
	3	$15.80 ($1.58×10)	$17.88 ($1.49×12)		$11.52 ($1.28×9)	$0	300
Units Requirements (std. hrs.)		150	150	350	250	30	930

method for determining the proper placement of the rows is to sum their respective contributions for comparable products, which are:

Machine 1:
$$\$16.20 + \$19.32 = \$35.52$$

Machine 3:
$$\$15.80 + \$17.88 = \$33.68$$

Machine 2:
$$\$15.40 + \$17.64 = \$33.04$$

Based upon inspection, columns are arranged in this sequence: B, A, D, C, and E. This rearrangement of rows and columns forms the first table for the stepping-stone method, using the Northwest Corner rule and inspection in Table 7-23.

Using the rules set forth under the stepping-stone method, the first table is not degenerate. The signs are to be treated differently, that is, a plus sign indicates further contribution is available, a minus sign indicates a decrease in contribution. The first table (Table 7-23) indicates more profits are available with the plus $0.09 in cell 3E. The second and final table for this problem is found in Table 7-24. The total monthly contribution from Table 7-23 is $11,649.90 based on standard hours of machine 2. Since 30 standard hours have been moved to increase profits by $0.09 per standard machine hour, this results in an increase in the contribution by $2.70. Adding this figure results in a total contribution of $11,652.60, the same figure shown in Table 7-24.

TABLE 7-23
Stepping-Stone Method Using the Northwest Corner Rule and Inspection (First Table)

Unit:	B	A	D	C	E	Capacity of Machines (hrs.)
Machine: 1	$19.32 150	$16.20 90			$0 −$.31	240
3	$17.88 −$1.04	$15.80 60	$11.52 240		$0 +$.09	300
2	$17.64 −$1.37	$15.40 −$.49	$11.61 10	$9.90 350	$0 30	390
Unit Requirements (hrs.)	150	150	250	350	30	930

Total monthly contribution $11,649.90.

TABLE 7-24
Stepping-Stone Method (Second Table)

Unit:	B	A	D	C	E	Capacity of Machines (hrs.)
Machine: 1	$19.32 150	$16.20 90			$0 −$.40	240
3	$17.88 −$1.04	$15.80 60	$11.52 210		$0 30	300
2	$17.64 −$1.37	$15.40 −$.49	$11.61 40	$9.90 350	$0 −$.09	390
Unit Requirements (hrs.)	150	150	250	350	30	930

Total monthly contribution $11,652.60.

Other Problems Utilizing the Transportation Model

One of the problems that utilizes the transportation model is assignment. For example, a firm has hired four men for four jobs. These four men and the four jobs can be shown in a table which indicates the scores obtained by analyzing the individual for each job. The rows pertain to the men

TRANSPORTATION METHODS

while the columns refer to the jobs. The problem is one of maximizing the scores in assigning the four jobs. The assumption is that a score made by the individual is directly proportional to the profit that the company would make if the man were placed in that job.

Another problem which utilizes the basic framework of the transportation model is the allocation of trucks to minimize operating costs. A firm operates nationally with trucks that are specially equipped to operate under specific climate conditions. The firm has divided the country into five geographic regions. Truck A is purchased and modified to operate efficiently in regions 1 and 2 while operating fairly well in regions 3 and 4. The same truck operates poorly in region 5. Gasoline, maintenance, and other direct costs of operations would be at a minimum in regions 1 and 2, average in regions 3 and 4, but high in region 5. This same information is available on the company's other trucks, namely, types B, C, and D.

At the start of each year, the five regional offices submit their requirements for new trucks. The corporate office plans to satisfy these demands in order to minimize the overall truck operating costs for the entire firm. The exact quantity of each truck required is not always available, resulting in substitutions being made. However, the problem can be solved with present information in terms of allocating the number of new trucks to the five regions. Many other problems of this type can be utilized within the framework of the transportation model for a solution. Some of these are presented in this chapter's problem section.

Distribution, a Part of the Total Company Model

When a firm decides to overhaul its distribution system, the first thing it does is set up a mathematical model of the firm. Despite the expense, it is easier and cheaper than getting locked into an unworkable system. This model must show more than the order processing, packaging, shipping, and storage costs. It must go all the way into the marketplace and find out what products sell, what the demands are, and where they originate. It must also go back into the factories and find the most efficient production lines for each product. The building of the model may take a year (or more).

Once the model is complete, the next step is to review company objectives. For example, it is possible to give every customer one-day service on every item at very high costs. Within limits that can be programmed into the model, the best service at the lowest cost can be determined by varying factors of number, size, and location for factories and warehouses as well as speeds and rates for different kinds of transportation. It is important to remember that transportation rates are not fixed, but vary from company to company and by size of load. They can often be lowered by negotiation. Building existing rates into the model when another rate may be applied can destroy the results of the model.

Once the model is correctly formulated in terms of the firm's objectives, it can bring to light warehouses serving wrong territories, territories with wrong boundaries, and products being made in the wrong plants. It can keep a company from adopting a distribution system its customers cannot use. If a customer cannot store a barge load of the products, there is no point in building a distribution system around barges. Once the computer model determines the tradeoffs and compromises that will most nearly achieve a firm's long-term objectives, the firm can start implementing the new system.

In most cases, it is best to install a new physical distribution system in a series of short steps. Trying to get there all at once will cause too many disruptions, upset too many existing capital investments, multiply the chances for mistakes, and endanger the success of the whole undertaking. Once the distribution system is producing better service to customers at lower cost, many firms find it is time to start over again since physical distribution needs constant attention and renewal. It should be remembered that fundamental changes are occurring so fast in every phase of distribution, that no system is permanent. The firm's competitor might be working on a better one. Besides, no going business can stand still. Growth can upset even the best designed distribution system through changes in products, outlets, diversification, and acquisitions.

While some firms have taken a comprehensive look at the entire distribution system, other firms have looked at some major phases of its distribution. One firm, for example, needs to maintain large amounts of supplies for its leased machines in the field. Formerly it worked out of 40 sales branches, each with its own inventories of paper, chemicals, and machine parts. The study of the firm's operations revealed that 80 percent of the items in the inventories were slow movers and that many could be stored at one location and air freighted as needed. At the end of the study, the firm determined that 92 percent of the company's customers could be served adequately from just 7 distribution centers in the United States and Canada. Another important result of the OR study was that supplies in the distribution pipeline were cut in half.

A few firms have found a distribution change can reduce transportation costs. For example, a manufacturer with many scattered production facilities found it would be much more profitable to buy (or lease) its own fleet of trucks. Now it can carry products, manufactured in the East, to the West Coast and return goods manufactured on the West Coast to the East. In addition, protective packaging requirements are less with its own trucks. Under these favorable conditions, overall distribution costs were reduced.

Transportation Application—American Products Corporation

The American Products Corporation operates four manufacturing plants, three of which are located in Buffalo, Cincinnati, and Cleveland. These factories supply several products (whose demand is declining) to three major warehouses located in Atlanta, Chicago, and New York. Transportation costs are as follows:

Buffalo to Chicago		$ .60/unit
Buffalo to New York		.30/unit
Buffalo to Atlanta		2.10/unit
Cincinnati to Chicago		.40/unit
Cincinnati to New York		.60/unit
Cincinnati to Atlanta		1.50/unit
Cleveland to Chicago		.70/unit
Cleveland to New York		.80/unit
Cleveland to Atlanta		1.90/unit

Buffalo can manufacture 3,000 units weekly while Cincinnati and Cleveland can supply 8,000 units and 10,000 units respectively on a weekly basis. The weekly requirements for Atlanta, Chicago, and New York are 5,000, 7,000, and 9,000 units, respectively.

Using the foregoing data, the problem can be solved by any of the methods set forth in the chapter. The first table per Table 7-25 employs the MODI method. The final shipping schedule on a weekly basis is given on the top of the next page.

Although weekly transportation costs have been calculated, management desires additional information about its physical distribution system. Due to the declining markets for products manufactured by these plants, it is considering what adjustments should be made to factory production in view of the fact that manufacturing costs are approximately the same. However, cost differences are caused by transportation costs. Warehouse require-

TABLE 7-25
First Table of the MODI Method Using the Northwest Corner Rule
(Arrows Indicate the Reassignment of Quantities to Take Place in Next Table)

From Factory	To Warehouse	$K_A = -2.10$ Atlanta	$K_B = -1.00$ Chicago	$K_C = -1.10$ New York	Weekly Factory Capacity
Buffalo $R_A = 0$		$2.10 3,000↑	$.60 −$.40	$.30 →−$.80	3,000
Cincinnati $R_B = +.60$		$1.50 2,000←	$.40 6,000↑	$.60 +$.10	8,000
Cleveland $R_C = +.30$		$1.90 +$.10	$.70 1,000←	$.80 ↓ 9,000	10,000
Weekly Warehouse Requirements		5,000	7,000	9,000	21,000

Buffalo to New York	3,000 units @ $ .30/unit = $	900
	3,000	
Cincinnati to Atlanta	5,000 units @ $1.50/unit =	7,500
Cincinnati to Chicago	3,000 units @ $ .40/unit =	1,200
	8,000	
Cleveland to Chicago	4,000 units @ $ .70/unit =	2,800
Cleveland to New York	6,000 units @ $ .80/unit =	4,800
	10,000	
Total weekly transportation costs		$17,200

ments, based on weekly sales forecasts one year hence, are estimated to be as follows:

Atlanta	4,000 units
Chicago	5,500 units
New York	6,500 units
	16,000 units

Utilizing the MODI method, the revised shipping schedule to keep overall transportation costs at a minimum next year is:

Buffalo to New York	3,000 units @ $ .30/unit = $	900
	3,000	
Cincinnati to Atlanta	4,000 units @ 1.50/unit =	6,000
Cincinnati to Chicago	4,000 units @ .40/unit =	1,600
	8,000	
Cleveland to Chicago	1,500 units @ .70/unit =	1,050
Cleveland to New York	3,500 units @ .80/unit =	2,800
	5,000	
Total weekly transportation costs (next year)		$12,350

Inspection of these values indicate that the American Products Corporation should reduce weekly production next year by 5,000 units at its Cleveland plant only in order to keep overall costs at a minimum.

Summary

Several optimal methods—stepping-stone, MODI, and linear programming—were presented to solve a transportation problem or similar type problem. An important consideration for any method utilized is that the transportation problem cannot always be isolated and solved within its own confines. Transportation is but one part of the entire company's distribution system. To solve the best transportation program in terms of service and lowest cost is difficult. This area requires continuous updating to reflect internal and external changes, resulting in a challenging task for any group of business researchers.

Questions

1. Explain why Vogel's approximation method does not always produce an optimal solution.
2. What approaches can be used for an initial solution using the stepping-stone method?
3. Discuss the similarities and differences between the stepping-stone method and the MODI method in solving a transportation problem.
4. Discuss the similarities and differences between the simplex method and the stepping-stone method in solving a transportation problem.

Problems

7-1 Three factories are operated by the Link Manufacturing Company of St. Louis, Missouri. Currently, the products manufactured are shipped to three different warehouses. The location and capacities of these warehouses are:

Warehouse	Capacity
Newark, New Jersey	1,200 units
Jacksonville, Florida	800 units
San Diego, California	1,000 units

The capacity of each factory together with the per unit freight rate from each factory to each warehouse are:

Factory	Capacity	Freight Rates To	Per Unit
1	600 units	Newark	$5
		Jacksonville	6
		San Diego	8
2	1000 units	Newark	4
		Jacksonville	7
		San Diego	7
3	1400 units	Newark	6
		Jacksonville	8
		San Diego	6

248 OPERATIONS RESEARCH MODELS—MATRIX ALGEBRA

Determine what factories should ship what quantities to the three warehouses in order to minimize freight costs.

7-2 The Jutson Manufacturing Company must ship from three factories to seven warehouses. The transportation cost per unit from factory to each warehouse, the requirements of each warehouse, and the capacity of each factory are:

Warehouse	Factories 1	Factories 2	Factories 3	Warehouse Requirements
A	$6	$11	$8	100
B	7	3	5	200
C	5	4	3	450
D	4	5	6	400
E	8	4	5	200
F	6	3	8	350
G	5	2	4	300
Factory capacity	700	400	1,000	

(a) Find the minimum cost transportation schedule using the stepping-stone method or the MODI method.
(b) If warehouse C is closed by the company, what procedures should be undertaken in order to find the minimum cost transportation schedule?
(c) How would you handle the case where the total warehouse requirements exceed total factory capacity?

7-3 The Austine Manufacturing Company has a current shipping schedule which is being questioned by top management as to whether or not it is optimal. The firm has three factories and five warehouses. The necessary data in terms of transportation costs, factory capacities, and warehouse requirements are as follows:

Warehouse	Factories A	Factories B	Factories C	Warehouse Requirements
1	$5	$4	$8	400
2	8	7	4	400
3	6	7	6	500
4	6	6	6	400
5	3	5	4	800
Factory capacity	800	600	1,100	2,500

Solve for an optimal shipping schedule in terms of lowest possible shipping costs using the simplex method of linear programming.

7-4 Building Products Company has a division made up of five separate plants scattered around the outskirts of a city. Railroad facilities are not available at any of the plant sites. The firm's own trucks carry all of the raw materials needed from suppliers. However, due to a strike of the firm's truckdrivers, several trucking companies have bid on the amounts they can carry to various plants. The prices quoted for this temporary situation are per 1000 pounds:

Plant	Requirements (weekly)	One Thousand Pound Rates Dalton	Doran	Riggs
A	800,000 pounds	$8	$6	$7
B	1,000,000 pounds	4	5	3
C	900,000 pounds	7	8	9
D	1,200,000 pounds	3	4	5
E	1,500,000 pounds	8	9	8
	5,400,000 pounds			

Hauling Capacities (weekly):
Trucking firm Dalton   2,000,000 pounds
Trucking firm Doran   1,800,000 pounds
Trucking firm Riggs   2,000,000 pounds

Determine the least cost program for the Building Products Company during this temporary situation (one week).

7-5 The Habsco Corporation has many manufacturing plants, three of which manufacture two principal products, a standard card table and a deluxe card table. A new deluxe card table will be introduced which must be considered in terms of selling price and costs. The selling prices are: standard $14.95; deluxe, $18.95; and new deluxe, $21.95.

Sales Requirements (units)	Plant A	Variable Costs Plant B	Plant C	Plant	Available Plant Capacities Weekly (units)
Standard 450	$8.00	$7.95	$8.10	A	800
Deluxe 1,050	8.50	8.60	8.45	B	600
New deluxe 600	9.25	9.20	9.30	C	700

Solve this problem for the greatest contribution using the stepping-stone method or MODI method.

7-6 Three classifications of workers (W_1, W_2, and W_3) can be used on three different jobs (J_1, J_2, and J_3) per an agreement with the union. Each man has a different cost for each job, which appears per the table on the top of the next page.

What is the best allocation of workers to the various jobs in order to minimize costs?

7-7 The Clover Transportation Company has four terminals, A, B, C, and D. At the start of a particular day, there are 8, 8, 6, and 3 tractors available at terminals A, B, C, and D, respectively. During the previous night, trailers were loaded at

Worker:	W₁	W₂	W₃	Workers Needed
Jobs:				
J₁	$4.00	$3.60	$3.75	5
J₂	$4.40	$3.50	$4.00	20
J₃	$4.60	$4.40	$4.60	10
Workers available	10	15	10	35

plants R, S, T, and U which were 2, 12, 5, and 6, respectively. The company dispatcher has come up with the distances between the terminals and plants which appear as follows:

Plant:	R	S	T	U
Terminal:				
A	22	46	16	40
B	42	15	50	18
C	82	32	48	60
D	40	40	36	30

Based upon the foregoing information, what tractors should the dispatcher send to which plants in order to minimize total distances?

7-8 The Arcose Company, having four plants and four warehouses, uses the stepping-stone method to minimize shipping costs. The tableau below was obtained after several iterations. The number in the upper left-hand corner of each cell in the table represents a cost while the circled numbers represent the current assignment.

Warehouse:	1	2	3	4	Capacity
Plant: A	$9	$8 (26)	$12	$10 (10)	36
B	$10	$10 (4)	$12 (40)	$14	44
C	$8 (12)	$9	$11	$11	12
D	$10	$10	$11 (20)	$12	20
Sales requirement	12	30	60	10	112

(a) Is this an optimal assignment? Prove it.
(b) If not optimal, what change would you make next? If optimal, is the solution unique? Why (either case)?

7-9 The Nielsen Printing Company has six orders for single-page advertising leaflets.

The quantities are: 28,000, 15,000, 15,000, 20,000, 38,000, and 44,000. The three presses available can produce 50,000, 70,000, and 60,000 sheets per day, respectively. The variable costs, per thousand in running the orders on the various presses, are given as follows:

Order:	1	2	3	4	5	6
Press:						
1	$4.48	$5.60	$6.40	$5.40	$6.42	$4.88
2	4.40	5.44	6.70	4.82	7.52	5.44
3	4.63	4.80	6.20	5.26	6.18	5.26

Determine the optimal assignment of orders to presses 1, 2, and 3.

7-10   The Precision Products Company has certain products that can be produced on several machines. However, there are differences of running speeds, selling prices, and costs which are as follows:

	Machines (output per hour)			Selling Price	Number of Products
	1	2	3		
Products:					
A	—	9.0	7.2	$3.05	1,620
B	7.5	10.0	8.0	$3.00	2,000
C	—	8.0	6.4	$2.85	1,800
D	7.5	10.0	8.0	$2.90	1,750
Monthly available time	320 hrs	400 hrs	320 hrs		

	Variable Costs per Machine		
	1	2	3
Products:			
A	—	$1.15	$1.25
B	$1.50	1.25	1.40
C	—	1.05	1.30
D	1.35	1.20	1.45

Find the optimum allocation of products to the three machines for the coming month.

Bibliography

R. L. Ackoff and M. W. Sasieni, *Fundamentals of Operations Research*, New York: John Wiley & Sons, 1968.

H. Bierman, C. P. Bonini, and W. H. Hausman, *Quantitative Analysis for Business Decisions*, Homewood, Ill.: Richard D. Irwin, 1973.

E. H. Bowman and R. B. Fetter, *Analysis for Production and Operations Management*, Homewood, Ill.: Richard D. Irwin, 1967.

E. S. Buffa, *Operations Management: Problems and Models,* New York: John Wiley & Sons, 1968.

F. S. Hillier and G. J. Lieberman, *Introduction to Operations Research,* San Francisco: Holden-Day, 1967.

N. K. Kwak, *Mathematical Programming with Business Applications,* New York: McGraw-Hill Book Company, 1973.

S. B. Richmond, *Operations Research for Management Decisions,* New York: The Ronald Press Company, 1968.

G. M. F. di Roccaferrera, *Introduction to Linear Programming Processes,* Cincinnati, O.: South-Western Publishing Company, 1967.

M. Simonnard, *Linear Programming,* Englewood Cliffs, N.J.: Prentice-Hall, 1966.

D. Teichroew, *An Introduction to Management Science, Deterministic Models,* New York: John Wiley & Sons, 1964.

Chapter EIGHT
Games and Strategies

The history of games dates from 1928 when von Neumann conceived its essential theory. Generally, his work went largely unnoticed until he coauthored with Morgenstern the first edition of the *Theory and Practice of Games and Economic Behavior* which appeared in 1944. This work had a major impact on the development of linear programming and Wald's statistical decision theory and started a new way of thinking about competitive situations.

The term "games" relates to conditions of business conflict over time. The participants are competitors who make use of mathematical techniques and logical thinking in order to arrive at the best possible strategy for beating their competitor(s). A marketing executive, for example, employs the concepts of game theory when he observes that if he raises his prices, his competitors might follow. On the other hand, if he cuts them, they certainly would.

Every game has a goal or end-state (winnings) for which the competitors strive by selecting appropriate courses of action. Even though the game may favor one over the other(s), each will do his best to maximize his profits or to minimize his losses. Within this chapter, only two-person games are discussed. Many business situations involve the participation of many competitors and are not examples of two-person games. The presentation of three-person and larger games is much too lengthy for inclusion here.

Two-Person Zero-Sum Games

In a two-person zero-sum game, the interests of the two competitors are opposed in that the sum of the gains for one exactly equals the sum of the losses for the other or the sum of the game adds up to zero. This can be illustrated by a game, as in Table 8-1, where competitors, X and Y, are assumed to be equal in ability and intelligence. X has a choice of strategy 1 or strategy 2 while Y can select strategy 3 or strategy 4. Both know the

TABLE 8-1
Two-Person Game

		Competitor Y		
		Strategy 3	Strategy 4	Minimum of Row
Competitor X	Strategy 1	+5	+7	5
	Strategy 2	+4	+6	4
	Maximum of column	5	7	

payoffs for every possible strategy. It should be noted that the game favors competitor X since all values are plus. Values that favor Y would be minus. Based upon these conditions, the game is biased against Y. However, since Y must play the game, he will play to minimize his losses. In the business world, there are times when short-run losses are inescapable and can be minimized by good strategy.

All of the possible strategies for both competitors are: (1) X wins the highest game value if he plays strategy 1 all the time since it has higher values than strategy 2; (2) Y realizes this situation and plays strategy 3 in order to minimize his losses since the value of 5 is lower than the value of 7 for strategy 4. The game value must be 5 since X wins 5 points while Y loses 5 points each time the game is played. The "game value" is the average winnings per play over a long number of plays. The game illustrated in Table 8-1 is a two-person zero-sum game since X wins 5 points in each play while Y loses the same amount.

Rules for Game Theory

The preceding two-person game (Table 8-1) can be easily solved due to the distribution of values within the game matrix. However, other two-person games, containing the same number or larger number of rows and columns, must employ orderly procedures to solve for their strategies and game values. The basic rules utilized in solving any type of two-person game are developed below.

Rule 1—Look for a Pure Strategy (saddle point)

A proper appraisal of the game in Table 8-1 indicates that there is one strategy for both X and Y. Perhaps, either or both competitors might have missed this one strategy at first, but eventually both would have seen it. The strategy for a game of this type is called a "pure strategy" since it is one played by both competitors all of the time. The point where each player plays his pure strategy is called a "saddle point" and is the game value.

Upon inspection of Table 8-1, a saddle point is easily recognizable since it is the lowest value in the row and the highest value in the column. Why is this so? Competitor X would like to have a payoff which is the highest value in any column while competitor Y would rather have as a payoff the smallest value in any row. Since there is one value, 5, which satisfies both of these conditions, each will be playing the game on an optimum basis if each one chooses the saddle point. In many cases, games will not have saddle points. An examination of the game matrix will reveal whether a saddle point is present by searching for the lowest value in the row and the highest value in the column rule.

On the top of the next page are several examples of games. Saddle points, if they exist, have been circled. Strategies and game values are also shown.

For larger payoff matrices, a fast method to determine if a saddle point exists is to circle the lowest value in each row and put a square around the

$$X\begin{pmatrix} Y \\ -5 & 4 \\ -4 & -8 \end{pmatrix}$$

No saddle point exists since there is no payoff which is both the lowest value in its row and the highest value in its column.

$$X\begin{pmatrix} Y \\ 2 & ①\\ -3 & -4 \\ -5 & -6 \end{pmatrix}$$

Strategies: X, row 1; Y, column 2. Game value: +1. The payoff of +1 is the lowest value in its row and the highest value in its column.

$$X\begin{pmatrix} Y \\ ② & 14 & 12 \\ -8 & 6 & -10 \\ 1 & -4 & 14 \end{pmatrix}$$

Strategies: X, row 1; Y, column 1. Game value: +2.

highest value in each column. Where a value has both a circle and square around it, a saddle point exists. This can be illustrated by the following example, where the saddle point is 8:

$$X\begin{pmatrix} Y \\ \boxed{18} & 6 & 2 & \boxed{16} & ⓪ \\ 12 & 10 & \boxed{⑧} & 12 & 14 \\ ④ & 8 & 6 & 10 & \boxed{16} \\ 10 & \boxed{12} & 4 & 4 & ② \end{pmatrix}$$

Rule 2—Reduce Game by Dominance

If no pure strategy exists, the next step is to eliminate certain strategies (columns and/or rows) by dominance. The resulting game can be solved by some mixed strategy.

Dominance can be illustrated by several examples. In the first example,

$$X\begin{pmatrix} Y \\ 2 & 6 \\ -1 & -2 \\ 3 & 1 \end{pmatrix}$$

competitor X will not play row 2 since this will give Y his only chance to win. It is evident that row 2 is dominated by row 1 or row 3 since these rows will always return to X a better payoff than the dominated strategy, regardless of Y's actions. The *dominance rule for rows* is: Every value in the dominating row(s) must be greater than or equal to the corresponding value of the dominated row. The resulting matrix is

$$X\begin{pmatrix} Y \\ 2 & 6 \\ 3 & 1 \end{pmatrix}$$

Another matrix that can be reduced by dominance is

$$X\begin{pmatrix} Y \\ -4 & -6 & 2 & 4 \\ -6 & -3 & 1 & 2 \end{pmatrix}$$

Competitor Y has more flexibility (giving it an advantage) since it has the ability to play four columns versus two rows for competitor X. Since column 3 and column 4 are X's only chances to win, Y will not play either one since these columns are dominated by columns 1 and 2. The *dominance rule for columns* is: Every value in the dominating column(s) must be less than or equal to the corresponding value of the dominated column. The new matrix is

$$X\begin{pmatrix} -4 & -6 \\ -6 & -3 \end{pmatrix}$$
(with Y labeling the columns)

It should be noted that a game reduced by dominance may disclose a saddle point which was not found in the original matrix under Rule 1 (look for a pure strategy or saddle point). This may have been caused by ignoring Rule 1 or incorrectly applying it. However, there is one word of caution. It is possible to have what appears to be a saddle point after reducing the game by dominance. This is not necessarily a true saddle point since it may not be the lowest value in its row and the highest value in its column per the original matrix. Therefore, this pseudo-saddle point is ignored.

Dominance can be illustrated by the following example of a company bargaining with its union over an upcoming wage contract. The management team of the Ross Manufacturing Company, Inc., has been delegated the task of developing a strategy to follow during the coming negotiations. Looking to past experience, the team has developed the following strategies for Ross:

C_1 = Expects extremely difficult bargaining with the union
C_2 = Considered to be realistic demands by the union
C_3 = Considered to be realistic demands by the union
C_4 = Wide swings of demands by the union

The union, based upon its past history, suggests that it is considering one of the following strategies:

U_1 = High cost demands by the union
U_2 = High cost demands by the union
U_3 = Average demands by the union
U_4 = Favorable demands to the company, not to the union

The question of what strategy the management team of Ross should use depends upon the strategy adopted by the union. However, with the aid of an outside mediator (brought in due to the prospects of an extremely difficult bargaining session with the union and the possibility of a prolonged strike), a conditional wage increase cost table was constructed by the management group (Table 8-2). The mediator indicated that the union has constructed a comparable table since he has provided them with the same information.

The conditional wage increase cost table is to be interpreted as follows: when the management of Ross adopts strategy C_1 and the union promotes strategy U_1, the final contract will read that a $0.25 per hour increase

TABLE 8-2
Conditional Wage Increase Cost Table (4×4 matrix)

		(Ross) Company Strategies			
		C_1	C_2	C_3	C_4
Union Strategies	U_1	+$0.25	+$0.14	+$0.15	+$0.32
	U_2	+ 0.40	+ 0.17	+ 0.13	+ 0.16
	U_3	+ 0.30	+ 0.05	+ 0.12	+ 0.15
	U_4	− 0.01	+ 0.08	+ 0.11	+ 0.03

will be granted by the company. The other entries in Table 8-2 have the same meaning. Given these figures, what will the bargainers do?

The first rule to follow in any game theory problem is to test for a saddle point. None exists in this example. Next, the matrix is examined for dominance. To ascertain dominance, a question can be raised, why should the union ever play U_4 since this would give the company a chance to win or agree on a smaller increase? Clearly, the union will never play row U_4 since the union can do much better by playing row U_1 or U_2. Thus row U_4 is dominated and it is discarded because one or more strategies will always return to the union a better payoff than the dominated strategy, regardless of the company's actions. When applying the dominance rule for rows in this problem, every item in rows U_1 or U_2 is greater than or equal to the corresponding item in row U_4. This reduces the original matrix (4×4) to the 3×4 matrix, shown in Table 8-3.

Further inspection reveals that column C_4 is dominated by column C_3 since the firm is trying to minimize its losses. Every item in Column C_3 is equal to or less than the corresponding item in Column C_4 according to the column rule. The new 3×3 matrix appears in Table 8-4.

TABLE 8-3
Conditional Wage Increase Cost Table (3×4 matrix)

		(Ross) Company Strategies			
		C_1	C_2	C_3	C_4
Union Strategies	U_1	+$0.25	+$0.14	+$0.15	+$0.32
	U_2	+ 0.40	+ 0.17	+ 0.13	+ 0.16
	U_3	+ 0.30	+ 0.05	+ 0.12	+ 0.15

TABLE 8-4
Conditional Wage Increase Cost Table (3×3 matrix)

		(Ross) Company Strategies		
		C_1	C_2	C_3
Union Strategies	U_1	+$0.25	+$0.14	+$0.15
	U_2	+ 0.40	+ 0.17	+ 0.13
	U_3	+ 0.30	+ 0.05	+ 0.12

TABLE 8-5
Conditional Wage Increase Cost Table (2 × 3 matrix)

		(Ross) Company Strategies		
		C_1	C_2	C_3
Union Strategies	U_1	+$0.25	+$0.14	+$0.15
	U_2	+ 0.40	+ 0.17	+ 0.13

TABLE 8-6
Conditional Wage Increase Cost Table (2 × 2 matrix)

		(Ross) Company Strategies	
		C_2	C_3
Union Strategies	U_1	+$0.14	+$0.15
	U_2	+ 0.17	+ 0.13

Inspection of Table 8-4 reveals that row U_3 is dominated by row U_2. Using the row rule, wage increases in row U_2 ($0.40, $0.17, and $0.13) are greater than or equal to the corresponding items in row U_3 ($0.30, $0.05, and $0.12). The new 2×3 matrix appears in Table 8-5.

The last opportunity for applying dominance is to column C_1. When applying the column rule, proposed increases, shown in column C_2 ($0.14 and $0.17), are equal or less than those in column C_1 ($0.25 and $0.40). The resulting matrix is 2×2 (Table 8-6). It should be noted that the dominance rule can be used to remove more than one row or one column in the same step. In the next section, the strategies and game values will be determined.

Rule 3—Solve for a Mixed Strategy
In cases where there is no saddle point and dominance has been used to reduce the game to a smaller matrix, competition will resort to a mixed strategy. Various methods will be shown to optimize the winnings for either player. Players X and Y must determine what proportion of the time to play each row (applies to X only) and each column (applies to Y only).

Mixed Strategies and Game Values (2 × 2 Games)

Three common methods used in finding optimum strategies for a 2×2 matrix are: arithmetic, algebraic, and matrix algebra. The last two methods, joint probability, subgames, and graphic solutions can be used for finding game values. The matrix algebra method will not be covered while the other methods for finding optimum strategies and game values are treated for a 2×2 matrix.

Arithmetic Method for Finding Optimum Strategies

The arithmetic method provides an easy method in determining the optimum strategies for each player in a 2×2 game. The first step is to subtract the smaller payoff in each row from the larger payoff. This same procedure is applied to the column. Referring to the previous example of the Ross Manufacturing Company, Inc., and the union, the results are:

$$U\begin{pmatrix} \$0.14 & \$0.15 \\ 0.17 & 0.13 \end{pmatrix} \begin{matrix} \$0.15-\$0.14=\$0.01 \\ \$0.17-\$0.13=\$0.04 \end{matrix}$$

$$\begin{matrix} \$0.17 & \$0.15 \\ -0.14 & -0.13 \\ \hline \$0.03 & \$0.02 \end{matrix}$$

The next step is to interchange each of these pairs of subtracted values:

$$U\begin{pmatrix} \$0.14 & \$0.15 \\ 0.17 & 0.13 \end{pmatrix} \begin{matrix} \$0.04 \\ \$0.01 \end{matrix}$$

$$\begin{matrix} \$0.02 & \$0.03 \end{matrix}$$

In order to determine the strategies for the company, add $0.02 and $0.03 and then place each over their sum. The same procedure is followed for the union, which is as follows:

$$U\begin{pmatrix} \$0.14 & \$0.15 \\ 0.17 & 0.13 \end{pmatrix} \begin{matrix} \dfrac{\$0.04}{\$0.04+\$0.01} \\ \dfrac{\$0.01}{\$0.04+\$0.01} \end{matrix} \qquad U\begin{pmatrix} \$0.14 & \$0.15 \\ 0.17 & 0.13 \end{pmatrix}\begin{matrix} \frac{4}{5} \\ \frac{1}{5} \end{matrix}$$

$$\begin{matrix} \dfrac{\$0.02}{\$0.02+\$0.03} & \dfrac{\$0.03}{\$0.02+\$0.03} \end{matrix} \qquad\qquad \begin{matrix} \frac{2}{5} & \frac{3}{5} \end{matrix}$$

Thus, the union will follow strategy U_1 80 percent of the time and strategy U_2 20 percent of the time while the company will follow strategy C_2 40 percent of the time and strategy C_3 60 percent of the time.

The accuracy of these arithmetic strategies will be verified by use of the algebraic method. The arithmetic technique is less complex than the algebraic method. Unfortunately, it cannot be applied to larger games.

Algebraic Method for Finding Optimum Strategies and Game Value

The starting point for the algebraic method is to let Q equal the fraction of the time that the union spends playing the first row and $(1-Q)$ the time it plays the second row. This same concept is applied to the company using P. Representation of the proportional distribution of time for the columns and rows is:

$$\begin{array}{cc} & \begin{matrix} C_2 & C_3 \\ P & 1-P \end{matrix} \\ \begin{matrix} U_1 \\ U_2 \end{matrix} & \begin{matrix} Q \\ 1-Q \end{matrix}\begin{pmatrix} \$0.14 & \$0.15 \\ 0.17 & 0.13 \end{pmatrix} \end{array}$$

GAMES AND STRATEGIES

Under this method, the union wants to divide its plays between the two rows in order that the expected winnings from playing the first row will be exactly equal to its winnings from playing the second row despite what the company does. In order to arrive at the correct strategies for the union when playing either row one or row two, it is necessary to equate the union's expected winnings when the company plays column 2 to the union's expected earnings when the company plays column 3. To do this, let $0.14Q + \$0.17(1-Q)$ equal $\$0.15Q + \$0.13(1-Q)$ and solve for Q:

$$\$0.14Q + \$0.17(1-Q) = \$0.15Q + \$0.13(1-Q)$$
$$\$0.14Q + \$0.17 - \$0.17Q = \$0.15Q + \$0.13 - \$0.13Q$$
$$\$0.05Q = \$0.04$$
$$Q = \frac{4}{5}$$

The above calculation indicates that the union will play the first row $4/5$ of the time and the second row $1/5$ of the time ($1-Q$ or $1-4/5=1/5$).

The same approach used by the union also applies to the company. The company wants to divide its time between the columns so that no matter what the union does, the firm will minimize its losses (costs). The company's choices of strategies between the columns can be set up in algebraic form. The company's expectations from playing its second column P of the time and its third column $(1-P)$ of the time is equated in this way: the company's expected losses when the union plays row 1 with the company's expected losses when the union plays row 2. The equation for this condition is:

$$\$0.14P + \$0.15(1-P) = \$0.17P + \$0.13(1-P)$$
$$\$0.14P + \$0.15 - \$0.15P = \$0.17P + \$0.13 - \$0.13P$$
$$5P = 2$$
$$P = \frac{2}{5}$$

This solution indicates that the firm will play column 2, $2/5$ of the time, and column 3, $3/5$ of the time ($1-P$ or $1-2/5=3/5$). The strategies which we have calculated for the union and company assume that both sides will play their strategies without using a set pattern. In this manner, the strategies set forth above represent the best possible divisions of time between the rows or columns. However, if one of the players in the game begins to notice a pattern in the plays of his opponent, he will adjust his strategy to take advantage of this disclosure.

Having solved for mixed strategies of a 2×2 game, attention is focused on solving for the game value that utilizes the algebraic method:

$$\begin{array}{cc} & \begin{array}{cc} C_2 & C_3 \\ \frac{2}{5} & \frac{3}{5} \end{array} \\ \begin{array}{c} U_1 \\ U_2 \end{array} & \begin{pmatrix} \$0.14 & \$0.15 \\ 0.17 & 0.13 \end{pmatrix} \begin{array}{c} \frac{4}{5} \\ \frac{1}{5} \end{array} \end{array}$$

The rationale used in developing the game value equation is: while the company plays column 2, $\frac{2}{5}$ of the time, the union wins a $0.14 increase $\frac{4}{5}$ of the time and $0.17 increase $\frac{1}{5}$ of the time; also while the company plays column 3, $\frac{3}{5}$ of the time, the union wins a $0.15 increase $\frac{4}{5}$ of the time and $0.13 increase $\frac{1}{5}$ of the time. The total expected winnings of the union are summed as follows:

$$\text{Game Value} = \frac{2}{5}\left[\$0.14\left(\frac{4}{5}\right) + 0.17\left(\frac{1}{5}\right)\right] + \frac{3}{5}\left[\$0.15\left(\frac{4}{5}\right) + \$0.13\left(\frac{1}{5}\right)\right]$$

$$= \frac{2}{5}\left(\frac{\$0.56}{5} + \frac{\$0.17}{5}\right) + \frac{3}{5}\left(\frac{\$0.60}{5} + \frac{\$0.13}{5}\right)$$

$$= \frac{2}{5}\left(\frac{\$0.73}{5}\right) + \frac{3}{5}\left(\frac{\$0.73}{5}\right)$$

$$= \frac{\$0.73}{5} \text{ or } \$0.146 \text{ increase}$$

The game value of $0.146 or $0.15 (rounded) is the increase the union can expect. As was pointed out earlier, the union must be the winner since the game value is positive. If the game value had been negative, the company would have won. However, in the original matrix, only one negative was present versus 15 positive values.

The solution for the game value could have been approached from the company's point of view. The rationale would be as follows: while the union plays row 1, $\frac{4}{5}$ of the time, the company loses $0.14, $\frac{2}{5}$ of the time, and $0.15, $\frac{3}{5}$ of the time; also while the union plays row 2, $\frac{1}{5}$ of the time, the company loses $0.17, $\frac{2}{5}$ of the time, and $0.13, $\frac{3}{5}$ of the time. Putting the foregoing into an equation, the game value is determined as follows:

$$\text{Game Value} = \frac{4}{5}\left[\$0.14\left(\frac{2}{5}\right) + \$0.15\left(\frac{3}{5}\right)\right] + \frac{1}{5}\left[\$0.17\left(\frac{2}{5}\right) + \$0.13\left(\frac{3}{5}\right)\right]$$

$$= \frac{4}{5}\left(\frac{\$0.28}{5} + \frac{\$0.45}{5}\right) + \frac{1}{5}\left(\frac{\$0.34}{5} + \frac{\$0.39}{5}\right)$$

$$= \frac{4}{5}\left(\frac{\$0.73}{5}\right) + \frac{1}{5}\left(\frac{\$0.73}{5}\right)$$

$$= \frac{\$0.73}{5} \text{ or } \$0.146 \text{ increase}$$

The game value for the company is the same as for the union and indicates the average winnings of the players over many plays. Analysis of this type can be applied yearly.

Joint Probability Method for Obtaining Game Value
Another method for obtaining the game value is the use of joint probability. The original game matrix and optimum strategies are reproduced below for convenience:

$$\text{Union} \quad \begin{array}{c} & \text{Company} \\ & \begin{array}{cc} C_2 & C_3 \\ \frac{2}{5} & \frac{3}{5} \end{array} \\ \begin{array}{c} U_1 \\ U_2 \end{array} & \left(\begin{array}{cc} \$0.14 & \$0.15 \\ 0.17 & 0.13 \end{array} \right) \begin{array}{c} \frac{4}{5} \\ \frac{1}{5} \end{array} \end{array}$$

Upon inspection of the matrix, the probability that the union will play row 1 is 4/5 with a 1/5 probability of playing row 2. Similarly, the probability the company will play column 2 is 2/5 with a 3/5 probability of playing column 3. Since the union and the company play independently of one another, the probabilities for the union are independent of the probabilities for the company.

The fact that both the union and the company play their chosen strategies establishes joint probability. For example, the probability that row 1 and column 2 in the example will be played at the same time is a joint probability under conditions of statistical independence or 4/5 times 2/5 equals 8/25. The probability that $0.14 will be a payoff after one play of the game is 8/25. The calculation for the game value of a $0.146 increase to the union is found in Table 8-7.

Method of Subgames for Finding Game Value

Procedures in this chapter for finding the game value have treated a solution for a 2×2 game only. Many larger games can be reduced by dominance to a 2×2 game. This, however, will not cover all cases.

For example, two airlines serve the same air route, both trying for as large a market share as possible. One of the airlines (A) appears more ag-

TABLE 8-7
Joint Probability Method for Obtaining Game Value

Payoff Value (a)	Strategies	Probability of Payoff (b)	Game Value (a) × (b)
$0.14	Row 1, Col. 2	$\frac{4}{5} \times \frac{2}{5} = \frac{8}{25}$	$\frac{\$1.12}{25} = \$0.0448$
0.15	Row 1, Col. 3	$\frac{4}{5} \times \frac{3}{5} = \frac{12}{25}$	$\frac{\$1.80}{25} = 0.0720$
0.17	Row 2, Col. 2	$\frac{1}{5} \times \frac{2}{5} = \frac{2}{25}$	$\frac{\$0.34}{25} = 0.0136$
0.13	Row 2, Col. 3	$\frac{1}{5} \times \frac{3}{5} = \frac{3}{25}$	$\frac{\$0.39}{25} = 0.0156$
		1.0	$\frac{\$3.65}{25} = \$0.1460$ increase

TABLE 8-8
Payoff Matrix (2×3) of Two Airlines

		Airline T		
		Does Nothing	Advertises Reg. and Special Rates	Advertises Special Features (i.e., Movies and Fine Food)
Airline A	Advertises reg. and spec. rates	300	−25	−50
	Advertises spec. features (i.e., movies and fine food)	150	155	175

gressive since its marketing department is more knowledgeable about local market conditions. Airline A realizes that if it has half of the available seats in a certain market, but they are available at the wrong time, its ability to exploit the market is very low. Just as important are special rates, movies, and fine food to attract and hold customers. Thus, Airline A must evaluate competition in every market, that is, will a competing airline add a flight and how should it respond to capture a good part of the market? Based on a certain market, monthly gains and losses are presented in Table 8-8 where positive values favor airline A and negative values favor airline T.

The 2×3 game set forth in Table 8-8 can be thought of as being three 2×2 games:

Subgame 1:

$$A\begin{pmatrix} 300 & -25 \\ 150 & 155 \end{pmatrix} \quad \text{Columns 1 and 2}$$

with T above the matrix.

Subgame 2:

$$A\begin{pmatrix} 300 & -50 \\ 150 & 175 \end{pmatrix} \quad \text{Columns 1 and 3}$$

with T above the matrix.

Subgame 3:

$$A\begin{pmatrix} -25 & -50 \\ 155 & 175 \end{pmatrix} \quad \text{Columns 2 and 3}$$

with T above the matrix.

Airline T, which has the choice of not playing one of the columns, is trying to determine the combination of a two-column strategy that is best for itself. The player with the most columns or rows has more flexibility, resulting generally in a better strategy. However, in this game, there are four plus values versus two minus values. In order to solve for airline T's best strategy,

GAMES AND STRATEGIES 265

all of the three 2×2 subgames must be solved for their strategies and game values. It should be noted that a column not being played is represented by a zero. This is demonstrated in the subgames that appear below. Any of the methods presented earlier for strategies and game values can be used.

Subgame 1:

$$A\begin{pmatrix} 300 & -25 \\ 150 & 155 \end{pmatrix} \quad T$$

Third column is not being played.

Strategies:

$$A = \frac{1}{66}, \frac{65}{66}$$
$$T = \frac{36}{66}, \frac{30}{66}, 0$$

Game value: 152.27

Subgame 2:

$$A\begin{pmatrix} 300 & -50 \\ 150 & 175 \end{pmatrix} \quad T$$

Second column is not being played.

Strategies:

$$A = \frac{1}{15}, \frac{14}{15}$$
$$T = \frac{9}{15}, 0, \frac{6}{15}$$

Game value: 160

Subgame 3:

$$A\begin{pmatrix} -25 & -50 \\ 155 & 175 \end{pmatrix} \quad T$$

First column is not being played.

Strategies:

$$A = 0, 1$$
$$T = 0, 1, 0$$

Game value: 155 (saddle point for this subgame)

Based upon the preceding computations, the lowest plus game value or subgame 1 is selected since airline T has more flexibility. While airline A must play either row, airline T does not have to play all three columns, but only two columns. Airline T's strategy is to play the first column $36/66$ of the time and the second column $30/66$ of the time. The third column will not be used by airline T. It can be proven that this strategy is optimum by looking at the original matrix:

		Airline T		
		T₁	T₂	T₃
Airline A	A₁	300	− 25	− 50
	A₂	150	155	175

The solution (game value of 152.27 in favor of airline A) indicates that A chooses its mixed strategy in such a manner that it wins (or loses) the same regardless of T's choice of columns. As stated in the earlier explanation of how a mixed strategy is determined, A's expectations from playing a mixed strategy (between its rows) are the same irrespective of what T plays. This point can be expressed algebraically by letting the game value of subgame 1 be equal to the column that T plays. This is shown as follows:

	A's expected winnings
T plays column 1	$300A_1 + 150A_2 \geq 152.27$
T plays column 2	$-25A_1 + 155A_2 \geq 152.27$
T plays column 3	$-50A_1 + 175A_2 \geq 152.27$

The preceding equations mean that A expects to win 152.27 customers regardless of T's choice. The $\geq$ sign means that A might gain more than 152.27 customers if T chooses a poor strategy. If the strategies we have found are optimum, they should satisfy the three inequalities developed above. Substituting values for A_1 ($1/66$) and A_2 ($65/66$), the results are:

Column 1:

$$300\left(\frac{1}{66}\right) + 150\left(\frac{65}{66}\right) \geq 152.27; \qquad 4.54 + 147.73 = 152.27$$

Column 2:

$$-25\left(\frac{1}{66}\right) + 155\left(\frac{65}{66}\right) \geq 152.27; \qquad -0.38 + 152.65 = 152.27$$

Column 3:

$$-50\left(\frac{1}{66}\right) + 175\left(\frac{65}{66}\right) \geq 152.27; \qquad -0.76 + 172.35 > 152.27$$
$$171.59 > 152.27$$

All three inequalities are satisfied by the values inserted for A's strategies. However, when T plays column 3, A gains more than 152.27 customers since this is a poor strategy for T. This is the reason why T will not play column 3. It gives A an additional advantage in a game that already favors A.

Having satisfied the requirements for A's strategies, we must look at T's strategies to determine whether they are optimum. T has chosen his strategies so that he will minimize his losses. This can be expressed algebraically by letting the game value of subgame 1 be equal to rows that A plays:

	T's expected earnings
A plays row 1	$300T_1 - 25T_2 - 50T_3 \leq 152.27$
A plays row 2	$150T_1 + 155T_2 + 175T_3 \leq 152.27$

The foregoing inequalities mean that T expects to lose 152.27 customers regardless of A's choice. The $\leq$ sign indicates that T may lose less if A chooses poor strategies. Again, if the strategies we have found are optimum, they should satisfy these two inequalities. Substituting values for T_1 ($^{36}/_{66}$), T_2 ($^{30}/_{66}$), and T_3 (0), the results are

$$300\left(\frac{36}{66}\right) - 25\left(\frac{30}{66}\right) - 50(0) \leq 152.27 \qquad 163.64 - 11.37 - 0 = 152.27$$

$$150\left(\frac{36}{66}\right) + 155\left(\frac{30}{66}\right) + 175(0) \leq 152.27 \qquad 81.82 + 70.45 + 0 = 152.27$$

Both inequalities are satisfied by the strategies which were determined in subgame 1, resulting in T's optimum strategies. Having picked the subgame with the lowest value, we have verified our decision that subgame 1 is an optimum one by satisfying all five inequalities. Without this verification, we would never have been certain that T had chosen correctly in refusing to play column 3.

Graphic Method for Determining Game Value

Another method for determining game values in the graphic method. The advantage of this method is that it is relatively fast.

In the example below, the graphic method will be used to solve for the game value:

$$X \begin{pmatrix} 19 & 6 & 7 & 5 \\ 7 & 3 & 14 & 6 \\ 12 & 8 & 18 & 4 \\ 8 & 7 & 13 & -1 \end{pmatrix}$$
$$\quad\quad\quad Y$$

The first step is to look for a saddle point (Rule 1). One does not exist in this problem. Next, the technique of dominance is used, indicating that column 2 dominates columns 1 and 3. The resulting matrix is:

$$\begin{array}{c} \\ X_1 \\ X_2 \\ X_3 \\ X_4 \end{array} \begin{pmatrix} Y_2 & Y_4 \\ 6 & 5 \\ 3 & 6 \\ 8 & 4 \\ 7 & -1 \end{pmatrix}$$

Further inspection indicates that row 3 dominates row 4. However, this dominance will be ignored for the time being.

If player X elects to play the first row (X_1), his winnings will be either 6 points or 5 points, depending upon Y's choice of columns. This is shown in Figure 8-1. Similarly, if X plays row 2 (X_2), his winnings will be either 3 points or 6 points, depending upon Y's choice of columns. Straight lines are drawn for X_1 and X_2. The remaining rows are constructed in like manner.

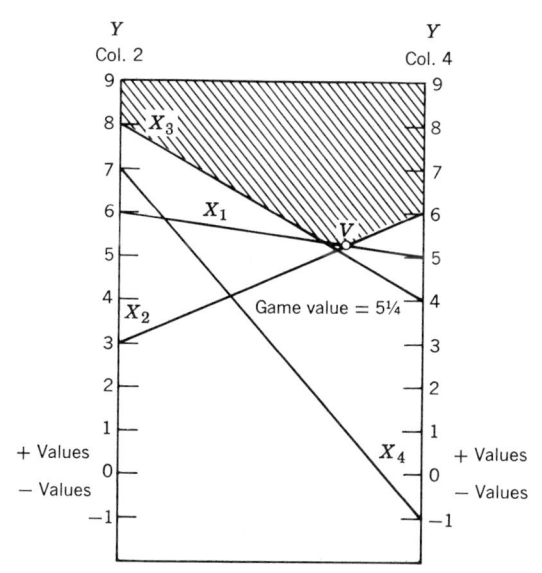

Figure 8-1 Graphic solution for a plus game value.

An examination of Figure 8-1 reveals that row X_4 is immaterial to the solution, graphically demonstrating the principle of dominance. Thus, it can be ignored in our further discussion of the graphic method. Another observation about the graph of the game is that it appears row X_3 offers X the best chance to win (8 points). However, one must remember that Y can shift to column 4. This would immediately reduce X's payoff to 4, the lowest value of the three rows, X_1, X_2, and X_3.

Assuming both players are rational and use intelligent approaches, the game would be played as follows:

1. If X plays row 3 (X_3), expecting to win 8 points, Y would immediately switch to column 4 to reduce X's winnings to 4 points.
2. As soon as X saw this happening, he would switch to row 2 (X_2) and win 6 points as long as Y continued to play column 4.
3. Y, realizing the situation, would switch to column 2 where X could win only 3 points.
4. As soon as X saw this happening, he would switch to row 1 (X_1) and win 6 points.
5. Player Y would see this and switch to column 4 where the winnings of X would be reduced from 6 points to 5 points.
6. Continue in the same manner.

The proportion of the time each player spends on his own strategies (rows or columns) can be determined by one of the methods previously covered.

The game value (point V) can be read from the graph in Figure 8-1; it is the lowest intersection point in the striped area. The importance of this lowest intersection is that it is the lowest level, on an average, at which Y can hold X's winnings. Similarly, it is the level at which X can hold Y to

GAMES AND STRATEGIES 269

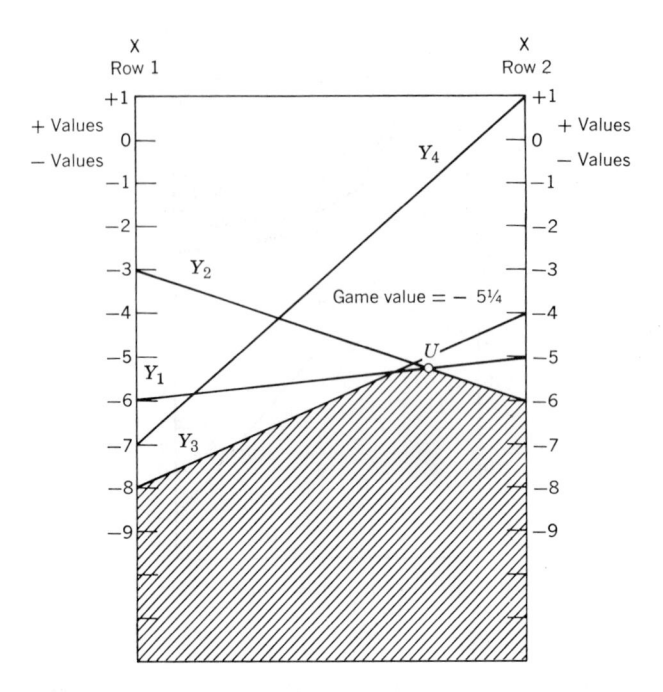

Figure 8-2 Graphic solution for a negative game value.

minimize his losses. In other words, the game value indicates just how far one player can go before he is restrained by his opponent's defensive strategy. It is the average payoff around which the game revolves.

Although the game value of $5\frac{1}{4}$ favors X, it is possible to have a game value that favors Y. The graphing of the preceding payoff matrix, where the matrix has been transposed and the signs have been changed, is

$$\begin{array}{c c} & \begin{array}{cccc} Y_1 & Y_2 & Y_3 & Y_4 \end{array} \\ \begin{array}{c} X_1 \\ X_2 \end{array} & \left(\begin{array}{cccc} -6 & -3 & -8 & -7 \\ -5 & -6 & -4 & +1 \end{array} \right) \end{array}$$

The basic difference between the payoff matrices when solving for the game value is this: in Figure 8-1, the lowest intersection point (V) in the striped area is the game value, whereas in Figure 8-2, the highest intersection point (U) in the striped area is the game value. The graphic method relates to the concept of an extreme point which was developed in the graphic method of linear programming. When applied to game theory, the highest or lowest intersection point represents the restraints on the game players.

The foregoing rules for solving two-person games are set forth in Figure 8-3. Although linear programming is utilized in the next section for solving 3×3 and larger games, it, too, can be used for solving 2×2 games. However, the preceding methods in the chapter are generally faster in ascertaining strategies and the final game value.

270 OPERATIONS RESEARCH MODELS—MATRIX ALGEBRA

Rule 1—Look for a Pure Strategy (saddle point)
   Look for a pure strategy or a saddle point—this represents a strategy that will be played by both competitors all of the time. It is easily recognizable since it is the lowest value in its row and the highest value in its column. Remember plus (row) values favor *X* while minus (column) values favor *Y*.

Rule 2—Reduce Game by Dominance
   Eliminate certain strategies—columns and/or rows—by dominance. Dominance rule for rows (*X*) is: every value in the dominating row(s) must be greater than or equal to the corresponding value of the dominated row. Dominance rule for columns (*Y*) is: every value in the dominating column(s) must be less than or equal to the corresponding value of the dominated column. If there is a legitimate saddle point, and rule 1 was ignored or was not correctly applied, the foregoing dominance procedures will highlight a pure strategy per the original game matrix.

Rule 3—Solve for a Mixed Strategy
   Solve the resulting game matrix using a mixed strategy. For a 2×2 matrix game, arithmetic, algebraic, and matrix algebra are useful in finding optimum strategies. The prior two methods, joint probability, subgames, and graphic solution can be employed for game values. For 3×3 or larger games, linear programming offers the best method for determining strategies and game values (to be explained in the next section).

Figure 8-3   Rules employed in determining two-person strategies and game values.

Mixed Strategies and Game Values (3×3 and Larger Games)

The preceding sections have developed various methods for determining mixed strategies and game values after consideration of saddle points and dominance. If there is no saddle point or dominance is unsuccessful in reducing the game matrix smaller than 3×3, linear programming offers the best method of solution. Computer programs are available to solve any 3×3 and larger size game.

Linear Programming
To illustrate linear programming, two competing large-volume service stations will be used. They are the most vigorous competitors in one section of a city. The Standard station and the Texas station are both trying to increase their market share at the expense of the other. The Standard station is considering the possibilities of decreasing price, giving free soft drinks on $4.00 purchases of gasoline and oil, or giving away a drinking glass with each 10-gallon purchase. It is obvious the Texas station's owners cannot ignore the Standard station's increased share of the market. In fact, the Texas station will counter with its own programs designed to increase its share of the market. Since the current price and quality of the competing products are the same, it is difficult to determine what to do. The Standard station has determined a payoff matrix (Table 8-9) from the viewpoint of increasing or decreasing market shares.

   Referring to a prior section (Methods of Subgames for Finding Game

TABLE 8-9
Payoff Matrix (3×3) of Two Service Stations

		Texas Station		
		Decrease Price	Free Soft Drinks on $4.00 Purchase	Free Drinking Glass on 10 Gallons or More
Standard Station	Decrease price	4%	1%	−3%
	Free soft drinks on $4.00 purchase	3	1	6
	Free drinking glass on 10 gallons or more	−3	4	−2

Value), we find the relationships which express the expectations of the Texas service station are the following:

$$4Y_1 + Y_2 - 3Y_3 \leq V \quad (V = \text{game value})$$
$$3Y_1 + Y_2 + 6Y_3 \leq V$$
$$-3Y_1 + 4Y_2 - 2Y_3 \leq V$$
$$Y_1 + Y_2 + Y_3 = 1 \quad \text{(Time spent playing all three columns sum to unity)}$$

$$\frac{4Y_1}{V} + \frac{Y_2}{V} - \frac{3Y_3}{V} \leq 1 \quad \text{(Divide each side by } V\text{)}$$
$$\frac{3Y_1}{V} + \frac{Y_2}{V} + \frac{6Y_3}{V} \leq 1$$
$$\frac{-3Y_1}{V} + \frac{4Y_2}{V} - \frac{2Y_3}{V} \leq 1$$

In order to remove Vs (in the denominator), it is necessary to define a new variable ($\overline{Y}_i$):

$$\overline{Y}_i = \frac{Y_i}{V}$$

We will solve the game in terms of $\overline{Y}$s so that when we are done, we can multiply the $\overline{Y}$s by V to determine the original Ys ($Y_i = \overline{Y}_i \times V$). The new inequalities are

$$4\overline{Y}_1 + \overline{Y}_2 - 3\overline{Y}_3 \leq 1$$
$$3\overline{Y}_1 + \overline{Y}_2 + 6\overline{Y}_3 \leq 1$$
$$-3\overline{Y}_1 + 4\overline{Y}_2 - 2\overline{Y}_3 \leq 1$$

The equation ($Y_1 + Y_2 + Y_3 = 1$) must also be restated in terms of $\overline{Y}$s as follows:

$$\frac{Y_1}{V} + \frac{Y_2}{V} + \frac{Y_3}{V} = \frac{1}{V}$$
$$\overline{Y}_1 + \overline{Y}_2 + \overline{Y}_3 = \frac{1}{V}$$

Thus, our four relationships per the above are

$$\overline{Y}_1+\overline{Y}_2+\overline{Y}_3=\frac{1}{V}$$
$$4\overline{Y}_1+\overline{Y}_2-3\overline{Y}_3\leq 1$$
$$3\overline{Y}_1+\overline{Y}_2+6\overline{Y}_3\leq 1$$
$$-3\overline{Y}_1+4\overline{Y}_2-2\overline{Y}_3\leq 1$$

We can state the foregoing equations in terms of a linear programming problem by solving for Y's optimum strategies and by adding a slack variable to each inequality. It must be remembered that Y's objective is to minimize the value of the game value (V) which is the same as maximizing 1/V:

$$\text{Maximize } \overline{Y}_1+\overline{Y}_2+\overline{Y}_3=\frac{1}{V}$$

Subject to:

$$4\overline{Y}_1+\overline{Y}_2-3\overline{Y}_3+\overline{Y}_4+0\overline{Y}_5+0\overline{Y}_6=1$$
$$3\overline{Y}_1+\overline{Y}_2+6\overline{Y}_3+0\overline{Y}_4+\overline{Y}_5+0\overline{Y}_6=1$$
$$-3\overline{Y}_1+4\overline{Y}_2-2\overline{Y}_3+0\overline{Y}_4+0\overline{Y}_5+\overline{Y}_6=1$$

where $\overline{Y}_4$, $\overline{Y}_5$, and $\overline{Y}_6$ are slack variables. The equation which we seek to optimize is known as the objective function while the inequalities which we have converted to equalities by the introduction of slack variables are known as constraint equations.

Because the simplex algorithm was treated at some length in other chapters, only the first tableau necessary to solve for Y's final strategies is shown in Table 8-10. The optimum $\overline{Y}$ strategies per the final tableau are:

$$\overline{Y}_1=\frac{27}{161}$$
$$\overline{Y}_2=\frac{62}{161}$$
$$\overline{Y}_3=\frac{3}{161}$$

TABLE 8-10
First Simplex Tableau for Solving Y Strategies

Tableau I

C_j	Mix	Quantity	1 $\overline{Y}_1$	1 $\overline{Y}_2$	1 $\overline{Y}_3$	0 $\overline{Y}_4$	0 $\overline{Y}_5$	0 $\overline{Y}_6$
0	$\overline{Y}_4$	1	4	1	−3	1	0	0
0	$\overline{Y}_5$	1	3	1	6	0	1	0
0	$\overline{Y}_6$	1	−3	4	−2	0	0	1
	Z_j		0	0	0	0	0	0
	C_j-Z_j		1	1	1	0	0	0
			↑ Opt. col.					

Note: Since there is a tie in the C_j-Z_j row, Column $\overline{Y}_1$ will be utilized initially.

It is necessary to convert $\bar{Y}_1$, $\bar{Y}_2$ and $\bar{Y}_3$ into real Y column strategies. This can be done by multiplying them by V. However, what we have actually maximized is $1/V$. If $1/V$ equals $4/7$ (the value in the quantity column in the last tableau or $\bar{Y}_1 + \bar{Y}_2 + \bar{Y}_3$), then V equals $7/4$. Substituting $7/4$ for V, the column strategies for Y are as follows:

$$Y_1 = \bar{Y}_1 \times V \qquad Y_2 = \bar{Y}_2 \times V \qquad Y_3 = \bar{Y}_3 \times V$$

$$Y_1 = \frac{27}{161} \times \frac{7}{4} \qquad Y_2 = \frac{62}{161} \times \frac{7}{4} \qquad Y_3 = \frac{3}{161} \times \frac{7}{4}$$

$$Y_1 = \frac{27}{92} \qquad Y_2 = \frac{62}{92} \qquad Y_3 = \frac{3}{92}$$

The procedure used above for calculating Y (Texas station) strategies (and game value) can be used for X (Standard station). The following inequalities represent X's expectations:

$$4X_1 + 3X_2 - 3X_3 \geq V \qquad (V = \text{game value})$$
$$X_1 + X_2 + 4X_3 \geq V$$
$$-3X_1 + 6X_2 - 2X_3 \geq V$$
$$X_1 + X_2 + X_3 = 1 \qquad \text{(Strategies add up to 1)}$$
$$\frac{4X_1}{V} + \frac{3X_2}{V} - \frac{3X_3}{V} \geq 1 \qquad \text{(Divide each side by } V\text{)}$$
$$\frac{X_1}{V} + \frac{X_2}{V} + \frac{4X_3}{V} \geq 1$$
$$\frac{-3X_1}{V} + \frac{6X_2}{V} - \frac{2X_3}{V} \geq 1$$
$$\frac{X_1}{V} + \frac{X_2}{V} + \frac{X_3}{V} = \frac{1}{V}$$

Defining a new variable $\bar{X}_i$, which equals X_i/V or $X_i = \bar{X}_i \times V$, we can restate the preceding inequalities and game value as follows:

$$\text{Minimize } \bar{X}_1 + \bar{X}_2 + \bar{X}_3 = \frac{1}{V}$$

Subject to:

$$4\bar{X}_1 + 3\bar{X}_2 - 3\bar{X}_3 \geq 1$$
$$\bar{X}_1 + \bar{X}_2 + 4\bar{X}_3 \geq 1$$
$$-3\bar{X}_1 + 6\bar{X}_2 - 2\bar{X}_3 \leq 1$$

These equations can be restated by adding slack variables and artificial variables. Player X desires to maximize V or minimize $1/V$. The equations for the initial tableau of the linear programming problem are

$$\text{Minimize } \bar{X}_1 + \bar{X}_2 + \bar{X}_3 = \frac{1}{V}$$

Subject to:

$$4\overline{X}_1+3\overline{X}_2-3\overline{X}_3-\overline{X}_4+0\overline{X}_5+0\overline{X}_6+\overline{X}_7+0\overline{X}_8+0\overline{X}_9=1$$
$$\overline{X}_1+\overline{X}_2+4\overline{X}_3+0\overline{X}_4-\overline{X}_5+0\overline{X}_6+0\overline{X}_7+\overline{X}_8+0\overline{X}_9=1$$
$$-3\overline{X}_1+6\overline{X}_2-2\overline{X}_3+0\overline{X}_4+0\overline{X}_5-\overline{X}_6+0\overline{X}_7+0\overline{X}_8+\overline{X}_9=1$$

where $\overline{X}_4$, $\overline{X}_5$, and $\overline{X}_6$ are slack variables and $\overline{X}_7$, $\overline{X}_8$, and $\overline{X}_9$ are artificial variables.

The simplex algorithm produces the following strategies:

$$\overline{X}_1=\frac{1}{7}$$
$$\overline{X}_2=\frac{2}{7}$$
$$\overline{X}_3=\frac{1}{7}$$

Since $X_i=\overline{X}_i\times V$, the resulting row strategies for X are:

$$X_1=\frac{1}{7}\times\frac{7}{4}; \quad X_1=\frac{1}{4}$$
$$X_2=\frac{2}{7}\times\frac{7}{4}; \quad X_2=\frac{1}{2}$$
$$X_3=\frac{1}{7}\times\frac{7}{4}; \quad X_3=\frac{1}{4}$$

Basic Limitations of Game Theory

The basic limitation of game theory is the inability of the players to determine accurate values for the payoff matrix rather than a lack of adequate methods to solve for strategies and game values. This limitation, although it may lack objective validity, must be considered. For example, in the bargaining application whether it is conscious or subconscious, every experienced bargainer makes certain assumptions about the commitment of his opponent to a given position. Only the willingness to reassign probabilities as bargaining commences gives this approach pragmatic value.

Incorrect figures in the matrix result in misleading output. It is not difficult to establish that one outcome is preferable to another, but it is quite another thing to state exactly how much more. Even though this point is true, a firm can, for example, rank the payoffs from the best to the worst in terms of appeal to its customers.

The idea of ranked payoffs can be illustrated with two firms (R and S), each having three products of a multiproduct line that are in direct competition with one another. The marketing department of the first company (R) has noticed over a period of time that the promotional effort for each of its products has varied from poor to exceptional. The market research department has determined the promotional effect from its displays of products A, B, and C, which are in competition with products D, E, and F of its competitor, as follows:

	Company S Displays		
	Products		
	D	E	F
Company R Displays — Product A	average	no opinion	poor
Product B	fair	very good	fair
Product C	poor	good	exceptional

Using the following ranking of exceptional, very good, good, average, fair, poor, and no opinion and values of 6, 5, 4, 3, 2, 1, and 0, respectively, the resulting payoff matrix is:

	Company S Displays		
	Products		
	D	E	F
Company R Displays — Product A	3	0	1
Product B	2	5	2
Product C	1	4	6

The foregoing payoff matrix, then, allows one firm (R) to relate mathematically its displays to another competitor (S).

Game Theory Application—American Products Corporation

The American Products Corporation presently has excess funds on hand which are available for investing in new production equipment or in marketable securities. Working in conjunction with the firm's finance department, the marketing department was surveyed as to the probability of good times and bad times. The consensus of opinion was that the probability of prosperity was low, that is, .25 and the probability of a recession was quite high, or .75. In addition, other essential data was collected by finance personnel. During good times, investment in production equipment is expected to yield a return of 20 percent since there is a great need for such equipment to satisfy expanded demand. A return of 6 percent is expected on marketable securities during prosperity. However, in case of a recession, new equipment is expected to produce a low return of 3 percent while marketable securities will yield a return of 4 percent. These data can be set forth in a 2×2 game matrix as follows:

	Economic Conditions	
Investment Alternatives	**Prosperity**	**Recession**
New production equipment	20%	3%
Marketable securities	6%	4%

Based on the foregoing data, indifference probabilities in the game can be determined by letting the prosperity probability factor be P and the recession probability factor be R. Thus, the return on each type of investment must be:

$$20P + 3R$$
$$6P + 4R$$

When these expressions are equated to each other, the return on new production equipment will be the same as the return on marketable securities. Solving for R in terms of P is as follows:

$$20P + 3R = 6P + 4R$$
$$R = 14P$$

Letting R equal $(1-P)$ where the sum of the probabilities $(P+R)$ equal 1.0, the above equation can be revised as:

$$1 - P = 14P$$
$$15P = 1$$
$$P = 0.067 \text{ and } R = 0.933$$

The resulting values mean that if the probabilities of prosperity and a recession are .067 and .933 respectively, then the firm is just as well off investing in new production equipment as investing in marketable securities. Thus, the problem can be stated as:

	Prosperity		Recession		
Forecasted probabilities	$P = .25$	+	$R = .75$	=	1.0
Indifference probabilities	$P = .067$	+	$R = .933$	=	1.0

Inspection of the preceding data indicates that finance personnel should choose the investment in new production equipment since it has a higher forecasted probability of prosperity than the indifference probability. On the other hand, if an investment is made in marketable securities, the indifference probability of prosperity is higher than the forecasted probability. Hence, this investment is not a good choice because it requires a probability greater than the forecasted one in order to be as attractive as the alternative investment in new production equipment.

Summary

Game theory, as presented in this chapter, assumes a dynamic environment where competitors are equal in ability and intelligence. The starting point for solving a game is looking for a pure strategy (saddle point). If this does not apply, dominance is recommended to reduce the game to a manageable size. After giving consideration to dominance, several methods are available for determining column and row strategies and solving for the game value. Linear programming will solve any size game. However, it must be pointed out that it is much easier to use one of the other methods on games less than 3×3 in size.

Game theory has not yet reached its full potential. As more firms employ computers to simulate their operations, game theory should gain in usage for solving OR marketing problems. The marriage of game theory with simulation to solve marketing management problems will give game theory the needed thrust to be an important tool for quantitative decision making.

Questions

1. What is game theory? Include in your answer various approaches in solving for strategies and game values.
2. Of what importance is dominance in reducing a game size?
3. How does a two-person game differ from three-person and larger games?
4. What are the principal difficulties with game theory? How can they be overcome?

Problems

8-1 Find the optimum strategies for X and Y as well as game value for the following:

(a)

$$X \begin{pmatrix} 11 & -3 & -4 \\ 8 & 7 & -8 \\ -5 & 5 & -6 \end{pmatrix}$$

Y above matrix.

(b)

$$X \begin{pmatrix} 4 & 4 & 3 \\ 8 & 1 & 7 \\ -1 & 2 & -1 \end{pmatrix}$$

Y above matrix.

8-2 Find the optimum strategies for X and Y, and the value of the game. Demonstrate that the optimum strategies satisfy the game inequalities.

$$X \begin{pmatrix} -8 & 8 & 9 \\ -3 & -4 & -5 \\ -3 & -4 & -6 \end{pmatrix}$$

8-3 Find the optimum strategies for Y and the value of the game.

$$X \begin{pmatrix} 6 & 1 & 6 & 1 & 4 \\ 4 & 4 & 5 & -2 & 4 \\ 3 & -1 & 3 & 2 & -2 \end{pmatrix}$$

8-4 Firm A has developed a sales forecasting function for its own products and those of its competitor B. If firm A employs strategy a_1 and firm B employs strategy b_1, there will be a resulting gain of $50,000 in quarterly sales revenue for firm A. Since there are 12 combinations of strategies available to A and B, the resulting increases or decreases in quarterly sales revenue for firm A can be represented in a payoff matrix, as follows:

278   OPERATIONS RESEARCH MODELS—MATRIX ALGEBRA

		Firm B			
		b_1	b_2	b_3	b_4
Firm A	a_1	$50,000	($20,000)	$120,000	($50,000)
	a_2	$60,000	$20,000	$ 70,000	$70,000
	a_3	($20,000)	$ 0	($ 40,000)	$75,000

What strategy should Firm A pursue?

8-5 Two separate firms (A and B) for years have been selling a competing product which is but a small part of both firms' total sales. The marketing executive of firm A raised the question, "What should the firm's strategies be in terms of advertising for the product in question?" The market research group of firm A developed the following data for varying degrees of advertising.
  (a) No advertising, medium advertising, and large advertising for both firms will result in equal market shares.
  (b) Firm A with no advertising: 40 percent of the market with medium advertising by firm B and 28 percent of the market with large advertising by firm B.
  (c) Firm A using medium advertising: 70 percent of the market with no advertising by firm B and 45 percent of the market with large advertising by firm B.
  (d) Firm A using large advertising: 75 percent of the market with no advertising by firm B and 47½ percent of the market with medium advertising by firm B.
Based upon the foregoing information, answer the marketing executive's question.

8-6 The RBM Corporation and the TSC Corporation compete in the sale of punched cards. RBM has a higher quality product, even though the prices are the same. The two critical factors—price decrease and quality increase—are available to both firms. If both companies decrease price, the first firm (RBM) will take away 10 percent of business from the second firm (TSC), whereas, if the first firm's price decrease is countered by the second firm's quality increase, then the first firm will lose 15 percent of its business to the second firm. On the other hand, if the first company chooses to increase quality even further and the second firm counters with a price decrease, the market is more sensitive to price than to an increase in the already high quality product. Thus the first firm will lose 15 percent of its business to the second firm. Finally, if the second firm attempts to counter a quality increase by the first firm with its own quality increase, the present higher quality of the first firm's punched cards will result in the first firm obtaining 20 percent of its business from the second firm. Find the strategies for both corporations and the game value. Discuss the results.

8-7 Steelcraft, Inc., is currently involved in negotiations with its union on its upcoming wage contract. With the aid of an outside mediator, the table below was constructed by the management group. The pluses are to be interpreted as proposed wage increases while a minus figure indicates that a wage reduction is proposed. The mediator informs the management group that he has been in touch with the union and that they have constructed a table that is comparable to the table developed by management. Both the company and the union must decide on an overall strategy before negotiations begin. The management group understands the relationship of company strategies to union strategies in the following table but lacks specific knowledge of game theory to select the best strategy (or strategies) for the firm. You have been called in to assist management on this problem. What game value and strategies are available to the opposing groups? Note that these strategies must be reappraised following each bargaining session.

| | | Additional Costs to Steelcraft, Inc. ||||
| | | Union Strategies ||||
		U_1	U_2	U_3	U_4
Steelcraft Strategies	C_1	+$0.25	+$0.27	+$0.35	−$0.02
	C_2	+ 0.20	+ 0.16	+ 0.08	+ 0.08
	C_3	+ 0.14	+ 0.12	+ 0.15	+ 0.13
	C_4	+ 0.30	+ 0.14	+ 0.19	0

8-8 Even though there are several manufacturers of vacuum cleaners, two firms control one market segment. If both manufacturers make model changes of the same type for this market segment in the same year, their respective market shares remain constant. Likewise, if neither makes model changes, their market shares also remain constant. If the Roover Company makes a major model change and its competitor, the Eura Corporation, does not, the Roover Company will be able to take a larger share of the market. If the Eura Corporation makes a major model change and the Roover Company does not, Eura will gain a larger market. The payoff matrix in terms of increased market shares under the various possible conditions is as follows:

| | | Eura Corporation |||
		No Change	Minor Change	Major Change
Roover Company	No change	0	−4%	−10%
	Minor change	+3%	0	− 5%
	Major change	+8%	−1%	0

(a) Find the game value.
(b) What change should the Roover Company consider if this information is available only to itself?
(c) What other data must be considered in reaching a final decision for the Roover Corporation?

8-9 Two major competitors—The Capco Corporation and The Kapon Corporation—in the plastic-bottle cap market have been plagued by diminishing returns on their investment for injection molding machines that produce bottle caps. Because the total market for their products are expected to remain static throughout the next year, the management of The Capco Corporation must decide whether to:

(A) Increase its profitability through the purchase of a new, low cost, high speed, injection molding machine.
(B) Increase its selling price.
(C) Lower its selling price.
(D) Launch an aggressive advertising campaign.

Because these same options are available to The Kapon Corporation, a strategy table has been constructed (based on the data from an outside market research company). The estimated gain or loss of each strategy has been rated on a scale of 0 through 6 where 6 is the greatest gain for The Kapon Corporation and −6 is the greatest gain for The Capco Corporation. From the table below, find the optimum strategies for The Capco Corporation and the resultant game value.

		The Capco Corporation			
		A	B	C	D
The Kapon Corporation	A	+2	+6	+2	−2
	B	+4	0	−4	−2
	C	−2	+4	+4	+4
	D	−1	−6	−1	−2

Bibliography

R. L. Ackoff and M. Sasieni, *Fundamentals of Operations Research*, New York: John Wiley & Sons, 1968.

H. Bierman, C. P. Bonini, and W. H. Hausman, *Quantitative Analysis for Business Decisions*, Homewood, Ill.: Richard D. Irwin, 1973.

E. Burger, *Introduction to the Theory of Games*, Englewood Cliffs, N.J.: Prentice-Hall, 1963.

M. Dresher, *Games of Strategy, Theory and Applications*, Englewood Cliffs, N.J.: Prentice-Hall, 1961.

A. M. Glickman, *An Introduction to Linear Programming and the Theory of Games*, New York: John Wiley & Sons, 1963.

F. S. Hillier and G. J. Lieberman, *Introduction to Operations Research*, San Francisco: Holden-Day, 1967.

R. Isaacs, *Differenial Games*, New York: John Wiley & Sons, 1965.

R. D. Luce and H. Raiffa, *Games and Decisions*, New York: John Wiley & Sons, 1958.

G. Owen, *Game Theory*, Philadelphia: W. B. Saunders Company, 1968.

M. F. Shakun, editor, *Game Theory and Gaming, Management Science*, Volume 18, No. 5, January, 1972.

M. Shubik, editor, *Game Theory and Related Approaches to Social Behavior*, New York: John Wiley & Sons, 1964.

S. Vajda, *An Introduction to Linear Programming and The Theory of Games*, New York: John Wiley & Sons, 1960.

J. D. Williams, *The Compleat Strategyst* (rev. ed.), New York: McGraw-Hill Book Company, 1966.

Chapter NINE

Markov Analysis

Markov analysis originated with the studies (1906–1907) of A. A. Markov on the sequence of experiments connected in a chain, and with the attempts to describe mathematically the physical phenomenon known as Brownian motion. The first correct mathematical construction of a Markov process with continuous trajectories was given by N. Wiener in 1923. The general theory of Markov processes was developed in the 1930s and 1940s by A. N. Kolmagorov, W. Feller, W. Doeblin, P. Levy, J. L. Doob, and others.

Markov analysis is a way of analyzing the current movement of some variable in an effort to forecast the future movement of that same variable. This method has come into use as a marketing research tool for examining and forecasting the behavior of customers from the standpoint of their loyalty to one brand and their switching patterns to other brands. It will be shown later that applications of this technique are not limited to marketing.

Procedure 1—Develop Matrix of Transition Probabilities

In order to illustrate the Markov process, a problem is presented in which the states of activities are brands and the transition probabilities forecast the likelihood of consumers moving from one brand to another. Assume that the initial consumer sample is composed of 1000 respondents distributed over four brands, A, B, C, and D. One further assumption is that the sample is representative of the entire group from the standpoint of brand loyalty and switching patterns from one brand to another. Consumers switch from one brand to another due to advertising, special promotions, price, dissatisfaction, etc.

In Table 9-1, most of the customers who initially purchased brand A remained with the brand in the second period. Nevertheless, 50 customers were gained while 45 customers were lost by brand A to other brands. Table 9-1 does not tell the complete story. A detailed analysis is needed

TABLE 9-1
Exchanges of Customers for One Month

Brand	Period One, No. of Customers	Changes During Period Gain	Changes During Period Loss	Period Two, No. of Customers
A	220	50	45	225
B	300	60	70	290
C	230	25	25	230
D	250	40	35	255
	1,000	175	175	1,000

that quantifies the rate of net gains and losses among the four brands. Without this type of analysis, we do not know to which brands the 45 customers lost by brand A switched nor from which brands the 50 customers gained had switched.

Before treating further the "switching component," attention is focused on the "hard core component" or the group that has not switched brands. It is necessary to compute transition probabilities for the four brands. Transition probabilities are defined as the probability that a certain brand (or seller) will retain its customers. Referring to our example, brand A lost 45 customers for a retention of 175 customers (220−45). To determine the probability factor, the customers retained for the period under review are divided by the number of customers at the beginning of the period, resulting in a retention probability of .796 ($175/220$) for brand A. The transition probabilities for B, C, and D are .767, .891, and .860, respectively.

For those customers who switch brands, it is necessary to show gains and losses among the brands in order to complete the matrix of transition probabilities. Data of this nature requires accurate statistical information, such as found in Table 9-2. It is possible to observe not only the net gains or losses for any of the four brands but also the interrelationships among the gains and losses of customers for each brand. Brand A gains most of its customers from brand B while losing many of its customers to the same brand. A more intelligent analysis of the facts, then, is available with Table 9-2 than with Table 9-1. In Table 9-2, zeros on the diagonals mean a brand incurs neither gains nor losses from itself. Also, the losses columns are transposes of the gains in the rows.

From the data developed, the next step is to convert the customer switching of brands so that all gains and losses take the form of transition probabilities. This is represented in Figure 9-1, where the arrows flowing in indicate increases while arrows flowing out represent losses. However, a more convenient form for ease of mathematical calculations is the use of a matrix of transition probabilities. This is found in Table 9-3 with the probabilities calculated to three decimal places.

The rows in the matrix show the retention of customers and the gain of customers while the columns show the retention of customers and the

TABLE 9-2
Brand Switching—Gains and Losses

Brand	Period One, No. of Customers	Gains From A	B	C	D	Losses To A	B	C	D	Period Two, No. of Customers
A	220	0	40	0	10	0	20	10	15	225
B	300	20	0	25	15	40	0	5	25	290
C	230	10	5	0	10	0	25	0	0	230
D	250	15	25	0	0	10	15	10	0	255
	1,000									1,000

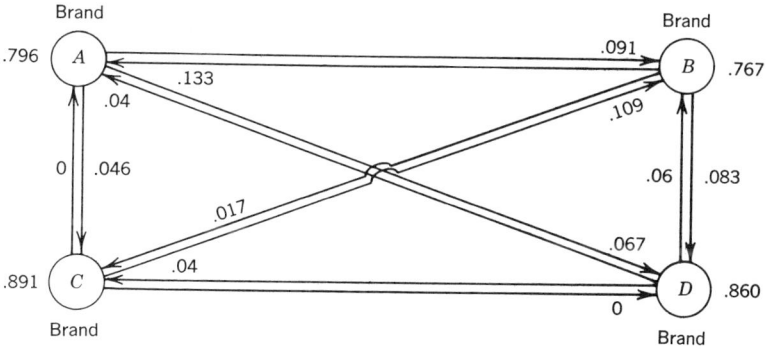

Figure 9-1 Brand switching by customers.

loss of customers. In Table 9-3, the first matrix is in terms of actual number of customers, whereas the second matrix is stated in terms of transition probabilities. It should be remembered that these probabilities are applicable to all customers since this is a representative sample of 1000 customers.

The calculations for the matrix probabilities in Table 9-3 are as follows:

$$\begin{array}{c} & \text{Brands} \\ & \begin{array}{cccc} A & B & C & D \end{array} \\ \begin{array}{c} A \\ B \\ C \\ D \end{array} & \begin{bmatrix} \dfrac{175}{220}=.796 & \dfrac{40}{300}=.133 & \dfrac{0}{230}=0 & \dfrac{10}{250}=.040 \\ \dfrac{20}{220}=.091 & \dfrac{230}{300}=.767 & \dfrac{25}{230}=.109 & \dfrac{15}{250}=.060 \\ \dfrac{10}{220}=.046 & \dfrac{5}{300}=.017 & \dfrac{205}{230}=.891 & \dfrac{10}{250}=.040 \\ \dfrac{15}{220}=.067 & \dfrac{25}{300}=.083 & \dfrac{0}{230}=0 & \dfrac{215}{250}=.860 \end{bmatrix} \end{array}$$

Examples of how to read the rows and columns are: row 1 indicates that brand A retains .796 of its customers while gaining .133 of B's customers and .040 of D's customers while gaining none of C's customers; column 1 indicates that brand A retains .796 of its customers while losing .091, .046, and .067 of its customers to brands B, C, and D, respectively. The same approach can be used to read the remaining rows and columns. The basic gain and loss relationships can be easily observed. Brand A gains most of its customers from brand B, and, at the same time, loses more to brand B than to brands C and D individually.

Several advantages accrue to marketing management through utilizing the data shown in the matrix. It can assist management in analyzing its promotional efforts in terms of the effect they have on the gain or loss of its market share. This data can forecast the rate at which a brand will gain or lose its market share in the future and can show the possibility of some market equilibrium in the future.

TABLE 9-3
Matrix of Transition Probabilities

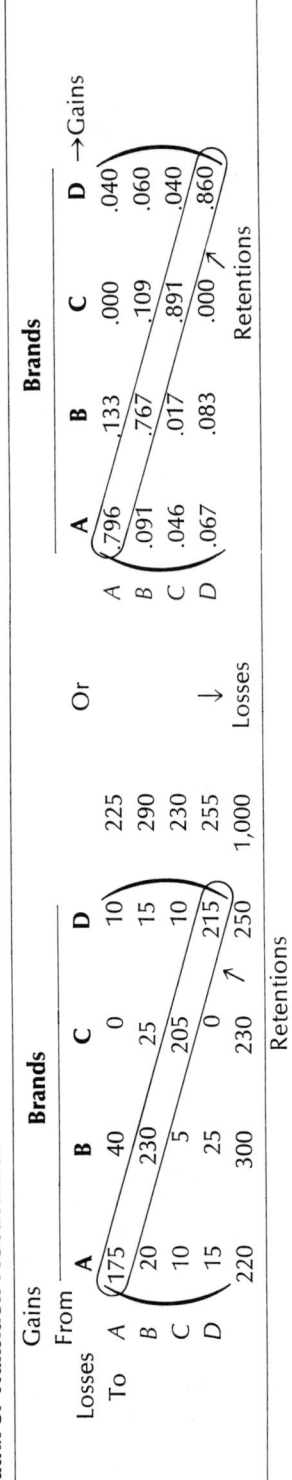

	Gains From	**Brands**				Or		**Brands**			
Losses		**A**	**B**	**C**	**D**			**A**	**B**	**C**	**D** →Gains
To	A	175	40	0	10	225	A	.796	.133	.000	.040
	B	20	230	25	15	290	B	.091	.767	.109	.060
	C	10	5	205	10	230	C	.046	.017	.891	.040
	D	15	25	0	215	255	D	.067	.083	.000	.860
		220	300	230	250	1,000					
			Retentions			↓ Losses			Retentions		

286 OPERATIONS RESEARCH MODELS—MATRIX ALGEBRA

First-Order and Higher-Order Markov Analysis

The preceding section was concerned with the "hard-core component" and "switching component" of customers in relation to one brand versus other brands. The basic assumption is that customers do not shift from one brand to another at random, but instead they buy brands in the future which reflect their choices made in the past.

The Markov process can be of different orders. The *first-order* considers only the brand choices made during this period for determining the probabilities of choice in the forthcoming period. A *second-order* Markov analysis assumes choices for a specific brand in the coming period depend upon the brand choices made by the customers during the last two periods. Similarly, a *third-order* Markov process looks to customer's preferences for the past three periods in order to forecast the next period's behavior toward particular brands by customers.

Many marketing research studies have shown that using first-order assumptions for forecasting purposes are valid. The data indicates that customer choices of brands follow a fairly stable pattern. In effect, the matrix of transition probabilities remains stable or very close to it over a period of time. Since first-order Markov analysis is not too difficult and has proven to be a reliable forecaster of future brand preferences for frequently purchased items, only first-order chains are treated in depth while higher-order chains are discussed briefly.

Procedure 2—Calculate Future Probable Market Shares

Returning to the example, the market shares for brands A, B, C, and D are now 22, 30, 23, and 25 percent, respectively, for period one. Management would benefit if they knew what market shares will be at some future period. Calculating the probable market shares for brands A, B, C, and D in period two is a matter of multiplying the matrix of transition probabilities by the market shares in the first period:

	Transition Probabilities					Period One, Market Shares		Period Two, Probable Market Shares
	A	B	C	D				
A	.796	.133	.000	.040		.22		.225
B	.091	.767	.109	.060	×	.30	=	.290
C	.046	.017	.891	.040		.23		.230
D	.067	.083	.000	.860		.25		.255
	1.0	1.0	1.0	1.0		1.0		1.0

Brand A's calculations (first row × first column):

1. A's ability to retain its own customers times A's share of the market:

$$.796 \times .22 = .175$$

2. A's ability to obtain B's customers times B's share of the market:

$$.133 \times .30 = .040$$

3. A's ability to obtain C's customers times C's share of the market:

$$0 \times .23 = 0$$

4. A's ability to obtain D's customers times D's share of the market:

$$.040 \times .25 = \underline{.010}$$

Brand A's share of market at period two: .225

Similar calculations are made for brands B, C, and D:

Brand B's calculation (second row × first column):

$$.091 \times .22 = .020$$
$$.767 \times .30 = .230$$
$$.109 \times .23 = .025$$
$$.060 \times .25 = \underline{.015}$$

Brand B's share of market at period two: .290

Brand C's calculation (third row × first column):

$$.046 \times .22 = .010$$
$$.017 \times .30 = .005$$
$$.891 \times .23 = .205$$
$$.040 \times .25 = \underline{.010}$$

Brand C's share of market at period two: .230

Brand D's calculation (fourth row × first column):

$$.067 \times .22 = .015$$
$$.083 \times .30 = .025$$
$$0 \times .23 = 0$$
$$.860 \times .25 = \underline{.215}$$

Brand D's share of market at period two: .255

After solving for period two, which takes into account starting market shares and the transition probabilities, period three can be determined in two ways. The first method is a continuation of the approach just set forth, that is, multiplication of the original matrix of transition probabilities by the second-period brand shares gives the results for the third period. The second method is squaring the matrix of transition probabilities for the desired number of periods and then multiplying the resultant matrix by the original market shares. The new market shares for period three using these methods are shown below.

First Method (Computations)
Matrix multiplication is again used to solve for the market shares of each brand. The detailed calculations are shown only for the first row and the first column.

	Transition Probabilities					Period Two, Probable Market Shares		Period Three, Probable Market Shares
	A	B	C	D				
A	.796	.133	.000	.040		.225		.228
B	.091	.767	.109	.060	×	.290	=	.283
C	.046	.017	.891	.040		.230		.231
D	.067	.083	.000	.860		.255		.258
	1.0	1.0	1.0	1.0		1.0		1.0

Brand A's calculation (first row × first column):

$$.796 \times .225 = .179$$
$$.133 \times .290 = .039$$
$$0 \times .230 = 0$$
$$.040 \times .255 = \underline{.010}$$
$$.228$$

Brand B's calculation (second row × first column):

$$.283$$

Brand C's calculation (third row × first column):

$$.231$$

Brand D's calculation (fourth row × first column):

$$.258$$

The advantage of this method is that changes, which occur from period to period, can be observed. However, management might desire market shares of its particular brand for some specified future period. If this is the case, the second method would be preferred. This method basically makes use of raising the matrix of transition probabilities to a power that represents the number of periods in the future. For example, the probable market shares for period three, which is two periods in the future, are calculated as follows:

	Transition Probabilities					Period One, Market Shares		Period Three, Probable Market Shares
	A	B	C	D				
A	.796	.133	.000	.040	^{2}	.22		.228
B	.091	.767	.109	.060	×	.30	=	.283
C	.046	.017	.891	.040		.23		.231
D	.067	.083	.000	.860		.25		.258
	1.0	1.0	1.0	1.0		1.0		1.0

Second Method (Computations)

Matrix multiplication is again used. The squaring of the matrix of transition probabilities means that new probabilities of retention, gain, and loss have to be calculated. The squared matrix of transition probabilities is multiplied by the original market shares. To illustrate, the various rows in the matrix of transition probabilities are multiplied by their corresponding columns to form a squared matrix of transition probabilities:

$$\begin{array}{c} \\ A \\ B \\ C \\ D \end{array} \begin{pmatrix} A & B & C & D \\ .796 & .133 & 0 & .040 \\ .091 & .767 & .109 & .060 \\ .046 & .017 & .891 & .040 \\ .067 & .083 & 0 & .860 \end{pmatrix} \times \begin{pmatrix} A & B & C & D \\ .796 & .133 & 0 & .040 \\ .091 & .767 & .109 & .060 \\ .046 & .017 & .891 & .040 \\ .067 & .083 & 0 & .860 \end{pmatrix}$$

$$= \begin{array}{c} \\ A \\ B \\ C \\ D \end{array} \begin{pmatrix} A & B & C & D \\ .6484 & .2112 & .0145 & .0742 \\ .1513 & .6073 & .1808 & .1056 \\ .0818 & .0375 & .7957 & .0729 \\ .1185 & .1440 & .0090 & .7473 \end{pmatrix}$$

Brand A's calculation (first row × first column):

$$\begin{pmatrix} A\text{'s ability to} \\ \text{retain its own} \\ \text{customers} \end{pmatrix} \times \begin{pmatrix} A\text{'s ability to} \\ \text{retain its own} \\ \text{customers} \end{pmatrix} = \begin{pmatrix} A\text{'s ability to retain its} \\ \text{original customers after} \\ \text{two periods} \end{pmatrix}$$

.796 × .796 = .6336

$$\begin{pmatrix} A\text{'s ability to} \\ \text{gain customers} \\ \text{from } B \end{pmatrix} \times \begin{pmatrix} B\text{'s ability to} \\ \text{gain customers} \\ \text{from } A \end{pmatrix} = \begin{pmatrix} A\text{'s regain of its} \\ \text{own customers} \\ \text{from } B \end{pmatrix}$$

.133 × .091 = .0121

$$\begin{pmatrix} A\text{'s ability to} \\ \text{gain customers} \\ \text{from } C \end{pmatrix} \times \begin{pmatrix} C\text{'s ability to} \\ \text{gain customers} \\ \text{from } A \end{pmatrix} = \begin{pmatrix} A\text{'s regain of its} \\ \text{own customers} \\ \text{from } C \end{pmatrix}$$

0 × .046 = 0

$$\begin{pmatrix} A\text{'s ability to} \\ \text{gain customers} \\ \text{from } D \end{pmatrix} \times \begin{pmatrix} D\text{'s ability to} \\ \text{gain customers} \\ \text{from } A \end{pmatrix} = \begin{pmatrix} A\text{'s regain of its} \\ \text{own customers} \\ \text{from } D \end{pmatrix}$$

.040 × .067 = <u>.0027</u>

The portion of A's original customers A retains
(sum of brand A's calculation) = .6484

The other 15 terms are calculated in a similar manner. The resulting squared matrix of transition probabilities is now multiplied by the original market shares. The results are shown on the top of the next page. The raising of a matrix to a much larger power is no easy task; however, computer programs are available.

$$\begin{array}{c}\text{Squared Matrix of} \\ \text{Transition Probabilities}\end{array} \qquad \begin{array}{c}\text{Original Market} \\ \text{Shares for} \\ \text{Each Period}\end{array} \quad \begin{array}{c}\text{Period Three,} \\ \text{Probable} \\ \text{Market Shares}\end{array}$$

$$\begin{array}{c}\;\;A\;\;\;\;\;B\;\;\;\;\;C\;\;\;\;\;D\\ \begin{array}{c}A\\B\\C\\D\end{array}\!\!\left(\begin{array}{cccc}.6484 & .2112 & .0145 & .0742\\ .1513 & .6073 & .1808 & .1056\\ .0818 & .0375 & .7957 & .0729\\ .1185 & .1440 & .0090 & .7473\end{array}\right)\\ \;\;\overline{1.0}\;\;\;\overline{1.0}\;\;\;\overline{1.0}\;\;\;\overline{1.0}\end{array} \times \left(\begin{array}{c}.22\\.30\\.23\\.25\end{array}\right) = \left(\begin{array}{c}.228\\.283\\.231\\.258\end{array}\right)$$

$$\overline{1.0} \overline{1.0}$$

Possible Market Shares (Higher Order)

The foregoing Markov chain analysis was of the first-order since the probability of the future event(s) depended upon the outcomes of the last period only. A higher-order Markov process depends upon the choices of consumers during the immediate preceding periods for predicting the probable future shares. Little or erratic brand loyalty patterns give rise to higher-order Markov chains. In essence, the degree of brand switching must be considered for predicting future periods more accurately.

A higher-order (third-order) Markov chain can be illustrated by utilizing the matrices of transition probabilities for three competing brands, shown in Table 9-4 during the last three time periods. The matrices are considered

TABLE 9-4
Past Matrices of Transition Probabilities in a Higher-Order Markov Chain Problem

		A	B	C
Period one (third last period)	A	.4	.3	.3
	B	.3	.5	.3
	C	.3	.2	.4
		1.0	1.0	1.0
Period two (second last period)	A	.3	.2	.3
	B	.5	.5	.4
	C	.2	.3	.3
		1.0	1.0	1.0
Period three (first last period)	A	.3	.2	.3
	B	.4	.3	.3
	C	.3	.5	.4
		1.0	1.0	1.0

representative of future market behavior. It should be noted that the transition probabilities are not equal since brand switching is taking place period by period. This is caused mainly by the introduction of slightly improved products, resulting in a state of disequilibrium. The problem is solvable

MARKOV ANALYSIS 291

TABLE 9-5
Probable Market Shares at the End of Period Three in a Higher-Order Markov Chain Problem (Based on Table 9-4)

Period one

	Transition Probabilities			Beginning of Period One, Market Shares	Ending of Period One, Probable Market Shares
	A	B	C		
A	.4	.3	.3	.3	.33
B	.3	.5	.3 ×	.4 =	.38
C	.3	.2	.4	.3	.29
	1.0	1.0	1.0	1.0	1.0

Period two

	Transition Probabilities			Beginning of Period Two, Probable Market Shares	Ending of Period Two, Probable Market Shares
	A	B	C		
A	.3	.2	.3	.33	.262
B	.5	.5	.4 ×	.38 =	.471
C	.2	.3	.3	.29	.267
	1.0	1.0	1.0	1.0	1.0

Period three

	Transition Probabilities			Beginning of Period Three, Probable Market Shares	Ending of Period Three, Probable Market Shares
	A	B	C		
A	.3	.2	.3	.262	.253
B	.4	.3	.3 ×	.471 =	.326
C	.3	.5	.4	.267	.421
	1.0	1.0	1.0	1.0	1.0

by starting with period one market shares and employing matrix multiplication for each of the three periods, illustrated in Table 9-5. Thus, probable period three market shares are contingent on the past matrices of transition probabilities.

Instead of demonstrating how other types of higher-order Markov chains are solved, the remainder of the chapter focuses on the first-order Markov chains under equilibrium conditions.

Procedure 3—Determine Equilibrium Conditions

The condition of equilibrium results only if none of the competitors alters the matrix of transition probabilities. It is reasonable to assume that a state of equilibrium might be reached in the future regarding market shares.

The exchange of customers in terms of retentions, gains, and losses would be static at the moment equilibrium is reached. In terms of marketing, what are the final or equilibrium market shares?

Several matrices of transition probabilities can be used to illustrate equilibrium conditions. The matrix of transition probabilities where A gains no customers but loses to B and C is:

$$\begin{array}{c|ccc} & A & B & C \\ A & .85 & 0 & 0 \\ B & .10 & .80 & .25 \\ C & .05 & .20 & .75 \\ \hline & 1.0 & 1.0 & 1.0 \end{array}$$

It is quite apparent that eventually B and C will take away all of A's customers since A loses .10 to B and .05 to C. But, more importantly, A gains no customers from B or C.

Another type of equilibrium that might occur is the condition under which A never loses any of its customers:

$$\begin{array}{c|ccc} & A & B & C \\ A & 1.0 & .10 & .05 \\ B & 0 & .80 & .05 \\ C & 0 & .10 & .90 \\ \hline & 1.0 & 1.0 & 1.0 \end{array}$$

Since A suffers no losses of its market, it is only a question of time until A has all of the customers of B and C. This is referred to as a "sink" or "basin of one state" since one firm eventually gets all the customers. In the first illustration, this is referred to as a "sink" or "basin of two states" since two firms eventually share all the customers.

The more common illustration occurs when no one firm gets all the customers, that is, no one firm or two firms out of three capture the entire market. Some final condition of equilibrium develops and continues based upon a stable matrix of transition probabilities. This can be illustrated by an example in the following section.

Simultaneous Equations Solution

The Gordon Company has two competitors in one market segment of its business. At the present time (this year), the market shares are as follows: Gordon Company (G), 30 percent; first competitor (A), 20 percent; and second competitor (B), 50 percent. The matrix of transition probabilities (first-order Markov chain), showing the flow of customers, is as follows:

	Gordon Co. (G)	First Competitor (A)	Second Competitor (B)
Gordon Co. (G)	.6	.2	.2
First Comp. (A)	.1	.6	.2
Second Comp. (B)	.3	.2	.6
	1.0	1.0	1.0

MARKOV ANALYSIS   293

The equation for the Gordon Company's share of the market at equilibrium equals .6 times the share Gordon had in the period immediately preceding equilibrium (or eq. − 1period) plus .2 times the share the first competitor had in equilibrium minus one period plus .2 times the share the second competitor had in equilibrium minus one period. This equation can be written as follows:

$$G_{eq.-1} = .6G_{eq.-1} + .2A_{eq.-1} + .2B_{eq.-1}$$

It should be noted that G's share of the market is labeled as some unspecified future period which we call the equilibrium period. The same type of equation can also be developed for both competitors.

In most Markov problems, the gains and losses are usually of a high magnitude in the early periods. However, as equilibrium is approached, the gains and losses become very small, as shown in Figure 9-2. The changes in the market shares between the equilibrium period and the period immediately preceding it are so small that they may be treated mathematically as equal. In the equation above, eq. equals eq. −1. The three equations in the example can be written as follows:

$G = .6G + .2A + .2B$	(Equation 9-1)
$A = .1G + .6A + .2B$	(Equation 9-2)
$B = .3G + .2A + .6B$	(Equation 9-3)
$1.0 = G + A + B$	(Equation 9-4)

A fourth equation is used to show that the total of the three market shares equals 1.0.

Since there are similar terms on both sides of the equation, the resulting equations which show the gains and losses for each firm are as follows:

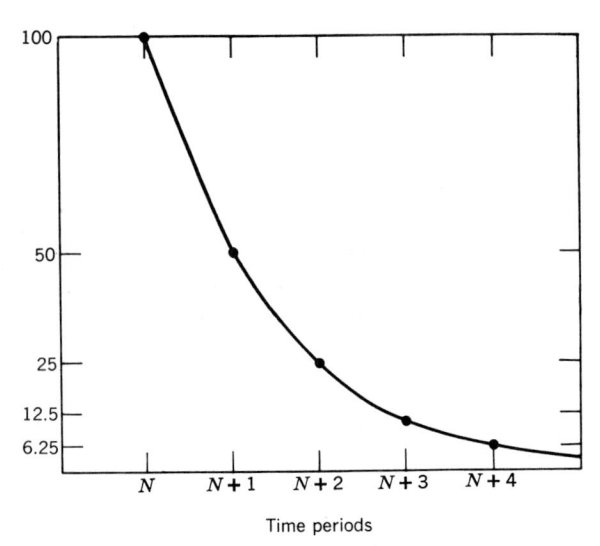

$$0 = -.4G + .2A + .2B \qquad \text{(Equation 9-5)}$$

Figure 9-2 Changes become smaller and smaller as equilibrium is reached.

$$0 = .1G - .4A + .2B \quad \text{(Equation 9-6)}$$
$$0 = .3G + .2A - .4B \quad \text{(Equation 9-7)}$$
$$1.0 = G + A + B \quad \text{(Equation 9-8)}$$

Having four equations and three unknowns, it is necessary to drop one equation (either Equation 9-5, 9-6, or 9-7, but not Equation 9-8) in order to have a one to one ratio between the number of equations and the number of unknowns. The reason one equation can be dropped is that the equations are mathematically interrelated, that is, the sum of $-.4G$ (Equation 9-5), $+.1G$ (Equation 9-6) and the $+.3G$ (Equation 9-7) equals zero. The ability to sum column G to zero is also applicable to columns A and B. Solving two equations (Equations 9-5 and 9-7) simultaneously and using Equation 9-8 for the equilibrium market shares is as follows:

(First set of simultaneous equations)

$$\begin{array}{ll} 0 = -.4G + .2A + .2B & \text{(Equation 9-5)} \\ \underline{0 = -.3G - .2A + .4B} \quad \text{(Change signs)} & \text{(Equation 9-7)} \\ 0 = -.7G + .6B & \end{array}$$
$$.7G = .6B$$
$$G = \frac{6}{7}B \quad \text{or} \quad .857B$$

(Second set of simultaneous equations)

$$\begin{array}{ll} 0 = -.4G + .2A + .2B & \text{(Equation 9-5)} \\ \underline{0 = +.4G + .267A - .533B} \quad \text{(Multiplied by } 1\frac{1}{3}) & \text{(Equation 9-7)} \\ 0 = .467A - .333B & \end{array}$$
$$.467A = .333B$$
$$A = \frac{333}{467}B \quad \text{or} \quad .715B$$

Substitute respective values for G and A:

$$1 = G + A + B \quad \text{(Equation 9-8)}$$
$$1 = .857B + .715B + 1.0B$$
$$1 = 2.572B$$
$$B = .389 \quad (B \text{ at equilibrium})$$

Determine values for G and A:

$$G = \frac{6}{7}B = \frac{6}{7}(.389) = .333 \quad (G \text{ at equilibrium})$$
$$A = \frac{333}{467}B = \frac{333}{467}(.389) = .278 \quad (A \text{ at equilibrium})$$

An effective way to prove that we have solved for equilibrium is to multiply the matrix of transition probabilities by the equilibrium market shares. This can be calculated by using matrix algebra and is shown as follows:

$$\begin{array}{c}\text{Matrix of Transition}\\ \text{Probabilities}\end{array} \qquad \begin{array}{c}\text{Equilibrium}\\ \text{Market Shares}\end{array}$$

$$\begin{array}{c}\quad G\quad A\quad B\\ \text{Gordon }(G)\\ \text{First Comp. }(A)\\ \text{Second Comp. }(B)\end{array}\begin{pmatrix}.6 & .2 & .2\\ .1 & .6 & .2\\ .3 & .2 & .6\end{pmatrix} \times \begin{pmatrix}.333\\ .278\\ .389\end{pmatrix} = \begin{pmatrix}.333\\ .278\\ .389\end{pmatrix}$$
$$\overline{1.0}\;\;\overline{1.0}\;\;\overline{1.0}\qquad\;\;\overline{1.0}\qquad\;\overline{1.0}$$

Determinants Solution

When dealing with a 4×4 matrix of transition probabilities (four unknowns and five equations) and current market shares, it is sometimes easier to use determinants to solve for the answer. Returning to the previous problem given in the chapter, determinants are employed in this last illustration for equilibrium conditions. Restating the problem for convenience is:

$$\begin{array}{c}\quad A\quad\;\; B\quad\;\; C\quad\;\; D\\ A\\ B\\ C\\ D\end{array}\begin{pmatrix}.796 & .133 & 0 & .040\\ .091 & .767 & .109 & .060\\ .046 & .017 & .891 & .040\\ .067 & .083 & 0 & .860\end{pmatrix} \times \begin{pmatrix}.22\\ .30\\ .23\\ .25\end{pmatrix} = \text{Equilibrium Shares}$$

Appendix A defines a determinant as an array of numbers, arranged in rows and columns, which has a numerical value. Expanding a determinant by a row simply means choosing any row, and then eliminating, in turn, each column which intersects that row. Likewise, expanding a column means choosing any column and eliminating, in turn, each row which intersects that column. This procedure will be shown in expanding the numerator and denominator to determine an equilibrium condition for A.

The algebraic sign of each step in the expansion depends upon the row and column eliminated. If the total of the row and column that are eliminated is an even number (for example, row 1 plus column 1 equals 2), the sign for that step is not changed. However, if the total of the row and column that are eliminated is an odd number (for example, row 1 plus column 2 equals 3), the sign is changed.

In using determinants, the value for each of the unknown variables—A, B, C, and D—is found by solving a particular set of two determinants which forms a fraction. The determinant that forms the denominator of the fraction remains the same and the determinant that forms the numerator of the fraction changes for each variable. The determinants which solve for A are given as follows:

$$A = \dfrac{\begin{vmatrix}0 & .133 & 0 & .040\\ 0 & -.233 & .109 & .060\\ 0 & .017 & -.109 & .040\\ 1 & 1 & 1 & 1\end{vmatrix}}{\begin{vmatrix}-.204 & .133 & 0 & .040\\ .091 & -.233 & .109 & .060\\ .046 & .017 & -.109 & .040\\ 1 & 1 & 1 & 1\end{vmatrix}} \begin{array}{l}\text{(numerator)}\\ \\ = \text{Equilibrium position for }A\\ \\ \text{(denominator)}\end{array}$$

An inspection of the determinant in the denominator reveals that it is nothing more than the coefficients of the four unknowns arranged in the same form as they would have appeared in the revision to the original equations, analogous to what we did with Equations 9-5, 9-7, and 9-8. One equation has been dropped for the same reason as in the previous problem dealing with the Gordon Company.

The determinant which forms the numerator of the fraction for A is identical to the determinant for the denominator, except the first column has been replaced by the values to the left of the equality signs, as they would have appeared in the revision of the original equations. Similarly, the determinant for the numerator of the fraction for the variable B is formed by eliminating the column of coefficients for the unknown B and replacing it with the values to the left of the equality sign in the revision of the original equations. The same procedure is used for the column coefficients of C and D.

The determinants for B, C, and D are as follows:

$$B = \frac{\begin{vmatrix} -.204 & 0 & 0 & .040 \\ .091 & 0 & .109 & .060 \\ .046 & 0 & -.109 & .040 \\ 1 & 1 & 1 & 1 \end{vmatrix}}{\begin{vmatrix} -.204 & .133 & 0 & .040 \\ .091 & -.233 & .109 & .060 \\ .046 & .017 & -.109 & .040 \\ 1 & 1 & 1 & 1 \end{vmatrix}} = \text{Equilibrium position for } B$$

$$C = \frac{\begin{vmatrix} -.204 & .133 & 0 & .040 \\ .091 & -.233 & 0 & .060 \\ .046 & .017 & 0 & .040 \\ 1 & 1 & 1 & 1 \end{vmatrix}}{\begin{vmatrix} -.204 & .133 & 0 & .040 \\ .091 & -.233 & .109 & .060 \\ .046 & .017 & -.109 & .040 \\ 1 & 1 & 1 & 1 \end{vmatrix}} = \text{Equilibrium position for } C$$

$$D = \frac{\begin{vmatrix} -.204 & .133 & 0 & 0 \\ .091 & -.233 & .109 & 0 \\ .046 & .017 & -.109 & 0 \\ 1 & 1 & 1 & 1 \end{vmatrix}}{\begin{vmatrix} -.204 & .133 & 0 & .040 \\ .091 & -.233 & .109 & .060 \\ .046 & .017 & -.109 & .040 \\ 1 & 1 & 1 & 1 \end{vmatrix}} = \text{Equilibrium position for } D$$

Using the rules for expanding a determinant, the first step is to expand the numerator determinant for A by its first column. Note that in the 4×4 determinant, when a row and a column are deleted, a 3×3 determinant remains in each case. This is apparent in steps a, b, c, and d.

Step a:

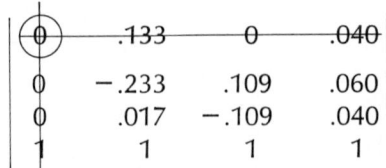

$$\begin{vmatrix} \boxed{0} & \cancel{.133} & \cancel{0} & \cancel{.040} \\ 0 & -.233 & .109 & .060 \\ 0 & .017 & -.109 & .040 \\ 1 & 1 & 1 & 1 \end{vmatrix}$$ 4×4 determinant

Step b:

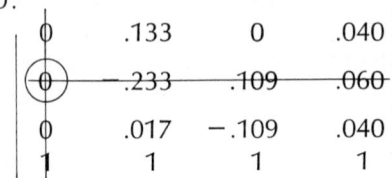

$$\begin{vmatrix} 0 & .133 & 0 & .040 \\ \boxed{0} & \cancel{-.233} & \cancel{.109} & \cancel{.060} \\ 0 & .017 & -.109 & .040 \\ 1 & 1 & 1 & 1 \end{vmatrix}$$ 4×4 determinant

Step c:

$$\begin{vmatrix} 0 & .133 & 0 & .040 \\ 0 & -.233 & .109 & .060 \\ \boxed{0} & \cancel{.017} & \cancel{-.109} & \cancel{.040} \\ 1 & 1 & 1 & 1 \end{vmatrix}$$ 4×4 determinant

Step d:

$$\begin{vmatrix} 0 & .133 & 0 & .040 \\ 0 & -.233 & .109 & .060 \\ 0 & .017 & -.109 & .040 \\ \boxed{1} & \cancel{1} & \cancel{1} & \cancel{1} \end{vmatrix}$$ 4×4 determinant

In steps a, b, and c, the value of the 4×4 determinants must be zero since the value of the 3×3 determinants is multiplied by the circled element zero. However, this is not true of step d, whose value is determined as follows:

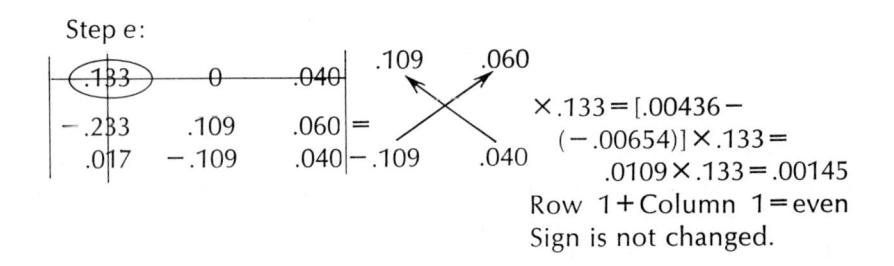

3×3 determinant $\begin{array}{c} \\ \\ \\ \end{array}\begin{vmatrix} \text{Col. 1} & \text{Col. 2} & \text{Col. 3} \\ .133 & 0 & .040 \\ -.233 & .109 & .060 \\ .017 & -.109 & .040 \end{vmatrix}\begin{array}{l} \text{Row 1} \\ \text{Row 2} \\ \text{Row 3} \end{array}$ Expand determinant by Column 1

Step e:

$$\begin{vmatrix} \boxed{.133} & \cancel{0} & \cancel{.040} \\ -.233 & .109 & .060 \\ .017 & -.109 & .040 \end{vmatrix} = \begin{vmatrix} .109 & .060 \\ -.109 & .040 \end{vmatrix} \times .133 = [.00436 - (-.00654)] \times .133 = .0109 \times .133 = .00145$$

Row 1 + Column 1 = even
Sign is not changed.

298 OPERATIONS RESEARCH MODELS—MATRIX ALGEBRA

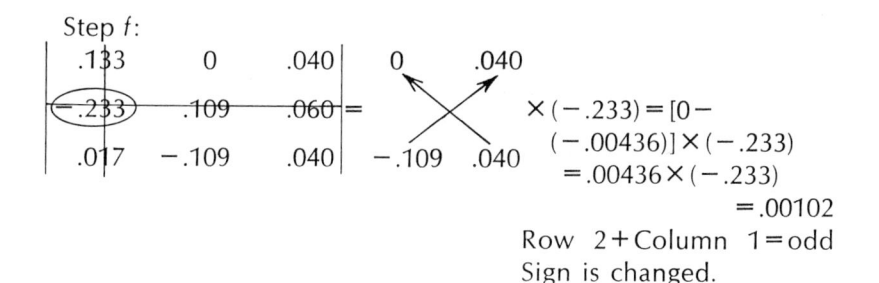

Step f:
$$\begin{vmatrix} .133 & 0 & .040 \\ \underline{-.233} & .109 & .060 \\ .017 & -.109 & .040 \end{vmatrix} = \begin{matrix} 0 & .040 \\ & \\ -.109 & .040 \end{matrix}$$

$\times (-.233) = [0 - (-.00436)] \times (-.233)$
$= .00436 \times (-.233)$
$= .00102$

Row 2 + Column 1 = odd
Sign is changed.

Step g:
$$\begin{vmatrix} .133 & 0 & .040 \\ -.233 & .109 & .060 \\ \underline{.017} & -.109 & .040 \end{vmatrix} = \begin{matrix} 0 & .040 \\ & \\ .109 & .060 \end{matrix}$$

$\times .017 = [0 - (.00436)] \times$
$.017 = -.00436$
$\times .017 = -.00007$

Row 3 + Column 1 = even
Sign is not changed.

Step d—sum of steps e, f, and g = +.00145 + .00102 − .00007
= .00240 (value of 3×3 determinant)

Value of step a = 0
Value of step b = 0
Value of step c = 0
Value of step d = −.00240 (Sums of steps e, f, and g = .00240 × 1)
Column 1 + Row 4 = odd
Sign is changed.

Value of determinant −.00240 (numerator for A)

Using the same procedure, the values for numerators B, C, and D are −.00282, −.00249, and −.00281, respectively. The same approach can be used for determining the denominator, its value being −.01052. A faster method is to expand the determinants using row 4, which amounts to adding determinant values for the numerators, A, B, C, and D (−.00240 −.00282 −.00249 −.00281 = −.01052). The resulting equilibrium shares for brands A, B, C, and D are:

$$A = \frac{-.00240}{-.01052} = 22.8\%$$
$$B = \frac{-.00282}{-.01052} = 26.8\%$$
$$C = \frac{-.00249}{-.01052} = 23.7\%$$
$$D = \frac{-.00281}{-.01052} = 26.7\%$$
$$\overline{100.0\%}$$

The solution to the preceding problem can be proven by multiplying the original matrix of transition probabilities by the equilibrium market shares.
It should be apparent that the nearer the initial market shares are to the

Procedure 1—Develop Matrix of Transition Probabilities

Determine the "hard-core component" or retentions (the groups that do not switch) and the "switching component" or gains and losses (the groups that do switch). In a matrix of transition probabilities, retentions are shown as values on the diagonal while gains become row values and losses become column values.

Procedure 2—Calculate Future Probable Market Shares

Calculate probable market shares for the next period (period two) by multiplying the original matrix of transition probabilities by the original market shares (period one). Similarly, multiplication of the original matrix of transition probabilities by period two market shares gives the results for period three. All remaining future probable market shares are calculated in a similar manner. An alternative method is raising the original matrix of transition probabilities to the desired power and multiplying by the original market shares. In such cases, computer programs are available for fast and accurate calculations.

Procedure 3—Determine Equilibrium Conditions

Changes in market shares between the equilibrium period and the period immediately preceding it are so small that they are treated mathematically as equal. Thus, equations can be developed for each row in the matrix of transition probabilities along with the addition of a final equation that sums all variables in the problem to 1.0. These equations can be solved simultaneously or by determinants.

Figure 9-3 Procedures utilized in Markov analysis of the first order.

final or equilibrium market shares, the faster equilibrium will be reached. If the beginning market shares are one-third each and the equilibrium shares are 30, 37, and 33 percent, it is obvious that equilibrium will be reached faster than if the initial market shares are 15, 55, and 30 percent.

The preceding procedures for determining probable future market shares with Markov chains of the first-order are summarized in Figure 9-3. Sometimes, the equilibrium state for market shares is not needed. In those cases, the third procedure is dropped. The procedures employed, then, are discretionary.

Management Uses of Markov Analysis

The preceding material treated the methodology of Markov analysis. Markov analysis is a marketing management tool for determining the appropriate marketing strategy of a firm. This can be illustrated by the following example where each firm has one-third of the market initially:

$$\begin{array}{c} \\ A \\ B \\ C \end{array} \begin{pmatrix} A & B & C \\ .5 & .3 & .1 \\ .2 & .6 & .2 \\ .3 & .1 & .7 \end{pmatrix} \begin{array}{l} \\ \text{Retention and gain} \rightarrow \\ \\ \text{Retention and loss} \downarrow \end{array}$$

Assuming the matrix of transition probabilities does not change, the equilibrium or long-run market shares of A, B, and C will be 27.8, 33.3, and 38.9 percent, respectively. Seller A, knowing that he expects to lose part of his market in the future, can do something about the situation today to prevent this unfortunate occurrence. A has two possible strategies available to him: he might try to retain more of his own customers (strategy 1) or he might direct his marketing efforts (advertising, personal selling, and promotion) at those customers who switch to B and C (strategy 2).

Referring to strategy 1, seller A might try to retain more of his customers, say from .5 to .7. This change assumes that A reduces his losses of customers to B and C. The new matrix of transition probabilities is:

$$\begin{array}{c} \\ A \\ B \\ C \end{array} \begin{pmatrix} A & B & C \\ .7 & .3 & .1 \\ .1 & .6 & .2 \\ .2 & .1 & .7 \end{pmatrix}$$

The new equilibrium market shares are: A, 38.6 percent; B, 27.0 percent; and C, 34.4 percent. Thus specific marketing efforts today have resulted in a more favorable position in the long-run for seller A.

The second strategy (or seller A directing his marketing efforts at those customers who switch to B and C) is shown in the revised matrix of transition probabilities:

$$\begin{array}{c} \\ A \\ B \\ C \end{array} \begin{pmatrix} A & B & C \\ .5 & .35 & .2 \\ .2 & .6 & .1 \\ .3 & .05 & .7 \end{pmatrix}$$

The calculation for the equilibrium market shares are: A, 32.6 percent; B, 19.0 percent; and C, 48.4 percent.

The question can be asked, what strategy is best for seller A? The cost factor of marketing efforts is the deciding factor, all things being equal. If the costs of the two strategies are the same, obviously strategy 1 is the better one. However, when the marketing cost factors are not the same, the choice of the appropriate answer will depend upon marginal analysis—the additional income versus the additional cost.

Other Uses of Markov Analysis

By no means is Markov analysis restricted to determining short-run and long-run market shares. Markov chains are being used by companies to aid in the analysis of its sales force manpower needs, such as illustrated for the American Products Corporation. Additional areas where Markov chains have been applied are estimation of the allowance for doubtful accounts in accounting and the introduction of a new product. Referring to the latter, a firm wants to judge how its new product, a bathroom cleaner, for example, will sell when placed on a supermarket shelf, beside a group of other bathroom cleaners. Some may be liquids in bottles, some powders in composite cans, some creams in plastic bottles, and some aerosols. This situation generally involves building mathematical models of how the customer's loyalty to a particular brand may switch or be switched. Actually, the firm's mathematicians will be explaining customer loyalty or lack thereof by building Markov chain models of consumer switching behavior.

Markov Analysis Application—American Products Corporation

Each year, the American Productions Corporation expects to lose a fraction of its manufacturing management through resignations, retirements, and deaths. It attempts to fill these vacant positions from within the firm before going to the outside for qualified personnel. In order to provide for a more orderly transition of replacing manufacturing management personnel, it has decided to employ Markov chains.

The initial procedure required for yearly manpower planning is to develop a matrix of transition probabilities—based on historical data of manufacturing management personnel. The transition probabilities are found by examining personnel records, noting each person's initial job and his job at the end of the year. For each manufacturing management position, the percentage of managers that remained in the same position for the whole year and the percentage that moved to other positions are calculated. Based on these historical data, a complete movement matrix is compiled for the first year per Table 9-6. The elements in each column give the probability that an individual will remain in the same position, move to another position, or leave the organization (exit category).

Since the matrix of transition probabilities is an estimate of manufacturing manpower movement for the next year, matrix multiplication can be used to predict future manpower movement. To determine expectations n years in the future, multiply the matrix by itself n times. In Table 9-7, the matrix of transition probabilities has been raised to the second power. This provides an estimate of where the original managers will be in two years. For example, a foreman has a .02 and .28 probability of being promoted to

TABLE 9-6
Matrix of Manufacturing Management Transition Probabilities for Year One—American Products Corporation

	Manufacturing Department Managers	Work Center Supervisors	Foremen	Exit from Firm
Manufacturing Department Managers	.95	.10	0	0
Work Center Supervisors	0	.75	.20	0
Foremen	0	.05	.65	0
Exit from Firm	.05	.10	.15	1.0
	1.0	1.0	1.0	1.0

TABLE 9-7
Matrix of Manufacturing Management Transition Probabilities for Year Two—
American Products Corporation

	Manufacturing Department Managers	Work Center Supervisors	Foremen	Exit from Firm
Manufacturing Department Managers	.9025	.1700	.0200	.0000
Work Center Supervisors	.0000	.5725	.2800	.0000
Foremen	.0000	.0700	.4325	.0000
Exit from Firm	.0975	.1875	.2675	1.0000
	1.0	1.0	1.0	1.0

manufacturing department manager and work center supervisor respectively in two years. Markov analysis, then, provides a basis for determining the likelihood of advancement as well as the number of individuals the firm must recruit each year to keep its positions filled.

Summary

This chapter has concentrated primarily on Markov chains of the first-order. The assumptions of stationary transition probabilities is critical to Markov brand-switching theory of the first-order. For the period during which the transition probabilities are stable, an equilibrium will result and can be calculated. However, if we know the transition probabilities will change due to internal or external conditions, these new figures can be used to calculate the equilibrium market shares. In this manner, Markov analysis can be used as a short-run, intermediate-run, or long-run marketing management tool.

Questions

1. What is Markov analysis?
2. Distinguish among Markov chains of the first-order, the second-order, and the third-order.
3. Describe the mathematical methods that are available for solving Markov chain problems.
4. Name additional business applications for Markov chains that are not set forth in the chapter.

Problems

9-1 Examine the matrices of transition probabilities and determine the equilibrium market shares for each firm. Explain your answer.

(a)

$$\begin{array}{c}\begin{array}{ccc}\text{Firm} & \text{Firm} & \text{Firm}\\ A & B & C\end{array}\\ \begin{array}{c}\text{Firm } A\\ \text{Firm } B\\ \text{Firm } C\end{array}\begin{pmatrix} .8 & 0 & 0\\ .1 & .8 & .4\\ .1 & .2 & .6\end{pmatrix}\end{array}$$

(b)

$$\begin{array}{c}\begin{array}{ccc}\text{Firm} & \text{Firm} & \text{Firm}\\ A & B & C\end{array}\\ \begin{array}{c}\text{Firm } A\\ \text{Firm } B\\ \text{Firm } C\end{array}\begin{pmatrix} 1.0 & .1 & .3\\ 0 & .8 & 0\\ 0 & .1 & .7\end{pmatrix}\end{array}$$

9-2 On January 1 (this year), Klosman Bakeries had 40 percent of its local market while the other two bakeries, A and B, have 40 percent and 20 percent, respectively, of the market. Based upon a study by a marketing research firm, the following facts were compiled. Klosman Bakeries retains 90 percent of its customers while gaining 5 percent of competitor A's customers and 10 percent of B's customers. Bakery A retains 85 percent of its customers while gaining 5 percent of Klosman's customers and 7 percent of B's customers. Bakery B retains 83 percent of its customers and gains 5 percent of Klosman's customers and 10 percent of A's customers. What will each firm's share be on January 1, next year, and what will each firm's market share be at equilibrium?

9-3 The Ribicoff Manufacturing Company is planning an extensive advertising campaign to increase the company's market share. Its executive committee is faced with the job of choosing between two campaigns that have been recommended. The committee has decided to test each proposal in two areas where the initial market shares of the competing firms and the initial transition probability matrices are the same. Also, the market shares are close to their national average, which are: brand R (Ribicoff), 28 percent; brand A, 39 percent; and brand B, 33 percent. In the two test areas, the initial market shares are: brand R, 30 percent; brand A, 40 percent; and brand B, 30 percent. The matrix of initial transition probabilities for both test areas is:

$$\begin{array}{c}\begin{array}{ccc}\text{Brand} & \text{Brand} & \text{Brand}\\ R & A & B\end{array}\\ \begin{array}{c}\text{Brand } R\\ \text{Brand } A\\ \text{Brand } B\end{array}\begin{pmatrix} .6 & .2 & .1\\ .3 & .7 & .1\\ .1 & .1 & .8\end{pmatrix}\end{array}$$

At the finish of the two different advertising programs in the two test areas, the transition probabilities, which were determined, are:

	Test Area 1			Test Area 2		
	Brand R	Brand A	Brand B	Brand R	Brand A	Brand B

$$\begin{array}{c} \text{Brand } R \\ \text{Brand } A \\ \text{Brand } B \end{array} \begin{pmatrix} .7 & .1 & .1 \\ .2 & .7 & .1 \\ .1 & .2 & .8 \end{pmatrix} \quad \begin{pmatrix} .8 & .1 & .2 \\ .1 & .7 & .1 \\ .1 & .2 & .7 \end{pmatrix}$$

(a) Using the initial matrix of transition probabilities, determine whether the test market shares at equilibrium for Ribicoff approach the national average.
(b) Assuming the advertising campaigns are equal in terms of cost, which advertising campaign gives the highest market share at equilibrium?

9-4 On July 1, the Hudson Chemical Company is competing with three other competitors in the area of a special chemical mixture. The market shares presently are: 24 percent for the Hudson Chemical Company, 29 percent for competitor A, 30 percent for competitor B, and 17 percent for competitor C. Over the past six months, the retentions and losses for the four firms are:

1. Hudson Chemical Company retains 70 percent of its customers while losing 20 percent to competitor A, 5 percent to competitor B, and 5 percent to competitor C.
2. Competitor A retains 65 percent of its customers while losing 15 percent to the Hudson Chemical Company, 10 percent to competitor B, and 10 percent to competitor C.
3. Competitor B retains 75 percent of its customers while losing 5 percent to the Hudson Chemical Company, 5 percent to competitor A, and 15 percent to competitor C.
4. Competitor C retains 70 percent of its customers while losing 10 percent to the Hudson Chemical Company, 10 percent to competitor A, and 10 percent to competitor B.

(a) What share of the total market is likely to be held by each company at the end of this year?
(b) Assuming no change in the rates of retention, gain, and loss, what is the long run market share for the Hudson Chemical Company?

9-5 On January 1, the Kummins Engine Company is competing with two other companies in the manufacturing of lightweight diesel engines. The market shares presently are: 61 percent for the Kummins Engine Company (A), 14 percent for competitor B, and 25 percent for competitor C. Over the past year, the percentage of retentions and losses for the three firms are:

	Customer Gains From			Customer Losses To		
Companies	A	B	C	A	B	C
Kummins	0%	5%	8%	0%	9%	6%
B	9	0	6	5	0	8
C	6	8	0	8	6	0

MARKOV ANALYSIS

Based upon the foregoing data, which is representative of future market movement, answer the following questions.
(a) What share of the total market is likely to be held by each company at the end of this year?
(b) Assuming no changes, what are the market shares for the three companies at the end of the following year?

9-6 The Racine Manufacturing Company has asked its advertising agency to develop two entirely different advertising programs to help one of the company's slow-moving product lines (floor wax). It was decided to use Columbus, Ohio, and Rochester, New York, as the test areas since both cities have a similar matrix of transition probabilities, that is, customer loyalty for the firm's product as well as gains and losses, for all practical purposes, are identical. The industry sales are $150 million. Racine has 30 percent of the market while its competitors have 40 percent (competitor A) and 30 percent (competitor B) of the total market. The net income as a percent of sales is a low 3 percent for Racine. The cost of advertising for test area number one (Columbus) is an additional $25,000 per year. Projected yearly sales in Columbus without additional advertising are $1.1 million. Cost of additional advertising in test area number two (Rochester) is $30,000. Comparable projected sales in Rochester without additional advertising are $1.2 million. The original matrix of transition probabilities for both test areas is:

$$\begin{array}{c c} & \begin{array}{ccc} \text{Racine} & \text{Comp. A} & \text{Comp. B} \end{array} \\ \begin{array}{c} \text{Racine} \\ \text{Comp. A} \\ \text{Comp. B} \end{array} & \begin{pmatrix} .75 & .15 & .10 \\ .15 & .80 & .10 \\ .10 & .05 & .80 \end{pmatrix} \end{array}$$

The new matrices of transition probabilities for several months which appear to be realistic for the entire year are:

	Columbus, Ohio			Rochester, N.Y.		
	Racine	Comp. A	Comp. B	Racine	Comp. A	Comp. B
Racine	.76	.20	.12	.75	.20	.11
Comp. A	.14	.77	.08	.13	.77	.07
Comp. B	.10	.03	.80	.12	.03	.82

Which of the two advertising programs appear best suited for the national market in terms of profits to Racine?

Bibliography

P. Billingsley, *Statistical Inference for Markov Processes*, Chicago: The University of Chicago Press, 1961.

K. L. Chung, *Markov Chains with Stationary Transition Probabilities*, Berlin: Springerverlag, 1960.

E. B. Dynkin, *Markov Processes*, Englewood Cliffs, N.J.: Prentice-Hall, 1965.

F. S. Hillier and G. J. Lieberman, *Introduction to Operations Research*, San Francisco: Holden-Day, 1967.

R. A. Howard, *Dynamic Probabilistic Systems* (two volumes), New York: John Wiley & Sons, 1971.

R. A. Howard, *Dynamic Programming and Markov Processes*, New York: John Wiley & Sons, 1960.

J. G. Kemeny and J. L. Snell, *Finite Markov Chains*, Princeton, New Jersey: Princeton University Press, 1960.

R. D. Luce and H. Raiffa, *Games and Decisions*, New York: John Wiley & Sons, 1957.

C. H. Springer, R. E. Herlihy, R. T. Mall, and R. I. Beggs, *Probabilistic Models*, Homewood, Ill.: Richard D. Irwin, 1968.

T. H. Williams and C. H. Griffin, *Management Information, A Quantitative Accent*, Homewood, Ill.: Richard D. Irwin, 1967.

4
Operations Research Models – Calculus

Chapter TEN
Classical Optimization Techniques

Business mathematical models are intended to be images of some portion of the real world. These representations enable the user to draw conclusions when translated back into the real world. Many of these mathematical models are flexible enough to allow alternative choices to be tested, either analytically or numerically. A model that accurately describes a portion of the business world not only adds to one's understanding of the problem, but also allows one to make a more reliable decision. Basically, the problem is to find the one best decision among many alternatives.

If the criterion is to choose the course of action that will produce the highest net profit, a model that predicts the likely profit for any action is of real value. The same rationale applies to those situations where an optimum selling price or lowest cost is desired. But what are the possibilities of building mathematical models which are capable of directly selecting the best choice without having to search through each and every alternative course of action? Such mathematical models can be constructed and take many forms.

In this chapter, we will optimize business problems using differential and integral calculus. For a brief review of their fundamentals, refer to Appendix B of this book. Likewise, the application of partial derivatives and the Langrange multiplier are demonstrated briefly for a typical business problem. This presentation represents a cross section of problems that can be solved using classical optimization techniques. In some of the subsequent chapters, basic OR models will employ some of these optimization techniques since other mathematical approaches fail either to solve the model or to give a satisfactory proof of the model.

Differentiation

Differentiation (differential calculus) is sometimes called the mathematics of change since it measures small changes in value. In the business problems illustrated within this chapter, attention is focused upon finding a point where the slope of the function to be optimized is zero or, stated another way, where a tangent to the curve is horizontal. The procedure for establishing a point of zero slope is to find the first derivative, set the first derivative equal to zero, and then solve the resultant equation. If a maximum point has been reached, the slope to the left is positive while the slope to the right is negative, illustrated in Figure 10-1a. Thus the slope changes from positive to negative as we traverse a maximum. Conversely, the slope changes from negative to positive as we traverse a minimum, shown in Figure 10-1b. As will be seen throughout the chapter, zero slope analysis not only is helpful in plotting curves, but more importantly in determining

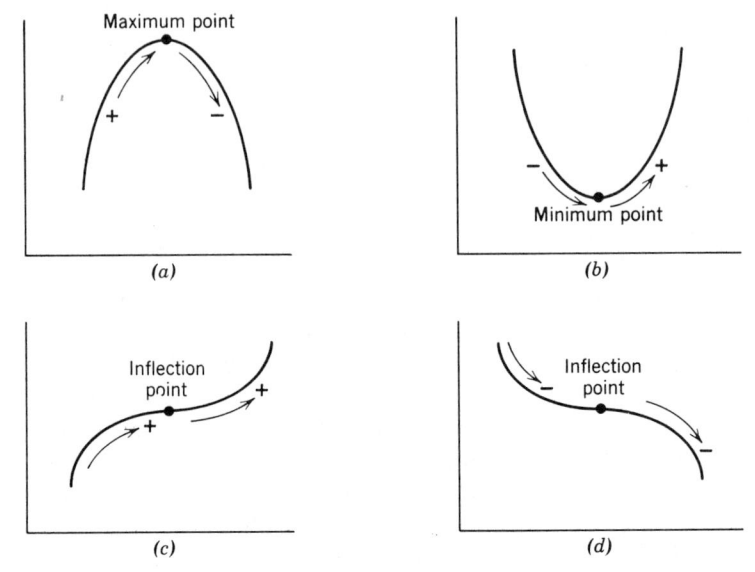

Figure 10-1 Zero slope analysis determines (a) the maximum value of a function, (b) the minimum value of a function, as well as (c) and (d) points of inflection.

the maximum and minimum values of a function, such as in maximizing profit or minimizing cost.

It should be noted than another condition—called an "inflection point"—exists when the slope starts either positively or negatively, levels off to zero, and then continues with the same slope with which it began. However, the condition of inflection points per Figure 10-1, c and d, will not be treated in this chapter.

Zero-slope analysis does not tell whether the point found is a maximum or a minimum. This can be established by finding the second derivative of the original function. The point of zero slope found is a maximum if the second derivative is negative. On the other hand, the point is a minimum if the second derivative at the point is positive. If the second derivative is zero, the test fails. It is then necessary to go back to the first derivative test and find points to the left and right so as to determine what condition exists. An inflection point or discontinuity may be present. As will be seen in this chapter and subsequent ones, the second derivative test will prove conclusively that maximum profits or minimum costs have been determined for the problem under study.

Differentiation Problem

An example may be helpful in demonstrating how differentiation is used in optimization of a business problem. Consider the total sales function where $S = -1000p^2 + 10,000p$ and the total cost function where $C = -2000p + 25,000$ (where p is the price of the new product). The problem is to find the optimal price for the new product. These equations for S and C

can be substituted into the profit equation [P (profits) equals S (total sales) minus C (total costs)] to determine the optimum price as follows:

$$P = S - C$$
$$P = -1000p^2 + 10{,}000p - (-2000p + 25{,}000)$$
$$P = -1000p^2 + 10{,}000p + 2000p - 25{,}000$$
$$P = -1000p^2 + 12{,}000p - 25{,}000$$
$$\frac{dP}{dp} = -2000p + 12{,}000 = 0 \quad \text{(first derivative)}$$
$$2000p = 12{,}000$$
$$p = \$6$$

Inspection of the above equation $P = -1000p^2 + 12{,}000p - 25{,}000$ reveals that the variable p in the first term is squared. The use of differentiation allows us to reduce the second power in this term by one.

Utilizing the formulas for differentiation, the approach to this problem is to employ the rules for the sum and difference of two functions. Whether formula 4 or 5 (Appendix B) is used, the essence of each formula is that the derivative of such an expansion $(-1000p^2 + 12{,}000p - 25{,}000)$ must be taken term by term. The first term, $-1000p^2$, can be differentiated by using the power formula 8 (Appendix B). The rule states that the derivative of a power is the original power (2) times a constant (-1000) with the new power being the value of the original power (2) minus one $(p^{2-1} = p)$. The first term after differentiating is $-2000p$. The second term, $12{,}000p$, can be differentiated by using formula 2 (and formula 3—Appendix B). Since C is a constant of 12,000 and p is analogous to x in the formula, the resulting value, after differentiation, is $+12{,}000$ ($12{,}000 \times 1$). The last term $(-25{,}000)$ requires the use of formula 1 (Appendix B) where the constant C is zero after differentiation. Finally, the whole equation is set equal to zero in order to solve for a maximum selling price or maximum point when graphed in terms of profits.[1]

Applying the second derivative test to determine whether we have actually solved for a maximum point, the value of the second derivative should be negative. The second derivative for this problem is as follows:

$$\frac{d^2P}{dp^2} = -2000(1) + 0$$

---

[1] This problem can be solved using algebra since the problem can be expressed as a quadratic. The quadratic formula is:

$$y = ax^2 + bx + c$$

Differentiating y with respect to x and setting the equation equal to zero for a point of zero slope, we get:

$$\frac{dy}{dx} = 2ax + b = 0$$

Thus,

$$x = \frac{-b}{2a} \quad \text{or} \quad p = \frac{-(+12{,}000)}{2(-1000)} = \frac{-12{,}000}{-2000} = \$6$$

CLASSICAL OPTIMIZATION TECHNIQUES

Using differentiation formula 2 (and formula 3—Appendix B), the value of the first term is −2000 while the constant +12,000 drops out after differention through the use of formula 1. The sign is negative. This indicates a maximum point on the profit (y axis) and price (x axis) curve has been reached and a selling price determined that will maximize profits for the firm.

This example raises several questions. For example, how was the total sales function determined, how was the total cost function determined, what would a graphical approach indicate, what is the optimum profit to be expected, and what is the quantity that can be expected to be sold at a price of $6? This problem was presented only to show how differential calculus can be used to solve a problem that ordinary algebra cannot. The example in the next section answers these questions.

Optimum Price and Profit Problem
Initially, some problems may have the outward appearances of being very difficult to solve. However, often an uncomplicated mathematical model can be constructed as the following example illustrates. The Lenox Manufacturing Company is considering marketing a new deluxe combination furnace-air conditioning unit for the better home market. Its market research department has forecasted demand and price relationships as follows:

Forecast	Proposed Selling Price	Estimated Demand—First Year
A	$1,000	6,000
B	2,000	4,000
C	3,000	2,000
D	4,000	0

The firm's cost accounting department in conjunction with its production control department has determined the annual fixed costs for the first year to be $100,000. This figure includes depreciation on proposed acquisitions of new machinery and equipment on a straight-line basis. The variable costs have been projected at $1000 per unit.

Based upon the preceding data, the problem can be solved by developing a mathematical model. The market forecast can be used to derive a market demand relation for the new product. The forecasted sales describes the interrelationship between the selling price (s) and expected unit sales (u). In Figure 10-2, expected unit sales (u) are plotted along the y axis while the selling price (s) is represented on the x axis. If forecast A is plotted, the point shown (for A) is located at the intersection of 6000 on the y axis and $1000 on the x axis. In like manner, forecasts B, C, and D are plotted in Figure 10-2. Obviously a linear relationship between demand and price exists.

The relationship between demand and selling price can be described in terms of an equation, the first step in developing the mathematical model. It can be said that demand is a function of price or demand is the dependent

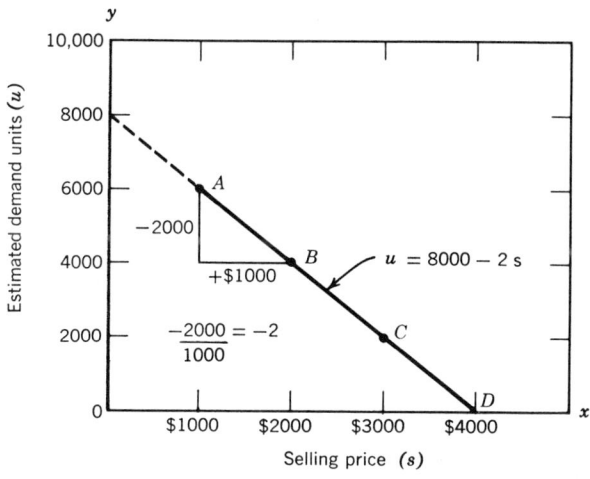

Figure 10-2 Forecasted demand—selling price relationship.

(endogenous) variable and price is the independent (exogenous) variable. Or to put it another way, demand will vary as price varies. Since we have a linear relationship, the equation for a straight line ($y = a + bx$) can be used where y is the dependent variable and x is the independent variable. The interrelationship between y and x is determined by a and b in the formula. Parameter a represents the intercept (the value of y when x equals zero) of the line while parameter b represents the slope of the line. Referring to Figure 10-2, the firm can expect to sell (or rather give away) 8000 units at a zero selling price (following the extended sloping line in Figure 10-2). Even though this demand relation exists only mathematically, being an extrapolation of the solid sloping line, it allows us to establish a value for "a" in the formula or 8000 units. Determining the value for "b," requires calculating the slope of the line, b. This can be calculated by using any two forecasts. Using forecasts A and B, the net change in price is plus $1000 (from $1000 to $2000) while the net change in demand is −2000 units (from 6000 units of 4000 units) for a slope of −2. This is in conformity with a basic principle of economics that there is an inverse relationship between demand and price. Substituting in the equation u and s for y and x, respectively, and 8000 and −2 for a and b, respectively, the resulting formula for demand and price is:

$$u = 8{,}000 - 2s \qquad \text{(Equation 10-1)}$$

The next step in developing the mathematical model is to determine an equation for new product cost—a relationship between fixed and variable costs. The firm's production control department estimates that it will cost $50,000 per annum for tooling costs in the form of depreciation on machinery and equipment. The firm's cost department estimates that other fixed costs will amount to $50,000 in the form of overhead (manufacturing, selling, general, and administrative expenses). The increased fixed costs of $100,000 for the new product is shown in Figure 10-3. The cost department

CLASSICAL OPTIMIZATION TECHNIQUES 315

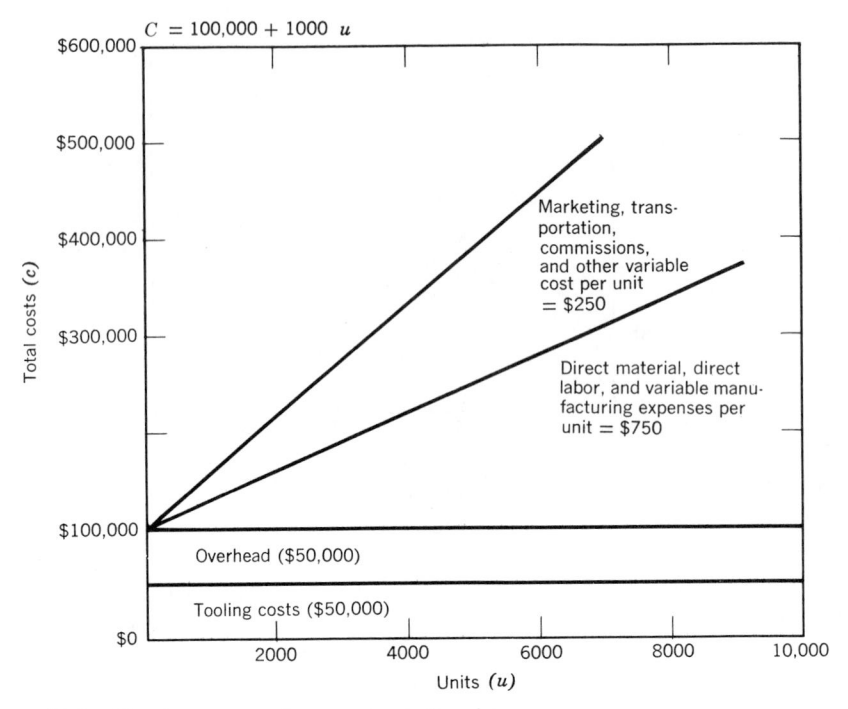

Figure 10-3 Firm's new product-cost relationship.

estimates that each deluxe furnace-air conditioning unit will cost $750 per unit in terms of direct manufacturing costs (direct material, direct labor, and variable direct manufacturing expenses) while the marketing, commissions, transportation, and other variable costs will be $250 per unit. The variable costs are $1000 per unit, shown in Figure 10-3. These cost estimates are combined to develop a new product total cost (C) equation as follows:

$$C = \$100{,}000 + \$1000u \qquad \text{(Equation 10-2)}$$

This expression means that if total sales are zero, the firm incurs $100,000 in fixed costs. Also, the firm spends $1000 per unit for variable costs. Using the equation for a straight line ($y = a + bx$), the parameter a equals $100,000 while parameter b equals $1000 per unit.

Having developed Equations 10-1 and 10-2, we can construct a mathematical model for the optimum pricing policy that will maximize the firm's total profits. Profits can be derived from the following expression:

$$P = S - C \qquad \text{(Equation 10-3)}$$

where

P = total profits
S = total sales
C = total costs

Referring to Equation 10-2, the total cost (C) equation was developed. How-

316 OPERATIONS RESEARCH MODELS—CALCULUS

ever, we still need an expression for the firm's total sales (S) which can be readily developed because:

$$S = u \cdot s \quad \text{(Equation 10-4)}$$

where

u = total demand
s = selling price per unit

In effect, Equation 10-4 defines total sales as the product of unit sales multiplied by unit selling price.

Combining Equations 10-4 and 10-1, the total sales (S) equation is as follows:

$$S = u \cdot s \quad \text{(Equation 10-4)}$$
$$u = 8000 - 2s \quad \text{(Equation 10-1)}$$
$$S = (8000 - 2s)s$$
$$S = 8000s - 2s^2 \quad \text{(Equation 10-5)}$$

Because Equation 10-5 is a quadratic function, the curve, plotted in Figure 10-4, is a parabola; it is symmetric with respect to the $2000 per unit selling price. Thus, as unit demand declines, the total sales will increase until a maximum point is reached at $2000 and will decline thereafter. Total dollar sales may also be calculated directly from Equation 10-4 (again demonstrating the maximum at $2000), as shown on the top of the next page.

Total profits (P), as defined in Equation 10-3, is shown in Figure 10-5. The total sales curve and the total cost curve correspond to the two curves

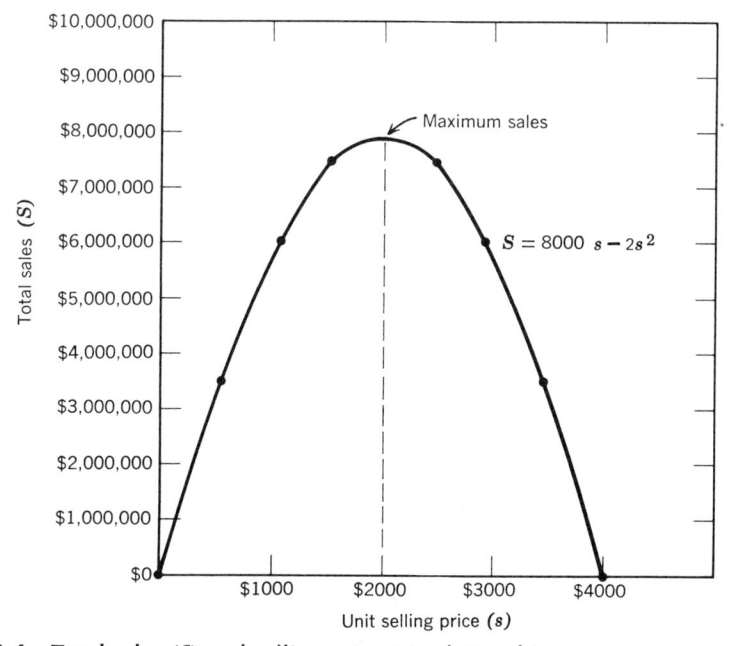

Figure 10-4 Total sales (S) and selling price (s) relationship.

CLASSICAL OPTIMIZATION TECHNIQUES 317

Selling Price (s)	×	Unit Sales (u)	=	Total Sales (S) (eq. 10-4)
$ 0		8,000		$ 0
500		7,000		3,500,000
1,000		6,000		6,000,000
1,500		5,000		7,500,000
2,000		4,000		8,000,000
2,500		3,000		7,500,000
3,000		2,000		6,000,000
3,500		1,000		3,500,000
4,000		0		0

in Figures 10-4 and 10-3, respectively. Two corresponding scales (unit sales and unit selling price) are shown on the x axis while dollar amounts (total sales and total costs) are shown on the y axis. This common vertical scale and double horizontal scale allow us to plot Equation 10-2 and Equation 10-5 on a single graph. The firm's profits are represented by the shaded area. There are breakeven price levels at points A and B, a selling price of less than $1000 or more than $4000 will yield a loss. The optimal profit point for the firm is that point at which the total sales curve is the greatest distance above the total cost curve. Graphically, the point of maximum profits is at a selling price of $2500.

While Figure 10-5 gives a graphic solution, the mathematical approach to the problem is easier to handle. We can use the profit maximization solution, or marginal revenue equals marginal cost solution. Initially, the optimal pricing (profit maximization) approach will be used. Equations 10-1 to 10-5,

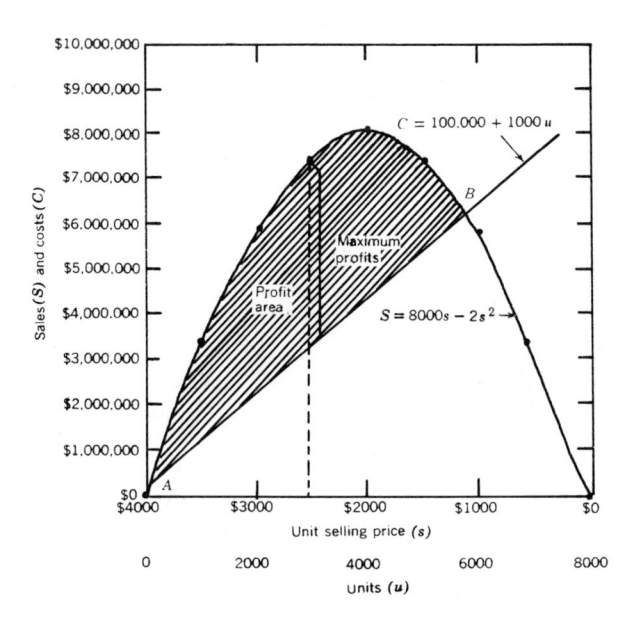

Figure 10-5 Total sales, total costs, and total profits.

which represent the complete pricing model, are reproduced below for convenience:

$$u = 8000 - 2s \quad \text{(Equation 10-1)}$$
$$C = 100{,}000 + 1000u \quad \text{(Equation 10-2)}$$
$$P = S - C \quad \text{(Equation 10-3)}$$
$$S = u \cdot s \quad \text{(Equation 10-4)}$$
$$S = 8000s - 2s^2 \quad \text{(Equation 10-5)}$$

Just as we developed Equation 10-5 from Equations 10-1 and 10-4, Equations 10-1 and 10-2 can be combined to produce a new equation for the total cost curve:

$$C = 100{,}000 + 1000(8000 - 2s)$$
$$C = 100{,}000 + 8{,}000{,}000 - 2000s$$
$$C = 8{,}100{,}000 - 2000s \quad \text{(Equation 10-6)}$$

Relating Equation 10-6 to Figure 10-5, the logic of this equation should be evident. If the firm's selling price is zero, total demand will be 8000 units [from Equation 10-1, $8000 - 2(0) = 8000$]. It will cost the firm $8,100,000 to produce and market the 8000 units [from Equation 10-2, $100{,}000 + 1000(8000) = 8{,}100{,}000$]. A one dollar increase in selling price will mean a decrease in demand by two units per Equation 10-1. A two unit decrease in demand will lead to a $2000 decrease in the firm's total variable cost [from Equation 10-2, $\$1000(-2) = -\$2000$]. Thus Equation 10-6 states an interrelationship between total cost and unit sales.

Now that all the necessary equations have been developed in the optimum pricing-maximum profits mathematical model, the final step is to substitute the appropriate equations into the profit equation as follows:

$$P = S - C \quad \text{(Equation 10-3)}$$
$$P = (8000s - 2s^2) - (8{,}100{,}000 - 2000s)$$
$$P = 8000s - 2s^2 - 8{,}100{,}000 + 2000s$$
$$P = -2s^2 + 10{,}000s - 8{,}100{,}000$$
$$\frac{dP}{ds} = -4s + 10{,}000 = 0$$
$$4s = 10{,}000$$
$$s = \$2500$$

In this solution, the basic concept of differential calculus is used, that is, we are concerned with the rate of change in the firm's profits (P) associated with a unit change in the firm's selling price (s). By making this rate of change equal to zero, we can solve for the maximum profits that results in an optimum pricing policy for the firm.

If the solution is not graphed as in Figure 10-5, how can we be sure that we have solved for an optimum selling price of $2500? Perhaps we have solved for a minimum selling price. Use of the second derivative test resolves this question:

$$\frac{d^2P}{ds^2} = -4 + 0$$

Since the second term becomes zero for its second derivative, the only remaining term is the first one. When this first term is differentiated for the second time, it becomes -4. A negative value, when evaluated from the results of the first derivative being set equal to zero, indicates that the slope has reached its maximum point and is declining. Thus this second derivative test is in agreement with Figure 10-5. Otherwise, if the sign were plus for the integer, it would have indicated that we had made an error in our calculations or we had solved for a minimum sales price. A positive answer in a second derivative test (evaluated for the result of the first derivative set equal to zero) indicates that the slope has reached its minimum point and is tending upward.

The second approach in solving this problem, marginal analysis, represents the net addition to the firm's total revenue and the cost resulting from the sale or production of one additional unit of output. Given the firm's total sales function and total cost function, the corresponding marginal revenue and marginal cost equations can be derived for the firm using differentiation. The firm's marginal revenue $\frac{dS}{ds}$ is the first derivative of the total sales relation:

$$S = 8000s - 2s^2 \qquad \text{(Equation 10-5)}$$
$$\frac{dS}{ds} = 8000 - 4s \qquad \text{(Equation 10-7)}$$

Similarly, the firm's marginal cost $\frac{dC}{ds}$ is the first derivative of the total cost relation:

$$C = 8,100,000 - 2000s \qquad \text{(Equation 10-6)}$$
$$\frac{dC}{ds} = -2000 \qquad \text{(Equation 10-8)}$$

The firm's profits will be at a maximum when marginal revenue $\frac{dS}{ds}$ equals marginal cost $\frac{dC}{ds}$ as follows:

$$\frac{dS}{ds} = \frac{dC}{ds}$$
$$8000 - 4s = -2000$$
$$4s = 10,000$$
$$s = \$2500$$

The optimum selling price is the same as that using the first approach.

Having determined the optimum selling price mathematically, the total maximum profits can be calculated by substituting the value for s (\$2500) in Equation 10-3 (modified) as follows:

$$P = (8000 - 2s)s - (8,100,000 - 2000s)$$

$$P = [8000 - 2(2500)]2500 - [8,100,000 - 2000(2500)]$$
$$P = (3000)2500 - (8,100,000 - 5,000,000)$$
$$P = 7,500,000 - 3,100,000$$
$$P = \$4,400,000$$

Profit (before federal income taxes) based on sales and cost estimates is $4,400,000 the first year.

In addition to profits, management would want to know the number of units that it should produce at a unit price of $2500. This can be calculated as follows:

$$u = 8000 - 2s \qquad \text{(Equation 10-1)}$$
$$u = 8000 - 2(2500)$$
$$u = 3000 \text{ units}$$

Although this problem can be solved graphically for optimum selling price, maximum profits, and expected demand, the mathematical solution is easier to handle and is more accurate since graphs are sometimes difficult to read accurately. If the firm chooses a selling price that is less than optimal, a decrease in total profits will result. Conversely, if the firm chooses a price that is greater than optimal, the increase in price will yield a decrease in total profits. Thus, only one selling price exists which yields a maximum total profit. This point is $2500 for the Lenox Manufacturing Company, the optimal pricing point.

Integration

Integration is often referred to as finding antiderivatives or procedures that reverse the process of finding derivatives. However, integration is generally defined as the process of summing the intervals under a curve. The process of summation used within this chapter requires the utilization of the definite integral, that is, the area(s) bounded by curves and lines are known within the problem. Indefinite integration differs from definite integration in that the limits of the integrals are not specified; thus, integration formulas given in Appendix B contain an arbitrary constant (C).

To illustrate the concept of integrating or summing, consider Figure 10-6 where the area under the curve between limits t_1 and t_2 is designated by S—the total sales over the period t_1 to t_2. Total sales are given by the following formula:

$$S = \int_{t_1}^{t_2} dA \qquad \text{(Equation 10-9)}$$

The elemental area dA is the area bounded by the rectangle, with sides dt and $f(t)$. This sales area is:

$$dA = f(t)\, dt \qquad \text{(Equation 10-10)}$$

CLASSICAL OPTIMIZATION TECHNIQUES

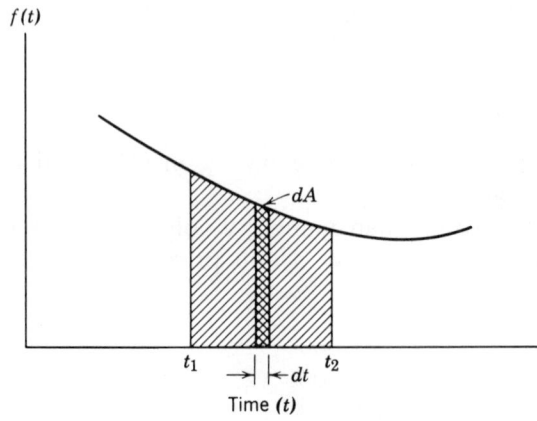

Figure 10-6 Areas by integration where sales are decreasing between limits t_1 and t_2.

Thus, the total sales area (shaded area in Figure 10-6) is given by the following formula:

$$S = \int_{t_1}^{t_2} f(t)\, dt \qquad \text{(Equation 10-11)}$$

which upon integration yields:

$$S = F(t) \Big|_{t_1}^{t_2}$$

Substituting the limits of integration to obtain the final formula for total sales gives:

$$S = F(t_2) - F(t_1)$$

(Equation 10-12, same as Equation B-13 in Appendix B)

This means that total sales for the period is equal to the difference between the total sales function evaluated at t_2 (end of the period) and the total sales function evaluated at t_1 (beginning of the period).

Integration Problem

The following example illustrates the use of integration. A firm is reviewing its current sales and past sales records for a particular product with the intention of forecasting its total sales for the coming year. The sales rate for this product at the start of the year was 160,000 units per year on an annual basis. This means that 160,000 units would be sold during the entire year if sales remained at the same level as during the start of the year.

An examination of the initial sales data for each of the past two years discloses, however, that sales (S) have not remained constant during the years, but have been growing in a nonlinear fashion. The sales rates (S') for this product were 130,000 units and 110,000 units for the last year and the preceding year, respectively, at the start of the year. These sales rates are shown in Figure 10-7. (Graphically, a sales rate at some time t can be defined as the slope of the tangent line to the sales curve at that point.)

The objective in the problem is to forecast total sales (S) for the current year—between year 2 and 3 in Figure 10-7. But before doing so, it is necessary to determine an equation for the sales rate (S'). The annual sales rate (S') is to be treated as a parabola, that is, $S' = A + Bt + Ct^2$ where t is time in years and A, B, and C are constants. The following is used in determining the unknown constants: when $t=0$, $S'=110,000$; when $t=1$, $S'=130,000$; and when $t=2$, $S'=160,000$. Substituting the above values into the original equation gives:

$$A = 110,000 \qquad A + B + C = 130,000 \qquad \text{and } A + 2B + 4C = 160,000$$

Using simultaneous equations (based on the last two equations) to solve for B and C, we find $B = 15,000$ and $C = 5000$ while $A = 110,000$ as given. Thus, the equation that gives an instantaneous rate for sales at time t is:

$$S' = 110,000 + 15,000t + 5000t^2 \qquad \text{(Equation 10-13)}$$

We can now predict the total sales for the current year (S_{2-3}, between $t=2$ and $t=3$) by utilizing Equation 10-13 as follows:

$$S_{2-3} = \int_2^3 S' \, dt$$

$$\int_2^3 S' \, dt = \int_2^3 (110,000 + 15,000t + 5000t^2) \, dt$$

$$S_{2-3} = \int_2^3 (110,000 + 15,000t + 5000t^2) \, dt$$

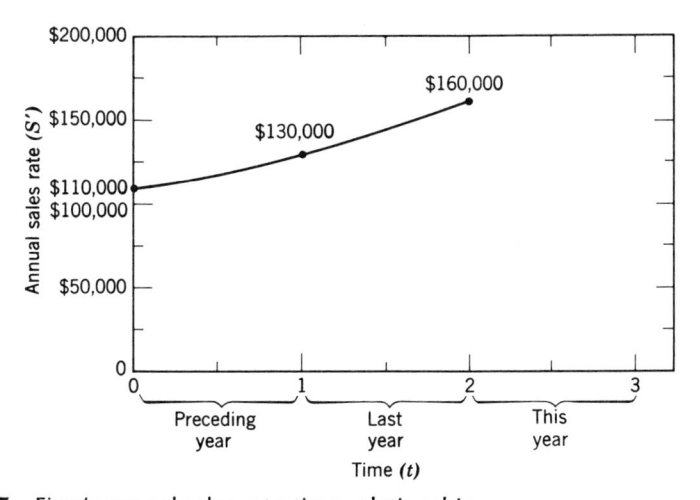

Figure 10-7 Firm's annual sales rate-time relationship.

CLASSICAL OPTIMIZATION TECHNIQUES 323

Referring to integration formula 4 (summation) in Appendix B, the preceding equation can be written as:

$$S_{2-3} = \int_2^3 (110{,}000)\, dt + \int_2^3 (15{,}000t)\, dt + \int_2^3 (5000t^2)\, dt$$

(Equation 10-14)

Using integration formulas 2 and 3 for the first term and integration formula 6 for the second and third terms from Appendix B, the equation is:

$$S_{2-3} = 110{,}000 t \Big|_2^3 + \frac{15{,}000 t^2}{2} \Big|_2^3 + \frac{5000 t^3}{3} \Big|_2^3$$

The last procedure in this problem is to use Equation 10-12 to determine a value when $t=2$ and $t=3$. The calculations are as follows:

$$S_{2-3} = \left[110{,}000\,(3) + \frac{15{,}000}{2}(3)^2 + \frac{5000}{3}(3)^3 \right]$$
$$- \left[110{,}000\,(2) + \frac{15{,}000}{2}(2)^2 + \frac{5000}{3}(2)^3 \right]$$

$S_{2-3} = 179{,}170$ units

The total sales during the year is therefore 179,170 units.

The sales rate at the start of the next year or the end of the current year can be calculated from Equation 10-13 as follows:

$$S' = 110{,}000 + 15{,}000(3) + 5{,}000(3)^2$$
$$= 110{,}000 + 45{,}000 + 45{,}000$$
$$= 200{,}000 \text{ units per year}$$

In summary, the product started the year with a sales rate of 160,000 units per year and should end the year with a sales rate of 200,000 units per year, with 179,170 units forecasted to be sold during the year. Illustrated in Figure 10-8 are the total sales for the coming year and all of the sales rates pertinent to the problem.

Equipment Investment Problem

When considering production equipment, two basic types of equipment are found in a firm, diminishing efficiency type and constant efficiency type. The first relates to durable goods whose lifetime can be extended almost indefinitely if their parts are replaced or repaired regularly (e.g., a lathe), whereas the second type of capital goods can produce some output at a given level until their productive life suddenly comes to an end (e.g., specialized machinery on automated production line). Our concern here is with equipment of the diminishing efficiency type, which tends to decline in productivity and/or increase in maintenance cost as it is used over time. If a piece of manufacturing equipment earns revenue (R) according to some function $R(t)$, it does so by incurring operating and maintenance expenses (E) according to some function $E(t)$ (excludes depreciation and interest on money). The value (V) of the investment to the firm can be given as follows:

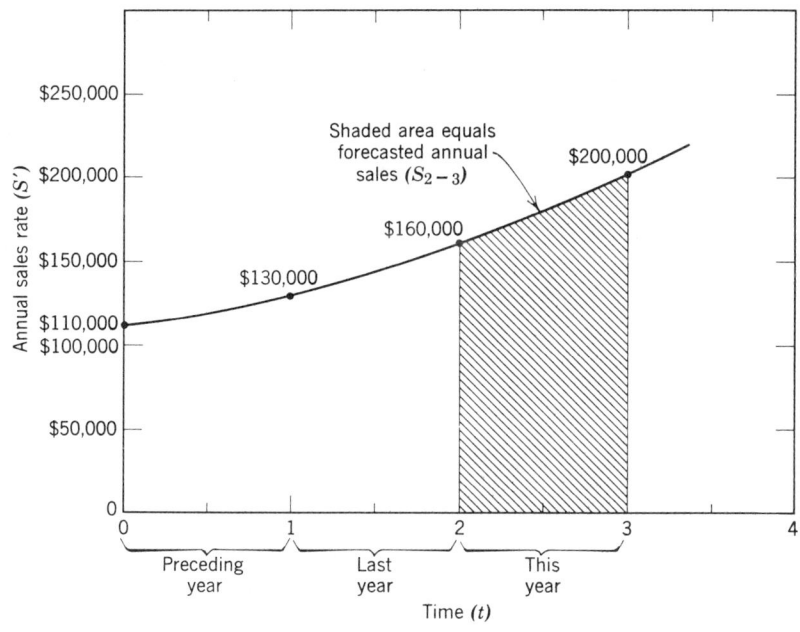

Figure 10-8 Firm's annual sales rate-time relationship showing forecasted sales.

$$V = \int_0^T [R(t) - E(t)]e^{-it}\,dt + S(T)e^{-iT} - C$$

(Equation 10-15)

where

V = present value of the equipment if salvaged or sold at time T

$\int_0^T R(t)e^{-it}\,dt$ = present or discounted value of the continuous stream of revenue, $t=0$ to $t=T$

$\int_0^T E(t)e^{-it}\,dt$ = present value of the continuous stream of operating and maintenance expenses, $t=0$ to $t=T$

$S(T)e^{-iT}$ = present value of the salvage or resale price at time T

C = initial purchase price of the equipment, freight cost, and installation cost

e^{-it} = present value factor when the annual rate of return i is discounted continuously over time t

$e = 2.71828$, the base of natural logarithms

i = annual rate of interest or the minimum rate of return which management expects to earn on this type of investment

Equation 10-15 gives the present value of a piece of equipment. It is equal to the sum of the discounted difference between revenues and expenses over its useful life (0 to time T) plus the discounted value of the equipment at time T, less its initial cost. The economic life of the asset (T) can be determined by setting the first derivative of V with respect to T in Equation 10-15 equal to zero per the following (first term, derivative of the integral, is equal to the function inside the integral; second term, differentiation formula 6; and third term, differentiation formula 1):

$$\frac{dV}{dT} = [R(T) - E(T)]e^{-iT} - iS(T)e^{-iT} + S'(T)e^{-iT} = 0$$

$$R(T) - E(T) = iS(T) - S'(T) \qquad \text{(Equation 10-16)}$$

In Equation 10-16, e^{-iT} divides out since this factor is common to all terms in the equation. The economic life of the equipment is reached when the difference between falling revenue and rising maintenance cost equals the interest on the salvage value plus the rate with which salvage value is declining [since rate $S'(T)$ is negative, a minus sign in front makes it positive]. Given the values for the functions in Equation 10-16, we can find the optimal economic life for the equipment by solving for T. The value for T can be substituted in Equation 10-15 and the appropriate value for V can be determined.

For example, the Argus Manufacturing Company has gathered data on a major new piece of machinery for its fabric coating department. The figures were obtained from the controller's office in conjunction with conferences from a supplier of this type machinery. The total cost of the new machine is $100,000 (C). The annual revenue (R) of $30,000 is expected to decrease at an exponential rate ($e^{-0.10t}$) while maintenance expenses are expected to be $1000 per year and operating expenses are $100 initially per year, increasing at an exponential rate ($e^{0.05t}$). The salvage value (S) is expected to fall exponentially ($e^{-0.02t}$). The minimum rate of return (i) which management expects to earn on this investment is 10 percent. The functions for Equations 10-15 and 16 are as follows:

$$R(t) = \$30,000e^{-0.10t}$$
$$E(t) = \$1000 + \$100e^{0.05t}$$
$$S(t) = \$100,000e^{-0.02t}$$
$$S'(t) = -.02(\$100,000e^{-0.02t})$$
$$i = .10 \text{ per year}$$

Substituting the preceding functions in Equation 10-16, the equation that solves for T is:

$$30,000e^{-0.10T} - (1000 + 100e^{0.05T})$$
$$= (0.10)(100,000e^{-0.02T}) - (-0.02)(100,000e^{-0.02T})$$
$$30,000e^{-0.10T} - 100e^{0.05T} - 12,000e^{-0.02T} = 1000$$

Using a table of exponential functions with a base e (see Appendix D), various values are substituted in the above equation for T. The value of 10 for T is shown as follows:

$$30,000(0.3679) - 100(1.6487) - 12,000(0.8187) = 1046$$

The optimal T equals approximately 10 years since the solution is approximately 1000 (1046) when T equals 10. Hence, the optimal economic life (T) means that at the end of the tenth year, the machine will have paid for itself while earning a 10 percent return on the investment of $100,000.

Having developed a value for T, we can determine the present cash value of the machine if it is used for 10 years. Substituting the functions given above and T=10 in Equation 10-15, the integrated equation is:

$$V(10) = \int_0^{10} [(30{,}000e^{-0.10t}) - (1000 + 100e^{0.05t})]e^{-0.10t} dt$$
$$+ (100{,}000e^{-0.02T})e^{-0.10T} - 100{,}000$$

$$V(10) = \int_0^{10} [(30{,}000e^{-0.20t}) - (1000e^{-0.10t}) - (100e^{-0.05t})] dt$$
$$+ 100{,}000e^{-0.12T} - 100{,}000$$

The next step is to integrate between the limits, 0 to 10, per Equation 10-12:

$$V(10) = \left[\left(\frac{30{,}000}{-0.20}e^{-0.20t}\right) - \left(\frac{1000}{-0.10}e^{-0.10t}\right) - \left(\frac{100}{-0.05}e^{-0.05t}\right)\right]_0^{10}$$
$$+ 100{,}000e^{-0.12T} - 100{,}000$$

$$V(10) = [-150{,}000e^{-2} - (-150{,}000e^0)] - (-10{,}000e^{-1} + 10{,}000e^0)$$
$$- (-2000e^{-0.5} + 2000e^0) + 100{,}000e^{-1.2} - 100{,}000$$

Using the table of exponential functions in Appendix D, we can determine a value for V:

$$V(10) = -150{,}000(0.1353) + 150{,}000 + 10{,}000 (0.3679) - 10{,}000$$
$$+ 2000(0.6065) - 2000 + 100{,}000(0.3012) - 100{,}000$$

$$V(10) = \$52{,}717$$

The present cash value is $52,717 if the equipment is salvaged or sold at the end of the tenth year. This illustration reflects the calculations for only one machine. Values for comparable machines could have been made to serve as a criterion for selecting the most profitable among alternative equipment investments. If a decision is to be made among several alternatives, the one yielding the greatest V would be selected. Thus Equation 10-15 can be called an equipment selection model and can be modified to determine the optimal replacement cycle for a group of machines. Also, this basic model can be modified as a minimum cost model for replacement of equipment.

Partial Derivatives

Partial derivatives are demonstrated in the next section on Lagrange multipliers and in the subsequent section on an optimization problem for the Cronin Manufacturing Company. They can be used in finding optimum solutions for problems but, many times, become intermediate procedures for solving optimization problems. This latter approach will be demonstrated in the next two sections. Utilization of partial derivatives will also be evident in the chapter on nonlinear programming.

Basic partial differentiation procedures provide a solution for problems that treat the effects of change in two variables on a third. The approach of partial differentiation is to act as though the variables in the problem are varying one at a time when applying the formulas for differentiation. Even though several variables are present in the problem, the formulas for differentiation can be used for one variable at a time, while considering the other variables as constants.

Consider the formula $Q = ax + by + c$ where x and y are independent variables while a, b, and c are constants. We desire to investigate how the quantity Q varies. If for the moment we consider y a constant and take the derivative of Q with respect to the variable x, we find what is called the partial derivative of Q with respect to x:

$$\frac{\delta Q}{\delta x} = a + 0 + 0 = a$$

(Differentiation formula 1, derivative of a constant is zero for second and third terms)

Similarly, letting x be a constant, the partial derivative of Q with respect to y is:

$$\frac{\delta Q}{\delta y} = 0 + b + 0 = b$$

The above symbol δ is used to distinguish a partial derivative from a total derivative. A partial derivative has meaning only when a function may contain more than one independent variable.

Having an understanding of partial derivatives, we can now write an expression for the total derivative which is:

$$dZ = \left(\frac{\delta Z}{\delta x}\right) dx + \left(\frac{\delta Z}{\delta y}\right) dy \qquad \text{(Equation 10-17)}$$

where $Z = f(x, z)$. Thus, the total differentiation in our example becomes:

$$dQ = a\, dx + b\, dy$$

Lagrange Multipliers

The differentiation method presented so far in the chapter has been rather straightforward. For example, the optimization problem, presented in the first part of the chapter for the Lenox Manufacturing Company, results in the development of a profit equation (Equation 10-3) in which all terms on the right hand side of the equation are the same. Hence, by taking the derivative of profits (P) with respect to selling price (s) and setting the slope equal to zero, we solved for the maximum profits and optimum selling price. However, when several terms and/or constraints appear on the right hand side of a profit equation, the procedures for solving this problem become long and drawn out, as will be demonstrated for the Cronin Manufacturing Company in the next section. A simplified approach, employing Lagrange multipliers, optimizes a function subject to these terms and/or constraints in which it is not necessary to incorporate the terms and/or constraints into the function to be optimized. This improved approach will be demonstrated for the Cronin Manufacturing Company.

The basics of Lagrange multipliers can be illustrated by considering the general problem of finding the extreme or boundary points of $z = f(x,y)$ subject to the constraint $g(x,y)$. Three equations,

$$\frac{\delta}{\delta x} f(x,y) = f_x(x,y) = 0 \qquad \frac{\delta}{\delta y} f(x,y) = f_y(x,y) = 0 \qquad g(x,y) = 0$$

must be satisfied by the pair of unknowns x and y. This system of equations is somewhat difficult to solve since there are more equations than unknowns. Using the Lagrange multipliers, and unknown λ (artificial), the Lagrangian expression for the general problem is:

$$L(x,y,\lambda) = f(x,y) + \lambda g(x,y) \qquad \text{(Equation 10-18)}$$

Inspection of Equation 10-18 indicates that L is a function of the three variables x, y, and λ. The necessary conditions for maximum or minimum points of this function are the three equations:

$$\frac{\delta L}{\delta x} = 0 \qquad \frac{\delta L}{\delta y} = 0 \qquad \frac{\delta L}{\delta \lambda} = 0$$

These three equations can be rewritten as:

$$\frac{\delta L}{\delta x} = \frac{\delta}{\delta x}(f + \lambda g) = f_x + \lambda g_x \qquad \text{or} \qquad f_x(x,y) + \lambda g_x(x,y) = 0$$

$$\frac{\delta L}{\delta y} = \frac{\delta}{\delta y}(f + \lambda g) = f_y + \lambda g_y \qquad \text{or} \qquad f_y(x,y) + \lambda g_y(x,y) = 0$$

$$\frac{\delta L}{\delta \lambda} = \frac{\delta}{\delta \lambda}(f + \lambda g) = g \qquad \text{or} \qquad g(x,y) = 0$$

The last equation above is actually the constraint equation. If an extreme point (x_m, y_m) of L is found, it will satisfy the constraint equation. Equation 10-18 can now be rewritten as:

$$L(x_m, y_m, \lambda) = f(x_m, y_m) + \lambda g(x_m, y_m) = f(x_m, y_m) \qquad \text{(Equation 10-19)}$$

where $g(x_m, y_m) = 0$. The values of L and f are the same at the maximum and minimum points of L.

Optimization Problem

The operations research team of the Cronin Manufacturing Company has been asked to investigate whether an increase in price from $1.00 to $1.10 will increase profits beyond the present level for its major product E. In addition, the team has been asked to determine and verify advertising and quality control costs that will maximize profits for the present price and if the price is increased.

The cost accounting department of the firm has been able to isolate the costs with a high degree of accuracy for this product. The annual total fixed costs, except for costs of quality control (Q) and advertising (A), are $15 million, while total variable costs, other than transportation charges (paid by customer), are $0.50 per unit times millions of units sold (N). The total cost (C) equation for product E, in terms of millions of dollars and units, can be written as:

$$C = 15 + 0.50N + Q + A \qquad \text{(Equation 10-20)}$$

The operations research team had a more difficult time with the total sales forecasting function (S) than it did with the cost function. After considerable experimenting with the relationship of sales, quality control, and advertising expenditures, it was able to develop the following relationships (where P equals selling price):

$$N = 150 - 15P + 0.2AQ + Q + 2A \qquad \text{(Equation 10-21)}$$
$$S = N \cdot P = 150P - 15P^2 + 0.2PAQ + PQ + 2PA \qquad \text{(Equation 10-22)}$$

The net profit function before federal income taxes ($P_n = S - C$), based upon Equations 10-20 to 10-22, is written as follows:

$$\begin{aligned}
P_n &= S - C \\
&= (150P - 15P^2 + 0.2PAQ + PQ + 2PA) - (15 + 0.5N + Q + A) \\
&= 150P - 15P^2 + 0.2PAQ + PQ + 2PA - 15 \\
&\quad - 0.5(150 - 15P + 0.2AQ + Q + 2A) - Q - A \\
&= 150P - 15P^2 + 0.2PAQ + PQ + 2PA - 15 \\
&\quad - 75 + 7.5P - 0.1AQ - 0.5Q - A - Q - A \\
&= -90 + 157.5P - 15P^2 + 0.2PAQ + PQ + 2PA \\
&\quad - 0.1AQ - 1.5Q - 2A \qquad \text{(Equation 10-23)}
\end{aligned}$$

The net profit for product E now can be thought of in terms of a function of three variables, P (selling price), Q (quality control cost), and A (advertising cost). In addition to the equations that have been developed, there is one more equation that is required. The budgetary constraint or the annual amount available for advertising and quality control of product E is $17.5 million. The budgetary constraint in millions of dollars is:

$$Q + A = \$17.5 \text{ million} \qquad \text{(Equation 10-24)}$$

The first question, whether the price increase will result in more profits, can be answered by solving when $P = \$1.00$ and $P = \$1.10$. The price variable can be removed from Equation 10-23 by substituting its actual value.

$$P_n = -90 + 157.5(1) - 15(1)^2 + 0.2(1)AQ + (1)Q + 2(1)A - 0.1AQ - 1.5Q - 2A$$
$$P_n = -90 + 157.5 - 15 + 0.2AQ + Q + 2A - 0.1AQ - 1.5Q - 2A$$

Now P_n is a function of two variables, Q and A. However, by restating Equation 10-24 in terms of Q as:

$$Q = 17.5 - A$$

330 OPERATIONS RESEARCH MODELS—CALCULUS

the P_n function becomes a function of one variable, A. The revised P_n equation is:

$$P_n = -90 + 157.5 - 15 + 0.2A(17.5 - A) + (17.5 - A) + 2A$$
$$-0.1A(17.5 - A) - 1.5(17.5 - A) - 2A$$
$$= -90 + 157.5 - 15 + 3.5A - 0.2A^2 + 17.5 - A + 2A$$
$$-1.75A + 0.1A^2 - 26.25 + 1.5A - 2A$$
$$= 43.75 + 2.25A - 0.1A^2 \qquad \text{(Equation 10-25)}$$

Maximum profit can be determined for the optimum level of advertising by finding the first derivative of Equation 10-25 and setting it equal to zero:

$$P_n = 43.75 + 2.25A - 0.1A^2 \qquad \text{(Equation 10-25)}$$
$$\frac{dP_n}{dA} = 2.25 - 0.2A = 0$$
$$0.2A = 2.25$$
$$A = \$11.25 \text{ million for advertising at a price of } \$1.00$$

The second derivative of the preceding equation is:

$$\frac{d^2 P_n}{dA^2} = 0 - 0.2$$

This indicates that a maximum has been found. The value for Q can be determined:

$$Q = 17.5 - A$$
$$= 17.5 - 11.25$$
$$= \$6.25 \text{ million for quality control}$$

The levels of advertising ($11.25 million) and quality control ($6.25 million) that will maximize profits with a unit price of $1 have been determined. The maximum expected profits is $56.4 million, calculated as follows from Equation 10-23 (when $P = \$1.00$, $A = \$11.25$ million, and $Q = \$6.25$ million):

$$P_n = -90 + 157.5P - 15P^2 + 0.2PAQ + PQ + 2PA - 0.1AQ - 1.5Q - 2A$$
$$= -90 + 157.5(1) - 15(1)^2 + 0.2(1)(11.25)(6.25) + (1)(6.25)$$
$$+ 2(1)(11.25) - 0.1(11.25)(6.25) - 1.5(6.25) - 2(11.25)$$
$$= -90 + 157.5 - 15 + 14.0625 + 6.25 + 22.50 - 7.03125 - 9.375 - 22.50$$
$$= \$56.4 \text{ million}$$

The same mathematical procedures can be used for the proposed selling price of $1.10, assuming that Equation 10-22 for the sales function will not be affected by the price increase of $0.10. The P_n equation becomes:

$$P_n = 58.10 + 2.70A - 0.12A^2 \qquad \text{(Equation 10-26)}$$

The first derivative of Equation 10-26 set equal to zero is:

$$\frac{dP_n}{dA} = 2.70 - 0.24A = 0$$
$$0.24A = 2.70$$
$$A = \$11.25 \text{ million}$$

The second derivative of the above equation is:

$$\frac{d^2 P_n}{dA^2} = 0 - 0.24 \quad \text{(Minus indicates a maximum has been reached.)}$$

Advertising (A) and quality control (Q) are again the amounts that will maximize profits for the firm. When the selling price is $1.10, advertising is $11.25 million, and quality control cost is $6.25 million, the net profits are $73.3 million. When compared with the present selling price of $1.00, an additional $16.9 million profit can be made.

Having answered management's initial question regarding product E, the firm's operations research team has been asked to verify that a price of $1.00 will result in advertising and quality control expenses of $11.25 million and $6.25 million respectively. Also, management has asked the OR team to verify that the price increase to $1.10 will result in advertising and quality control expenses ($17.5 million) remaining the same. The Lagrange multiplier method will be utilized below to answer these questions.

For the sake of convenience, the net profit equation (Equation 10-23), a function of three variables, is reproduced below:

$$P_n = -90 + 157.5P - 15P^2 + 0.2PAQ + PQ + 2PA - 0.1AQ - 1.5Q - 2A$$
(Equation 10-23)

subject to the constraint Equation 10-24:

$$Q + A = 17.5 \quad \text{(Equation 10-24)}$$

Equations 10-23 and 10-24 can be rewritten, following the format of Equation 10-18 as:

$$L(P,A,Q,\lambda) = P_n(P,A,Q) + \lambda(Q + A - 17.5) \quad \text{(Equation 10-27)}$$

The necessary conditions for extreme points, based upon Equation 10-27, are given as follows:

$$\frac{\delta L}{\delta P} = 157.5 - 30P + 0.2AQ + Q + 2A = 0 \quad \text{(Equation 10-28)}$$

$$\frac{\delta L}{\delta A} = -2 + 0.2PQ + 2P - 0.1Q + \lambda = 0 \quad \text{(Equation 10-29)}$$

$$\frac{\delta L}{\delta Q} = -1.5 + 0.2PA + P - 0.1A + \lambda = 0 \quad \text{(Equation 10-30)}$$

$$\frac{\delta L}{\delta \lambda} = Q + A - 17.5 = 0 \quad \text{(Equation 10-31)}$$

Having found partial derivatives, the next step is to eliminate the λs. Subtracting Equation 10-30 from 10-29 provides a way to accomplish this elimination, thereby forming Equation 10-32:

$$\begin{aligned}
-2 + 0.2PQ + 2P - 0.1Q + \lambda &= 0 \\
+1.5 - 0.2PA - P + 0.1A - \lambda &= 0
\end{aligned}$$

(Equation 10-29)
(Equation 10-30—multiplied by a minus)

$$-0.5+0.2P(Q-A)+P+0.1(A-Q)=0$$
$$-0.5+[0.2(Q-A)+1]\,P+0.1(A-Q)=0$$
(Equation 10-32)

Since the selling price is given as $1.00 and quality control expenses Q are $17.5-A$, Equation 10-32 can be stated only in terms of A and is solved as follows:

$$-0.5+0.2(Q-A)+1+0.1(A-Q)=0$$
$$-0.5+0.2[(17.5-A)-A]+1+0.1[A-(17.5-A)]=0$$
$$-0.5+3.5-0.2A-0.2A+1+0.1A-1.75+0.1A=0$$
$$-0.2A+2.25=0$$
$$A=\$11.25 \text{ million}$$

Substituting this value into Equation 10-24 yields:

$$Q+A=17.5 \qquad \text{(Equation 10-24)}$$
$$Q+11.25=17.5$$
$$Q=\$6.25 \text{ million}$$

Having answered the question regarding the verification of Q and A expenses for a $1.00 selling price, we can use the Lagrange multiplier method to show that the price increase of $1.10 will result in the same amount ($17.5 million) for advertising and quality control expenses. Utilizing Equation 10-32 (derived from Lagrange Equations 10-29 and 10-30), we can substitute $1.10 for P as follows:

$$-0.5+[0.2(Q-A)+1]1.10+0.1(A-Q)=0$$
$$-0.5+0.22(Q-A)+1.1+0.1(A-Q)=0$$
$$-0.5+0.22Q-0.22A+1.1+0.1A-0.1Q=0$$
$$+0.12Q-0.12A+0.6=0$$
$$0.12(Q-A)=-0.6$$
$$Q-A=-5$$

Substituting 17.5—A for Q in the foregoing expression, it becomes:

$$(17.5-A)-A=-5$$
$$17.5-2A=-5$$
$$A=\$11.25 \text{ million}$$
$$Q=\$6.25 \text{ million}$$

When comparing differentiation and the Lagrange multiplier, fewer calculations are required for the Lagrange multiplier. This is evident in problems that contain numerous variables and constraints. In addition to being faster, the Lagrange multiplier method provides additional information, having determined a value for λ. The value for λ can be calculated by using Equation 10-29 or Equation 10-30 given previously. Its value (λ) is actually the additional profits that could be obtained if an additional amount were added to the constraint equation ($Q+A=17.5$). Solving for λ per Equation 10-29 is:

$$-2+0.2PQ+2P-0.1Q+\lambda=0$$
$$-2+0.2(1.10)(6.25)+2(1.10)-0.1(6.25)=-\lambda$$

CLASSICAL OPTIMIZATION TECHNIQUES 333

$$-2+1.375+2.20-0.625 = -\lambda$$
$$3.575-2.625 = -\lambda$$
$$-\lambda = \$.95 \text{ million}$$

Thus, if the firm spent a combined $18.5 (the original $17.5 plus an additional $1) million on advertising and quality control, profits would increase by $0.95 million, assuming that all other conditions remained constant in the problem.

Calculus Application—American Products Corporation

The American Products Corporation plans to market a new novelty plastic product whose life is estimated to be one year. However, the Board of Directors has recently adopted a policy that only those short-life products which show a 10 percent return on sales can be marketed. In order to undertake this product venture, the marketing group is proposing the purchase of five automatic molding machines, valued at $10,000 each. After consulting with the cost department, all variable costs of manufacturing and marketing the product are expected to be $3.00 per unit. All overhead costs for the coming year have been allocated to the present product lines. The marketing research group has determined a demand and selling price relationship to be:

$$u = 10,000 - 400s$$

where u = demand
s = selling price

The foregoing data has been turned over to the operations research group for answers to the following questions. What should the optimal selling price be to maximize profits? What profits or losses can be expected during the one year life? If losses are anticipated based upon the calculated selling price, what is the optimum number of machines to purchase in order to reverse this unfavorable condition such that profits are equal to or better than 10 percent of sales?

The first question regarding an optimum selling price can be readily solved by differentiating total profits with respect to selling price. First, total sales and total costs equations must be developed, shown as follows:

$$\text{Total Sales } (S) = s \cdot u$$
$$S = s(10,000 - 400s)$$
$$S = -400s^2 + 10,000s \qquad \text{(Equation 10-33)}$$

$$\text{Total Costs } (C) = (3.00 \cdot u) + 50,000$$
$$C = 3(10,000 - 400s) + 50,000$$
$$C = -1200s + 80,000 \qquad \text{(Equation 10-34)}$$

Next, the selling price is determined where P = total profits:

$$P = S - C$$
$$P = -400s^2 + 10,000s - (-1200s + 80,000) \qquad \text{(Equation 10-35)}$$
$$P = -400s^2 + 11,200s - 80,000$$

$$\frac{dP}{ds} = -800s + 11{,}200 = 0$$
$$800s = 11{,}200$$
$$s = \$14.00$$

Thus, an optimum selling price is $14.00.

The second question regarding profits or losses for one year can be solved by substituting the optimum selling price into Equation 10-35. The loss is determined to be:

$$P = -400(14)^2 + 11{,}200(14) - 80{,}000 \qquad \text{(Equation 10-35)}$$
$$P = -78{,}400 + 156{,}800 - 80{,}000$$
$$P = -\$1600$$

Since the purchase of five machines will result in a loss of $1600, the marketing group must reconsider the number of machines to purchase based on the $14.00 selling price. One approach is to decrease the rate of production by reducing the capital equipment expense. For this approach, it is necessary to solve for profits at a 10% rate of return on sales which is:

$$P = .10S$$
$$P = .10[-400(14)^2 + 10{,}000(14)] \qquad \text{(Equation 10-36)}$$
$$P = .10(-78{,}400 + 140{,}000)$$
$$P = \$6160$$

The ten percent return on sales of $6160 is equated to total sales minus total costs in order to determine the required capital investment.

$$P = S - (TVC - TFC) \qquad \text{(Equation 10-37)}$$

where TVC = total variable costs
TFC = total fixed costs

Calculations are as follows:

$$6160 = 61{,}600 - [3[10{,}000 - 400(14)] + TFC]$$
$$TFC = \$42{,}240$$

The maximum capital investment to show a 10 percent return on sales is $42,240. Thus, the purchase of four machines only at a total cost of $40,000 is warranted to meet the recently adopted return on sales policy. The rate of return on sales (based on a $14.00 selling price) that can be expected with four machines is calculated to be 13.6 percent, shown per the following:

$$P = 61{,}600 - 13{,}200 - 40{,}000 \qquad \text{(Equation 10-37)}$$
$$P = \$8400$$

$$\text{Rate of return on sales} = \frac{\$8{,}400}{\$61{,}600} = 13.6 \text{ percent}$$

CLASSICAL OPTIMIZATION TECHNIQUES

Summary

The use of higher mathematics—differential calculus, integral calculus, partial derivatives, and the Lagrange multiplier—enables operations researchers to solve complex business problems that cannot be solved with algebraic approaches. Models in this chapter have used the classical method of calculus where the first derivative of a differential function is set equal to zero. In case of a multivariable function, partial derivatives are taken with respect to each of the n variables. When constraints are imposed, Lagrange multipliers are introduced, one for each constraint so that the number of independent equations and the number of unknowns are identical. Thus to use the analytical method of calculus, a function must be in a mathematical form and must be differentiable.

Models based on calculus are deterministic, having the inherent characteristic of producing a unique solution by precise and direct mathematical operations. This approach can be contrasted with the iterative models presented previously, such as linear programming and transportation methods which required selecting an initial set of values for variables in the problem to produce a trial solution and then modifying these values in a prescribed manner so that each successive solution will be closer to the optimum answer.

Questions

1. (a) Distinguish between differentiation and integration.
   (b) Distinguish between partial derivatives and the Lagrange multiplier.
2. What does a second derivative test tell you when applied to the statement of a business problem?
3. In what ways is calculus superior to algebra for business problems?

Problems

10-1 Develop a generalized pricing formula (to maximize profits) applicable to any situation in which a linear demand function and a linear cost relation are present.

10-2 The Smith Arms Manufacturing Company is considering the advisability of marketing several new products, one in particular. Its market research group has calculated demand and price for this new product to be as follows:

Price	Demand for First Year
$100	9,000
200	6,000
300	3,000
400	0

The firm's accounting department, in conjunction with its production department, has developed the estimated costs of the new product to be as follows:

Fixed costs $100,000
Variable costs per unit $75

(a) Determine the optimum selling price that will maximize profits for the firm during the first year.
(b) Determine that the selling price is maximum.
(c) Determine how many units should be produced in the first year to maximize profits for the firm.
(d) What are the expected optimum profits for the firm's new product in its first year?

10-3 A new product is under consideration by the Champion Company. Its marketing department has estimated the relationship of sales volume and price as follows:

Price	Demand per Year
$ 2	2,000
4	1,500
6	1,000
8	500
10	0

The cost function per unit has been developed by the firm's cost department based upon a similar product which is as follows:

$$C \text{ (per unit)} = \frac{\$1000}{u} + \$0.80$$

The first term in the equation is fixed costs and the second term is variable costs.
(a) Calculate the expected number of units during the first year for optimum profits.
(b) Calculate the optimum profits (losses) for the first year.

10-4 The Silvercreat Company, Inc., a manufacturer of professional photographic supplies, has compiled the following information on a proposed new product—an enlarger. The firm estimates that it can sell 900 enlargers at $30 each, 600 at $60 each, and 300 at $90 each. In addition, estimated costs are as follows:

Direct Material—variable	$ 8/enlarger
Direct Labor—variable	$12/enlarger
Manufacturing Expenses—variable	$ 2/enlarger
Manufacturing Expenses—fixed	$4000 for next year
Commissions—variable	$ 5/enlarger
Administrative and Selling Expenses—fixed	$8000 for next year

Given the foregoing data, what are the maximum expected profits for next year?

CLASSICAL OPTIMIZATION TECHNIQUES

10-5 The Regis Company has determined the relationship between sales (S) and advertising cost (x) for one of its products to be

$$S = \frac{20{,}000\,x}{500+x}$$

The firm has also determined that net profit before advertising cost is 20 percent of total revenue. Thus the equation for net profit (P) as a function of sales and advertising costs is

$$P = \frac{1}{5}S - x$$

(a) Find the amount to spend on advertising for this one product to maximize net profit.
(b) Show that we do get maximum profit by finding the second derivative of the net profit function.

10-6 The Atlas Battery Company has an advertising budget problem for the coming year. It can set up an arbitrary sum, spend an amount representing a certain percentage of sales, or match its competitors' outlays. The firm has determined that forecasted sales for its batteries is 550,000 for this year. In addition, the derived profit function (P) is equal to $20u - 10{,}000{,}000$ where u is the number of units. If actual sales equaled the forecasted sales, the firm would make a profit of $1,000,000 before federal income taxes. The vice president in charge of marketing feels that the advertising budget of its competitors should be considered. The market research department has revealed that its competitors plan to spend $300,000 on an average and forecasted industry sales are 2,000,000 batteries. All variable costs amount to $15 per battery. The operations research consultant has decided to use the following terms in his first equation: let x be the unknown advertising outlay of the Atlas Battery Company, let y equal the average unknown budget of its competitors, and let Q be the forecasted potential sales volume in units for the entire industry. The OR man is assuming that total industry sales are independent of the total amount spent on advertising and that the firm's shares of sales is proportional to its share of the total industry advertising budget. Based upon the foregoing, the company's expected sales volume will be equal to

$$Q\left(\frac{x}{x+y}\right)$$

(a) Using the preceding simplifying assumptions (which are relatively realistic when describing the competitive battery market of the firm), what recommendation should the OR man make regarding the optimal advertising budget for the Atlas Battery Company?
(b) What other factors should be considered in arriving at a final decision for the firm?

10-7 The Searle Company sells many products in several states. The firm has decided to take a closer look at a typical item, product E. It is sold in two states, one of which imposes a $2.00 per unit sales (consumer) tax on this item, whereas the other state has no tax of this type. The vice president in charge of marketing has asked their operations research man from the Systems Analysis group what prices the firm should charge in each state in order to maximize profits for the firm. The revenue and cost functions have been determined as follows:

$$S = 9{,}000 - 90p \qquad \text{(Unit sales function of product E)}$$
$$TC = 25{,}000 + 50S \qquad \text{(Total cost function of product E)}$$

where p equals selling price

10-8 The Kline French Company has developed a new product for which a patent had been obtained several years ago. The product has been on the market for three years. Its sales rates have been as follows: first year, 50,000 units; second year, 65,000 units; and third year, 90,000. An examination of these sales rates for the past three years indicates that sales are growing in a nonlinear rather than a linear fashion. The firm assumes this same type of increase will be applicable to the coming year due to the increasing popularity of the product. What will be the forecasted sales over the fourth year of operation?

10-9 The Ajax Company has one product in its major product line which is experiencing a declining sales rate of 2 percent per month. If the sales rate is presently $40,000 (monthly basis), what can the firm expect for sales in the twelfth month? Your answer will be of help in deciding the future of this product. It should be noted that the rate of change of sales with respect to time (months) is to be treated as a quadratic function.

10-10 The Sincor Machine Tool Company is considering a special machine tool for its manufacturing facilities, valued at $10,000. The annual return on savings (R) from using this special type of equipment is estimated to be:

$$R = \frac{30{,}000}{(t+5)^2}$$

If t is the number of years after purchase, will the special piece of equipment pay for itself after five years?

10-11 The newly formed Ace Reproducing Company manufactures copying machines. It has requested your OR consulting firm to determine the first five years of sales. The company will use this data to determine its sales and service personnel requirements. One member of your OR team has researched the market and has estimated the annual sales to be:

$$\$100{,}000\,(1.0 - e^{-.70t})$$

For the first five years, find the yearly sales.

10-12 The operations research team of the Photon Copying Company (rents copying machines) has been asked to settle a heated argument that has arisen in the marketing department. The problem revolves around the advertising campaign for the coming months. The vice president in charge of marketing wants an answer regarding the dispute. Half of the marketing group feels that $3,000 a month should be spent on advertising for a two-month period, whereas the other half feels that better results would accrue to the firm if the campaign were extended from two to three months for a monthly expenditure of $2,000. Monthly income from renting copying machines is $30,000 while about 5 percent of monthly income is lost by nonrenewals. Thus it is necessary to spend $600 per month to attract a sufficient number of new customers to maintain the $30,000 monthly revenue.

The operations research group was able to determine that as monthly sales increased, the effectiveness of advertising would probably decrease because the ratio of customers to potential customers would increase and those remaining would be harder to sell. The group, after two days of developing various models for the problem, feels the following two integrals most accurately represent the conditions prevailing:

Total sales revenue (for two-month advertising program) is:

$$\int_0^2 \left[\frac{(60{,}000)(3000)}{600+3000}(1-e^{-(0.0001 \times 3000+0.05)t}) + 30{,}000 e^{-(0.0001 \times 3000+0.05)t} \right] dt$$

Total sales revenue (for three-month advertising program) is:

$$\int_0^3 \left[\frac{(60{,}000)(2000)}{600+2000}(1-e^{-(0.0001 \times 2000+0.05)t}) + 30{,}000 e^{-(0.0001 \times 2000+0.05)t} \right] dt$$

Based upon the data given, what advertising campaign is the most effective one in terms of total sales revenue?

10-13 Jarvis Manufacturing, Inc., has been considering raising the price of its principal product from $2.00 to $2.10 since many of its competitors had done so last week. Costs for this product were relatively easy to isolate since its major plant is devoted exclusively to this product. The main office overhead was allocated to this product based upon its contribution to total sales. Thus the recent cost study presents a current realistic picture of costs related to present selling price. The firm has calculated total fixed costs, exclusive of advertising and personal selling expenses (salesmen are on a salary basis), to be $6 million. Due to its tight cash position, the budget committee has allocated $6 million to advertising and personal selling for the year. Its variable costs are 45 percent of selling price. The firm, after considerable work on its forecasting function, has determined the number of units that can be sold is best described by the equation

$$N = 100 - 25P + 0.15AS + S + 0.5A$$

where
N = millions of units that can be sold
P = selling price per unit
A = total advertising cost
S = total personal selling cost

(a) What is the present profit and the expected profit with the price increase? What would be the increase in profits if the price is raised?
(b) Prove advertising and personal expenses are correct using the Lagrange multiplier.
(c) If the budget for advertising and personal selling costs is increased by $0.5 million at the current price of $2.00, what additional profits can be expected if all other conditions remain the same?

(d) Based upon (c), what rate of return on the additional investment of $0.5 million for advertising and personal selling can be expected?

Bibliography

R. L. Ackoff and M. W. Sasieni, *Fundamentals of Operations Research*, New York: John Wiley & Sons, 1968.

M. Aoki, *Introduction to Optimization Techniques*, New York: MacMillan Company, 1971.

M. Aoki, *Optimization of Stochastic Systems*, New York: Academic Press, 1967.

A. V. Balakrishnan and L. W. Neustadt, *Computing Methods in Optimization Problems*, New York: Academic Press, 1964.

E. K. Bowen, *Mathematics with Applications in Management and Economics*, Homewood, Ill.: Richard D. Irwin, 1972.

E. H. Bowman and R. B. Fetter, *Analysis for Production and Operations Management* (3rd ed.), Homewood, Ill.: Richard D. Irwin, 1967.

G. J. Brabb, *Introduction to Quantitative Management*, New York: Holt, Rinehart and Winston, 1967.

E. R. Caianiello (Ed.), *Functional Analysis and Optimization*, New York: Academic Press, 1966.

L. T. Fan, *The Continuous Maximum Principle*, New York: John Wiley & Sons, 1966.

G. Leitmann, (Ed.), *Topics in Optimization*, New York: Academic Press, 1967.

C. W. Merriam, III, *Optimization Theory and the Design of Feedback Control Systems*, New York: McGraw-Hill Book Company, 1964.

S. B. Richmond, *Operations Research for Management Decisions*, New York: The Ronald Press Company, 1968.

W. A. Spivey and R. M. Thrall, *Linear Optimization*, New York: Holt, Rinehart and Winston, 1970.

C. H. Springer, R. E. Herlihy, and R. I. Beggs, *Advanced Methods and Models*, Homewood, Ill.: Richard D. Irwin, 1965.

D. Teichroew, *An Introduction to Management Science, Deterministic Models*, New Jersey: John Wiley & Sons, 1964.

H. B. Wagner, *Principles of Operations Research with Applications to Managerial Decisions*, Englewood Cliffs, N.J.: Prentice-Hall, 1969.

D. J. Wilde, *Optimum Seeking Methods*, Englewood Cliffs, N.J.: Prentice-Hall, 1964.

Chapter ELEVEN

Inventory Control Models

Beginning about 1915, attention was focused on the development of mathematical approaches designed to aid the decision maker in setting optimum inventory levels. Since that time, increasingly sophisticated analytical tools have been brought to bear on the problems of inventory management. The reason for greater attention to inventory is that this asset, for many firms, is the largest one appearing on the balance sheet. Inventory problems of too great or too small quantities on hand can cause difficulties. If a manufacturer experiences a stockout of a critical inventory item, production halts can result. Moreover, a shopper expects the retailer to carry the item wanted. If an item is not stocked when the customer thinks it should be, the retailer loses a customer not only on that item but on many other items in the future. The conclusion one might draw is that effective inventory management can make a significant contribution to a company's profit as well as have a decided impact regarding its return on total assets.

Functions Performed by Inventories

The basic function of inventories, whether they be raw materials, work-in-process, or finished goods, is to *decouple*. This allows the successive stages in the purchasing, manufacturing, and distribution process to operate somewhat independently of one another. The decoupling function may be performed in at least four ways. First, process and movement inventories, sometimes called pipeline stocks, are necessary where significant amounts of time are required to transport goods from one location to another. For example, an inventory representing an average week's demand would be needed in movement if one week were required to ship the goods from a manufacturer's warehouse to a retail outlet. Second, there is a lot size inventory where more units are purchased or manufactured than are needed for present use. The rationale is that economies may be realized from larger lots versus smaller lots through quantity discounts or lower total setup costs. Third, when demand for an item is known to be variable or seasonal, it may be more economical for a firm to absorb some of the fluctuation by permitting its inventories rather than its level of production to oscillate. Many firms find it more economical to stabilize production since the costs of acquiring and training new workers, unemployment compensation, and overtime work to meet periods of peak demand are higher than the carrying costs of inventory. Last, fluctuation inventories may be required if an adequate supply of items is to be available for the consumer when he wants them and stockouts are to be minimized. In effect, safety or buffer stocks are necessary so that fluctuations above average demand can be met.

While the foregoing are legitimate functions of inventories, too often inventories are wrongly used as a substitute for management. For example, if finished goods inventories are too large, inaccurate sales forecasting by marketing management may never be apparent. Similarly, a production foreman who saturates his department with large in-process inventories can hide poor planning because there is always something to manufacture.

Basic Inventory Decisions

A fundamental concern of management is developing inventory policies that will minimize the total operating costs of the firm. Thus, two basic inventory decisions must be made: the quantity to order at one time and when to order this quantity. In approaching these two decisions, one path is ordering large amounts to minimize ordering costs. The other path is ordering small amounts to minimize inventory carrying costs. Either course pushed too far will have an unfavorable effect on profits. The best course in terms of profit and return on total assets is a compromise between the two extremes. The subject matter for this chapter is the development of inventory control models under stipulated operating conditions.

Inventory Costs

The costs a firm may incur as a result of established inventory levels can be grouped into three categories. The first two costs—ordering costs and inventory carrying costs—are equated to one another in the basic inventory models. The third cost—outage—is the loss realized by the firm if stockouts of items occur. Sales may be lost if inventories are not adequate to meet consumer demand, or production may come to a halt if the critical inventories are insufficient to meet its need. The first two costs are our concern initially since stockouts are assumed not to occur in the basic inventory models.

Ordering Costs or Acquisition Costs

Costs related to acquisition of purchased items are those of getting an item into the company's inventory. Ordering costs, incurred each time an order is placed, start with the purchase requisition. Other costs include issuing the purchase order, follow-up, receiving the goods, quality control, placing them into inventory, and paying vendors.

Acquisition costs pertaining to company-manufactured items include several of the above-mentioned items, but they also comprise other categories. A sample list of costs for both conditions is found on the top of the next page. Very often, determination of these costs must be made by special study. Because the incremental cost per order is needed, costs estimates for the purchasing, receiving, and accounting departments are determined at different levels of ordering for the year. For example, if 1000 additional

Purchased Items	Manufactured Items
Requisitioning	Requisitioning
Purchase order (includes expediting)	Setup
Trucking	Receiving and inspection
Receiving and inspection	Placing in storage
Placing in storage	Accounting and auditing:
Accounting and auditing:	Inventory
Inventory	Product costs
Disbursements	

orders are estimated to cost $20,000 for these departments, the incremental cost per order is $20.

Some caution is necessary in assuming that manufacturing costs may be directly replaced by purchasing costs when considering how much to purchase rather than how much to manufacture. First, reordering costs are usually less than setup costs. Second, external considerations surround the purchase decision. Items, such as short-term interest rates, price speculation, and labor stability of suppliers make the amount to purchase somewhat less straightforward than the internal considerations involved in deciding to manufacture.

Inventory Carrying or Inventory Holding Costs

Carrying or holding costs of inventory are those incurred because the firm has decided to maintain inventories. Of course, a firm cannot operate without a certain amount of process and movement inventories, as stated earlier. In arriving at these costs, it is best to consider those items that meet the following two tests: out-of-pocket expenditures and foregone opportunities for profit.

An example of applying these tests would be the consideration of warehouse space costs—only to the extent that additional facilities would need to be acquired or that unused space could be rented for profit. Also, these rules would indicate that interest is considered from the standpoint of foregone profit opportunity only when sufficient capital existed in the business and need not be borrowed to finance inventories.

These costs, like ordering costs, are somewhat difficult to determine precisely because the required records do not always exist. The following composite of data, taken from various references, gives representative ranges for these costs:

Item	Approximate Range
Interest (on money invested in inventory)	6–14%
Insurance	1–3
Taxes	1–3
Storage (may include heat, light, or refrigeration)	0–3
Obsolescence and depreciation	4–16

Carrying costs for most manufacturing firms are normally about 20 to 25 percent. Obviously, any extreme situation may fall outside the ranges shown. These costs are stated on an annual basis and are expressed as a percent of average inventory value. This percentage can be obtained in much the same manner as was used to obtain the incremental cost per order, that is, by estimating total carrying costs at two different inventory levels.

Outage Costs

This category of costs is mentioned primarily because it exists, and not because definitive rules can be set forth for computing outage costs. Outages result in decreased customer service level, less efficient production operations, and high costs resulting from "crash" procurements. Since outages affect the items just named, the unanswered question in most cases is by "how much?" Unless some very direct relationships exist, the cost of an outage is difficult to quantify. The fact that answers to the determination of outage costs are approximate and arbitrary in nature does not necessarily mean that their significance should be ignored. Knowledge of cost alternatives enables the application of enlightened judgment to produce satisfactory answers to the problem of just how great an outage rate is acceptable.

Concept of Average Inventory

Before developing the economic lot size inventory model, certain assumptions must be made regarding the purchase of a single item of inventory. First, demand for the item is at a constant rate and is known to the decision maker in advance. Second, the lead time, which is the elapsed time between the placement of the order and its receipt into inventory, or the time necessary for acquiring an item is also known. Although these assumptions are rarely valid for inventory problems in the business world, they do permit us to develop a simplified model into which more realistic, complicating factors can be introduced.

If we let Q be the order size under the preceding assumptions, it can be shown in Figure 11-1 that the number of units in inventory is equal to Q when each new order is physically received into inventory and that the inventory is gradually depleted until it reached zero just at the point when the next order is received. It is observed that the average inventory ($Q/2$) is equal to one-half the number of units in the lot size. As illustrated in Figure 11-1, the average inventory is effected by the order quantity and the number of orders per year. Furthermore, each new order is received into inventory at exactly the time at which the previous order is depleted, resulting in no stockouts.

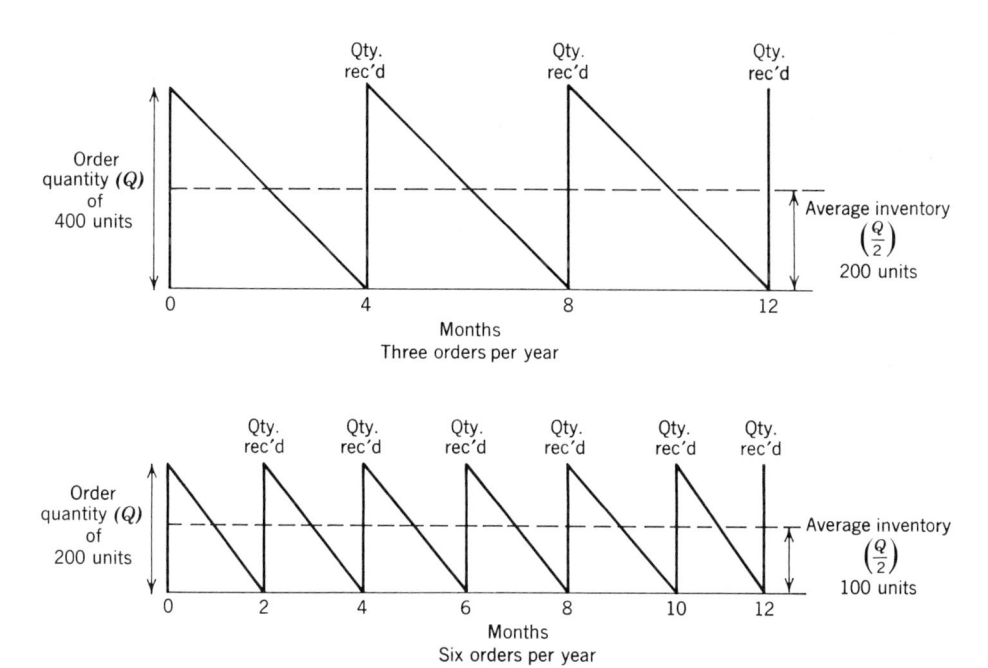

Figure 11-1 Concept of average inventory (Q/2) and the effect of order quantity (Q) and orders per year on average inventory level.

Economic Ordering Quantity

Now that the methods for determining incremental ordering costs, carrying costs, and average inventory have been set forth, the next step is the development of an inventory model in terms of economic ordering quantity. A key feature of this model, first developed by F. Harris in 1916, is that management is confronted with a set of opposing costs—as the lot size increases, the carrying charges will increase while the ordering costs will decrease. On the other hand, as the lot size decreases, the carrying costs will decrease, but the ordering costs will increase. (In the cases under discussion in this chapter, only minor deviations from these trends are assumed to occur.) Economic ordering quantity (EOQ) is that size order which minimizes total annual (or other time period as determined by individual companies) cost of carrying inventory and cost of ordering. Again, we are assuming conditions of certainty and that annual requirements are known.

Tabular Approach

One approach for solving the EOQ is by trial and error. The method is as follows: (1) select a number of possible lot sizes to purchase; (2) determine total costs for each lot size chosen; and (3) select the ordering quantity which minimizes total cost. Table 11-1 illustrates this approach.

In the example, annual requirements equal 8000 units, ordering cost per order is $12.50, 20 percent per year is the carrying cost of average inven-

TABLE 11-1
Tabular Approach to EOQ

Orders Per Year	Lot Size	Average Inventory	Carrying Charges 20% Per Year	Ordering Costs $12.50 Per Order	Total Cost Per Year
1	8,000	4,000	$800.00	$ 12.50	$812.50
2	4,000	2,000	400.00	25.00	425.00
4	2,000	1,000	200.00	50.00	250.00
8	1,000	500	100.00	100.00	200.00
12	667	333	66.00	150.00	216.00
16	500	250	50.00	200.00	250.00
32	250	125	25.00	400.00	425.00

tory, and the cost per unit is $1.00. The table indicates that an order size of 1000 units will result in the lowest total cost of the seven alternatives evaluated. Note that this minimum total cost occurs when carrying costs are equal to ordering costs. In this example we were fortunate in determining the lowest possible cost. Suppose the computation for eight orders per year had not been made. We could choose only among the six remaining alternatives for the lowest cost solution. This points up a serious limitation of the tabular approach. In many cases, a relatively large number of alternatives must be computed before the best possible least cost combination is determined.

Graphic Approach

The preceding data can be graphed to show the nature of the opposing costs involved in an EOQ problem. Figure 11-2 shows that annual total

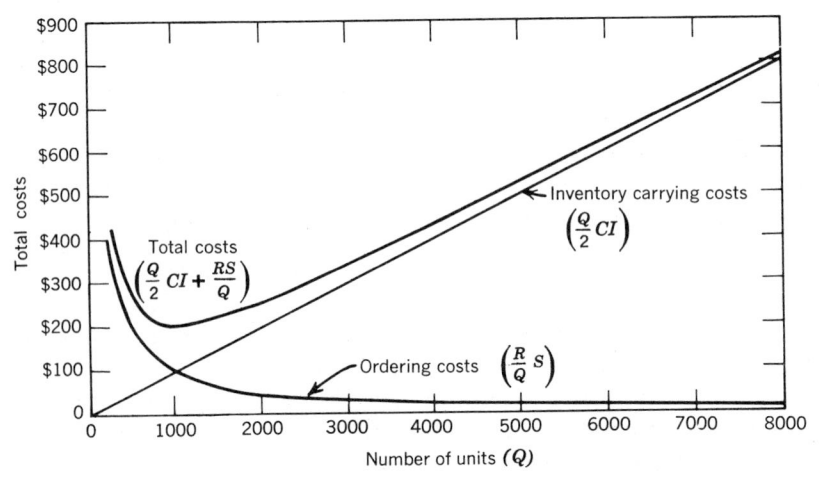

Figure 11-2 Economic ordering quantity graph.

costs of inventory carrying costs and ordering costs first decrease, then hit a low point where inventory carrying costs equal ordering costs, and finally increase as the economic ordering quantity increases. Our basic objective is to find a numerical value for EOQ that will minimize the total variable costs on the graph. However, without specific costs and values, an accurate plotting of the carrying costs, ordering costs, and total costs is not feasible.

In actual practice, few firms have found it economically sound to calculate the costs for each inventory item. Inventory, however, can be grouped by similarities. The economic ordering quantity logic is then applied to these groups. Many purists may decry this lack of rigor but examination of their curves, as in Figure 11-2, indicate a relatively flat area around the minimum cost point. This means that certain cost assumptions may be in error by as much as ±10 percent (based on the authors' consulting experience) and not significantly affect the economic ordering quantity.

Algebraic Approach

As discussed previously, the most economical point in terms of total inventory cost is where the inventory carrying cost equals ordering cost. This is the basis of the algebraic approach. In order to derive the EOQ model, the following definitions are needed:

Q = economic ordering quantity or optimum number of units per order to minimize total cost for the firm
C = cost value of one unit
I = inventory carrying costs, expressed as a percentage of the value of average inventory
R = total annual quantity requirements
S = ordering costs per order placed (or set-up costs per run).

Total inventory carrying costs are derived in the following manner:

$$\underbrace{\frac{Q}{2}}_{\begin{array}{c}\text{Average}\\\text{inventory}\\\text{quantity}\end{array}} \times \underbrace{C}_{\begin{array}{c}\text{Cost of}\\\text{one}\\\text{unit}\end{array}} \times \underbrace{I}_{\begin{array}{c}\text{Inventory}\\\text{carrying cost}\\\text{percentage}\end{array}} = \underbrace{\frac{Q}{2}CI}_{\begin{array}{c}\text{Total inventory}\\\text{carrying}\\\text{costs}\end{array}}$$

Note that the term CI could have been written as simply as I. However, it would have to be defined differently from the above, that is, I would be the annual inventory carrying cost of one unit.

Total annual ordering costs are determined as follows:

$$\underbrace{\frac{R}{Q}}_{\begin{array}{c}\text{Number of orders}\\\text{per year}\end{array}} \times \underbrace{S}_{\begin{array}{c}\text{Ordering cost}\\\text{per order}\end{array}} = \underbrace{\frac{R}{Q}S}_{\begin{array}{c}\text{Total ordering}\\\text{costs}\end{array}}$$

Equating total annual inventory carrying costs to total annual ordering costs results in the following:

INVENTORY CONTROL MODELS 349

$$\frac{Q}{2}CI = \frac{R}{Q}S$$
$$QCI = \frac{2RS}{Q}$$
$$Q^2CI = 2RS$$
$$Q^2 = \frac{2RS}{CI}$$
$$Q = \sqrt{\frac{2RS}{CI}} \qquad \text{(Equation 11-1)}$$

The EOQ model may be illustrated by taking the same set of data as used previously with the tabular and graphic examples where $C = \$1.00$, $I = 20$ percent, $R = 8000$ units, and $S = \$12.50$:

$$\begin{aligned} Q &= \sqrt{\frac{2(8000)(\$12.50)}{\$1.00(20\%)}} \\ &= \sqrt{\frac{(16{,}000)(12.50)}{0.20}} \\ &= \sqrt{\frac{200{,}000}{0.20}} \\ &= \sqrt{1{,}000{,}000} \\ &= 1000 \text{ units} \end{aligned}$$

Substituting the value for Q in the original terms of the model, total inventory carrying costs $= (Q/2)CI$ or $(1000/2)(\$1) \times 20\% = \$100$, and total ordering costs $= (R/Q)S$ or $(8000/1000)(\$12.50) = \$100$. These costs can be compared with those obtained by the tabular approach. The adding of the two costs equals the lowest minimum cost per year of $200 for the economic ordering quantity.

This analysis demonstrates that we have solved for a minimum cost. But how can we be sure? This will be determined by the last approach for solving the EOQ inventory model.

The equating of inventory carrying costs to ordering costs can likewise be applied to the optimum number of orders per year and to the optimum number of days' supply per order. It should be noted that the answer for the number of orders per year can be converted to ordering every so many days.

For the optimum number of orders per year, the following terms are needed:

$N =$ optimum number of orders per year to minimize total costs for the firm
$A =$ total dollar amount of annual usage
$S =$ ordering costs per order placed (or set-up costs per run)
$I =$ inventory carrying costs, expressed as a percentage of the value of average inventory

Total inventory carrying costs are derived as follows:

$$\frac{A}{N} \times \frac{1}{2} \times I = \frac{AI}{2N}$$

$$\begin{pmatrix}\text{Dollar amount}\\\text{per order}\end{pmatrix} \times \begin{pmatrix}\text{Average}\\\text{inventory}\\\text{under con-}\\\text{stant usage}\end{pmatrix} \times \begin{pmatrix}\text{Inventory}\\\text{carrying}\\\text{cost}\\\text{percentage}\end{pmatrix} = \begin{pmatrix}\text{Total}\\\text{Inventory}\\\text{carrying}\\\text{costs}\end{pmatrix}$$

Total order costs per year $= N \times S = NS$

Again, equating total inventory carrying costs to total ordering costs, the formula is:

$$\frac{AI}{2N} = NS$$
$$2N^2S = AI$$
$$N^2 = \frac{AI}{2S}$$
$$N = \sqrt{\frac{AI}{2S}} \quad \text{(Equation 11-2)}$$

By using the data from the illustration, N, the optimum number of orders to be placed per year, is calculated as follows:

$$N = \sqrt{\frac{\$8000 \times 20\%}{2(\$12.50)}} = \sqrt{\frac{\$1600}{\$25}} = \sqrt{64} = 8 \text{ orders per year}$$

or

1 order every 45.6 days

Another way of solving for N is to divide the total annual quantity requirements (R) by the economic ordering quantity (Q). Thus, a simplified formula for determining the optimum number of annual orders to be placed is:

$$N = \frac{R}{Q} \quad \text{(Equation 11-3)}$$

Applying the data developed above, the calculation for Equation 11-3 is:

$$N = \frac{8000}{1000}$$
$$N = 8 \text{ orders per year}$$

Having developed the inventory model for the optimum number of orders, we can now develop a formula for the optimum days' supply per order, based upon 365 days per year. In the model, the following terms are used:

    D = optimum number of days' supply per order in one year
    R = total annual quantity requirements
    S = ordering costs per order placed (or set-up costs per run)
    I = inventory carrying costs, expressed as a percentage of the value of average inventory
    C = cost value of one unit
    365 = calendar days per year

Again, total inventory carrying costs per year equal ordering costs per year:

$$\frac{RC}{365/D} \times \frac{1}{2} \times I = \frac{RCI}{730/D}$$

$$\begin{pmatrix}\text{Dollars}\\ \text{per order}\end{pmatrix} \times \begin{pmatrix}\text{Average}\\ \text{inventory}\\ \text{under constant}\\ \text{usage}\end{pmatrix} \times \begin{pmatrix}\text{Inventory}\\ \text{carrying}\\ \text{cost}\\ \text{percentage}\end{pmatrix} = \begin{pmatrix}\text{Total}\\ \text{inventory}\\ \text{carrying}\\ \text{costs}\end{pmatrix}$$

Total ordering costs per year:

$$\frac{365}{D} \times S = \frac{365S}{D}$$

$$\begin{pmatrix}\text{Number of orders}\\ \text{per year}\end{pmatrix} \times \begin{pmatrix}\text{Ordering cost}\\ \text{per order}\end{pmatrix} = \begin{pmatrix}\text{Total}\\ \text{ordering}\\ \text{costs}\end{pmatrix}$$

$$\frac{RCI}{730/D} = \frac{365S}{D}$$

$$\frac{RCID}{730} = \frac{365S}{D}$$

$$D^2 RCI = 266{,}450S$$

$$D^2 = \frac{266{,}450S}{RCI}$$

$$D = \sqrt{\frac{266{,}450S}{RCI}} \text{ or } D = 365\sqrt{\frac{2S}{RCI}} \quad \text{(Equation 11-4)}$$

Returning to our illustration, the number of days' supply per optimum order is 45.6 or 46 days, computed as follows:

$$D = \sqrt{\frac{266{,}450 \times \$12.50}{8000 \times \$1 \times 20\%}} = \sqrt{\frac{3{,}330{,}625}{1600}} = \sqrt{2082} = 45.6 \text{ days or about 46 days' supply per optimum order}$$

A simplified formula for determining the number of days' supply per optimum order is dividing 365 days by the optimum number of orders (N). Thus, the equation is:

$$D = \frac{365}{N} \quad \text{(Equation 11-5)}$$

Inserting the N value of 8 in the sample problem, the value for D is:

$$D = \frac{365}{8}$$

$$D = 45.6 \text{ days}$$

Differentiation Approach

The last approach for solving the economic ordering quantity utilizes differentiation. This is the best approach since it does not suffer from the limitations of the prior approaches.

From Figure 11-2, the slope of the total cost curve is the sum of the slopes of the other two lines. Starting with the left-hand portion of the graph, the inventory carrying cost has a positive slope while the ordering cost has a negative slope. As the quantity Q increases on the x axis, a point is reached where the negative slope of the ordering cost line has decreased to the same value as that of the inventory carrying cost line (slopes numerically equal but opposite) so that their total, the slope of the total cost line, is zero. In the EOQ model, the rate of change for the total cost with respect to Q, the economic ordering quantity, is zero when the total cost curve has a zero slope.

To review, the equation developed under the algebraic method is:

$$\frac{Q}{2}CI = \frac{R}{Q}S$$

Restating the equation in terms of total costs (TC), the equation is:

$$TC = \frac{Q}{2}CI + \frac{R}{Q}S$$

Differentiating the preceding equation, the resulting expression is the slope of the total cost curve:

$$\frac{d(TC)}{d(Q)} = \frac{CI}{2} - \frac{RS}{Q^2}$$

The first derivative is set equal to zero in order to determine where the rate of change of the total cost curve relative to Q is zero:

$$\frac{CI}{2} - \frac{RS}{Q^2} = 0$$
$$Q^2 CI = 2RS$$
$$Q^2 = \frac{2RS}{CI}$$
$$Q = \sqrt{\frac{2RS}{CI}} \qquad \text{(Equation 11-1)}$$

The above solution yields the same formula (Equation 11-1) as the algebraic method. However, this does not say whether total costs are at a minimum or maximum with respect to the economic ordering quantity. The use of the second derivative test will resolve this problem:

$$\frac{d^2(TC)}{d(Q)^2} = +\frac{2RS}{Q^3}$$

A minimum total cost point rather than a maximum total cost point with respect to the EOQ is indicated by a plus sign in the second derivative test. The plus sign indicates that the total cost curve is increasing upward.

EOQ and the Computer

Under the assumptions of the EOQ model (constant usage and constant lead time), the placing of an order for 1000 units with a weekly demand of 154

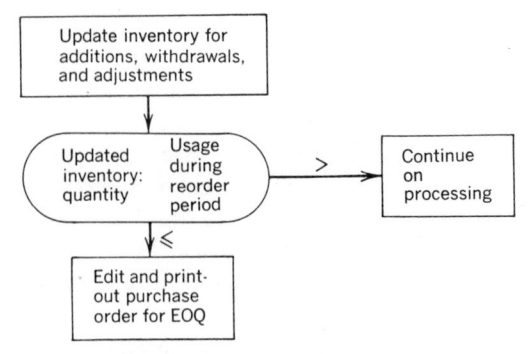

Figure 11-3 Subroutine for computer inventory program.

units in the example requires a lead time of one week. Each reorder would be placed one week before the depletion of the existing inventories or when the inventory level has fallen to the level of 154 units. This number represents usage during the delivery period and assumes a condition of certainty relative to delivery predictability.

Since numerical values can be used for acquisition lead time, this method is easily adaptable to a computer program. As the inventory is updated daily or on some other periodic basis, a comparison can be made between the balance on hand and the quantity necessary for the acquisition lead time. In Figure 11-3 this comparison of a greater than condition means nothing is to be done. However, an equal to or a less than condition signals for a printout of the economic order quantity. In effect, a purchase order for the number of EOQ units, in this example 1000 units, can be prepared automatically by a single comparison of the new updated inventory to the acquisition lead time in units. The computer can also be used annually (or on some other time basis) for computing new economic ordering quantities on each inventory item since the current annual usage can be added and stored with a minimum of cost. All the other factors for computing EOQ's should not be too difficult to obtain.

Since the EOQ model can be readily programmed, it appears convenient to keep all inventory items on-line within a computer system. However, it may not always be practical for a computer system to handle all of them. Hence it is helpful to divide the many component parts that must be handled by the computer into three categories (A, B, and C), based on annual dollar usage and number of items. The relationship of annual dollar usage and number of inventory items for a typical manufacturing firm is shown in Table 11-2. The A items are valuable enough to justify close control by the computer as well as inventory management. In some companies, A items may not be ordered until the customer's order is actually received. The particular circumstances would dictate the best approach for the individual firm. The B and C items, being more numerous and less costly, are also ideal candidates for computer control. When the reorder point has been reached, the EOQ is automatically placed without further management intervention. However, some C items might be so insignificant in cost that

TABLE 11-2
Importance of Inventory Items

Inventory Distribution by Value	A	B	C
Annual dollar usage	65%	20%	15%
Number of inventory items	15%	35%	50%

they may be ordered quarterly or on some other logical time basis. The cost of ordering nuts, bolts, and like items might exceed their value. Again, the attendant circumstances must be examined.

Quantity Discounts

The EOQ model, as set forth at this point, does not take into account the factor of quantity discounts. Buying in large quantities has some favorable and some unfavorable features. The advantages of buying in large quantities are: lower unit cost, lower ordering costs, fewer stockouts, and lower transportation cost. On the other hand, quantity buying presents these disadvantages: higher inventory carrying costs, more capital required, greater chance of deterioration and depreciation of inventory, and older stock.

Cost Comparison Approach
Three approaches are presented for evaluating quantity discounts. Again, the demand and acquisition lead time are constant and known in advance by the decision maker. The first one, widely used due to its simplicity, is the cost comparison approach. The present total annual inventory costs, using an optimum purchase basis or economic ordering quantity, is compared to the proposed total annual inventory cost conditions which qualify the buyer for the quantity discount. The formula for total annual inventory costs (an extension of the basic EOQ equation) is:

$$T = RC + \frac{Q}{2}CI + \frac{R}{Q}S \qquad \text{(Equation 11-6)}$$

where T = total annual inventory costs
R = total annual quantity requirements
C = cost value of one unit at the appropriate price break level
Q = economic ordering quantity or optimum number of units per order to minimize total costs for the firm
I = inventory carrying costs, expressed as a percentage of the value of average inventory
S = ordering costs per order placed

To illustrate the cost comparison approach, the Precision Company purchases solenoid valves for use in its line of spot welders. Precision buys at least 400 of these valves annually. With a cost of $50 each, inventory carrying costs are 20% of average inventory and ordering costs are $20 per order. The firm has received a proposal from the Ross Valve Company which offers Precision a 2 percent discount on purchases of 100 or more valves.

The initial step is to calculate EOQ without taking the 2 percent quantity discount. Using Equation 11-1, the result is 40 units:

$$Q = \sqrt{\frac{2RS}{CI}} = \sqrt{\frac{2(400)(\$20)}{\$50(20\%)}} = \sqrt{\frac{\$16,000}{\$10}} = \sqrt{1600} = 40 \text{ units per order}$$

The annual total cost of purchasing the Ross valves is 400 units times $50 per unit or $20,000. Inventory carrying costs are 20% of the average inventory of $1000 (40 units × $50 per unit = $2000 ÷ 2 = $1000) or $200. Ordering costs are $20 per order times 10 orders for the year or $200. The present cost is given in Table 11-3.

The final step is to compute the total annual costs with the proposed 2 percent discount. The cost of the valves is the annual cost times 98 percent. The method for computing inventory carrying costs and ordering costs are the same as above, except consideration must be given to average inventory at the discounted price. Based upon the data in Table 11-3, the Precision Company should take advantage of the quantity discount offered since total annual costs will be reduced by $230.

Another way of approaching this method is to first calculate the savings because of the discount. In the illustration, savings of $1 ($50×2%) will be realized on each unit. For 400 units, total savings are $400. Next, the total costs of present inventory carrying and ordering costs are subtracted from the total costs for the proposal. From the above data, $400 ($200+$200) from $570 ($490+$80) is $170. Last, a comparison is made between the total discount amount and the additional cost of the proposed costs. If the total discount is greater than the additional proposed costs, the offer should be accepted. If the situation results in a less than condition, the offer should be refused. The total discount of $400 is greater than the additional cost of $170, for a net gain of $230, the same answer as the earlier one.

TABLE 11-3

Present Annual Inventory Costs	
Cost of valves ($50 × 400)	$20,000
Inventory carrying costs (20% × $\frac{40 \times \$50}{2}$ av. inv.)	200
Ordering cost (10 × $20)	200
Total annual costs of Ross valves	$20,400
Proposed Annual Inventory Costs	
Cost of valves ($50 × 400 × 0.98)	$19,600
Inventory carrying costs (20% × $\frac{100 \times 0.98 \times \$50}{2}$ av. inv.)	490
Ordering cost (4 × $20)	80
Proposed annual costs of Ross valves	$20,170

Price Change Approach
Another approach for evaluating quantity discounts is to determine the point where the reduction in ordering cost and unit price is equal to the additional carrying cost which results from purchasing in larger amounts. Stated another way, the problem is one of finding a solution for the largest order quantity, expressed in dollars, that it is economical to order at the price offered with the discount. The following terms are used in the development of this model:

> X = largest order quantity, in dollars, that it is economical to order
> D = discount, expressed as a percentage of A
> A = old annual requirements in dollars
> P = ordering cost per order
> Q = economic order quantity in dollars previous to discount price offer
> I = annual carrying cost, expressed as a percentage of average inventory

The first step is to determine the reduction in ordering cost. This is found by subtracting the new ordering cost from the ordering cost which prevailed before taking the quantity discount. The present ordering cost is the old annual dollar usage (A) divided by the economic ordering quantity in dollars (Q) times the ordering cost per order (P) or (A/Q)P. The new ordering cost is the new annual usage in dollars or $A(1-D)$ divided by X, the dollar size of new orders, multiplied by P, the ordering cost per order, or $A(1-D)P/X$. Thus the present ordering cost, AP/Q, minus the proposed ordering cost $[A(1-D)/X]P$, is the resultant decrease in ordering cost. The reduction in total cost of units due to the lower unit price must be calculated to complete the left side of the equation. This is nothing more than the discount (D) times the annual requirement in dollars (A), or DA. The resultant left-hand side of the equation for the reduction in ordering cost and unit price is:

$$\frac{AP}{Q} - \frac{A(1-D)}{X}P + DA$$

The other side of the equation expresses the additional carrying cost that results from buying in larger amounts. The starting point is an expression for the carrying cost of the proposed plan. This is obtained by taking the largest order quantity to order at a reduced price (X) and dividing by 2; the resultant figure is multiplied by the carrying cost (I) percent or ($X/2$)I. The carrying cost, under the economic ordering quantity before the discount, is next formulated. EOQ in dollars before discount (Q) divided by 2 times the carrying cost (I) is ($Q/2$)I. The additional carrying cost is:

$$\frac{X}{2}I - \frac{QI}{2}$$

Having developed both sides of the equation, we can now equate the savings in ordering cost and the reduction in total purchasing price with the additional carrying cost and solve for X:

INVENTORY CONTROL MODELS

$$\frac{AP}{Q} - \frac{A(1-D)}{X}P + DA = \frac{XI}{2} - \frac{QI}{2}$$

For conversion to the general algebraic quadratic formula ($ax^2 + bx + c = 0$), both sides of the equation must be multiplied by X:

$$\frac{XAP}{Q} - A(1-D)P + XDA = \frac{X^2 I}{2} - \frac{XQI}{2}$$

$$\frac{X^2 I}{2} - \frac{XQI}{2} - XDA - \frac{XAP}{Q} + A(1-D)P = 0$$

$$\frac{X^2 I}{2} + X\left(-\frac{QI}{2} - DA - \frac{AP}{Q}\right) + A(1-D)P = 0$$

In the equation above, the terms for the quadratic formula are:

$$a = \frac{I}{2} \quad b = -\left(\frac{QI}{2} + DA + \frac{AP}{Q}\right) \quad c = A(1-D)P$$

Next, the preceding terms are substituted in the quadratic formula:

$$X = \frac{-b \pm \sqrt{b^2 - 4ac}}{2a}$$

$$X = \frac{\frac{QI}{2} + DA + \frac{AP}{Q} \pm \sqrt{\left[-\left(\frac{QI}{2} + DA + \frac{AP}{Q}\right)\right]^2 - 4\frac{I}{2}[A(1-D)P]}}{2\frac{I}{2}}$$

$$X = \frac{\frac{QI}{2} + DA + \frac{AP}{Q} + \sqrt{\left[-\left(\frac{QI}{2} + DA + \frac{AP}{Q}\right)\right]^2 - 2IAP(1-D)}}{I}$$

(Equation 11-7)

Solving for X in this equation yields the largest order quantity economical to order in dollars at the lowest unit price. It should be noted that the minus sign in front of the square root sign has been dropped since we are interested in the maximum X value.

In order to apply this model, the data set forth in the cost comparison approach is used. It is already known that the 2 percent discount should be accepted. If the reverse situation were true, that is, if the offer should not be accepted by the Precision Company, what quantity in total dollars should they purchase at a time in view of the discount offered? Equation 11-7 would give the answer. However, in view of the present results, the firm may still want to know what the largest quantity of Ross valves in total dollars it should buy at a time in order to get the 2 percent quantity discount offered.

The values for terms in the quantity discount model are:

D = discount offered (2%)
Q = optimum ordering quantity ($2000)

A = annual requirements in dollars ($20,000)
P = ordering cost per order ($20)
I = carrying costs per annum (20%)
X = largest quantity to buy at one time to get discount (2%), expressed in dollars

Then

$$X = \frac{\frac{\$2000 \times 20\%}{2} + (2\% \times \$20,000) + \frac{\$20,000 \times \$20}{\$2000} + \sqrt{-\left[\frac{\$2000 \times 20\%}{2} + (2\% \times \$20,000) + \frac{\$20,000 \times \$20}{\$2000}\right]^2 - 2(20\% \times \$20,000 \times \$20)(100\% - 2\%)}}{20\%}$$

$$X = \frac{\$200 + \$400 + \$200 + \sqrt{[-(\$200 + \$400 + \$200)]^2 - \$160,000(98\%)}}{20\%}$$

$$X = \frac{\$800 + \sqrt{[-(\$800)]^2 - \$156,800}}{20\%}$$

$$X = \frac{\$800 + \sqrt{\$640,000 - \$156,800}}{20\%}$$

$$X = \frac{\$800 + \sqrt{\$483,200}}{20\%}$$

$$X = \frac{\$800 + \$696}{20\%} = \frac{\$1496}{20\%}$$

$$X = \$7480$$

Thus $7480 is the largest quantity of Ross valves the company should buy at one time in order to reap the benefits of the 2 percent quantity discount. Since $7480 is greater than the $4900 purchase quantity necessary to get the discount, it will pay the Precision Company to take advantage of the offer.

Price Break Approach

The two previous approaches to quantity discount were limited to the case where only one discount price is offered. Instead, it is possible to determine the economic order quantity with any number of successive discounts taking effect as the purchase quantity increases. These are known as price breaks, the last approach to quantity discounts.

To examine this approach consider the Randall Company. This company has been offered a discount schedule for the purchase of a small bracket used in the production of the firm's principal product. The term PB_{n-1} ($PB_{n-2}, PB_{n-3}, \ldots$) in parentheses in the discount schedule below relates to price breaks, starting with the lowest price. The cost of ordering is $25, the annual average inventory carrying cost is 20 percent, and annual usage is 30,000 brackets. These figures plus the varying unit prices are used in calculating EOQ_n ($EOQ_{n-1}, EOQ_{n-2}, \ldots$). The discount schedule offered by a vendor along with corresponding economic order quantities is:

INVENTORY CONTROL MODELS 359

EOQ for Each Price	Price Break Quantity	Unit Price
7,454 (EOQ_n)	9,001 and over (PB_{n-1})	$0.135
6,955 (EOQ_{n-1})	7,001–9,000 (PB_{n-2})	0.155
6,646 (EOQ_{n-2})	5,001–7,000 (PB_{n-3})	0.170
6,284 (EOQ_{n-3})	3,001–5,000 (PB_{n-4})	0.190
5,975 (EOQ_{n-4})	1–3,000 (PB_{n-5})	0.210

Inititially a series of comparisons are made between the economic order quantities and the lowest quantity offered for sale at each price break. In Figure 11-4, EOQ_{n-2} is 6646 brackets and is greater than the 5001 brackets or PB_{n-3}—the first greater than condition. Next, it is necessary to compute the annual inventory costs (utilizing Equation 11-6) for the selected number of units, as shown in Figure 11-4. Thus, total costs must be computed for the following: 6646 items (EOQ_{n-2}), 7001 items (PB_{n-2}), and 9001 items (PB_{n-1}). The resultant values in Table 11-4 indicate that the economic ordering quantity for lowest cost is 9001 brackets at $0.135 each.

All of the foregoing quantity discount approaches lend themselves to real-time and time-sharing computer systems. Programs can be written easily and quickly. Similarly, the costs of implementing and using quantity discount computer packages are minimal.

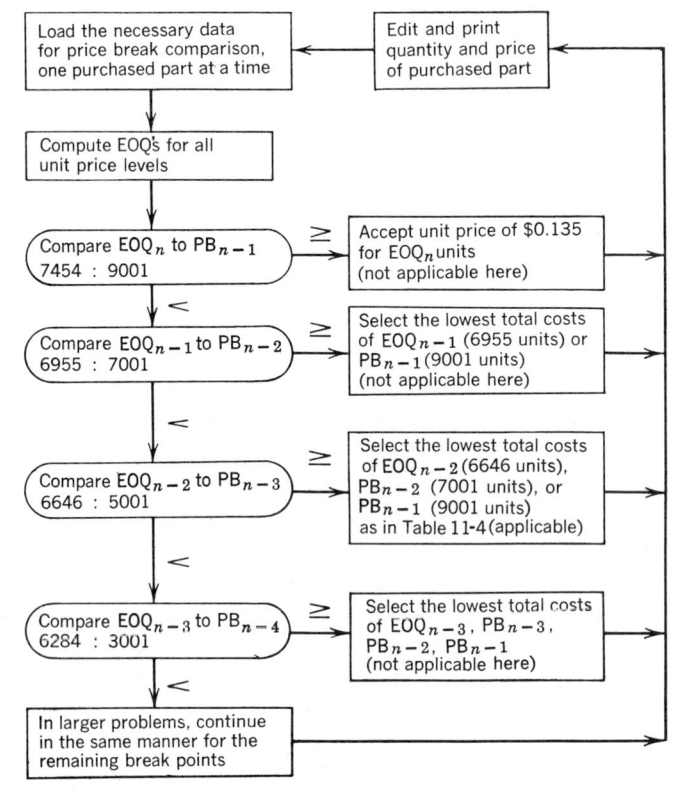

Figure 11-4 Subroutine for computer price break inventory program.

TABLE 11-4
Computations for Total Costs for Selected Quantities and Prices

Number of Units	Cost of Goods, 30,000 Annual Units × Unit Price	Inventory Carrying Costs, 20 Percent × Average Inventory	$25 Ordering Costs × Average Orders Per Year	Total Costs Per Year
6,646	× ($0.170 each) = $5,100.00 +	× ($564.91) = $112.98 +	× (4.51) = $112.75	= $5,325.73
7,001	× ($0.155 each) = $4,650.00 +	× ($543.22) = $108.64 +	× (4.28) = $107.00	= $4,865.64
9,001	× ($0.135 each) = $4,050.00 +	× ($608.11) = $121.62 +	× (3.33) = $ 83.25	= $4,254.87

Reorder Point and Safety (Buffer) Stock

The obvious problem of the prior inventory models is that certainty does not exist in most inventory situations. Both usage and acquisition lead-time usually fluctuate in a manner not completely predictable. In cases where these two factors are relatively constant and known, the previous inventory models provide us with a close approximation of reality. Another problem that may be encountered in the application of inventory models is that accurate cost information may be difficult to obtain. However, relatively good approximations should be obtainable from a proper study of costs. Close watch should be maintained on all cost factors whose change could affect results greatly.

The assumptions dealing with economic ordering quantities per Figure 11-5 are not applicable to all inventory situations. Demand or usage of inventory items can be greater or less than anticipated due to external and internal factors, such as weather change and power failures. Similarly, the acquisition lead time can also vary from favorable to unfavorable due to supplier(s) and/or transportation carrier(s).

If inventory is not available when needed due to any internal or external factor, a stockout occurs. This situation can lead to a noticeable decrease in

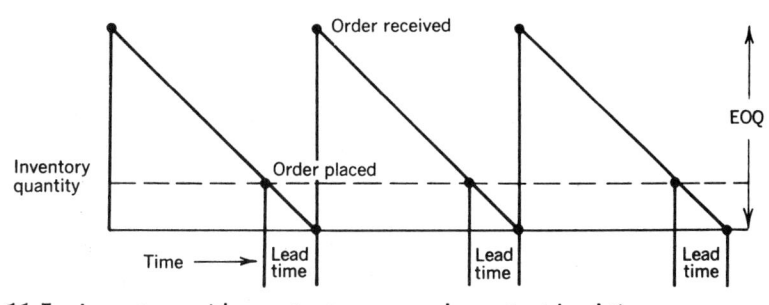

Figure 11-5 Inventory with constant usage and constant lead time.

INVENTORY CONTROL MODELS

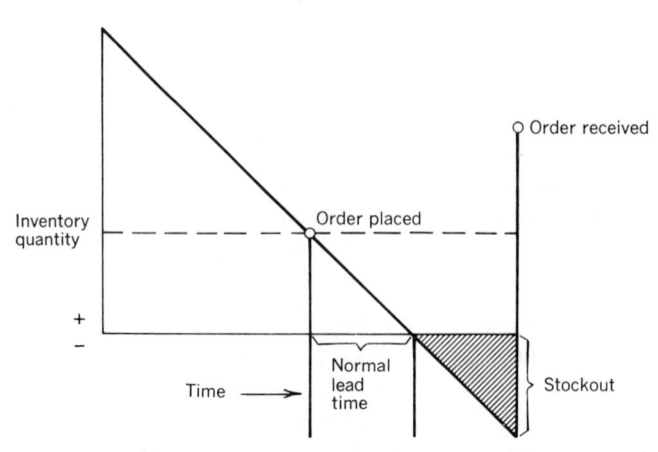

Figure 11-6 Inventory level with no safety stock, resulting in stockout.

profits and possibly losses. Figure 11-6 shows the problem of no stock when needed. It should be noted that the inventory level does not return to its original point as in Figure 11-5 since back orders must be filled.

The reorder point is defined as a condition that signals someone, usually a purchasing agent, that a purchase order should be placed to replenish the inventory stock of some item. Thus the two variables (usage and lead time) mentioned previously as a source of potential trouble are an integral part of the reorder point. The computation for the reorder point (R) is the result of multiplying usage (U), expressed in terms of number of units per day, times the lead time in days (L). However, what must a firm do to provide for stockouts? The calculation for the reorder period must be adjusted to provide for stockouts, resulting in the addition of buffer or safety stock (B) to the above computation. Thus:

$$R = (U \times L) + B$$
$$\text{(Reorder point)} = \left[\begin{pmatrix}\text{average daily}\\\text{usage}\end{pmatrix} \times \begin{pmatrix}\text{lead time}\\\text{in days}\end{pmatrix}\right] + \begin{pmatrix}\text{buffer or}\\\text{safety stock}\end{pmatrix}$$

(Equation 11-8)

The term *safety stock* refers to extra inventory held as a buffer or protection against the possibility of a stockout. As was pointed out previously in this chapter, a larger inventory of safety stock means higher inventory carrying costs. On the other hand, safety stock will decrease stockout costs. The decision on how much safety stock to carry in order to provide minimum total costs to the firm is not an easy one. One of the best approaches is the use of probabilities.

The first step, utilizing the probability approach, is to analyze past inventory records in order that a probability percent can be assigned to the various quantities of usage during the reorder period. For example, the Brown Manufacturing Company has compiled data for a purchased flange (Table 11-5). The company has found the economic ordering quantity to be 250 units with an average daily usage of 5 units. Lead time for this purchased flange is 21 days. Based upon the data in Table 11-5, the firm could

TABLE 11-5
Probabilities of Usage During Reorder Period

Usage During Reorder Period	Number of Times This Quantity Was Used	Usage Probability
90 units	7	7/100 or .07
95 units	10	10/100 or .10
100 units	25	25/100 or .25
105 units	50	50/100 or .50
110 units	6	6/100 or .06
115 units	2	2/100 or .02
	100 times	1.00

reorder 250 units when the level of its stock falls to 105 units [5 (average daily usage) × 21 (lead time in days)], but it will be out of stock 8 percent of the time (.06 + .02). What should management do about this condition of 8 percent stockouts? The answer may or may not be a certain level of safety stock. A procedure for determining safety stock is needed.

Obviously, management desires to pick that level of stock which will yield the lowest total cost for stockouts and inventory carrying costs of safety stock. Since the firm's reorder point is 105 units, the following safety stocks are considered: 5 units for a usage of 110 units and 10 units for a usage of 115 units. Five units of safety stock would cover a usage of 110 units during the reorder period, resulting in the firm being out of stock .02 of the time. Ten units of safety stock would take care of all usage during the reorder period, thereby, never having a stockout occur.

The next step is to construct a table reflecting, for each level of safety stock, the total annual stockout costs. In order to do this, the cost of being out of stock for each unit must be calculated. For the example, the cost is $30 per item. Also, consideration must be given to the number of times per year the company reorders since a firm will be in danger of running out of stock that many times during the year. In the example, the EOQ formula indicates that five orders per year is optimum. The costs of being out of stock for each level is shown in Table 11-6.

TABLE 11-6
Costs of Being Out of Stock

Stock Safety	Probability of Being Out of Stock	Number Short	Expected Annual Cost (No. Short × Prob. of Being Short × Cost of Being Out Per Unit × No Orders/Yr.)	Total Annual Stockout Costs
0	.06 when use is 110	5	5 × .06 × $30 × 5 = $45	
	.02 when use is 115	10	10 × .02 × $30 × 5 = 30	$75
5	.02 when use is 115	5	5 × .02 × $30 × 5 =	$15
10	0	0	0	$ 0

INVENTORY CONTROL MODELS

The final step after determining the total annual stockout costs is to calculate the annual carrying costs per year. In this example, the cost per year of carrying each flange in inventory is $4.00. Table 11-7 gives total costs

TABLE 11-7
Costs of Safety Stock

Safety Stock	Cost of Being Out of Stock Per Table 11-6	Annual Carrying Costs (No. Carried × Cost/Year)	Total Costs/Year (Stockout Costs Plus Carrying Costs)
0	$75	0	$75
5	$15	5 × $4 = $20	$35
10	$ 0	10 × $4 = $40	$40

of safety stock. The lowest total cost in this table is $35 for a safety stock of 5 flanges. The present reorder point of 105 units must be increased to provide for the safety stock of 5 units. Thus the reorder point is 110 flanges.

Inventory and Uncertainty

In many cases, the decision maker may have no idea whatever of what variations to expect between the variables of demand and lead time. If this is the case, we are confronted with decision making under uncertainty. Two approaches commonly employed for inventory control where demand varies are: (1) holding the lot size constant by using the EOQ formula while varying the time between the placement of orders or (2) holding the time between the placement of orders constant while varying the lot size.

Fixed Quantity-Variable Cycle

The first approach considers buying fixed lot sizes at varying intervals, as seen in Figure 11-7. Note that the fixed quantity may be determined by the use of the EOQ formula or on some other basis as circumstances warrant. Both cases require provision for safety stock (as shown in Figure 11-7). One method of handling safety stock has been discussed previously; another approach for computing safety stock is given below for the fixed quantity-variable cycle inventory system that utilizes the EOQ model.

Initially, it is necessary to calculate the economic ordering quantity. In the example, the EOQ is 1160 units with average daily requirements of 75 purchased parts. The acquisition lead time is 30 days while stockouts are allowed only once a year. Since the plant operates only 250 days a year, the average daily requirements times 250 days gives annual requirements of 18,750 units. Distribution is approximately normal for the 75 parts per day with a standard deviation of 25 units.

The next procedure is to calculate the standard deviation of distribution of demand during the acquisition lead time. The standard deviation in

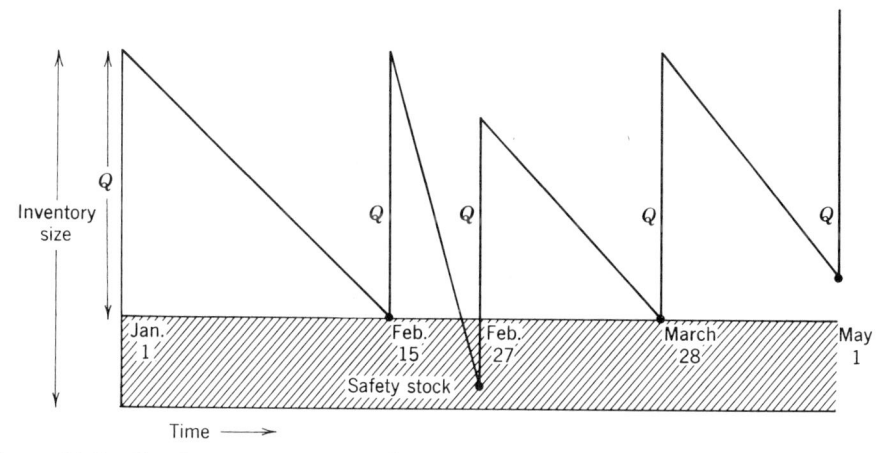

Figure 11-7 Fixed quantity size-variable cycle.

units for the acquisition lead time (σ_t) is the square root of the acquisition lead time (L) times the square of the standard deviation (D). The square root sign is used to establish an equitable basis for wide variations in usage. Using the example data, calculations are as follows:

$$\sigma_t = \sqrt{L \times D^2}$$
$$= \sqrt{30(25)^2} = \sqrt{30(625)} = \sqrt{18{,}750} = 137 \text{ units (approx.)} \quad \text{(Equation 11-9)}$$

For this type of problem, the number of allowable stockouts during the year must be stated and is given as one per year. The calculation for exposures to stockouts is annual usage, 18,750, divided by the economic ordering quantity, 1160, or 16.2 times per annum in the example. The allowable probability of a stockout is stated as a percent and subtracted from 100 percent to determine the probability of no stockout. In the illustration, the allowable probability of one stockout a year is 6.2 percent (100 percent ÷ 16.2 ordering times per year). The probability of no stockout is therefore 93.8 percent. Referring to Appendix C for areas under a normal curve, the probability of no stockout for a 93.8 percent assurance of reliability is represented by the value 1.54.

The last step before calculating the reorder point per Equation 11-8 is to multiply the area under the curve (which allows for one stockout per year) times one standard deviation in units for the required safety stock. The safety stock, in the above example, is 1.54 times 137 units, or 211 units. The reorder point is 75(30) plus 211 units, or 2461 units.

In addition to the method just set forth for calculating safety stock under a fixed quantity-variable cycle inventory system for a reliable reorder point, the two-bin system has been used for certain items. The items are placed in two bins. The first bin contains the number of items for the average expected demand during the acquisition lead time and the necessary safety stock. Initially, items needed are drawn from the second bin. The depletion of the second bin signals it is time to place an order. This approach is useful for a large number of low value items. However, there is need of a periodic review in order to make adjustments as changes take place.

Fixed Cycle-Variable Quantity

The second approach used in controlling inventories under risk and uncertainty is the fixed cycle-variable quantity stock control system. It is necessary to vary the lot size as demand changes while keeping the interval for placement of orders constant. This approach is illustrated graphically in Figure 11-8. The fixed intervals might be quite lengthy in some cases, whereas in others it might be on a daily basis, depending upon the prevailing conditions.

The mechanics of this method may be illustrated by the example used earlier for the fixed quantity-variable cycle inventory system. The review period is the economic ordering quantity divided by the average usage per day (1160/75), or 15.4, that is, approximately 15 days in our illustration. In order to find the level of safety stock for one stockout a year, the safety stock in terms of days must be determined. This is the review period (15 days in the example) plus the acquisition lead time in days (30 days), or 45 days. Returning to the standard deviation formula for acquistion lead time (Equation 11-9), the calculation for the standard deviation in units is:

$$\sigma_t = \sqrt{45(25)^2} = \sqrt{45(625)} = \sqrt{28,125} = 168 \text{ units (approx.)}$$

It should be noted that the 168 units is higher than 137 units in the last approach. This is caused by the addition of the 15 days for the review period.

The procedure for determining the probability of no stockouts and the area under a normal curve used in the preceding section is repeated here. Since the review period has already been established as 15 days, the last step is to multiply the distance under the curve (1.54) times one standard deviation in units (168). The required safety stock is 259 units for a fixed cycle, variable quantity stock control system.

For this approach, the reorder point quantity is not determined since this method recognizes that quantity will vary when reordering, as indicated in Figure 11-8. However, mathematical and statistical techniques are used to determine the frequency of the acquistion intervals.

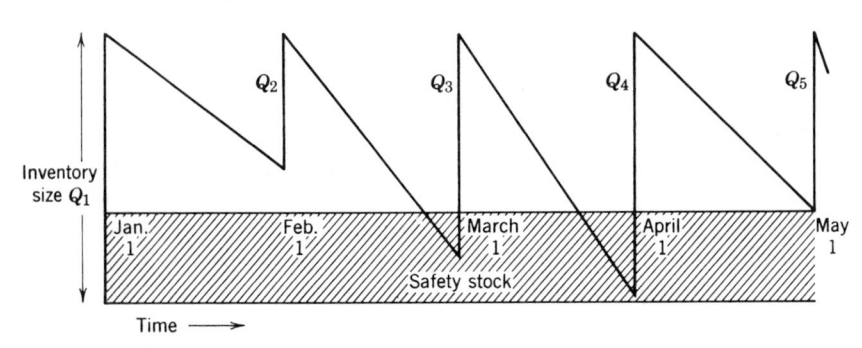

Figure 11-8 Fixed reorder time-variable quantity.

Comparison of Methods

When comparison is made between the two approaches in controlling inventories, it is possible to provide tighter and more frequent control over inventories with the fixed cycle method. Since inventories may have to be reviewed quite frequently, this approach is often used for control of high value, critical, and rapidly depreciable inventory items where close control is a must. Also, this method is applicable in those situations where shipping costs can be reduced by ordering a number of items jointly from one supplier.

The fixed order size approach is most often used for medium and low value items where lesser control is allowable. This method permits the use of the EOQ formula or some other logical basis for reordering. The EOQ model is used more frequently for the medium value items than the lower value items since the costs involved in applying it to the latter are more than offset by any savings. For example, what are the inventory carrying costs and ordering costs for bolts and nuts that are worth only a few mils? In essence, the decision maker must weigh the costs of gathering and applying information against the potential savings.

EOQ Applied to Production

Heretofore all purchased items were treated as being received into inventory at one time. However, when a firm manufactures the items, there is a continuous flow into the inventory as units are completed, illustrated graphically in Figure 11-9. Formulas for determining the optimum run size may be developed in much the same manner as the previous inventory models.

Many companies produce certain items in production lots or batches since sales are not sufficient to warrant a continuous, year-long run. If this is the case, these firms incur set-up costs each time a production lot is started. Set-up costs are similar to the ordering costs per order. Included in set-up costs is the time to set up and tear down the machine for the batch being run, production control cost, and the ordering cost to provide raw materials for the batch order.

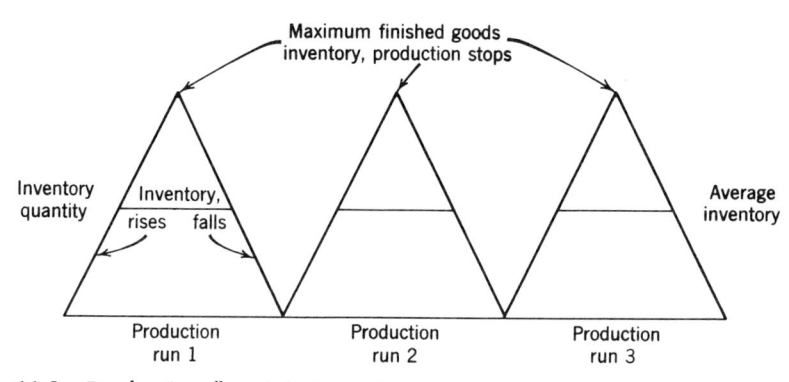

Figure 11-9 Production flow into inventory.

Just as inventory carrying costs were determined for our previous economic ordering formula, the same holds true for a production batch order. A firm incurs carrying costs on the finished product from the time it is manufactured until it is sold. The carrying charges will be higher on finished goods than raw materials since the finished goods inventory is a composite of direct material, direct labor, and variable-fixed manufacturing expenses.

Production for Stock

The basic concept for an optimum number of production lots is similar in theory to that used for purchased parts. Three approaches are set forth, the first being a case where finished goods are to be placed in stock and sold at a constant rate until some low level of finished goods inventory is reached. At that point, another production lot is run. The approach for finding the optimum annual batch runs is the same as for the optimum number of orders per year, that is, the symbols of the equation are the same, but the descriptions have been changed. The symbols with the appropriate descriptions are:

$N=$ optimum number of runs per year (was optimum number of orders per year)
$A=$ annual sales of item at factory cost (was total dollar amount of annual usage)
$S=$ set-up cost per production run (was ordering cost)
$I=$ inventory carrying cost expressed as a percentage of the value of average inventory—finished goods (same, except for average inventory—raw materials)

For example, the Hobart Manufacturing Company manufactures many parts for its products, many of which are stocked while sales are at a constant rate. Part #624 is an example of the items stocked. The firm sells $10,000 (at factory cost) worth of this part with average carrying costs on finished goods of 25 percent per annum. The set-up costs have been determined to be $50 per production run. Using the formula for the optimum number of orders per year (Equation 11-2), the results are:

$$N = \sqrt{\frac{AI}{2S}} = \sqrt{\frac{\$10{,}000 \times .25}{2 \times \$50}} = \sqrt{\frac{\$2{,}500}{\$100}} = \sqrt{25} = 5 \text{ runs per annum}$$

It should be noted that we could use other inventory models, developed previously, for the optimum number of units per run and the optimum number of month's sales per run.

Simultaneous Sales and Production for One Item

The second case where the concept of an optimum production lot size can be applied is the simultaneous sales and production of the finished goods. Referring again to Figure 11-9, the inventory of finished goods does not build up immediately to its maximum point as was the case with the optimum order of purchased parts. Rather, it builds up gradually since goods are being produced faster than they are being sold. The mathematical derivation of this formula is given below. First, the terms are defined:

Q = optimum number of units per production run
R = total annual quantity requirements
S = set-up costs per production run
U = usage (or sales rate) in units per day
P = production rate in units per day
C = cost value of each unit
I = inventory carrying costs, expressed as a percentage of the value of average finished goods inventory
D = number of days in the production run

The set-up costs, referred to previously as ordering costs in the purchase-size model, utilizes the same expression $(R/Q)S$. This is the total annual requirement divided by the number of units per run or the number of production runs times the set-up costs per run for the total annual set-up costs of production.

The inventory carrying costs on finished goods inventory is a more complex mathematical expression. Referring to Figures 11-1 and 11-9, average inventory and, in turn, inventory carrying costs are different when there is a continuous flow of items into the finished goods inventory than when the entire lot is received at once. In the production run model, inventory is at its maximum size at the time each production run is completed (Figure 11-9). The maximum point is equal to the number of days in the run (D) times the daily production rate in units (P) minus the daily usage rate (U), or $D(P-U)$. The average inventory, then, is $D(P-U)/2$. The number of days in the run (D) is equal to the optimum number of units per run (Q) divided by the production rate in units (P), or $D = Q/P$. Substituting this foregoing term for D in the equation $D(P-U)/2$ gives $[(Q/P)(P-U)]/2$. Using the same reasoning as in the economic ordering quantity model, average inventory, or $[(Q/P)(P-U)]/2$, times the cost of one unit (C) times the inventory carrying percent of average finished goods (I) gives the inventory carrying costs of $[(Q/P)(P-U)/2](CI)$.

After determining the proper mathematical expressions for set-up costs and inventory carrying costs, it should be apparent from our previous derivation of inventory models that manufacturing costs are at their minimum when these sets of cost are equal. Equating these expressions results in the following:

$$\frac{RS}{Q} = \frac{(Q/P)(P-U)}{2} CI$$

$$\frac{RS}{Q} = \frac{Q}{2}\left(\frac{P-U}{P}\right) CI$$

$$Q^2\left(\frac{P-U}{P}\right) CI = 2RS$$

$$Q^2 = \frac{2RS}{CI(1-U/P)}$$

$$Q = \sqrt{\frac{2RS}{CI(1-U/P)}} \qquad \text{(Equation 11-10)}$$

Equation 11-10 can be solved, using differentiation, in the same manner as the economic ordering quantity. Again, the first derivative is set equal to zero in order to determine the optimal point. The mathematical derivation is as follows:

$$TC = \frac{RS}{Q} + \frac{Q}{2}\left(\frac{P-U}{P}\right)CI$$

$$\frac{d(TC)}{d(Q)} = -\frac{RS}{Q^2} + \frac{CI}{2}\left(\frac{P-U}{P}\right) = 0$$

$$\frac{RS}{Q^2} = \frac{CI}{2}\left(\frac{P-U}{P}\right)$$

$$Q^2\left[CI\left(\frac{P-U}{P}\right)\right] = 2RS$$

$$Q^2 = \frac{2RS}{CI(1-U/P)}$$

$$Q = \sqrt{\frac{2RS}{CI(1-U/P)}}$$

Applying the second derivative test to the statement of the model,

$$\frac{d^2(TC)}{d(Q)^2} = +\frac{2RS}{Q^3}$$

The plus sign indicates that a minimum total cost point has been reached with respect to the optimum number of units per production run.

It should be noted that this model gives a lower total cost for the firm than when the entire purchased quantity is received into inventory at once. The rationale is that the production of a continuous flow into inventory brings about an increase in the optimum lot size and thus fewer runs. Furthermore, a decrease in the size of the average inventory results in smaller finished goods carrying costs. This can best be illustrated by comparing costs for the two models. The original data ($C=\$1.00$, $I=20\%$, $R=8000$ units, and $S=\$12.50$) must be modified for the two new terms, U and P. Daily production is 44 units per day (p) while the usage rate is 22 units per day, based on a 365 day per year (plants operate seven days a week), which approximates a yearly demand of 8000. The preceding formula gives the following results:

$$Q = \sqrt{\frac{2(8000)(\$12.50)}{(\$1)(.20)(1-22/44)}} = \sqrt{\frac{200,000}{.10}} = \sqrt{2,000,000} = 1414 \text{ units}$$

The average number of runs that should be scheduled is 8000 units divided by 1414 or 5.6 while the comparable number of orders for the purchase order model is 8000 units divided by 1000 (EOQ) or 8. The total ordering and carrying costs for the simplified formula are $200 while the comparable costs for the optimum quantity per production run are as follows:

$$TC = \frac{RS}{Q} + \frac{Q}{2}\left(\frac{P-U}{P}\right)CI$$

$$TC = \frac{8000 \times \$12.50}{1414} + \frac{1414}{2}\left(\frac{44-22}{44}\right)\$1 \times .20$$

$$TC = \$70.70 + \$70.70 = \$141.40$$

Thus total costs are minimized with the optimum lot size production model.

Simultaneous Sales and Production for Two or More Items

Some manufacturing firms have purchased special machinery whose entire production is allocated to two products. Having developed the preceding model for the optimum number of units per production run, we now may modify the formula for this condition. Thus, it is possible to determine the number of units required for each production run in order to minimize costs for the firm.

The basic approach to setting an economical cycle length is the same as in the case of one product, that is, to find the cycle length or number of cycles per month or year which will make the total set-up (or changeover costs) and inventory costs a minimum. The changeover costs increase with more cycles in a given period while inventory costs tend to fall because of more frequent cycles. The resulting formula is very similar to that for a one-product condition.

The starting point for the model is: the number of cycles per year (N) equals annual usage requirements (R) divided by the economic ordering quantity per production run (Q), or $N = R/Q$. Substituting Equation 11-10 for Q, the following model is:

$$N = \frac{R}{\sqrt{\frac{2RS}{CI(1-U/P)}}} = \sqrt{\frac{R^2}{\frac{2RS}{CI(1-U/P)}}}$$

$$N = \sqrt{\frac{R^2 CI(1-U/P)}{2RS}} = \sqrt{\frac{RCI(1-U/P)}{2S}}$$

The preceding equation reflects only the quantities and costs for one part produced on the machine. In order to reflect the same for the second part, the model must be modified for this addition:

$$N = \sqrt{\frac{R_1 C_1 I_1 (1 - U_1/P_1) + R_2 C_2 I_2 (1 - U_2/P_2)}{2(S_1 + S_2)}} \quad \text{(Equation 11-11)}$$

Notice the use of the subscript one for the first part and subscript two for the second part.

In order to apply this formula, the following example is used for two pistons, parts K and L, produced on an automatic machine. Data from the production and accounting records are:

	Part K	Part L
Production rate	2,000 parts/day	1,500 parts/day
Usage or sales rate	1,000 parts/day	500 parts/day
Changeover cost	$200 (L to K)	$100 (K to L)
Cost per part	$0.20	$0.40
Inventory carrying costs	25%	25%
Average number of working days per year = 250 days		

Based upon the foregoing data, how many runs per year should the firm consider to minimize costs for each part?

INVENTORY CONTROL MODELS 371

$$N=\sqrt{\frac{(1000)(250)(\$0.20)(0.25)(1-1000/2000)}{2(\$200+\$100)}+(500)(250)(\$0.40)(0.25)(1-500/1500)}$$

$$N=\sqrt{\frac{250{,}000\times 0.05(1-1/2)+125{,}000\times 0.10(1-1/3)}{2(300)}}$$

$$N=\sqrt{\frac{12{,}500(0.5)+12{,}500(0.667)}{600}}$$

$$N=\sqrt{\frac{14{,}588}{600}}=\sqrt{24.3}=4.9 \text{ (approx.) number of runs per year for each part}$$

Another question can be raised: What quantities per run should be manufactured for parts K and L during the year? This is easily determined. The ordering quantities per production run for each part is the annual usage of the particular part divided by the number of production runs annually for each product. In the illustration the required units per production run for part K is 250,000 divided by 4.9 or 51,020 parts. For part L, the number of units per run is 25,510 units. If the number of production days for each run is desired, this can be obtained by taking the order quantities and dividing by the daily production rate. The number of continuous production days for K is about 26 days (51,020 divided by 2000) and approximately 17 days for part L.

The preceding formula (Equation 11-11) is not restricted to two products. It can be expanded to include several products. Written in compact notation, the equation becomes:

$$N=\sqrt{\frac{\Sigma R_j C_j I_j (1-U_j/P_j)}{2\Sigma S_j}} \qquad \text{(Equation 11-12)}$$

where j represents values for each product. Equation 11-12 can be illustrated for several products by using the paper-making industry. It is normally desirable to go from fine to coarser grades on the same paper-making machine. The data for this example is found in Table 11-8. It should be noted that the production rate is based upon 250 working days a year. This yearly basis will be used in computing U_j/P_j below.

TABLE 11-8
Rate of Production, Usage, Cost, Inventory, and Changeover Costs Based on 250 Working Days

Product	Units-Production Rate/Day	Days-Yearly Usage Rate	Units-Yearly Usage	Cost Per Piece	Inventory Carrying Costs	Changeover Costs
1	800	100	80,000	$0.10	20%	$16.00
2	1,100	100	110,000	0.15	20	22.00
3	800	50	40,000	0.08	20	36.00
		250 days				

TABLE 11-9
Length of Production Cycle per Year for Three Products

Product	$R_j C_j I_j$	U_j/P_j	$1 - U_j/P_j$	$\Sigma R_j C_j I_j (1 - U_j/P_j)$	Change-Over Costs, ΣS_j
1	80,000 × $0.10 × 20% = $1,600	100/250 = 0.4	1 − 0.4 = 0.6	$ 960	$16
2	110,000 × $0.15 × 20% = $3,300	100/250 = 0.4	1 − 0.4 = 0.6	1,980	22
3	40,000 × $0.08 × 20% = $640	50/250 = 0.2	1 − 0.2 = 0.8	512	36
				$3,452	$74

$$N = \sqrt{\frac{\$3,452}{2 \times \$74}} \; \sqrt{23.3} = 4.8 \text{ (approx.) or about 5 cycles per year}$$

The calculations, using Equation 11-12, are shown in Table 11-9. The least cost operation is approximately 5 runs per year, each run lasting 50 days (250 days divided by 5 runs) in order to produce one-fifth of the usage or sales requirements.

Future Inventory Methods

Inventory control recently has gained momentum due to the increased number of computers. Inventory models developed in this chapter lend themselves to this new technology. Many manufacturers have data links between their sales offices, plants, distribution and shipping points for computerized inventory control. Some firms currently are working with computed managed inventories that tie the customer and supplier together through a data communications network. The customer's computer determines what, how much, and when to buy and the order is transmitted from the customer's data processing center to the supplier's data processing center. As this method gains favor, the next step may well be a tie with the transportation companies. Thus, as stocks near a predetermined reorder level, the chain's computers would not only alert the producer, they would also alert the railroad or trucker to have equipment ready at the loading dock. The computer then would follow the boxcar or trailer across the country, making reports on its whereabouts until the goods are delivered. Of course, the customer's computer is updated for the receipt of materials and the inventory computer process continues again in the prescribed manner.

Inventory Application—American Products Corporation

Inventory procedures for the three manufacturing plants of the American Products Corporation do not operate in a vacuum but are an integral part of the firm's computerized management information system. From this broad viewpoint, sales are initially forecasted by exponential smoothing. This method which is explained below is the beginning module in a series of computerized program modules that ultimately results in purchasing parts and materials as well as manufacturing products on an optimum basis.

Exponential Smoothing Method
The exponential smoothing method develops a forecast of sales for the next period by taking a weighted average of sales in the current period and the sales forecast made in the current period. The weighted values must total one. If the weight for actual current sales is set at .1, then the weight for the forecast made in the current period would have to be .9. The selection of the weighting factor (A) is of crucial importance. Experience for the firm has shown that setting A at .2 leads to favorable results. This setting smoothes the extremes of current sales while allowing for definite fluctuations in sales trends.

The basic exponential smoothing formula is: new sales forecast for the coming period equals A times the actual sales during the current period plus (1−A) times the forecasted sales determined in the current period. This formula is written as follows:

$$\bar{S}_t = AS_t + (1-A)\bar{S}_{t-1} \qquad \text{(Equation 11-13)}$$

where $0 \leq A \leq 1$
$\bar{S}_t$ = new sales forecast (in units) for the coming period, made at the end of period t.
A = the weighting factor, some number between 0 and 1.
S_t = actual sales for period t.
$\bar{S}_{t-1}$ = sales forecast for period t made in period $t-1$, that is, one period before it.

Equation 11-13 assumes that average sales over the year will be approximately constant or there will be no upward or downward trend and no seasonal influence. For the American Products Corporation, these assumptions are unrealistic. Therefore, the forecast method must be adjusted for both.

Seasonal factors where B is the seasonal smoothing parameter are updated according to the formula:

$$F_t = B\left(\frac{S_t}{\bar{S}_t}\right) + (1-B)F_{t-N} \qquad \text{(Equation 11-14)}$$

where $0 \leq B \leq 1$
F_t = seasonal factor for period t (ratio of actual sales to smoothed sales).
B = seasonal smoothing factor, some number between 0 and 1.
S_t = actual sales for period t.
$\bar{S}_t$ = nonseasonal sales forecast for the coming period, made at the end of period t.
N = number of periods for seasonal effect (ordinarily 12 months).

Trend adjustment adds a small amount to each forecast if there is a rising trend or subtracting a small amount if there is a declining trend. Experimentation with the trend weighting factor (C) for the firm has shown that good results are obtained when it approximates A. The basic trend adjustment formula is:

$$R_t = C(\bar{S}_t - \bar{S}_{t-1}) + (1-C)R_{t-1} \qquad \text{(Equation 11-15)}$$

where $0 \leq C \leq 1$
R_t = the trend adjustment (in units).
C = trend weighting factor, some number between 0 and 1.
$\bar{S}_t$ = nontrend sales forecast for the next period, made at the end of period t.
$\bar{S}_{t-1}$ = nontrend sales forecast for period t made in period t−1, that is, one period before t.
R_{t-1} = trend adjustment for period t made in period t−1, that is, one period before t.

After solving for values $\bar{S}_t$, F_t, and R_t, the last step in this initial program module is to compute the revised forecasts ($\bar{S}_t$ is adjusted for seasonal and trend adjustments) by using the formula

$$\bar{\bar{S}}_{t,T} = (\bar{S}_t + TR_t)F_{t-N+T} \qquad \text{(Equation 11-16)}$$

where $T = 1, 2, \ldots N$.

Purchasing and Manufacturing on an Optimum Basis

Once the *sales forecasting module* has determined finished goods requirements for the forthcoming sales period, the next computer program module —the *finished goods-production schedule module*—adjusts the forecasted sales for current finished goods on hand in order to calculate the quantities to be manufactured during the coming period. It is important to note that perpetual finished goods inventories stored on-line by the computer system have been adjusted to actual units on hand to insure accurate output for this program module.

The next major part of the computer program is the *materials planning by periods module* which multiples the quantity needed of each component times the number of final products that are to be manufactured. This module also places the component requirements in the appropriate planning period since certain parts and materials will be needed before others. Another name often given to this program module is "exploding bills of materials" which refers to the process of multiplying the component parts times the quantities set forth by the bills of materials.

Continuing with this modular computer program, the output of the material requirements by future planning periods becomes input for the *materials availability and EOQ module* which can take two paths. One is the purchasing of parts and raw materials from outside vendors while the other is the manufacturing of parts within the plants. The outside raw materials provide the basic input for manufacturing specific parts used in the assembly of the finished products. Likewise, outside purchased parts are used in the assembly of the final product. This program module employs the price break approach (includes basic EOQ formula—Equation 11-1) for purchasing from the outside. On the other hand, the number of runs per annum approach (modified number of orders per year formula—Equation 11-2) is utilized for manufacturing within the firm. Before materials are purchased or manufactured, this computer program module determines if present inventory and materials on order are sufficient to meet the firm's needs for future planning periods. Like with finished goods inventory, perpetual raw materials and parts inventory stored on-line have been adjusted to reflect physical counts for accurate output.

The foregoing computer program modules for sales forecasting through economic ordering can be summarized as follows. Sales forecasting serves as input for finished goods product requirements which is input for exploding bills of materials which forms the basis for materials requirements by future planning periods. In turn, this information is employed for placing orders with outside vendors and within the firm's manufacturing plants. This input/output modular program provides a basis for day-to-day scheduling of production orders through the manufacturing work centers.

Summary

Although inventory decisions are being made more routine with the computer, the fundamental decision criterion on which all approaches, methods, and models center is the minimization of total inventory costs. The reason is obvious if one examines the annual reports of manufacturing, wholesaling, and retailing firms. The subject matter of this chapter has focused upon the analysis of the key decision variables and their interelationships in order that they may be used in decision making by the various levels of inventory management. The material presented is a sampling of current inventory models. Other excellent inventory tools and models are available to management, such as ordering tables and nomographs (Figure 11-10). For more details on inventory, consult the bibliography of this chapter.

Questions

1. What function do inventories serve? What is the function of safety stock?
2. How is the EOQ formula derived? Use either algebra or calculus methods.
3. Discuss the similarities and differences between the EOQ derived for purchasing raw materials and producing finished goods.
4. What is the relationship of inventory models to computers?

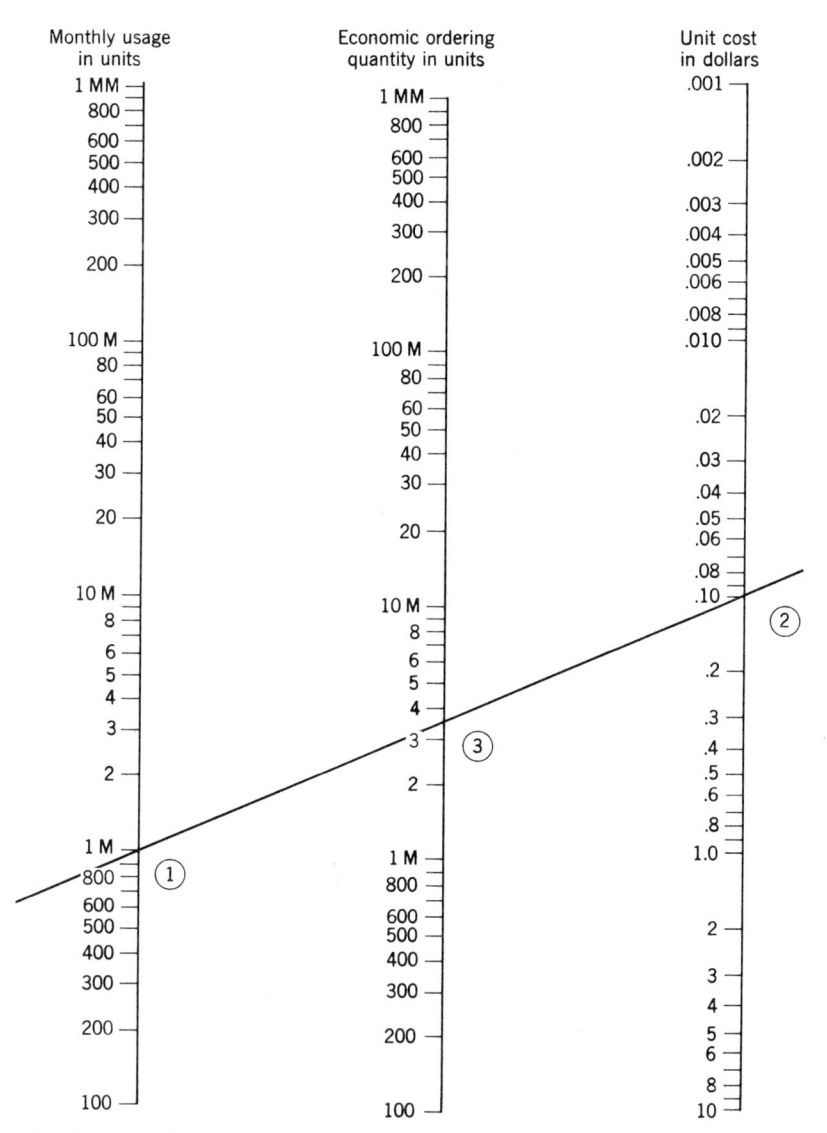

Figure 11-10 Sample EOQ nomograph for $10.00 ordering costs. To find the EOQ, place one end of a ruler on the appropriate point of the monthly usage scale (1) and the other end on the unit cost scale (2), then read the EOQ in units on the center scale (3).

Problems

11-1 Simplify the basic EOQ formula for the following:
  (a) Cost of placing an order is the same for all items in inventory.
  (b) Carrying charges are the same for all items in inventory.
  (c) Carrying charges and ordering costs are the same for all items in inventory.

INVENTORY CONTROL MODELS   377

11-2 Derive a formula for each of the following:
(a) The optimum number of orders to place monthly.
(b) The economic ordering quantity on a quarterly basis.

11-3 The Harmon Manufacturing Company has determined, from an analysis of its accounting and production data for part number 625, that its cost to purchase is $35 per order and $2.20 per part. Its inventory carrying charge is 18 percent of the average inventory. The firm currently purchases $22,000 of this part per year.
(a) What should the economic ordering quantity be?
(b) What is the optimum number of days' supply per optimum order?
(c) What is the optimum number of orders per year to minimize the firm's costs?

11-4 The Jarmon Shoe Company has found its purchases a large amount of industrial tapes for production of its shoes. Currently, it purchases $40,000 a year of the various sized tapes from the O'Donnell Company. A proposal was made by its supplier, whose offer consists of a 1¼ percent discount if Jarmon places an order quarterly. Jarmon has calculated the cost to purchase at $22.50 per order and inventory carrying costs at 22 percent. Should Jarmon accept the discount offer from O'Donnell? If the answer is no, what counteroffer should be made in terms of a discount?

11-5 The Lister Corporation finds itself in a tight cash position and is attempting to do something about it. The firm currently has an optimum purchasing policy, but it has been offered a 1 percent discount if they purchase twice a year. The firm purchases $50,000 of castings per year; administrative charge is $50 per purchase and carrying charge is 20 percent of the average inventory.
(a) Should the offer be accepted?
(b) If not, what counteroffer should be made in terms of discount or purchase amount?

11-6 The Wilcox Electric Company is considering the feasibility of changing suppliers for coupling hardware. Presently the firm has an optimum purchasing policy with Ace Hardware at a 1 percent discount. Current yearly purchases are $81,000. The administrative charge is $125 per purchase and the carrying charges are 25 percent of the average inventory level. Bids received from other suppliers are: Nutz, Inc. offers a 5 percent discount if ordered twice a year and Grabbers, Inc. offers a 3 percent discount if ordered four times a year. Which of the proposed offers should be accepted or should the present supplier be retained?

11-7 Arco, Inc., has a monthly usage for part #L25241 of 125 units. Inventory carrying costs are 25 percent of average inventory and ordering costs are $15 per order. Each part cost $2.00 and its economic ordering quantity is 300 units. The freight on a shipment of 300 units is $95. If 500 units are shipped, the freight is $122. Should a quantity of 500 be purchased in order to effect the savings in freight?

11-8 The QM Company uses Part No. 1150 at an average rate of 110 units per day, 250 days per year. It buys the part from the Marmo Manufacturing Corporation in Nashville for $75. The firm is contemplating using air freight instead of motor freight since it would reduce lead time from 10 days to 4 days. Ordering costs are $40 per order; Part No. 1150 weighs 15 lb; and inventory carrying costs are

25 percent of product cost. Air freight cost is $388 per ton, and motor freight is $110 per ton. Assume that there is no safety stock in the problem.
(a) What is the economic ordering quantity?
(b) What is the optimum orders per year?
(c) Do savings during the first year for reduced inventory investment and carrying costs justify the additional costs for air freight?

11-9 The Coca-Cola Company buys a large number of pallets every year which it uses in the warehousing of its bottled products. A vendor has offered them the following discount schedule for pallets:

Order Quantity	Price Per Unit
1–500	$10.00
501–1000	9.50
1001–1500	9.15
1501–over	9.00

The average yearly replacement for the past two years has been 1650 pallets, which looks realistic for this year. The cost per order is $12.50 and its carrying costs are 18 percent of average inventory. What quantity should be ordered?

11-10 The Jones Manufacturing Company has been incurring out of stock problems lately, which has caused a slow up in the company's shipments. Management has approached you to study the inventory items critical to its manufacturing operations. You have selected at random from this group part #3516, which has a long lead time. Your data, compiled from production records, are:

Usage During Past Reorder Period	Percent of Times This Quantity Was Used
1,200	0.02
1,225	0.10
1,250	0.15
1,275	0.20
1,300	0.30
1,325	0.10
1,350	0.07
1,375	0.04
1,400	0.02

Other information compiled is:

Normal lead time = 53 days
Average use per day = 25 units
Optimum number of orders per year = 5
Cost to store one unit per year = $4.00
Cost of being out of stock per unit = $30.00

What is the reorder point?

INTEGER AND NONLINEAR PROGRAMMING

11-11 A municipal water treatment plant purchases 100-lb bags of lime for use in the water treatment process. The number of bags used per day varies with the water consumption and past records have yielded the following data:

Usage During Past Reorder Period	Number of Times This Quantity Was Used
225	9
300	20
375	15
450	3
525	2
600	1

The normal lead time is 15 days and the average usage per day is 25 bags. Inventory cost is $2.00 per bag per year and being out of stock necessitates buying at the regular price of $5.00 per bag. The optimum orders per year are 15. As a consulting engineer for the municipality, you are asked to determine the reorder point.

11-12 The Ajax Manufacturing Company has compiled the following information concerning purchased part #5643. The average usage is 120 units per day with a standard deviation of 50 units based upon the plant operating 250 days per year. The acquisition cost per order is $20. Inventory holding cost is $1.00 per year and the acquisition lead time is 10 days, which is constant. The company has determined the allowable stockouts per year to be one.
(a) Calculate the economic ordering quantity.
(b) Using a fixed quantity-variable cycle inventory control system, calculate the required safety stock and the reorder point.
(c) Using a variable quantity-fixed cycle inventory control system, calculate the length of the review period and the required safety stock.

11-13 Use the information developed in Problem 11-12 except for inventory holding cost, which is $0.25 for each unit per year, and reasonable demand estimates which are given in the following table:

Working Days	Demand (Units) Minimum	Demand (Units) Average	Demand (Units) Maximum
1	40	100	160
5	366	500	634
10	810	1,000	1,190
15	1,268	1,500	1,732
20	1,732	2,000	2,268
25	2,200	2,500	2,800
30	2,670	3,000	3,330
35	3,146	3,500	3,854

Answer (a), (b), and (c) of Problem 11-12 using this new data. Ignore the allowable stockouts per year to be one in this problem.

11-14 The Margo Company manufactures part B-2000 on a special lathe for use in a continuous assembly. The assemblies that use B-2000 are manufactured at a slower rate. This allows time for doing odd jobs on the special lathe when it is not being used for part B-2000. When parts are being run, deliveries are made to the assembly area; otherwise, the assembly department draws parts from inventory. The following information is given for part B-2000:

> Production rate = 4000 pieces per day
> Assembly requirements = 1200 pieces per day
> Inventory holding cost per piece = $0.02 per year
> Set-up cost = $110
> Acquisition lead time = 10 working days
> Use a 250 working day year.

(a) Calculate the economic ordering quantity.
(b) Determine the reorder point.
(c) Suppose the use rate fluctuates. Would your answer to question (b) be altered? How?

11-15 The Margo Company has decided to expand its product line. All the odd jobs (as explained in Problem 11-14) have been taken off the special lathe. Instead, production on this lathe will be allotted to parts B-2000 (see Problem 11-14 for data) and F-1000 (part for a new product). The estimated figures for F-1000 from the production and accounting departments are:

> Production rate = 8000 pieces per day
> Assembly requirements = 5000 pieces per day
> Inventory holding cost per piece = $0.01 per year
> Changeover cost from F-1000 to B-2000 = $110
> Changeover cost from B-2000 to F-1000 = $90

(a) Calculate the optimum number of cycles per year.
(b) Determine the length of run for each part.

11-16 The Hudson Chemical Company manufactures dyes for the textile industry. Several of these products are manufactured on the same equipment. As inventory control manager, the production superintendent has requested you to determine how many cycles per year are needed to minimize cost. The accounting department has supplied you with the following data:

Product	Production Rate— Lbs/Day	Daily Usage Rate	Lbs per Year	Cost per Lb	Inventory Carrying Cost	Changeover Cost
Yellow	2000	50	100,000	$1.20	20%	$250
Red	4000	50	200,000	$1.43	20%	$160
Blue	500	150	75,000	$6.50	20%	$320
		250				

INVENTORY CONTROL MODELS

11-17 The Regis Paper Company has investigated the purchase of a new piece of machinery which is capable of producing several grades of paper. Before a decision can be reached on its purchase, management desires some additional information. To be specific, it wants to know the least cost operation in terms of production runs per year and the number of days for each run. The facts are given below to assist you in determining the information needed.

	Paper Grade			
	#1	#2	#3	#4
Daily production rate	10,000 lbs	4,000 lbs	2,000 lbs	4,000 lbs
Daily sales requirements	2,000 lbs	960 lbs	400 lbs	1,400 lbs
Inventory holding cost per pound	$1.00/M lb	$0.80/M lb	$0.60/M lb	$0.40/M lb
Cost per pound	$0.005	$0.004	$ 0.003	$ 0.002
Changeover costs	$5.00	$8.00	$10.00	$11.00
Inventory carrying cost:	20%	20%	20%	20%

Sales and production rate, based upon 250 day year

Bibliography

R. H. Bock and W. K. Holstein, *Production Planning and Control,* Columbus, O.: Charles E. Merrill Books, 1963.

E. H. Bowman and R. B. Fetter, *Analysis for Production and Operations Management,* Homewood, Ill.: Richard D. Irwin, 1967.

J. Buchon and E. Koeningsberg, *Scientific Inventory Management,* Englewood Cliffs, N.J.: Prentice-Hall, 1963.

E. S. Buffa, *Operations Management: Problems and Models,* New York: John Wiley & Sons, 1968.

N. L. Enrick, *Management Operations Research,* New York: Holt, Rinehart and Winston, 1965.

G. Hadley and T. M. Whitin, *Analysis of Inventory Systems,* Englewood Cliffs, N.J.: Prentice-Hall, 1963.

F. Hanssmann, *Operations Research in Production and Inventory Control,* New York: John Wiley & Sons, 1962.

F. S. Hillier and G. J. Lieberman, *Introduction to Operations Research,* San Francisco: Holden-Day, 1967.

D. W. Miller and M. K. Starr, *Executive Decisions and Operations Research,* Englewood Cliffs, N.J.: Prentice-Hall, 1969.

M. K. Starr and D. W. Miller, *Inventory Control: Theory and Practice,* Englewood Cliffs, N.J.: Prentice-Hall, 1962.

R. Stockton, *Basic Inventory Systems: Concepts and Analysis,* Boston: Allyn and Bacon, 1965.

Chapter TWELVE

Integer and Nonlinear Programming

Prior chapters have treated problems whose equations and inequalities are expressed as linear relationships. This chapter concentrates on OR techniques for solving integer linear programming problems and nonlinear or curvilinear programming problems. Nonlinear relationships may occur in the constraints, in the objective function, or in both simultaneously. Presently, a general overall approach for solving nonlinear programming problems does not exist, although certain specialized types can be solved.

Specialized Types of Integer and Nonlinear Programming Problems

Integer and nonlinear programming problems are difficult to solve because only a small number of computational procedures have been developed. Some of those that can be solved will be studied along with the appropriate techniques of analysis. No attempt will be made to study in detail the great variety of business problems that can be formulated as nonlinear programming problems.

One of the easiest ways for solving integer and nonlinear programming problems is to transform the problem into a form that permits application of linear programming. The nature of the transformation required to change a nonlinear programming problem into an acceptable form for the simplex method varies with the type of problem being studied. While some cases require no approximation, others do. In any event, these should be as accurate as possible. The simplex algorithm proves to be one of the most powerful devices for solving nonlinear programming problems.

A class of programming problems which is obtained from the general linear programming model by imposing the additional requirements that the variables can take on only integral values is referred to as *integer linear programming*. It is adaptable to problems that allow only whole numbers for the final solution. For example, assume that an optimum production plan requires buying several different types of machines. Obviously, only whole machines can be bought. Other applications include allocation of salesmen to sales districts, capital budgeting for research and development, and optimum location of warehouses.

A variation of integer programming is *mixed integer linear programming*. This technique applies to problems in which some of the variables are continuous while other have only integer values. For example, a container manufacturer must cut various sizes of blanks from sheet stock with minimum waste. One of the restrictions is that whole blanks must be cut from sheets. Thus, mixed integer linear programming is more applicable for this kind of problem than linear programming is. This OR technique has been applied to production planning, investment analysis, and similar problems.

Nonlinear programming problems which have been studied extensively are those in which the constraints are linear and the objective function is nonlinear. Consider, for example, a durable consumer product whose production time remains the same as volume is increased. However, in order to sell more and more of the product, the price must be reduced, resulting in a nonlinear objective function. Other problems of this type include promotion expenditures, advertising campaign expenditures, and distribution analyses. For many of these type problems, the objective function is written as the sum of a linear form plus a quadratic form, that is, the objective function contains squared terms. Computational procedures for finding optimal solutions have been developed when the objective function has certain properties. In some cases, calculus methods can be employed to solve the problem. In other cases, *quadratic programming* procedures are more effective in solving the problem. Fortunately, the simplex method can be modified for quadratic programming problems.

Other problems that are solvable by nonlinear programming methods include those whose objective function and constraints are nonlinear. In addition to a nonlinear objective function for a durable consumer product, the production constraints may exhibit nonlinear characteristics, caused by working the manufacturing departments overtime. As production line personnel work longer hours each day, their efficiency decreases, resulting in nonlinear constraints rather than linear constraints within the problem.

Specialized Nonlinear Programming Computational Procedures
The specialized types of nonlinear programming problems mentioned in the preceding section are only some of the major ones for which computational procedures have been developed. For the nonlinear programming problem, the computational procedures may not always yield an optimal solution in a finite number of steps. One must settle for procedures that provide only an approximate optimal solution or may require an infinite number of steps for convergence. This is in contrast with the simplex algorithm of linear programming in which an optimal answer is obtained within a finite number of steps.

To insure that an optimal solution for problems with nonlinear constraints can be obtained, stringent restrictions must be placed on both the constraints and the objective function. One technique for solving problems which have nonlinear constraints is the *classical optimization method*. This technique, based on calculus and the Lagrange multiplier, is a theoretical tool. Classical optimization techniques can be generalized to handle cases in which the variables are required to be non-negative and the constraints may be inequalities. These generalizations are primarily of theoretical value and do not usually constitute computational procedures. Another technique to solve this class of problems is searching for a *tangency case* and employing calculus methods for a final solution.

Not only are the simplex algorithm, calculus, and the Langrange multiplier used for solving nonlinear programming problems, but also other computational procedures are employed, such as dynamic programming and gradient type methods. *Dynamic programming* refers to business problems where changes occur over time and hence time must be considered explicitly. However, dynamic programming is not always used in this sense but frequently as a computational method involving recurrence relationships in which time is in no way relevant. This latter definition of the term relates to its narrow viewpoint. Dynamic programming is used in its broad and narrow sense in Chapter 15.

The *gradient method* or the steepest ascent (descent) method, like the simplex method, is an iterative process which moves from one feasible solution to another in order to improve the value of the objective function. If the objective function is envisioned as a surface in space, this method takes steps in the locally steeped direction that lead either up or down the curved surface until a peak, valley, or some upper or lower constraint is reached. As with ordinary maxima-minima, this process is not limited to the three-dimensional slopes that can be visualized. Calculus techniques, computing what is called the gradient vector, can lead through iterative steps to reach a solution. The gradient method differs from the simplex method since it does not guarantee that each successive solution will be nearer the optimum and may require an infinite number of iterations for convergence. This method, which is designed for use on computers, can be used when both the objective function and the constraints contain nonlinearities.

Integer Linear Programming

Integer linear programming will be the first of the techniques explored in this chapter. An integer linear programming problem is actually a variation of a linear programming problem which requires that the variables appearing in the final solution be non-negative whole numbers (0, 1, 2, . . .). This OR technique recognizes that many resources are indivisible, such as machinery and the assignment of men to jobs, and solves the problem on that basis.

It is tempting to round off noninteger solutions in problems involving indivisible resources, especially if the rounding is small relative to the values of the variables involved. However, such rounding can result in solutions far from the optimal integer solution, as shown in Figure 12-1 for two products. The best solution in the noninteger problem is at point A while point B represents the rounded solution (the closest integer point to point A). Nevertheless, point C produces the best contribution on an integer programming basis.

In Figure 12-2, the best convex region of a linear programming problem is shown. When the integer restriction is imposed, the feasible solution set contains only the critical points. By adding new restraining lines connecting the outside integer points, we can pretend the entire convex set of points, bounded by the axes and the new constraints, is a new problem. Its characteristics are such that the feasible region contains all integer points contained in the original feasible region and that every extreme

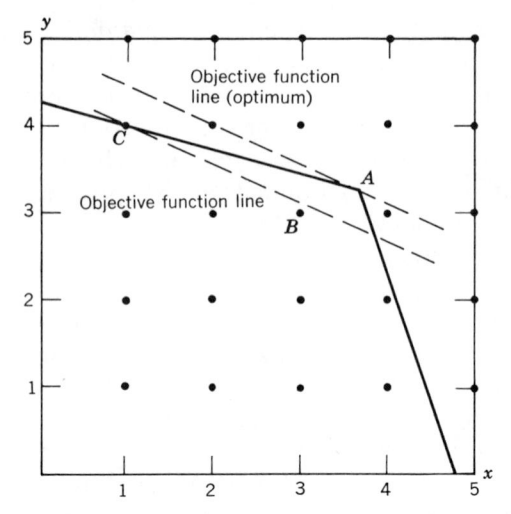

Figure 12-1 Linear programming problem with possible integer solutions.

point of the new feasible region is an integer point. From previous chapters, it was demonstrated that optimal solutions occur at extreme points. Thus, this section proceeds basically in the same manner to find the optimum.

Step 1. Integerize the Constraints

The first step in an integer linear programming problem is to "integerize" the original constraints. This involves transforming the constraints so that all of the coefficients are whole numbers. As a sample problem, the fractions in the constraint inequality $\frac{3}{8}P_1 + \frac{1}{2}P_2 \leq 2\frac{2}{5}$ can be converted into whole

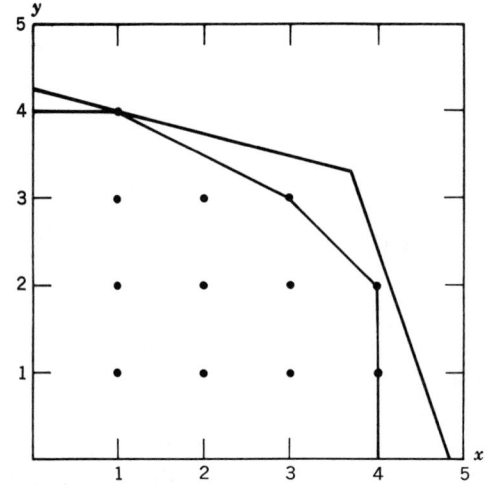

Figure 12-2 Linear programming problem with integer restrictions imposed.

386 OPERATIONS RESEARCH MODELS—CALCULUS

numbers by multiplying by the least common denominator, 40. The resulting constraint inequality, $15P_1+20P_2\leq 96$, can then be converted to an equality by adding a slack variable or $15P_1+20P_2+P_3=96$. The problem is to maximize the objective function, $Z=\$10P_1+\$5P_2$, subject to this constraint equation.

Step 2. Solve Using the Simplex Method

The next step is to solve the problem using the simplex method of linear programming. This gives as the optimal solution P_1 equals $6\frac{2}{5}$ and P_2 equals 0. The graph of this problem and the contribution lines are shown in Figure 12-3.

Step 3. Develop a Cutting Plane

Having solved for the best linear programming solution in the second step, the third step is to select the equation from the final tableau corresponding to the variable which has the largest fractional part. In the example, the equation selected from the tableau (Table 12-1) is:

$$P_1+1\frac{1}{3}P_2+\frac{1}{15}P_3=\frac{96}{15}$$

$$P_1=\frac{96}{15}-1\frac{1}{3}P_2-\frac{1}{15}P_3$$

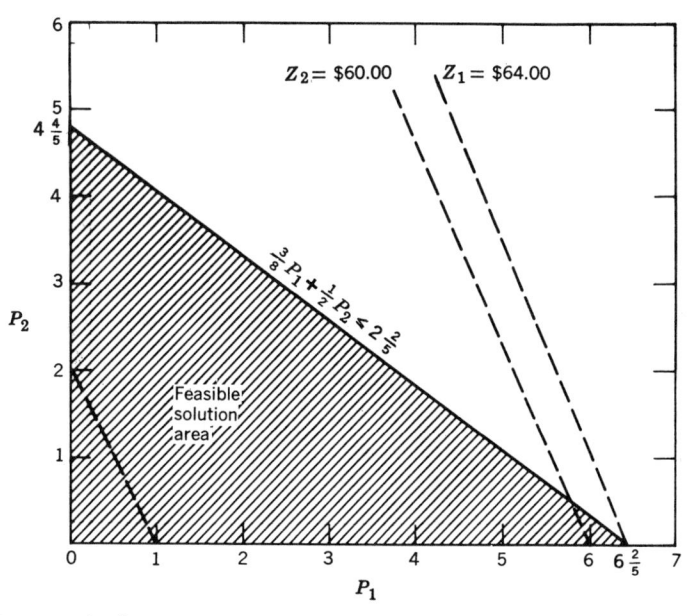

Figure 12-3 Graph showing optimum solution (Z_1) and integer solution (Z_2).

This equation serves to express the basic variable P_1 as a function of the variables P_2 and P_3. Using a prime (') to indicate integer values, the preceding equation becomes:

$$P'_1 = \frac{96}{15} - 1\frac{1}{3}P'_2 - \frac{1}{15}P'_3$$

Since P'_1 is a whole number (left-hand side of the equation), the right-hand side of the equal must be an integer (I) which can be written:

$$1\frac{1}{3}P'_2 + \frac{1}{15}P'_3 - \frac{96}{15} = I$$

Of course, we do not know whether this integer will be positive, negative, or zero. If we changed the coefficients of P'_2 and P'_3 as well as $96/15$ by some integer amount, the difference would still be an integer which is shown as follows:

$$\left(1\frac{1}{3} \pm I_1\right)P'_2 + \left(\frac{1}{15} \pm I_2\right)P'_3 - \left(\frac{96}{15} \pm I_3\right) = I$$

Suppose we change each coefficient and $96/15$ by those integer amounts that will leave the smallest non-integer number as the new value. This is shown as follows:

$$1\frac{1}{3} - 1 = \frac{1}{3}$$
$$\frac{1}{15} - 0 = \frac{1}{15}$$
$$\frac{96}{15} - 6 = \frac{6}{15} \quad \left(\text{remember } 6 = \frac{90}{15}\right)$$

The resulting equation is:

$$\frac{1}{3}P'_2 + \frac{1}{15}P'_3 - \frac{6}{15} = I$$
$$\frac{1}{3}P'_2 + \frac{1}{15}P'_3 = I + \frac{6}{15}$$

The left side of the new equation must be positive because all Ps are non-negative (P' is always an integer value of a P); their coefficients were adjusted to the smallest non-integer number possible. The value on the right-hand side of the last equality must be a positive whole number. Thus we can write the equality as an inequality $\frac{1}{3}P_2 + \frac{1}{15}P_3 \geq \frac{6}{15}$, which is our new constraint. This is sometimes referred to as a cutting plane or Gomory's technique. Adding a new slack variable P_4 with a coefficient of -1 (caused by a greater than and equal to condition) gives an equality constraint equation which is added to the original constraint to form a new linear programming problem. The equality constraint is:

$$\frac{1}{3}P'_2 + \frac{1}{15}P'_3 - P_4 = \frac{6}{15}$$

Step 4. Add Cutting Plane and Solve Using the Simplex Method

The fourth step is to add the equality constraint (Gomory's cutting plane) as a new row under that of the P_1 row in the modified tableau, shown in Table 12-1. Also, an additional column must be added for P_4. In this modi-

TABLE 12-1
Modified Tableau for Integer Linear Programming Problem

C_j	Product Mix	Quantity	$10 P_1	$5 P_2	$0 P_3	$0 P_4
$10	P_1	$\frac{96}{15}$	1	$1\frac{1}{3}$	$\frac{1}{15}$	0
	?	$\frac{6}{15}$	0	$\frac{1}{3}$	$\frac{1}{15}$	−1
?	Z_j	$64.00	(This row need not be copied for this step.)			
	$C_j − Z_j$		$0	−$8.33	−$0.66	$0

fied tableau, we have a problem with two constraints. Notice that P_4 cannot enter the solution at this step for it has a coefficient of −1 and its value would be −6/15 (not feasible.) The choice of a new basic variable is P_2 or P_3. The value of $C_j − Z_j$ row for P_3 is the smallest negative amount of P_2 and P_3. Bringing P_3 into the solution will reduce the value of the objective function less than by bringing in P_2. This is accomplished in Table 12-2. The solution is $P_1 = 6$, $P_2 = 0$. All variables are integers and the $C_j − Z_j$ row has no variables outside the solution that can improve on this solution. Thus we have solved for the optimal integer solution. The steps for solving an integer linear programming problem are set forth in Figure 12-4.

Illustrative Problem of Integer Linear Programming

The Excell Machinery Company manufactures three machines (products P_1, P_2, and P_3) with a contribution per unit as follows: P_1 of $200, P_2 of $400, and P_3 of $300. Each of these products pass through three production centers. Time required per center to produce each of the three products is shown on the bottom of the next page. Time available in the three production centers for the next week is: Center 1, 600 hours; Center 2, 400 hours; and Center 3,

TABLE 12-2
Final Tableau (Optimal) for Integer Linear Programming Problem

C_j	Product Mix	Quantity	$10 P_1	$5 P_2	$0 P_3	$0 P_4
$10	P_1	6	1	1	0	1
$ 0	P_3	6	0	5	1	−15
	Z_j	$60.00	$10	$10	$0	$10
	$C_j − Z_j$		$0	−$5	$0	−$10

INTEGER AND NONLINEAR PROGRAMMING

Step 1—Integerize the Constraints

Transform the constraints so that all of their coefficients are whole numbers, that is, integerize the constraints in the problem. Note: this step tends to simplify the problem when developing a cutting plane per step (3) below.

Step 2—Solve Using the Simplex Method

Solve the problem using the simplex method of linear programming. The final tableau will show either nonintegers or a combination of integers and nonintegers for values in the problem, such as products to be manufactured. Ignore fractional answers for slack variables since they represent unused resources, such as departmental time.

Step 3—Develop a Cutting Plane

Select the equation from the final simplex tableau corresponding to that variable, such as products to be manufactured, which has the largest fractional part. If there are two or more product variables with the same largest fractional part, select the equation which has the lowest contribution for a maximization problem or the highest cost for a minimization problem. Next, for each coefficient, subtract an integer amount that will leave the smallest non-integer number as the new value. All whole number coefficients, along with their variables, are dropped. Adding a new slack variable with a coefficient of minus one to these fractional coefficients and their corresponding variables in a maximization problem results in a new equation, called Gomory's cutting plane. A similar type cutting plane can be developed for a minimization problem.

Step 4—Add Cutting Plane and Solve Using the Simplex Method

Add the cutting plane as a new row in the final simplex tableau and solve using the simplex method of linear programming for this modified tableau. When the coefficients of the variables are negative in the new row, they must be ruled out as is the case with any simplex method problem. In addition, the first step of the simplex method must be modified. For a maximization problem, the smallest negative value (of the feasible variables) is selected while the smallest plus value (of the feasible variables) is selected for a minimization problem. Note if desired variables in the problem fail to become integers, repeat this last procedure.

Figure 12-4 Steps employed in integer linear programming—Gomory's cutting plane algorithm.

Product	Production Center 1	Production Center 2	Production Center 3
P_1	30 hr/unit	20 hr/unit	10 hr/unit
P_2	40 hr/unit	10 hr/unit	30 hr/unit
P_3	20 hr/unit	20 hr/unit	20 hr/unit

800 hours. How many machines of each type are required to maximize contribution in the next week if there are no sales limitations?

The problem becomes:

$$\text{Maximize } Z = \$200P_1 + \$400P_2 + \$300P_3$$

Subject to:
$$30P_1 + 40P_2 + 20P_3 \leq 600 \text{ hours}$$
$$20P_1 + 10P_2 + 20P_3 \leq 400 \text{ hours}$$
$$10P_1 + 30P_2 + 20P_3 \leq 800 \text{ hours}$$

Since all coefficients are already integers, the first step is not necessary. The second step is to solve the problem, using the simplex method of linear programming. The third and optimal linear programming simplex tableau is shown in Table 12-3, which contains noninteger variables.

If one considers rounding off the noninteger values of P_2 and P_3, the rounded solution is: P_2 equals 7 machines and P_3 equals 17 machines. Since these answers would exceed the constraints, we must continue our search for the optimal solution by developing Gomory's cutting plane, the third step of integer linear programming. This consists of choosing the equation corresponding to the element under the quantity column which has the largest fractional part in Table 12-3. The third tableau discloses that all three equations have the same fractional part, $2/3$. In this case, P_3 row is selected because it has the lowest contribution of the products in the final solution. Row P_6 should not be selected since it is unused time.

Starting with the P_3 equation, $5/6 P_1 + P_3 - 1/60 P_4 + 1/15 P_5 = 50/3$, we get the cutting plane:

$$\frac{5}{6}P_1 - \frac{1}{60}P_4 + \frac{1}{15}P_5 \geq \frac{2}{3}$$

Adding a surplus variable or slack variable P_7 with a coefficient of -1 for a greater than and equal to condition, this equation becomes:

$$\frac{5}{6}P_1 - \frac{1}{60}P_4 + \frac{1}{15}P_5 - P_7 = \frac{2}{3}$$

This equation is added to the optimal linear programming tableau as a new row, the fourth step in our computational procedure. This appears in Table 12-4, the modified tableau.

Adding a new constraint requires bringing a new variable into the

TABLE 12-3
Third Tableau (Optimal) of Linear Programming Problem

C_j	Product Mix	Quantity	$200 P_1	$400 P_2	$300 P_3	$0 P_4	$0 P_5	$0 P_6
$400	P_2	$\frac{20}{3}$	$\frac{1}{3}$	1	0	$\frac{1}{30}$	$-\frac{1}{30}$	0
$300	P_3	$\frac{50}{3}$	$\frac{5}{6}$	0	1	$-\frac{1}{60}$	$\frac{1}{15}$	0
$0	P_6	$\frac{800}{3}$	$-\frac{50}{3}$	0	0	$-\frac{2}{3}$	$-\frac{1}{3}$	1
	Z_j	$7,667	$383	$400	$300	$8.33	$6.66	$0
	$C_j - Z_j$		$-$183	$0	$0	$-$8.33	$-$6.66	$0

TABLE 12-4
Fourth Tableau (Table 12-3 Modified) of Illustrative Integer Linear Programming Problem

C_j	Product Mix	Quantity	$200 P_1	$400 P_2	$300 P_3	$0 P_4	$0 P_5	$0 P_6	$0 P_7
$400	P_2	$\frac{20}{3}$	$\frac{1}{3}$	1	0	$\frac{1}{30}$	$-\frac{1}{30}$	0	0
$300	P_3	$\frac{50}{3}$	$\frac{5}{6}$	0	1	$-\frac{1}{60}$	$\frac{1}{15}$	0	0
$0	P_6	$\frac{800}{3}$	$-\frac{50}{3}$	0	0	$-\frac{2}{3}$	$-\frac{1}{3}$	1	0
$0	P_7	$\frac{2}{3}$	$\frac{5}{6}$	0	0	$-\frac{1}{60}$	$\frac{1}{15}$	0	-1
	Z_j	$7,667	$383	$400	$300	$8.33	$6.66	$0	$0
	$C_j - Z_j$		$-$183	$0	$0	$-$8.33	$-$6.66	$0	$0

solution—which shall it be? The smallest decrease in the $C_j - Z_j$ row is related to P_5, which will be brought into the solution. Using the simplex method, the resulting tableau (Table 12-5) is optimal with respect to the cutting plane.

In Table 12-5, note that P_2, P_3, P_5, and P_6 have attained integer values. Since all entries in the $C_j - Z_j$ row are zero or negative, the fifth tableau represents the optimal solution to our problem of the Excell Machinery Company. It is not necessary for P_5 or P_6 to be integer values since they do not represent the actual products of the firm, but are only slack variables. If the tableau in Table 12-5 had not given us integers for the products manufactured, it would have been necessary to continue with additional tableau(s) by introducing into the solution the variable which now has the lowest negative value.

The optimal answer for this problem (from Table 12-5) is a contribu-

TABLE 12-5
Fifth Tableau of Illustrative Integer Linear Programming Problem (Optimal for First Cutting Plane)

C_j	Product Mix	Quantity	$200 P_1	$400 P_2	$300 P_3	$0 P_4	$0 P_5	$0 P_6	$0 P_7
$400	P_2	7	$\frac{3}{4}$	1	0	$\frac{1}{40}$	0	0	$-\frac{1}{2}$
$300	P_3	16	0	0	1	0	0	0	1
$0	P_6	270	$-12\frac{1}{2}$	0	0	$-\frac{3}{4}$	0	1	-5
$0	P_5	10	$12\frac{1}{2}$	0	0	$-\frac{15}{60}$	1	0	-15
	Z_j	$7,600	$300	$400	$300	$10	$0	$0	$100
	$C_j - Z_j$		$-$100	$0	$0	$-$10	$0	$0	$-$100

392   OPERATIONS RESEARCH MODELS—CALCULUS

tion of $7600. Seven P_2 machines and sixteen P_3 machines should be manufactured next week to maximize contribution. No P_1 machines should be manufactured. The question can be raised, were our calculations of any help? Based upon rounding figures that appeared in Table 12-3 ($P_2=7$ machines and $P_3=17$ machines), we would have erred on the number of P_3 machines to manufacture. This combination would have exceeded the constraints. Comparison of results in this case is not bad. However, other situations might have different results.

Nonlinear Objective Function and Linear Constraints

Nonlinear programming, in some cases, treats problems in which the objective function involves nonlinear expressions. This is basically a condition where the forces of supply and demand interact on one another. The following example is used where the objective function for one of two products is nonlinear.

The Keco Manufacturing Company produces two products, K and L. The linear constraints, shown in Figure 12-5, are:

$$x + 0.429y \leq 150$$
$$x + 0.750y \leq 175$$

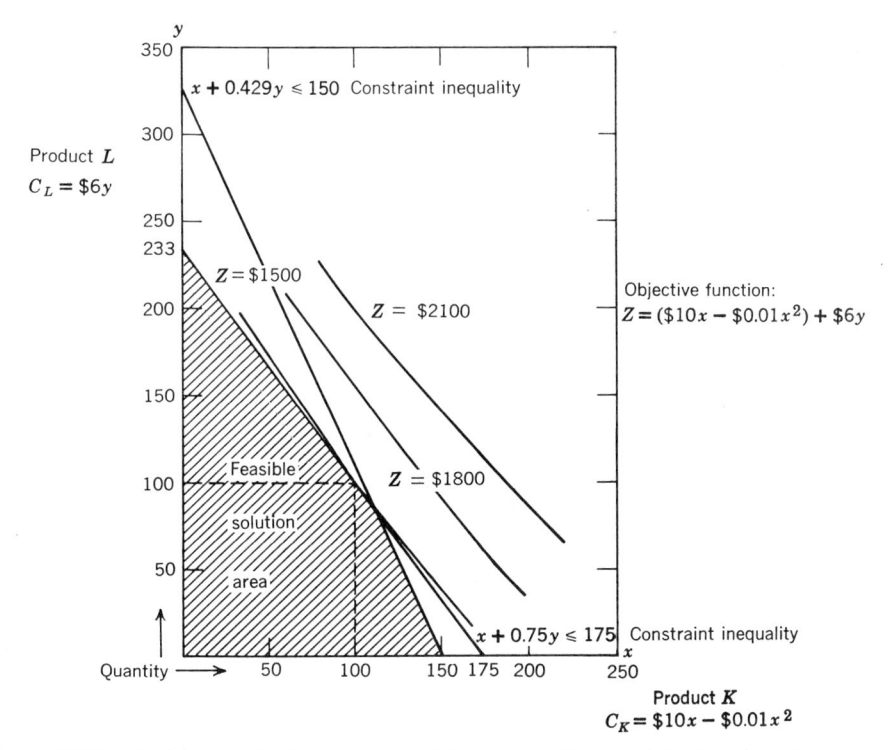

Figure 12-5 Problem with linear constraints and nonlinear objective function.

INTEGER AND NONLINEAR PROGRAMMING 393

The contribution for each unit of product L sold is $6.00; the total contribution of product L can be expressed as a linear equation: $C_L = \$6y$, where y equals the number of L units sold. The contribution for product K declines as additional units are marketed. The equation for the unit contribution of K is $C_K = \$10 - \$0.01x$, where x equals the number of K units sold. The foregoing expression was derived in this manner: if 100 units of K are offered for sale, the per unit contribution is $\$10 - (\$0.01)(100)$ or $9; if 200 units are offered for sale, the per unit contribution is $\$10 - (\$0.01)(200)$ or $8; and so forth. The total contribution obtained from any number of units will equal x times the unit contribution ($\$10 - \$0.01x$) or $x(\$10 - \$0.01x)$. This can be simplified as $\$10x - \$0.01x^2$. The total contribution for products K and L is: $Z = (\$10x - \$0.01x^2) + \$6y$ (where the total product contributions are separable.) Any number of contribution curves can be graphed in two-dimensional space as shown in Figure 12-5.

The majority difficulty one encounters in trying to solve a problem of this type is that the optimum solution will not be found by testing the corners, as is the case with the graphic method of programming. Although this problem can be solved graphically for 100 units of product K and 100 units of product L (illustrated in Figure 12-5), a mathematical method will give the most accurate solution. Also it will verify the graphical answer.

Upon inspection of Figure 12-5, the optimal solution occurs at the point where the contribution curve of the objective function (where Z equals a constant) touches the constraint line. The constraint line has a slope of -1.333 ($^{-233}\!/_{175}$). In order to solve the problem mathematically, it is necessary to take the first derivative of the objective function (where Z is a constant.):

$$Z = (10x - 0.01x^2) + 6y$$
$$Z - 6y = 10x - 0.01x^2$$
$$\frac{Z}{6} - y = \frac{10x - 0.01x^2}{6}$$
$$y = -\frac{10x - 0.01x^2}{6} + \frac{Z}{6}$$
$$y = -\frac{10x}{6} + \frac{0.01x^2}{6} + \frac{Z}{6}$$
$$\frac{dy}{dx} = -\frac{10}{6} + \frac{0.01x}{3}$$

Since we have a tangency case (the tangent to the contribution curve of the objective function is the same as the tangent to the line of the constraint), it is necessary to equate the two slopes:

$$-1.333 = -\frac{10}{6} + \frac{0.01x}{3}$$
$$-1.333 = -1.666 + 0.00333x$$
$$0.00333x = 0.333$$
$$x = 100 \text{ units of product K}$$

Substituting x back into the contraint equation, a value for y can be calculated:

$$x + 0.75y = 175$$
$$100 + 0.75y = 175$$
$$0.75y = 75$$
$$y = 100 \text{ units of product } L$$

Upon substitution of these values into the objective function, the optimum contribution is $1500, shown as follows:

$$Z = (\$10x - \$0.01x^2) + \$6y$$
$$Z = \$10(100) - \$0.01(100)^2 + \$6(100)$$
$$Z = \$1000 - \$100 + \$600$$
$$Z = \$1500$$

Many nonlinear programming problems with a nonlinear objective function can be solved by use of an approximation method. This technique is used in conjunction with the simplex method of linear programming. The basic approximation technique is that of replacing the functions (must be separable) in the problem by polygonal approximations (a set of lines joined together which approximate a curve), thereby reducing the problem to a form that can be solved by the simplex method. Several firms have developed computer programs which permit application of the simplex method for this nonlinear form.

Nonlinear Objective Function and Nonlinear Constraint

Nonlinear programming problems deal not only with nonlinear objective functions but also with nonlinear constraints. In the following illustrative problem, the objective function and constraint are:

$$\text{Maximize } Z = (\$7.34x - \$0.02x^2) + \$8y$$

Subject to:

$$2x^2 + 3y^2 \leq 12{,}500$$

All functions appearing in the above problem are separable. The term $2x^2$ is separate from $3y^2$ and $\$7.34x - \$0.02x^2$ is distinct from $\$8y$. The feasible region is a convex set of points corresponding to the preceding inequality and the objective function is concave. This is shown in Figure 12-6.

The optimum solution can be found graphically. The optimum units of x is 50 and y is 50. This point (shown in Figure 12-6) can be determined mathematically as the point where the slope of the constraint is equal to the slope of the contribution curve of the objective function. It is necessary initially to find the first derivative of the objective function (where Z is a constant):

$$Z = \$7.34x - \$0.02x^2 + \$8y$$
$$Z - 8y = 7.34x - 0.02x^2$$
$$-y = \frac{7.34x - 0.02x^2}{8} - \frac{Z}{8}$$
$$y = \frac{-7.34x}{8} + \frac{0.02x^2}{8} + \frac{Z}{8}$$
$$\frac{dy}{dx} = -0.917 + 0.005x$$

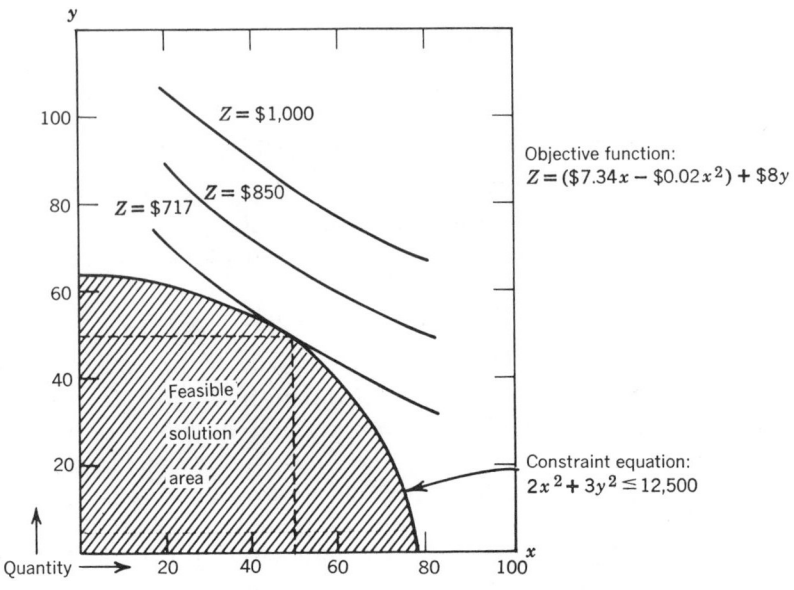

Figure 12-6 Problem with nonlinear constraint and nonlinear objective function.

In addition to the above derivative, the first derivative must be found for the constraint equation:

$$2x^2 + 3y^2 = 12{,}500$$
$$3y^2 = 12{,}500 - 2x^2$$
$$y^2 = \frac{12{,}500}{3} - \frac{2}{3}x^2$$
$$\frac{d}{dx}(y^2) = \frac{d}{dx}\left(\frac{12{,}500}{3} - \frac{2}{3}x^2\right)$$
$$2y\frac{dy}{dx} = -\frac{4}{3}x$$
$$\frac{dy}{dx} = -\frac{2}{3}\frac{x}{y}$$

Next, equating the slope of the constraint to the slope of the objective function, the resulting equation is:

$$-\frac{2}{3}\frac{x}{y} = -0.917 + 0.005x$$
$$\frac{1}{y} = -\frac{3}{2x}(0.917 + 0.005x)$$
$$y = \frac{-2x}{3(-0.917 + 0.005x)}$$

Substituting the preceding equation into the constraint equation gives:

$$2x^2 + 3\left[\frac{-2x}{3(-0.917 + 0.005x)}\right]^2 = 12{,}500$$
$$2x^2 + 3\left[\frac{(2)^2 x^2}{3^2(-0.917 + 0.005x)^2}\right] = 12{,}500$$

396 OPERATIONS RESEARCH MODELS—CALCULUS

From the graph, it can be seen that the optimal value of x will be some value near 50. The quantity of 50 units will be substituted for x in order to determine if the preceding equation equals 12,500:

$$2(50)^2 + 3\left[\frac{4(50)^2}{3^2(-0.917 + 0.005 \cdot 50)^2}\right] = 12,500$$

$$2(2500) + 3\left[\frac{10,000}{9(-0.667)^2}\right] = 12,500$$

$$5000 + 3\left[\frac{10,000}{9(0.444)}\right] = 12,500$$

$$5000 + 3(2500) = 12,500$$

$$12,500 = 12,500$$

Since an x value of 50 does satisfy the equation, x can be substituted into the constraint equation. A value for y can be determined as follows:

$$2x^2 + 3y^2 = 12,500$$
$$2(50)^2 + 3y^2 = 12,500$$
$$5000 + 3y^2 = 12,500$$
$$3y^2 = 7500$$
$$y^2 = 2500$$
$$y = 50 \text{ units}$$

Upon substitution of values for x and y into the objective function, the optimum contribution is $717:

$$Z = \$7.34x - \$0.02x^2 + \$8y$$
$$Z = \$7.34(50) - \$0.02(50)^2 + \$8(50)$$
$$Z = \$367 - \$50 + \$400$$
$$Z = \$717$$

The problem can also be solved by an approximation method discussed in the previous section; this method would give a solution that is quite close to the optimal solution. The reader is urged to consult the bibliography of this chapter for sources that explore the intricacies of this method.

Quadratic Programming

As stated previously, a quadratic programming problem is a nonlinear problem having linear constraints and an objective function which is the sum of a linear and a quadratic form. The importance of having a systematic method for solving quadratic programming problems is that many problems for which a linear programming approximation would not be adequate can be better approximated by a model containing a quadratic objective function. Further, existing linear programming computer programs need only slight changes to enable them to handle these quadratic problems. It should be noted that the following procedures are only applicable when the objective function is concave. Other methods are available for solving a convex objective function, but these are not presented in this chapter.

A quadratic objective function in n variables in matrix notation can be written as:

$$f(X) = B^T X + \tfrac{1}{2} X^T C X$$

where B is an $(n \times 1)$ vector, X is an $(n \times 1)$ vector, and C is an $(n \times n)$ matrix. The superscript (T) on the vectors B and X stands for the transpose of those vectors. For example, if the vector X is an $(n \times 1)$ vector, the transpose of X is a $(1 \times n)$ vector. The term $X^T C X$ is the quadratic part of the objective function. When expressing the strictly quadratic part of the quadratic function in matrix form, the matrix must always be made symmetric. It should be noted that a transpose of a symmetric matrix is the same matrix:

$$\left[\text{example}: \begin{pmatrix} 1 & 2 \\ 2 & 1 \end{pmatrix}^T = \begin{pmatrix} 1 & 2 \\ 2 & 1 \end{pmatrix} \right].$$

Quadratic programming can be illustrated by the following problem:

$$\text{Maximize } Z \text{ or } f(x,y) = 12x + 12y + 4xy - 4x^2 - 4y^2$$

Subject to:

$$3 - y \geq 0$$
$$6 - x - y \geq 0$$
$$x, y \geq 0$$

In order to find the stationary points (maximum, minimum, or inflection points) of the objective function, it is necessary to set the first partial derivatives of the objective function equal to zero (where Z is a constant):

$$\frac{\delta f(x,y)}{\delta x} = 12 - 8x + 4y = 0$$

$$\frac{\delta f(x,y)}{\delta y} = 12 + 4x - 8y = 0$$

Solving this set of equations simultaneously, the values $x = 3$ and $y = 3$ represent the relative maximum of the objective function (where Z is a constant). Since we have solved only for stationary points, we cannot be sure that we have solved for a maximum. A method will be given below to resolve this difficulty.

By referring to matrix notation, the objective function can be written in the proper matrix form for the illustrative problem:

$$f(X) = B^T X + \frac{1}{2} X^T C X = (12, 12) \begin{pmatrix} x \\ y \end{pmatrix} + \frac{1}{2}(x, y) \begin{bmatrix} -8 & 4 \\ 4 & -8 \end{bmatrix} \begin{pmatrix} x \\ y \end{pmatrix} \quad \text{(Equation 12-1)}$$

The values obtained for the first term $(B^T X)$ are the constant terms from the first partial derivatives of the objective function. Similarly, the values for the second term $(\tfrac{1}{2} X^T C X)$ are the second partial derivatives with respect to x and y of the objective function.

A method is needed at this point to determine whether the stationary point is a relative maximum, a relative minimum, or an inflection point. We know the values (second partial derivatives of the objective function) of f_{xx} ($=f_{11}$), f_{xy} ($=f_{12}$), f_{yx} ($=f_{21}$), and f_{yy} ($=f_{22}$), which are the following constants:

$$f_{11} = -8 \qquad f_{21} = 4$$
$$f_{12} = 4 \qquad f_{22} = -8$$

A differentiable function $f(X)$ is concave in a neighborhood of the point X^0 if the following conditions are met:

$$f_{11}(X^0) < 0$$

$$\begin{vmatrix} f_{11}(X^0) & f_{12}(X^0) \\ f_{21}(X^0) & f_{22}(X^0) \end{vmatrix} > 0$$

$$\begin{vmatrix} f_{11}(X^0) & f_{12}(X^0) & f_{13}(X^0) \\ f_{21}(X^0) & f_{22}(X^0) & f_{23}(X^0) \\ f_{31}(X^0) & f_{32}(X^0) & f_{33}(X^0) \end{vmatrix} < 0$$

etc.

If the indicated determinants alternate in sign as shown above, where f_{ij} is a second-order partial derivative evaluated at the point X^0, the function $f(X)$ is strictly concave in a neighborhood of the point X^0. Otherwise, the function $f(X)$ is convex in a neighborhood of the point X^0 if all the expressions are positive. In the example, X^0 equals (3,3) for a starting point, as shown in Figure 12-7.

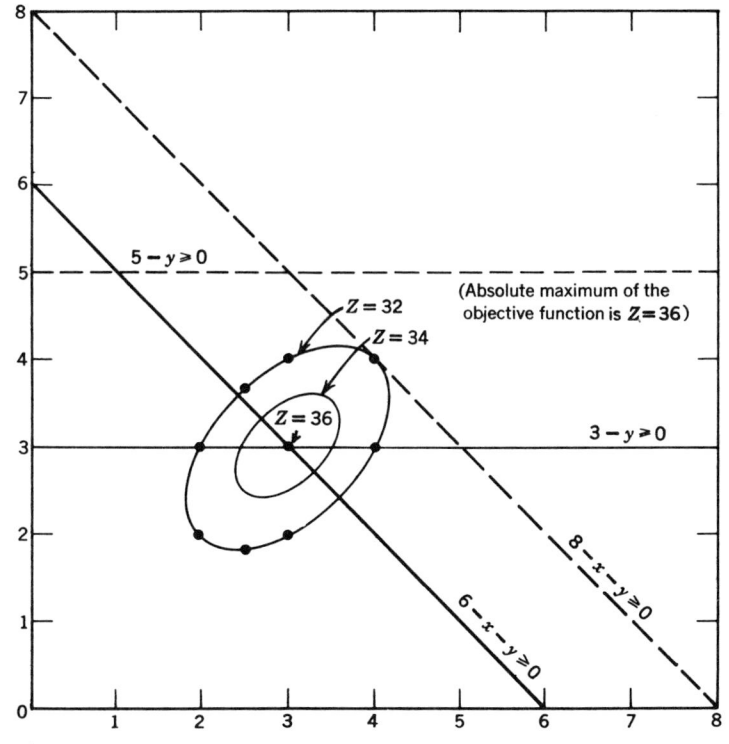

Figure 12-7 Absolute maximum of the objective function for quadratic programming problem.

$$f_{11}(3,3) = -8 < 0$$

$$\begin{vmatrix} f_{11}(3,3) & f_{12}(3,3) \\ f_{21}(3,3) & f_{22}(3,3) \end{vmatrix} = \begin{vmatrix} -8 & 4 \\ 4 & -8 \end{vmatrix} = 64 - (16) = 48 > 0$$

By the preceding mathematical rule, we know that $x=3$ and $y=3$ is a point where f attains a relative maximum since f is strictly concave. Having established that the objective function is concave, the matrices and vectors for the illustrative problem are:

$$A = \begin{bmatrix} 0 & 1 \\ 1 & 1 \end{bmatrix}, \quad B = \begin{pmatrix} 12 \\ 12 \end{pmatrix}, \quad C = \begin{bmatrix} -8 & 4 \\ 4 & -8 \end{bmatrix}, \quad I = \begin{bmatrix} 1 & 0 \\ 0 & 1 \end{bmatrix}, \quad Q = \begin{pmatrix} 3 \\ 6 \end{pmatrix}$$

$$\begin{bmatrix} \text{matrix of} \\ \text{coefficients} \\ \text{for} \\ \text{constraints} \end{bmatrix} \begin{pmatrix} \text{vector} \\ \text{of} \\ \text{constants} \\ \text{for} \\ \text{objective} \\ \text{function} \end{pmatrix} \begin{bmatrix} \text{matrix of 2nd-} \\ \text{order partial} \\ \text{derivatives for} \\ \text{the objective} \\ \text{function} \end{bmatrix} \begin{bmatrix} \text{identity} \\ \text{matrix} \end{bmatrix} \begin{pmatrix} \text{vector} \\ \text{of} \\ \text{constants} \\ \text{for} \\ \text{constraints} \end{pmatrix}$$

The detached coefficient form, as used for the initial simplex tableau, is as follows:

$$\begin{array}{cccccc} X & U & V & W & Z_1 & Z_2 & Y \end{array}$$
$$\begin{bmatrix} C & -A & I & 0 & I & -I & 0 \\ A & 0 & 0 & I & 0 & 0 & I \end{bmatrix} = \begin{bmatrix} -B \\ Q \end{bmatrix} \quad \text{(Equation 12-2)}$$

where Equation 12-2 is given without mathematical proof.[1]

Replacing the appropriate vectors and matrices set forth above for the terms in Equation 12-2, the first simplex tableau of the illustrative problem is shown in Table 12-6. The first two rows have been multiplied by a -1 in order to have positive B values in Equation 12-2. This permits the use of the simplex method without extensive modification.

In the first simplex tableau, the starting basis for the rows consists of the artificial variables, z_{12}, z_{22}, y_1, and y_2. It should be noted that these variables form an identity matrix. These variables, assigned pseudo objective function coefficients (each with the value 1), provide a starting computational basis for this minimization problem. The objective is to eliminate two artificial variables z_{12} and z_{22} from the solution and replace them with x and y values. In Table 12-6, the largest negative value is -6 for column y, the basis for the most negative criterion. The necessary changes for the second tableau are found in Table 12-7. Just as we used 1s for the artificial variables in the C_j row and column, we use the same approach for the y variable in order to facilitate computations.

Using the rules of linear programming for a minimization problem, we find the column with the largest negative value in the second tableau is x. The row that will be replaced is z_{12}. The changes are reflected in the third tableau (Table 12-8) where a value of 1 is inserted for the x variable.

Inspection of the third tableau (Table 12-8) shows there are still a few

---

[1] Reference for the proof is C. R. Carr and C. W. Howe, *Quantitative Decision Procedures in Management and Economics*, New York: McGraw-Hill Book Company, 1964.

TABLE 12-6
First Simplex Tableau for Quadratic Programming Problem with Concave Objective Function

C_j			0	0	0	0	0	0	0	0	0	0	1	1	1	1
	Basis	B / Q	x	y	u_1	u_2	v_1	v_2	w_1	w_2	z_{11}	z_{21}	z_{12}	z_{22}	y_1	y_2
1	z_{12}	12	8	−4	0	1	−1	0	0	0	−1	0	1	0	0	0
1	z_{22}	12	−4	8	1	1	0	−1	0	0	0	−1	0	1	0	0
1	y_1	3	0	1	0	0	0	0	1	0	0	0	0	0	1	0
1	y_2	6	1	1	0	0	0	0	0	1	0	0	0	0	0	1
	Z_j	33	5	6	1	2	−1	−1	1	1	−1	−1	1	1	1	1
	$C_j − Z_j$		−5	−6	−1	−2	1	1	−1	−1	1	1	0	0	0	0

TABLE 12-7
Second Simplex Tableau for Quadratic Programming Problem with Concave Objective Function

C_j			0	1	0	0	0	0	0	0	0	1	1	1	1
Basis	B Q	x	y	u_1	u_2	v_1	v_2	w_1	w_2	z_{11}	z_{21}	z_{12}	z_{22}	y_1	y_2
1 z_{12}	18	6	0	$\frac{1}{2}$	$1\frac{1}{2}$	-1	$-\frac{1}{2}$	0	0	-1	$-\frac{1}{2}$	1	$\frac{1}{2}$	0	0
1 y	$1\frac{1}{2}$	$-\frac{1}{2}$	1	$-\frac{1}{8}$	$-\frac{1}{8}$	0	$-\frac{1}{8}$	0	0	0	$-\frac{1}{8}$	0	$-\frac{1}{8}$	0	0
1 y_1	$1\frac{1}{2}$	$\frac{1}{2}$	0	$-\frac{1}{8}$	$-\frac{1}{8}$	0	$\frac{1}{8}$	1	0	0	$\frac{1}{8}$	0	$-\frac{1}{8}$	1	0
1 y_2	$4\frac{1}{2}$	$1\frac{1}{2}$	0	$\frac{3}{8}$	$1\frac{3}{8}$	-1	$-\frac{3}{8}$	0	1	0	$-\frac{3}{8}$	0	$\frac{3}{8}$	0	1
Z_j	$25\frac{1}{2}$	$7\frac{1}{2}$	1	$\frac{3}{8}$	$1\frac{3}{8}$	-1	$\frac{3}{8}$	1	1	-1	$-\frac{3}{8}$	1	$\frac{3}{8}$	1	1
$C_j - Z_j$		$-7\frac{1}{2}$	0	$-\frac{3}{8}$	$-1\frac{3}{8}$	1	$\frac{3}{8}$	-1	-1	1	$\frac{3}{8}$	0	$\frac{5}{8}$	0	0

402 OPERATIONS RESEARCH MODELS—CALCULUS

TABLE 12-8
Third Simplex Tableau for Quadratic Programming Problem with Concave Objective Function

C_j			1	1	0	0	0	0	0	0	0	0	1	1
	Basis	B Q	x	y	u_1	u_2	v_1	v_2	w_1	w_2	z_{11}	z_{21}	z_{12}	z_{22}	y_1	y_2
1	x	3	1	0	$\frac{1}{12}$	$\frac{1}{4}$	$-\frac{1}{6}$	$-\frac{1}{12}$	0	0	$-\frac{1}{6}$	$-\frac{1}{12}$	$\frac{1}{6}$	$\frac{1}{12}$	0	0
1	y	3	0	1	$\frac{1}{6}$	$\frac{1}{4}$	$-\frac{1}{12}$	$-\frac{1}{6}$	0	0	$-\frac{1}{12}$	$-\frac{1}{6}$	$\frac{1}{12}$	$-\frac{1}{6}$	0	0
1	y_1	0	0	0	$-\frac{1}{6}$	$-\frac{1}{4}$	$\frac{1}{12}$	$\frac{1}{6}$	1	0	$\frac{1}{12}$	$\frac{1}{6}$	$-\frac{1}{12}$	$-\frac{1}{6}$	1	0
1	y_2	0	0	0	$-\frac{1}{4}$	$-\frac{1}{2}$	$\frac{1}{4}$	$\frac{1}{4}$	0	1	$-\frac{1}{4}$	$-\frac{1}{4}$	$-\frac{1}{4}$	$-\frac{1}{4}$	0	1
	Z_j	6	1	1	$-\frac{1}{6}$	$\frac{1}{4}$	$-\frac{1}{12}$	$-\frac{1}{6}$	1	1	$\frac{1}{12}$	$\frac{1}{6}$	$-\frac{1}{12}$	$-\frac{1}{6}$	1	1
	$C_j - Z_j$		0	0	$\frac{1}{6}$	$\frac{1}{4}$	$-\frac{1}{12}$	$-\frac{1}{6}$	-1	-1	$-\frac{1}{12}$	$-\frac{1}{6}$	$1\frac{1}{12}$	$1\frac{1}{6}$	0	0

minus figures. A closer examination reveals that the possible rows to replace are y_1 and y_2, and not x and y. Since we cannot replace row x or y, we have reached the final solution. To review, the original objective function and constraints are reproduced below for convenience:

$$\text{Maximize } Z = 12x + 12y + 4xy - 4x^2 - 4y^2$$

Subject to:

$$3 - y \geq 0$$
$$6 - x - y \geq 0$$
$$x - y \geq 0$$

Inserting the values ($x=3$, $y=3$, $y_1=0$ and $y_2=0$) from the final tableau into the objective function, the results are:

$$\text{Maximize } Z = 12(3) + 12(3) + (4)(3)(3) - 4(3)^2 - 4(3)^2$$
$$Z = 36 + 36 + 36 - 36 - 36$$
$$Z = 36$$

Two partial derivatives (set to zero) based upon the objective function are:

$$\frac{\delta f(x,y)}{\delta x} = 12 - 8x + 4y = 0$$
$$12 - 8(3) + 4(3) = 0$$
$$12 - 24 + 12 = 0$$

$$\frac{\delta f(x,y)}{\delta y} = 12 + 4x - 8y = 0$$
$$12 + 4(3) - 8(3) = 0$$
$$12 + 12 - 24 = 0$$

The problem is subject to these constraints:

$$3 - y \geq 0$$
$$3 - 3 \geq 0$$
$$0 = 0 \text{ (per } y_1 \text{ in the final tableau)}$$
$$6 - x - y \geq 0$$
$$6 - 3 - 3 \geq 0$$
$$6 - 6 \geq 0$$
$$0 = 0 \text{ (per } y_2 \text{ in the final tableau)}$$
$$x, y \geq 0$$
$$3, 3 > 0$$

The answers for x and y are graphed in Figure 12-7.

It should be noted that if the constraints are changed for this problem, the optimal solution will be somewhere within the area of feasible solutions. For example, if the constraints are changed from $6 - x - y \geq 0$ to $8 - x - y \geq 0$ and from $3 - y \geq 0$ to $5 - y \geq 0$, the optimum solution lies within the feasible area ($Z = 36$). (The dotted lines in Figure 12-7 indicate this condition). The reason is that the global maximum of the objective function is unique and will never change. The calculated values for the objective function (Z) on the graph indicate this condition.

Nonlinear Programming Application—American Products Corporation

The American Products Corporation which produces a wide variety of consumer products has additional manufacturing time available on its second shift in Department 22 of its largest plant. Management is considering the production of two new products—RX and SY—which can be manufactured completely in this department. However, management needs the assistance of the OR group in deciding what quantities of each should be produced weekly to maximize profits assuming all products manufactured can be sold. The weekly unused time on three types of production machines is given as follows:

Injection machines	550 hours
Molding machines	600 hours
Assembly machines	1200 hours

Thus, considerable time is available weekly on the second shift.

In addition to the foregoing data, the OR group has obtained all relevant input from the marketing and production departments. The market research group has concluded that the per unit contribution for product RX is $18 per unit while the comparable contribution for product SY is $20−$.005x where x equals the number of units sold. The production department has estimated that the manufacturing time (hours) for these two new products is:

Machine	RX	SY
Injection	2.50	2.50
Molding	1.75	2.00
Assembly	4.00	3.00

Plotting the foregoing data in Figure 12-8 indicates that injection machines are the constraining ones in the problem; therefore, the other two machine constraint lines are ignored. Inspection of this illustration indicates a tangency case, that is, the tangent to the objective function (contribution) curve is the same as the tangent to the constraint line. Hence, it is necessary to equate the two slopes.

Before equating the slope of the constraint line to the objective function, the derivatives of both must be determined. The first derivative of the constraint equation

$$2.5y + 2.5x = 550$$

is a −1. Similarly, the first derivative of the objective function, equation

$$Z = 18y + (20x - .005x^2)$$

is a $-\frac{10}{9} + \frac{.005}{9}x$. Equating the two first derivatives

$$-1 = -\frac{10}{9} + \frac{.005}{9}x$$

INTEGER AND NONLINEAR PROGRAMMING

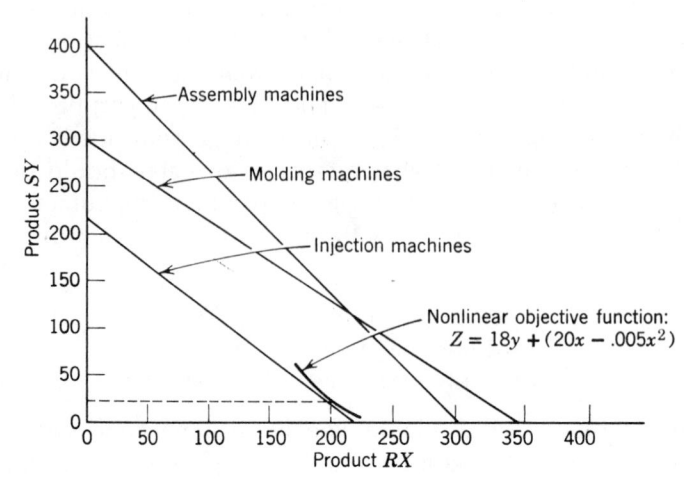

Figure 12-8 Linear production constraints for all machines and nonlinear objective function.

results in an x value of 200 units for product RX. Substituting this value for x in the constraint equation gives a value of 20 units for product SY. These two values can be verified graphically, as shown in Figure 12-8. Finally, these values are substituted in the objective function equation for a weekly contribution of $4160.

Summary

This chapter has presented some of the more easily understood concepts found in the literature on integer and nonlinear programming. These have included integer linear programming, nonlinear objective functions and constraints, and quadratic programming. One should not get the impression that once the foregoing material has been understood, he (she) has mastered integer and nonlinear programming. In reality, he has only scratched the surface. Some of the computational techniques presented may be superseded by more efficient and less complex ones in the near future. As in the past, one of the most powerful techniques for solving nonlinear programming problems is to transform the objective function and constraints by some means into a form which allows utilizing the simplex method of linear programming.

Questions

1. (a) What are the similarities and differences between a linear programming problem and a integer linear programming problem?

(b) What are the similarities and differences between a linear programming problem and a nonlinear programming problem?

2. Describe briefly the methods presented in this chapter to solve nonlinear programming problems.

Problems

12-1 The Dumont Corporation, a manufacturer of television sets, sells portable models in its color line. The problem is to determine the optimal product mix of its portable color television line. This line consists of three models: wood, plastic, and metal. The objective is to maximize contribution to fixed costs and profit based upon the following data (applicable to this line only):

	Wood	Plastic	Metal	Manhours Available for Next Week
Wood Cabinet Department	2.0	0	3.0	550
Plastic Cabinet Department	0	1.8	0.2	440
Chassis Assembly Department	2.0	2.0	2.0	400
Final Assembly Department	1.25	1.25	1.33	360
Contribution per set	$55	$50	$60	

Assuming the firm can sell everything it can manufacture next week, what quantities (integers only) of wood, plastic, and metal color TV sets should be produced?

12-2 The Cutting Department of the Eastman Company requisitions from the Stock Control Department a plastic film of 85 feet (fixed stock unit length) which can be cut according to two different cutting patterns. Pattern 1 will cut each stock length into two 35 feet lengths with 15 feet of scrap film. Pattern 2 will cut each stock length into one 35 feet piece and two 25 feet pieces. Presently, a customer order is for eight pieces of 35 feet length and six pieces of 25 feet length. What is the smallest number of stock units required to fill this order, that is, what number of stock units should be cut according to each pattern in order to minimize trim loss?

12-3 The Grosse Manufacturing Company produces a wide range of products in its many factories scattered around the country. In three departments of one plant, products A and B are manufactured whose linear constraints are as follows:

	Hours Required		Hours Available
Department	Product A	Product B	Weekly
15	2.5	2.5	600
17	1.75	2.0	600
21	4.0	3.25	1200

The per unit contribution for product A is $18.00 while the contribution for product B is subject to the quantity that is sold. The per-unit contribution for product B is $20.00 − $0.005X where X equals the number of units sold.

Assuming the firm can sell all products A and B that it can manufacture, what is the maximum contribution the firm can expect weekly?

12-4 The Loomis Manufacturing Company produces a wide range of products. One plant currently produces two products D and E for which the linear constraints are as follows:

	Hours Required Product D	Hours Required Product E	Manhours Available Daily
Machinery Department	3.0	3.0	600
Electrical Department	1.75	2.0	500
Assembly Department	4.0	3.0	1,000
Painting Department	0.25	0.25	100

The contribution for each unit of product D is $20 while the contribution for each unit of product E is subject to the quantity that is sold. The per unit contribution for product E has been determined to be $21—$0.005x where x equals the number of units sold. The decrease in contribution is based upon the fact that more units can be sold at a lower price. Total contribution for any number of E units sold equals $21x − $0.005x². Assuming the firm can sell all it can manufacture, what quantities of products D and E should it manufacture to maximize its contribution?

12-5 The Dalton Manufacturing Company has a condition where both the objective function and the constraints are nonlinear for two products F and G produced in one department of its manufacturing plant. The systems analysis group has been able to determine on a daily basis the mathematical requirements of the problem which are:

$$\text{Maximize contribution} = \$5.60x - \$0.02x^2 + \$8y$$

Subject to:
$$6x^2 + 12y^2 \leq 28{,}800$$
$$x, y \geq 0$$

Based upon this data, what maximum daily contribution and quantities can the firm expect to make?

12-6 The operations reasearch team of the Arcose Company has come up with the mathematical data (daily basis) needed for two products which the firm manufactures. It also has determined that this is a nonlinear programming problem, having linear constraints and an objective function which is the sum of a linear and a quadratic form. The pertinent data, gathered by the OR team, is:

Maximize:

$$\text{Contribution} = \$15x + \$20y + \$1xy - \$2x^2 - \$2y^2$$

Subject to:

$$10 - y \geq 0$$
$$12 - x - y \geq 0$$
$$x \geq 0$$
$$y \geq 0$$

Find the maximum contribution and number of units that can be expected for these two products which are a part of the firm's total output.

12-7 Suppose both constraints in Problem 12-6, namely $10 - y \geq 0$ and $12 - x - y \geq 0$, are changed to $8 - y \geq 0$ and $10 - x - y \geq 0$, respectively, while all other values in the problem are unchanged. Find the maximum contribution and number of units that can be expected for these two products which are a small part of the firm's total output. In what way(s) do the solutions for Problems 12-6 and this problem differ?

Bibliography

W. J. Baumol, *Economic Theory and Operations Analysis*, Englewood Cliffs, N.J.: Prentice-Hall, 1965.

J. C. G. Boot, *Quadratic Programming*, Chicago: Rand McNally and Company, 1964.

J. Bracken and G. P. McCormick, *Selected Applications of Nonlinear Programming*, New York: John Wiley & Sons, 1968.

R. S. Garfinkel and G. L. Nemhauser, *Integer Programming*, New York: John Wiley & Sons, 1971.

H. Greenberg, *Integer Programming*, New York: Academic Press, 1971.

G. Hadley, *Nonlinear and Dynamic Programming*, Reading, Mass.: Addison-Wesley Publishing Company, 1964.

F. S. Hillier and G. J. Lieberman, *Introduction to Operations Research*, San Francisco: Holden-Day, 1967.

D. M. Himmelblau, *Applied Nonlinear Programming*, New York: McGraw-Hill Book Company, 1972.

R. W. Llewellyn, *Linear Programming*, New York: Holt, Rinehart and Winston, 1964.

O. L. Mangarsarian, *Nonlinear Programming*, New York: McGraw-Hill Book Company, 1969.

T. L. Saaty and J. Bram, *Nonlinear Mathematics*, New York: McGraw-Hill Book Company, 1964.

H. M. Wagner, *Principles of Operations Research with Applications to Managerial Decisions*, Englewood Cliffs, N.J.: Prentice-Hall, 1969.

W. I. Zangwill, *Nonlinear Programming: A Unified Approach*, Englewood Cliffs, N.J.: Prentice-Hall, 1969.

5
Operations Research Models – Simulation Techniques

Chapter THIRTEEN
Queuing Models

The theory of queues or waiting-line theory has its origin in the work of A. K. Erlang, starting in 1909. He experimented on a problem dealing with the congestion of telephone traffic. During busy periods, intending callers experienced some delay because the operators were unable to handle the calls as rapidly as they were made. The original problem Erlang treated was the calculation of this delay for one operator, and in 1917 the results were extended to the case of several operators. This was the year that Erlang published his well-known work, *Solution of Some Problems in the Theory of Probabilities of Significance in Automatic Telephone Exchanges*. Development in the field of telephone traffic continued largely along the lines initiated by Erlang, and the main publications were those of Molina in 1927 and Thornton D. Fry in 1928. It was not until the end of World War II that this early work was extended to other general problems involving queues or waiting lines.

Initially, this chapter concentrates on the mathematical derivations of the formulas for a single-channel queuing problem. Mathematical models for multichannel queuing problems are given without mathematical proof. Next, the Monte Carlo method is presented. Basically, it is a simulation technique in which statistical distribution functions are created by using a table of random numbers. It is used for solving single-channel and multichannel waiting line problems.

Use of Arrival Rates and Service Rates

Queuing theory, like most mathematical techniques, has its own set of terms. The term queue or waiting line discipline refers to the condition in which arrivals are selected for service. The procedure in this chapter is that arrivals take their place in the waiting line on a first-come first-served basis. In the same manner, arrivals in line will be serviced on a next in line-next served basis. Although some priority could change this pattern of servicing, the analysis does not consider this possibility.

Arrivals can be uniform over a period of time or they can be at random. The arrival rate can take the form of employees arriving at the firm's tool crib or, in another situation, the number of customers waiting to eat. The *arrival rate* is generally stated as the number of arrivals per unit of time. If the arrival rate is random, the customers arrive in no logical pattern or order over time. This represents most cases in the business world. In situations where the arrivals are randomly distributed, their average can be used provided that the data was accumulated over a sufficiently long time period.

The *service rate* treats the manner in which the servicing facility can handle the incoming demands and is expressed as a rate per unit of time. For instance, servicing rate might indicate the number of orders that are processed per hour by the parts department. Service time may also be uniformly or randomly distributed. More cases of a uniform service rate will be found in business problems than for the uniform arrival rate.

Queuing Applications

Waiting line or queuing theory has been applied to a great variety of business situations. A brief description of a few applications is helpful in suggesting problems where queuing can be applied. A large chain of supermarkets has used queuing to determine the number of checkout stations needed to secure smooth and economic operation of its stores at various times throughout the day. Another use is to analyze delays at the toll booths of bridges and tunnels. A study of this kind concerns the number and scheduling of toll booths required on a 24-hour basis in order to minimize cost at a given level of service. Other areas where a customer is involved would be the waiting lines of restaurants, cafeterias, gasoline service stations, airline counters, department stores, and the scheduling of patients in clinics. In all cases, a certain acceptable level of service is expected by the customer while the firm expects to keep its costs at a minimum.

Not only is waiting line theory applicable to retail and wholesale establishments, it is also widely used by manufacturing firms. One popular application of queuing theory is in the area of tool cribs. Foremen are continually complaining that their men wait too long in line for tools and parts. Though plant managers are under pressure to reduce overhead, assigning more attendants can actually reduce overall manufacturing costs since plant personnel will be working instead of standing in line.

Another problem which has been successfully solved by waiting line theory is the proper determination of the number of docks to be constructed for trucks or ships. Since both dock costs and demurrage costs can be very great (the former cost decreasing as the latter mounts and vice versa), the number of docks constructed should minimize the sum of these two costs.

Several manufacturing firms have attacked the problem of machine breakdowns and repairs by utilizing queuing methods. The problem deals with a battery of machines that break down individually and at random times. This application, however, will violate our "first come—first served" rule since the most critical machine must be serviced first. This practice is known as pre-emptive priority, that is, service on a lower priority machine stops when a higher priority machine breaks down. Without pre-emptive priorities, the presence of a lower order has no effect on the higher order—either on waiting time or service time, hence the theory discussed is applicable. In effect, the machines that break down form a waiting line for repairs by maintenance personnel. It is desirable to employ the number of repair personnel which makes the sum of the cost of the production loss from down time and the cost of repairmen a minimum.

Queuing theory has been extended to study wage incentive plans. For example, some production line personnel have been assigned to operate two machines while others have been assigned to operate four machines.

Since all machines are the same, the men are paid the same base rate, but the incentive bonus for production in excess of quota is half as much per unit for operators with four machines as for men with two machines. On the surface, this arrangement seems fair. However, a study of downtime for repairs reveals that while the two machines run by one man would lose about 12 percent of its scheduled time, the four machines run by one man would lose about 16 percent of its scheduled operating time. The problem is that two (or more) machines can break down at once in the four-machine group which is generally not true for the two-machine group. Thus, the individual operating the group of four machines had to operate at a higher efficiency than the operator of a two-unit machine group in order to earn the same incentive. The problem was solvable by paying the operators of the four-machine battery at a higher base rate—determined basically by using the probabilities computed from queuing theory.

By no means do the foregoing areas exhaust the possible applications of waiting line theory. It can be extended to include the staffing of clerical operations and the balancing of material flow in a job shop. Also, queuing can have an impact on the design of inventory and production control systems.

Uniform Arrival and Service Times

The handling of uniform arrival and service times in terms of solving for minimum cost can be illustrated. A manufacturing firm operates several tool rooms within one of its large plants. Currently one of these tool rooms, staffed by one attendant, is under observation by the systems analysis group to determine if additional staffing is justified. The machinists arrive for service at a uniform rate of one every 6 minutes while the tool room attendant handles these requests at a uniform rate of one every 7 minutes. Would costs be reduced by increasing the number of attendants? The tool room attendant is paid $3.00 per hour and the machinists are paid $4.00 per hour. Both rates include fringe benefits.

The problem is calculated initially on a 4-hour basis since the shop personnel work from 8 A.M. to 12 A.M. and then go to lunch. The final results are calculated on an 8-hour basis. Based upon the data—uniform arrival rate of one every 6 minutes and a uniform service rate of one every 7 minutes—the problem can be solved by utilizing the formula for the sum of an arithmetic series. If the first man arrives at 8 A.M., he has no waiting time. Before the first arrival has been serviced, the second machinist arrives and becomes the first person to wait in line. His waiting time is 1 minute (7 minutes − 6 minutes) before being serviced.

Once we know the waiting time for the first machinist, it is necessary to calculate the waiting time of the last man in the initial 4 hours. Since 40 (10 men per hour × 4 hours) machinists arrive and the first man does not wait, we can calculate the waiting time for this thirty-ninth machinist or 39 machinists times 1 minute equals 39 minutes. Because the increase in

QUEUING MODELS   415

TABLE 13-1
Simulated Behavior of Tool Crib Based Upon Uniform Arrival and Uniform Service Rates

	Number of Attendants		
	1	2	3
Uniform arrival of machinists—4 hours	40	40	40
Average time each machinist spends waiting for service	20 min.	—	—
Total time lost by machinists during 4 hours	20 min. × 39 men = 780 minutes	—	—
Machinists' average hourly pay (including fringe benefits)	$4	$4	$4
Tool crib attendant's average hourly pay (including fringe benefits)	$3	$3	$3
Value of machinists' lost time during 4 hours	$52	—	—
Pay of tool crib attendants during 4 hours	12	$24	$36
Total cost for 4 hours	$64	$24	$36
	×2	×2	×2
Total cost for 8 hours (machinists' lost time plus tool crib attendant's pay on an 8-hour basis)	$128	$48	$72

waiting time for each additional machinist is linear, we can average the waiting time of the second and fortieth arrival. Average waiting time per machinist equals 1 minute plus 39 minutes divided by 2, or 20 minutes. Table 13-1 summarizes this information. (The probability that the last arrivals will not wait in line, since the lunch hour is approaching, has not been considered, although normally it would be.) Inspection of the data reveals that using two attendants minimizes cost. In contrast to uniform rates, most business problems are concerned with random rates of arrival and service. These require a different solution procedure, which will be the subject matter for the remainder of the chapter.

Single-Channel Queuing Theory

In the previous section, uniform arrival and service rates were considered. Attention is now focused on random arrival and service rates for a single-channel (single-station) queuing problem. A single-channel queuing problem results from random arrival and service times at a single service station. The random arrival time can be described mathematically with a probability distribution. The probability distribution used depends upon the pattern of the arrivals as shown by observed data and the nature of the operation. One of the most common distributions found in queuing problems is the Poisson distribution. This is used in single-channel queuing problems for random arrivals where the service provided is exponentially distributed. Although the mathematics needed for deriving the solution to this problem is not simple, an attempt to comprehend the theory should be made. However, the models (Equations 13-19 to 13-22) presented later in the chapter may be used without a complete comprehension of their derivation. The focal point of advanced operations research is in developing models of this type. This section gives the reader an insight into the true nature of operations research—the difficulties of developing OR models, the need for logical assumptions, and the utilization of higher mathematics.

Model for Arrivals (Poisson Distribution)

A *Poisson distribution* is a discrete probability distribution that predicts the number of arrivals in a given time. The Poisson distribution involves the probability of the occurrence of an arrival and is independent of what has occurred in preceding observations. It is similar to a normal distribution but is skewed to one side (Figure 13-1). The Poisson assumption indicates the arrivals occur at random as represented by the constant λ. The constant λ is the number of arrivals per unit of time (or mean arrival rate) while $1/\lambda$ is the length of the time interval between two consecutive arrivals (t and $t+\Delta t$).

The Poisson distribution (curve with parameter λT), where n is the number of arrivals within the T interval, the parameter λ is the probability of an arrival, and T is the total time period under consideration, is:

$$f(n,\lambda,T) = \frac{(\lambda T)^n \cdot e^{-(\lambda T)}}{n!} \quad \text{(Equation 13-1)}$$

The symbol (!) after n is n factorial (that is, if n is 4, then $n!$ is $4\times3\times2\times1$) while e (value of 2.71828) is the base of the natural logarithm. In the formula, the expected number of arrivals in the interval T is λT when the arrivals fol-

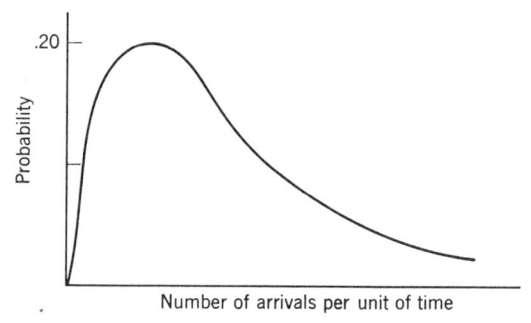

Figure 13-1 Poisson distribution (approximates a normal distribution but is skewed to one side) describes those cases in which there is a much greater probability of few arrivals per unit of time than there is of very many arrivals per unit of time.

low a Poisson distribution. Taking Equation 13-1 and assigning the value of 1 to T, the equation becomes:

$$f(n,\lambda) = \frac{\lambda^n \cdot e^{-\lambda}}{n!} \qquad \text{(Equation 13-2)}$$

The expression of the exponential distribution (density function of T) is:

$$f(T,\lambda) = \lambda e^{-\lambda T} \qquad \text{(Equation 13-3)}$$

Since the single-channel queuing models make use of a Poisson distribution, one can test the assumption that arrivals do follow a Poisson distribution. This is accomplished by picking a fixed interval of time and counting the number of units arriving in an interval. This is performed for a sample of the arrivals. The mean number of arrivals is then computed. The observed data can be plotted in the form of a histogram or bar chart. An appropriate statistical test can be used to determine how well the data fits a Poisson distribution.

Model for Service Time (Exponential Distribution)
Service time is that interval between the beginning of service and its completion. The mean service rate (μ) is the number of customers served per time unit while average service time ($1/\mu$) is time units per customer. Service time delivered is given by an exponential distribution (referred to by many authors as a negative exponential distribution) when the servicing of a customer takes place between the time t and $t+\Delta t$. It should be noted that the Poisson distribution cannot be applied to servicing. There is usually some idle time on the part of the attendant. The Poisson distribution holds for a fixed time interval of continuous servicing, but we can never be sure this will occur in all situations. For this reason, the (negative) exponential distribution is used. When graphed, it slopes downward and to the right from its maximum (Figure 13-2).

Substituting μ for λ in Equation 13-1 and calling n the number of poten-

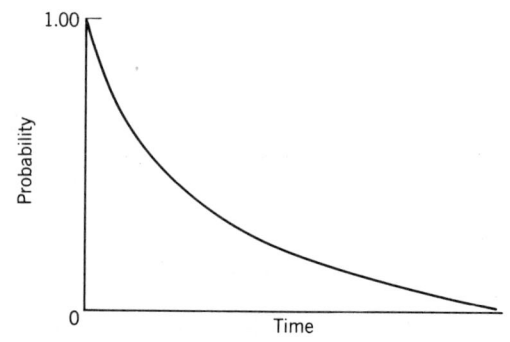

Figure 13-2 Exponential distribution (slopes downward and to the right) describes the probability distribution function of service times.

tial services that can be performed in the interval T, the Poisson formula for servicing rates is:

$$g(n,\mu,T) = \frac{(\mu T)^n \cdot e^{-(\mu T)}}{n!}$$ (Equation 13-4)

Replacing μ for λ in Equation 13-3, the probability that service is completed on a unit by time T for the exponential distribution is:

$$g(T,\mu) = \mu e^{-\mu T}$$ (Equation 13-5)

The assumption that service times are distributed exponentially can be verified by applying the appropriate statistical test to data collected through standard study methods.

Single-Channel Poisson Arrivals with Exponential Service

A single-channel Poisson arrivals with exponential service problem treats a condition where one unit is delivering the service. The inputs, such as customers and jobs, are considered to arrive in a Poisson manner. The exponential servicing rate is independent of the number of elements in line. Arrivals are handled on a first-come first-served basis. Also, a very important assumption is made about the arrival rate (λ) and the service rate (μ) —the service rate is greater than the arrival rate.

A logical starting point for developing single-channel queuing models under the foregoing conditions is to list the mathematical notation that will be used.

λ = mean arrival rate or number of arrivals per unit of time
$\lambda \Delta t$ = probability that an arrival enters the system between t and $t+\Delta t$ time interval
$1-\lambda \Delta t$ = probability that no arrivals occur within interval Δt plus higher order terms[1] in Δt
μ = mean service rate per channel (station)
$\mu \Delta t$ = probability of a service completion between t and $t+\Delta t$ time interval
$1-\mu \Delta t$ = probability of no one being serviced during the interval Δt plus higher order terms[1] in Δt
n = number of units, such as customers, in the system (waiting line and service facility) at time t
$P_n(t)$ = probability of n units in the system at time t
$P_{n+1}(t)$ = probability of having $n+1$ units in the system at time t
$P_{n-1}(t)$ = probability of having $n-1$ units in the system at time t
$P_n(t+\Delta t)$ = probability of having n units in the system at time $(t+\Delta t)$

In order to determine the properties of the single-channel system, it is necessary to find an expression for the probability of n units in the system at time t or $P_n(t)$. Why? If we knew $P_n(t)$ and its mathematical expression, we could calculate the expected number of units in the system. In place of writing an expression for $P_n(t)$, one for $P_n(t+\Delta t)$, will be developed initially.

[1] Higher order terms in Δt are so small that they are insignificant.

TABLE 13-2
Four Events for the Expression $P_n(t+\Delta t)$ Where n is Greater Than Zero

Event	Probability of n Units In Line At Time t	Arrivals In Interval, t to t +Δt	Units Serviced In Interval, t to t +Δt	Units In Line At Time t+Δt
1	P_n	0	0	n
2	P_{n+1}	0	1	n+1
3	P_{n-1}	1	0	n−1
4	P_n	1	1	n

If n is greater than zero in the expression $P_n(t+\Delta t)$, the event can occur in four mutually exclusive and exhaustive ways (only one of these events could occur and one must occur) (Table 13-2). Note that each of these elements is actually a compound event composed of three simple events.

Since one and only one of the four events must happen, we can obtain $P_n(t+\Delta t)$ where n is greater than zero by adding the probabilities for each of the separate but compound events found in Table 13-2. This is done as follows:

$$P_n(t)(1-\lambda \Delta t)(1-\mu \Delta t) + P_{n+1}(t)(1-\lambda \Delta t)(\mu \Delta t)$$
$$+ P_{n-1}(t)(\lambda \Delta t)(1-\mu \Delta t) + P_n(t)(\lambda \Delta t)(\mu \Delta t) = P_n(t+\Delta t)$$

$$P_n(t)(1-\lambda\Delta t - \mu\Delta t) + P_{n+1}(t)(\mu \Delta t) + P_{n-1}(t)(\lambda \Delta t)$$
$$+ (\Delta t)_1 + (\Delta t)_2 + (\Delta t)_3 + (\Delta t)_4 = P_n(t+\Delta t)$$

In this equation, $(\Delta t)_1$, $(\Delta t)_2$, $(\Delta t)_3$, and $(\Delta t)_4$ are terms with higher order powers of Δt. When the limit of Δt approaches zero, these become so small that they may be disregarded. The new equation is:

$$P_n(t+\Delta t) = P_n(t)(1-\lambda \Delta t - \mu \Delta t) + P_{n+1}(t)(\mu\Delta t) + P_{n-1}(t)(\lambda \Delta t) \quad \text{(Equation 13-6)}$$

Expanding the first term $[P_n(t)]$ on the right-hand side of the equation, the result is:

$$P_n(t+\Delta t) = P_n(t) - P_n(t)(\lambda \Delta t + \mu \Delta t) + P_{n+1}(t)(\mu \Delta t) + P_{n-1}(t)(\lambda \Delta t)$$

Next, we subtract $P_n(t)$ from both sides of the equation and divide by Δt, which results in the following equation:

$$\frac{P_n(t+\Delta t) - P_n(t)}{\Delta t} = -(\lambda+\mu)P_n(t) + \mu P_{n+1}(t) + \lambda P_{n-1}(t)$$

By definition,[2] the derivative of P_n with respect to t is:

$$\frac{dP_n(t)}{dt} = \lim_{\Delta t \to 0} \frac{P_n(t+\Delta t) - P_n(t)}{\Delta t}$$

---
[2] General definition of the derivative (from Appendix B):

$$\frac{dy}{dx} = \lim_{\Delta x \to 0} \frac{f(x+\Delta x) - f(x)}{\Delta x}$$

When Δt approaches zero, the following differential equation (Equation 13-7) can be stated to express the relationship among the probabilities (P_n, P_{n+1}, and P_{n-1} at time t), the mean arrival rate (λ), and the mean service rate (μ):

$$\frac{dP_n(t)}{dt} = \lambda P_{n-1}(t) + \mu P_{n+1}(t) - (\lambda + \mu) P_n(t) \qquad \text{(Equation 13-7)}$$

where $n > 0$.

After solving for $P_n(t+\Delta t)$ where n is greater than zero, it is necessary to solve for n where it is equal to zero. If n is zero, only two mutually exclusive and exhaustive events can occur as shown in Table 13-3.

TABLE 13-3
Two Events for the Expression $P_0(t+\Delta t)$ Where n is Equal to Zero

Event	Probability of n Units In Line At Time t	Arrivals In Interval, t to t +Δt	Units Serviced In Interval, t to t +Δt	Units In Line At Time t+Δt
1	P_0	0	—	0
2	P_1	0	1	0

The probability that no units will be in line at the time $t+\Delta t$ is given by adding the probabilities for each of the separate events found in Table 13-3. This is shown as follows:

$$\left.\begin{array}{l} P_0(t)(1-\lambda\,\Delta t) \\ + P_1(t)(1-\lambda\,\Delta t)(\mu\,\Delta t) \end{array}\right\} = P_0(t+\Delta t)$$

$$P_0(t)(1-\lambda\,\Delta t) + P_1(t)[\mu\,\Delta t - \lambda\mu(\Delta t)^2] = P_0(t+\Delta t)$$

Neglecting the terms with higher order powers of Δt as before, the new equation is:

$$P_0(t+\Delta t) = P_0(t)(1-\lambda\,\Delta t) + P_1(t)(\mu\,\Delta t) \qquad \text{(Equation 13-8)}$$

This can be rewritten as:

$$\frac{P_0(t+\Delta t) - P_0(t)}{\Delta t} = +\mu P_1(t) - \lambda P_0(t)$$

When Δt approaches zero, the differential equation which indicates the relationship among the probabilities (P_0 and P_1), the mean arrival rate (λ), and the mean service rate (μ), is:

$$\frac{dP_0(t)}{dt} = +\mu P_1(t) - \lambda P_0(t) \qquad \text{(Equation 13-9)}$$

where $n = 0$.

Equations 13-7 and 13-9 provide relationships involving the probability density function $P_n(t)$ for all values of n. However, these equations do not allow us to solve for the probability density function. Let us assume that $P_n(t)$ is independent of t since we are not actually interested in what happens to the probabilities over time. Our interest is in what happens when the waiting line settles down, that is, to the steady state. (The transient case is treated in more advanced analysis.) With this fact in mind, Equation 13-7 becomes:

$$\frac{dP_n(t)}{d(t)} = 0 \qquad \text{(Equation 13-10)}$$

and $P_n(t)$ is just P_n in the equations below.

By virtue of Equation 13-10, Equation 13-7 reduces to:

$$0 = \lambda P_{n-1} + \mu P_{n+1} - (\lambda + \mu) P_n \qquad \text{(Equation 13-11)}$$

where $n > 0$. Likewise, Equation 13-9 becomes:

$$0 = \mu P_1 - \lambda P_0 \qquad \text{(Equation 13-12)}$$

where $n = 0$.

Now that we have converted Equations 13-7 and 13-9 into difference equations (the difference between sequential terms) by Equations 13-11 and 13-12, we need an uncomplicated expression for P_n [formerly $P_n(t)$]. From Equation 13-12, the following equation is obtained:

$$P_1 = \frac{\lambda}{\mu} P_0 \qquad \text{(Equation 13-13)}$$

where P_1 is the probability of having one unit in line excluding the one being served.

The following relationships are obtained from Equation 13-13 by substituting for each P_n the preceding P_{n-1} up to P_0:

$$P_n = \frac{\lambda}{\mu} P_{n-1} \qquad \text{where } n = 1, 2, \ldots$$

$$P_2 = \frac{\lambda}{\mu} P_1 = \frac{\lambda}{\mu}\left(\frac{\lambda}{\mu} P_0\right) = P_0\left(\frac{\lambda}{\mu}\right)^2 \qquad \text{where } n = 2$$

$$P_3 = \frac{\lambda}{\mu} P_2 = P_0\left(\frac{\lambda}{\mu}\right)^3 \qquad \text{where } n = 3$$

It now is evident that a certain pattern is emerging:

$$P_n = \left(\frac{\lambda}{\mu}\right)^n P_0 \qquad n \geq 0 \qquad \text{(Equation 13-14)}$$

Equation 13-14 is almost what we have been searching for in terms of an expression for the probability density function. The only difficulty is that the expression contains P_0, which is unknown at this point. We do know a property of the probability density function that may allow us to determine P_0. If x is a random variable with a probability density function, $P(x)$ can be stated:

$$\Sigma P(x) = 1$$

This is in accordance with the fundamental concept that the summation of all probabilities is equal to 1.

From this property of a probability distribution function, it follows that 1 equals $P_0 + P_1 + P_2 + P_3 \cdots$ or:

$$\sum_{n=0}^{\infty} P_n = 1$$

Substituting Equation 13-14 in the preceding summation for the term P_n, the new expression is:

$$\sum_{n=0}^{\infty} \left(\frac{\lambda}{\mu}\right)^n P_0 = 1$$

$$P_0 \sum_{n=0}^{\infty} \left(\frac{\lambda}{\mu}\right)^n = 1 \qquad \text{(Equation 13-15)}$$

In all situations where the waiting line does not grow without bound, λ/μ will be less than one. For such cases, the terms of the sum in Equation 13-15 is a converging geometric series. The sum of an infinite series is given by the formula:

$$S_\infty = \frac{a}{1-r}$$

where a is the first term and r is the common ratio ($\neq 1$). Equation 13-15 reduces to:

$$1 = P_0 \frac{1}{1 - \lambda/\mu} \quad \text{or} \quad P_0 = 1 - \frac{\lambda}{\mu} \qquad \text{(Equation 13-16)}$$

the probability that the facility is idle. By substituting the expression $(1 - \lambda/\mu)$ for P_0 in Equation 13-14, we have finally obtained a fully defined mathematical expression for P_n when n is equal to or greater than zero. The equation for P_n is:

$$P_n = \left(\frac{\lambda}{\mu}\right)^n \left(1 - \frac{\lambda}{\mu}\right) \qquad n \geq 0 \quad \text{(Equation 13-17)}$$

Having solved for P_n, we can now write an expression for the expected or average number being served and waiting in the system, $E(n)$:

$$E(n) = \sum_{n=0}^{\infty} n P_n$$

Substituting Equation 13-17 for P_n, the resulting equation is:

$$E(n) = \sum_{n=0}^{\infty} n \left(\frac{\lambda}{\mu}\right)^n \left(1 - \frac{\lambda}{\mu}\right)$$

$$E(n) = \left(1 - \frac{\lambda}{\mu}\right) \sum_{n=0}^{\infty} n \left(\frac{\lambda}{\mu}\right)^n \qquad \text{(Equation 13-18)}$$

The sequence of terms in Equation 13-17 is of the form $0, a, 2a^2, 3a^3, \ldots, xa^x, \ldots$. This series can be rewritten where each term is shown as the sum of an infinite series. In the case where a (a constant) is less than 1, this sequence converges to the sum given by the formula:

$$S_\infty = \frac{a}{(1-a)^2}$$

Bringing the constant $(1-\lambda/\mu)$ from Equation 13-18 and replacing the infinite series $\left[\sum_{n=0}^{\infty} n(\lambda/\mu)^n\right]$ in the same equation with the foregoing formula $[S_\infty = a/(1-a)^2$ where $a = \lambda/\mu]$, the formula for the average number of units (both waiting and being served) in the system is:

$$E(n) = \left(1 - \frac{\lambda}{\mu}\right) \frac{\lambda/\mu}{(1-\lambda/\mu)^2}$$

$$E(n) = \frac{\lambda/\mu}{1 - \lambda/\mu}$$

$E(n)$ average number in the system $= \dfrac{\lambda}{\mu - \lambda}$ \qquad (Equation 13-19)

In order to determine the average number of customers waiting to be served, it is necessary to use a different notation from the $E(n)$ above. $E(w)$ will be used to designate the average number of customers in the system before entering the service facility. Because there can be only one unit in the service facility at any time, the average number of units (both waiting and in service) or $E(n)$ less the one being serviced (λ/μ) must be the average number of customers waiting to be served. Thus the equation is:

$$E(w) = E(n) - \frac{\lambda}{\mu} = \frac{\lambda}{\mu - \lambda} - \frac{\lambda}{\mu}$$

$E(w)$ average queue length $= \dfrac{\lambda^2}{\mu(\mu - \lambda)}$ \qquad (Equation 13-20)

From Equations 13-19 and 13-20, other waiting line models can be derived. For example, the average time a customer spends in the system can be determined. The mathematical notation used is $E(v)$. During the time period $E(v)$, the average number of customers arriving is $\lambda E(v)$. This is also the average number of customers in the system or $E(n)$. Equating these terms, the equation for the average time a customer spends in the system is:

$$E(n) = \lambda E(v)$$

$$E(v) = \frac{1}{\lambda} E(n) = \frac{1}{\lambda}\left(\frac{\lambda}{\mu - \lambda}\right)$$

$E(v)$ average time in the system $= \dfrac{1}{\mu - \lambda}$ \qquad (Equation 13-21)

The last model for single-channel queuing relates to the average time a customer waits before being served. The notation for this condition is $E(y)$. The average time a customer spends in the system includes both his service and waiting time. $E(v)$, minus the average service time $(1/\mu)$, must equal the average time a customer spends before being served or his average waiting time. The model for this condition is:

$$E(y) = E(v) - \frac{1}{\mu} = \frac{1}{\mu - \lambda} - \frac{1}{\mu}$$

$E(y)$ average waiting time for service $= \dfrac{\lambda}{\mu(\mu - \lambda)}$ \hfill (Equation 13-22)

Applying Equations 13-19 to 13-22 to a sample problem, we will assume that the data is representative of customers arriving in a single station service facility. The mean arrival rate (λ) is one customer every 4 minutes and the mean service time (μ) is 2½ minutes. The calculations for arrival and service times in minutes and, on the basis of an hour, are as follows:

$\lambda = \dfrac{1}{4} = 0.25$ arrivals per minute or 15 arrivals per hour

$\mu = \dfrac{1}{2.5} = 0.4$ service time per minute or 24 service times per hour

1. Using Equation 13-19, the average number of customers in the system is:

$$E(n) = \frac{\lambda}{\mu - \lambda} = \frac{0.25}{0.4 - 0.25} = \frac{0.25}{0.15} = 1.66 \text{ customers}$$

$$\frac{15}{24 - 15} = \frac{15}{9} = 1.66 \text{ customers}$$

2. Using Equation 13-20, the average number of customers waiting to be served or average queue length is:

$$E(w) = \frac{\lambda^2}{\mu(\mu - \lambda)} = \frac{(0.25)^2}{0.4(0.4 - 0.25)} = \frac{0.0625}{0.06} = 1.04 \text{ customers}$$

$$\frac{(15)^2}{24(24 - 15)} = \frac{225}{216} = 1.04 \text{ customers}$$

Calculation for the average number being served:

1.66 (average number in system) − 1.04 (average queue length)
= 0.62 (average number being served)

Proof:

15 arrivals/hour ÷ 24 service times/hour = 0.62 customers

3. Using Equation 13-21, the average time a customer spends in the system is:

$$E(v) = \frac{1}{\mu - \lambda} = \frac{1}{0.4 - 0.25} = \frac{1}{0.15} = 6.66 \text{ minutes}$$

$$\frac{1}{24 - 15} = \frac{1}{9} = 0.111 \text{ hour}$$

QUEUING MODELS   425

4. Using Equation 13-22 the average time a customer waits before being served is:

$$E(y) = \frac{\lambda}{\mu(\mu-\lambda)} = \frac{0.25}{0.4(0.4-0.25)} = 4.16 \text{ minutes}$$

$$\frac{15}{24(24-15)} = \frac{15}{216} = 0.07 \text{ hour}$$

Proof:

6.66 minutes (average time in system)
$$-2.5 \text{ minutes (average service time)} = 4.16 \text{ minutes}$$

Single-Channel Minimum Cost Service Rate

As demonstrated earlier (Table 13-1), the expected total cost is the sum of the expected waiting cost for the arrivals per period (WC) and the expected facility cost (basically salary and fringe benefits) of service personnel per period (FC). This can be written as follows (m=mean):

$$TC_m = WC_m + FC_m \qquad \text{(Equation 13-23)}$$

The expected waiting cost per period (WC_m) is the product of unit waiting cost (C_w) for an arrival per period and the mean number of units in the system $E(n)$ during the period:

$$WC_m = C_w[E(n)]$$
$$= \frac{C_w \lambda}{\mu - \lambda}$$

The expected service cost per period (FC_m) is the product of the cost of servicing one unit (C_f) and the service rate in units per period (μ):

$$FC_m = C_f(\mu)$$

Restating Equation 13-23, the expected total system cost per period becomes:

$$TC_m = \frac{C_w \lambda}{(\mu - \lambda)} + C_f(\mu)$$

A minimum cost service rate can now be found by differentiating total cost with respect to μ, setting the result equal to zero, and solving for μ as follows:

$$\frac{dTC_m}{d\mu} = -C_w \lambda (\mu - \lambda)^{-2} + C_f = 0$$
$$(\mu - \lambda)^2 C_f = \lambda C_w$$
$$(\mu - \lambda)^2 = \frac{\lambda C_w}{C_f}$$
$$\mu - \lambda = \pm \sqrt{\frac{\lambda C_w}{C_f}}$$
$$\mu = \lambda \pm \sqrt{\frac{\lambda C_w}{C_f}} \qquad \text{(Equation 13-24)}$$

Note that a plus sign and a minus sign appear before the square root sign. A $-\mu$ is not a possible answer in the real world. This can be seen in the example where λ is 0.25 arrivals per minute and μ is 0.4 persons serviced per minute. The waiting cost is $0.05 per unit per minute and the cost for servicing one unit is $0.04. Substituting these figures into Equation 13-24 results in the minimum cost service rate of 0.81 units per minute and not -0.31 units per minute, calculated as follows:

$$\mu = 0.25 \pm \sqrt{\frac{(0.25)(\$0.05)}{\$0.04}}$$

$$\mu = 0.25 \pm \sqrt{\frac{\$0.0125}{\$0.04}}$$

$$\mu = 0.25 \pm 0.56$$

$\mu = 0.81$ units per minute or $\mu = -0.31$ units per minute (not a feasible solution)

Single-Channel Poisson Arrivals with Nonexponential Service

The preceding section has assumed that the number of arrivals follows a Poisson distribution. Substantial evidence exists and intuitive considerations support this assumption since arrival rates are usually independent of time, queue length, or any other property of a waiting line system. Evidence in support of the exponential distribution of service durations is not as strong. In the previous section, this type of distribution was assumed for mathematical convenience. When the service time distribution is nonexponential, the development of decision models is difficult.

This section will treat mathematical models with a Poisson distribution for arrivals that have service times which are constant and service times with any distribution. The assumption is retained that the service rate (μ) is greater than the arrival rate (λ). Due to the complexity of developing these models, they will be presented without mathematical proof.[3]

In situations where the service time is automated by mechanical means or where the service station is mechanically paced, the service time will be a constant. This results in the service time distribution having a variance of zero. The model for the mean number of units in the system is:

$$n_m = \frac{(\lambda/\mu)^2}{2[1-\lambda/\mu]} + \frac{\lambda}{\mu} \qquad \text{(Equation 13-25)}$$

$$= \frac{\lambda^2}{2\mu(\mu-\lambda)} + \frac{\lambda}{\mu}$$

The mean waiting time is:

$$w_m = \frac{\lambda/\mu}{2\mu[1-(\lambda/\mu)]} + \frac{1}{\mu} \qquad \text{(Equation 13-26)}$$

$$= \frac{\lambda}{2\mu(\mu-\lambda)} + \frac{1}{\mu}$$

---

[3] Reference for this proof is W. J. Fabrycky and P. E. Torgersen, *Operations Economy, Industrial Applications of Operations Research*, Englewood Cliffs, N.J.: Prentice-Hall, 1966.

Using Equation 13-23 ($TC_m = WC_m + FC_m$), the expected total system cost per period is the sum of the expected waiting cost and the expected facility cost per period. The expected waiting cost per period (WC_m) is the result of multiplying the cost of the waiting for a unit per period and the mean number of units in the system during the period. This is similar to an equation in the last section:

$$WC_m = C_w(n_m)$$
$$= C_w\left[\frac{\lambda^2}{2\mu(\mu-\lambda)} + \frac{\lambda}{\mu}\right]$$

The expected facility cost per period is the product of the cost of servicing one unit and the service rate in units per period. This is the same equation used in the last section:

$$FC_m = C_f(\mu)$$

Substituting the preceding expressions for WC_m and FC_m in Equation 13-23, the expected total cost per period for constant service time is:

$$TC_m = C_w\left[\frac{\lambda^2}{2\mu(\mu-\lambda)} + \frac{\lambda}{\mu}\right] + C_f(\mu) \qquad \text{(Equation 13-27)}$$

In some cases, it is desirable to have models for Poisson distribution arrivals that have any service time distribution. If σ^2 is the variance of the service time distribution, the mean number of units in the system is:

$$n_m = \frac{(\lambda/\mu)^2 + \lambda^2\sigma^2}{2[1-(\lambda/\mu)]} + \frac{\lambda}{\mu} \qquad \text{(Equation 13-28)}$$

The mean waiting time is:

$$w_m = \frac{(\lambda/\mu^2) + \lambda^2\sigma^2}{2[1-(\lambda/\mu)]} + \frac{1}{\mu} \qquad \text{(Equation 13-29)}$$

Using Equation 13-23 for the expected total system cost per period, the cost equation for any service time distribution is:

$$TC_m = C_w\left(\frac{(\lambda/\mu)^2 + \lambda^2\sigma^2}{2[1-(\lambda/\mu)]} + \frac{\lambda}{\mu}\right) + C_f(\mu) \qquad \text{(Equation 13-30)}$$

An illustration of Equation 13-30 will help clarify its usefulness. The number of arrivals has a Poisson distribution with a mean of 0.4 units. The cost of waiting per employee on an hourly basis is $5.00 and the cost of servicing one arrival is $3.00. A decision must be made between two policies, the first being a service rate of 0.8 units per hour with a service time variance (σ^2) of 2 hours. The second policy is a service rate of 0.9 units per hour with a service time variance (σ^2) of 3 hours. The expected total system cost of the first policy is:

$$TC_m = \$5.00\left(\frac{(0.4/0.8)^2 + (0.4)^2(2)}{2[1-(0.4/0.8)]} + \frac{0.4}{0.8}\right) + \$3.00(0.8)$$
$$= \$5.35 + \$2.40$$
$$= \$7.75$$

The total expected system cost of the second policy is:

$$TC_m = \$5.00\left(\frac{(0.4/0.9)^2 + (0.4)^2(3)}{2[1-(0.4/0.9)]} + \frac{0.4}{0.9}\right) + \$3.00(0.9)$$
$$= \$5.25 + \$2.70$$
$$= \$7.95$$

Based upon the foregoing results, the first policy is better in terms of cost. Additional policies in the problem could have been considered other than the two presented.

Multichannel Queuing Theory

Before discussing a multichannel problem, it is helpful to discuss a system consisting of two or more stations where the arrivals cannot pass from one line to another. This type of waiting-line problem is really a single-channel one rather than a multichannel problem. Once an arrival has selected a particular line, he becomes a part of that single service facility. For example, on a toll road, each pay station is placed next to a specific route which has different destinations, from the other routes. Obviously, an automobile waiting for one station cannot switch to a pay station for a different route.

Multichannel queuing theory treats the condition where several service stations are in parallel and each element in the waiting line can be served by more than one station. Each service facility is prepared to deliver the same type of service and is equipped essentially with the same type of facilities. The arrival selects one station without any external pressure. When a waiting line is formed, a single line usually breaks down into shorter lines in front of each of the service stations.

Multichannel Poisson Arrivals with Exponential Service

Problems treating multichannel queuing are composed of a number of parallel stations (k) where the state of the system (n, number of elements in the system at a certain moment) can assume one of two values: there is no queue because all arrivals are being serviced ($n \leq k$) or a queue is formed because the service demanded by the arrival(s) is greater than the capabilities of the service stations in the problem ($n > k$). The first case presents no problem, whereas the second does. The multichannel formulas for when n is greater than k are presented with little mathematical proof.[4] Their derivation is more complex than the comparable formulas for a single-channel station.

The utilization factor (P_k) for the whole system describes the probability of a given station being in use; it is the ratio between the mean arrival rate

---

[4] Reference for this proof is P. M. Morse, *Queues, Inventories, and Maintenance*, New York: John Wiley & Sons, 1958.

(λ) and the maximum possible service rate (μ) of all k channels. This can be stated as follows:

$$P_k = \frac{\lambda}{\mu k}$$

The probability that there are n elements in the system, when it is equipped with two or more stations and n is less than k, is (refer to Equation 13-14):

$$P_n = \frac{1}{n!}\left(\frac{\lambda}{\mu}\right)^n P_0$$

where $n = 0, 1, 2, \ldots, k-1$ or $n < k$. When the number of elements is equal to or greater than the number of stations k, the probability becomes:

$$P_n = \frac{1}{k! k^{n-k}}\left(\frac{\lambda}{\mu}\right)^n P_0 \qquad \text{(Equation 13-31)}$$

where $n \geq k$. The probability of having no elements in a multichannel system is given as follows:

$$P_0 = \frac{1}{\left[\sum_{n=0}^{k-1} \frac{1}{n!}\left(\frac{\lambda}{\mu}\right)^n\right] + \left[\frac{1}{k!}\left(\frac{\lambda}{\mu}\right)^k \frac{\mu k}{\mu k - \lambda}\right]} \qquad \text{(Equation 13-32)}$$

The preceding formulas are applicable only if $\mu k > \lambda$ or $P_k < 1$. In all other cases where $\mu k \leq \lambda$ and $P_k \geq 1$, the waiting lines increase indefinitely in size.

For the general case of k servicing stations, the probability that an arrival has to wait coincides with the probability that there is no servicing station available in the system. The probability is given as:

$$P_n' = \frac{\mu(\lambda/\mu)^k}{(k-1)!(\mu k - \lambda)} P_0 \qquad \text{(Equation 13-33)}$$

The average queue length or the mean length of the waiting line is the result of multiplying Equation 13-33 by the ratio $\lambda/(\mu k - \lambda)$, which results in the following:

$$E(w) \text{ average queue length} = \frac{\lambda \mu (\lambda/\mu)^k}{(k-1)!(\mu k - \lambda)^2} P_0$$

$$\text{(Equation 13-34)}$$

The model for the average number of units in a multichannel system is:

$$E(n) \text{ average number in the system} = \left[\frac{\lambda \mu (\lambda/\mu)^k}{(k-1)!(\mu k - \lambda)^2} P_0\right] + \frac{\lambda}{\mu}$$

$$\text{(Equation 13-35)}$$

This equation is the same as Equation 13-34, except for the addition of the term λ/μ. This represents an arrival being serviced.

The average waiting time of an arrival before being served is given as follows:

$$E(y) \text{ average waiting time for service} = \frac{\mu(\lambda/\mu)^k}{(k-1)!(\mu k - \lambda)^2} P_0$$

(Equation 13-36)

The last model is the average time an arrival spends in the system, which is given as follows:

$$E(v) \text{ average time in the system} = \left[\frac{\mu(\lambda/\mu)^k}{(k-1)!(\mu k - \lambda)^2} P_0\right] + \frac{1}{\mu}$$

(Equation 13-37)

Equation 13-37 is the same as Equation 13-36 plus $1/\mu$, which represents the average service time. The average waiting time of an arrival plus the average service time equals the average time an arrival spends in the system (Equation 13-37).

Multichannel queuing models can be illustrated as follows. The Internal Revenue Service has four stations in an office to receive people who have problems and complaints about their income taxes. Arrivals average 80 persons in an 8-hour service day. Each tax adviser spends an irregular amount of time servicing the arrivals which have been found to have an exponential distribution. The average service time is 20 minutes.

Before entering the known data into the foregoing multichannel models, it is necessary to find the value of P_0 (Equation 13-32) which expresses the probability of having no elements in the system. P_0 is calculated thus:

$$P_0 = \frac{1}{\left[\sum_{n=0}^{k-1} \frac{1}{n!}\left(\frac{\lambda}{\mu}\right)^n\right] + \left[\frac{1}{k!}\left(\frac{\lambda}{\mu}\right)^k \frac{\mu k}{\mu k - \lambda}\right]}$$

$$= \frac{1}{1 + \frac{\lambda}{\mu} + \frac{1}{2}\left(\frac{\lambda}{\mu}\right)^2 + \frac{1}{6}\left(\frac{\lambda}{\mu}\right)^3 + \frac{1}{4!}\left(\frac{\lambda}{\mu}\right)^4 \frac{\mu k}{\mu k - \lambda}}$$

$$= \frac{1}{1 + \frac{10}{3} + \frac{100}{18} + \frac{1000}{162} + \left(\frac{10{,}000}{1944}\right)\left(\frac{12}{2}\right)}$$

$$= \frac{1}{46.91} = 0.0213$$

In the above equation, $n!$ where $n=0$ is 1, that is, $0! = 1$.

Based upon the multichannel models (Equations 13-34 to 13-37), the results are as follows (where $\lambda = 10/\text{hour}$, $\mu = 3/\text{hour}$, $k = 4$ service stations, and $P_0 = 0.0213$):

1. Average number of customers in the system:

$$E(n) = \left[\frac{\lambda\mu(\lambda/\mu)^k}{(k-1)!(\mu k - \lambda)^2} P_0\right] + \frac{\lambda}{\mu} \quad \text{(Equation 13-35)}$$

$$= \frac{(10)(3)(10/3)^4}{(4-1)!(3 \times 4 - 10)^2} 0.0213 + \frac{10}{3}$$

$$= \frac{(30)(123.4)}{(6)(4)} 0.0213 + 3.33$$

$$= (154.2)(0.0213) + 3.33 = 6.61 \text{ customers}$$

2. Average number of customers waiting to be serviced or average queue length:

$$E(w) = \frac{\lambda\mu(\lambda/\mu)^k}{(k-1)!(\mu k-\lambda)^2}P_0 \qquad \text{(Equation 13-34)}$$

$$= \frac{(10)(3)(10/3)^4}{(4-1)!(3\times 4-10)^2}0.0213$$

$$= \frac{(30)(123.4)}{(6)(4)}0.0213$$

$$= 154.2 \times 0.0213$$

$$= 3.28 \text{ customers}$$

Calculation for average number being served:

6.61 (average number in the system) − 3.28 (average queue length)
= 3.33 customers (average number being served)

Proof:

10 arrivals per hour ÷ 3 service times per hour = 3.33 customers

3. Average time a customer spends in the system:

$$E(v) = \left[\frac{\mu(\lambda/\mu)^k}{(k-1)!(\mu k-\lambda)^2}P_0\right] + \frac{1}{\mu} \qquad \text{(Equation 13-37)}$$

$$= \frac{3(10/3)^4}{(4-1)!(3\times 4-10)^2}0.0213 + \frac{1}{3}$$

$$= \frac{(3)(123.4)}{(6)(4)}0.0213 + \frac{1}{3}$$

$$= \frac{370.2}{24}0.0213 + \frac{1}{3}$$

$$= 0.328 + 0.333$$

$$= 0.661 \text{ hour or about 40 minutes}$$

4. Average time a customer waits before being served:

$$E(y) = \frac{\mu(\lambda/\mu)^k}{(k-1)!(\mu k-\lambda)^2}P_0 \qquad \text{(Equation 13-36)}$$

$$= \frac{(3)(10/3)^4}{(4-1)!(3\times 4-10)^2}0.0213$$

$$= \frac{(3)(123.4)}{(6)(4)}0.0213$$

$$= \frac{370.2}{24}0.0213$$

$$= 0.328 \text{ hour or about 20 minutes}$$

Proof:

40 minutes (average time in the system)
− 20 minutes (average service time) = 20 minutes

Having solved for the various values in the problem, we can ask further questions. First, how many hours each week does a tax counselor spend performing his job? To answer this question, it is necessary to compute the utilization factor (P_k) given in this section:

$$P_k = \frac{\lambda}{\mu k} = \frac{10}{(3)(4)} = 0.833$$

The expected time spent in servicing customers during an 8-hour day is $0.833 \times 8 = 6.66$ hours. On an average, a tax adviser is busy 33.3 hours based on a 40 hour week.

Second, what is the probability that a tax counselor is waiting for a customer? Referring to Equation 14-33, the probability that one of the counselors will be idle is:

$$\begin{aligned} P_n' &= \frac{\mu(\lambda/\mu)^k}{(k-1)!(\mu k - \lambda)} P_0 \\ &= \frac{3(10/3)^4}{(4-1)!(3 \times 4 - 10)} 0.0213 \\ &= \frac{(3)(123.4)}{(6)(2)} 0.0213 \\ &= \frac{370.2}{12} 0.0213 \\ &= (30.85)(0.0213) \\ &= 0.6571 \end{aligned}$$

Third, what is the expected number of idle counselors at any specified moment? Presently, we know that the probability of no customers with four counselors waiting is 0.0213 (P_0). In order to obtain the figures for one, two, and three counselors waiting, it is necessary to refer to an earlier model in this section where the probability of arrivals is less than the number of servicing stations ($n < k$). The formula is:

$$P_n = \frac{1}{n!}\left(\frac{\lambda}{\mu}\right)^n P_0$$

$$P_1 = \frac{1}{1!}\left(\frac{10}{3}\right) 0.0213 = (3.33)(0.0213) = 0.0709$$

$$P_2 = \frac{1}{2!}\left(\frac{10}{3}\right)^2 0.0213 = (5.55)(0.0213) = 0.1182$$

$$P_3 = \frac{1}{3!}\left(\frac{10}{3!}\right)^3 0.0213 = (6.17)(0.0213) = 0.1314$$

The expected number of idle counselors (E_c) is calculated as follows:

$$\begin{aligned} E_c &= 4P_0 + 3P_1 + 2P_2 + 1P_3 \\ &= 4(0.0213) + 3(0.0709) + 2(0.1182) + 1(0.1314) \\ &= 0.0852 + 0.2127 + 0.2364 + 0.1314 \\ &= 0.666 \end{aligned}$$

This calculated value means that we can expect to have less than one (exactly 0.666) counselor idle on the average which can be proven by referring to the answers obtained previously. The number of customers in the system (6.61 customers) minus the average queue length (3.28 customers) equals the average number being served (3.33 customers). Four counselors minus 3.33 customers being served equals 0.666 counselor idle.

Another question can be raised: Could we get along with the three advisers if we have about one person idle? This means taking the original data and coming up with new answers for the multichannel models since the k factor is now 3 versus 4 in the illustration.

Monte Carlo Approach to Queuing

In many cases, the observed distributions for arrival and service times cannot be fitted to certain mathematical distributions (Poisson and exponential). In addition, the first in and first out assumption may not be valid for a particular queuing problem. Similarly, in multichannel queuing, departures from one queue may form the arrivals for another. Under these conditions, the Monte Carlo method is extremely useful since none of the previous queuing models perform adequately.

Basically, the Monte Carlo method is a simulation technique in which statistical distribution functions are created by using a series of random numbers. This approach can develop many months or years of data in a matter of a few minutes on a digital computer. It allows manipulation of those factors that are subject to control, such as adding another service station without actually having to incur the expense of installing one. Changes can be tried without disrupting the actual process.

Single-Channel Arrival and Service Time Distributions

Even though Monte Carlo analysis does not require that the arrival and service time distributions obey certain theoretical forms, it does demand that the form and parameters of these distributions be set forth. The cumulative distributions which can then be developed are used as a means for generating arrivals and service times. The following problem illustrates Monte Carlo analysis.

A firm has a single-channel service station which has the following characteristics based upon empirical data: the time between arrivals has a mean of 6.0 minutes (A_m) while the service time has a mean of 5.5 minutes (S_m). These arrival and service time distributions are found in Figure 13-3.

In Figure 13-3 the probabilities associated with each value of A_x and S_x are shown. In order to determine the cumulative arrival and service time distributions, the individual probabilities are totaled, starting from left to right. These cumulative distributions, shown in Figure 13-4, are the basis for generating arrival and service times in conjunction with a table of random numbers.

Single-Channel Monte Carlo Method Using Random Numbers

In the illustration, the queuing process begins at 8:00 A.M. and continues for approximately 2 hours. An arrival moves immediately into the service facility if it is empty. Otherwise, if the service station is busy, the arrival

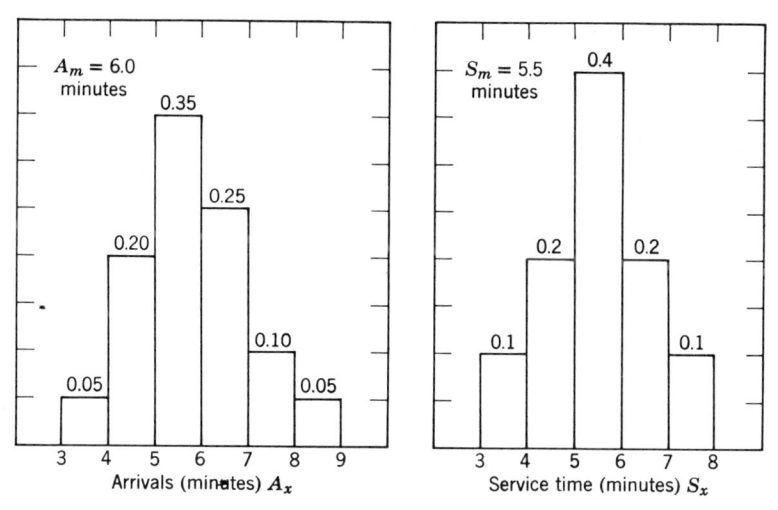

Figure 13-3 Arrival and service time distributions in minutes.

will wait in a queue. Units in the waiting line will enter the service facility on a first come, first served basis. Instead of using a computer program for solving the problem, a worksheet will serve the same purpose (Table 13-4).

The arrival and service times for the simulation worksheet of Table 13-4 are developed in the following manner. A table of random numbers (a group of numbers which occur in no order with no one number more likely to occur than any other number), found in Appendix E, is utilized. The random numbers for arrival times are taken from the second last group column

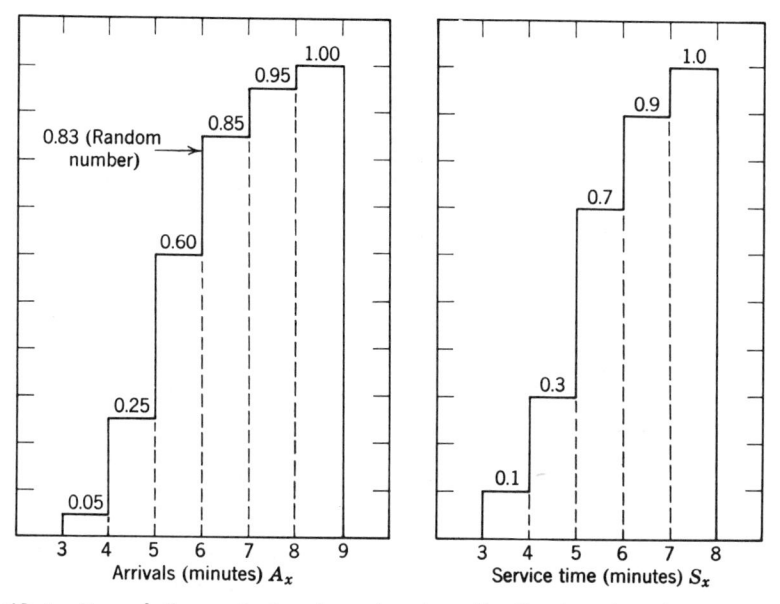

Figure 13-4 Cumulative arrival and service time distributions in minutes.

QUEUING MODELS 435

TABLE 13-4
Simulation Worksheet for Arrival Time, Service Time, and Waiting Time

Random Number	Time Till Next Arrival (Min.)	Arrival Time (A.M.)	Service Begins (A.M.)	Random Number	Service Time (Min.)	Service Ends (A.M.)	Waiting Time Attend. (Min.)	Waiting Time Cust. (Min.)	Length of Line
83	6	8:06	8:06	46	5	8:11	6	—	—
70	6	8:12	8:12	64	5	8:17	1	—	1
06	4	8:16	8:17	09	3	8:20	—	1	—
12	4	8:20	8:20	48	5	8:25	—	—	—
59	5	8:25	8:25	97	7	8:32	—	—	1
46	5	8:30	8:32	22	4	8:36	—	2	1
54	5	8:35	8:36	29	4	8:40	—	1	1
04	3	8:38	8:40	01	3	8:43	—	2	—
51	5	8:43	8:43	40	5	8:48	—	—	—
99	8	8:51	8:51	75	6	8:57	3	—	—
84	6	8:57	8:57	10	4	9:01	—	—	—
81	6	9:03	9:03	09	3	9:06	2	—	—
15	4	9:07	9:07	70	6	9:13	1	—	1
36	5	9:12	9:13	41	5	9:18	—	1	1
12	4	9:16	9:18	40	5	9:23	—	2	1
54	5	9:21	9:23	37	5	9:28	—	2	—
97	8	9:29	9:29	21	4	9:33	1	—	—
00	9	9:38	9:38	38	5	9:43	5	—	—
49	5	9:43	9:43	14	4	9:47	—	—	—
44	5	9:48	9:48	32	5	9:53	1	—	1
13	4	9:52	9:53	60	5	9:58	—	1	1
23	4	9:56	9:58	31	5	10:03	—	2	—
22	116				103		20	14	9

(first two digits) and the service times are taken from the last group column (first two digits). The random numbers are related to Figure 13-4, (cumulative arrival and service time distributions). For example, the first random number for arrival time is 83. Inspecting Figure 13-4, 83 (or 0.83) lies between 0.60 and 0.85. The vertical line that intersects the x-axis for the value 0.83 indicates a simulated arrival time of 6 minutes. All simulated arrival and service times are determined in the same manner.

Having generated arrival and service times from a table of random numbers, the next step is to list the waiting time in the appropriate column. Since the first arrival comes in 6 minutes after the starting time, the clerk has waited 6 minutes. This time is written in the column, Waiting Time—Attendant while the column, Waiting Time—Customer is blank due to zero waiting time on the part of the first customer. The simulated service time for the first arrival is 5 minutes, which results in the service ending at 8:11. Looking at the next line, we see the next arrival comes at 8:12, which indicates no one has waited in line. Therefore the last column is blank for the first line.

The second arrival comes at 8:12 while the attendant has waited 1 minute from 8:11 to 8:12. The service time of 5 minutes results in the service ending at 8:17. Before the attendant can finish servicing the second arrival, a third arrival comes at 8:16, which means that a customer is waiting The last column, Length of Line, indicates one person in line. When the attendant does service the third arrival, the individual has waited 1 minute. The column Waiting Time—Customer is used to indicate the 1 minute of waiting time from 8:16 to 8:17. The same procedure is used throughout Table 13-4.

Based upon the simulated period for about 2 hours, several questions can be asked. (1) What is the average length of the waiting line? (2) What is the average time a customer waits before being served? (3) What is the average time a customer spends in the system? (4) Would it pay to add another attendant? The first question can be answered by taking the number of customers in line for the 2-hour period and dividing by the number of arrivals, or 0.41 people (9 divided by 22) is the average length of the waiting line. The answer to the second question can be obtained by taking the waiting time of the customers (14 minutes) and dividing by the number of arrivals (22) for 0.64 minutes, the average time a customer waits before being served.

In order to answer the third question of how much time a customer spends in the system, it is necessary to calculate the average service time. Total service time of 103 minutes divided by 22 arrivals equals 4.68 minutes. It should be noted that this average service time is far short of the 5.5 minutes originally set forth in the problem. The sample is much too small; in fact, many weeks of simulated data would be needed to bring it back in line. (This is where the benefits of the computer are apparent.) Nevertheless, the average time a person spends in the system is the summation of average service time (4.68 minutes) and average waiting time (0.64 minutes) for 5.32 minutes.

Regarding the feasibility of adding another attendant, it is necessary to compare the cost of one attendant and customer waiting time to the cost of two attendants and no waiting time (simulated analysis for the two attendants indicates no customer waiting time) to answer the fourth question. Using the cost of $3.00 for the attendant's wages plus fringe benefits and $6.00 for customer waiting time, the results are:

Two Hour (Approx.) Period	One Attendant	Two Attendants
Customer waiting time (14 minutes × $6.00/hour)	$1.40	—
Attendant's cost (2 hours × $3.00/hour)	6.00	$12.00
Total cost of two-hour (approx.) period	$7.40	$12.00

Assuming this analysis is representative of the actual situation over many months rather than for approximately two hours, the cost for one attendant is lower than for two attendants.

This example illustrates the single-channel Monte Carlo method, which utilizes random numbers for originating data. The random numbers are used in creating hypothetical data for a problem whose behavior is known from past experience. If no past data is available, the individual must decide whether the variables in the phenomenon under study can be assumed to act at random. The use of the cumulative probability distribution for arrival and service time should closely parallel the real world.

Multichannel Monte Carlo Method Using Random Numbers

In multichannel problems using random numbers for simulated arrivals and service times, the prior method could have been utilized. However, an approach silghtly different from the preceding one is set forth. Consider a manufacturing plant which has a tool crib located in the center of the plant. Currently, two attendants (hourly wage rate plus fringe benefits is $2.50) are assigned to issue tools and parts to plant personnel. The plant superintendent notices that a waiting line of production workers (average hourly rate is $5.00 including fringe benefits) forms several times a day. The superintendent is questioning whether two attendants assigned to the tool room are adequate to keep overall factory costs at a minimum.

Empirical data has been gathered on the problem. It indicates the average time between requests for tools and parts is five minutes while the length of service time has the following distribution:

6 minutes	.10
7 minutes	.20
8 minutes	.30
9 minutes	.30
10 minutes	.10
	1.00

With this information and a random number table (Appendix E), the arrival and service times can be simulated.

The first task is to simulate the arrivals of the production workers at the tool crib. Since we are dealing with 10 digits (0 through 9) in a table of random numbers, we can select one of these to represent an arrival. Since the number 5 (or any other number) appears on the average once in each group of 10 digits, it represents the chance of an arrival. Using the table of random numbers (start in upper left-hand corner), the number of 5s in each 10-digit random number represents the arrival during that period. Shown in Table 13-5 are arrivals for a 2-hour period or 24 5-minute periods.

After simulating the arrivals at the tool crib, it is necessary to simulate the service time that is required by each of the arrivals. Service times can be distributed as follows:

1. Let 0 represent the probability of a service time of 6 minutes since we have a .1 probability of this amount of service time.
2. Let 1 and 2 represent the probability of a service time of 7 minutes since we have a .2 probability of this amount of service time.

TABLE 13-5
Simulated Arrival and Service Times

Period Number	Number of Arrivals	Service Time (Minutes)
1	1	8 ①
2	1	6 ②
3	—	—
4	1	9 ③
5	1	9 ④
6	2	8 ⑤ 9 ⑥
7	2	9 ⑦ 9 ⑧
8	2	8 ⑨ 8 ⑩
9	3	9 ⑪ 10 ⑫ 8 ⑬
10	—	—
11	2	6 ⑭ 9 ⑮
12	—	—
13	—	—
14	—	—
15	—	—
16	1	7 ⑯
17	2	9 ⑰ 8 ⑱
18	1	7 ⑲
19	1	9 ⑳
20	1	8 ㉑
21	2	10 ㉒ 8 ㉓
22	—	—
23	1	8 ㉔
24	2	8 ㉕ 9 ㉖

3. Let 3, 4, and 5 represent the probability of a service time of 8 minutes since we have a .3 probability of this amount of service time.
4. Let 6, 7, and 8 represent the probability of a service time of 9 minutes since we have a .3 probability of this amount of service time.
5. Let 9 represent the probability of a service time of 10 minutes since we have a .1 probability of this amount of service time.

The simulated service times are shown in Table 13-5. This time the random numbers are found in the last row of Appendix E.

Now that arrivals and service times have been simulated, we want to determine the optimum number of attendants in the tool crib. The first in, first out rule will be observed. Notice that the number of simulated arrivals exceeds the number of time periods by 2. The sample is too small, causing the inequality between the arrivals and time periods.

In order to establish a method for arrivals within each 5-minute period, the following rule will be observed. If there is 1 arrival, we will assume that the production worker arrives at the beginning of the 5-minute period. If 2 arrivals occur within a 5-minute period, one will be assumed to arrive at the beginning of the period, and the other to arrive at the end of the third minute during the period. If 3 arrive, one will be assumed to arrive at the beginning of the period, the second man to arrive at the end of the third minute, and the third man to arrive at the end of the fifth minute. Ideally, the distribution of arrivals should be based upon observed patterns. For a conservative point of view, all men can be assumed to arrive at the beginning of the period.

The simulated behavior of the problem in Figure 13-5 is a 2-hour period. Time is represented on the left-hand margin. To make it easier for referencing arrivals in Table 13-5, the same circled numbers are assigned in Figure 13-5. The following symbols are used:

$$\text{Arrival} \quad \bigcirc$$
$$\text{Being served} \quad \longmapsto\!\!\longleftarrow$$
$$\text{Waiting} \quad \longmapsto\text{-----}\longleftarrow$$

Based upon Figure 13-5, the total waiting time is read from the graph for 93 minutes or an average waiting time per arrival of 3.6 minutes (93 minutes divided by 26 arrivals). If the average time between arrivals is 5 minutes, the number of arrivals for an 8-hour day is 96 (8 hours per day times 12 arrivals per hour). Also, if the average waiting time is 3.6 minutes, total waiting time is 345.6 minutes (96 arrivals times 3.6 minutes) or 5.8 hours of lost time per day for production workers.

Before computing the total cost for two attendants in the problem, it is necessary to simulate the problem with three attendants. This is shown in Figure 13-6, except three solid lines exist simultaneously because three production men can be serviced at one time. The total waiting time is calculated to be 12 minutes or 0.5 minute (12 minutes divided by 26 arrivals) lost per production worker. With 96 arrivals in an 8-hour day, the total time lost is 0.8 hour of lost time per day (96 arrivals times 0.5 minute).

A cost comparison for two, three, and four attendants per Table 13-6 is used to determine the optimum number of servicemen that minimizes the total cost of the plant operation. The cost for three attendants results in lower total costs. Again, a larger sample is needed to finalize the results of the problem.

TABLE 13-6
Cost Comparison of Two, Three, and Four Attendants

	Two Attendants	Three Attendants	Four Attendants
Customer waiting time	5.8 hours	0.8 hour	—
Cost per hour	$5	$5	$5
Waiting time cost (waiting time × cost per hour)	$29.00	$ 4.00	—
Attendant's cost (8-hour basis × $2.50 per hour)	40.00	60.00	$80.00
Total daily cost	$69.00	$64.00	$80.00

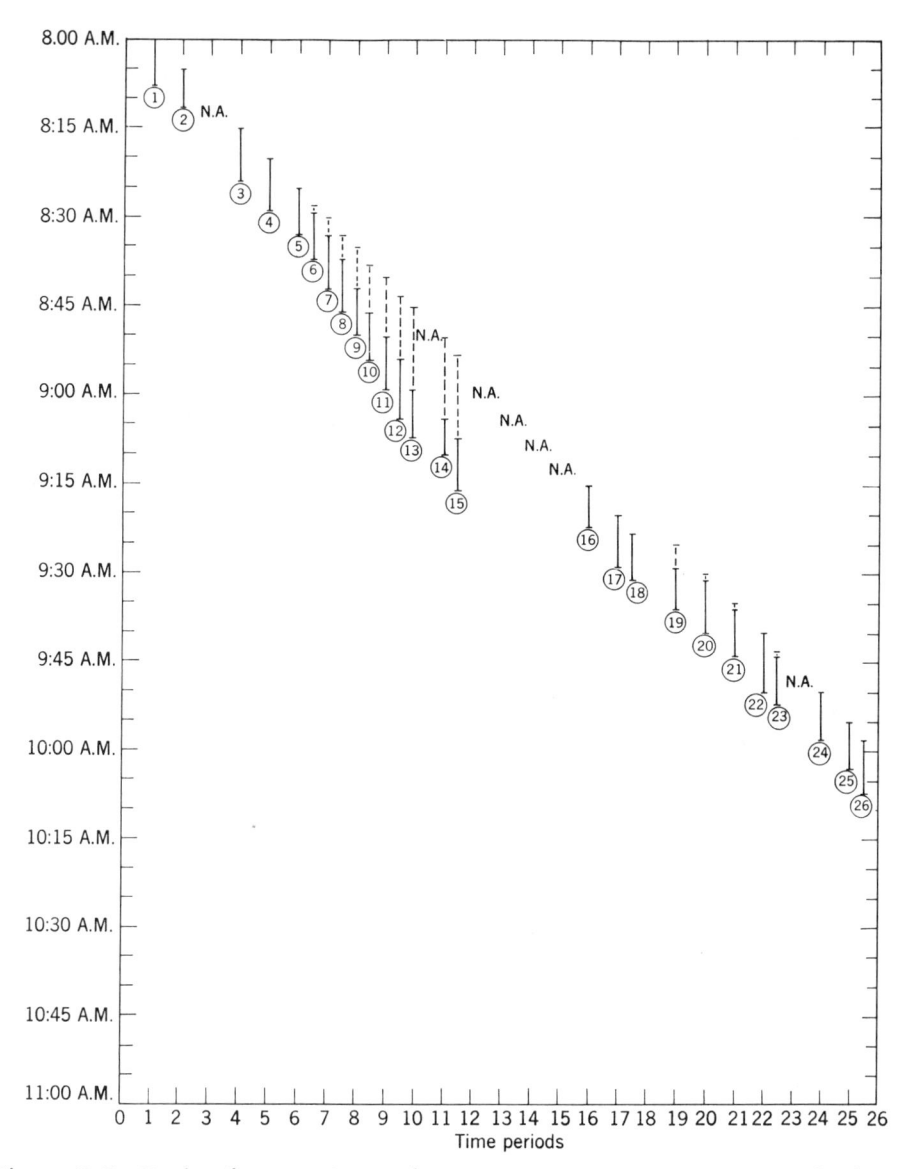

Figure 13-5 Tool crib operation with two servicemen. N.A. = no arrivals during five-minute period.

Queuing (Servicing) Application—American Products Corporation

The American Products Corporation has special machinery (temperature recorders) for one of its plants serviced by the Leeds & Northrop Company. The firm has been offered three different service plan proposals on a three year basis whereby the cost of emergency service is $20.00 per hour, and the cost of the contract service is $15.00 per hour. Each service call averages 4 hours in length. The probability distributions set forth below for each of the three plans represent the need for emergency service.

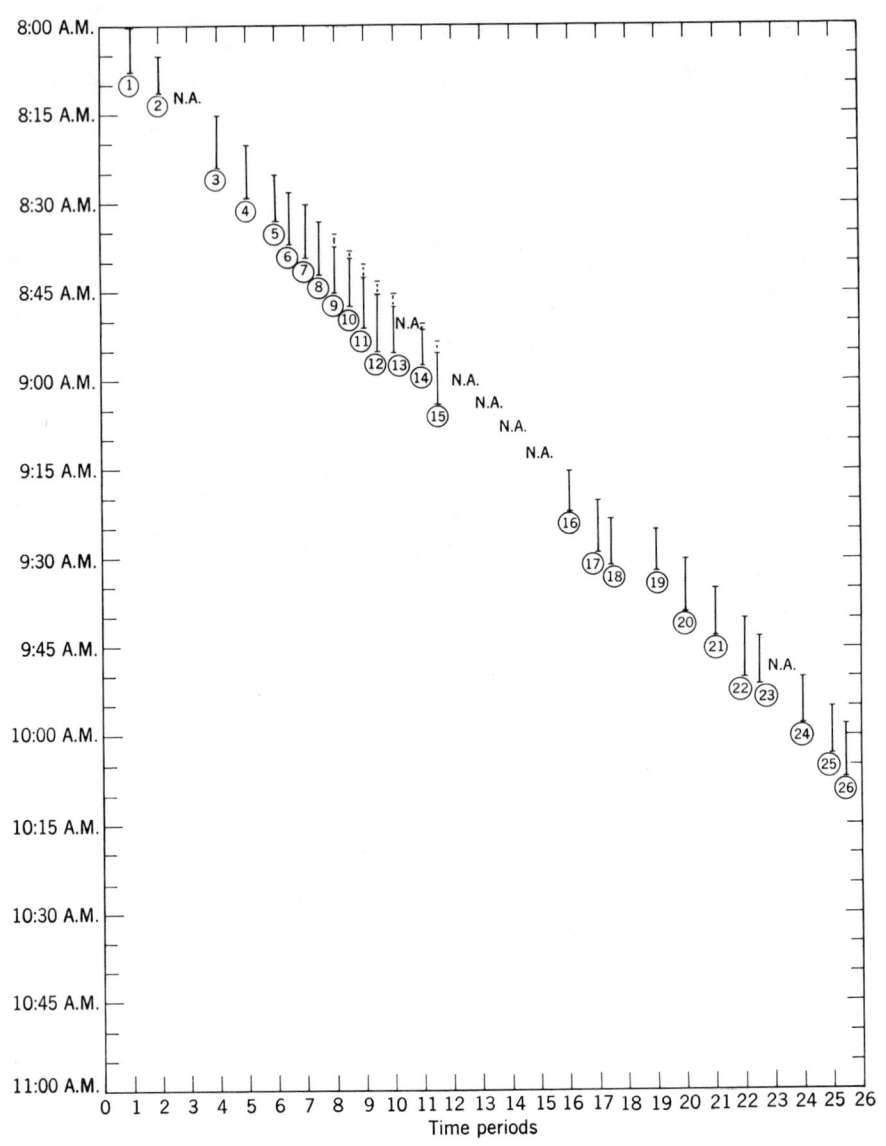

Figure 13-6 Tool crib operation with three servicemen. N.A. = no arrivals during five-minute period.

Plan A No contract service calls—3-year basis

Month	Probability
1st month	.05
2nd month	.15
3rd month	.30
4th month	.20
5th month	.15
6th month	.15
	1.00

442 OPERATIONS RESEARCH MODELS—SIMULATION TECHNIQUES

Plan B Four contract service calls—3-year basis

Month	Probability
2nd month	.10
4th month	.10
6th month	.30
8th month	.20
10th month	.20
12th month	.10
	1.00

Plan C Eight contract service calls—3-year basis

Month	Probability
4th month	.05
8th month	.10
12th month	.30
16th month	.30
20th month	.20
24th month	.05
	1.00

Based on the need for emergency service given by the above data, the production manager has asked a member of the OR group to resolve the problem of what service plan is lowest in cost. Using a random numbers table, the operations research analyst simulated the problem on a 3-year basis. The following costs were determined:

Plan A
  11 emergency service calls @ $20.00/hour for 4 hours   = $880.00

Plan B
  7 emergency service calls @ $20.00/hour for 4 hours   = $560.00
  4 contract service calls @ $15.00/hour for 4 hours   =   240.00
                                                             $800.00

Plan C
  3 emergency service calls @ $20.00/hour for 4 hours   = $240.00
  8 contract service calls @ $15.00/hour for 4 hours   =   480.00
                                                             $720.00

Inspection of the simulated emergency and contract service data indicates that Plan C provides the lowest cost service over the three year period.

QUEUING MODELS   443

Summary

The treatment of queuing theory in this chapter is a cross section of various waiting line models and methods. These were presented for single-channel and multichannel problems, allowing for the application of queuing theory to many business areas: the factory, the office, the sales floor, and public places. The reader can readily identify other areas where queuing discipline can be utilized by using his imagination and experience. In many cases, a firm can realize considerable cost savings without making a substantial investment in the queuing study itself. Operations research groups should give considerable thought to the use of this technique for high return projects.

Questions

1. What is queuing theory?
2. What are the similarities and differences in the techniques for single-channel and multichannel queuing models?
3. What are the advantages of the Monte Carlo method for single-channel and multichannel queuing problems over earlier models?

Problems

13-1 The Midland Manufacturing Company operates several tool rooms within one of its major manufacturing plants. The arrival of its production men is observed to be at a uniform rate of 30 men per hour while the tool room service attendant is observed to handle these requests at the uniform rate of 24 per hour.
 (a) What is the waiting line likely to be at the end of 4 hours?
 (b) Would it be profitable for the company to add another attendant assuming the time of the production men to be worth $4.50 per hour (wage rate plus fringe benefits) and the attendant's time costs $2.50 per hour (wage rate plus fringe benefits) based on an 8-hour day?
 (c) Suppose the uniform service rate increases to 40 per hour for one attendant. Would it pay to add another one?

13-2 The Newcomb Corporation must make a decision regarding its policy of hiring a repairman to fix machines which break down at an average rate of 4 per hour according to a Poisson distribution. Nonproductive time on any of the machines is costing the firm $10.00 per hour. The firm can hire two different types of repairmen, one slow but inexpensive ($2.50 per hour), the other fast but expensive ($4.50 per hour). The slow repairman can repair machines exponentially at an average rate of 6 per hour while the fast repairman can repair machines exponentially at the rate of 8 per hour. Based upon the foregoing data, which repairman should be hired?

13-3 Trucks are known to arrive at a dock in a Poisson manner at the rate of 8 per hour. Service time distribution is approximated exponentially with an average rate of 5 minutes. The cost of waiting is $10.00 per hour while the cost of servicing is $4.00 per unit.
 (a) Calculate the average number of trucks in the system.
 (b) Calculate the average time a truck spends in the system.
 (c) Calculate the average queue length for the trucks.
 (d) Calculate the average time a truck waits before being served.
 (e) Calculate the minimum cost service rate.

13-4 A stenographer has 5 persons for whom she performs stenographic services. Arrival rate is Poisson and service times are exponential. Average arrival rate is 4 per hour with an average service time of 10 minutes. Cost of waiting is $8.00 per hour while the cost of servicing is $2.50 each.
 (a) Calculate the average waiting time of an arrival.
 (b) Calculate the average length of the waiting line.
 (c) Calculate the average time which an arrival spends in the system.
 (d) Calculate the minimum cost service rate.

13-5 Incoming materials arrive at a receiving dock at an average rate of 5 per hour (Poisson distribution). The material is handled by a lift truck whose service time is exponential with an average service rate of 7 loads per hour. Production management desires to know (a) the average number of loads waiting on the docks to be moved, (b) the average length of time that an arriving load will spend waiting for service, and (c) what would the lift truck average service rate have to be in order to have an expected waiting time of 20 minutes for a load. [Hint for first part: average length of nonempty waiting line $=\mu/(\mu-\lambda)$.]

13-6 The manager of a Capital Finance loan office has to make a decision regarding its service rate on new loans. One service rate is 0.5 unit per hour with a service time variance of 3 hours and another is a service rate of 0.4 unit per hour with a service time variance of 2 hours. The difference in rate per hour represents explaining to the customer the other services offered by the firm if the customer should have need of these services sometime in the future. The cost of waiting per employee for an hour is estimated to be $3.00 while the cost of servicing one arrival is $1.50. The number of arrivals has a Poisson distribution with a mean of 0.3 units per hour. What should the manager do?

13-7 The Citizens Savings and Loan has 4 tellers for saving accounts. It has found that the service time distributions are exponential with mean service time of 6 minutes per customer. Customers are found to arrive in a Poisson manner throughout the day with a mean arrival rate of 30 per hour.
 (a) Calculate the average number of customers in the system.
 (b) Calculate the average time a customer spends in the system.
 (c) Calculate the average queue length.
 (d) Calculate the average time a customer waits before being served.
 (e) Calculate how many hours a week each employee spends performing his job.
 (f) Calculate the probability that an employee is waiting for a customer.
 (g) Calculate the expected number of idle employees at any specific moment.

13-8 The Lincoln Insurance Company has 3 claims adjusters in one of its large midwestern offices. Customers are found to arrive in a Poisson manner at an average rate of 32 per 8-hour day for claims against the company. The service time is found to have an exponential distribution with a service time of 30 minutes. Claimants are processed on a first come, first served basis.
(a) How many hours a week can an adjuster expect to spend with the claimants?
(b) Management also desires to know how much time a claimant spends in the firm's office on the average.

13-9 Twenty production machines of the Ward Manufacturing Company are serviced by three repairmen. Breakdowns and service rates follow the Poisson distribution and the exponential distribution, respectively. The average breakdown rate is 88 per 8-hour shift and the mean repair time is 2 hours.
(a) Determine the average waiting time of a machine.
(b) Determine the average number of machines running on an hourly basis.

13-10 In the machine shop of the Lodge and Shapely Company, 4 overhead cranes serve a number of production machines. If all cranes are busy and one machinist must wait for service, the waiting time cost is $4.50 per hour (wage rate, fringe benefits, and nonproduction costs). On the other hand, the overhead cost of the crane is $5.80 per hour (wage rate, fringe benefits, and other costs). Empirical data gathered indicates that the number of machinists' requests for crane service follows the Poisson distribution with an average rate of 5 calls per hour. The average service time is exponentially distributed with a time of 20 minutes per call. The cranes serve the machinists on a first come, first served basis. The vice president in charge of manufacturing wants to know how many cranes are needed to keep the machinists' cost of waiting time and the overhead cost of the cranes at a minimum. Use an 8-hour day in your calculations.

13-11 The Askcraft Machine Company operates a warehouse which services its foremen. The foremen arrive at a random rate of 6 per hour. The warehouse attendant is is able to service these arrivals at a uniform rate of 4 per hour. If the attendant's cost is $3.50 per hour and the foremen's cost per hour is $5.00, use the simulation method to determine the optimum number of attendants to assign to the warehouse in order to minimize cost. Use a 2-hour period for your decision. Assume any foreman in line will be serviced.

13-12 A sample of 300 arrivals (customers) at a checkout counter of a store indicates that an average time between arrivals is 5 minutes. A study of the time required to service the customer, that is, adding up the bill, receiving payment, cashing checks, giving stamps, and the like, yields the following distribution:

Service Time (Minutes)	Frequency
1.5	10%
2.0	20%
2.5	30%
3.0	20%
3.5	10%
4.0	10%

Using a simulated sample of 20 arrivals, calculate (a) the average customer waiting time, (b) the idle time of the checkout clerk, and (c) the average time a person spends in the system. Assume all arrivals come at the beginning of each 5-minute period.

13-13 A single-service gasoline station has determined the following arrival and service times:

Between Time Arrivals (Minutes)	Percent of Cases	Service Time (Minutes)	Percent of Cases
0	3	1	6
1	4	2	12
2	8	3	17
3	11	4	19
4	16	5	17
5	14	6	12
6	10	7	8
7	9	8	5
8	8	9	3
9	5	10	1
10	4		
11	3		
12	2		
13	1		
14	1		
15	1		

Simulate the operation of this service station from 8:00 A.M. to 10:04 A.M. (time for last arrival). Assume that any customer(s) in the line at 10:00 A.M. will be serviced. Determine (a) the average length of the waiting line, (b) the average time a customer waits before being serviced, and (c) the average time a customer spends in the system. (d) Also determine whether or not it would pay to add another attendant if the attendant's cost is $2.50 per hour and the customer's time is valued at three times that amount. (Note: treat random number 00 as 100.)

13-14 The General Service Company has made a study of the average time for requests of its two office copiers. Requests were found to total 12 times an hour for both machines. The time it takes to run off the desired copies has the following distribution:

Service Time (Minutes)	Frequency
6	10%
7	20%
8	30%
9	30%
10	10%

QUEUING MODELS 447

The office manager is wondering if another machine might help alleviate the apparent traffic jam at the two machines. He has assigned the problem to you and suggested that a two-hour period be used for a preliminary analysis of the situation. (If the third machine appears warranted, the problem will be simulated on the firm's IBM 370/145 for a conclusive answer.) Assume that the waiting time of the average office employee is $3.00 per hour and the hourly cost of the machine with materials to be $2.50 per hour. Are the present two office copiers adequate?

Bibliography

R. L. Ackoff and M. W. Sasieni, *Fundamentals of Operations Research*, New York: John Wiley & Sons, 1968.

H. Bierman, C. P. Bonini, and W. H. Hausman, *Quantitative Analysis for Business Decisions*, Homewood Ill.: Richard D. Irwin, 1973.

C. W. Churchman, R. L. Ackoff, and E. L. Arnoff, *Introduction to Operations Research*, New York: John Wiley & Sons, 1957.

D. R. Cox and W. L. Smith, *Queues*, New York: John Wiley & Sons, 1961.

W. J. Fabrycky and P. E. Torgersen, *Operations Economy, Industrial Applications of Operations Research*, Englewood Cliffs, N.J.: Prentice-Hall, 1966.

L. W. Hein, *The Quantitative Approach to Managerial Decisions*, Englewood Cliffs, N.J.: Prentice-Hall, 1967.

F. S. Hillier and G. J. Lieberman, *Introduction to Operations Research*, San Francisco: Holden-Day, 1967.

P. M. Morse, *Queues, Inventories, and Maintenance*, New York: John Wiley & Sons, 1958.

C. M. Paik, *Quantitative Methods for Managerial Decisions*, McGraw-Hill Book Company, 1973.

J. A. Panico, *Queuing Theory*, Englewood Cliffs, N.J.: Prentice-Hall, 1969.

N. U. Prabhu, *Queues and Inventories*, New York: John Wiley & Sons, 1965.

T. L. Saaty, *Elements of Queuing Theory*, New York: McGraw-Hill Book Company, 1961.

Chapter FOURTEEN

Simulation

The technique of simulation has long been an important tool of the designer. Scale models of machines have been used for many years to simulate plant layouts. Simulation, as used initially by operations research, had its origin in the work of John von Neumann and Stanislaw Ulam in the late 1940s. Using Monte Carlo analysis in conjunction with a mathematical technique, they solved nuclear shielding problems that were either too expensive for experimentation or too complex for analysis. With the advent of digital computers in the early 1950s, simulation has made substantial progress. Countless business problems are being solved since computer simulation is the only economical and fast way of performing the vast amount of calculations required.

In this chapter the important variants of simulation—the operational gaming method, the Monte Carlo method (treated in the previous chapter), and the system simulation method—and a systematic approach to the study of systems using simulation methods are discussed. The advantages and limitations of simulation then are set forth. Finally, application of simulation methods to the functional areas of a firm is illustrated.

Simulation Defined

Simulation is useful in solving a business problem where many values of the variables are not known or partly known in advance and there is no easy way to find these values. The problem is likened to the sequence for which no ready-made formula is known for the nth (last) term. The only known fact is a rule (recursion relation) which allows us to find the next term from the previous terms. Basically, the only way to discover the nth term is to apply the same rule over and over again until the nth term is reached. Simulation utilizes a method of finding these successive states in a problem by repeatedly applying the rules under which the system operates. This successive linking of one particular state to a previous state is a distinguishing characteristic of simulation. Thus it should be apparent why simulation models are stated in the form of recursion relations.

For the most part, simulation involves the construction of some type of mathematical model that describes the system's operation in terms of individual events and components. Further the system is divided into the elements and the interrelationships of those elements with predictable behavior, at least in terms of a probability distribution, for each of the various possible states of the system and its inputs. Simulation is a means of dividing the model building process into smaller components parts and combining them in their natural, logical order. This then allows computer analysis of the effects of their interactions on one another. Due to statistical error, it is impossible to guarantee that the optimal answer will be found, but the answer should be at least near optimal if the problem is simulated correctly. In essence, the simulation model performs experiments on the sample input data rather than on the entire universe (statistically speaking), since the latter would be too time consuming, inconvenient, and expensive.

Simulation has been defined as the use of a system model that has the desired characteristic of reality in order to reproduce the essence of the actual operations. It has also been defined as a representation of reality through the use of a model or other device which will react in the same manner as reality under a given set of conditions. None of these definitions include all of its fundamental characteristics, namely, the use of mathematical models, computers, statistics or stochastic processes, facts, assumption, and alternative courses of action. A more general and inclusive definition of simulation is: a quantitative technique that utilizes a computerized mathematical model in order to represent actual decision making under conditions of uncertainty for evaluating alternative courses of action based upon facts and assumptions.

Operational Gaming Method

Before examining the essential characteristics of Monte Carlo and system simulation, operational gaming (the first method of simulation) is examined. This refers to those situations involving conflict of interest among players or decision makers within the framework of a simulated environment. The two most widely used forms of operational gaming are military games and business management games (mostly computer oriented). Military gaming is essentially a training device for military leaders, enabling them to test alternative strategies under simulated war conditions. On the other hand, participants of business games must make decisions based upon historical information. These decisions then influence and create the environment under which subsequent decisions must be made. Its characteristics are sequential decisions, rapid feedback, and new responses.

Military Games

Military games for amusement, and for the physical and mental preparation of war, are as old as civilization. Andrew Wilson, in his book, *The Bomb and the Computer,* traces war games back to the Chinese game *weich'i* which appeared about 3000 B.C. The names translates literally as "envelopment." It was played with colored stones on a map.

Historically, European war gaming goes back to the game of chess—the first so-called "modern" version of which was invented by a Prussian in the seventeenth century. The game was played with 30 different pieces and 14 various moves on an enlarged board. In 1824 another Prussian, von Reisswitz, put the game on a plaster relief model of a countryside and substituted color-coded blocks, representing troop units, in place of chess pieces. Called Kriegsspiel (literally war game in German), it was quickly picked up by the military in other countries and used in testing operational plans.

By World War I, virtually every major world power was employing war games to determine its strategies. The subsequent history of war gaming is a story in itself and is marked by a number of outstanding successes. Today the military services conduct extensive war gaming to evaluate equipment, to test strategy and plans, and to train commanders and combat staffs. The individual services operate their own independent gaming establishments. One example is the United States Army's Fort Leavenworth War Games Facility, for which Booz, Allen Applied Research, Inc. gaming teams assist in evaluating problems.

Business Games

Management games have gained wide acceptance in business and education. The first such business game, which Booz, Allen & Hamilton helped develop, was known as "Top Management Decision Simulation." It was introduced by the American Management Association in 1957. Since then, management games of various kinds and levels of sophistication have been developed all over the world. Growth in the number of games and participants has been tremendous because computer capabilities have increased many fold.

The primary use of management games is to help the participants, be they executives in industry or students in business schools, develop their ability to make difficult interdependent business decisions in real life, evaluate new ideas, and introduce new techniques of decision making—all in a simulated environment. These games offer the participants a high degree of personal involvement and competitive spirit. The results gained are in direct proportion to the skills of the participants.

The use of management games in the business world is in some sense equivalent to the use of laboratory experiments in the physical sciences. The outcome of good or bad decisions can be examined quickly and without fear of real loss. Simulations of business environments provide valuable experience in conceptualizing ideas and in logical thinking. Furthermore, games can be used to introduce operations research techniques and give participants training in model building and analysis. A sophisticated, but not necessarily complex management game, can also serve as a stepping-stone for development of information processing systems and corporate behavior models.

With the advent of interactive computing, the use of management games as a teaching, training, or research device is even more feasible. The decision-making process is enhanced by operations research because it affords the user an opportunity to utilize the techniques interactively on various sample data via remote terminals. Data retrieval and manipulation are simplified to a great extent. Thus, advancements in computers and utilization of OR techniques have led to the development of interactive management games—a new direction in business games.

Modeling the Business Game

The essence of a business simulation model is one that accepts input, analyzes or processes it according to a set of rules or formulas, and generates

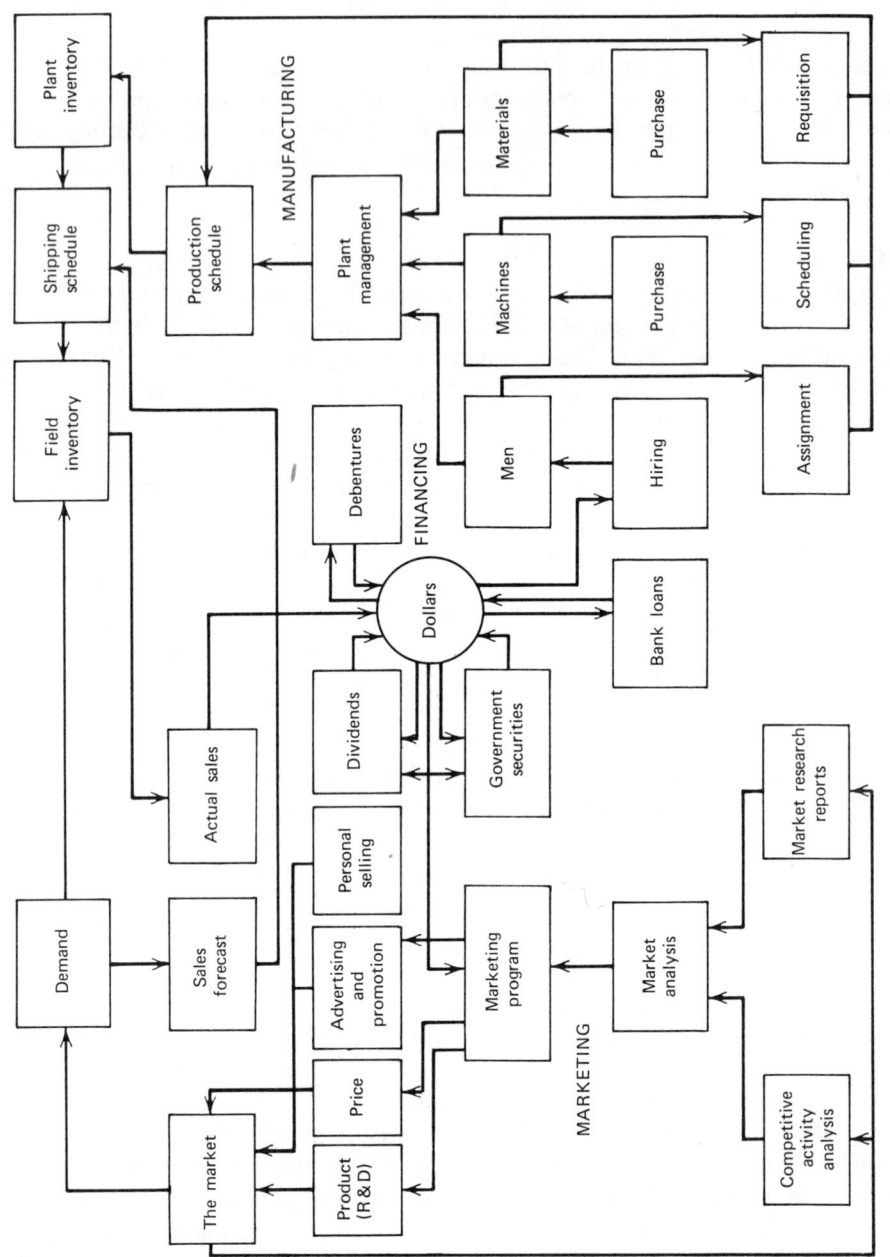

Figure 14-1 Major modules—marketing, manufacturing, and financing—for firms operating in a simulated business game environment.

an outcome per the analysis. Figure 14-1 illustrates a typical business game consisting of three modules: marketing, manufacturing, and financing.

The *marketing module* simulates the behavior of customers in response to price and product availabilities, their preferences being modified by the firm's personal selling, advertising, sales promotion, and research and development activities. Basically, the market consists of two types of customers: the "loyal" customers, who do not switch brands unless price varies and the "switchers," who can be lured away by personal selling, advertising, sales promotion, and research and development activities of the firm.

A firm may not be able to supply all the demand in a market region if it is "out-of-stock." A percentage of the excess demand (the really loyal customers) may be back ordered, and the rest is redistributed among the other firms to the extent that they can supply the excess beyond their original market share. The rest of the unsupplied demand, if any, is assumed to be lost.

The effects of personal selling, advertising, sales promotion, and research and development activities are cumulative and lag over time. These activities have both competitive and cooperative aspects. For convenience, they are referred to as "effective advertising and research." Product promotion and product development are necessary to stimulate the demand. Hence, the marketing module determines:

- Market share for each product in each region.
- Actual sales versus demand.
- Back orders, if any.

Within the *manufacturing module*, each firm has a plant, a work force, and raw materials which form the three basic factors of production. The products that a firm manufactures require different combinations of these factors. The scarcity of the three factors limits production. Production changes are proportional to the quantities ordered. Finished goods can be stored at the plant or shipped to the market region warehouses. Thus, the manufacturing module:

- Determines actual production schedules subject to the constraints of machines, work force, and raw materials.
- Modifies shipping schedules, if necessary.
- Updates factory and warehouse inventories.

Costs are incurred in manufacturing, shipping to warehouses, and storing inventory. Inventory costs are charged on average inventory during the period. All costs are linear and each firm has the same internal cost structure.

The *financing module* summarizes the results of all activities and actions undertaken during a given period. Each period, the firms must make financial decisions relative to investment in government securities, payment of dividends, issuing of debentures, and purchase of new equipment. Other financial revenues and obligations arise as the result of activities in the production and marketing of a firm's products. Bank loans that partially cover the cash obligations for a firm are automatically drawn as required and are paid back when possible. Inability to meet the financial obligations beyond the outstanding line of bank credit can result in the firm's bankruptcy.

The cash transactions simulate the continuous flow of receipts and payments such that the income from operations offset the expenses. The financing module uses standard cost accounting for manufacturing operations and computer cost variances. It calculates the working relationship between incomes, expenses, and cash flows of each firm.

The business game reports to the teams the outcome of their decisions and actual activities that took place during the simulation. These reports are the basis for making decisions in the following period(s). They can be grouped in various ways depending on the information required and ease of interpretation. The usual standard reports are:

- Market reports.
- Competitive performance reports.
- Finished goods and production report.
- Factory and warehouse status report.
- Profit-and-loss statement.
- Balance sheet.
- Cash-flow statement.

To aid effective decision making during the simulation exercise, the decision-assisting tools of operations research are available to the teams. These tools demonstrate to the participants the role of operations research techniques in decision making and expose them to model building and analysis. For example, linear programming can procure and allocate production resources effectively during the simulation exercise. The linear programming model optimizes the production decisions subject to the constraints and criterion of optimization. Markov analysis can explain the movement and retention of customers among firms. Also, multiple regression techniques can establish relationships between different variables in the market place. Regression analysis of the latest market data can help forecast demands of products and assist in pricing and product promoting decisions.

Monte Carlo Method

For a complete understanding of the Monte Carlo method (the second method of simulation), it is necessary to refer to the work of von Neumann and Ulam mentioned earlier in this chapter. During World War II, physicists at the Los Alamos Scientific Laboratory were puzzled by the behavior of neutrons. The two mathematicians suggested a solution which amounted to submitting the problem to a roulette wheel. Step by step, the probabilities of the separate events were merged into a total picture which gave an approximate but workable answer to a problem. Von Neumann gave it the code name "Monte Carlo" for the secret work of Los Alamos. The Monte Carlo method, which is actually the study of the laws of chance, was so successful on neutron diffusion problems that its popularity spread and is now an important operational research technique.

Even though the Monte Carlo approach suggests the use of roulette wheels or dice, random numbers are used. This method can solve probability dependent problems where physical experimentation is impracticable and where the creation of an exact formula is impossible. Basically, we are studying problems with a long sequence of probability-determined steps or events. Although we can write mathematical formulas for the probability of a given step or event, we are often unable to write a useful equation for the probabilities of all steps or events.

With this brief background of the Monte Carlo method, a definition will help clarify its meaning. The Monte Carlo method is simulation by sampling techniques, that is, instead of drawing samples from a real population, they are obtained from a theoretical counterpart of the actual population. Monte Carlo involves determining the probability distribution of the variable under consideration and then sampling from this distribution by means of random numbers to obtain data. In effect, a set of random numbers generates a set of values that have the same distributional characteristics as the real population.

The Monte Carlo method can be used to solve several different classes of problems. The first are problems that involve some kind of stochastic process while the second are deterministic mathematical problems that cannot be solved easily or at all by deterministic methods. For the first problem type, Monte Carlo methods have been developed for simulating data based upon probability distributions. For the second class of problems, approximate solutions may be possible by simulating a stochastic process whose cumulative distribution function satisfies the functional relationships and the solution requirements of the deterministic problem.

Any waiting line problem of the previous chapter is a likely candidate for Monte Carlo simulation since both the arrival and service times can be simulated where they are probabilistic and their distributions are known. A special case of Monte Carlo simulation, known as model sampling, is helpful where some complicated stochastic process is too difficult to analyze by standard statistical procedures. In these cases, repeated application of the Monte Carlo process may enable one to collect a set of data concerning the system and to estimate its statistical properties. Other logical business areas for Monte Carlo simulation are: order flow, maintenance policies, inventory levels, and assembly operations. These last three areas will be illustrated in this chapter. Monte Carlo simulation has also been used to determine the number of airport runways and the flow of automobile traffic. The military has used it to solve Air Force logistics problems.

System Simulation Method

System simulation (the third method of simulation) is a process in which real world data—useful in the analysis of a complex problem—is processed through a model which reproduces the operating environment. The simulation model allows an analysis of the system response to alternative management actions, providing a sound basis for decision.

System simulation differs from the Monte Carlo approach in several respects. This method generally draws samples from a real population instead of drawing samples from a table of random numbers (or some special model). No theoretical counterpart of the actual population is used in system simulation. Another distinction is that the simulation method makes use of a mathematical and/or logical model which can be analytically solved to assist an individual in reaching a decision. However, when situations are complex and do not lend themselves to analysis by a mathematical model (which can be analytically solved), the technique of Monte Carlo is the answer. An example of this is the condition of an uncontrollable input to a system whose probability distribution is known and can be handled analytically, but whose sequential pattern cannot be adequately expressed for an analytical solution.

The distinction between these two basic techniques (Monte Carlo and system simulation) is actually not great. A system simulation example might help highlight the basic difference in the two approaches. In this problem, the prediction of consumer reaction to new products, without extensive and costly surveys, is desired. The model exposes some 500 hypothetical individuals with certain characteristics to a set of communication channels, each of which carries a particular message. During each simulated week, an individual is subjected with varying probabilities of exposure to several communication channels and to particular corrections made in these channels. Predetermined rules decide if an assertion is accepted, depending on the individual's attitudes toward the communication source, previous acquaintance, acceptance of the assertion, and previous position on similar messages. As one might guess, a model of this kind is complex since it incorporates reasonable hypotheses regarding human behavior. This system simulation problem points out at least two basic differences—need for data not found in random tables and the use of a sophisticated model.

Advantages and Limitations of Simulation Techniques

Simulation techniques are extremely useful since they allow experimentation with a model of the system rather than the actual operating system. Experimenting with the system itself could prove too costly and, in many cases, far too risky. For example, a member of an OR team suggests that a certain process be expanded to overcome scheduling difficulties. After a considerable outlay of cash, the situation has not improved. This problem can be simulated on a computer without interfering with the system itself. From past history of the system and the frequency of occurrence with certain events, the OR team can generate the operation and observe how the system would react to changes under various operating conditions. By changing one input or variable at a time, it is possible to evaluate the behavior of the system in order to determine the pertinent parameters governing it and to set forth recommendations that will improve the overall performance of the system. Simulation techniques allow the group to manipulate a replica of the actual system for trial runs before committing the firm to large outlays of cash. This is an important advantage of simulation.

Computer simulation allows one to incorporate time into an analysis. In a computer simulation of business operations, one can compress the results of several years or periods into a few minutes of running time. A computer simulation study is completely repeatable, that is, the user exercises complete control over development of the model and the use of simulation routines. It is ideal for the collection and processing of quantitative data and free from physical limitations on the system being studied since the system is represented in purely symbolic terms. Simulation languages are available, which mean lower programming costs, thereby widening their application to new business problems. These languages offer a conceptual view of a system, which should facilitate the construction and programming of simulation models and techniques.

The nontechnical manager can comprehend simulation more easily than a complex mathematical model. Simulation does not require simplifications and assumptions to the extent required in analytical solutions. In fact, less work may be required in development. Generally, a simulation model is easier to explain to management personnel since it is in essence a description of the behavior of some system or process. If comprehension is easier with simulation than a comparable complex mathematical model, the chances of success are greatly improved. No manager wants to implement and work day by day with a model he is not capable of understanding. Even if a complex mathematical model is used, simulation sometimes can be used to check the adequacy of an analytic solution to insure management that the OR solution is accurate.

The introduction of new machinery and equipment into a plant may produce unforeseen bottlenecks and problems. Simulation can be used to foresee these upcoming difficulties. It enables production management to focus attention on problems that otherwise might be ignored. Simulation studies are a valuable and convenient way of breaking down a complicated system into its subsystems. Each subsystem may, in turn, be simulated individually or jointly with other subsystems. This type of simulation also allows the observer to gain increased knowledge of what makes the system operate. It permits one to observe a cause and effect relationship which can result in suggestions for improvement in the system and its related subsystems.

In many cases where complex relationships of a predictable and random nature occur, a simulated process is easier to use than developing an elaborate mathematical model. Even where an activity can be affected by numerous random influences where each influence can be separately examined, the calculation for the probability of the combined sequence of activities spilling over and interacting may be too difficult to incorporate efficiently into a mathematical model. Here, the use of random numbers will be just as effective as the utilization of some elaborate model. Many other cases that cannot be solved directly by standard analytical methods can be approximated by simulation. This also applies to certain classes of nonprobabilistic mathematical equations.

Simulation that utilizes some mathematical model of the system enables one, by trial and error, to determine the controlled variable values that will generate the best results for the firm. In some cases, the experience of designing a computer simulation model may be more valuable than the actual simulation itself. The knowledge obtained in designing a simulation study many times suggests changes in the system being simulated. The effect of these changes can then be tested by simulation before imposing them on the real system.

The use of business games has been extremely beneficial for the training of management personnel at all levels. It allows the player to observe the interaction of his decisions on corporate objectives and policies under conditions of uncertainty. Executive simulation provides opportunities for the practice and application of skills under dynamic conditions with a high degree of experienced realism. It permits the participants to quickly ascertain their capabilities and their weaknesses. This kind of simulation creates a high degree of self-motivation and self-learning because feedback provides a basis for self-evaluation and self-correction. It allows the individual participant to test alternative courses of action before making a final decision. Since most business games are computer oriented, they provide the participants with some familiarity with electronic data processing.

As is the case with all OR techniques, simulation does have limitations that should be recognized. It does not produce optimum solutions. Each simulation run is like a single experiment conducted under a given set of conditions as defined by a set of values for the solution. Because simulation requires a number of successive runs, it can be time consuming. As the number of variables increases, the difficulty in finding the optimum values increases considerably. This necessitates careful design of experimental runs and optimum research methods to avoid lost time and additional cost.

Simulation can be a more direct method than a complex mathematical model to the solution of an OR problem. As the ability to employ simulation increases, a tendency may develop to rely on this technique too often because of its relative ease of application. This might result in substituting simulation for mathematical analytical techniques which are better suited. The focus may center on applying techniques rather than solving problems.

When referring to a mathematical model used in a computer simulation program, quantifying all the variables that affect the behavior of the system may be impossible or the number of variables under review may exceed the capacity of the available computer. In addition, all known inputs may not be included in the model due to errors of omission or commission. Some input and output relationships may not be known or may be impossible to ascertain. Also, the relationships among the variables in the system may be so involved that they cannot be expressed in the form of one or more mathematical equations. Simulation, then, can suffer from the same deficiencies as other mathematical models.

Executive simulation suffers from several shortcomings. The overly simplified simulation makes the participant feel that management is overrated since it is so simple to make decisions and show a reasonable profit. The problem is one of not being able to incorporate all the pertinent variables to make it completely realistic. In most cases the participant does not act as he would act in a real life situation. He has a tendency to consider the simulation artificial to the point where his involvement is related to winning rather than learning. He is concerned with finding the key to success, such as the right combination of price, advertising, and number of salesmen as set up by the game model. The point of winning in terms of total assets and profits overshadows the possible learning experience.

Systematic Computer Approach to Simulation

The foregoing material provides a background for a systematic approach to the study of systems that utilize simulation. The planned approach, set forth in this book for an OR project, is also applicable to simulation. However, constructing the computer model, using a random number generator, and analyzing the data should be explained for a better understanding of simulation.

After the observation phase (first step), which leads to a formulation of the real problem under study (second step), collection and processing of data follows. Because a certain amount of data must have been collected and processed before the real problem is defined, the medium on which data are recorded in the initial step of the planned approach may not be the most efficient medium for use in the later stages of computer processing. The conversion of the data from one medium to another may play an important role in determining data processing efficiency. Information that is handwritten, acceptable in the observation phase, must be converted to punched card, to magnetic tape, disk, or some other computer input medium.

The third step of the planned approach, when applied to simulation, is formulation of the computer model by determining how many variables to include in the model. Very little difficulty is encountered with the output variables since these endogenous variables are determined at the outset. The real difficulty arises in the choice of the input variables. Too few exogenous variables may lead to invalid or incomplete models, whereas too many may result in no computer simulation because of insufficient computer memory capacity. Moreover, too many input variables will cause unnecessarily complicated computational methods.

Computer programming time is an important consideration in formulating mathematical models for computer simulation. The time required for writing a computer program depends upon the number of variables used in the model and the model's complexity. When variables of the model are stochastic in nature, both programming time and computation time are likely to increase. Reductions in the amount of programming time must be balanced against model validity and the computer's computational speed. The programmer should give serious thought to simulation languages, discussed in a later section of this chapter. The gain in time savings from use of these languages might mean the difference between success and failure from a timing aspect. Other considerations in the formulation of mathematical models for simulation are computational efficiency and compatibility with the data that has been collected.

An examination of the basic designs used in formulating mathematical models for computer simulation reveals that they are either generalized or modular (building block). The first type attempts to predict the operation of an entire system. The simulation of some segment of our economic system is an example of this generalized approach. The difficulty here is the vast number of interrelationships and related complexities which make the task almost impossible. Even though these models might be useful in formulating initial hypotheses in the third step of the planned approach, they seldom hold up when subjected to rigorous statistical testing procedures. For this reason, the modular approach to computer models is largely used for OR problems. The advantage of working with models which are block recursive is that computers are able to perform their operations in a sequential fashion. The use of a block recursive model in a simulation study reduces the computational time required to generate the time paths of the output variables. It should be remembered for the planned approach that more than one mathematical model can be and usually is formulated in this third step.

Having formulated a set of mathematical models describing the behavior of the system under study and having set forth their parameters for operating characteristics, we can now make an initial judgment concerning the adequacy of the models. This testing phase is the fourth step of the planned approach. Prior to actual computer runs, the inputs and assumptions of the simulation models are tested. We are interested in applying tests that determine how well a given hypothetical probability distribution fits the system under study. These tests may include: those concerning variances, such as chi-square tests; those based on count data, such as tests of goodness of fit; and those concerning means and nonparametric tests. (These tests are basically taken from statistics.) At this point, one or more of the models will fail to meet the test requirements, leaving at least one promising model to formulate into a computer program.

Flow charting and/or decision tables is the initial step in outlining the logical sequence of events for the selected computer model. This serves as the basis for writing the actual computer program. Programming can take any one of three directions: (1) use computer machine language; (2) write in a general purpose language—FORTRAN, ALGOL, COBOL, or PL/1; or (3) utilize one of the special-purpose simulation languages. Once the model has been programmed and errors deleted from the program, initial values must be assigned to the model's variables and parameters before simulation of the system can begin. This initializing of the model often requires trial and error methods.

An important part of the computer program is the development of techniques for generating data. Data can be read in from punched cards, but preferably from computer storage devices because they are faster, or it can be generated internally by special subroutines. This last method will be covered in a subsequent section, dealing with random number generation.

The last consideration in the computer programming steps is determining the type of output reports needed. Programming languages impose no restriction on the format of the output records. However, the special simulation languages require adherence to the output requirements of that particular language.

Having formulated, programmed, and debugged the optimum model computer program as part of the fourth step of the planned approach, the computer simulation model must be validated. This is the most difficult task because it involves a large number of practical, theoretical, statistical, mathematical, and philosophical complexities. In general, two tests can validate a simulation model. How well do the simulated values of the output variables compare with available historical data? Secondly, how reliable are the simulation model's predictions of the behavior of the real system in the future?

Once the validation of the computer model is complete, the fifth step of the planned approach seeks a complete verification of the model. To conduct these actual simulation experiments, we must focus our attention on questions of experimental design. We must select factor levels and combinations of levels as well as the order of experimentation. Within our factors and combinations, we must ensure that the results are reasonably free from error. The computer output, generated for the system being simulated, requires analysis prior to a final managerial decision. This analysis is considerably more difficult to interpret than analysis of real world data. The problems of randomness, the assumptions set forth, the dynamic nature of business today and in the future, the large number of variables and parameters, to name the more important ones, cause this difficulty. For these reasons, the sixth and final step of the planned approach requires establishing proper controls to detect how changes may affect the current simulation model. What might be the best simulation model today may not be best tomorrow. This is why one cannot say a simulation model is either true or false; rather, one can only say it is relevant to the current state of the system.

General Simulation Languages

Development of simulation languages has simplified the task of writing simulation programs for different types of models and systems. The simulation languages that have been developed are: GPSS, SIMSCRIPT, GASP, SIMPAC, DYNAMO, and SIMLATE. The objectives of these simulation languages are to furnish a generalized structure for designing simulation models and to speed the conversion of a simulation model to a computer program. The reason for several simulation languages is that they can be applied to different type problems which make their simulation procedures more automatic for the user. For example, DYNAMO and SIMLATE were designed primarily for simulating large-scale economic systems that have been formulated as econometric models, consisting of large sets of equations. GPSS, SIMSCRIPT, and GASP are well suited for scheduling and waiting line problems. Although programming time can be reduced by using a simulation language, there are the usual problems of reduced model flexibility and increased computer running time.

GPSS

The General Purpose Systems Simulator (GPSS) can be applied to a broad class of systems while maintaining a relatively fixed set of procedures for carrying out the simulation automatically. Substantial experience accumulated in the use of this program has led to an improved version, GPSS II; the latest version is GPSS III. Improvements include greater ability to sense the current state of the system and to implement decisions based upon that state, the ability to associate a greater amount of information with each transaction in the form of parameters, and generally faster computer execution.

In constructing a model using GPSS, the analyst must initially concern himself with four entities which form the foundation of the language: transactions, facilities, storages, and blocks. Understanding these entities and how they function is essential to the understanding of how GPSS works and what it does. *Transactions* represent physical units flowing through the system. Each transaction (a large system may involve thousands) interacts with the other transactions by competing for the resources (described below) of the system studied. Examples of transactions are: one message in the study of a computer system; one vehicle in the case of a study of traffic flow on a principal highway, or one shop order in the case of a model studying the operations of a factory.

In GPSS there are two types of resources, that is, facilities and storages. *Facilities* represent a resource capable of handling only one transaction at a time, such as the central processing unit of a computer system, a toll booth, or a particular machine in a factory. *Storages* are capable of handling many transactions simultaneously, up to a specified maximum. Examples of this would be core storage in a computer, a lane of traffic, or a group of identical machines in a factory.

In defining resources, ambiguity sometimes arises. For example, machines in a factory can be modeled as facilities if they are to be considered individually or as a storage if several machines are identical and the machine actually used by the transaction is immaterial. The system under study determines the exact nature of transactions, facilities, and storages. The analyst assigns meaning to each when constructing the model.

Finally, the structure of the system being modeled and its logic (decision rules) are described by means of GPSS *blocks*. Each block represents a command for the transaction to perform in a certain manner as it passes through the model. The analyst uses these blocks to construct a system flowchart; each block becomes one punched card in coding a GPSS program. The flowchart constructed with these blocks, along with various definition and control cards, such as the one used to control the length of the simulation run, constitutes the GPSS model. The concept of a transaction flowing through blocks and competing for resources (storages and facilities) is unique to GPSS. However, other aspects of GPSS are common to all discrete-event simulation languages.

SIMSCRIPT

SIMSCRIPT, developed by the Rand Corporation, is an outgrowth of work originated within the General Electric Company. Since that time, SIMSCRIPT has evolved into several more powerful versions: SIMSCRIPT I.5, SIMSCRIPT II, and SIMSCRIPT II.5. The basis of this language is a description of systems in terms of concepts denoted by entity, attribute, set, status, and event, as defined below.

An *entity* is a class of objects described by a fixed collection of parameters called *attributes*. Individual members of an entity class have specific numerical values assigned to their parameters. For example, in a machine shop, entities are the machines themselves, the skilled personnel running the machines, or a unit of demand flowing through the shop. On the other hand, only certain workers have the desired attributes or skills to operate certain machines or only certain machines can be used to fill a specified unit of demand. These attributes are defined by the modeler. Random numbers can specify the value of the attributes for a given entity.

Sets are collections of individual entities having certain common properties. The *status* of the model at any given instant is completely described by the current list of individual entities, their attributes, and set memberships. The dynamics of the system are represented by changes of status, that is, addition or deletion of individual entities, change of attributes, set memberships, or some combination of these. These changes which take place instantaneously at discrete points in simulated time are called *events*. The time an event is to occur is most frequently prescribed by SIMSCRIPT programming as current time plus some increment. At the conclusion of any event, simulation time is automatically increased to the time of the next event. Although this may seem cumbersome and difficult to understand at first reading, experience with the language will make the going considerably easier. When SIMSCRIPT is compared to GPSS, the former is considered more flexible, but assumes a knowledge of FORTRAN. Conversely, GPSS can be learned more quickly with no prior knowledge of programming, but it is less flexible and somewhat slower in execution than SIMSCRIPT. GPSS is best suited for "queuing" and other simpler problems; it has a rigidly defined "data structure" which makes modeling quite easy if the system under study fits the structure of the language. SIMSCRIPT is recommended for studies of more complex systems which cannot be neatly mapped in the predefined structure of GPSS.

DYNAMO

DYNAMO is similar to SIMSCRIPT, except that it simulates continuous models rather than models involving individual events. It was developed at M.I.T. Computation Center to simulate mathematical models. It allows computer output in both tabular and graphical form. The program contains extensive error checking for logical inconsistencies peculiar to simulation.

It also contains many subroutines convenient for testing models under different conditions.

GASP

GASP, developed by Philip J. Kiviot, represents a different concept in simulation languages because it is written in FORTRAN. It can be recompiled using any FORTRAN compiler. Basically, GASP is a FORTRAN compiled set of 23 subroutine programs and function subprograms linked and organized by a main program known as the GASP EXECUTIVE. Once the components, variables, parameters, and functional relationships for the simulation study have been specified, a small set of special symbols and GASP-oriented flow-charting conventions can be used to write flowcharts describing the behavior of the system. Flowcharts written with these GASP conventions are easily translatable into FORTRAN statements. Four different concepts are embodied in GASP flow charts: operations, decisions, transfers, and control.

Random Number Generator

Random numbers are useful in many types of computation, such as those found in the preceding chapter on queuing problems. The remainder of this chapter discusses other applications. One of the simplest methods for determining a set of random numbers for a uniform distribution involves the use of 10 balls, chips, or like items which are identical except for their numbering—0 to 9. By selecting these objects in an unbiased manner (one at a time with replacement), we can expect to obtain a set of random digits. A record of a very large set of these numbers could be kept so that one need not return to the physical objects to obtain random numbers.

Another approach to generating random numbers uses mechanical or electronic devices. The mechanical devices usually use a spinning device, divided into equal numbered sections, with some method for randomly interrupting and selecting one of the sections. Electronic devices utilize a random noise which is converted into pulses for driving a cyclic counter. Interruptions at fixed intervals produce random numbers. Of these approaches—mechanical and electronic—the electronic device of uniformly inspecting a randomly activated counter is preferred.

In 1939, Kendall and Babington-Smith published 100,000 random digits read from a spinning disk illuminated by a flash lamp. More recently (1955), the Rand Corporation published 1,000,000 digits produced by monitoring a random frequency pulse source (electronic device). Despite this large number of random numbers, a computer will often consume large quantities of numbers at such rapid rates that reading from storage or tape becomes inadequate. Likewise, the monitoring of physical devices, in addition to being slow, has the disadvantage that the numbers generated are not reproducible. Calculations cannot be identically repeated as required in debugging. Thus a strong emphasis has been on arithmetic generators since von Neumann and Metropolis proposed their mid-square method around 1946.

The arithmetic methods, such as the mid-square method and the multiplication method, are generally based on some sort of recurrence relations involving integers, that is, each new number is generated from the previous one. The output is randomly drawn from a finite population of integers so that the machine can produce an initial value which is required to start the recurrence relationship. At some point, a number that has already occurred will be produced, thus forming a closed-loop sequence, which continuously cycles from that point on. The length of this loop sequence is called the period of the generator and, hopefully, is equal to or nearly equal to the total integer population of the machine. (The period can be greater if a recurrence relation involving more than one previous number is used.) The problem is to find a relation that produces a sufficiently random sequence of numbers for a long period and with a minimum of computer time. Computer generated numbers that manage to pass statistical tests for randomness are called pseudo-random numbers even though produced by a completely deterministic process.

Ideally, the output of the random number generator should have statistical properties for the problem under study. Kendall and Babington-Smith (in 1938) proposed four widely used tests: the frequency, serial, poker, and gap to check on the accuracy of the solution. The frequency test counts how often each digit occurs in the sequence. The serial test tallies the frequencies of occurrence of all possible combinations of two digits, such as 42, 84, 01, ... The poker test counts how often various poker hands occur. And the gap test totals the number of digits that appear between repetitions of a particular test. The results then can be compared with theoretically expected values by some statistical test.

Actually, it is possible to perform many other tests that have since been developed. If too many tests are used, one would never get around to using a random number generator. In essence, exhaustive tests are impractical. Probably, it is best to choose a generator that passes the more conventional tests, such as the frequency and serial tests, plus those tests that are relevant to the problem at hand. An important test would be a sample computation on a problem in which the answer is known. A final precaution to insure that the generator has not produced a wrong answer is to rerun the problem using a different random number generator.

Simulation in the Firm

Simulation has been applied to many functional areas of the firm which will be evident in the following sections. This is a cross section of current applications and should not be construed as an all inclusive grouping of OR simulation studies. New applications are being discovered periodically, adding a new dimension to our understanding of this dynamic OR tool.

Marketing Simulation
Simulation has made great gains in marketing. It was mentioned previously how simulation has been used in predicting consumer reaction to new

products. In another area of marketing, numerous consumer flow models have been designed to predict the expected product market share. These are commonly referred to as brand shifting or brand loyalty models. They basically take the form of Markov, learning, or other probabilistic models. Generally, these models suffer numerous deficiencies, largely because their use requires assumptions which are unrealistic. Many times they exclude relevant factors, such as sales promotion, advertising, and competition. The real promise of simulation for these models lies in its capacity to consider complex but realistic conditions which minimize the need to make unwarranted simplifying assumptions.

Many companies are showing an increasing interest in developing total marketing decision models rather than separate ones for each area. An appropriate name for these total models is market simulator. Marketing management, today, must define the proper level, mix, allocation, and timing of diverse marketing efforts for its products. To do this, some aggressive firms are constructing computerized models of their markets to serve as a creditable basis for testing and predicting response to alternative marketing programs without incurring the usual high test costs.

Advanced market simulators are microbehavioral. They include a representative sample of customers who are distributed graphically and a representative group of retailers and wholesalers. Actually, the market simulator encompasses the firm's marketing structure, its particular characteristics, and its market behavior. For the most part, the mathematical formulation is based on data obtained through a representative sample of customers and subsequent analysis. For the remainder, marketing management reports a feel for the nature of the response. The value of the market simulator lies in its ability to search out a new marketing strategy that fits the market segment best. Alternative strategies are tried on the simulator along with expected events and responses to yield a "best" marketing strategy over time to maximize sales and minimize costs.

A few of these market simulators are an outgrowth of marketing games which became more complex so as to reflect the realities of the business world. Other market simulators are still in the development stage. They need to undergo further refinement and testing before they are ready for practical application. When these market simulators become operational and reflect the true conditions, marketing decisions will rise to a new level of performance. Firms that operate without market simulators are skating on thin ice. They may be very sincere and determined in their approach based upon intuition and hunch, but how can they effectively compete in the long run with other firms who know more about the market through simulation and related quantitative techniques? Aggressive marketing managers will remedy the quantitative information gap within their firms.

Physical Distribution Simulation
Simulation has been successfully applied to a firm's physical distribution system. It has enabled the firm to operate a physical distribution program at the lowest possible cost consistent with satisfactory customer service. In order to accomplish this task, basic questions must be asked. How many

warehouses should the firm use? What are their locations and sizes? Which markets should the warehouses serve? Which products should be made at what plants and in what quantities? Which plants should serve what warehouses? Should an additional plant be constructed? What customer service levels are desirable and at what costs? Simulation of a physical distribution system, as described below, takes into account answers to some of these vital questions.

In order to simulate a physical distribution problem that centers around determining the optimum number of warehouses, data must be gathered in five groupings. The first is market location. This considers customer location, order size, ordering patterns, shipment types, and product mix. In some cases, sales data by product class and customer may be converted into sales totals for each county in a problem covering the United States. These counties, in turn, can be grouped into metropolitan trading areas which account for the bulk (70-85 percent) of total sales. These can be designated as major markets. The remaining sales (15–30 percent) can be totaled by state and assigned to the next largest trading area within each state. In this manner, the total number of market locations can be reduced from several thousands to several hundred or less without significantly misrepresenting the actual geographical dispersion of the markets.

Once the location of the firm's markets has been studied, data must be gathered on the kinds of goods that can be supplied from any given factory point to the warehouse, the quantities that can be supplied, and location of factories and warehouses. The relationship among the factories, warehouses, and customers can now be expressed in terms of freight costs for the second group of data needed. Since many different rates are applicable to the same city, a regression line, using the method of least squares, can result in one realistic cost for a certain distance from one location to another. This is an assignment for the computer. Again, realistic simplifications are necessary to make the problem manageable.

Having calculated the appropriate freight costs, we must consider the number of times each warehouse must be supplied by the plants (plant) to keep stock at a desired level with the smallest investment in inventory. Data for the annual weight of product for each shipment—*CL* (car load), *LCL* (less than car load), *TL* (truck load), and *LTL* (less than truck load)—are determined. The computer is again used to calculate this third data group— the annual volume of shipments in pounds for each plant and warehouse combination.

The fourth group of data is an extension of the preceding computer runs. Computer output is directed toward calculating transportation costs based on units times weight times the appropriate freight rates. The fifth and last group of data to be determined is warehousing costs. This too is a difficult problem since unit costs vary with the annual volume for each warehouse. This problem can be overcome by developing standard cost curves for each warehouse at varying volumes.

Now that the required data have been developed (which may take considerable time), attention is focused on the warehousing aspect of the problem. If all customers were large and gave sufficient lead time when ordering, and if all factories produced the full line of products, all shipments could be made directly to ultimate customers. However, this does not always occur. The reasons for warehouses are obvious: customers are not all large enough to warrant direct shipments; they do not all give sufficient lead time when ordering; and each factory does not always produce a full line.

In view of these facts, the model can be further simplified in one of these areas by initial computer testing to see which customers are large enough to justify direct shipments. Direct shipments from producing factories have no effect on the optimal placement of warehouses since they are eliminated from consideration. An initial computer run will remove all the direct shipment volumes. After this first elimination run, the information relating to transportation costs, warehousing costs, location of customers, factory locations, factory output, and poundage by customers can be stored on magnetic tape, disk, or other computer medium. The basic process in the second computer run is the utilization of a simulation program to vary warehouse configurations so as to compare the resultant effects on distribution costs. These millions of comparisons ultimately result in an output listing of the warehousing and transportation costs for each warehouse. In effect, the computer simulates the many combinations of plants, warehouses, and markets. The solution provides each and every market with its requirements at minimum cost. A plotting of the output data indicates generally that a specific number of warehouses results in the lowest physical distribution costs. In making the final choice of which number of warehouses is best, experience, judgment, and knowledge of local market conditions are necessary.

Manufacturing Simulation
Many firms use simulation to test new ideas in production scheduling. Every production control manager knows that the methods and priority rules used in scheduling jobs in the plant have an important bearing on the utilization of men and machines as well as on how smoothly the production flows and serves the customer. In a production control model, factory operations are simulated to test the decision rules which actually are the scheduling system. Policies and procedures concerning machine loading, scheduling, and dispatching are tested in terms of inventory costs, idle machine (man) time, flexibility, and cost of the scheduling itself. In this way, the trial and error method of actually trying for the best approach is avoided.

A special subset of scheduling problems, known as the job shop problem, has been the subject of numerous simulation studies since the early days of computer simulation. In its simplest form, it consists of the random arrival of jobs requiring work to be done in some sequence by a set of manufacturing facilities. The manufacturing times associated with each facility are different and usually assumed to be random variables. Job shop simulations are generally concerned with experiments of various queue disciplines and priority rules as a means of optimizing some performance index. Therefore, the underlying theoretical structure of a job shop production system is basically a queuing model with two or more sequential servers which lends itself to computer simulation.

Improving Assembly Operations
An interesting manufacturing application is the simulation of an assembly line. The need for assembly line design occurs when a new product is to be assembled, increased production requirements exceed the capacity of the existing line, assembly methods must be changed because of product design changes, or costs can be reduced by improving the existing line. Thus, the extent of the design effort is dependent on the problem.

There are several steps in the design process. The first is to establish a clear definition of the objectives or requirements. To design an assembly line, the engineer must know the assembly line's job, the production requirements, and the flexibility required. In addition to establishing the objectives, a clear definition of any factors which will constrain or limit alternatives must be established. In defining constraints, the designer should keep an open mind, avoiding limitations of historic operational modes.

The second step is to describe one or more alternative assembly line designs. The third step is to evaluate each proposed design and determine whether it meets the requirements. After the proposed assembly line is described, it can be simulated. The engineer will then know whether the proposed line will meet the production requirements. Also, he can tell whether any facilities will be underutilized. The engineer can iterate steps two and three. By examining the results of step three, he may modify the proposed designs. The results may suggest other alternatives which were not apparent at the outset.

The assembly line simulation model is based on a collection of many assumptions; each assumption relates to only a small part of the assembly line. Examples are: the probability that a unit will fail at a certain station; and the probability that a station will not complete a unit in the given cycle time. The accuracy of the model is dependent upon the accuracy of the assumptions. Where changes to an existing line are being simulated, the assumptions can be quite accurate. The operation times can be observed and for each station, the distribution of those times can be determined from a time study. Where a new product line is simulated, the distributions may be assumed to be the same as those found on lines with similar operations. Where a new type of operation is being evaluated, the engineer can assume the best and the worst conditions, and thereby, bracket the expected performance. The confidence which is placed in the simulation results can be no greater than the confidence which is placed on the individual assumptions.

Finally, the fourth step of the process compares the alternatives and makes a selection. The engineer must consider not only the production capability, but also the costs of installing and operating the line. Simulation results give the assembly, repair, and utility labor requirements, but does not specify equipment, space, or installation costs (including the cost of interrupting or disrupting the existing operations).

Determining Size of the Maintenance Force

One area of manufacturing that has received considerable attention in simulation studies is determining the size of a maintenance force. The Monte Carlo approach to simulation for this problem is certainly a lot less costly than experimenting in the plant. With actual experimentation, there is no assurance that an improvement will be realized, not to mention the lost production and poor labor relations that can result. The following section presents a problem for determining the size of a maintenance crew. The question of the lowest cost maintenance policy is of utmost importance.

The manufacturing management of the Ace Tool and Manufacturing Company, after considerable bargaining with its union, must now employ maintenance personnel to service its machinery. The previous method of having the machine operators service the machines is no longer permissible. Hence, the company wants to determine the optimum employment of new maintenance personnel to minimize production losses caused by downtime on machinery. The number of men required is a primary consideration since their wages and fringe benefits must be balanced against the expected idle machine and operator's cost.

The starting point in the study is to compile data on machines as they now operate. This can be done by recording the total number of incidents where equipment needs service each hour and the time required to perform the service. All service times greater than full minutes have been assigned the next full minute, resulting in a conservative approach to the problem. The data for this study are shown in Tables 14-1 and 14-2. Table 14-1 shows the delays per hour while Table 14-2 indicates the service time for machine downtime in the plant (based on present machine operators).

Data in Tables 14-1 and 14-2 are plotted in Figures 14-2 to 14-5. The first two figures are histograms, Figure 14-2 showing the distribution of all machine operation delays per hour and Figure 14-3 depicting the distribution of downtime in minutes for each time service is required (based on present machine operators). The cumulative distribution of machine delays

TABLE 14-1
Delays per Hour on Machinery in the Plant

Delays per Hour	Number of Occurrences	Relative Frequency (percent)	Cumulative Frequency (percent)
17 and under	19	5	5
18	35	9	14
19	40	10	24
20	74	19	43
21	95	24	67
22	70	18	85
23	45	10	95
Over 23	20	5	100

TABLE 14-2
**Service Times for Downtime of Machinery in the Plant
(Based on Present Machine Operators)**

Minutes	Number of Occurrences	Relative Frequency (percent)	Cumulative Frequency (percent)
Under 7	18	5	5
7 to 8	82	25	30
8 to 9	136	40	70
9 to 10	82	25	95
Over 10	16	5	100

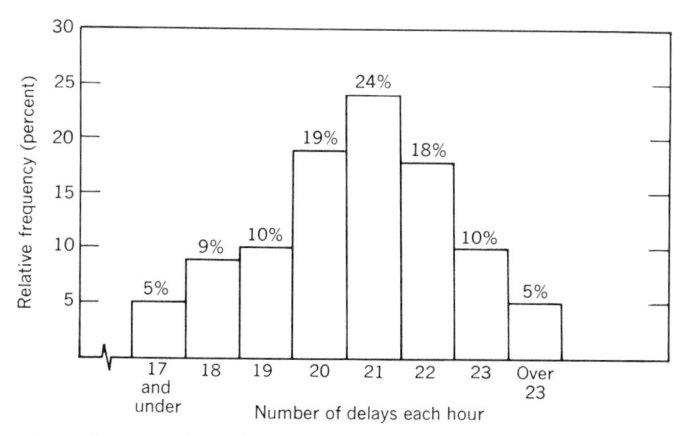

Figure 14-2 Distribution of machine delays per hour.

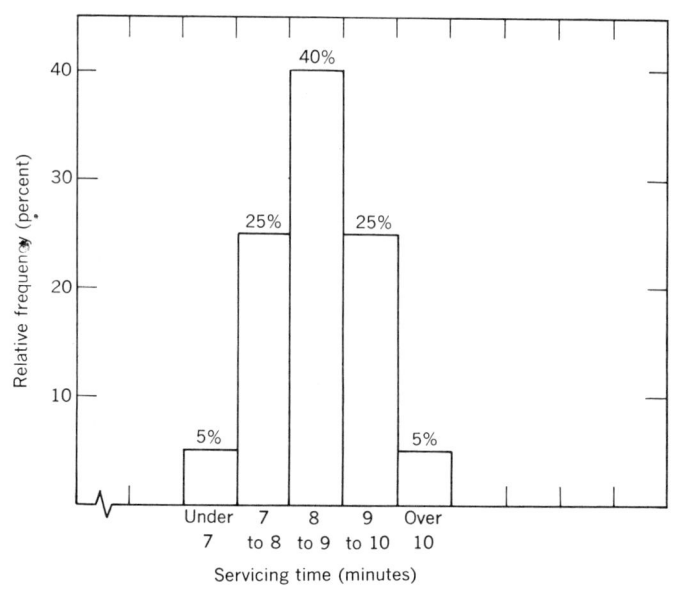

Figure 14-3 Distribution of downtime (minutes) for each time service is needed (based on present machine operators).

SIMULATION 471

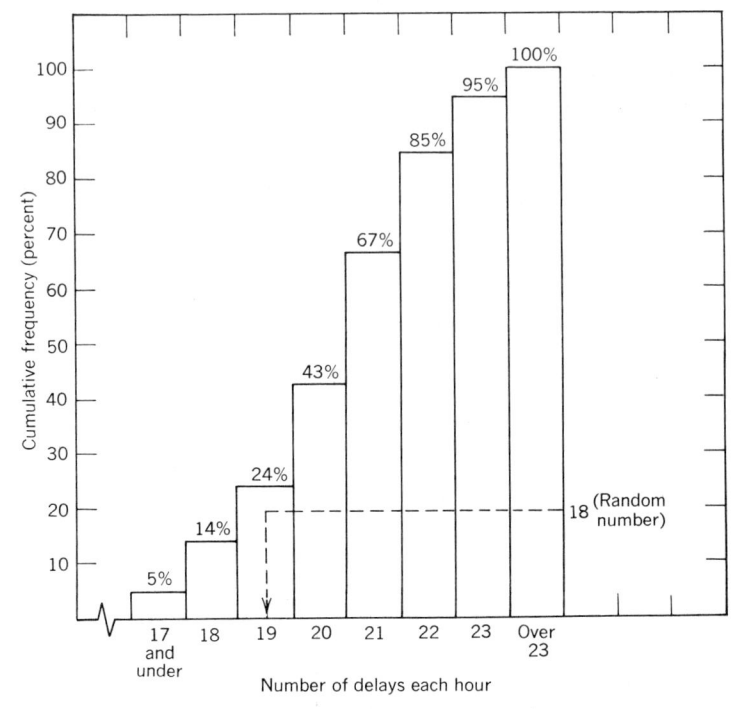

Figure 14-4 Cumulative percent of machine delays per hour.

from Figure 14-2 is graphed in Figure 14-4. Similarily, the graph of Figure 14-5 is taken from Figure 14-3, the cumulative distribution of service time per breakdown (based on present machine operators). For these last two graphs (Figures 14-4 and 14-5), the accumulated frequencies are constructed by starting with the lowest number of events, summing the frequencies, and plotting them. Thus, a percentage or probability scale is developed.

Events for this study can now be simulated through the use of a random number table (Appendix E). The random numbers will represent probabilities, shown as percents in Figures 14-4 and 14-5. They are used to obtain machine delays and servicing time values in the problem. For example, random number 18 is selected to represent delays per hour in Figure 14-4. Starting at the right side of the chart, a horizontal line is drawn until it intersects the distribution curve. A vertical line is then dropped down to the x axis (see dashed line on the graph). In this example, the delays per hour would be 19 for the first hour. Simulating in this manner from the cumulative distribution gives us the machine delays that are close to actual operating conditions. The same type of simulation is applicable in determining service times. A random number is selected for each delay and the service time is obtained from Figure 14-5. A conservation approach is used, that is, a random number of 20 is interpreted as 8 minutes (see dashed line on the graph). For any hour of the study, the number of service calls is dependent upon the delays. In the first hour, 19 service times must be simulated since this number of delays was experienced through the use of random numbers. A simulated sample of three hours of machine servicing time is shown in Table 14-3.

472 OPERATIONS RESEARCH MODELS—SIMULATION TECHNIQUES

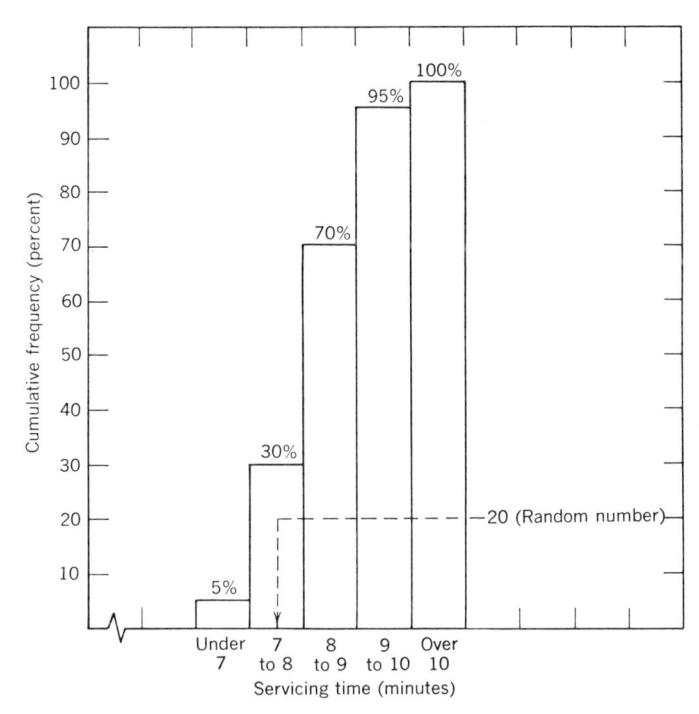

Figure 14-5 Cumulative percent of service time per breakdown (based on present machine operators).

TABLE 14-3
Simulation Sample of Three Hours of Machine Servicing Time (Based on Present Machine Operators)

Simulation of Delays in One Hour		Simulation of Individual Servicing Time per Hour		Total Hourly Servicing Time
Random Number	Delays in Hour	Random Numbers	Individual Service Time in Minutes	Expressed in Minutes
18	19	20,68,57,79,84	8,9,9,10,10	
		72,95,08,85,79	10,10,8,10,10	
		34,40,67,24,86	9,9,9,8,10	
		54,35,81,07	9,9,10,8	175
09	18	88,30,90,90,88	10,8,10,10,10	
		72,22,75,69,86	10,8,10,9,10	
		45,48,32,63,00	9,9,9,9,7	
		32,74,13	9,10,8	165
41	20	68,65,99,76,66	9,9,11,10,9	
		12,72,59,02,72	8,10,9,7,10	
		75,97,69,07,00	10,11,9,8,7	
		01,46,29,64,88	7,9,8,9,10	180

SIMULATION 473

TABLE 14-4
Activity of Service Maintenance Men (An allowance of ten minutes of each serviceman per hour for personal time is included in the activity before he is considered idle.)

Hour of Study	Total Servicing Minutes Required	Three Servicemen				Four Servicemen			
		Busy Time	Idle Time	Operators Waiting Time	Cumulative Operators Waiting Time	Busy Time	Idle Time	Operators Waiting Time	Cumulative Operators Waiting Time
		In Minutes				In Minutes			
1	137	167	13	—	—	177	63	—	—
2	129	159	21	—	—	169	71	—	—
3	140	170	10	—	—	180	60	—	—
4	167	180	—	17	17	207	33	—	—
5	119	149	31	—	—	159	81	—	—
6	179	180	—	29	29	219	21	—	—
7	105	135	45	—	—	145	95	—	—
8	130	160	20	—	—	170	70	—	—
9	150	180	—	—	—	190	50	—	—
10	166	180	—	16	16	206	34	—	—
11	141	171	9	—	7	181	59	—	—
12	155	180	—	5	12	195	45	—	—
					81 minutes				0 minutes

474 OPERATIONS RESEARCH MODELS—SIMULATION TECHNIQUES

The simulated sample in Table 14-3 is based on the present machine operators performing the required repairs. However, consideration must be given to the fact that maintenance men should have more skill and familiarity with machinery than machine operators. Thus, maintenance personnel should reduce the present service time (based on machine operators' service time) on each machine delay, say by two minutes. This fact is incorporated into Table 14-4 based on three and four servicemen. Even though 12 hours were utilized in the simulation study, a computer could easily simulate the problem for a longer period (say a couple of years), resulting in greater reliability of final results.

The operators' waiting times in Table 14-4 for three servicemen were calculated in the following manner. The total servicing time required for the first hour of the study is 175 minutes (Table 14-3) which must be adjusted for faster service time of 38 minutes (2 minutes per service call × 19 delays) and personal time allowance of 30 minutes (10 minutes for each serviceman per hour × 3 men) during the first hour. The servicing time of 175 minutes less 38 minutes for greater efficiency plus 30 minutes for personal time totals 167 minutes for three servicemen. Thus, servicemen are not busy throughout the first hour, which means their busy time is 167 minutes with 13 minutes of idle time. Similarly, the operators are not waiting. The same type of calculations applies to all other rows. When moving to the columns representing four servicemen, 40 minutes of personal time must be considered.

Based upon an hourly wage including fringe benefits of $4.00 for maintenance personnel and $15.00 per hour for an idle automatic machine (rate includes profit lost in not producing parts and idle operator cost), the OR study indicates the employment of three service maintenance men is best as shown in Table 14-5. Even though this problem was worked manually, it would have been better to utilize a computer for a larger sample, resulting in a more reliable answer. Nevertheless, the method used here gives a picture of what the computer program would be doing.

Simulation is equally applicable to other maintenance problems. In particular its use can be helpful in determining an optimum policy for replacing machine parts, motors, tubes, transistors, light bulbs, and the like. Sev-

TABLE 14-5
Cost Analysis of Using Maintenance Men Based on Service by Maintenance Men

	Number of Maintenance Personnel	
	Three	Four
Total time lost by machines (operators) per Table 14-4	81 min.	—min.
Idle machine (operator) cost	$15/hour	$15/hour
Value of machines' (operators') lost time	$ 20.25	$—
Total pay of maintenance personnel for 12 hours ($48 per man)	144.00	192.00
Total cost (idle machine and maintenance)	$164.25	$192.00

eral maintenance procedures are available to the firm: (1) repair or replace the item when it fails, (2) repair or replace all items of the same kind when the first one fails, (3) repair or replace all items of the same kind and items that are comparable to the ones that failed, and (4) repair or replace the items after so many hours or weeks of use based on an estimated average service life. For these conditions, cumulative probability distributions are determined in order that random numbers, representing probability values, can be utilized to simulate experience. The simulation method set forth above can be used for these problems.

Inventory Simulation

For many years, Monte Carlo simulation has been applied repeatedly to inventory systems under uncertainty. In the inventory chapter, probability of usage during the reorder period, based upon past experience, was used to determine the cost of being out of stock. For each level of safety stock, total annual stockout costs were calculated. This cost plus the annual carrying cost of the safety stock were totaled for an optimum safety stock policy that minimized the firm's overall inventory costs.

To determine usage during lead time, computer program reads as many random numbers as there are days in the lead time period to simulate demand during lead time. An adequate sample is needed for simulating lead time. The output from the computer run would be a probability distribution and a cumulative probability of demand during lead time. This output serves as input for calculating annual stockout costs and inventory costs for each level of safety stock. Finally, the computer calculates an optimum level of safety stock for all inventory items.

Determining Production-Inventory Levels

Simulation can not only be applied to certain phases of inventory, such as setting reorder points and determining usage during the reorder period, but also is rightfully applicable to integrating production scheduling models and inventory control models for a combined production-inventory system. The interaction of these two areas makes for a more involved simulation problem, requiring several steps.

The first step is a general decision model to forecast demand. After forecasting sales, the next step is to compute production rates according to some rule set forth by the OR group. The purpose of this decision rule is to specify an inventory position in which the manufacturing manager would like to find himself. This means that the production man, at a point in time nearest to the present and still within his control, would like to make a decision which will come as close as possible to a desired inventory position, subject to any technical constraints or changes in the production rate. This decision rule for calculating the desired inventory could be simple in form but, at the same time, must be flexible enough in its outcome. For example, inventory could be maintained at one-half month's forecasted sales. Once the desired inventory has been established, an initial value for the production rate is used. However, the rate is checked against the absolute limits (upper and lower) of manufacturing. It may have to be reset if it exceeds manufacturing limits. Also the production rate is checked against any relative upper and lower limits specified by the previous rate set. If exceeded, the production rate is reset. This rate is stored for use in the appropriate period during simulation.

The simulation model proceeds to generate demands for each day of the current manufacturing period. The generation of demand is under the control of the user since he has specified the seasonal and trend factors plus the actual forecasts. He has the ability to vary the forecasts in order to determine the effect on the inventory decision rule. Daily production is added to inventory while demand is subtracted from inventory. Back orders are recorded when they occur and are filled from production, upon availability. Through simulation, average inventory is tabulated as well as demand. At the end of a period, say a week, two weeks, or a month, control is given to the decision model for a new rate to be set, based upon the current factors. Thus this simulation model allows the firm to relate the current factors of supply to demand.

The simulation model uses cost values for carrying costs of inventory, cost of being out of stock, and stockout costs to determine a near optimal solution. The term "near" is used since the model is only as good as its forecasting ability, its inventory decision rule, and its cost factors, which may be only good estimates. However, the demand generator in a simulation model allows the user to control error in forecasting so that its effect on the model can be predicted. Only by testing with such models can one fit a decision rule to given conditions that will give the lowest cost basis to the firm and best service criterion to customers.

Minimize Total Inventory Cost

To illustrate a straightforward inventory system using Monte Carlo simulation, attention must be focused initially on the objective of the inventory system. The aim of management is to operate the business such that total costs are at a minimum—the least total cost curve is the sum of the ordering costs, carrying costs, and lost revenue. Application of the Monte Carlo method requires that an event occur according to some probability density distribution for each variable that is to be sampled. First, the density function for demand (units) and delivery time (weeks) must be determined (illustrated in Tables 14-6 and 14-7 respectively) along with their cumulative probabilities. Likewise, corresponding random numbers are assigned that reflect the frequency of an event in the cumulative probability distribution. During the simulation process, random numbers are generated for demand and delivery time according to the Monte Carlo numbers assigned in Tables 14-6 and 14-7.

A manual simulation of this problem is illustrated in Table 14-8. Fourteen weeks of operation were arbitrarily selected although several years of simulated data using a computer is recommended. For the simulation process, the reordering point level is set at 15 units and the ordering quantity variable is 20 units. Inventory carrying costs have been computed to be $10

TABLE 14-6
Cumulative Probability Distribution and Distribution of Random Numbers for Customer Demand (units)

Demand (Units)	Frequency	Cumulative Probability Distribution	Distribution of Random Numbers
0	2	2	00–01
1	8	10	02–09
2	22	32	10–31
3	34	66	32–65
4	18	84	66–83
5	9	93	84–92
6	7	100	93–99

TABLE 14-7
Cumulative Probability Distribution and Distribution of Random Numbers for Delivery Time (weeks)

Delivery Time (Weeks)	Frequency	Cumulative Probability Distribution	Distribution of Random Numbers
1	23	23	00–22
2	45	68	23–67
3	17	85	68–84
4	19	94	85–93
5	6	100	94–99

per unit per week, and the cost of placing an order is $25. Also, the lost revenue (selling price less costs) per unit of stockout is $100 per day.

To illustrate the simulation process per Table 14-8, we will start with an inventory on hand of 20 units at the beginning of the first week. Based on a simulated demand of 4 units (random number 68 represents 4 units of demand per Table 14-6) in the first week, the balance at the end of the first week is 16 units (20 units less 4 units) which is still higher than the reordering point level of 15 units. For the second week, demand is simulated to be 3 units, resulting in an ending inventory of 13 units. Since the balance is below the reordering level, the delivery time of two weeks (random number 50 represents a delivery time of two weeks per Table 14-7) is generated. Hence, delivery is expected in two weeks. As indicated in the fourth week, 20 units are received into inventory. The rest of the table follows the foregoing simulation procedures.

Moving on to the inventory carrying costs, ordering costs, and lost revenue columns in Table 14-8, calculations are made in the following manner. In the first week, 16 units on hand is multiplied by the weekly carrying costs of $10 per unit which totals $160 for the first week. Similarly, the calculated carrying costs for the second week is $130 plus the ordering

478   OPERATIONS RESEARCH MODELS—SIMULATION TECHNIQUES

TABLE 14-8
Fourteen Week Simulation of Demand, Delivery, Inventory, and Total Costs

Week	Demand Random Number	Demand (Units)	Delivery Random Number	Delivery (Weeks)	Units Rec'd	Bal. on Hand	Inventory Carrying Costs	Ordering Costs	Lost Revenue	Total Costs
0						20				
1	68	4				16	$160			$160
2	52	3				13	130			155
3	90	5	50	2		8	80	$25		155
4	59	3			20	25	250			250
5	08	1				24	240			240
6	72	4				20	200			200
7	44	3				17	170			170
8	95	6	85	4		11	110			
9	81	4				7	70	25		135
10	93	6				1	10			70
11	28	2				0				10
12	89	5			20	15	150		$100	100
13	60	3	15	1		32	320	25		175
14	3	1			20	31	310			320
										310

Average weekly cost $169.64

SIMULATION 479

costs of $25, totaling $155. All other weeks are calculated in this manner. However, demand during the eleventh week cannot be met, resulting in an out-of-stock condition. The result of not being able to meet the demand of one unit is $100 of lost revenue for the week. Based upon averaging the total cost column in Table 14-8, the problem has been solved in terms of an average weekly inventory cost of $169.64.

There are other important factors in this inventory problem. Utilizing a computer, management can reevaluate its total inventory costs by varying the carrying cost per unit, the ordering cost, and the lost revenue. Thus, management can ask, "What would the result be if . . ." and expect a reasonably accurate answer employing simulation procedures.

Accounting Simulation

Simulation has been put to great use in accounting, especially in the area of budgeting. Initially, the existing budgeting system will have to be examined and translated into mathematical terms for each sub-budget. A consideration is the desirability of improving the present budgeting system. The model, at this point, will consist of several hundred simultaneous equations that reflect the variables, parameters, and the model structure. The budget model can now be translated into computer machine language through some symbolic coding system. Values must be assigned to the exogenous variables and to the parameters, based on empirical data estimates, forecasting techniques, etc.

After preparatory work, computation by the computer can be carried out. The output should yield the budgeting data of the firm simulated under certain selected conditions. The computer output can be arranged to print a sales budget, a manufacturing budget, a cash budget, and related budgets for the most satisfactory choice or a limited number of the better alternatives. The output also includes the projected income statement.

The foregoing approach has not been too concerned with the individual departments. If the budgeting activity is on a departmental basis, it is necessary to incorporate these elements in the model. Many of the previous exogenous variables will have to be converted into endogenous variables. As a result, a long array of new exogenous variables will emerge. This increases considerably the number of simultaneous equations and complicates the program. If departmental optimization models are to be used, it may be advantageous to compute these departmental optima independently from and prior to the overall budget model. However, this approach is not the best since it generally does not lead to overall optimization.

Finance Simulation

Decisions that relate to investigating large amounts of capital, reducing production cost, or increasing plant capacity are among the most challenging problems that financial management has to face. The risk associated with a large investment may be minimized if more is learned about the effects of the many factors by evaluating alternative courses of action. If these alternatives involve many parameters and interactions with large volumes of data, a situation exists where the human mind cannot digest and analyze all of these relevant facts. Under these conditions, financial simulation offers a great deal of help by reducing the complexities in such cases.

Simulation of alternative investments as well as the appropriate methods to be used with each investment will become routine. The reason is that the tremendous pressure on profits these days will apply equally in the future. No firm can afford to make a mistake when investing large sums of money. Both highly profitable and poor investments show up in a much sharper focus when they are properly simulated. Simulation also allows the firm to calculate more accurately its return on investment or payback of each project. Every company has a minimum rate of return it is willing to accept for each class of projects. By simulating an investment with all its possibilities, the financial structure of the firm should be strengthened in the short, intermediate, and long run.

The more aggressive companies employing operations research techniques are experimenting with financial simulation for the entire firm. A financial simulation model can be defined as a formal statement of the relationships among the elements of a firm's financial structure. The total model consists of a set of submodels, one for each of the management units in a firm. Each of these management units has its output expressed. The overall model follows a logical sequence which depends on the structure of the business. The output of certain submodels forms the input for others. These relationships reflect the cause and effect that exists within the firm itself and between the firm and its specific market segments. In defining cause and effect in the model, there are two considerations—the intermodel relationship and the intramodel detail. The former refers to the factors that determine the ordering (relationship) between the submodels, whereas the latter refers to the level of detail essential in structuring one of the submodels.

The intermodel relationship of marketing to manufacturing will help illustrate its importance in the overall model. Because the marketing divisions are organized on a geographic basis (each area handles the full product line), there is no direct interdivisional relationship influencing the ordering of the marketing models. However, the submodels must specifically describe the form by which marketing demands are translated into production requirements. Any decision made by the marketing organizations which affects demand rate will influence in varying degrees each of the manufacturing divisions, even though the decision might affect only one product in a wide product line. To go a step further, the output of both the marketing model and the manufacturing model provides input to the financial management model in which we determine cash inflow, cash outflow, taxes, and like items.

In this financial simulation model, the manufacturing interdivisional relationship can be accomplished by having the demand for all product lines sent to each manufacturing plant. The marketing demand interacts with the manufacturing submodel in terms of manufacturing constraints and inventory policy in order to generate what is to be produced and when it is to be produced. When the number of units have been met, goods are provided to satisfy demand. Marketing policies determine revenues which affect the capital position and debt level of the firm. The capital position, then, defines the money available for marketing activity. This feedback ability of the financial simulation model allows for some checking on its reasonableness.

The level of detail necessary in such a model can be illustrated by tracing the impact of an input change. Suppose we want to evaluate the change in sales force for one of the marketing divisions. Demand forecast has been structured to be a function of the amount of direct selling by salesmen and productivity. For this change, we also evaluate the impact of the demand change on equipment and services revenue, cost of sales, and finished goods inventory. The change in demand, together with an inventory policy, permit us to determine cost of sales and finished goods inventory. The same change in demand together with an inventory policy allow us to determine the resultant requirements of manufacturing, which is an input in calculating the in-process inventory. The determination of in-process inventories permits us to calculate the subassembly and parts requirements for manufacturing. These requirements are then related to variable and fixed costs of manufacturing, which affect the firm's ability to absorb burden. Marketing expenses, commissions, freight out, and similar items are brought into the analysis. The change in sales manpower affects net profits, income taxes, accounts receivables, and ability to pay off short-term and long-term debts. It ultimately determines dividends, which are a function of net profit. Thus it is necessary to evaluate the proposed marketing change in terms of cash flow.

The preceding example illustrates what happens when a single change is made. These complex relationships are the result not only of functional interaction but also of the time factor. The nature of these relationships changes as time passes. Expenditures for research are not expected to produce revenue in the immediate period since they are investments in future revenue. Administrative expenses may follow changes in revenue and, in other cases, could lag. It is essential that the time relationships used in the model be adequately representative of the firm's own processes. Also, the simulation model must be consistent with the financial practices of the firm in order to reflect the plans, policies, and procedures of management.

Other Simulation Applications

There have been numerous applications of simulation in industry and the military. Simulation studies have included steelmaking operations to evaluate changes in operating practices, capacity, and configuration of the facilities. Simulation has been used by the airlines to test changes in company policies and practices. These include the amount of maintenance capacity, berthing facilities, and spare parts needed. The telephone companies have used simulation to determine the capacity of the respective components that would be required to provide satisfactory service at the most economical level. Another application includes simulation of a developed river basin in order to determine the best configuration of dams, power plants, and irrigation works. This data would provide information on the desired level of flood control and water resource development.

At present, the insurance industry employs simulation in analyzing investment portfolios and in the operating control of company administration. Wall Street has embarked upon computer simulation models that test the performance of a stock under various market conditions. Experimenting with a simulation model of a system allows one to design the best management information system for the firm.

Simulation has been adopted by the military to evaluate defensive and offensive weapon systems in medium- and large-scale battles. It has proven to be an invaluable tool in space-oriented studies. In the field of economics, simulation of the U.S. economy or some segment has been used to predict the effect of economic and fiscal policy decisions. Engineering and scientific fields also have been beneficiaries of this OR technique, not to mention the behavioral and social sciences. The virtual explosion of simulation applications will provide the necessary thrust for an even wider application to theoretical and practical problems.

Simulation Application—American Products Corporation

The American Products Corporation operates four manufacturing plants, one of which is in the state of being highly mechanized. Before installing the highly mechanized equipment, the manufacturing manager of this plant has turned to the operations research group to determine the optimum number of personnel at each work station on the various assembly lines. Rather than detailing data on all work stations, the first project problem is examined below.

The specific problem involves the number of operators to place at a work station where two operations are performed on coils—a transformer subassembly. Data from the previous operation indicates that the time between coil arrivals—0.5, 1.0, 1.5, and 2.0 minutes—occur with equal probability. Knowing the mix of various types of coils, and the time standards for the two operations for each type of coil, the following time variables are:

First Operation Time (minutes)	Product Mix (%)	Second Operation Time (minutes)	Product Mix (%)
0	50	0	34
1.5	5	1.5	34
2.0	8	3.0	10
3.0	27	4.0	22
3.5	7		100%
4.0	3		
	100%		

In determining the number of operators required, excessive backup of the line (queue) with too few operators must be balanced with excessive idle time caused by too many operators.

Examination of the foregoing data indicates that this project is a natural application for Monte Carlo simulation, using random numbers for generating arrival times and processing times for the two operations. Also, as the project study developed, it became apparent that an "all-purpose" method was needed to handle this project and all remaining assembly line balancing projects. Thus, time-sharing was employed, because of its speed and the availability of a stored random number generator. The computer program was designed to handle the following parameters:

1. Number of operators: one to four.
2. Number of variables: one to four.
   (a) One variable is the arrival time.
   (b) Remaining variables are the operation times.

The time-sharing system generated random numbers from 0–99, making the following distribution necessary (based on previous data):

Variable	Minutes	Distribution of Random Numbers
Arrival time (rate)	0.5	0–24
	1.0	25–49
	1.5	50–74
	2.0	75–99
First operation time	1.5	0– 4
	2.0	5–12
	3.0	13–39
	3.5	40–46
	4.0	47–49
	0	50–99
Second operation time	4.0	0–21
	3.0	22–31
	1.5	32–65
	0	66–99

For these three variables, it was necessary to determine the idle time and the work ahead of each operator (queue) at the end of a shift, which was 8 hours less 24 minutes per shift or 456 minutes in duration.

Upon entering the time-sharing program, all that is required for input is the number of operators planned at the work station. For the illustrated problem, one to four operators were entered. The results are based on 372 arrivals (an 8-hour shift):

Number of Operators	Total Queue Time (minutes)	Total Idle Time (minutes)
1	726.0	1.5
2	276.5	8.5
3	93.0	191.5
4	3.0	648.0

From an analysis of the data, the proper number of people required to minimize idle time, and at the same time prevent excessive backup on the line, is two to three people. Upon closer examination, management should plan for two permanent operators and a third at this station for two hours each morning and each afternoon.

Summary

A major stimulant to the utilization of simulation lies in its ability to deal with complex, dynamic, and interacting phenomena. If the process or phenomena permit quantitative description, it can be modeled and experiments can be simulated. Unlike analytical optimization solutions, simulation models tend to be better descriptions of reality. The availability of more powerful and less costly computer systems has and will continue to hasten the growth of simulation.

The method of conducting a simulation study revolves around the planned approach. The most critical step in the study is the construction of a model which is simple enough to permit experimentation and yet complete enough to capture the relevant aspects of the business situation being simulated. The test of a simulation model is its ability to capture the essence of reality with a minimum of details. A prerequisite for model construction is a clear definition of the objective for the study. An increasingly important phase of any simulation model is using random numbers or a random number generator to simulate the process of the real world. It should be remembered that new knowledge about the real world, caused by the dynamic nature of business, can be a basis for reevaluating the simulation study.

Monte Carlo is only one of the simulation techniques that has been utilized in the business world. It has been applied to numerous problems in practically all industries, as is evident from the vast outpouring of published material. It should be recognized that the Monte Carlo approach is no panacea since many problems are too complex for its use. Problems that cannot be handled by this approach possibly can be solved by the system simulation approach. This latter method makes extensive use of complex models and historical data. As with any other OR technique, refinements and new developments will be forthcoming in the future. The continual upgrading of special simulation programming languages will extend their acceptance and application.

Questions

1. What are the various techniques associated with simulation?
2. It has been said that certain types of business problems can be solved more

easily by using OR techniques other than simulation. What problem types may they be and why?
3. How practical are large-scale simulation models of the firm? Explain.
4. In addition to those areas where simulation is now being applied, that are mentioned in the chapter, where else can it be applied in the business world?

Problems

14-1 The King Manufacturing Corporation is concerned about its solvency if a recession should hit the firm. The risk of cash insolvency can be defined as the probability that the firm's cash balance will fall below zero at the end of a recession. Using the assumption that the firm's outstanding debt can be successfully refunded at maturity, the firm's cash balance at the end of the recession (C_e) is given as follows:

$$C_e = C_b + \tilde{R} - \tilde{V} - F - I - \tilde{T}$$

where C_b = cash balance at beginning of recession (initial cash balance of $350,000)
R = collections on accounts receivable during recession
V = total variable cash expense during recession, excludes federal income taxes ($0.60 on $1 of sales)
F = total fixed cash expenses during recession, excludes interest ($20,000 = daily fixed cash expenses and $2,000 = daily fixed noncash expenses)
I = total interest payment during recession (rate of 0.03 percent per day) on a debt of $2,500,000 in its capital structure
T = total federal income tax payments during recession (50 percent rate)

Since the sales volume is a random variable, the ~ sign is used to distinguish random variables from constants. The probability distributions of recession sales and recession collection periods are given below:

Probability Distribution of Daily Sales During Recession

Sales	Probability
$80,000	.1
70,000	.4
60,000	.4
50,000	.1

486 OPERATIONS RESEARCH MODELS—SIMULATION TECHNIQUES

Probability Distribution of Increment in Collection During Recession (S = Daily Sales During Recession)

Increment in Collection Period	Probability S=$80,000	S=$70,000	S=$60,000	S=$50,000
10 days	.5	.4	.1	.1
20 days	.2	.3	.2	.2
30 days	.2	.2	.3	.2
40 days	.1	.1	.4	.5

Since we know the probability distributions of recession sales and recession collection periods, the equation to determine the firm's risk of cash insolvency (the probability that the firm's ending cash balance is negative) can be used.

Based upon a recession during the next 360 days (one year), what is the probability that the firm will become insolvent? Rather than simulating the problem, determine what steps would be involved in solving the problem.

14-2 Electron Manufacturing, Inc. is a manufacturer of specialized electrical measuring devices. The lead time of obtaining the needed materials for production is shown in Table 1. The probability of material shortages during the past year is given in Table 2. For the 20 devices just placed into production, what is the average delay that can be expected because of material shortages? Assume that the past will be representative of the future.

Table 1

Lead Time/Materials	Probability	Cumulative Probability
1 week	.10	.10
2 weeks	.15	.25
3 weeks	.20	.45
4 weeks	.25	.70
5 weeks	.25	.95
6 weeks	.05	1.00

Table 2

Material Shortages	Probability	Cumulative Probability
5 items	.10	.10
4 items	.20	.30
3 items	.20	.50
2 items	.30	.80
1 item	.10	.90
0 item	.10	1.00

14-3 The Public Service Commission is considering the employment of an additional filing clerk in its Motor Carrier Insurance Department. The filing clerk is responsible for processing insurance filings for truck owners so that they may legally transport commodities in this state. Each clerk works 8 hours per day, being paid at the rate of $2.50 per hour. There are presently two clerks. Since the work being performed is a public service, the idle time of truck owners waiting to have their insurance filed is determined to be $5.00 per hour. Waiting time should be computed in excess of 8 hours in order to complete the processing of the filings for that day.

Given below are the number of filings per day and the processing times along with their respective frequencies:

Number of Filings Per Day	Frequency	Processing Times—Minutes Per Filing	Frequency
60	30	6	10
70	10	8	25
80	15	10	35
90	10	21	20
100	35	14	10

Based on the foregoing data, should another clerk be hired?

14-4 The Automatic Machinery Company receives a different number of orders each day and the orders vary in the time required to process them. The firm is interested in determining how many machines it should have in the department to minimize the combined cost of machine idle time and order waiting time. In addition, the firm knows the average number of orders per day and the average number of hours per order. However, the number of machines that will result in minimum total variable costs cannot be analytically determined because analytical approaches do not take into account the sequential pattern of the number of orders or the sequential pattern of the number of hours to process an order. The firm has turned to you with the following data for a solution:

Probability Distribution—No. of Orders	
No. of Orders	Probability
0	.10
1	.15
2	.25
3	.30
4	.15
5	.05

488 OPERATIONS RESEARCH MODELS—SIMULATION TECHNIQUES

**Probability Distribution—
No. of Hours Per Order**

Hours/Order	Probability
5	.05
10	.05
15	.10
20	.10
25	.20
30	.25
35	.15
40	.10

Cost/hour of idle machine time = $4.00/hour
Cost/hour for orders backordered per day = $6.00/hour
What is the best approach for solving the problem? Solve using this approach.

14-5 The Orlando Manufacturing Company has a large machine which contains three identical vacuum tubes that are the major cause of downtime. The current practice is to replace the tubes as they fail. A proposal has been made to replace all three tubes whenever any one of them fails in order to reduce the frequency with which the equipment must be shut down. The objective, then, is to compare these alternatives on a cost basis. Presently, the equipment must be shut down for one hour to replace one tube or for two and one quarter hours to replace all three tubes. The total cost associated with shutting down the equipment and replacing the tubes is $30.00 an hour in terms of lost production. The cost of each vacuum tube is $10.00. The probability distribution between breakdowns, based upon past experience for replacing one tube, is given as follows:

Hours Between Breakdowns Before Replacing Each Tube	Probability
20	.05
40	.10
55	.30
70	.30
85	.20
100	.05

The probability distribution between breakdowns, based upon limited experience for three tubes, is given as follows:

SIMULATION   489

Hours Between Breakdowns Before Replacing Three Tubes	Probability
170	.10
175	.20
180	.40
185	.20
190	.10

Simulating this problem, what is the best policy for the firm—replace one or all three vacuum tubes at a time? Outline alternative approaches to the solution of the problem.

14-6 The Progressive Manufacturing Company has 20 machines which are basically alike and run 8 hours per day. These machines break down from time to time despite the preventive maintenance practices of the firm. Four repairmen are on duty during the eight hours. The machines are such that only one repairman can work on them at a time. Sometimes more than four machines are down simultaneously while at other times all repairmen are idle. Even more frequently, two and three men are idle. Management is questioning the need for four repairmen. The data compiled by the operations research analyst indicates there is one chance in ten that a machine will break down in any given hour. A study of the necessary repairs discloses this probability distribution:

Time Required to Repair Each Machine	Probability
20 min.	.05
25 min.	.25
30 min.	.35
35 min.	.30
40 min.	.05

The cost of idle machine time to the firm is $8.00 an hour while the repairman hourly rate, including fringe benefits, is $4.00 an hour. Allow 10 minutes per hour for each repairman's personal time. Based upon the foregoing data, what is the optimum number of repairmen for the firm?

Bibliography

D. C. Basil, P. R. Cone, and J. A. Fleming, *Executive Decision Making Through Simulation*, Columbus, O.: Charles E. Merrill, 1965.

C. P. Bonini, *Simulation of Information and Decision Systems in the Firm,* Englewood Cliffs, N.J.: Prentice-Hall, 1963.

E. H. Bowman and R. B. Fetter, *Analysis for Production and Operations Management,* Homewood, Ill.: Richard D. Irwin, 1967.

D. N. Charafas, *Systems and Simulation,* New York: Academic Press, 1965.

G. W. Evans, G. F. Wallace, and G. L. Sutherland, *Simulation Using Digital Computers,* Englewood Cliffs, N.J.: Prentice-Hall, 1967.

G. Gordon, *System Simulation,* Englewood Cliffs, N.J.: Prentice-Hall, 1969.

P. S. Greenlaw, L. W. Herron, and R. H. Rawden, *Business Simulation: In Industrial and University Education,* Englewood Cliffs, N.J.: Prentice-Hall, 1962.

F. S. Hillier and G. J. Lieberman, *Introduction to Operations Research,* San Francisco: Holden-Day, 1967.

C. McMillan and R. F. Gonzalez, *Systems Analysis, A Computer Approach to Decision Models,* Homewood, Ill.: Richard D. Irwin, 1968.

R. Meier, W. T. Newell, and H. L. Pazer, *Simulation in Business and Economics,* Englewood Cliffs, N.J.: Prentice-Hall, 1969.

J. H. Mize and J. G. Cox, *Essentials of Simulation,* Englewood Cliffs, N.J.: Prentice-Hall, 1968.

T. H. Naylor, J. L. Balintfy, D. S. Burdick, and D. Chu, *Computer Simulation Techniques,* New York: John Wiley & Sons, 1966.

C. H. Springer, R. E. Herlihy, and R. I. Beggs, *Advanced Methods and Models,* Homewood, Ill.: Richard D. Irwin, 1965.

K. D. Tocher, *The Art of Simulation,* London: The English Universities Press, 1963.

T. H. Williams and C. H. Griffin, *Management Information, A Quantitative Accent,* Homewood, Ill.: Richard D. Irwin, 1967.

6

Operations Research Models—Advanced Topics

Chapter FIFTEEN

Dynamic Programming

Linear programming problems have one common characteristic: they are static. Problems are stated and solved in terms of a specific situation occurring at a certain moment. When a problem is concerned with variations over time, another OR technique must be utilized which includes the time element. Such a technique, called dynamic programming, is an extension of the basic linear programming technique.

Characteristics of Dynamic Programming

Dynamic programming was developed by Richard Bellman and G. B. Dantzig. Their important contributions on this quantitative technique were first published in the 1950s. Initially, dynamic programming was referred to as stochastic linear programming or linear programming problems dealing with uncertainty. Today, dynamic programming has been developed as a quantitative technique to solve a wide range of problems. Within the chapter, this quantitative technique will be applied to production smoothing, distribution of salesmen to various marketing areas, purchasing under uncertainty, and planning advertising expenditures.

Dynamic programming is based on the "principle of optimality" which states that an optimal policy consists of optimum subpolicies. It can be defined as a mathematical technique which solves for a series of sequential decisions, each of which affects future decisions. This is important since we rarely encounter an operational situation where the implications of a decision do not extend into the future. Thus the executive faces situations that require him to make a series of decisions with the outcome of each depending on the results of a previous decision(s) in the series.

A production manager, for example, might neglect plant maintenance in order to obtain a higher output today rather than some time in the future. The total return resulting from all decisions may not be optimal if each decision is considered by itself. Instead, a sacrifice of some gain in making the first and subsequent decisions, resulting in the need of suboptimization for each decision, may produce a higher total return. The technique of dynamic programming, then, is used to determine the possibilities of modifying decisions that may exist over a period of time.

Dynamic programming is also concerned with problems in which time is not a relevant variable. For example, a decision must be made which involves an allocation of a fixed quantity of resources among a number of alternative uses. This type of problem can be solved by breaking it down into several steps. In this manner, the final decision is handled as if it were a series of dependent decisions over time. Even though this type of problem is not concerned with the time factor per se, it still adheres to the fundamental characteristic of dynamic programming—a multistage process of decision making. Some of the problems in this chapter are basically of this type.

Besides the essential characteristic of sequential decision making, dynamic programming problems have other properties. Only a small number of items need be known at any stage in order to describe the problem. In effect, dynamic programming problems are characterized by the dependence of the outcome of decisions on a small number of variables. Another characteristic is that the result of a decision at any stage alters the numerical values for the small number of variables relevant to the problem. The actual decision neither increases nor decreases the number of factors on which outcomes depend. Thus for the next decision in the sequence, the same number of variables must be considered.

In a dynamic programming problem, a series of decisions must be made in a certain sequence. When this is accomplished, an optimal policy is pursued. No matter what the initial state(s) and decision(s) were, the remaining decisions will constitute an optimal policy with regard to the state resulting from the first decision. For example, if wrong decisions have been made for the first week and second week, this does not prevent one from making the right decisions in the future—third week, fourth week, and remaining weeks. Dynamic programming enables one to arrive at optimal decisions for the periods or stages that still lie ahead despite the bad decisions made in the past.

Structure of Dynamic Programming

Dynamic programming shares some concepts with other quantitative methods while others are unique. The first concept is a "state variable" whose value specifies the condition of the process. The values of these variables tell us all we need to know about the system for the purpose of making decisions. For example, in a production problem, we might require state variables that relate to plant capacity and present inventory. Although the number of state variables can be large, the difficulty in solving a problem increases considerably as the number of these variables increase. It is to our advantage to minimize their number.

Included in the structure of a dynamic programming problem is the concept of a "decision" which is an opportunity to change the state variables (possibly in a probabilistic manner). The net change in the state variables over some time period is subject to considerable uncertainty. The returns generated by each decision depend on the starting and ending states for that decision, thereby adding up as a sequence of decisions. The task is to make decisions that maximize total return.

The last concept for the structure of dynamic programming is the ability to make decisions about the problem at various "stages" or points in time. At each step in the problem, a decision is made to change the state and thereby maximize the gain. At the next stage, decisions are made using the values of the state variables that result from the preceding decision, and so forth. Thus the time component is considered in only two ways: the present and its immediate preceding period. This approach is shown as follows:

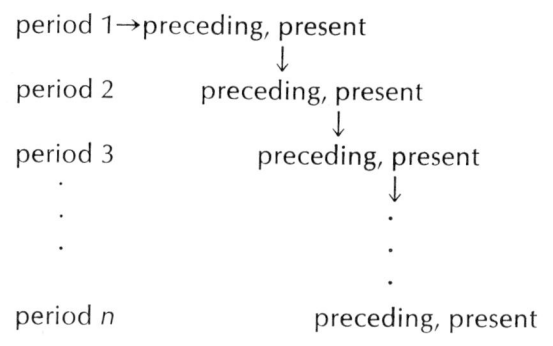

period 1 → preceding, present
↓
period 2   preceding, present
↓
period 3   preceding, present
↓
.
.
.
period n   preceding, present

The foregoing is based on the mathematical notion of *recursion*, found in continued fractions. A number plus a fraction in which the denominator is a number plus a fraction is called a continued fraction. It may have a finite or an infinite number of terms: the former is called a terminating continued fraction while the latter is non-terminating. An example of a continued fraction is

$$a_1 + \cfrac{b_2}{a_2 + \cfrac{b_3}{a_3 + \cfrac{b_4}{a_4 + \cfrac{b_5}{\text{etc.}}}}}$$

Production Smoothing Problem

The first example of dynamic programming is a production scheduling and inventory control problem that determines the best plan for producing a seasonal product. The basic costs involved are the cost of production and the cost of storage for this nonperishable product. As always, management wants to minimize the total operational costs for the period.

The production smoothing aspect of the problem looks to a leveling of the valleys and peaks in the production process. The time period in this problem is well defined just as is demand, production (supply), and storage factors. The cost factors are known: (1) cost of production in terms of regular time and overtime and (2) cost of storage in terms of quantity stored. The task of dynamic programming is to minimize the sum of these two costs—those due to fluctuation and output and those due to inventories.

There are three basic approaches to the dynamic programming problem in which demand varies within a fixed period of time. The first approach manufactures the product in accordance with the amount desired in each time period. Sales requirements, production, and inventory are not the same for each time period, resulting in wide swings of volume for each period.

Thus, costs for the seasonal product will be very high during the peak sales period unless major inventories had been accumulated during prior periods. These high costs result from hiring and training short term help, excessive overtime, and equipment purchases.

The second approach utilizes a constant production rate. When demand is light, inventory is accumulated. When demand is heavy, the inventory "cushion" minimizes its impact upon production. The difficulty with this approach is the determination of the beginning inventory. If the initial inventory is too small, stockouts will occur initially and stock overages eventually. If the initial inventory is too large, excess carrying costs will be experienced through the entire year. The value of this approach varies directly with the accuracy of prediction of the initial inventory and the general assumption that inventory carrying costs are relatively low.

The last approach compromises these two approaches allowing the production manager to plan production in a manner to meet demand and, at the same time, minimize both production and storage costs. This production smoothing problem utilizes linear programming to produce an optimum solution and allows for regular time and overtime.

For example, the production manager has a product, part #5050, which must be produced to meet a fluctuating demand. He knows the monthly requirements are: 900 for the first month, 700 for the second month, 1100 for the third month, and 1000 for the fourth month. The part can be produced either on regular time or on overtime. However, two restrictions imposed by technical conditions are: regular production cannot exceed 900 items per month and overtime production cannot exceed 500 items per month. Manufacturing cost per item during regular hours varies each month: $3 in the first month, $4 in the second month, $2.50 in the third month, and $3 in the fourth month. This cost varies due to the anticipated volume for each month. The manufacturing costs for overtime are: $4 in the first month, $5 in the second month, $3.50 in the third month, and $4 in the fourth month. Monthly storage cost is $2 per unit. Items manufactured but not distributed during the month are stored for distribution in the following month. Since the time period is limited, no inventory is to remain at the end of the period (fourth month). The number of units produced must equal the number demanded and distributed.

Based on this information, the "state variables" are: monthly requirements, monthly plant capacities (regular and overtime), and zero inventory at the end of the period. The "stages" within the problem are the four monthly periods. "Decisions" concerning monthly production schedules must be made on a regular and an overtime basis.

Since the problem is to minimize the objective function in terms of production costs and storage costs, it can be approached as a transportation model. The unused capacity has a value of 1900 items or $(900 \times 4) + (500 \times 4) - (900 + 700 + 1100 + 1000)$. The costs associated with unused capacity is zero. The costs of an item produced in a given month is its production cost (regular or overtime). However, the cost of the same item in subsequent months is its production cost plus its monthly storage costs. These figures appear in Table 15-1.

TABLE 15-1
Cost Factors for Production Smoothing (Scheduling) Problem

		Units	First Month	Second Month	Third Month	Fourth Month	Unused Capacity
First month	Regular production	900	$3	$5	$7	$9	$0
	Overtime production	500	4	6	8	10	0
Second month	Regular production	900	—	4	6	8	0
	Overtime production	500	—	5	7	9	0
Third month	Regular production	900	—	—	2.50	4.50	0
	Overtime production	500	—	—	3.50	5.50	0
Fourth month	Regular production	900	—	—	—	3.00	0
	Overtime production	500	—	—	—	4.00	0
Monthly Requirements			900	700	1,100	1,000	1,900

DYNAMIC PROGRAMMING 499

Since the costs increase progressively within each row, the lowest cost for the first row lies to the extreme left. Thus the Northwest Corner rule (modified) can be used. Table 15-2 is the initial table for this production smoothing problem. Using the basic formula for the rim requirements $(m+n-1)$, the initial solution is degenerate since the rim requirements of $12(8+5-1)$ does not equal the filled cells. Thus, one artificial variable (ε) is needed for evaluation of all unused cells. Applying the rules of the steppingstone method, all pluses in the unused cells indicate the best solution in terms of costs has been reached in Table 15-2 and that the solution

TABLE 15-2
Production Smoothing Problem

	First Month	Second Month	Third Month	Fourth Month	Unused Capacity	Available Capacities
First month	$3 / 900	$5 / +$1	$7 / +$3.50	$9 / +$5	$0 / ε	900
	$4 / +$1	$6 / +$2	$8 / +$4.50	$10 / +$6	$0 / 500	500
Second month	—	$4 / 700	$6 / +$2.50	$8 / +$4	$0 / 200	900
	—	$5 / +$1	$7 / +$3.50	$9 / +$5	$0 / 500	500
Third Month	—	—	$2.50 / 900	$4.50 / +$1.50	$0 / +$1	900
	—	—	$3.50 / 200	$5.50 / +$1.50	$0 / 300	500
Fourth month	—	—	—	$3 / 900	$0 / +$1	900
	—	—	—	$4 / 100	$0 / 400	500
Monthly requirement	900	700	1,100	1,000	1,900	5600

is unique. The total production cost plan during the next four months for part #5050 is computed as follows:

First month	900 items × $3 (R)	=	$2,700
Second month	700 items × $4 (R)	=	2,800
Third month	900 items × $2.50 (R)	=	2,250
Third month	200 items × $3.50 (O)	=	700
Fourth month	900 items × $3 (R)	=	2,700
Fourth month	100 items × $4 (O)	=	400
	3,700 items		$11,550 total cost

where (R) = regular time and (O) = overtime. In this solution which minimizes total costs, the production manager can utilize the excess capacity for manufacturing other parts.

Distribution of Salesmen for Various Marketing Areas

Initially this section will investigate the distribution of salesmen for two marketing areas and then extend this analysis to three marketing areas. The problem is how to distribute a given number of salesmen among marketing areas to achieve maximum profit. In Figure 15-1, the profit for two marketing areas is given as a function of sales effort expended. Inspection of this data indicates that sales actually drop when too many salesmen antagonize the customers.

Using six salesmen in two sales areas produces seven possible combinations: allocate all six to sales area 1 and none to sales area 2, five salesmen to sales area 1 and one salesman to sales area 2, and the like. This is summarized in Table 15-3. The mathematical notation is: $f_1(x)$ denotes profit in sales area 1, $f_2(x)$ denotes profit in sales area 2, and x equals the number of salesmen employed in a sales area.

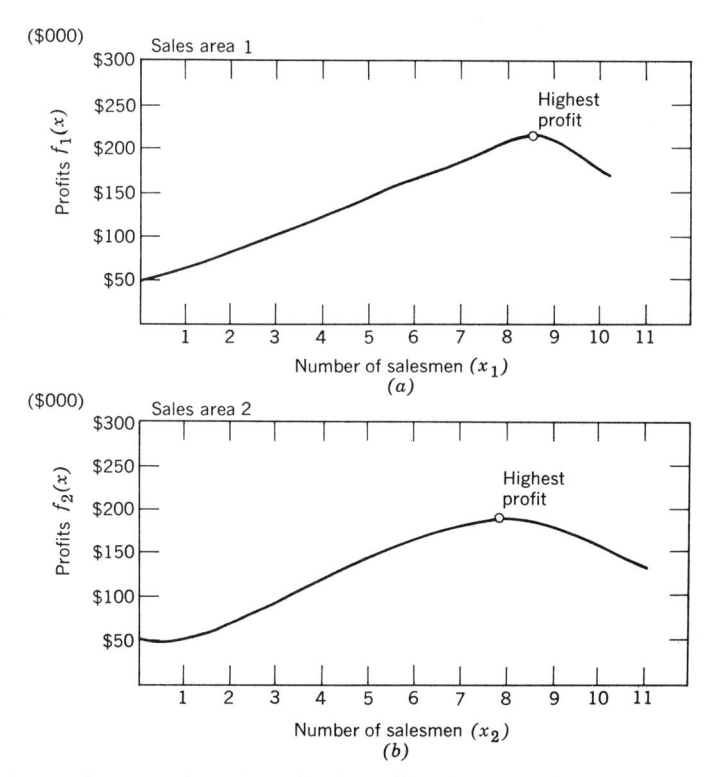

Figure 15-1 Profits as a function of sales effort for (a) sales area 1 and (b) sales area 2.

DYNAMIC PROGRAMMING

TABLE 15-3
Profits Available in Both Sales Areas

Number of Salesmen	x (area 1) x (area 2)	6 0	5 1	4 2	3 3	2 4	1 5	0 6
Profit in sales area	$f_1(x)$ $f_2(x)$	$150,000 50,000	$130,000 65,000	$115,000 85,000	$105,000 110,000	$80,000 140,000	$60,000 160,000	$50,000 175,000
Total Profit		$200,000	$195,000	$200,000	$215,000	$220,000	$220,000	$225,000

The last row in Table 15-3 indicates the total profit for each of the seven alternatives. The best allocation is six salesmen in sales area 2 and none in sales area 1 for a maximum profit of $225,000. Data in Table 15-3 can be written in mathematical form as follows:

$$Z = f_1(0) + f_2(6)$$
$$Z = f_1(1) + f_2(5)$$
$$Z = f_1(2) + f_2(4)$$
$$Z = f_1(3) + f_2(3)$$
$$Z = f_1(4) + f_2(2)$$
$$Z = f_1(5) + f_2(1)$$
$$Z = f_1(6) + f_2(0)$$

where Z equals total profit. What we need at this point is a formula for obtaining the best allocation of salesmen for optimum profit. Based upon the above mathematical notation, a maximum profit equation is determined as follows:

$$Z = F(A) = \max_{0 \leq x \leq A} [f_1(x) + f_2(A-x)] \qquad \text{(Equation 15-1)}$$

where x is the number of salesmen for one sales area, (FA) is the maximum profit that can be made if A salesmen are allocated in an optimum manner between the two sales areas. Also, A is a state variable in this problem.

The optimum equation for six salesmen is:

$$F(6) = \max_{0 \leq x \leq 6} [f_1(x) + f_2(6-x)] \qquad \text{(Equation 15-2)}$$

It should be remembered that other values for the state variable, not just 6, could have been used in the preceding equation.

An alternative method is to compute the profit for a certain number of salesmen assigned to the first sales area and a given number of salesmen allocated to the second sales area. This is shown in Table 15-4, the source data being Figure 15-1. For example, if four salesmen are assigned to the first area and one salesman is assigned to the second area, the profit realized will be $180,000 or $115,000 for four salesmen in sales area 1 and $65,000 for one salesman in sales area 2. Another example for 11 salesmen is an optimum profit of $310,000 where profit from utilizing six men is $150,000 in the first sales area while profit from using five men in the second sales area is $160,000. Inspection of Table 15-4 reveals that optimum profits are starred (*) amounts on the diagonals for the various number of salesmen. This data is plotted in Figure 15-2. Thus $F(A)$, which is the maximum profit for a combined number of A salesmen assigned to two marketing areas, can be easily determined.

Having treated two marketing areas, we can now consider the interrelationship of profit and salesmen for three sales areas. Just as we plotted profit as a function of sales effort for the first two sales areas, the same method can be continued for sales area 3 as shown in Figure 15-3. However, the addition of another sales area makes the problem much more complex. Six salesmen can be allocated 28 different ways while 11 salesmen can be

TABLE 15-4
Profits for Sales Efforts in Two Sales Areas

Number of Salesmen	Profits ($000)	Sales Area 1											
		0	1	2	3	4	5	6	7	8	9	10	11
		$50	$60	$80	$105	$115	$130	$150	$165	$185	$200	$195	$185
Number of Salesmen Sales Area 2	0 $50	$100*	$110	$130	$155	$165	$180	$200	$215	$235	$250	$245	$235
	1 $65	115*	125	145	170	180	195	215	230	250	265	260	
	2 $85	135*	145	165	190	200	215	235	250	270	285		
	3 $110	160*	170	190	215	225	240	260	275	295			
	4 $140	190*	200	220	245*	255	270	290	305				
	5 $160	210*	220	240	265*	275	290	310*					
	6 $175	225*	235	255	280*	290	305						
	7 $190	240	250	270	295*	305							
	8 $200	250	260	280	305								
	9 $195	245	255	275									
	10 $193	243	253										
	11 $190	240											

* Profits are the maxima along each diagonal.

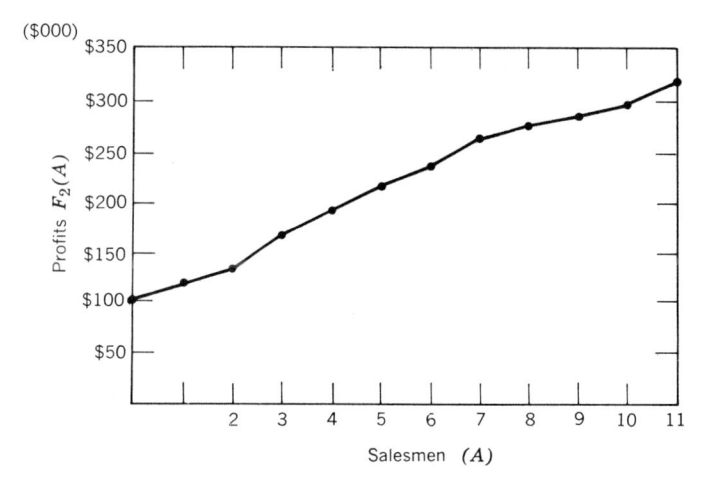

Figure 15-2 Maximum profits from optimum allocation of salesmen between two sales areas.

allocated in 78 ways. Obviously, the method of preparing a table for all possible combinations requires quite a few calculations. Expressing this problem mathematically, the equation for determining the maximum profit is:

$$F_n(A_n) = \max_{0 \leq x_n \leq A_n} [f_1(x_1) + f_2(x_2) + f_3(x_3) + \cdots f_n(x_n)]$$ (Equation 15-3)

where *n* is the number of marketing areas.

The solution to this problem for optimum allocation of salesmen in three marketing areas requires a somewhat different point of view. For example, we could solve the problem of allocating the six salesmen with the understanding that two salesmen will be allocated to the first two sales areas and that the other four will be in sales area 3. Upon modification of Equation 15-3, we can say that the profit by using two salesmen in the first

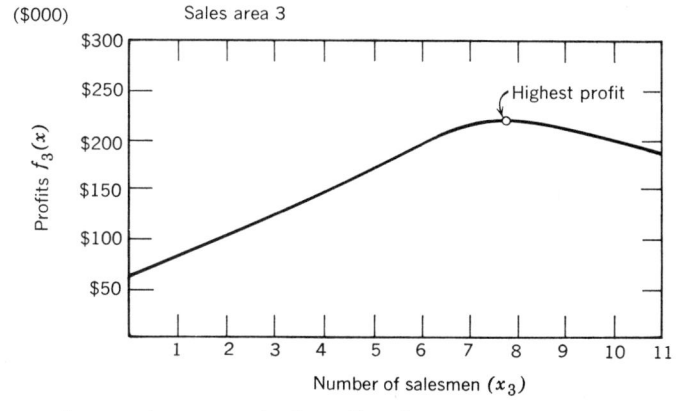

Figure 15-3 Profits as a function of sales effort for sales area 3.

DYNAMIC PROGRAMMING 505

two sales area is $F(2)$ and the profit from allocating four salesmen to the last sales area is $f_3(4)$. Therefore profit is:

$$Z = F(2) + f_3(4) \qquad \text{(Equation 15-4)}$$

However, there is no logical reason to allocate exactly two salesmen to the first two areas. Since this is the case, it is necessary to drop this assumption and try to allocate 0 salesman, 1 salesman, and so forth, to the first two sales areas. The problem can now be seen as one of trying to select the largest of the following (based upon Equation 15-4):

$$Z = F(0) + f_3(6)$$
$$Z = F(1) + f_3(5)$$
$$Z = F(2) + f_3(4)$$
$$Z = F(3) + f_3(3)$$
$$Z = F(4) + f_3(2)$$
$$Z = F(5) + f_3(1)$$
$$Z = F(6) + f_3(0)$$

Equation 15-4 can be restated so that we can solve the problem in terms of optimum profit for three marketing areas, which is as follows:

$$F_3(A_3) = \max_{0 \le x \le A_3} [F_2(x) + f_3(A_3 - x)] \qquad \text{(Equation 15-5)}$$

In Equation 15-6, $F_2(A_2)$ is used to denote the optimum profit that can be realized by allocating salesmen between the first two marketing areas. This is the same function that we denoted by $F(A)$ in Equation 15-1. In fact, both sides of the equation are essentially unchanged:

$$F_2(A_2) = \max_{0 \le x_1 \le A_2} [f_1(x_1) + f_2(A_2 - x_1)] \qquad \text{(Equation 15-6)}$$

The maximum profit that can be realized by allocating a number of salesmen among the three marketing areas is denoted by $F_3(A_3)$. The equation is:

$$F_3(A_3) = \max_{0 \le A_2 \le A_3} [F_2(A_2) + f_3(A_3 - A_2)] \qquad \text{(Equation 15-7)}$$

The term $F_2(A_2)$ in Equation 15-7 is actually Equation 15-6. Thus Equation 15-7 considers all three sales areas for optimum profits.

The problem can be stated in a tabular form (as previously shown) by adding the profits of two sales areas to the profits of the third sales area. This is shown in Table 15-5. The top row shows the combined number of salesmen in sales areas 1 and 2 while the second row indicates the maximum profit, $F_2(A_2)$, that can be realized by allocating the salesmen between the first two sales areas. This second row is from Table 15-4, the profits marked with asterisks on the diagonals. The columns to the left of Table 15-5 are the number of salesmen and profits for sales area 3. The second column (profits) is based upon the data found in Figure 15-3. The entire table shows the combined profits of all three salesmen. Again, we must follow the diagonals and select the maximum values which are marked with asterisks.

TABLE 15-5
Profits for Sales Efforts in Three Sales Areas

Sales Areas 1 and 2

Number of Salesmen	Profits ($000)	0	1	2	3	4	5	6	7	8	9	10	11
0	$60	$100	$115	$135	$160	$190	$210	$225	$245	$265	$280	$295	$310
1	$75	$160*	$175*	$195	$220*	$250*	$270*	$285	$305	$325	$340	$355	$370
2	$100	175*	190	210	235	265	285	300	320	340	355	370	
3	$120	200*	215	235	260	290*	310*	325	345*	365*	380		
4	$135	220*	235	255	280	310*	330*	345*	365*	385*			
5	$150	235	250	270	295	235	345*	360	380				
6	$175	250	265	285	310	340	360	375					
7	$190	275	290	310	335	365*	385*						
8	$205	290	305	325	350	380							
9	$202	305	320	340	365								
10	$200	302	317	337									
11	$195	300	315										
		295											

Sales Area 3 labels rows 5–7; "Salesmen" labels rows 2–4.

* Profits are the maxima along each diagonal.

DYNAMIC PROGRAMMING

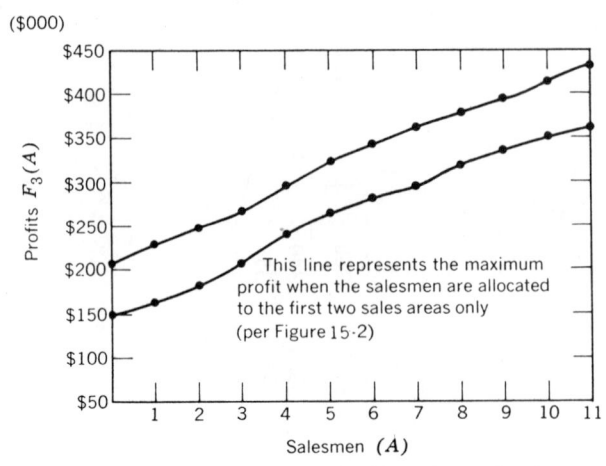

Figure 15-4 Maximum profits from optimum allocation of salesmen among three sales areas.

These maximum profits refer to the term $F_3(A_3)$ in Equation 15-7. Figure 15-4 shows a graphical representation of $F_3(A_3)$ or the maximum profit that can be realized when considering the three sales areas.

Referring to the earlier example where only six salesmen are available, the problem is how to allocate these six men in three sales areas for maximum profit. Inspection of Table 15-5 (on the diagonal) reveals that a profit of $290,000 is available with four salesmen in sales areas 1 and 2 plus two salesmen in sales area 3. Table 15-4 then determines the breakdown between sales areas 1 and 2. The maximum profit on the diagonal for four salesmen is $190,000, which results in allocating four salesmen to sales area 2 and none to sales area 1. Thus both tables had to be consulted for the proper allocation of salesmen.

This problem can be expanded to include more than three sales areas. If four sales areas are being considered, the equation for optimum profits is:

$$F_4(A_4) = \max_{0 \leq A_3 \leq A_4} [F_3(A_3) + f_4(A_4 - A_3)] \qquad \text{(Equation 15-8)}$$

The term $F_3(A_3)$ in Equation 15-8 is the same as Equation 15-7. Again, an appropriate table can be prepared. Based upon the material presented in this example, we can obtain maximum profits for any number of sales areas (where $n = 2, 3$, etc.) by using the following recursion formula:

$$F_n(A_n) = \max_{0 \leq A_{n-1} \leq A_n} [F_{n-1}(A_{n-1}) + f_n(A_n - A_{n-1})] \qquad \text{(Equation 15-9)}$$

This approach to the dynamic programming problem made use of an algorithm since a solution was not obtained at once, but was obtained step by step. Each successive step utilized the results obtained in the preceding steps. From the first step we obtained the solution for the first two sales areas in the form of a table. This table was used in constructing a second table for determining the maximum profit where there are three sales areas.

When additional sales areas make the job too cumbersome for manual methods, a computer is used. Although step-by-step optimization may produce a "true" optimum, additional areas or changed conditions may require that the present optimized solution be reevaluated to reflect accurately the real world.

Purchasing Under Uncertainty

An optimum purchasing policy that will minimize the cost of obtaining raw materials is solvable by dynamic programming. For example, suppose that during the next four weeks, raw material prices for a particular purchased item are expected to vary week-by-week per the following probability factors:

Price	Probability
$150	.25
170	.35
200	.40
	1.00

Utilization of these values is illustrated in Figure 15-5 for the alternatives faced weekly by purchasing. If the purchasing agent buys the raw material at the end of the first week, the price that is paid is the price that is prevailing in that week. However, if he decides to delay his purchase until one of the three remaining weeks, he must pay the prevailing price for that week. Should the purchasing agent not purchase the material prior to the fourth week, production requirements will force him to buy at the end of the fourth week.

An approach for this problem is to start with the fourth or final week and work our way back to the first week since the material must be purchased before the end of the fourth week. The fourth-week decision can be expressed as:

$$F_4(X_4) = X_4 \qquad \text{(Equation 15-10)}$$

where $F_n(X_n)$ = lowest expected cost if purchase price observed in week n is X_n and an optimal policy is pursued for the four-week period
X_n = purchase price observed in week n
n = week number, that is 1, 2, 3, or 4

In Equation 15-10, n is referred to as the "stage" number while X is the "state variable."

For the third week, an equation can be written which is:

$$F_3(X_3) = \min\ [\overset{Act}{X_3},\ \overset{Wait}{(\$150)(0.25) + (\$170)(0.35) + (\$200)(0.40)}]$$
$$\text{(Equation 15-11)}$$

DYNAMIC PROGRAMMING 509

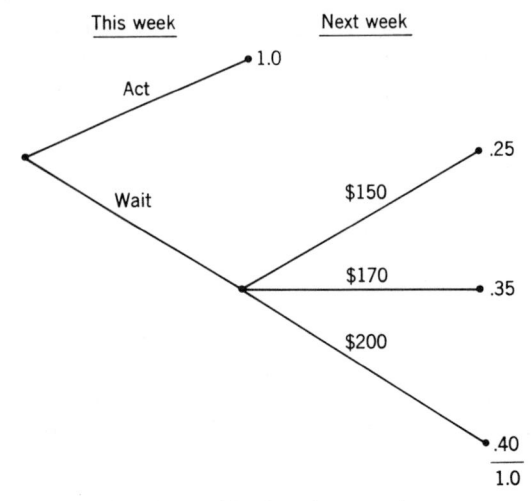

```
                    This week              Next week
                                    • 1.0
                        Act
                                                        • .25
                              Wait       $150
                                    
                                         $170
                                                        • .35
                                         $200

                                                        • .40
                                                        ───
                                                        1.0
```

Figure 15-5 Alternatives faced weekly by the purchasing agent during the four week period.

The foregoing equation has this meaning: in the third week, the purchasing agent can *Act* on the basis of price X_3 or *Wait* for the expected value of the price in the fourth week. Thus, Equation 15-11 can be expressed as:

$$F_3(X_3) = \min[\overset{Act}{X_3}, \overset{Wait}{F_4(\$150)(0.25) + F_4(\$170)(0.35) + F_4(\$200)(0.40)}]$$
(Equation 15-12)

To determine a break-even point between the *Act* and *Wait* alternatives, it is necessary to restate Equation 15-12 such that the values of these two alternatives are equal to each other. For a break-even X_{3be} value, Equation 15-12 becomes:

$$X_{3be} = (\$150)(0.25) + (\$170)(0.35) + (\$200)(0.40) \quad \text{(Equation 15-13)}$$
$$= \$37.50 + \$59.50 + \$80.00$$
$$= \$177.00$$

Thus, if the material price is below the expected purchase price of $177.00, that is, at $150.00 or $170.00, the purchasing agent should make the purchase. On the other hand, if the price is above this value of $177.00, the purchase should be delayed for the fourth week.

The calculation for the minimum expected cost in the third week (refer to Equation 15-10), then, is:

$$F_3(X_3) = \begin{bmatrix} \$150 \text{ if } X_3 = \$150 \\ \$170 \text{ if } X_3 = \$170 \\ \$177 \text{ break-even} \end{bmatrix} \quad \text{(Equation 15-14)}$$

For the second week, a comparable equation to Equation 15-12 is developed, which is:

$$F_2(X_2) = \min[\overset{Act}{X_2}, \overset{Wait}{F_3(\$150)(0.25) + F_3(\$170)(0.35) + F_3(\$177)(0.40)}]$$
(Equation 15-15)

Substitution of the values from Equation 15-14 into the foregoing equation allows a calculation of a break-even between the *Act* and *Wait* alternatives (as in the third week). The break-even point for X_{2be} at which the two alternatives have equal value is:

$$X_{2be} = (\$150)(0.25) + (\$170)(0.35) + (\$177)(0.40)$$
$$= \$37.50 + \$59.50 + \$70.80 \qquad \text{(Equation 15-16)}$$
$$= \$167.80$$

If the purchase price in the second week is under the expected price of $167.80, that is, at $150.00, the purchasing agent should initiate an order. But, if the price is greater than the calculated $167.80, the purchase can be delayed. Thus, the minimum expected cost for the second week is:

$$F_2(X_2) = \begin{bmatrix} \$150 \text{ if } X_2 = \$150 \\ \$167.80 \text{ break-even} \end{bmatrix} \qquad \text{(Equation 15-17)}$$

In the first week, the problem can be expressed mathematically as:

$$\overset{Act}{F_1(X_1)} = \min\ [X_1, \overset{Wait}{F_2(\$150)(0.25) + F_2(\$167.80)(0.35) + F_2(\$167.80)(0.40)}]$$
(Equation 15-18)

The break-even value calculates to be:

$$X_{1be} = \$163.35 \qquad \text{(Equation 15-19)}$$

The lowest cost, then, in the first week is:

$$F_1(X_1) = \begin{bmatrix} \$150 \text{ if } X_1 = \$150 \\ \$163.35 \text{ break-even} \end{bmatrix} \qquad \text{(Equation 15-20)}$$

An analysis of the foregoing values for an optimum purchasing policy under uncertainty indicates the following results: If the price in the first or second week is $150, the purchasing agent should acquire the materials; otherwise, he should wait. If the purchase price in the third week is either $150 or $170, the purchase should be made; otherwise, wait. If no purchase is made by the fourth week, the purchase must be made at the prevailing price in the fourth (final) week.

It should be noted that generalized equations can be developed for this purchasing problem under uncertainty. For any number of weeks, Equations 15-10 and 15-12 can be solved recursively by working backward.

Other Dynamic Programming Areas

Many other applications can be found for this OR technique in the industrial firm. In the production area, dynamic programming has been employed for smoothing production employment in an environment of widely fluctuating demand. Scheduling methods for routine and major overhauls on machinery have been developed. In a similar manner, optimal new equipment replacement policies have been determined. This OR technique has been successfully employed for computing the maximum output from production processes of varying efficiencies.

Dynamic programming has been employed in finance to determine the most profitable investment of resources or alternative opportunities as well as a long-range strategy for replacing depreciating assets. It is also extremely useful in capital budgeting for allocating scarce resources to new ventures. In addition, finance officers have turned to dynamic programming for the proper determination of short-to-long-range dividend policies.

An examination of the foregoing applications plus those illustrated in the chapter indicates the potential of dynamic programming. The ability to solve many different and difficult problems is generally limited only by the capability of the user—not by the technique itself. Dynamic programming is an art as much as a science in problem solving.

Comparison of Dynamic Programming and Linear Programming

The problems presented in this chapter are not sophisticated examples of dynamic programming, but they do present some of its basic concepts. Although both linear programming and dynamic programming make use of an algorithm, the techniques are different.

The basic characteristic of dynamic programming involves a multi-stage process of decision making where there are generally time intervals. However, these stages may be only an order in which the problem is solved. On the other hand, linear programming gives a solution as of one time period based upon certain capacity, quantity, and contribution (or cost) constraints.

Wrong decisions in the past, under dynamic programming, do not prevent the making of correct decisions now and in the future. In essence, regardless of earlier decisions, dynamic programming enables one to find optimal decisions for future periods. Conversely, linear programming requires constant updating that reflects the current constraints for an optimal answer.

Several additional comparisons are possible between these two quantitative techniques. Dynamic programming is more powerful in concept, but computationally less so than linear programming. This should be apparent in the sample problems. Dynamic programming is similar to calculus, whereas linear programming is analogous to solving sets of simultaneous linear equations. Tables 15-4 and 15-5 are examples of the similarity to calculus from the viewpoint of finite differences on the diagonals. Dynamic programming is quite different in form from linear programming. While certain rules must be followed in the iterative process of linear programming, dynamic programming utilizes the appropriate mathematics necessary for the problem's solution.

Dynamic Programming Application—American Products Corporation

The American Productions Corporation has decided to try marketing experiments in one of its test markets. The firm wants to determine the best combination of advertising media and frequency. During the past two years, the market research group has collected data about the relationship of sales to the frequency of the advertisement. Figures are based upon conservative market conditions which appear in Table 15-6. The cost of using advertising

TABLE 15-6
Estimated Units Sold under Conservative Conditions with Three Different Advertising Media Based on Frequency of Advertising per Period

		Estimated Units Sold Under Conservative Conditions Using Advertising		
		R	S	T
Frequency per Period	1	125	140	225
	2	200	240	275
	3	225	265	310
	4	250	300	350

R, S, and T is $3000, $5500, and $9000, respectively. The total advertising budget is $22,000 for the period of the test. Since the several combinations of expenses may be equal to or less than the budget, the technique of dynamic programming allows us to determine the optimum combination of frequencies and media that will maximize expected unit sales. The first step is to construct a table (Table 15-7) to reflect expected unit sales

TABLE 15-7
Total Expected Sales Under Conservative Conditions for Advertising Frequencies in Media R, S, and T

Frequency of R's Advertisement	How Often S's Advertisement Appears While T's Advertisement Does Not Appear					How Often S's Advertisement Appears While T's Advertisement Appears Once				
	0	1	2	3	4	0	1	2	3	4
0	0	140	240	265	300	225	365	465	490	525
1	125	265	365	390	425	350	490	590	615	650
2	200	340	440	465	500	425	565	665	690	725
3	225	365	465	490	525	450	590	690	715	750
4	250	390	490	515	550	475	615	715	740	775

under conservative market conditions for the various types of advertising.

The basis for data in Table 15-7 is Table 15-6. An example of how the figures are used would be a decision to advertise three times with R (225), twice with S (240), and none with T (0), which totals 465, estimated units sold. Another example would be to advertise four times with R (250), three

TABLE 15-8
Total Advertising Costs Using the Various Advertising Media of R, S, and T

Frequency of R's Advertisement	How Often S's Advertisement Appears While T's Advertisement Does Not Appear					How Often S's Advertisement Appears While T's Advertisement Appears Once				
	0	1	2	3	4	0	1	2	3	4
0	$0	$5,500	$11,000	$16,500	$22,000	$9,000	$14,500	$20,000	$25,500	$31,000
1	3,000	8,500	14,000	19,500	25,000	12,000	17,500	23,000	28,500	34,000
2	6,000	11,500	17,000	22,500	28,000	15,000	20,500	26,000	31,500	37,000
3	9,000	14,500	20,000	25,500	31,000	18,000	23,500	29,000	34,500	40,000
4	12,000	17,500	23,000	28,500	34,000	21,000	26,500	32,000	37,500	43,000

times with S (265), and once with T (225), which results in a total of 740 units. The reason that the frequency of T's advertisement appears no more than once in Table 15-7 is the cost factor of $9000 versus $3000 and $5500 for R and S, respectively. Table 15-8 shows the total costs involved when choosing various frequency combinations of R, S, and T.

An examination of Table 15-8 reveals that certain combinations are not feasible because they have violated the budgetary constraints. Since they violate the basic conditions under which the problem is formulated, such combinations are not considered. Based on Table 15-8, feasible combinations from $14,000 up to and including $22,000 are shown below:

\multicolumn{3}{c}{Frequency}	Total Cost	Total Expected Sales
R	S	T		
3	1	0	$14,500	365
4	1	0	17,500	390
1	2	0	14,000	365
2	2	0	17,000	440
3	2	0	20,000	465
0	3	0	16,500	265
1	3	0	19,500	390
0	4	0	22,000	300
2	0	1	15,000	425
3	0	1	18,000	450
4	0	1	21,000	475
0	1	1	14,500	365
1	1	1	17,500	490
2	1	1	20,500	565
0	2	1	20,000	465

The criterion for a decision in the problem is the maximization of total sales within the budget constraint of $22,000. Examination of the above figures reveals that advertising twice with media R and once each for media S and T will yield the highest expected sales of 565 units.

Summary

Dynamic programming is structured somewhat differently from other OR techniques. It divides the problem into a number of subproblems or decision stages. General recurrence relations between one stage and the next stage describe the problem. The stage usually refers to a time period but need not necessarily represent time. Finally, the state of the system is described by one or more state variables.

A dynamic programming approach is helpful in solving sequential decision problems where a sequence of decisions that affect future decisions must be made. Even though incorrect or less than optimal decisions have been made in the past, dynamic programming still enables one to make correct decisions for future periods. This technique is one of the newer tools of operations researchers. As more researchers master the subject matter of dynamic programming, it will find wider application. Imaginative OR personnel are required if this technique is to reach its full potential.

Questions

1. What are the essential characteristics of a dynamic programming problem?
2. Compare the essentials of dynamic programming to linear programming.
3. In what areas of the firm can dynamic programming be applied?

Problems

15-1 The Newcomb Manufacturing Company has compiled the following data for future monthly production requirements and costs:

Month	Quantity	Regular Costs per Unit	Overtime Costs per Unit
January	820	$4	$6
February	1,000	5	7
March	1,000	5.50	7.50
April	920	5.20	7.20
May	800	5	7
June	500	5	7

On December 31, there are 400 units in stock at a cost of $5.00 each. Regular production cannot exceed 650 units, overtime production cannot exceed 300 units. Storage costs are $1.50 per month for each unit. What is the optimal production schedule and total related costs? Assume no inventory is desired at the end of six months.

15-2 The Sperry Corporation has a problem of determining the number of units for each of three items to put in a military repair kit whose total cost cannot exceed $390. Part 23 costs $40; part 56, $60; and part 42, $100. The utility (usefulness) in the field for each part decreases as more are added, as shown in the schedule below. (The utility of the repair kit is based upon multiplying the value in use by the probability of use in the field.) The problem is to determine the number of each type part (23, 56, and 42) to pack in a field kit to maixmize its usefulness. At least one unit of part 23 and 56 must be contained in the repair kit.

No. of Parts In Kit	Utility of Part 23	Utility of Part 56	Utility of Part 42
1	60	140	200
2	120	200	300
3	180	250	380
4	230	290	440
5	275	320	480
6	310	345	510
7	345	365	540
8	375	380	560

15-3 The Monsot Manufacturing Corporation has nine salesmen who presently sell in three separate sales areas of the United States. The profitability for each salesman in the three sales areas is as follows:

No. of Salesmen
	0	1	2	3	4	5	6	7	8	9
Area 1	0	1	2	3	4	5	6	7	8	9
Area 2	9	8	7	6	5	4	3	2	1	0
Area 3	0	1	2	3	4	5	6	7	8	9

($000) Profitability
Area 1	$20	$32	$47	$57	$66	$71	$82	$90	$100	$110
Area 2	135	125	115	104	93	82	71	60	50	40
Area 3	50	61	72	84	97	109	120	131	140	150

Determine the optimum allocation of salesmen in order to maximize profits.

15-4 The Dandy Diaper Delivery Company presently has seven delivery trucks. Based on a number of complaints about poor pickup and delivery service, the owner of the company has hired you to determine the proper distribution of the trucks within the four districts it serves. You have conducted a survey on the pickup rates per day that could occur in a given district for the various number of trucks. Given this survey data (shown below), you are to determine the distribution of seven trucks within the four districts that will result in the maximum number of pickups.

Survey Data

Number of Trucks

District		0	1	2	3	4	5	6	7
1	P	0	1000	2000	2800	3700	4200	5000	5500
2	i	0	900	1900	3000	4000	4300	4800	5000
3	c	0	1200	1900	2200	2400	3000	3800	5000
4	k	0	1100	1500	2000	2800	3700	4900	5800
	u								
	p								
	s								

15-5 The LaCrosse Manufacturing Company has $2 million in additional funds available for investing during the next five months. The return on each monthly investment is a random variable distributed according to the probabilities below:

Annual Return on Investment (%)	Probability
20	.5
30	.4
40	.1
	1.0

At the start of each month, the company's treasurer is presented an opportunity to invest the entire $2 million which he must accept or reject. If the investment is rejected, the opportunity is withdrawn. If the treasurer has not invested the money by the fifth month, he must invest it at the return available during that month. In what month(s) should the treasurer invest the $2 million?

15-6 The Litto Corporation has had a relatively fixed policy in the past regarding its dividend policy. However, due to a rapidly expanding market (caused by its introduction of many new products), the firm's board of directors is asking how much money should be paid out as dividends and how much should be retained for the firm's expansion. The firm has asked you to determine a payment policy which is best suited for stockholders who desire maximum dividends in the coming years, in particular, on a one-year basis, on a two-year basis, and on a three-year basis. The anticipated earnings are $500,000 per year before consideration for the reinvestment of earnings, which are as follows:

Amount Reinvested	Rate of Return
$0– $99,999	0.50
$100,000–$199,999	0.45
$200,000–$299,999	0.40
$300,000–$399,999	0.30
$400,000–$499,999	0.25
$500,000 and over	0.22

This table shows that the return on invested money decreases as the size of the reinvestment increase. This is because the more profitable projects are undertaken first. An assumption in this problem is that the return on invested money for the various levels continues at the same rate over the years. Also consider the fact the company has $500,000 available at the beginning of the first year for dividends, reinvestment in the company, or a combination of both. It will be further assumed that the company pays a dividend only once a year.

Bibliography

R. I. Ackoff and M. W. Sasieni, *Fundamentals of Operations Research*, New York: John Wiley & Sons, 1968.

R. E. Bellman, *Dynamic Programming*, Princeton, N.J.: Princeton University Press, 1957.

R. E. Bellman and S. E. Dreyfus, *Applied Dynamic Programming*, Princeton, N.J.: Princeton University Press, 1962.

U. Bertele and F. Brioschi, *Nonserial Dynamic Programming*, New York: Academic Press, 1972.

S. E. Dreyfus, *Dynamic Programming and the Calculus of Variations*, New York: Academic Press, 1965.

G. Hadley, *Nonlinear and Dynamic Programming*, Reading, Mass.: Addison-Wesley Publishing Company, 1964.

F. S. Hillier and G. J. Lieberman, *Introduction to Operations Research*, San Francisco: Holden-Day, 1967.

R. A. Howard, *Dynamic Programming and Markov Processes*, New York: John Wiley & Sons, 1960.

N. K. Kwak, *Mathematical Programming with Business Applications*, New York: McGraw-Hill Book Company, 1973.

G. L. Nemhauser, *Introduction to Dynamic Programming*, New York: John Wiley and Sons, 1966.

D. Teichroew, *An Introduction to Management Science, Deterministic Science*, New York: John Wiley and Sons, 1964.

H. M. Wagner, *Principles of Operations Research with Applications to Managerial Decisions*, Englewood Cliffs, N.J.: Prentice-Hall, 1969.

D. J. White, *Dynamic Programming*, San Francisco: Holden-Day, 1969.

Chapter SIXTEEN

Heuristic Programming

Although this book has concentrated on "well-structured" business problems (all of the constraints and variables are set forth with quantified values in a mathematical model) that have been successfully solved by OR groups, there is a growing trend to solve problems that are "poorly structured," sometimes called "ill-structured." Unfortunately, the most difficult and pressing problems facing managers tend to be poorly structured—ones that cannot be stated in a precise mathematical model with appropriate values for solution. The approach used in their solution involves programming them on a computer "heuristically." This means employing rules of thumb to explore the most likely paths in arriving at a conclusion rather than examining all of the possible alternatives to find the optimum one. In this chapter, heuristic programming is presented in its present state of development.

Definition of Heuristic Programming

Heuristic is derived from the Greek word *heuriskin* meaning "serving to discover." The mathematician G. Polya credits Pappus (lived around 300 A.D.), René Descartes (1596–1650), and Bernard Bolzano (1781–1848) with the first important contributions on this subject. According to Polya, heuristic "was the name of a certain branch of study, not very clearly circumscribed, belonging to logic, or to philosophy or to psychology, often outlined, seldom presented in detail, and as good as forgotten today."[1] The aim of heuristic is to study the methods and rules of discovery and invention.

Heuristic programming, as it is known in OR literature, has its roots in the artificial intelligence research of Herbert Simon of Carnegie Institute of Technology, together with Allen Newell of Carnegie and J. C. Shaw of the Rand Corporation. Their goal in artificial intelligence research is to write programs instructing the computer on how to behave in a way that, in human beings, would be called intelligent. The workers proceed on the assumption that human nervous systems process information in the act of thinking. Given enough observations, experiments, analysis, and modeling, they can instruct a digital computer to process information as humans do. In other words, this approach allows one to analyze problems that can be solved by human intelligence and to write a computer program that will solve the problem.

Herbert Simon has made the following observation concerning heuristics:

---

[1] G. Polya, *How to Solve It*, Garden City, N.Y.: Doubleday & Company, Inc., 1957, pp. 112-113.

> "... rules of thumb, that allow us to factor, approximately, the complex perceived world into highly simple components and to find, approximately and reasonably reliably, the correspondences that allow us to act on that world predictably."[2]

Also, he stated that heuristic programming is:

> "... a point of view in the design of programs for complex information processing tasks. This point of view is that the programs should not be limited to numerical processes, or even to orderly systematic non-numerical algorithms of the kinds familiar from the more traditional uses of computers, but that ideas should be borrowed also from the less systematic, more selective, processes that humans use in handling those many problems that have not been reduced to algorithm."[3]

About the same time, another operations researcher, Geoffrey Clarkson, provides an additional dimension to the heuristic concept.

> "When the rules or heuristics for processing information yield results consistent with those obtained by human subjects, the model is said to have 'simulated' the decision process—that is, the set of heuristics is sufficient to 'simulate' the behavior of the subject."[4]

Examination of the foregoing definitions indicates differences in defining the subject matter. These differences can be explained by the applications of heuristics under study. Polya, in addition to not having the benefit of computer processing, was emphasizing the usefulness of heuristics in mathematical instruction. On the other hand, Simon and Clarkson realized the importance of computers in duplicating rules of thumb employed by human decision makers. The latter point of view, then, is the one found in this chapter.

A simplified definition of heuristic programming that utilizes the computer as a major tool of analysis is given as follows:

> Heuristic programming utilizes rules of thumb or intuitive rules and guidelines and is generally under computer control to explore the most likely paths and to make educated guesses in arriving at a problem's solution rather than going through all of the possible alternatives to obtain an optimum one.

Although this definition differs somewhat from the prior ones, it does set forth the essentials of heuristic programming in its current state of development.

---

[2] Herbert A. Simon and Allen Newell, "Simulation of Human Thinking," in *Management and the Computer of the Future*, Martin Greenberger, editor, New York: John Wiey & Sons, Inc., 1962, p. 113.

[3] Herbert A. Simon, *The New Science of Management Decision*, New York: Harper & Row Publishers, 1960, p. 30.

[4] Geoffrey P. E. Clarkson, *Portfolio Selection: A Simulation of Trust Investment*, Englewood Cliffs, N.J.: Prentice-Hall, Inc., 1962, p. 4.

Characteristics of Heuristic Programming

For years, businessmen have developed and followed various heuristics in their operations without realizing it. When inventory for a particular part gets down to a certain level, that is the time to reorder. Value inventory items at the lower of cost or market; or on a first-in, first-out basis. Job scheduling is placed on a first-come, first-served basis or schedule the rush jobs first. Similarly, management should handle only the exceptions while subordinates should decide routine matters.

Although the foregoing heuristics may not lead to the best solution in every case, experience over time has proven their general usefulness in finding solutions to recurring problems with a minimum of effort. In addition, the above heuristics could be improved by further elaboration in order to take into account exceptional conditions or additional information. The inventory rule could, for example, take into consideration recent trends in usage rates and expectations of future demand for every stocked item. Thus, instead of a simple heuristic, a combination of heuristics might be better for optimizing the problem under study.

Based on the foregoing heuristic examples, one might be prompted to ask this question: Why resort to heuristic programming? Why not employ other OR techniques set forth earlier in the book to solve a firm's problems? There are several reasons for employing heuristics to solve problems. First, heuristics simplify the environment of the decision maker by permitting him to make decisions quickly without considering the number of ways that each decision can be made. They limit the search by reducing the number of alternatives to a manageable size. Second, many problems are so complex that, although the essence of the problem may be stated in a mathematical framework, the computations required are not feasible, even on the largest computer. Third, planning and policy problems with which top management must come to grips are so difficult to quantify and ill structured that a mathematical model cannot capture their most important characteristics. Judgment, intuition, creativity, and learning are important elements of the problem and its solution—these variables are qualitative rather than quantitative. Fourth and last, although a mathematical model may be successfully employed, the work prior to the model and subsequent to the modeling must be such that it can be understood by those who will utilize the model. Many problems encountered in the real world fall into one or more of the preceding categories and often can be solved through the use of heuristics. On the other hand, the most economical and practical approach, sometimes, is a combination of standard OR models and heuristics.

Due to their complexity, most heuristic programming problems rely heavily on computers. Such heuristic programs take the form of a set of instructions for directing the computer to solve a problem—the way the user might do it if he had enough time. To cover all contingencies likely to occur in a problem, generally a group of heuristics are needed which are much too difficult to follow at the user's pace of problem solving. Hence, the need for a computer is paramount in heuristic programs to identify and evaluate alternatives quickly and accurately.

A computer heuristic program, like a computer algorithm, terminates in a finite number of steps. However, a heuristic program produces a *good* answer while an algorithm gives an *optimal* one. Although an algorithm appears better on the surface than a heuristic approach, many so-called algorithms end up in actual practice as heuristic programs because judgments have to be made by the user in their application which negate their optimality. Their principal difference is that a heuristic program can be constructed rather freely in a common-sense, intuitive manner. On the other hand, an algorithm must be constructed based on a mathematical model so that its optimality proofs can be substantiated. Thus, a computerized heuristic program, in reality, appears preferable to an algorithm for many of the poorly structured and well-structured problems facing the firm. In the remaining sections of the chapter, this distinction should be apparent for the many applications of heuristic programming presented.

Locating Warehouses

A heuristic computer program has been developed to determine near optimal locations of regional warehouses in order to minimize distribution costs. The program permits consideration of a large number of potential warehouse sites and customers, various mixes of product orders by customers, actual shipping costs, warehouse operating costs, delays in shipping, and so forth. The problem is to determine the geographical pattern of warehouse locations that will be most profitable to the firm by equating the marginal cost of warehouse operation with the transportation cost savings and incremental profits resulting from more rapid delivery.

This heuristic program for locating warehouses consists of two parts—the main program and the bump and shift routine.[5] The main program locates warehouses one at a time until no additional warehouses can be added to the firm's distribution network without increasing total costs. Three principal heuristics are used in the main program. The first states that warehouse locations with promise will be at or near concentration of demand. Second, warehousing systems are generally developed by locating warehouses one at a time, adding at each step of analysis that warehouse which produces the greatest cost savings for the entire system. Finally, only a small subset of all possible warehouse locations need be evaluated in detail at each stage of the analysis to determine the next warehouse site to be added.

The bump and shift routine (entered after processing in the main program is complete) evaluates the profit implications of dropping individual warehouses or shifting them from one location to another. Then this routine modifies the solutions reached in the main program in two ways. First, it

---

[5] Alfred A. Kuehn and Michael J. Hamburger, "A Heuristic Program for Locating Warehouses," *Management Science*, July, 1963, pp. 643-666.

eliminates or bumps any warehouse which is no longer economical because the firm's customers can better be serviced by another warehouse. Second, it insures that the warehouse selected by the computer technique is the most economical to service the territory by shifting each warehouse from its currently assigned location to the other potential sites within its territory.

Experience with the program indicates that a heuristic approach to this class of problems is quite profitable in practice, producing near optimal solutions within acceptable limits of computer time. The use of heuristics in solving this problem has two distinct advantages over the currently available linear programming quantitative techniques. It has computational simplicity, which results in less computer time, and permits the treatment of large-scale problems. Second, the heuristic approach has flexibility with respect to the underlying cost functions, eliminating the need for restrictive assumptions. In addition, it represents an important extension for the simulation approach of locating warehouses since the heuristic approach generates at least one near optimal solution without reducing flexibility in the modeling of the problem.

Traveling Salesman Problem

One of the first applications of heuristic programming was the "traveling salesman problem" which asks the best route a salesman might take from some starting point in making a number of calls and returning home (to his original starting point). The best route is one that produces the minimum distance traveled, minimum time on the road, minimum cost, or optimizes some other criterion. The difficulty of the problem is entirely computational since the number of routes is generally quite large. Enumeration of all routes (N) is a discouraging process for a problem of any size since there are (N-1)! routes. Doubling the size of a problem from 5 to 10 cities multiplies the number of routes by about 15,000.

Mathematical programming approaches have had rather limited success with this problem. For a 20-city problem, integer programming requires 8000 variables and 440 constraints while dynamic programming is limited to a 13-city problem. Beyond these limits, time and storage requirements go up very rapidly. Also, the traveling salesman problem has been studied within the framework of linear programming, but the method is somewhat cumbersome in application and requires a great deal of computer time as integer programming.

The heuristic programming approach in solving a complex problem, such as visiting the 50 capitals of the United States or visiting 40 or 50 cities, makes use of two heuristics.[6] The first heuristic starts by constructing an initial route tour for three randomly chosen cities; it then adds the remaining cities one at a time to form a sequence of partial routes, the last one having all N cities in it. This is accomplished by the following three steps:

[6] P. J. Mudar, "Heuristic Programming," *Chemical Engineering*, Vol. 65, No. 12, December, 1969, pp. 20-24.

1. Choose any three cities to form an initial route of length 3. They can be listed in any order.
2. Choose any city from the list of remaining cities and try inserting it between each pair of the cities on the route of length 3 in order to compute the length of the resulting route. Select that route on 4 cities that has the shortest length.
3. Select any city from the list of remaining cities and insert it between each pair of cities on the route of length 4 in order to compute the length of the resulting route. Select that route on 5 cities that has minimum length and so forth.

This process will construct a variety of routes depending upon the order in which new cities are introduced within the process. For example, to start a problem, choose a random order in which to introduce the cities and repeat the process a number of times, say 100, saving the shortest one as the answer.

Although the above heuristic works well on small problems, it becomes too time-consuming on large ones. Therefore, a second heuristic is needed to cut off the extreme ends of the route and then solve the smaller problem defined with the remaining cities. The second heuristic is as follows:

1. Run the first heuristic 100 times saving the best route found.
2. For the best route, locate one of the extreme ends and determine a cut that will eliminate some of the cities.
3. Run the first heuristic 100 times more on the reduced problem saving the best route found.
4. In the best route, locate one of the extreme ends and make another cut.

This second heuristic is continued until no further cutting is possible. By eliminating cities, subproblems of smaller size are created, thereby making the problem easier to solve. This process allows the first heuristic a better chance of obtaining a good answer. The computer program itself makes all the cuts and defines all the subproblems that it works on. In a sense, it learns from its own computational experience. It can learn well or badly, depending on how much time is given to applying the first heuristic after a subproblem has been defined.

In summary, the foregoing heuristic programming approach focuses on solving a complex situation where the salesman's itinerary includes many cities and alternatives. As each city is added, the computer evaluates all of the alternative ways it can be incorporated into the current network. The computer program calculates the effect of inserting the salesman's call between each pair of cities that are visited in sequence at the previous stage of analysis. It chooses the most desirable point in the salesman's route at which to make the call, given that the balance of routing remains unchanged. This procedure is repeated indefinitely, starting each time with a random set of three cities and proceeding until a solution is reached.

The traveling salesman problem can be extended to more than one salesman. For example, the multiple salesmen formulation is appropriate in the problem of bank messenger scheduling. In this problem, a crew of messengers picks up deposits at branch banks and returns them to the central office for processing. This problem is exactly the m-salesman problem for a crew of m messengers and n branch banks. Thus, the multiple salesmen problem may be stated as follows. Given m salesmen and n cities, find m sorties such that every city (except the home city) is visited exactly once by only one salesman, so that the total distance traveled by all the salesmen is minimum. This is a generalization of the traveling salesman problem and can be solved by a branch and bound algorithm.[7] (Branch and bound algorithm is an iterative, structured search of feasible solutions to a problem.)

Project Scheduling

Another application is a heuristic program for project scheduling.[8] The basic heuristic program, shown in Figure 16-1, is based on three heuristics:

1. Allocate resources (men) serially in time. This means to start on the first day and schedule all jobs possible, then, do the same for the second day, and so forth.
2. Give preference to jobs with the least slack when several jobs compete for the same resources.
3. Reschedule noncritical jobs, if possible, in order to free resources for critical jobs having no slack.

To demonstrate how these three heuristic rules operate per the computer program, they will be applied to one part of the main project. This sub-section of the project consists of jobs, each of which requires a certain amount of time and a given number of men (Table 16-1). The assumptions for this group of jobs are: all eight men are interchangeable; jobs are undertaken only if sufficient manpower is available for the entire week; and certain jobs must be completed before others can begin. For example, job 8 in Table 16-1 cannot begin until jobs 5 and 6 have been completed.

The subsection under study can be illustrated as a network diagram in which each job appears as an arrow and each connection (small circles) indicates the predecessor relationship. This is depicted in Figure 16-2, where a horizontal time scale indicates the period during which the job is active. It should be noted that all jobs are started as early as their predecessors will allow. Dashed lines indicate slack time in the network. The number above each arrow indicates the job number; the number in brackets shows the number of men required. The manpower requirements in Figure 16-2 were calculated by summing vertically the crew size of all jobs active during a

---

[7] Joseph A. Svestka and Vaughn E. Huckfeldt, "Computational Experience with an M-Salesman Traveling Salesman Algorithm," *Management Science*, March, 1973, pp. 790-799.

[8] The source for material in this section is: Jerome D. Wiest, "Heuristic Programs for Decision Making," *Harvard Business Review*, Sept.-Oct., 1966, pp. 140-143.

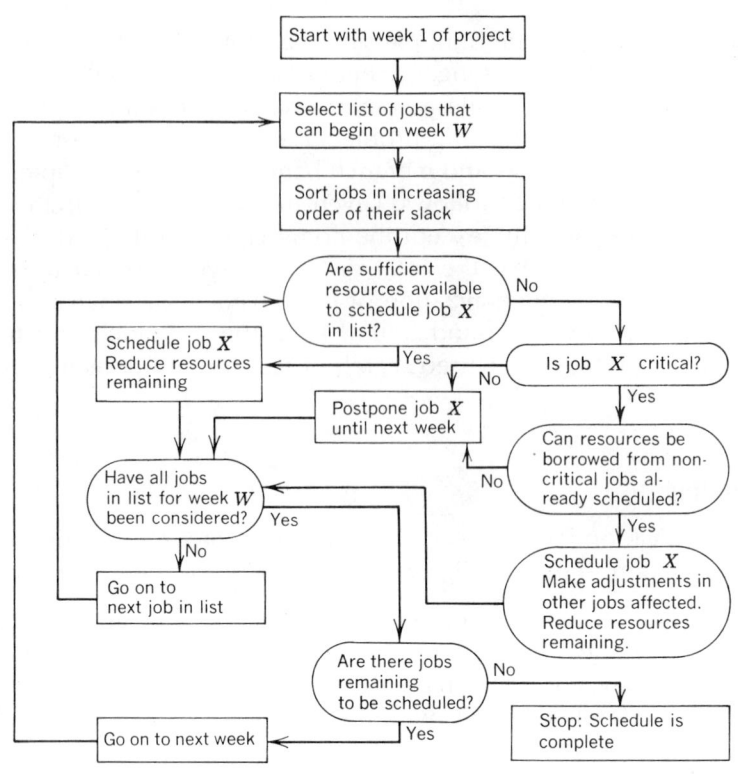

Figure 16-1 Heuristic program for scheduling a project. (*Note*: Week W is week under consideration; job X is job under consideration.)

specific week. For example, manpower requirements for the fourth week are 5 men for job 5 plus 4 men for job 6 plus 5 men for job 7, or 14 men.

Since we have only eight men available to assign to the project in any one week, we will have a problem from the beginning of the second scheduled week through the end of the fifth scheduled week. The problem is how to allocate the men in order to complete the project as soon as possible.

TABLE 16-1
Subsection of a Larger Project—Time and Men Required

Job Number	Preceding Jobs	Time (weeks)	Number of Men Required
1	—	1	8
2	1	2	4
3	1	2	2
4	1	1	4
5	4	3	5
6	3	2	4
7	2	2	5
8	5 and 6	1	8
9	8	2	8

528   OPERATIONS RESEARCH MODELS—ADVANCED TOPICS

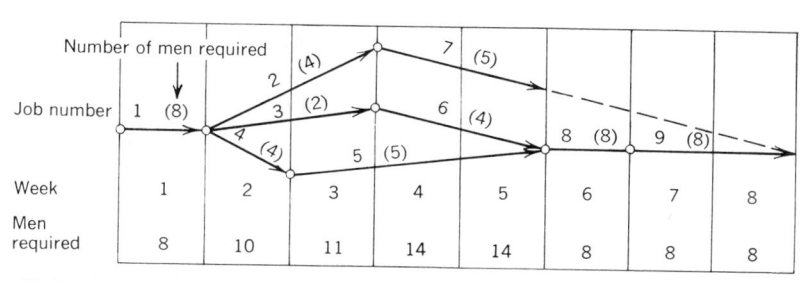

Figure 16-2 Network diagrams for subsection of a larger project—time and men required.

One way to find the shortest feasible schedule would be to enumerate all possible schedules. For the first week, there is only one possible choice of jobs (job 1), whereas for the second week, with three jobs available, there are several possible combinations. Each of these combinations represents a branch on a tree diagram and multiple choices fan out from each of these on succeeding weeks. A tree of all possible schedules is very large even for this small subsection of the project. The heuristic program trims this tree significantly since it selects just one branch at each decision point. Occasionally, the heuristic program will retrace its steps to see if a better branch can be found.

Starting with the first week and using the first heuristic (allocate men serially in time), only job 1 is available to start in this period. There are sufficient men to schedule it, that is, eight men required for job 1 during the first week of the project equals the eight men available. Slack is zero since it is a job on the critical path. For the second week, three jobs, jobs 2 through 4, can be started. However, not enough men are available to schedule these three jobs since they require ten men. The second heuristic calls for scheduling jobs with the least slack first or jobs 3 and 4 in the second week. Since job 2 has three weeks slack, jobs 3 and 4 will take first preference, followed by job 2. The calculations for the second week are:

Schedule job 4 (slack=0): 8−4=4 men remain
Schedule job 3 (slack=0): 4−2=2 men remain
Postpone job 2 (slack=3): Job 2 must be postponed since 2 men cannot start on a job that requires the use of four men at a time

In the problem, we assume that jobs cannot be interrupted once started. In the third week, 11 men are required (Figure 16-2), although only 8 men are available. The scheduling for the third week is as follows:

Continue job 3 (slack=0): 8−2=6 men remain

The third heuristic is now brought into play—noncritical jobs, still active, can be postponed if they do not delay the project. Job 2 satisfies this rule. This allows us to start job 5 in the third week which has no slack, making it critical.

HEURISTIC PROGRAMMING 529

Schedule job 5 (slack=0): 6−5=1 man remains
Postpone job 2 (slack=2): Job 2 again must be postponed since four men are needed at one time

The updated network diagram appears in Figure 16-3 at the end of the third week. In this figure, the men required for the remaining weeks is recomputed.

The scheduling for the fourth week is given as follows:

Continue job 5 (slack=0): 8−5=3 men remain
Postpone job 6 (slack=0): Need 4 men
Postpone job 2 (slack=1): Need 4 men

At the beginning of the fifth week, all jobs are critical, except job 2. Notice that at this point, the project has been delayed by one week due to the fact that job 6 was not started. The scheduling for the fifth week is as follows:

Continue job 5 (slack=0): 8−5=3 men remain
Postpone job 6 (slack=0): Need 4 men
Postpone job 2 (slack=1): Need 4 men

The scheduling for the sixth and seventh weeks is the same:

Schedule job 6 (slack=0): 8−4= men remain
Schedule job 2 (slack=1): 4−4=0 men remain

The network diagram for seven weeks is found in Figure 16-4. At this point, the project is two weeks behind schedule, the result of not starting job 6 on time.

The program decisions for the remaining weeks of the project are:

Eighth week—   Schedule job 8 (slack=0): 8−8=0 men remain
Ninth week—   Schedule job 9 (slack=0): 8−8=0 men remain
Tenth week—   Continue job 9 (slack=0): 8−8=0 men remain
Eleventh week—   Schedule job 7 (slack=1): 8−5=3 men remain
Twelfth week—   Continue job 7 (slack=0): 8−5=3 men remain

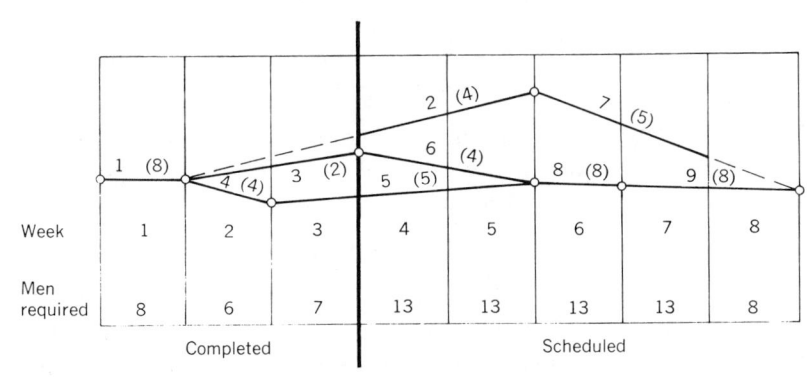

Figure 16-3 Network diagram after three weeks—subsection of a larger project.

530 OPERATIONS RESEARCH MODELS—ADVANCED TOPICS

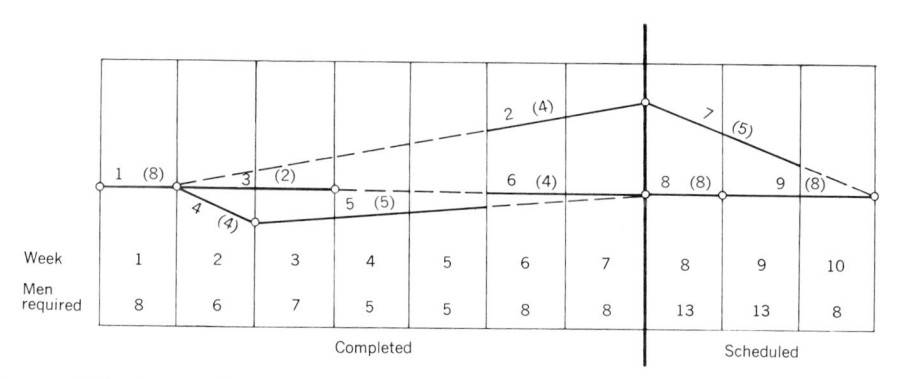

Figure 16-4 Network diagram after seven weeks—subsection of a larger project.

The final scheduling of all jobs appears in Figure 16-5. The manpower limit of eight men has resulted in a four-week increase in the project's length. The heuristic program has found an acceptable schedule even though other feasible schedules exist. None are shorter than the one found.

Other Heuristic Applications

In addition to the preceding heuristic programming examples, other heuristic applications that serve to discover or to stimulate investigation are set forth for functional areas of the firm. These examples illustrate the difficulty where all unknowns cannot be defined exactly or where several alternative actions appear to be equally desirable or undesirable. Likewise, they further demonstrate the procedural rules which are based both on intuitive judgment and on experience.

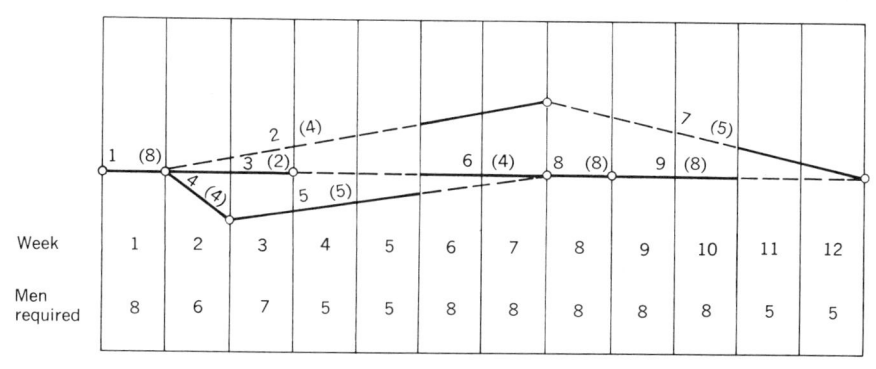

Figure 16-5 Completed network diagram after 12 weeks—subsection of a larger project.

HEURISTIC PROGRAMMING 531

Marketing

Heuristic programming has wide application in marketing. A systematic approach for generating new product ideas is important since 80 percent of new products fail. When the firm lacks a well-structured program, the timing of idea inputs will be random. Thus, the firm may be forced to develop poor ideas merely to keep people busy. All relevant concepts (factors) must be located such that they can be associated with a given product area. A total set of ideas is a set of all possible combinations. In the food processing industry, for example, a brownie mix is composed of sugar, chocolate, flour, walnuts, mix, and a box. The results are related to what, how, when, and why. Since the number of possibilities is enormous, heuristics can eliminate sets of alternatives less likely to yield good results.[9]

Several heuristics that have been developed for idea generation in this industry attempt to find combinations that have high positive interaction. For example, in generating "snack food" ideas, three factors which could be considered are chip, shake, and potato. Individually evaluated, each factor rates relatively low, but the combination potato and chip rates very high while the combination potato and shake appears marginal. In the first case, the interaction effect was positive, in the second negative. Without reviewing every possible combination of factors, some idea might be overlooked which indicates a strong positive interaction effect.

Although the use of heuristics only generates ideas and does not screen them, they do considerably reduce screening time. One heuristic is based on the observation that a majority of the positive interaction effects are at the two-factor level: that is, the *heart* of most food ideas can be described in a two-word combination (toaster tart) even though the idea is incomplete (e.g., it lacks flavors, ingredients, shape, and packaging).

A second heuristic is that certain cross classifications yield more interesting ideas than others. Different technologies applied to the various food forms often produce more meaningful concepts than combinations such as vegetables with fruits. Some specific heuristics for the food industry suggest cross classifications:

1. Kitchen appliances applied to various foods (toaster waffles).
2. Foods adapted to a different meal (breakfast milkshake).
3. Dessert words applied to nondessert foods (rice flakes cereal).
4. Gaps in consumer benefits applied to existing food forms (nutritious coffee).

To simplify usage, the more interesting cross classifications from the food industry application are arranged in matrix form.

In order to utilize the idea-generating grid, the creator is instructed to review each cell in the grid, place an X on the number of every word combination that represents an existing item on the market, and circle the number of any combination that might have market potential. After analyzing a grid, the creator should write a short statement about each interesting

[9] Edward M. Turner, "HIT: Heuristic Ideation Technique—A Systematic Procedure for New Product Search," *Journal of Marketing*, January, 1972, pp. 58-61.

combination, describing how he sees the product, its use, etc. Experience has shown that varying results are obtained from the same grid due to differences in background, knowledge, perception, task, and innate creativity. Since the combinations are incomplete ideas, visualizing the product requires imagination.

Another interesting marketing application of heuristic programming focuses on the introduction of a new product. Marketing management operates within such constraints as keeping the investment within a certain budget, the size of the factory capacity, and the size of the sales force. However, it does not have ample time to evaluate the many possible ways for introducing a new product. A heuristic program allows evaluation of many promising introductory solutions. Thus a heuristic approach can free the marketing manager to concentrate on developing a total program around one or more of the skeleton programs proposed by the heuristic program.

Heuristic programming has also been employed successfully by media and advertising personnel who have developed various heuristics or rules of thumb to use in reacting to competitive media strategies.[10] Initially, a predictive model is developed to evaluate expected market response due to an advertising media schedule considering the anticipated schedule of competitors as well as other major advertising phenomena. Heuristic search routines are used to select and schedule media with the objective of maximizing market response subject to budget limitations. The market response model divides people into market segments which are characterized by product class sales potential. Advertisements placed by competing firms cause people to be exposed to this advertising and thereby create a level of exposure value which decays over time in the absence of new exposures. The individual's response during a time period is a function of his retained exposure value for each competing firm and his market segment. Summing over time to obtain total market response is approximated analytically using media coverage and overlap data.

Manufacturing

A heuristic decision procedure for solving large-scale, single-machine trim problems has been developed for the paper industry.[11] When paper is sold as finished rolls of specific width and diameter, the problem is to formulate cutting patterns from the order rolls which will fit the stock rolls so that minimum side waste occurs. The following heuristic procedures are used in solving a problem of this kind:

1. Estimate the potential cost per roll for each order width with regard to trim waste.
2. Arrange the order width in a priority table according to current cost

---

[10] Leonard M. Lodish, "Considering Competition in Media Planning," *Management Science*, February, 1971, pp. B-293–B-306.

[11] Edwin C. Johns, "Problem Solving in the Paper Industry Through Operations Research," *Tappi*, May, 1966, Vol. 49, No. 5, pp. 137A-138A, and Robert W. Haessler, "A Heuristic Programming Solution to a Nonlinear Cutting Stock Problem," *Management Science*, August, 1971, pp. B-793–B-802.

estimates so that combinations involving order widths with high potential trim waste will be generated first.
3. Generate combinations involving the order widths with the highest cost until a combination is found with a trim waste equal to a lower boundary value.
4. Accept the combination that removes the highest potential trim and waste from the problem and schedule production rolls according to this pattern.
5. Update the cost estimates of the order rolls involved in the scheduled combinations and then go to Step 2 given above.

Using a computer, these heuristics have been utilized to solve problems with up to 100 different widths.

The problem of job shop scheduling can be characterized as a continuous flow of jobs into a plant where each job requires one or more operations to be performed on one or more machines. The problem is to schedule operations on the machines in order to minimize idle machine time, total time on jobs in the system, or some other criterion. Computer heuristic rules are used to decide which jobs will be scheduled, on what machines, and at what time. Each machine in the plant can be viewed as a service facility with a waiting line of jobs to be serviced. The simplest heuristic for determining the order of jobs in the first-in, first-out basis. Other heuristics can be applied where the longest jobs are scheduled first or jobs that can be finished first are the initial ones to be scheduled. Scheduling programs use these heuristic rules or some combination of them to take into account the constraints of the problem, such as machine capabilities, priority jobs, and sequencing constraints.[12] All are integrated into a program which specifies the order in which jobs are to be processed and on what machines.

When products are assembled on a conveyor line, there is a problem of assembly line balancing.[13] Ideally, each work station is manned by a single operator where the sum of the time at each station is equal to all other stations. However, an out of balance line usually results from the first attempt. The use of heuristics attempts to duplicate the procedures utilized by a human being. One current technique capitalizes on the speed of a computer to generate many solutions on a trial and error basis. The solutions are not completely random samples from the set of all possible combinations, but are biased in favor of the more promising combinations, the basic approach of the heuristic method.

Numerous heuristic techniques for minimizing costs in inventory problems have been developed. Many of these start with the basic EOQ formulas and proceed to highly sophisticated models. Despite the availability of precise inventory models, many firms, with thousands of different inven-

[12] Herbert G. Campbell, Richard A. Dudek, and Milton L. Smith, "A Heuristic Algorithm for the *n* Job, *m* Machine Sequencing Problem," *Management Science*, June, 1970, pp. B-630–B-637.

[13] Heskia Heskiaoff, "An Heuristic Method for Balancing Assembly Lines," *Western Electric Engineer*, October, 1968, pp. 9-16.

tory items, find it difficult to fit these models to their requirements and conditions because the assumptions of the model are not rightfully applicable; demand patterns are extremely unpredictable; accurate data is difficult to obtain; or the sheer magnitude of the problem frustrates attempts at analytical solutions. As a result of these problems, heuristic inventory rules are being employed. Computerized systems that contain analytical and heuristic elements are used for complex and somewhat poorly structured inventory problems. Since inventory decisions are directly related to marketing, manufacturing, and finance functions, the managers of these functions should have some say in establishing the heuristics that underlie the inventory control system.

A computerized heuristic model that creates a cost minimizing schedule for shortening the critical path of a PERT activity network to a desired length has been developed.[14] The model follows a series of systematic, logical steps similar to those an experienced analyst might follow. Some of the factors included in the model are: the amount of time that each alternate path in the network needs to be shortened (if any); the cost per unit of shortening each activity; the maximum amount that each activity can be shortened; and so forth. This model develops reduction schedules similar to those produced by alternative methods, such as linear programming.

Finance

As in marketing and manufacturing, finance is well suited for the application of heuristic models. A computer heuristic program, used in the selection of stocks for a portfolio, operates in the following manner.[15] A working list of stocks from which the investment officer will make all his portfolio selections is established and stored in the computer's memory. This preference list of stocks is designed to cover the various economic conditions and is updated periodically. Various data for each stock is also stored in memory. These include such items as price, growth rate, dividends paid, price/earnings ratio, and expected earnings. From this list of stocks, a portfolio is generated based on heuristics or rules of thumb which relate information about the client, the securities market, and the economy in the selection of stocks. The heuristics are compiled and based upon the study of the past decisions of the trust officer. The program keeps a history (in memory) of its past decisions and modifies its future behavior by eliminating unsuccessful procedures. In effect, the program learns from its past experience, thereby paralleling the human learning process.

Heuristic programming can be employed by most banks since they receive a large number of overdrafts or bad checks each day.[16] The building of the heuristic model begins by drawing up an initial list of variables that

[14] N. Siemens, "A Simple CPM Time-Cost Trade Off Algorithm," *Management Science*, February, 1971, pp. B-354–B-363.
[15] G. P. E. Clarkson, *Portfolio Selection: A Simulation of Trust Investment*, Englewood Cliffs, N.J.: Prentice-Hall, Inc., 1962.
[16] Hugh J. Watson, "Simulating Human Decision Making," *Journal of Systems Management*, May, 1973, pp. 24-27.

are important in deciding how to handle an overdraft. After empirical data has been gathered on these variables, it becomes evident that many of the variables initially suggested are relatively unimportant or can be grouped together. For example, to whom the check is written does not matter and is dropped from the model. Considerations, such as the depositor's income level and whether or not he maintains a savings account, are handled by a single "credit worthiness" variable. The resulting variables—type of account, number of overdrafts, credit worthiness, account balance, and amount of overdraft—are incorporated into a heuristic model which is programmed for computer processing. A few minutes of daily computer time can save hours of manual work for the firm's employees.

Advantages and Limitations of Heuristic Programming

Examination of the numerous heuristic programming applications presented in the chapter indicates several distinct advantages for this OR technique. Heuristic programs can be developed to solve specific problems while mathematical programming techniques are formalized into generalized programs to handle specific types of problems. In essence, heuristic procedures can be constructed rather freely, that is, in a common sense, intuitive manner. Essentially their programs are simulations of how a man might search for a good solution if he had precise rules for evaluating alternatives. Many times, heuristic programs run faster than equivalent mathematical programming formulations, allowing their use in a dynamic scheduling environment. Similarly, a considerable advantage in terms of developing and executing computerized heuristic programs is their low cost. With heuristics, programs which more accurately define the problem can be generated. This is particularly true with the handling of fixed and setup costs and when attention must be given to provisions of union contracts.

The foregoing advantages far outweigh the primary disadvantage of heuristic programming—it does not guarantee optimality. Basically, in the real world, we are not usually seeking optimal solutions, but "good" solutions. In fact many so-called algorithms end up in actual practice as heuristics because judgments have to be made which negate optimality. We often find that the *good* solutions generated by heuristic programs are better than the *best* solutions of optimizing routines because of more realistic problem definition. Thus, this limitation is not an important one when considering the foregoing factors.

Heuristic Programming Application—American Products Corporation

The American Products Corporation is currently reviewing the location of its fifteen company-owned warehouses throughout the country. Management desires a geographic pattern of warehouse locations which is most profitable to the firm subject to specific constraints of delivery time which is three days from the receipt of the order. Due to the nature of the problem, it was immediately given to the operations research group who decided to employ heuristic programming in the problem's solution.

After examining and isolating the important factors in the problem, the OR group decided to utilize the following heuristics in the computer program:

1. Consider only the obvious locations for warehouses, that is, locations near large centers of demand.
2. Add one warehouse at a time such that adding that warehouse produces the greatest cost savings.
3. After an initial assignment of warehouses, reevaluate them to determine if one or more have become uneconomical as the result of later assignments. Also try shifting each warehouse to other potential sites located near large demand centers.

The employment of the above heuristics produced a listing of warehouses quite different from the present structure. The computer printout indicated that lowest warehouse costs are achieved by closing several small warehouses throughout the country and reassigning their requirements to large warehouses located near large centers of demand. Overall costs of storing and transporting goods from a remotely located warehouse were higher than from a large, centrally located warehouse. The basic reason is the expansion of the interstate highway system over the past years, thereby reducing the costs from large, centrally located warehouses.

Summary

Heuristic methods of decision making have made inroads into many poorly structured problems that do not lend themselves to mathematical equations and well-structured problems that are difficult to solve. Operations researchers are showing that some decision processes can be formalized and described in terms of heuristic decision rules. To date, heuristic programs generally have been tailored to specific and narrowly defined problems. What the future will be in this area is open to discussion. Some see no limit to the use of heuristics, whereas others see a slower advancement in this area. The latter approach seems more realistic since new computer problem solvers will have to be developed, better programming languages will be needed, and more clever heuristics will be necessary. There is also the problem of acceptance by operating personnel. Heuristics (and any other quantitative method) yields computer outputs which have to be combined and tempered with managerial judgment for a final decision. In short, the combination of man, heuristics, and the computer can lead to accomplishments that none of them is capable of performing alone.

Questions

1. How does heuristic programming differ from other mathematical programming methods?
2. What is the principal limitation of heuristic programming?
3. List additional applications for heuristic programming not found in the chapter.

Problems

16-1 Develop a set of heuristics for vendor selection that can be utilized by purchasing agents employed in a large manufacturing firm. Not only will these rules of thumb be computerized, but they also will serve as a basis for judging how effective the firm's purchasing agents are performing their jobs.

16-2 Develop a set of heuristics for smoothing production in a large manufacturing plant that produces special orders on a short- to long-term basis. Consider overtime and moving production dates ahead to meet anticipated production completion dates.

16-3 The City of Huntswood currently has 40 trucks to handle its garbage disposal. Each garbage truck has a three-man crew that services approximately 500 residences daily. The mayor has been talking to other cities (of similar size) which employ fewer trucks than his own. The feedback that the mayor has received relates to applying OR techniques in solving the waste disposal problem, particularly, heuristic programming. He has asked you, a municipal consultant, to set up a list of heuristics that can be programmed by his computer staff. Admittedly, efficient routing requires both skill and aptitude. However, guided by these heuristics and a combination of your experience and their own, the mayor is expecting a more efficient routing system than present in order to reduce the cost of garbage disposal for the City of Huntswood.

16-4 The National Bank of Akron receives a large number of overdrafts, that is, checks written against insufficient funds. The number is usually between 150 and 300 per day. These "bad checks" are handled personally by a vice president who decides whether to pay or not to pay the check or to postpone the decision until the depositor has been contacted by phone. Approximately half of the vice-president's time is spent each day on this activity.

This vice-president that has hired you to computerize this phase of his job wants you to solve his problem by utilizing heuristic programming. Your analysis indicates that the final computer heuristic model must contain these variables:

1. Type of account—either regular or special (held by depositors who carry small balances and write few checks; thus overdrafts are seldom paid).
2. Account balance—either positive (multiple overdraft) or negative (nonmultiple overdraft) prior to receiving the bad check.
3. General credit worthiness of the depositor—either good, bad, or unknown as evaluated by the bank vice-president.
4. Amount of check—either small or large.

Based on the foregoing data, develop a heuristic program flowchart that can be converted to a computer program which will relieve the vice president of deciding whether to accept or reject bank overdrafts. In your flowchart, assume the cut off period for accepting overdrafts on regular, good accounts that are nonmultiple overdrafts to be $50.00 or less.

16-5 The Greenup Manufacturing Company has received a subcontract to manufacture a specialized piece of equipment for one of its customers. Requirements are such that each event in the order requires a certain amount of time and a given number of men to complete it. An important consideration in the problem is that each event cannot be undertaken unless there is sufficient manpower available for the entire week. (This condition is a part of the firm's contract with the union.) Also, the events must be undertaken in sequential order. The events, number of weeks, and number of men required are given as follows:

Event Number	Preceding Event	Time (Week)	Number of Men Required
1	—	1	6
2	1	2	2
3	1	3	4
4	3	2	4
5	4	1	5
6	2	3	6
7	5 and 6	2	4
8	7	2	6

Assuming six men are interchangeable and available at the beginning, determine the minimum time to complete the order given the above data. Also, develop appropriate heuristics that are used in the problem's solution.

Bibliography

J. S. Aronofsky, *Progress in Operations Research,* Volume III, New York: John Wiley & Sons, 1969.

E. H. Bowman and R. B. Fetter, *Analysis for Production and Operations Management,* Homewood, Ill.: Richard D. Irwin, 1967.

R. C. Meier, W. T. Newell, and H. L. Pazer, *Simulation in Business and Economics,* Englewood Cliffs, N.J.: Prentice-Hall, 1969.

D. W. Miller and M. K. Starr, *Executive Decisions and Operations Research,* Englewood Cliffs, N.J.: Prentice-Hall, 1969.

D. B. Montgomery and G. L. Urban, *Management Science in Marketing,* Englewood Cliffs, N.J.: Prentice-Hall, 1969.

F. M. Tonge, *A Heuristic Program for Assembly Line Balancing,* Englewood Cliffs, N.J.: Prentice-Hall, 1961.

F. Zwicky, *Discovery, Invention, Research Through the Morphological Approach,* New York: The MacMillan Company, 1969.

Chapter SEVENTEEN
Behavioral Models

Emphasis in the prior chapters has been on solving well-structured and poorly structured problems that are encountered by management and nonmanagement personnel. Beyond this dichotomy of problem structure, there are problems that are "behavioral" in nature. These problems focus on human behavior as found in the disciplines of psychology, sociology, political science, and, upon occasion, in economics. Hence, a multidisciplinary approach is needed to solve this class of problems. Although such an approach was encouraged in the 1950s, it was seldom used.

Behavioral problems present new challenges as well as obstacles to operations researchers. Recognition of the human element poses the question of how and when to include this element in an operations research model. How does the OR practitioner build "human constraints" into the model like mathematical constraints found in OR models? One school of thought ignores the human factor in modeling. The late Dr. Norbert Weiner, the communications theorist, cautioned: "There is much we must leave, whether we like it or not, to the 'unscientific.'" On the other hand, the more positive approach is to include the human constraints (if necessary) before completing the OR model. Dr. B. F. Skinner of Harvard University, a behavioral psychologist, has suggested that all human behavior can ultimately be interpreted in the rigorous language of mathematics. This latter viewpoint is studied in this chapter, particularly for a firm's customers and its employees.

Definition of Behavioral Models

The term "behavioral science" came into popular usage during the 1950s although it had been applied to business firms much earlier, starting with the Hawthorne experiments of Elton Mayo and F. J. Roethlisberger at Western Electric from 1927 to 1932. It was used as a shortened description for a six-year Ford Foundation program on individual behavior and human relations. Further popularization of this approach occurred with the establishment of the Foundation for Research on Human Behavior in 1952. Its objective was the support of behavioral research in business, government, and other organizations.

The science of behavioral research from the 1950s to the present day has been and continues to be concerned with three levels of analysis. First, the accent is on the behavior of the individual, that is, research is directed toward such topics as personality, motivation, attitudes, learning, coping with change, and leadership style. Second, the focus is on the behavior of the group. Such research of group behavior treats interaction patterns, group conflict, problem solving, emergent leadership, and group norms.

The third and last level of behavioral research deals with the organization as a whole. The effects on human behavior as related to the design of the firm's total system and comparison of organizations are examples of this last level of analysis. These three levels of behavior, then, have become the domain of researchers taking the behavioral science approach.

Before defining behavioral models, a contrast of the important differences between behavioral research and operations research might be helpful. Although both study the operation of organizations, the behavioral scientists are primarily interested in how decisions are made while operations researchers are concerned with how they ought to be made. However, both research methodologies are problem oriented. Behavioral research is generally inductive since it tends to draw from statistics, psychology, and sociology while operations research is largely deductive, drawing largely from nonstatistical OR techniques. In essence, behavioral scientists are concerned with describing the nature of operations while operations researchers are interested in prescribing their nature.

Despite these differences and the fact that the behavioral sciences have had little or no impact on operations research, there is a great need to integrate behavioral research into the discipline of OR. The motivation and satisfaction of the employee have a profound effect on the way functions are performed as well as the way in which decisions are made. The usefulness of a custom-made mathematical model which optimizes the firm's goals and objectives is severely limited if it ignores the human problems that directly affect the model. A firm's success depends on its functioning as a coordinated unit, one that melds the human element with its environment.

Based on the integration of these disciplines, researchers need to construct behavioral models which explain and quantify the behavior of the human element. These models can be defined as the study of observable and verifiable human behavior that employ scientific procedures, such as the experimental method and the planned approach. They are largely inductive with special focus on why customers or employees behave as they do whether as an individual, a member of a small or large group, or a member of a market segment or firm.

Underlying Theory of Many Behavioral Models

The underlying theory of many behavioral models is based upon satisfying customer and employee needs. Although customer satisfaction from a product or service differs from employee job satisfaction, they have similarities in terms of the varying levels of satisfaction and a hierarchy of needs as postulated by Maslow. Maslow's hierarchy, ranging from the lowest level to the highest, is:

1. Physiological—the needs of survival, food, clothing, shelter, sex, etc.
2. Security—the needs for safety from danger, threat, and deprivation.
3. Affiliation—the needs of socializing with fellow members for friendship and love.

4. Esteem—the needs of being held in high regard by oneself as well as by friends and associates.
5. Self-actualization—the needs for self-fulfillment through the development of skills, powers, and creativity.

Basically, he hypothesized that once a lower order need was satisfied, only appeal to the next higher need could motivate an individual.

Based upon Maslow's hierarchy of needs, both customer satisfactions and employee needs can be classified further. Customer satisfactions can be summarized into three major categories (from the lowest to the highest):

- Economic
- Physical
- Psychological

Similarly, employee needs can be set forth within three major categories (again from the lowest to the highest):

- Economic
- Social
- Ego

Customer Satisfactions

The first level of customer satisfactions (economic) is governed by the stated price of the product or service. If the price is too high in relation to the satisfaction expected by the customer, the seller has a high probability of losing the sale. Regarding the second level (physical), the customer asks himself or herself: Will the product or service add to my physical well being? Will the end result of buying the product or service enhance the individual in a physical way? If the answer is yes, the seller has a chance to profit from the sale. The third and final level (psychological) of customer satisfaction is much more complex than the prior two. Customer behavior at this level (mental versus physical of the prior level) focuses on a large number of psychological factors, such as attention, attitude, motive, overt search, which intervene between the marketing stimuli and the customer's response. Similarly, social class, cultural background, hereditary factors, and peer groups also are determinants of customer responses on the psychological level.

The foregoing three levels of customer satisfaction can be applied to any product or service. Unless a given product or service can legitimately claim that it does a better job than its competitors in providing one or more of these consumer satisfactions, it has not really established its right to be represented in the marketplace. Although this principle has always been true for products and services in abundant supply, it operates more noticeably today due to product dynamics, that is, life cycles of products have become shorter. The causes of shorter life cycles are:

- Increasing consumer sophistication resulting from higher education levels, and changes in income distribution which permit more people to exercise greater brand choice.

- Proliferation of consumer choice, both within and between product categories.
- More effective mass-media advertising.
- Increased sophistication of retailers aided by computerization which is reflected in quicker decisions about a given brand's viability.

Thus, the degree of customer satisfaction for one or more of the three levels determines the potential salability of a given product or service.

Employee Needs

Employee needs, like customer satisfactions, are an essential part of behavioral models. The first category (economic) focuses on the individual's need to provide for himself or herself and family obligations through periodic wage or salary payments. The next higher need level (social) recognizes man as a social being, that is, the social need for working in groups, the necessity to lean on others for support and encouragement, and reassurance as to job security. The highest level of needs (ego) is directed toward status in the eyes of coworkers as well as a need for recognition, attention, and affection. This last level is the individual's accomplishment of short- to long-range goals. To state it another way, the accent is on self-realization in his or her endeavors.

To illustrate the effect of the three need levels on an individual, consider a systems change from a manually oriented environment to one that employs operations research models in a real-time computer environment. In such a situation, research has indicated that the individual has a natural tendency to resist changes, tends to believe rumors versus facts, needs continuous motivation, is concerned with his or her short- to long-range plans within the firm, and is influenced by key employees. In such a changing environment, the individual is more concerned about social and ego needs as opposed to economic needs. Social acceptance in a new environment by his fellow workers is of great importance. Will new working conditions mean isolation from the individual's present friends? Similarly, how will the new job meet his or her ability and talents? Will the newly created position present too much of a challenge or will it mean that the individual must look elsewhere for work since he or she lacks the appropriate skills? Thus, the three levels of needs take on important dimensions for the individual and affect his or her behavior. The individual's varying levels of behavior serve as input to behavioral models.

Designing Behavioral Models

Designing behavioral models is similar to developing any OR mathematical model. Using the six steps of the planned approach (updated scientific method), the model designer begins by studying the underlying behavioral facts, opinions, and symptoms concerning the problem (first step). A thorough understanding of the behavioral process leads to a definition of the real problem (second step). Depending on the nature of the problem, it could be customer dissatisfaction with specific products or poor morale within certain departments. In other cases, the real behavioral problem might be focused on the "power" structure of the physical distribution system or on the firm's relationship with its creditors. No matter the source of the real problem, it must be defined clearly and objectively.

Before attempting to formulate tentative hypotheses or alternative solutions to the behavioral problem (third step), some fundamental law or established theory should be employed to provide an underlying structure or logical framework for developing hypotheses or solutions. For example, in certain marketing problems, "carryover effects" which can be defined as the effects that current marketing expenditures have on sales beyond the current period should be an integral part of the marketing behavioral model. Similarly, certain employee behavioral models that relate to need levels and corresponding satisfactions thereof should include Maslow's hierarchy of needs. Thus, the third step of the planned approach links the problem to be solved with some underlying law or theory when developing tentative behavioral models or hypotheses.

Next, the model designer studies the behavioral process in some detail. Based on an ample number of observations, he summarizes the data and tests the observed data according to the hypotheses. The modeler lists the variables that appear to play an important role in the behavioral environment being studied. Thus, he begins with some behavioral notion of what affects these variables and runs statistical tests of how in actual practice each has correlated with the elements for which he is trying to find valid relationships.

Having arrived at a list of important variables, he structures the variables in a logical, mathematical way. As the model builder develops different behavioral models based on selected hypotheses, he drops and downgrades the variables that have lesser importance. Similarly, he eliminates those models (built on the selected hypotheses) that appear least promising by testing them against the observed data. Finally, he selects the most promising behavioral model that conforms as closely as possible to the observed data (fourth step). Although the final mathematical model need not have the extreme complexities of the real world, its structure must follow reality so that the results parallel the real world.

Using the concept that the model is only an approximation of the real behavioral environment, the decision maker wants an accurate and workable solution. In effect, he employs the computer to focus on what is most likely to occur, then selects a safe range around it. Desiring that range to be as narrow as possible, he will try to make good decisions relative to it. Throughout the implementation phase (fifth step), the computer is assisting the decision maker—not replacing him—in verifying the optimum behavioral solution.

Because a behavioral model is dynamic and depicts a situation over time, the model builder must be alert to shifts that take place in an ever-changing world. Thus, there must be provision for periodic evaluation which insures that the model is still representative of the real world (sixth step).

The preceding material has emphasized the underlying aspects of behavioral models, with special reference to customer satisfactions and employee needs. The remainder of the chapter centers on developing sample applications of marketing behavioral models and employee behavioral models. By no means do these few examples exhaust the possible applications of behavioral operations research.

Marketing Behavioral Models

Marketing behavioral theory, like other functional behavioral theory, occurs at both a theoretical and a practical level. From a theoretical standpoint, the more and different implications that can be derived from a behavioral theory, the more credible or reliable is that theory. Marketing offers numerous opportunities for testing existing theories of human behavior as well as offering new opportunities for abstracting new behavioral theories.

In addition to common theoretical concerns, there are common practical or implemental concerns with which the marketing manager must contend. He must promote the acceptance or continued use of a product or service among some specified market segment under conditions of limited resources and competing influences. To do this, he must differentiate his own ideas, products, or services from those of his competitors. He is faced with the common task of understanding the relevant wants of particular groups and developing an appropriate offering and strategy when communicating to the public.

Marketing, more than other social action disciplines, appears to have developed a more systematic approach to the study of its activities. Marketing concepts, such as product differentiation, service offerings, competitive strategies, promotion, and distribution, are tools which enable marketing managers to better utilize their knowledge of human behavior in order to accomplish the desired changes. Marketing, then, has the capacity to integrate marketing knowledge within behavioral models to attain the desired response in the marketplace.

Customer Buying Behavioral Model

Before presenting a sample problem, a brief discussion of the distinct stages through which a potential customer passes before purchasing a brand-new product should be helpful. The "hierarchy of effects" model, proposed by Lavidge and Steiner in their studies of advertising effects, postulates six stages. Awareness (first stage) is followed by knowledge (second stage) of the product, resulting in a liking (third stage) for the item. Preference (fourth stage) can lead to a conviction (fifth stage) about the desirability of the product and a resulting purchase (sixth stage). Thus, each stage leads to another and, in many cases, to a purchase.

The foregoing stage-by-stage approach and other comparable schemes assume that there is a unidirectional passage through which the customer passes. Although this may describe the experience of the average individual, Palda[1] and other marketing theorists have pointed out that some of these six stages may actually be reversed. For example, a shopper may become aware of an item in a store, buy it without really assessing its benefit, and only then experience a preference for it. In this case, preference follows purchase rather than preceding it.

Since we will be discussing a problem revolving around buying habits for brand-new products, there is a tendency for the innovators or first buyers to have certain characteristics. They tend to have a higher educational level and a higher income; they tend to be more cosmopolitan and trend setters. The innovators are followed by the early adopters, the early majority, the late majority, and finally, the laggards. This generalized theory will be evident in the following problem.

The illustrative problem involves the evaluation of women's buying habits for three new cosmetics introduced via TV advertisements during a 10-week, one-half hour documentary series, "Woman and Her World." Following this time period, 600 women, classified as to the following education levels—college, graduate; college, 3 to 4 years; college, 1 to 2 years; high school; and grade school—were asked how many purchases they had made for each product and their reason for purchase: price, need, or attention. The anticipated result is that exposure to TV commercials for new products causes different buying patterns based on the educational level of the viewers. In effect, exposure to TV advertisements about a new cosmetic gives women of varying educational background a different message about the desirability of the product, thereby, leading to its purchase for differing reasons: price, need, and attention.

Due to the diverse educational levels desired for the sample population, telephone calls were made prior to the documentary series in order to classify them within the desired educational categories. The respondents in each group were promised a check for $5.00 if a summary (Table 17-1) of

TABLE 17-1
Forms Mailed and Completed by Participants

Fill In the Number of Purchases During the 10-Week Period for the Reasons Given

Cosmetic Sales Based Upon:	Ten-Week Period		
	Product 1	Product 2	Product 3
Price (equal or lower in price than competition)			
Need (adds to physical appearance)			
Attention (attracts attention of others—men and women)			

[1] Kristian S. Palda, "The Hypothesis of a Hierarchy of Effects: A Partial Evaluation," *Journal of Marketing Research*, February, 1966, pp. 13-24.

their purchases was properly completed and mailed on time (within two weeks at the close of the documentary). Because some participants did not comply with the stated conditions, usable replies were received from approximately 100 women in each education group. For ease of comparison, the first 100 respondents in each group were used.

A summary of usable replies, set forth in Table 17-2, centers on why purchasers bought the cosmetic products. Comparison of the three reasons for buying product 1 only are illustrated in Figure 17-1 by education level. Comparable bar diagrams could be drawn for products 2 and 3. However, the following discussion focuses on product 1 only.

Examination of Figure 17-1a reveals that the number of purchases for product 1, based on price (equal or lower in price than competition), tends to cluster together regardless of the educational level. Similarly, the same clustering effect is found in Figure 17-1b for need (adds to physical appearance). However, the last scatter diagram relating to attention (attracts

TABLE 17-2
Summary of Cosmetic Sales During 10-Week Period for 500 Participants

Educational Level	Product 1	Product 2	Product 3	Totals
Grade School				
Price	24	21	20	65
Need	29	26	25	80
Attention	23	27	25	75
High School				
Price	28	25	32	85
Need	26	22	32	80
Attention	31	29	25	85
College—1 to 2 years				
Price	25	30	25	80
Need	23	27	25	75
Attention	36	30	34	100
College—3 to 4 years				
Price	16	14	15	45
Need	30	22	28	80
Attention	55	45	40	140
College—Graduate				
Price	22	15	18	55
Need	28	26	26	80
Attention	45	48	42	135
Totals				
Price	115	105	110	330
Need	136	123	136	395
Attention	190	179	166	535
	441	407	412	1260

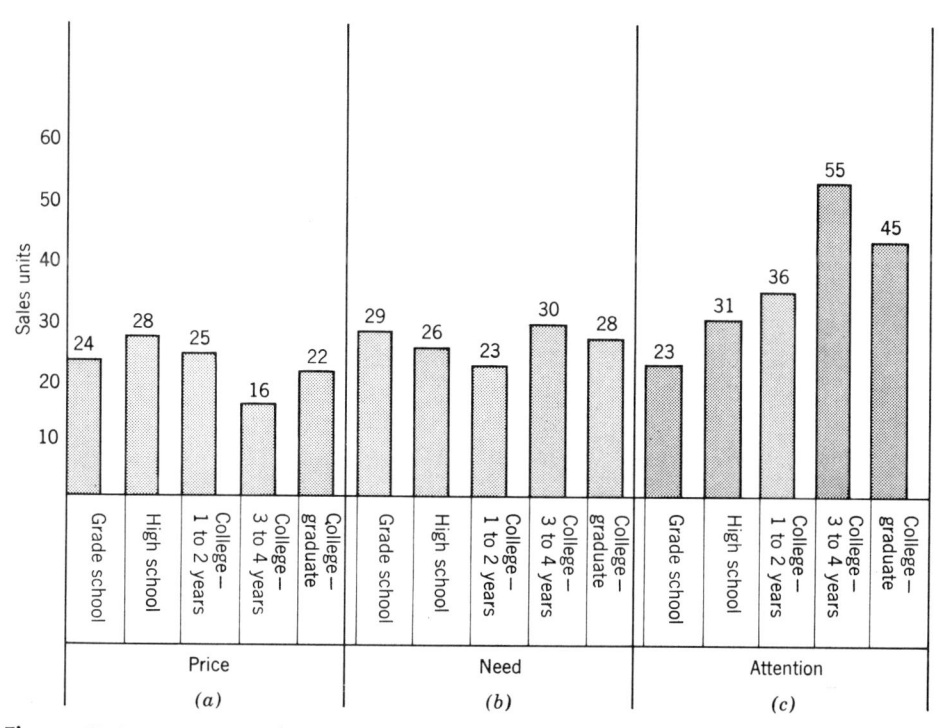

Figure 17-1 Bar groups for cosmetic sales of product 1 only—based upon fulfilling three customer satisfactions.

attention of others—men and women) indicates that graduate and college-educated women find this a much more important factor than high-school and grade-school women. Referring to our earlier discussion, this study establishes the fact that the higher educated tend to be more of the innovators than their lower educated counterpart for the attention factor. In summary, buying patterns when related to the three variables—price, need, and attention—differ depending on the educational level, especially for the attention variable, but less so for the price and need variables. Also, analysis of product 1 (comparable analyses are found with products 2 and 3) indicates that the more important variable in the documentary series for selling the most products is the one focusing on customer attention (sales—190 units) as opposed to price (sales—115 units) and need (sales—136 units).

Now that the behavioral aspects have been illustrated, the technique of dynamic programming can be applied to analyze the problem further. Within the framework of dynamic programming, an equation that expresses the maximum number of units sold for products 1, 2, and 3 for various educational levels during the test period can be developed. It is given as follows:

$$F_3(A_3) = \max_{0 \leq A_2 \leq A_3} [F_2(A_2) + f_3(A_3 - A_2)] \quad \text{(Equation 17-1)}$$

BEHAVIORAL MODELS 549

where

$F_2(A_2)$ = maximum number of products 1, 2, and 3 sold to various educational levels during the test period for one (or more) factors
$F_3(A_3)$ = maximum number of products 1 and 2 sold to various educational levels during the test period for one (or more) factors
$f_3(A_3 - A_2)$ = maximum number of product 3 sold to various educational levels during the test period for one (or more) factors

The term $F_2(A_2)$ in the above equation can be stated in tabular form, as in Table 17-3. Inspection of this table reveals, based on the attention factor only for products 1 and 2, that the optimum number of units sold to various educational levels is the starred(*) amounts for each column. In a similar manner, the term $F_3(A_3)$, based on the various educational levels, is represented by the starred items in Table 17-4. Since our interest is directed to

TABLE 17-3
Number of Cosmetic Sales for Products 1 and 2 Based on Attention Factor Only

		Product 1—Educational Level				
		Grade School	High School	College— 1 to 2 yr	College— 3 to 4 yr	College— Graduate
Number of Units Sold		23	31	36	55	45
Product 2—Educational Level						
Grade school	27	50	58	63	82	72
High school	29	52	60	65	84	74
College—1 to 2 yr	30	53	61	66	85	75
College—3 to 4 yr	45	68	76	81	100	90
College—graduate	48	71*	79*	84*	103*	93*

* Number of units sold are the maxima for each column.

TABLE 17-4
Number of Cosmetic Sales for Products 1, 2, and 3 Based on Attention Factor Only

		Products 1 and 2—Educational Level				
		Grade School	High School	College— 1 to 2 yr	College— 3 to 4 yr	College— Graduate
Number of Units Sold (Per Table 17-3)		71	79	84	103	93
Product 3—Educational Level						
Grade school	25	96	104	109	128	118
High school	25	96	104	109	128	118
College—1 to 2 yr	34	105	113	118	137	127
College—3 to 4 yr	40	111	119	124	143	133
College—graduate	42	113*	121*	126*	145*	135*

* Number of units sold are the maxima for each column.

that combination of educational levels which results in the highest number of products sold based on the attention factor only, reference must be made to Table 17-4 first. The highest starred value in the table is 145 units, denoting the college—graduate level for product 3 and the college—3-to-4 years level for products 1 and 2. Examination of Table 17-3 indicates that the optimum combination is the college—3-to-4 years level for product 1 and the college—graduate level for product 2. Thus, the following combination is the maximum sale for each product given the various educational levels in the problem (for attention factor only):

Educational Level	Product	Number of Units Sold
College—3 to 4 years	1	55
College—graduate	2	48
College—graduate	3	42
		145

It should be noted that the preceding analysis has reached the same result as indicated earlier, that is, TV documentary advertising was more effective in reaching the higher-educated women than the lower-educated ones.

In addition to solving the problem using dynamic programming, a statistical technique, such as chi-square, could have been employed for determining the pattern of numbers.

Sales—Advertising Behavioral Model

Marketing theorists and practitioners have an underlying maxim that an increase in the advertising expenditures for a product should produce a corresponding increase in sales. However, several important questions must be answered. Do sales always respond to an increase in advertising? And if so, by how much will sales respond to an increase in advertising? To answer these questions, progressive marketers have turned to operations research.

Early attempts to solve these problems employed statistical techniques to determine the relationship between sales and advertising. However, the results were unreliable and left marketing researchers with inadequate methods for finding a relationship that they were convinced existed. Toward the late 1950s, Vidale and Wolfe[2] integrated behavioral science with OR to make these problems amenable to solution. They found that a model based on three behavioral characteristics reliably predicted the effect of increased advertising on sales.

The first characteristic in the model is the market potential or saturation level (M). This is simply the number of available consumers with a need that the product can satisfy. The factor is certainly necessary since, as the market becomes saturated thereby leaving few potential customers, a sub-

---

[2] M. L. Vidale and H. C. Wolfe, "An Operations-Research Study of Sales Response to Advertising," *Operations Research*, June, 1957, pp. 370-381.

stantial increase in advertising expenditures (A) will have little effect on the level of sales (S). Secondly, a sales decay constant (λ) is included in the model. Since an individual's needs are dynamic, some of those who purchased in previous periods will discontinue buying in the upcoming period(s). (This is sometimes referred to as product obsolescence.) The last characteristic to be included in the model is the sales response constant (r). This represents the responsiveneses of consumers to advertising for the product in question.

With these three characteristics, the Vidale and Wolfe model for changes in the sales level is:

$$\frac{dS}{dt} = \left[rA \frac{(M-S)}{M} \right] - \lambda S \qquad \text{(Equation 17-2)}$$

An important function of this model is to determine a level of advertising expenditures required to maintain a given sales level. If no change in sales level is desired, the first derivative of sales (d S/d t) is set equal to zero. Thus, the revised equation is:

$$\frac{dS}{dt} = \left[rA \frac{(M-S)}{M} \right] - \lambda S = 0$$

$$\frac{rA(M-S)}{M} = \lambda S$$

$$A = \left(\frac{\lambda}{r}\right) \frac{SM}{(M-S)} \qquad \text{(Equation 17-3)}$$

To illustrate Equation 17-3, suppose a company wants to maintain sales of $10,000 per month (S) in a market that has potential sales of $20,000 per month (M). We will assume that $5 in sales is generated by $1 in advertising (r) when S=0. The sales constant decay (λ) is 5 percent per month. Hence, the amount of advertising required to maintain a $10,000 sales level per month is $200, calculated as follows:

$$A = \left(\frac{.05}{5}\right)\left(\frac{\$10,000 \times \$20,000}{\$20,000 - \$10,000}\right)$$
$$A = .01 \times \$20,000$$
$$A = \$200$$

If sales (S) are $15,000 and all other variables remain the same, the advertising (A) must be $600. Both advertising amounts ($200 and $600) are shown in Figure 17-2. The resulting curve shows the decreasing effectiveness of advertising expenditures. Numerous test cases have established the reliability of this model.

In summary, the formulation of this sales-advertising model introduces behavioral aspects whereas earlier models relied solely on quantitative aspects.

Employee Behavioral Models

Examination of the underlying human behavioral factors on the job is the focal point of employee behavioral models. In some cases, the important

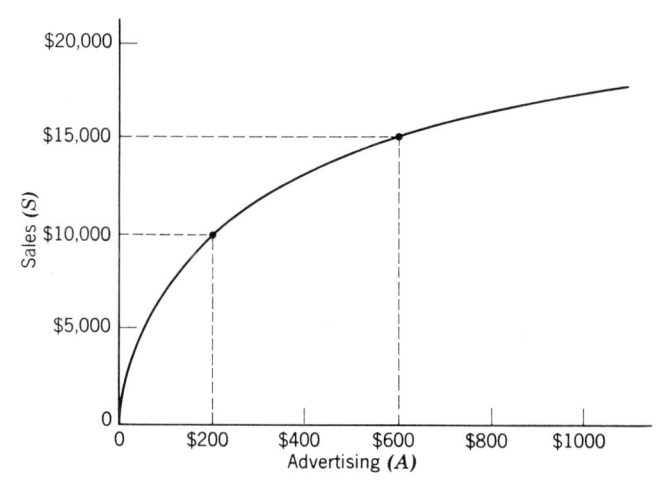

Figure 17-2 Effectiveness of advertising expenditures decreases as they approach the market saturation level.

factors are the environment of the work place and the individual's needs (Maslow's hierarchy of needs). In other situations, the underlying factors for desirable or undesirable behavior go beyond the firm and are influenced by demands from the home and sometimes the neighborhood. No matter what the source of human behavior, the objective of employee behavioral models within the firm is to determine what these factors are and, where there are deficiencies of human behavior on the job, to isolate them so that these human problems can be remedied. Thus, the application of the employee behavioral models is a challenging job for any group of behavioral operations researchers.

Evaluation of employees within the framework of behavioral models can start with their reasons for working. Most often, the principal initial objective is the satisfaction of basic needs, particularly self-maintenance (food, clothing, and shelter) and self-perpetuation (sex), noted previously as economic needs. As a consequence of these universal needs, the individual's internal drives and motivation provide him with a capacity for either a positive or negative evaluation of this objective. After the individual's economic needs have been met, more important factors come into play. Specifically, social needs and ego needs on the job as well as the home interact and affect the individual's performance positively or negatively. Based on the individual's perception of these internal and external factors, specific values and guidelines are formulated for obtaining specific needs on the job. The individual's perceived nature of these needs determines the type of behavioral response: good, bad, or indifferent. In essence, the employee's perception of his or her needs plus the internal and external environmental factors determine the behavioral response of the individual on the job.

Although the foregoing behavioral response process may appear to be somewhat straightforward, it is actually a very complex process. For example, when two people decide to marry, generally their values change drastically, resulting in a new set of needs on the job. Also, the rearing of children again results in a new set of values and resultant needs. Similarly, the entry and exit of personnel from a firm with different sets of values and needs cause never-ending changes within the firm. The ever-changing external environment affects life-styles and, consequently, the resulting needs of the firm's employees. This constant interchange among these factors can cause rapid changes in behavioral responses. The need for employee behavioral models in a fast-changing environment, then, is quite obvious.

Motivation Theory Behavioral Model
Maslow's theory, as described earlier, assumes five broad levels of needs: physiological, security, affiliation, esteem, and self-actualization. Since his theory has been so widely publicized, one may get the impression it represents a law so fundamental as not to be challenged. However, a number of "caveats" must be explored that represent areas of possible challenge.

Maslow's original work presented very little research methodology or data to support the motivation theory. He himself stated that his postulation on motivation was to serve as a conceptual framework on which more substantive research should be performed. Also, he admitted that many of the needs, although they may exist, exist at the subconscious level. A further difficulty exists since one assumes that all behavior is "motivated" (i.e., to seek good or avoid evil). If guided by this theory, one must seek another theory to explain worker behavior that is by definition "unmotivated." In other words, to build on Maslow's theory leaves one with two alternatives. The first is to assume that all behavior is motivated and therefore presumed to be within the conceptual boundaries of Maslow. The second is to seek a theoretical structure to explain unmotivated behavior. It was perhaps unfortunate that following close on the "heels" of Maslow, McGregor published his Theory X and Theory Y ideas which were based on the Maslow theory and were so eagerly accepted as dogma. Perhaps the existence of so little empirical research gives testimony to the difficulty that one finds in applying Maslow's theory.

One may ask why a theory that was admittedly based on little research and has been subsequently subjected to few studies is so universally embraced. There are several reasons. The most attractive aspect is that it intuitively seems real—it makes sense. The second reason, related to the first, is its multidimensional structure—it seems practical. So therein lies the problem. Because it seems to represent a portion of the real world as most people view it, it also contains the unpredictability of the real world and the people in it. Maslow's theory, therefore, does not lend itself to simplistic, univariate structuring.

The following example, proposed by Chung,[3] will demonstrate that although some social scientists decry quantification as an attempt to emulate

[3] Kae H. Chung, "A Markov Chain Model of Human Needs: An Extension of Maslow's Need Theory," *Academy of Management Journal*, Volume 12, No. 2, June, 1969, pp. 223-234.

the physical sciences, many meaningful overlaps exist that can provide meaningful insights for future managers. Unlike many previous theories that relate motivation to need fulfillment, the model presented is dynamic and probabilistic in nature. It is *dynamic* in that it does not see a specific set of gratifications linearly related to a comparable set of needs, but recognizes the uniqueness of the interrelated nature of satisfactions. It is *probabilistic* since both needs and values to satisfy them are related to some prior state of being. In addition, it is probabilistic in that it recognizes the heuristic nature of our being, that is, new values are sought as prior needs are satisfied. Similarly, these values are predictable.

As explained in an earlier chapter, Markov chains involve dynamic, probabilistic, and multivariate variables which assume that the characteristics of a given state are dependent on the activity of the immediately preceding period. Therefore, to apply Markov chains to Maslow's theory, we must determine the initial state of the need system. This can be undertaken by asking an individual how much time is spent satisfying his needs at each level and then express them as percentages. In the sample illustration, we will assume that a person has the following needs at the time of his change in states: physiological, security, affiliation, esteem, and self-actualization.

$$N^0 = \begin{pmatrix} .15 \\ .20 \\ .30 \\ .25 \\ .10 \end{pmatrix}$$

The transition probabilities can be calculated by asking or even observing how an individual will reallocate his time between the needs he is attempting to satisfy. If a given state (N^t) is dependent on the outcomes of the previous state (N^{t-1}), the movements from one state to another can be expressed as the transition probabilities (P). The matrix of transition probabilities is shown in Table 17-5 where N_1 through N_5, going from the lowest level to the highest level, represents Maslow's hierarchy of needs.

If the change in states is represented by the (P) values in Table 17-5, the following states can be predicted since $N^t = (P)(N^{t-1})$. Using matrix multiplication, the calculated state values for the next period or N^1 are given below:

N_1 row $\times N^0$
.40 × .15 = .0600
.15 × .20 = .0300
.10 × .30 = .0300
.05 × .25 = .0125
.00 × .10 = .0000
   .1325

N_2 row $\times N^0$
.25 × .15 = .0375
.35 × .20 = .0700
.15 × .30 = .0450
.10 × .25 = .0250
.05 × .10 = .0050
   .1825

N_3 row $\times N^0$
.20 × .15 = .0300
.25 × .20 = .0500
.35 × .30 = .1050
.25 × .25 = .0625
.15 × .10 = .0150
   .2625

N_4 row $\times N^0$
.15 × .15 = .0225
.20 × .20 = .0400

N_5 row $\times N^0$
.00 × .15 = .0000
.05 × .20 = .0100

TABLE 17-5
Matrix of Transition Probabilities (P) Based on Maslow's Hierarchy of Needs

	Physiological N_1	Security N_2	Affiliation N_3	Esteem N_4	Self-Actualization N_5
Physiological N_1	.40	.15	.10	.05	.00	→ Gains
Security N_2	.25	.35	.15	.10	.05	↓ Losses
Affiliation N_3	.20	.25	.35	.25	.15
Esteem N_4	.15	.20	.25	.40	.30	↙
Self-Actualization N_5	.00	.05	.15	.20	.50
	1.0	1.0	1.0	1.0	1.0	Retentions

$$.25 \times .30 = .0750$$
$$.40 \times .25 = .1000$$
$$.30 \times .10 = \underline{.0300}$$
$$.2675$$

$$.15 \times .30 = .0450$$
$$.20 \times .25 = .0500$$
$$.50 \times .10 = \underline{.0500}$$
$$.1550$$

Thus, the problem can be stated for period N^1 as follows:

	Transition Probabilities (P)					This Period—Needs at the Time of Change in States	Next Period—Calculated State Values
	N_1	N_2	N_3	N_4	N_5	N^0	N^1
N_1	.40	.15	.10	.05	.00	.15	.1325
N_2	.25	.35	.15	.10	.05	.20	.1825
N_3	.20	.25	.35	.25	.15	.30	.2625
N_4	.15	.20	.25	.40	.30	.25	.2675
N_5	.00	.05	.15	.20	.50	.10	.1550
	1.0	1.0	1.0	1.0	1.0	1.0	1.0

A comparison of the foregoing N^0 and N^1 values reveals that when a change in a need state shifts to a higher level, the potency of lower needs drops over the two time periods. Similarly, need levels change over time to a higher level as one approaches the steady state (equilibrium or the long run), as noted per the following:

	N^1 (per the above)	N^2	N^3	N^4	N^5
N_1	.1325	.1200	.1128	.1089	.1069
N_2	.1825	.1709	.1644	.1610	.1592
N_3	.2625	.2541	.2515	.2504	.2498
N_4	.2675	.2755	.2798	.2820	.2832
N_5	.1550	.1795	.1915	.1977	.2009
	1.0	1.0	1.0	1.0	1.0

Interpreting the above results in terms of the real world, a younger person who is promoted conjures up all sorts of higher needs in terms of perceiving his or her new role. The model indicates that his or her motivations will be most acutely felt in the period immediately following the promotion.

Sensitivity analysis finds a few difficulties with this application. The most noticeable is that the process reaches an "absorbing" state, which when carried to the ultimate means that self-actualization cannot be replaced by a higher level. Thus, those persons who have reached their highest need level tend to go back down the hierarchy need levels and rely on current stimuli to satisfy a rediscovered lower need (either real or imagined). For example, in one of the few empirical studies on this topic, Porter[4] found

---

[4] L. W. Porter, *Organizational Patterns of Managerial Job Attitudes*, New York: American Foundation for Management Research, 1964.

in a multinational study that, regardless of the country or managerial level, those needs (irrespective of position in the hierarchy) which managers perceive to be least satisfied tended to be the most important. This study, confirms Maslow's conclusion that a satisfied need was not a motivator; but disproves the hierarchial assumption which states a need must be relatively satisfied before interest in the next is in evidence. Finally, the assumption that transition probabilities are most affected by the outcomes of a prior state at least reflects the maxim that we respond most dramatically to our most recent stimuli. The exact long-term impact of stimuli in the face of new stimuli is yet to be determined exactly.

Personnel Behavioral Application—American Products Corporation

The data processing director of the American Products Corporation is concerned about the fulfillment of data processing personnel needs on the job. Being in charge of 200 data processing personnel, he knows that each of his employees, like other employees in the firm, is searching for a balance of needs which will yield the greatest satisfaction. The data processing professional is presumed to be striving toward the higher level of needs per Maslow, that is, more esteem and self-actualization, and is slightly less interested in affiliation. Also assumed is that the data processing professional has satisfied most physiological and security needs on the job.

Using the above hypothesis, the data processing director wants to determine if this is true. If so, he will use various techniques to motivate his subordinates which will satisfy their needs. To prove or disprove this hypothesis, forms which are structured on Maslow's hierarchy of needs were distributed to all 200 data processing personnel. A sample form where only one box is to be checked is illustrated in Table 17-6. To insure accuracy of input data, managers of each section were instructed that only one box was to be checked, resulting in 100 percent usable responses. Summary results are set forth in Table 17-7 by the five major personnel categories: data processing manager, operations researcher, systems analyst, programmer, and data entry operator.

TABLE 17-6

Form Completed by Data Processing Personnel—American Products Corporation

Need Deemed Most Important in Present Position

(check one box only)
1. Physiological (basic physical factors)
2. Security (assurance of job)
3. Affiliation (accepted by others)
4. Esteem (recognition by others)
5. Self-actualization (intellectual fulfillment)

Position: _____ (data processing manager, operations researcher, systems analyst, programmer, or data entry operator)

TABLE 17-7
Summary of Completed Forms by Data Processing Personnel—
American Products Corporation

	Need Deemed Most Important in Present Position					
Position	Physiological	Security	Affiliation	Esteem	Self-Actualization	Totals
Data processing manager	—	—	—	1	9	10
Operations researcher	—	—	1	5	4	10
Systems analyst	—	2	5	9	4	20
Programmer	3	10	14	8	5	40
Data entry operator	22	38	29	21	10	120
Totals	25	50	49	44	32	200

Examination of the results indicates that various data processing position levels have different needs. As shown in Table 17-7, the higher-level positions tend toward esteem and self-actualization while the lower-level positions cover all need levels. The action required by the data processing director of the American Products Corporation to motivate the five levels differs, resulting in the rejection of the hypothesis set forth above for all data processing positions. However, the hypothesis is true for data processing managers and operations researchers.

Rather than pursue all position categories and their related need levels, only the operations research position will be explored as related to the need level of "esteem." Esteem is closely related to recognition which is one of the approaches available to a manager to motivate his employees. Recognition is also an important factor to OR personnel with their immediate peers. Along with recognition is the use of identification as a motivator. If an individual can identify himself (or herself) with the OR group, the leader, or some cause, he is in effect saying that goals and values associated with the cause have become his own. So another method of motivation open to the OR manager is to try and get the person to identify with the various OR projects he is currently undertaking.

Another idea related to both recognition and identification is the value of commitment to an OR project. If a person has a high desire to be recognized, which most professionals have, and can identify with a project, then he commits to the success of the project. Once an individual has committed himself to organizational objectives, his potential is greater—provided that his own goals and those of the firm have been allowed to influence each other. Thus, in order to keep an operations researcher motivated toward the successful completion of a specific project, the OR manager must establish the importance of the project and the recognition that it will bring on successful completion. In addition, the manager must try to keep the goals of the project and the goals of the professional related so as to allow identification with the project.

Since the desire for esteem (recognition) is a characteristic of OR personnel (thereby giving the OR manager a method of providing motivation), there are several ways other than salary by which recognition may be accomplished. Some operations researchers need to be involved in a situation to get certain satisfactory recognition. Similarly, OR personnel resent doing something that they have no part in planning. Hence, any project that justifies the use of PERT should have a built-in recognition factor. If the project is so large and complex as to warrant a PERT/Time or PERT/Cost system, the OR worker should see that the successful completion of the project would benefit him in order that he can be recognized both by his professional peers and by his manager.

Once the operations researcher has seen the worth of the project and realizes what it can do for him, the OR manager aligns the goals of the individual with the goals of the project. The idea of participation is very important in maintaining the alignment between the goals of OR personnel and those of the firm. With the PERT network, the OR professional can see where he is going and also see how he is progressing in relation to his fellow workers. Each participant can see his relative position and understand the timing and relationship of his responsibilities to other participants on the program team.

In summary, if PERT is used properly by the OR manager for planning and controlling his many projects, it can be very helpful in recognizing the contributions of his subordinates. PERT/Time and PERT/Cost is a successful way to get employees involved in the planning and goal-setting of the project. The involvement should be enough to cause a sense of identification with the project. If the assumption that recognition and identification will lead to commitment is true, and the assumption that commitment is the way to motivate the OR professional is true, then PERT, or any similar type of PERT technique is an effective management tool for motivation.

Summary

Before behavioral models can become widespread in usage, there is an urgent need for OR practitioners to be trained in "behavioral operations research." Specifically, management scientists must study the behavioral sciences and learn how to use this knowledge in OR projects. This implies knowing how to incorporate behavioral variables into OR models as well as when to effect revisions to behavioral models as conditions change. Although behavioral aspects of an OR problem tend to be qualitative, appropriate methods can be employed, as illustrated in the chapter, to quantify these factors.

Not only have the behavioral qualitative factors been ignored by most

OR groups in the past when solving individual, group, and organization problems, but they also have been ignored directly or indirectly by econometricians whose job is to model some part of the economy or the entire economy. Why, for example, have individuals chosen to save an abnormal amount of their incomes when theory says that the anticipation of inflation should make them want to get rid of cash? Or why have union leaders fought so stubbornly—and successfully—for large wage increases in the face of rising unemployment? Obviously, econometric models need to incorporate more sophisticated thinking in such areas as union politics, family budget practices, and corporate financial techniques. The path to better forecasting of what the economy as a whole will do lies in a better understanding of what individual consumers and organizations will do in specific situations.

New ways of explaining behavioral patterns of individuals, groups, firms, and the entire economy, then, are necessary if behavioral problems are to be solved. Behavioral operations research, enriched by psychology, sociology, and any other discipline, from which OR analysts can borrow, must provide the building blocks for a new and a more complete way of structuring problems facing the firm and the economy.

Questions

1. (a) How do behavioral problems differ from well-structured problems? Explain.
   (b) How do behavioral problems differ from poorly structured problems? Explain.
2. What is the most difficult part of a behavioral model? Explain.
3. In addition to the areas given in the chapter for behavioral operations research, specify other areas that are logical candidates for behavioral study.

Problems

17-1 The Lane Mail Order House, Inc., which sells men's and women's clothes through its quarterly fashion catalog, has experienced a tremendous increase in its credit sales over the last two years. Currently, when a customer requests a credit account, the following criteria are used to determine whether or not the account should be opened: total monthly income, total monthly obligations, number of dependents, and years with present employer. For each of these criteria, a certain point value is assigned based upon the prospective customer's answer. For example, if the total monthly income is $401 to $500, a value of 5 points is given; similarly, if income is $501 to $600, a point value of 6 is assigned; and so forth. If the customer scores above 20 points for these four criteria, the firm accepts the individual as a credit customer. Otherwise, the individual is advised that orders are acceptable only on a check or a money order basis.

(a) In addition to the foregoing critreia, what other criteria might be used for evaluating credit customers?

(b) What operations research (or statistical) techniques could be used to determine a valid, point-value system that reflects the experience of the firm in its credit operations (accounts that have been paid on time and accounts that have been charged off)?

17-2 The top management of the King Manufacturing Company is currently evaluating leadership capabilities of its middle-management level. Top management has noticed that middle managers, on occasion, permit and even encourage involvement in decisions by their subordinates. At other times, their decisions are made unilaterally, thereby resulting in direct orders to their subordinates. After talking with many of its middle-level managers about their differing leadership styles, top management concluded that the appropriate way depends on the circumstances, that is, leadership is situational.

(a) Enumerate the various ways in which a middle manager can obtain the most desirable responses from his subordinates through effective leadership.

(b) Assuming that the answer to (a) above is set forth in some type of rating scale form and leadership data are compiled and summarized on this basis, what operations research (or statistical) techniques could be employed to determine an accurate leadership evaluation of the firm's middle management?

17-3 In a certain test market, Fragrance, Inc. mailed free samples of a new deodorant (product 1) and a new soap (product 2), both scented with a nationally known perfume. Samples were mailed only to middle-income families. However, within this middle-income bracket, certain areas of the test market were considered to be lower-middle, middle-middle, and upper-middle. Hence, the firm compiled information on the basis of this family income structure. Using several sales researchers, the firm's marketing research group had them canvass the test market door-to-door and fill out the form below for the two scented products. Thus, both products were evaluated on the basis of cost, hygiene, appeal, and combined hygiene and appeal factors.

Suburb_____	Lower-middle income group ☐
Name_____	Middle-middle income group ☐
	Upper-middle income group ☐

Basis for Future Purchase:

	Scented Deodorant	Scented Soap
Cost	☐ Attractive price for scented deodorant	☐ Attractive price for scented soap
Hygiene	☐ Stops perspiration more effectively than ordinary deodorants	☐ Cleans better than ordinary soaps
Appeal	☐ Smells more pleasing than ordinary deodorants	☐ Smells more pleasing than ordinary soaps
Combined hygiene and appeal	☐ Serves as an effective deodorant and smells more pleasing than ordinary deodorants	☐ Serves as an effective soap and smells more pleasing than ordinary soaps

Based on the following 750 usable responses, 250 in each income category, the data is summarized as follows for both products:

Basis for Future Purchases	Lower-Middle Income Group Product 1	Lower-Middle Income Group Product 2	Middle-Middle Income Group Product 1	Middle-Middle Income Group Product 2	Upper-Middle Income Group Product 1	Upper-Middle Income Group Product 2
Cost	34	25	31	38	33	45
Hygiene	76	29	92	48	100	62
Appeal	75	105	60	100	40	65
Combined hygiene and appeal	65	91	67	64	77	78
	250	250	250	250	250	250

(a) To achieve the largest sales volume possible, should both products be advertised together for a given income group if the above sample is representative of the total population?

In addition to the foregoing market testing, two other new products—scented powder (product 3) and scented makeup (product 4)—have been tested in another market. These products are comparable to the prior products; hence, they can possibly be advertised together. Data on both of these products is given below:

Basis for Future Purchases	Lower-Middle Income Group Product 3	Lower-Middle Income Group Product 4	Middle-Middle Income Group Product 3	Middle-Middle Income Group Product 4	Upper-Middle Income Group Product 3	Upper-Middle Income Group Product 4
Cost	33	62	29	55	22	48
Hygiene	59	28	72	37	78	45
Appeal	76	105	55	95	40	82
Combined hygiene and appeal	82	55	94	63	110	75
	250	250	250	250	250	250

(b) To achieve the largest sales volume possible, should all products be advertised together for a given income group if the above sample is representative of the total population?

17-4 The Babcox Manufacturing Company wants to maintain a sales level of $25,000 per month for a certain product in a market that has potential sales of $55,000. Based upon the firm's past experience, sales for this product are assumed to decay at the rate of 2 percent per month. Also, the firm assumed that $1.00 of advertising will generate $6.50 of sales. Using the Vidale and Wolfe model, what advertising amount should be expended to maintain sales at $25,000? Answer this same question for maintaining sales at $35,000 and $45,000.

17-5 Nucleonics International is a rapidly expanding firm in the electronics field. Six months ago, 20 college graduates were hired by the various operating departments. The personnel department is attempting to evaluate their need requirements in the short and long run. In order to evaluate their forthcoming need levels (physiological, security, affiliation, esteem, and self-actualization), the recent graduates were asked to estimate as accurately as possible how much time is being spent on satisfying their needs for each of Maslow's five levels. Although the personnel department is interested in evaluating each person separately, the personnel manager felt a logical starting point is to obtain average values initially and compare each individual to the average. The average times, expressed as percentages, are as follows:

	This Period (N^0)
Physiological (N_1)	10%
Security (N_2)	20
Affiliation (N_3)	35
Esteem (N_4)	30
Self-actualization (N_5)	5
	100%

Similarly, average times were obtained for the matrix of transition probabilities which are:

$$\begin{array}{c c} & \begin{array}{c c c c c} N_1 & N_2 & N_3 & N_4 & N_5 \end{array} \\ \begin{array}{c} N_1 \\ N_2 \\ N_3 \\ N_4 \\ N_5 \end{array} & \begin{pmatrix} .40 & .15 & .05 & .05 & .00 \\ .25 & .45 & .15 & .10 & .05 \\ .20 & .20 & .40 & .25 & .10 \\ .15 & .15 & .25 & .45 & .35 \\ .00 & .05 & .15 & .15 & .50 \\ \hline 1.0 & 1.0 & 1.0 & 1.0 & 1.0 \end{pmatrix} \end{array}$$

(a) Calculate the next period or short-run condition for the five need levels.
(b) Calculate the steady state or long-run condition for the five need levels.

Bibliography

J. S. Aronofsky, *Progress in Operations Research, Volume III,* New York: John Wiley & Sons, 1969.

J. Beishon and G. Peters, *Systems Behaviour,* New York: Harper & Row, Publishers, 1972.

J. M. Dutton and W. H. Starbuck, *Computer Simulation of Human Behavior,* New York: John Wiley & Sons, 1971.

J. F. Engel, D. T. Kollat, and R. D. Blackwell, *Consumer Behavior,* New York: Holt, Rinehart and Winston, 1968.

H. Guetzkow, P. Kotler, and R. L. Schultz, *Simulation in Social and Administrative Science,* Englewood Cliffs, N.J.: Prentice-Hall, 1972.

J. H. B. M. Huysmans, *The Implementation of Operations Research*, New York: John Wiley & Sons, 1970.

P. Kotler, *Marketing Decision Making—A Model Building Approach*, New York: Holt, Rinehart and Winston, 1971.

C. McMillan, R. F. Gonzalez, and T. J. Schriber, *Systems Analysis, A Computer Approach to Decision Models*, Homewood, Ill.: Richard D. Irwin, 1973.

D. W. Miller and M. K. Starr, *Executive Decisions and Operations Research*, Englewood Cliffs, N.J.: Prentice-Hall, 1969.

M. K. Starr, *Management: A Modern Approach*, New York: Harcourt Brace Jovanovich, 1971.

7
Future of Operations Research

Chapter EIGHTEEN
Operations Research– Present and Future

Operations research will take on new directions in the future since more quantitative techniques are being developed that will add to the number of available quantitative tools. Not only will the present "tools of the trade" be expanded to solve "well-structured" business problems, but also there will be an expansion of present OR techniques and the addition of new ones to resolve "poorly structured" problems. Similarly, behavioral models will become more fully developed. The present state of the art, centering on well-structured OR problems, was covered in Chapters 1 through 15 while poorly structured problems and behavioral problems were treated in Chapters 16 and 17 respectively.

In addition to these emerging and dynamic directions of operations research, a most important trend is currently developing in business. It involves the combining of different OR methods to produce new quantitative techniques. Instead of being concerned with the maximization of profits or minimization of costs in one selected area, the trend is to include many or all functional relationships in a system. For example, operations research groups are building mathematical models to include the entire life cycle of a new product in order to maximize profits in the long run. This basic approach to new and established business ventures will become more prevalent in the future and will undoubtedly provide a new thrust in solving operations research problems. It will lead to optimization for the entire firm rather than optimization in one area which, many times, leads to overall suboptimization. Sample applications of these combined OR methods in marketing, physical distribution, manufacturing, finance, accounting, and corporate planning will be explored in the final chapter. Also, other OR approaches not found in the previous chapters will be presented for the foregoing functional areas of the firm. An overview of operations research presently and in the future concludes the book.

Current Quantitative Marketing Models

In the past, businessmen have generally accepted the increasing use of quantitative methods in the various areas of business, except marketing. Most marketing decisions are still made on the basis of intuitive judgment, unaided by any quantitative techniques. The rationale is that marketing men feel information in their area of business is never adequate, competition is too difficult to state precisely, customers are unpredictable, and marketing effects are highly conditional. However, headway is being made by many firms through their operations research groups. Real-time and time-sharing computer systems, coupled with advanced mathematical models, are changing marketing concepts and practices.

Comprehensive Marketing System Model

One of the most extensive and sophisticated mathematical marketing models that employs combined OR methods centers around a comprehensive model of the entire marketing system. A diagram of such a model for the gasoline market is found in Figure 18-1.[1] Inspection of this illustration indicates that it is divided into six major components:

1. The *market environment* or those forces in the environment that affect gasoline demand, such as population, income, and price.
2. The *marketing-mix decision model* that relates to the company and its competitors.
3. The *marketing decision variables* that focus on the major categories of decision making in the market, that is, product quality, pricing, distribution, point-of-sale promotion, mass-media advertising, product mix, distribution mix, and advertising mix.
4. The *productivity of marketing factors* that the company utilizes for its products, in particular, network of outlets and advertising theme.
5. The *consumer behavioral model* which shows customer response to the activities of the product, distribution, and advertising mixes as well as to the environment.
6. The *output: sales and profit* that reflect total industry sales and market shares for the company and its competitors as well as profits.

The various arrows in the illustration depict the flows which interconnect

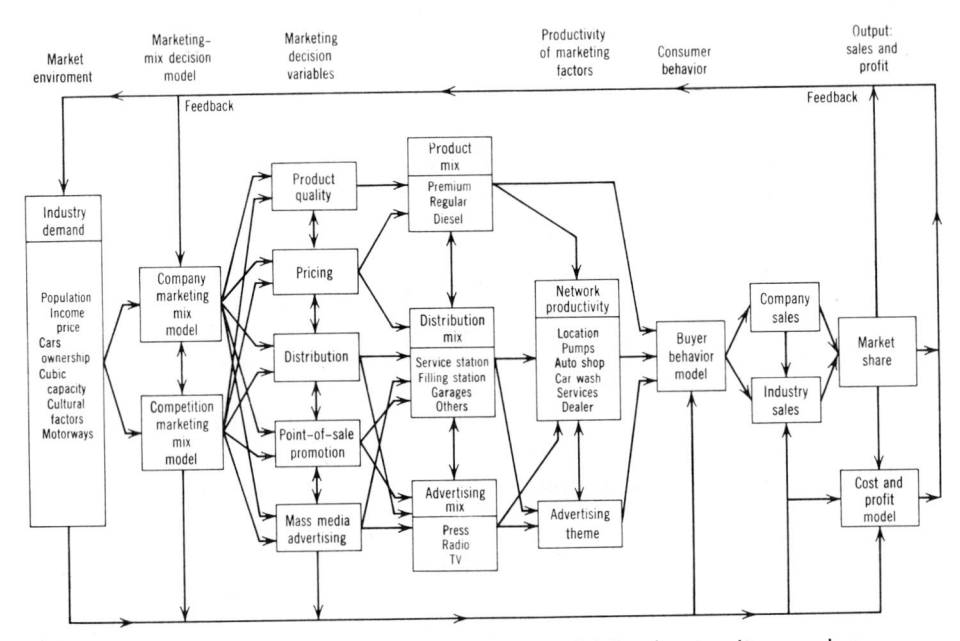

Figure 18-1 Computer on-line marketing mix model for the gasoline market.

[1] Jean-Jacques Lambin, "A Computer On-Line Marketing Mix Model," *Journal of Marketing Research*, May, 1972, pp. 119-126.

570 FUTURE OF OPERATIONS RESEARCH

the major elements in the marketing system. The output of (6) provides feedback for components (1) and (2).

Once the overall marketing system model has been developed, the marketing system is further defined by preparing outputs which relate to either trade decisions or consumer decisions. To influence trade decisions, the company uses the wholesale price, trade allowances, sales calls, advertising, credit policy, and delivery policy. To influence consumer decisions, the company uses product characteristics, retail price, consumer deals, and consumer advertising.

Having identified the major decision outputs, management lists the various inputs and influences on these decisions. These fall into one of four groups: (1) the company's long- and short-range goals for sales growth, return on sales, and return on investment, (2) forecastable factors in the environment, such as population growth, disposable personal income, price, and car ownership, (3) various assumptions about the sales effectiveness of different marketing instruments, (4) as well as expectations concerning competition. The next step traces how these data feed into and out of other parts of the marketing system, that is, how the outputs of one component become the inputs to others. This determines the functional relationships between key elements. For example, product quality, retail price, and mass media advertising can affect consumer buying decisions for gasoline. The real task, then, is to measure by how much.

The next logical step in developing a comprehensive marketing system model is to bring the various functional relationships together in a model that analyzes sales and profit consequences of a proposed marketing plan. For instance, a functional relationship shows that gasoline sales tend to increase with populaton growth but at a decreasing rate. This relationship, plus many others developed within the problem's framework, is the starting point for stating a series of equations that describe the entire marketing system in terms of the pertinent variables. Typical equations focus on industry sales, company market shares, and company profits. Once these equations have been developed, they are brought together to form the overall marketing system model. Once formulated, the resultant model must be fitted and updated according to the best available information and statistical techniques. Objective data is preferred but, when not available, carefully collected subjective data is used. The effect of uncertain data inputs on the results can be tested through sensitivity analysis.

Finally, the marketing system model is computer programmed and made available to management on an on-line basis. Using an input/output terminal, marketing planners can enter the latest research data along with specific proposed settings of the marketing decision variables, and thereby retrieve an estimate of the plan's expected sales and profits. The computer program should also contain a subroutine which can search for the best marketing plan possible.

In addition to developing a comprehensive marketing system model, a feedback control program for adjusting marketing mix variables to changes in sales and profits can be employed. A drop in sales would lead to changes in price, advertising and distribution effort in order to restore sales or profits to their previous levels. The optimality of the program can be tested against the real world by utilizing a market simulator.

Allocation of Sales Effort

A classical marketing management problem involves, "Where should salesmen be spending their *call* time on present and potential customers?" While there certainly are exceptions, most salesmen do not follow an optimal call frequency policy. Because of time pressures, most salesmen do not organize their activities very well. They spend a lot of time "firefighting" emergency calls from customers. Also, salesmen like to call where they are comfortable or appreciated—it is easier to call on a friend than a tough but potentially profitable new account.

Suppose a salesman has as few as 20 clients, each in a different geographic area, each taking a different amount of time to reach, each taking a different amount of time per call, each responding differently, and each with different profitability; the resultant task of maximizing sales subject to the salesman's limited time becomes an impossible task to solve by hand. Dr. Leonard Lodish, professor at the University of Pennsylvania's Wharton School of Finance, set to work on this difficult problem. The result is CALLPLAN,[2] a computer based system that aids sales staffs in deciding how to allocate call time among each client or prospect. The salesman supplies such inputs as the number of clients and prospects, the geographic location of each, the length of an average call, his current call policy (number of calls, say, in three months), his total time available for selling and travel, and most important, his estimates of sales at different call levels.

Using the salesman's own estimates, CALLPLAN supplies the salesman with an optimal call frequency policy. It takes into account travel expenses and travel time and gives him anticipated sales at both his present and optimal call policy. This system seems to work well in repetitive selling situations where more calls to a particular account bring more sales and fewer calls bring less. The average CALLPLAN user has seen sales increases of 5 percent to 30 percent which the salesman himself has attributed to CALLPLAN. Actually, this OR approach gives him the ability to consider more alternatives and factors, and to consider tradeoffs which he could not previously have contemplated.

CALLPLAN is presented in a two-day seminar in which the salesmen prepare their inputs and are shown how to use the model. These seminars are usually conducted for 8 to 12 salesmen at a time. Programming is performed on a time-sharing basis wtih portable computer terminals. The salesman supplies three kinds of input data: (1) geographical data showing his present call policy, area destination of trips, average trip cost, and one-half hour units consumed by each trip; (2) account data, that is, number of calls made on each account per a three-month period, average time per call, and an "adjustment factor" for weighting expected sales (it could refer

---

[2] Leonard M. Lodish, "CALLPLAN: An Interactive Salesman's Call Planning System," *Management Science*, December, 1971, pp. 25-40.

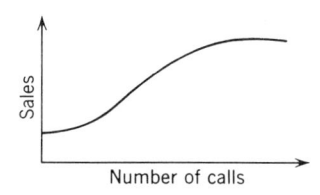

Figure 18-2. CALLPLAN sales response curve to the number of calls.

to sales commissions and profit margins); and (3) sales response relationship data, that is, the salesman's best estimate of the dollars he will generate according to the number of calls in a three-month period. Also, he is asked to estimate what would happen to his sales volume if he made zero calls, one-half the present number of calls, his present number of calls, 50 percent more calls, and at saturation—called as much as was physically possible. If the account is a prospect, he first indicates the likelihood of converting to a buying customer and then the appropriate sales response.

Fed the foregoing salesman's information, the computer converts the probabilities into numerical values and fits a sales response curve for each account and prospect, as shown in Figure 18-2. The computer weighs each of these curves against all the others within the constraint of the total time available for selling. At the same time, such factors as travel time and the point of diminishing returns with regard to incremental sales per additional call are weighed. The output is a call policy that specifies the number of calls that should be made on each account to produce the maximum total anticipated sales for a specific time period. The salesman can either accept the initial recommended policy or make certain changes to see what alternative plans might produce. He could, for instance, reallocate the time spent among specific accounts or change some of the probability estimates to weigh the impact on total sales. Hence, one or more outputs can be generated to reflect the changed conditions.

Marketing "What-If" Games
Several advertising agencies have been developing specialized marketing "what-if" games for their clients. The need for such games should be somewhat apparent. In spite of the growing sophistication in marketing and research, no perceptible improvement has been made in the success ratio of new products over the last decade. For example, N. W. Ayer & Sons, Inc., a New York-based advertising agency, has a "new product model."[3] Under development for six years, it draws on case studies of nearly 120 new-product introductions and is designed to predict within 5 percent the initial purchase levels during the first 13 weeks of a product's introduction.

Currently, Ayer is refining the next logical step: a model to project repeat purchases and longer-term sales. Progress is far enough along that Ayer

---

[3] Special Report, "New Products: The Push Is on Marketing," *Business Week*, March 4, 1972, p. 77.

can play the "what-if" game. What if competitors move in with X advertising dollars and Y sampling techniques in three months or six months? What if an established competitor boosts his advertising budget 30 percent or reduces prices by 5 percent or 10 percent? The computer determines dollar projections on net sales, cost of goods sold, gross margin, marketing costs, depreciation, and even by how much the new product might detract from other products in the company's line. The resultant "net contribution" of the product is converted to an estimated cash flow after taxes and payback period. However, the model is not a crystal ball; it has made mistakes and is only as good as the input data.

Computer Optimization and Simulation Modeling for Operating Supermarkets

COSMOS, which is an acronym for Computer Optimization and Simulation Modeling for Operating Supermarkets (a computer program), was jointly developed by NCR and the National Association of Food Chains working with several management consulting firms over a four-year period.[4] Since net profits after taxes in supermarkets have in recent years been falling below one percent, COSMOS was conceived to attack this problem in a scientific and practical way.

A store report produced by COSMOS indicates the direct profitability of each shelf item. Based on this profitability factor and turnover, the report recommends which items should receive greater or less display, the best locations for display, and which items should be discontinued. A second COSMOS report, called the merchandiser report, summarizes all store reports and recommends price changes, promotional efforts, and deletions by item for all stores in a supermarket chain. The system uses a mathematical model for each store of the chain. The order billing file constitutes the data base for COSMOS. COSMOS can be programmed to reflect the different policies of various supermarket chains and also such variable factors as ethnic neighborhood preferences and other demographic characteristics.

Current Quantitative Physical Distribution Models

Considerable management attention has been focused on improving traditional physical distribution practices. Physical distribution is an integrative field which combines transportation, inventory, warehouse operations, order communication, and material handling as components of a single system. The structure of the system is determined by the number, size, and geographical arrangement of warehouse facilities that serve to integrate the above components. The planning objective in physical distribution is to isolate the operating system structure and procedures which most satisfactorily contribute to the firm's profit goals.

Physical distribution performance is measured by the relationship be-

---

[4] National Association of Food Chains, *COSMOS I Training and Instruction Manual*, Case and Company, Inc., 1969.

tween customer service capability and associated cost. Customer service measurement relates to the speed and consistency of servicing orders. Cost measurement constitutes asset values and operational expenditures required to support the desired customer service level. Each potential level of customer service has an associated distribution system that will result in least total cost.

Long Range Environmental Planning Simulator

A dynamic simulation model, called LREPS (Long Range Environmental Planning Simulator), has been developed for improving the physical distribution system of a manufacturing firm engaged in national distribution of packaged goods.[5] The model's purpose is to assist management in physical distribution system design. LREPS utilizes a multilevel structure. The first level comprises the manufacturing plants and adjacent warehouses. Each plant may be designated as either a partial or full product line producer. The second level consists of distribution centers which may stock any inventory assortment. If desired, distribution centers can be stacked in product flow sequence and thus become primary and remote facilities. An additional feature is the capability to simulate shipping points solely for the purpose of consolidating transportation tonnage. The final level represents demand units—individual and/or aggregations of customers.

The operation of the model embodies several steps. First, daily orders by demand units are generated. This is achieved by randomly selecting blocks of actual orders to satisfy the daily sales requirements of each demand unit. An overall sales forecast is allocated to demand units on the basis of independent market variables. Initial activity is performed by the model's demand and environmental subsystem.

Second, actual processing of orders is simulated. The order cycle between demand units and the servicing distribution center is simulated, and appropriate elapsed times are computed. The operations subsystem of LREPS performs this processing function and thereby constitutes the model's system structure. As orders are processsed at each distribution center, inventories are appropriately reduced. If goods are unavailable, products are back ordered. As reorder points or periods are reached at one level, replenishment orders are dispatched to the next level. There, time delays are computed and inventory replenishment decisions are made.

Third, all of the above information is used to compute target variable values. Total cost is measured on the basis of cost parameters and mathematical transformations related to each component of the system. Fixed facility investment cost by size and type of facility is based on an annual depreciated amount. Order processing costs for each distribution center are calculated using regression analysis with different cost factors based upon size and location of facility. Communication costs are calculated using regression equations where the independent variables are the number of

---

[5] Donald J. Bowersox, "Coping: Dynamic Simulation of PD," *Distribution Worldwide*, December, 1972, pp. 24-31.

orders and lines processed. Inventory carrying costs and reorder costs are calculated for all inventories. Inbound transportation costs to distribution centers are calculated on specific point-to-point rates. Outbound transportation costs to demand units are calculated from sets of regression equations based on distance. This subsystem provides necessary measurement for evaluation of system performance.

As a generalized simulation model, LREPS does not incorporate many simplifying assumptions common to other physical distribution simulators, such as a single product, one manufacturing location, or a single channel distribution. The development of cost functions based on historic corporate data and representation by regression equations reduces the need to assume a variety of data relationships.

Distribution System Simulator

The Distribution System Simulator is another modeling tool which produces a mathematical representation of a firm's distribution system.[6] The user of DSS responds to a true/false questionnaire in which he specifies the options and characteristics of his desired model. The options take into account each of the major factors involved in the operation of a distribution system: the characteristics of customers' demand for products, buying patterns of customers, order-filling policies, replenishment policies, emergency replenishment policies, redistribution policies, transportation practices, distribution channels, factory locations, production capabilities, and other significant elements. In addition to these options which are essentially inventory and product movement oriented, DSS provides the capability, through user functions, to incorporate other vehicle scheduling algorithms, forecasting techniques, production schedules, and pricing mechanisms.

Using the answers to the questionnaire described above, the DSS program: (1) generates a computer program whose logic is described by the options chosen on the questionnaire, (2) specifies the data required by the simulation program, and (3) specifies the information required for the output analysis. The user need not be familiar with any elements of computer programming. However, he must have a thorough understanding of the distribution system, modeling, and management science.

Concluding Comments on Marketing and Physical Distribution Models

The foregoing OR models, though not exhaustive, indicate the kind of marketing and physical distribution problems that can be solved. The future will bring increased efforts to build models for large and complex processes, interrelated courses of action, and predominating nonlinearities in marketing problems. In essence, they will be total systems simulations that encompass all components of the marketing mix. Extension of statistical decision theory and mathematical programming will deal with dynamic, multistage problems under uncertainty. Models of search, rule of thumb procedures,

---

[6] M. M. Connors, C. Coray, C. J. Cuccaro, W. K. Green, D. W. Low, and H. M. Markowitz, "The Distribution System Simulator," *Management Science*, April, 1972, pp B-425–B-453.

and model validation will become more common. Joint optimization models will encompass the producer, distributor, and consumer sequence in an effort to assign inventory levels and distribution arrangements that will produce lower costs for the entire marketing chain. Investigation of the properties in optimal models will be made for conditions where competitors employ similar techniques and interact. The marketing problem facing the firm becomes more difficult when the competitor is as smart or smarter. There will be increased research on the development of behavioral theories of the firm and the relationship of the firm to its environment.[7]

The potential gain from using marketing and physical distribution OR models is currently being felt in many medium and large size firms. These OR models will gradually filter down to smaller firms as soon as there is recognition of the gains available. Marketing people acknowledge that the cost of doing business is basically the cost of marketing. This means spending large sums to market new products or maintain present products and establishing or maintaining the channels of distribution. Instead of spending these large sums in a haphazard way, the marketing department is able to channel these outlays in a more optimum manner. Thus any quantitative technique that sheds some light on where dollars should be spent and what will be achieved will receive the support and backing of management. These factors alone will provide the impetus necessary to initiate OR marketing studies within the firm. In the long run, a firm will suffer if its marketing effort is based on intuition alone while its competitors adopt an operations research approach. Output from marketing OR models plus intuition and judgment form a sound basis for a marketing decision at any time, whereas intuition or "flying by the seat of your pants" may lead to poor or average decisions from which the firm may never recover to recapture its lost markets.

Current Quantitative Manufacturing Models

As compared with marketing, manufacturing is characterized by the fact that it is more wholly within the control of management. More of the relevant variables in this area are subject to the control of the decision maker. In manufacturing decision problems, the objective and constraints are more likely to be expressible and the necessary cost information will generally be available with more accuracy. Even though this dissimilarity exists between marketing and manufacturing, there are some very important interactions between these two functions. The manufacturing process has a direct effect on product quality and manufacturing costs, which, in turn, have an impact on product prices. Marketing similarly influences inventories since the products must be manufactured for shipment or stock. This interaction between marketing and manufacturing also brings into play the finance function of the firm. It is difficult, then, to construct a meaningful

---

[7] P. E. Green and R. E. Frank, *A Manager's Guide to Marketing Research*, New York: John Wiley & Sons, 1967, pp. 151-164.

OR model without some reference to the requirements of marketing demand and financial considerations. This is evident in many of the present-day models.

Production Planning through Goal Programming

Goal programming can be classified in the category of combined OR methods. It is a special application of linear programming, capable of handling a single goal with multiple subgoals, or multiple goals with multiple subgoals. In this sense, conventional linear programming is a special case of goal programming which consists of a single goal with single or multiple subgoals. In conventional linear programming method, the objective function must be unidirectional—either to maximize profits (or effectiveness) or to minimize costs. It is this unidirectional quality of the objective function that limits the application of the simplex method to aggregate production planning.

Since goal programming is capable of handling multiple goals in multiple dimensions, conversion of various factors to costs or profits may no longer be necessary. In other words, two hours of idle time in work group A or two hours of overtime in work group B do not have to be expressed in terms of estimated costs. Since the multiple goals are often achieved only to the detriment of one another, a hierarchy of importance among these goals is required. This allows consideration of low-order goals only after higher-order goals are fulfilled. Therefore, various kinds of problems can be solved if management provides a ranking of goals in terms of their contribution or importance to the organization.[8]

Management, for instance, might consider the costs of shortages to be higher than costs of changing the employment level, and the latter costs to be higher than inventory costs, thus establishing three separate goals (the levels of production, employment, and inventories). The hierarchy among these incompatible multiple goals may be set in such a way that those with lower priorities are considered only after higher-priority goals are satisfied or have reached points beyond which they cannot be improved under the given conditions. This implies that there could be deviations from some or all goals, although the aim is to get as close to these goals as possible within the given constraints.

If shortages of one product are considered more critical than shortages of some other product, the largest weight should be assigned to the *deviational variables* for that product. In other words, we can assign differential weights to each variable within the same hierarchial order group, provided that they are in the same dimension.

The same reasoning can be applied to all variables. If it is more important to avoid underemployment in some groups than in others, different weights could be assigned to variables in the various groups. Similarly, different weights could be assigned to deviations from goals in the

---

[8] Sang Lee and Veekko Jaaskelainen, "Goal Programming: Management's Math Model," *Industrial Engineering*, February, 1971, pp. 30-35.

lowest order group representing excess inventories. In order to minimize the capital employed in production, goal programming minimizes the sum of each of the deviational variables in the objective function multiplied by the weights assigned to these variables.

In the simplex method, deviations from goals are designated as slack variables and are used only as dummy variables. In goal programming, these deviations, either positive or negative, are real variables and the objective function is expressed only by these variables. Once the goal programming model is developed, the computational algorithm is almost identical to the procedure followed in the simplex method.

To illustrate goal programming, consider a manufacturing plant which has a current operational capacity of 500 hours a day. With this capacity, the company produces two products: A and B. Production of either product requires one hour in the plant. Because of the limited sales demand, only 300 units of product A and 400 units of product B can be sold. The profit from the sale of product A is $10 whereas the profit from product B is $5.

The president of the company has listed the following goals in order of importance:

1. Avoid underutilization of production capacity.
2. Sell as many units as possible; however, since the profit from the sale of product A is twice that of product B, he is doubly anxious to achieve the sales goal for product A relative to product B.
3. Reduce overtime.

He must choose a strategy which will achieve all of his goals as nearly as possible.

Since overtime is allowed, production may take more than 500 hours of operating time. The operational capacity may be expressed as follows:

$$x_1 + x_2 + d_1^- - d_1^+ = 500$$

where x_1 = the number of product A to be manufactured
x_2 = the number of product B to be manufactured
d_1^- = idle time when production of products A and B does not exhaust production capacity
d_1^+ = overtime operation

The number of products that can be sold for A and B is expressed as follows:

$$x_1 + d_2^- = 300$$
$$x_2 + d_3^- = 400$$

where d_2^- = underachievement of sales goals for product A
d_3^- = underachievement of sales goals for product B

In addition to these variables and constraints, priority factors must be assigned to the deviations from the goal as follows:

P_1—the highest priority assigned by management to the underutilization of production capacity: d_1^-.

P_2—the priority factor assigned to the underutilization of sales capacity: d_2^- and d_3^-. Also, management wishes to assign twice the importance to d_2^- as that assigned to d_3^-.

P_3—the priority factor assigned to the overtime in the production operation: d_1^+.

Based on the foregoing constraints, the goal programming model can be formulated per Figure 18-3. The objective is the minimization of deviations from goals. Hence, the objective function is expressed only in terms of the deviational variables. The deviational variable associated with the highest preemptive priority must first be minimized to the fullest possible extent. When no further improvement is possible in the highest priority order group, the deviations associated with the next highest priority are minimized. The optimal solution to the above problem can be obtained by applying the simplex method of linear programming.

Employment and Production Planning Using the Universal Front End

For the most part, attempts to facilitate the design and execution of simulation programs for employment and production planning (or any other area) have centered on writing subroutines to carry out various record-keeping and output-format functions. The Universal Front End takes just the opposite approach. It assumes that the manager wants to try alternative inputs, see what effect or outputs they produce, and then experiment further with possible variations of inputs.[9] Using the front end (the part of the system that is visible to him), management tries different inputs either in a systematic way or by hunch and intuition. Any variable in the program, whether it was originally defined as a control variable or as a cost coefficient, can be changed. Using his knowledge and understanding, the manager instructs the computer about different values that he knows are possible in order to learn the consequences of the changed variable or variables.

To illustrate the Universal Front End, consider a production manager who has the task of devising an employment and production plan to fit an expected pattern of demand. He wants to determine when and how much he should increase his work force and when he should schedule overtime. He would like a plan which takes into account the costs of hiring and training workers, storage of the product, overtime production, and failure to satisfy demand.

$$\begin{aligned}
\text{Minimize:} \quad & Z = P_1 d_1^- + 2P_2 d_2^- + P_2 d_3^- + P_3 d_1^+ \\
\text{Subject to:} \quad & x_1 + x_2 + d_1^- \qquad\qquad - d_1^+ = 500 \\
& x_1 \qquad\quad + d_2^- \qquad\qquad\quad = 300 \\
& \quad\ x_2 \qquad\qquad + d_3^- \qquad\quad = 400 \\
& x_1,\ x_2,\ d_1^-,\ d_2^-,\ d_3^-,\ d_1^+ \geq 0
\end{aligned}$$

Figure 18-3 Goal programming model for the production of products A and B.

---

[9] Curtis H. Jones, "At Last: Real Computer Power for Decision Makers," *Harvard Business Review*, Sept.-Oct., 1970, pp. 75-89.

Since the manager knows he will have this problem many times in the future, he asks a member of the OR staff to recommend a relatively simple program. The model builder utilizes the technique called Parametric Production Planning which allows four numbers, each ranging from zero to one, to determine useful employment and overtime patterns. Parameter A determines the speed with which the employment is adjusted to meet changes in demand. Parameter B determines the relative weights to be placed on each of the upcoming period demands in estimating the average demand. Parameter C determines the amount of overtime to be worked in response to demands above the straight-time capacity of the production facility. Parameter D weighs the future forecasts for this overtime calculation.

Searching through the zero-to-one range of Parameters A, B, C, and D, say in increments of .25, the Universal Front End finds the best pattern, and the on-line computer terminal device displays simulated results, such as those trials which produced the highest net profits. The production manager can then rerun the simulation with varying input data to search for a better solution. With this simulated information as a starting point, he notices the temporary layoff and hire position during the year as well as the temporary hire and layoff in the peak demand months. By moving the cursor (a lighted spot on the terminal screen) to the desired point on the graph and depressing a key, he can change the number stored in computer memory for the variable in that period.

After the manager has developed an employment pattern, that is better suited to his goals, he adjusts the employment graph. He can work with the weekly hours in order to make similar adjustments in overtime so as to reduce inventories or stockouts. These changes, too, can be made by sliding the cursor to the desired points. Similar analysis can be made to answer other questions relating to employment and production planning.

Optimizing Blends Using Linear Programming

An excellent OR manaufacturing model that is part of a continuing operation (as opposed to one-time solutions) is one found in a petroleum refinery for optimizing gasoline blends, refinery settings, and purchases using linear programming.[10] Some of the elements that must be known are: the cost and capacities of running the refineries to produce a multitude of intermediate products, inventories, product requirements, and the range of acceptability for each of these and the qualities of each of the intermediate products that can be blended to manufacture them. This application is in widespread use.

Before any segment of the problem can be run, a great deal of research is necessary to bring the technology to the point of application. For example, before blending can be optimized, it is necessary to develop the constraints for each characteristic as well as the characteristics themselves. These include octane, vapor pressure, and percent off at different distillation temperatures. In many cases, these criteria do not exist and certainly are not needed so

---

[10] Harry Stern, "Informative Systems in Management Science," *Management Science*, February, 1969, pp. B-325–B-330.

long as blending is done by formula and not by feasible region. Having developed the required criteria, it is then necessary to cost each of the components. In order to accomplish this, the refinery process must be understood thoroughly.

The petroleum companies employ the largest computers available and have spent millions of dollars to develop these models. However, this investment can be more than justified by the savings of a fraction of a cent on each gallon produced. Any optimization of a process takes an in-depth understanding of that process and the building of this understanding can be, and usually is, costly. It can only be justified in very specific instances such as this. In addition to solving the technical problems, it often means admitting that, what was thought to be an art, is quantifiable.

Inventory and Order Entry System
With an on-line, real-time computer system, a firm can install a highly advanced order entry and inventory control system connecting all its sales offices, plants, and warehouses by means of a leased teletype network. As soon as a salesman receives a customer order, the information is teletyped to the central computer where a check is made for the order's completeness and accuracy, the customer's credit standing, and the availability of the required product in the nearest warehouse(s) (or factory). If everything checks, a shipment order is transmitted to the warehouse(s) (or factory) where applicable. If the particular shipment causes inventory levels to fall below a specified reorder point, the computer also orders replenishment stocks and, if need be, enters a factory production order to manufacture more of the items. Finally, the computer sends a confirmation of the order to its originating sales office, describing the shipment and its point of origin. Often this confirmation is received within a few minutes of order placement. Even during peak load periods, the delay may be no longer than 15 minutes (subject, of course, to computer breakdown). A system of this type lays the groundwork for a comprehensive management information system for controlling the performance of manufacturing and distribution activities.[11]

For a small company, it would not be economical to lease a teletype network and utilize an on-line, real-time computer system full time. However, with time sharing now available, orders, as they arrive within the firm, can be sent over the dial telephone network into a time-shared computer. Hence, order entry and inventory control systems are feasible for smaller firms.

Concluding Remarks on Manufacturing
The trend in operations research is to merge the basic functions of the firm —marketing, manufacturing, and finance—into one comprehensive mathematical model, known as corporate planning models. This subject will be covered in a subsequent section of this chapter.

---

[11] Felix Kaufman, "Data Systems That Cross Company Boundaries," *Harvard Business Review*, Jan.-Feb., 1966, pp. 141-155.

Operations research is not content to stay within the confines of the firm. Manufacturing OR problems are now being extended to interact with other firms. For example, the linking of the manufacturer's computer with its suppliers' computers could allow the manufacturer to receive periodic progress reports on suppliers' production of his orders and information regarding delivery status. Moreover, a considerable reduction in ordering time of goods needed for production could result. There is no reason why, in most cases, this cannot be done within the prevailing complex of competitive and regulatory constraints. An example of this approach is in the food industry where orders are received through a teletype network by a food manufacturer from the various supermarket chains.

Not only is vertical integration possible in computer-to-computer communications between manufacturer and suppliers or some other combination, but also applicable is horizontal integration. This can be illustrated best by a department store which may not have a certain appliance model desired by a customer. With a horizontally integrated system, the salesman could direct his computer console to interrogate records of other department stores in the surrounding area for the desired model. The computer would have to be programmed so that valuable competitive information would not be available. Such security is easily within the realm of programming and is realistic since the airlines are doing much the same thing today.

Current Quantitative Finance Models

The choice of capital investment alternatives, such as whether to buy or not to buy, and if to buy, which purchase is best, is a tough problem for management. Managers are on the alert for new products, new processes, and new equipment where risks are low and a high return on the investment can be expected. However, there is evidence that profitable investment opportunities are being passed up by management with resultant losses in terms of higher costs and lost markets. This is a high price to pay for less than optimal capital investment policies. Current quantitative finance models are available to resolve difficult financial problems facing management.

Venture Analysis

One of the most extensive and sophisticated mathematical models that utilizes combined OR methods for assessing uncertainty and risk is called "venture analysis." This is an integrated investment planning system for firms. Its purpose is to analyze, logically and quickly, any investment opportunity that may be offered. For example, a company might consider introducing a new product (Figure 18-4), acquiring another company, building a new plant, or modernizing its distribution system. Whatever the objective, the computer evaluates the interactions of all the factors that might influence the project and the company's cash flow. With answers that the computer provides, a company is better able to maximize its profit at minimal risk.

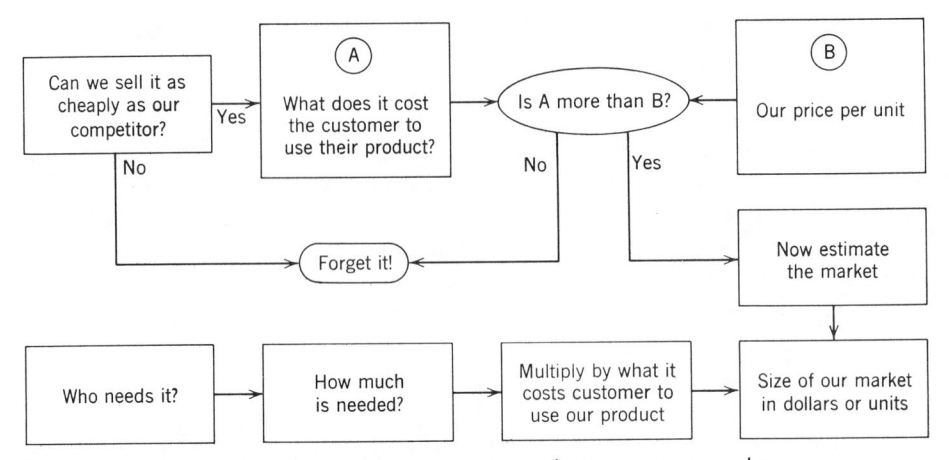

Figure 18-4 Venture analysis—basic steps in marketing a new product.

When considering the introduction of a new product, several problem areas are troublesome to the manager—troublesome in the sense that they engender a desire to delay decisions until a firmer basis can be developed for choosing among the many alternatives. The major ones are (1) the complexity of the market plus investment and cost factors influencing profitability of the venture, (2) the multitude of alternatives to be evaluated quantitatively before selecting a course of action, (3) the risks introduced by forecast uncertainties, and (4) the possible counteractions by customers and competitors.

Based on these foregoing problems, venture analysis evaluates alternate strategies, thereby permitting more explicit consideration of the risks introduced by the forecast uncertainties and the potential counteractions of customers and competitors (who must adjust their tactics in the face of a new factor in the market). Thus, for the commercialization of a new product, venture analysis is extremely helpful for developing decisions in the early stages of planning. As might be expected, this type of analysis relies heavily on computer programming and processing.

A typical venture analysis model is a simulation model.[12] All inputs are communicated to the model through a dialogue between management-user and the computer time-sharing system. The dialogue consists of answering a series of questions posed by the model. The answers form the data base for a particular analysis. A teletyped keyboard or video display terminal may be used for purposes of the dialogue.

The basic inputs to the model are of two types: probabilistic (i.e., uncertain) and deterministic (i.e., assumed known). Sales, cost of sales, capital purchases, engineering expenses, and general and administrative expenses are treated as probabilistic quantities, that is, uncertainty is considered. Interest rate, corporate assessment rate, number of years to be considered, depreciation life, depreciation type, and the like are considered to be de-

[12] Franz Edelman and Joel S. Greenberg, "Venture Analysis: The Assessment of Uncertainty and Risk," *Financial Executive*, August, 1969, pp. 56-62.

584 FUTURE OF OPERATIONS RESEARCH

terministic, or known precisely. The probabilistic data conveys to the model management's assessment of the uncertainty associated with each of the key variables. It consists of management's subjective estimates of the likelihood that the variables will attain specified values.

A set of standard financial computations are performed, thereby determining values of profit, cash flow, return on assets, and similar items. These computations are repeated a large number of times employing different combinations of values for the key variables, as described by management's uncertainty assessments. Each repetition of the computation produces new values (profit, cash flow, etc.). This information establishes the risk profiles of the performance measures. The risk profiles—the model outputs —are printed on the same teletype keyboard or video display used to supply the input data. The outputs are available within a few minutes of entering the data. Upon management review and evaluation, necessary input changes can be made and the computations repeated.

The values of key input variables and their uncertainty profiles are functions of many factors. For example, revenue is a function of selling price, total market, and market share. Thus, these factors may be interrelated; market share is a function of relative selling price, total market is a function of selling price, selling price may be related to manufacturing cost, and manufacturing cost may be a function of quantity manufactured, which is related to market size. No attempt has been made here to define these complex interrelationships within the model. Instead, it is assumed that meaningful estimates, based on a detailed analysis performed outside of the venture analysis model, can be made for all pertinent data.

The venture analysis model, in essence, is a management laboratory in which managers can experiment before the fact with a variety of investment alternatives. One experiment may consist of choosing a set of specific values for the key input variables, then utilizing these values to compute after-tax profit, cash flow, indebtedness, payback period, return on assets, and present worth (discounted cash flow). In each experiment, the choice of values for key variables is based upon random sampling of the variables' probability distribution—the uncertainty profiles. The experiment is then repeated a large number of times, each time choosing, from the specified uncertainty profiles, a new set of values for the key variables and computing an after-tax profit. In this manner, frequency distributions—the number of times the computed results fall within specific intervals—are created for each of the computed quantities. The risk profiles are obtained directly from the frequency distributions and represent the chance that the committed quantity will exceed various specified values.

Investment Decision Model
A financial simulation model represents complex interactions of marketing and manufacturing with finance.[13] It would be next to impossible for the human mind to think through all of the ramifications demanded for proper

---

[13] E. H. Khoury and H. W. Nelson, "Simulation in Financial Planning," *Management Services*, March-April, 1965, pp. 13-20.

financial planning without the assistance of simulation. The simulation model definitely lessens the magnitude of the problem through the definition and quantification of the relationships within the system. Another benefit of simulation is the flexibility that makes it possible to generate a number of different plans quickly, easily, and cheaply. By forcing management to define and quantify the relationships and interactions existing within the system, it brings into focus the hidden determinants of policy and practice. The financial simulation model provides the potential for the development of feedback within a management information system.

A financial simulation model has been put to good use at both divisional and corporate levels of Burroughs. At the divisional level, it has been used to understand the combined influence of independent decisions and to improve decision-making ability by making several test runs before preparing detailed forecasts. At the corporate level, this model permits management to see the effect on the firm of a proposed divisional plan as well as to evaluate corporate decision alternatives. An evaluation of divisional profit plans can be undertaken with respect to alternative plans that reflect the firm's growth objectives, asset management, profit maximization, and cash flow. Lastly, the model at the corporate level allows management to prepare long-range financial plans.

Decision Model For Portfolio Selection

Just as investment decision models can be developed internally for the firm, so too can mathematical models be constructed for investment decisions in the stock market.[14] Dr. John Kuark at the University of Denver has been researching the stock market and models for investment decision making. After much theorizing and testing, he has developed a portfolio selection model.

Every investor would like to experience the greatest increase in value possible with each dollar invested, and do so with the greatest amount of assurance (minimum risk). Maximization of expected future payoffs is facilitated by means of selecting those volatile stocks with relatively wide price fluctuations which have shown consistent per-share earnings growth in the past and are forecasted by the "experts" to continue to grow in the future. Risk potential is minimized by calculating Bayesian posterior probabilities (probabilities of an event based upon the best knowledge of what is to come). The stocks which are selected by the above method are timed for purchase or sale, based on the investors' objective return and chart analysis.

As a first step in selecting stocks, it is necessary to survey those which have desirable price fluctuations, good earnings growth, and are forecasted to continue to have good earnings growth. The foregoing process is necessary because of the amount of research which must go into the analytical phase of computing probabilities.

Next, the probabilities of a stock going up (bullish) or going down (bearish) must be computed using the following variables: (1) the two states

---

[14] John Y. T. Kuark, "Business Decision Model for Portolio Selection," *Interface*, August, 1972, pp. 63-65.

of possible outcomes (bullish or bearish), (2) the ratio of historical price earnings multiple to current price earnings multiple, (3) the historical earnings per share and forecasted earnings per share, (4) the trading volume, the number of shares outstanding, and the short interest ratio, (5) the rating of management capabilities and the financial condition of the firm, (6) the current business and economic conditions, (7) the course of monetary and fiscal policies, and (8) governmental and legislative actions, public opinions, political and social developments, both domestic and international, which would have an impact on individual stocks as well as the entire stock market. With this information the posterior probability that the stock will increase (p) and the probability that the stock will decrease (q) can be computed ($q = 1 - p$). It should be noted that when q is much larger than p, short selling may be in order.

As a final step in allocating a fixed amount of capital to various stocks for which probabilities have been computed, a linear programming model is used to maximize the expected Bayesian return subject to these conditions. (1) The sum of the returns from the stocks selected is greater than or equal to an objective—for example, 30 percent. (2) The proportion of capital allocated to any stock is greater than or equal to zero. (3) The sum of the proportions of capital allocated to all stocks is less than or equal to one. The decision model has been tested at the University of Denver.

Current Quantitative Accounting Models

Not only can there by less than optimal decisions in making financial investments, there can also be less than optimal procedures for handling the firm's financial data. Accounting information systems should provide managers with information for planning the actions of the firm. To be accepted as a basis for making decisions, the information should appear in a form that is familiar to managers. This consideration is taken into account for those quantitative accounting models set forth below.

Simulating An Accounting Information System Model

Simulation of an accounting system has as its objective the generation of projected accounting statements. The accounting information system model is probabilistic, that is, it recognizes uncertainty by accepting input data and estimating key factors as probability distributions rather than as point values.[15] Furthermore, it consists entirely of equations and inequalities that relate the various factors involved in the accounting process. It explicitly incorporates decision rules that may easily be altered to determine the effect upon the criterion. It is computer programmed so that a large variety of alternative plans can be feasibly considered. Building an accounting information system, model that is sufficiently comprehensive and realistic as well as probabilistic is not easy, quick, or inexpensive. Several man-years by high-salaried analysts may be required.

[15] Bernard M. Davall and Joseph W. Wilkinson, "Simulating An Accounting Information System Model," *Management Accounting*, January, 1971, pp. 26-35.

Planning effectively with the model requires that some systematic method be adopted that allows features of the model to be varied. Sensitivity analysis is one suitable method of experimentation. By measuring the effects of systematic changes in the structure of the model, or to the values of the various factors in the model, sensitivity analysis isolates the key factors that affect the business firm. It also measures the sensitivity of a criterion such as net income to alternative courses of action, to errors in the estimates of the factor values to changes in assumptions, and to changes in decision rules. Sensitivity analysis thus provides a better understanding of the uncertainty involved in making decisions affecting the future, the relative influences of the various factors in the model, and the consequences of alternative courses of action.

The model consists of a series of equations plus several inequalities and "if-then" statements that express operating relationships. These relationships involve the factors encompassed by the accounting information system and are based upon accounting principles as well as the operations conditions of the company.

As a starting point, the model uses the past monthly demand trend to forecast the expected units of product to be demanded in the first month of the coming year. Planned production is geared to this forecasted demand, as adjusted by expected losses, back orders, and replenishment of the safety stock. Actual sales volume is based on the lesser of (1) the units of product demanded and (2) the units available for sale. If the units demanded are less than the units available, then the sales volume equals the units demanded. However, if the units available are less than the units demanded, then the units sold are equal to the units available and sales are lost. (The cost of lost sales, if any, is a function of the quantity of lost sales and the estimated unit cost of a lost sale.) The month's cost of goods sold equals the variable manufacturing costs (direct material, direct labor, factory supplies, etc.), as adjusted by the work in process and finished goods inventories. Thus, the model relates the appropriate variable and nonvariable costs in computing the contribution margins, net operating income, and net income after taxes for the first month. After repeating the procedure for each of the following eleven months, the model contains the data for the projected income statement and supporting schedules for the year.

In addition to relating the cost and revenue factors that underlie the income statement, the model relates the factors revelant to inventory management and to idle capacity. The model can be validated by using actual past values as input data and observing the extent to which the output values approximate the actual results achieved by the business firm.

Accounting System Structured on a LP Model

An interesting OR application is an accounting system which is structured on a linear programming model.[16] This can be illustrated as applied to a particular industry, petroleum. To get an idea of the problem involved, a

---

[16] J. Demski, "An Accounting System Structured on a Linear Programming Model," *The Accounting Review*, October, 1967, pp. 701-712.

certain refinery must produce a specified amount of gasoline and oil with certain quality specifications. To accomplish this objective, the refinery has at its disposal certain processing units and a number of raw materials. The problem is to select that combination of raw materials and processing sequences which minimize the total cost of meeting the stipulated market requirements. In terms of size, the model contains approximately 125 equations with 300 variables and slightly fewer than 3000 nonzero elements.

The internal accounting system of the refinery is responsibility-oriented using standard costs. The refinery is structured by divisions, each having departments with individual responsibility centers. Total costs are segregated into variable and fixed components. For each refinery, the firm has a mathematical model which is used for varied economic analysis. Actual blended and product quantities are inserted into the model and an adjusted "optimum" budget is determined—reflecting the standard cost of producing the end products actually produced during the quarter. Actual results and budgeted figures are then compared in an effort to review the particular quarter's performance. The quarterly accounting system, in effect, is merely a flexible budgeting arrangement in which actual cost incurred in the production of a set of end products is compared with the standard cost for that set of end products. The standard is determined by optimizing the linear programming model with these end product quantities. Hence this OR approach to accounting allows comparison of what the firm accomplished with what it should have accomplished using linear programming standards in order to determine accounting variances.

Concluding Remarks on Finance and Accounting

Just as newer OR quantitative methods and refinements to existing OR models have been developed for other functional areas of the firm, the same is true in the finance function and in the methods of compiling accounting data. A linear programming model for budgeting and financial planning, cost finding through multiple correlation analysis, use of matrix accounting, concepts of statistical techniques in auditing, capital budgeting, and game theory are a few examples of the various directions operations research has taken. By no means have finance and accounting been restricted to problems within the firm. OR techniques have been utilized to help management in mergers and acquisitions as well as in determining the feasibility of leasing from the outside. As experience with new and improved financial and accounting methods is gained, higher levels of sophistication will be incorporated into quantitative models to further the profitability of the firm.

Current Quantitative Corporate Planning Models

Corporate planning models are highly complex and fully integrated models of the total corporate structure which can be employed as part of the planning process. These models represent, in detail, the physical operations of the company, the financial practices followed, and the response to investment in key areas. They furnish management with decision-oriented information on marketing, research and development, finance, cost estimating, competitive bidding, plant expansion, and long-range planning. It answers the many "what if" questions that are constantly occupying the minds of executives. Corporate modeling may well become one of the great milestones of modern management.

Corporate planning models play an important role in three areas of planning. First, they give the planner the ability to test the effect of an assumption not only in one area but over the company as a whole. For example, a particular construction project may look best from an engineering standpoint, but after testing the effects of that project on financing, taxes, and earnings per share of the company, perhaps another alternative would be more suitable. Using the real-time capabilities of computers, the total effect of a decision can be received within seconds. Second, the system can be employed to test the effect of today's decisions on future plans. For instance, in floating stock and bond issues, the type and amount are considered not only for current needs, but also to insure the ability to float the proper issue in the future. A corporate planning system bridges the gap between short- and long-range plans. Third, and last, the system serves as a basis for increasing communication in the decision-making process. Because the logic of the model is defined and documented, it is easy to retrace the outputs back to the underlying assumptions, making it easier for the manager to understand the output. The quick turn-around time, combined with the ease of handling, means up-to-date reports and company decisions all based on uniform information.

From a more general standpoint, the most unpublicized benefit of building a corporate planning system is the educational aspect produced during the development of the models. To stand back and analytically define the operations of a company gives management an unparalleled understanding of how the organization functions. The knowledge is already there, but management can now formally evaluate the interrelationships among the firm's functional areas.

General Corporate Model
The basic structure of a general corporate model allows management to raise a host of "what if" questions and receive immediate answers showing the impact of the proposed operational change on cash flow, income statement, balance sheet, production schedule, manpower schedule, and other critical factors. The general system program calls on specified logic from the corporate planning model for the problem at hand, using pertinent information from a bank of general and specific data.[17] The general system program also utilizes rapid computations from a time-shared computer. In a few moments the effects of the proposed change are printed for the manager's inspection. The new information may lead then to a decision by the manager

---

[17] James B. Boulden and Elwood S. Buffa, "Corporate Models: On-Line, Real-Time Systems," *Harvard Business Review*, July-August, 1970, pp. 65-83.

to ask questions concerning additional alternatives. Typical "what if" questions are:

- If products and/or service prices are changed, what will be the effect on cash flow as well as on net profits before federal income taxes?
- If proposed new equipment is purchased or leased, what will be the effect on cash flow and net profits before federal income taxes?
- If wage increases are granted, what will be the effect on productivity, amount of overtime, and the entire production program?

The main components of the general system program in relation to the data files and the corporate planning model logic are illustrated in Figure 18-5. The business series data file and the corporate planning model logic are unique to the particular enterprise while the economic series data file and the general system program are common to all applications.

Stored in the business series data file are proprietary data of the particular company, including sales, costs, and other information. These data and the corporate model logic are accessible to authorized personnel. On the other hand, the economic series data file contains a wide variety of national and industry economic series, such as gross national product, indexes of industrial production, and housing starts. These data series are maintained and updated by the operators of the general system.

In using the system, it is necessary to manipulate the raw data contained in the business and economic series files in meaningful ways so

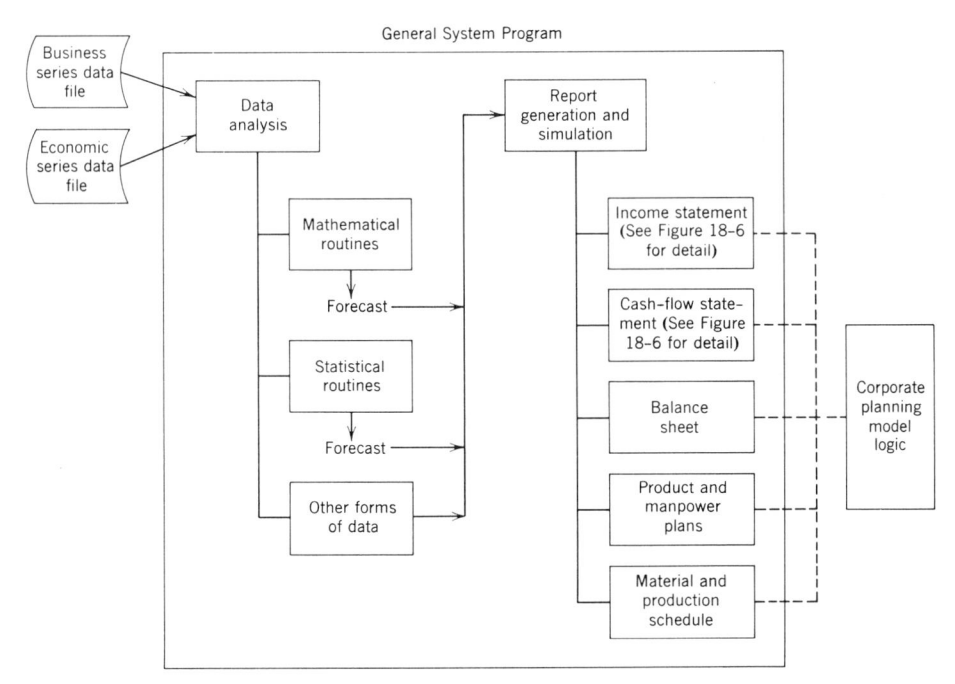

Figure 18-5 Interrelationships of a general system program to the corporate planning model logic and the data files.

as to forecast future sales or other aspects of performance. An analyst might take raw sales data from the business file and smooth them by removing seasonal and cyclical variations. The final result of his analysis is a forecast which becomes an input to the report generation and simulation phase, as illustrated in Figure 18-5. He may wish to employ more than one forecast (for example, expected, optimistic, and pessimistic forecasts) in the simulation phase to see how they reflect on the income statement, cash-flow statement, and balance sheet. The important fact concerning the data analysis phase is the integrated nature of the general system program which makes it possible to carry effects computed by one subprogram into another subprogram.

The next phase (report generation and simulation) is where the manager can test the different assumptions and ideas he has. This is the part of the system in which businessmen are most interested. Sample manipulation and output possible in corporate financial analysis is shown in Figure 18-6 for the income statement and the cash flow statement. Any form of operating report can be generated, including facility utilization, manpower requirements, and raw materials flow.

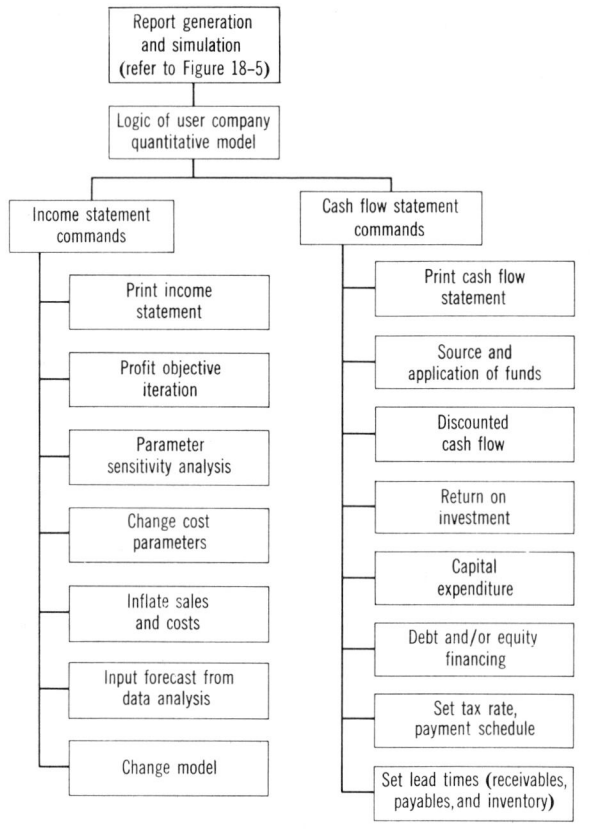

Figure 18-6 Corporate financial analysis—income statement and cash flow statement (elaboration of Figure 18-5).

592 FUTURE OF OPERATIONS RESEARCH

Raising "what if" questions of the type mentioned earlier, the manager determines the effect of various actions and events on income and cash statements. The corporate planning model logic works in conjunction with the general system program to produce these reports (printed in a form specified by the manager). Thus the manager can try many alternate sets of assumptions and see almost immediately the effects of the proposed changes.

Corporate Simulation Model
Numerous corporate simulation models have been developed for various sized firms. One such model is called CORSIM (CORporate SIMulation), developed for a relatively small firm in the capital goods industry.[18] The CORSIM model has been utilized successfully in four types of situations:

1. Capacity planning—timing of plant expansion and capital equipment purchase. Expansion of plant capacity often can be delayed by utilizing subcontractors and/or allowing backlogs and delivery lead times to increase. However, as demand on the production system continues to increase, these become increasingly expensive alternatives to capital investment. The CORSIM model provides a means to compare these alternative costs and cash flows.
2. Budgeting—testing alternative budgets for the coming budget period. Many alternative budgets for various assumed sets of conditions now can be explored, whereas in the past only a few possibilities could be evaluated due to the time required for manual calculations.
3. Inventory planning—testing alternative inventory strategies. Reduction of a firm's investment in inventories is an inevitable topic of discussion from time to time in any firm. The CORSIM model provides a means to analyze this question by evaluating alternative means of accomplishing inventory reduction (e.g., by decreasing lot sizes and/or safety stocks) and the effect of each upon customer service and company profits.
4. Aggregate production planning—planning of alternative aggregate levels of work force, production, and subcontracting. Again, the CORSIM model provides a means for management to evaluate alternative decisions and to determine their effects upon the firm.

In each of these situations, the dominant consideration is the interrelationship which exists among the decision variables and the performance of the firm, and a means of analyzing these decision problems is an aggregrate-level simulation model of the firm. The procedure used calls for management to develop a set of decisions, to incorporate these decisions into the model, and to determine their expected impact upon the firm from the model using the proposed decision variables.

For the purposes of model building, the firm is considered to be a set of modules, as shown in Figure 18-7, with the assumption that for each

---
[18] William B. Lee, "Corporate Simulation Models and Purchases Decision-Making," *Journal of Purchasing*, November, 1972, pp. 4-16.

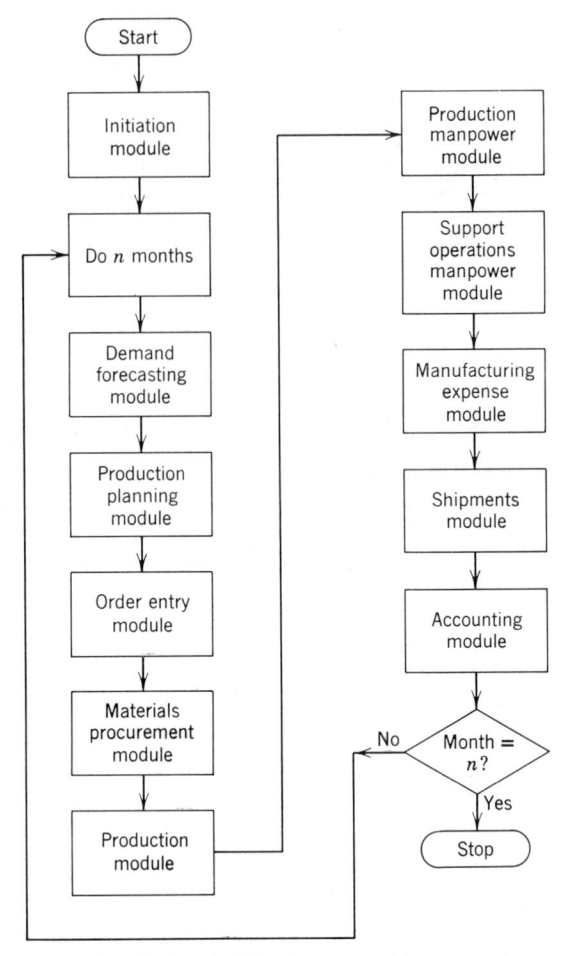

Figure 18-7 Corporate simulation (CORSIM)—modular flowchart.

month of the simulation run the tasks structured into these modules are accomplished in the sequence shown. The demand forecasting module in the illustration provides the forecast of future demand for use in the production planning module which contains decision rules to plan production, work force, subcontracting, and inventories for succeeding months in the simulation run. Through the use of appropriate subroutines, any of several decision rules can be utilized to accomplish this planning function, or the experimenter can incorporate his own set of decisions. The performance of alternative sets of decisions and of alternative means of arriving at decisions, thus, can be evaluated. The order entry module simulates the receipt of new orders from customers each month. Then the operation of the firm is simulated for the month, based on the demand forecast, the production plan, and the simulated orders entered. The materials procurement module simulates the purchasing of the appropriate materials, and the production module simulates production for the month. The production manpower module, the support operations manpower module, and the manufacturing expense module contain dependent variables and thus simulate the consequences of the decisions and actions taken in the previous modules. The shipments module simulates the shipment of finished good per customers' orders, and the accounting module is utilized to gather the data produced during the course of the simulation run and to print the appropriate accounting statements. Standard accounting formats utilized by the firm are prepared, including the income statement, balance sheet, and analysis of various expense categories. Other statements and analyses which currently may not be available but which potentially have usefulness to the management of the firm can be prepared. An important side benefit is the capability to evaluate proposed new information prior to expending resources for its development.

Concluding Remarks on Corporate Planning
The focus of a corporate model is on an entire company, not just on a division or functional area. This feature encourages a global or overall viewpoint in the analysis of problems and enhances the likelihood of capturing the full financial impact of a proposed course of action. Planning in large companies tends to focus along departmental responsibilities and, as a result, plans sometimes lack overall coordination and the underlying assumptions may be inconsistent. A corporate model demands companywide effort to take advantage of the knowledge and expertise in all departments of a company. It is a tool for executive management, not just for the controller's department.

A corporate model emphasizes the financial dimension of a company's operations. The model may contain details concerning marketing, production, personnel, or other factors, but the ultimate objective is the financial result implied by these items. Nonfinancial factors may form an important part of a corporate model, but only because of their ultimate impact on the projected financial results.

Unlike financial reporting, the object of which is to disclose what has occurred in the past, financial projection, and correspondingly, corporate models are future oriented. Historical data provides useful insight into past relationships which, as a first approximation, may be forecasted into the future. Planning, by its very nature, is primarily concerned with the future.

Operations Research—An Overview

Operations research and management science journals abound with material found in this book. Unfortunately, much of this material requires a greater understanding of OR techniques than can be obtained from an introductory text. Nevertheless, knowledge of OR methods can provide the reader with a deeper appreciation and understanding of the quantitative approach to business problems. After all, students of operations research today will be tomorrow's important managers. An understanding of the basic concepts will advance the application of operations research.

Operations Research at Present

The current direction of operations research within the firm has been treated in this book. The reader should have noticed the similarity of problems being solved by different OR techniques. For example, inventory problems have utilized EOQ models, dynamic programming, simulation, or some combination. One firm might be able to solve a specific problem by one method, whereas another firm might need an entirely different approach to solve its problem. No matter what approach is undertaken by the OR group, there is one basic direction—enabling management to make better, and hopefully, optimal decisions.

The basis for an optimum solution utilizing any OR quantitative method is predicated upon using accurate costs and taking into account all the relevant factors. Cost estimates, generally, are available if a cost accounting system is operating. Wherever reliable cost systems are operating, accurate figures for manufacturing and finance can be developed since these areas are somewhat static. In the area of marketing, less reliable data is available since this is a more dynamic area and least understood by the cost accountants.

Not only must the OR group develop reliable cost data and take into account the appropriate factors affecting the problem, but it must determine the interactions among the numerous factors in the problem. The failure to set forth the interrelationships in the mathematical model can only lead to incorrect or approximate solutions. This is easier to accomplish in the areas of manufacturing and finance than in marketing. The reason for this is that many major marketing decisions have factors that are not under the control of the decision maker, that is, they depend on factors outside the firm itself. An optimum or near optimum OR marketing solution attempts to unravel the interrelationships of the various factors and, even then, usually requires some important assumptions. The problem of costs and interacting factors make OR solutions somewhat less reliable in the marketing functions versus other functions.

Within the past few years, there has been a concerted effort on the part of OR groups to develop some type of mathematical model for the entire firm. Basically, these have been large-scale simulation models of the firm. Primary emphasis is placed on the behavior of the firm as a whole rather than on some particular area. The purpose in constructing these large-scale models is to learn how managerial activity, particularly decision making and control, can be explicitly modeled. The reduction of organizational concepts to precise formulation and the requirement to specify decision rules and procedures is an education not only for the model builders but also for people interested in large-scale simulation models.

A further extension of large-scale simulation models is joint large-scale simulation models. Using modeling techniques that extend to the supplier-manufacturer-distributor-customer sequence, the manufacturer, for example, can assign inventory and distribution arrangements in such a way as to produce lower costs for the whole sequence of firms involved. At present, these types of joint optimization models are under consideration by progressive firms. The potential return to all firms in such an arrangement cannot but help relieve the ever-increasing pressure on profits. Not only is vertical integration possible to firms, but horizontal integration also is feasible.

The increasing use of quantitative methods of operations research is currently having a dramatic effect on the human element, namely lower and middle management. Many of the present decision making activities of these managerial levels are capable of being programmed. Computers can perform the necessary operations and, in turn, feed to these levels the optimum answer or courses of action. Examples were shown throughout the book, some of which are control of inventories—raw materials, work in process, and finished goods; optimum scheduling; and best routing of shipments. Once the problem has been programmed, it is no longer necessary for the manager to give as much time and thought in reaching decisions on the firm's problems. Instead of being bogged down with the routine decisions of his department, he can now relegate these to a management information computer system. Thus lower and middle management can now spend time planning for their respective areas, training their personnel, and, perhaps for the first time, getting their respective jobs "under control."

The impact of quantitative methods on top management has likewise been dramatic. While the primary functions of lower and middle management are organizing, directing, and controlling the firm's activities, the primary concern of those at the highest level is planning the objectives, policies, and procedures that provide a framework for guiding the firm in a changing environment. Computer feedback from a management information system that utilizes the "management by exception" concept allows top management to review and evaluate all significant deviations (favorable and unfavorable) from the present profit plan. This information is instrumental in formulating the future plans of the firm. The use of computer models, then, has freed management from routine work in order to concentrate on the overall direction of the firm. However, there are a growing number of problems that are too complex for present quantitative methods or too time consuming for solution. The freeing of top management from some routine tasks will allow them to concentrate on these more difficult problems.

No matter what level of management is involved in operations research, it must help the OR group isolate and clarify the variables that have a bearing on the solution. Management must carefully consider the soundness of the quantitative information gathered about these variables and be able to assist OR personnel in assigning realistic weights to the variables. In most cases, managers need all of the assistance of quantitative methods that are available to them in order to cope with the complexity of their positions.

Operations Research in the Future
The dynamics of the business world today, but more so in the future, are forcing companies to concentrate on the planning process, in particular,

planning for change and planning necessitated by change. The dynamics of products (the shortened life of products), markets (technically superior products displace established products in the marketplace here and abroad), industrial processes (the shortened and changing state of manufacturing processes), and government and society (legal and social constraints imposed on the firm which are continually changing) will be causing firms to plan carefully for the short, medium, and long range. In addition, the entry of more sophisticated computers, with their ability to handle unbelievable amounts of data, the continuing trend toward growth by merger and acquisition, and the growing problems with labor unions will highlight the need for effective planning. It will be only through the use of optimum plans which consider all the relevant changing factors that the firm can benefit rather than its competition. The planning function, then, is and will continue to be a logical candidate for quanitative study since operations research actually uses a planned approach in problem solving. Several OR methods are available for planning, some of which were indicated throughout this book.

Tomorrow's managers will be affected by organization structure changes. This will be particularly noticeable in the middle management area. It is becoming more and more important for firms to innovate with the market as the focus. This means that the marketing department takes preference over the other areas of the firm. To state it another way, firms must bring their products to the right market at the right time in order to satisfy a particular market segment. This may necessitate a change in market structure. For example, direct shipments may eliminate the need for a middle manager since such transactions can be handled by a computer.

The dynamics of business will cause changes at the top management level. There will be the employment of numerous staff specialists to advise top management on special aspects of their jobs. Most of these specialists will have direct access to the computer through input/output terminal devices that allow them to use some mathematical model in order to solve a pressing management problem. The president may have attached to his office a planning staff—an operations research specialist, an economist, a marketing research specialist, and a scientific adviser. Similarly, the marketing, manufacturing, finance (and accounting), engineering, R & D and personnel executives will be served by staff specialists so that knowledge from many disciplines will be used to solve complex business problems. By no means will computer mathematical models be limited to the OR group in the future. Many disciplines will have taken up the planned approach in solving complex well structured or poorly structured problems as well as behavioral problems.

The methods of operations research that will be developed in the future will arise out of the necessity to solve particular problems. Among these will be the construction of a mathematical model for the entire firm. This model will demonstrate interrelationships of all its parts more clearly than they have ever been understood before. It might, for example, permit management to make far more accurate judgments about the potential value of a possible acquisition and its resultant effect in the long run on the firm. This model might enable management to gauge in advance the probable impact on the firm of the various external conditions, such as development of new technology, and to take action accordingly. Newer on-line, real-time computers with massive storage facilities should be capable of handling such mathematical models for most firms. It is hoped that future computers will have the hardware to simulate the supplier-manufacturer-distributor-retailer relationship model in a routine manner. Thus, large-scale OR models will not be restricted to the firm but will be available to all phases of business activity.

Conclusion

The increasing managerial use of quantitative methods, backed up by the use of computers, is now considered a major turning point in the traditional way of viewing managerial functions of the firm. This revolution has given management at all levels improved information for decision making. The very structure of the firm has been changed to allow the optimum use of these OR computer techniques. The resulting answers from OR methods, models, and techniques have helped to liberate management so it can spend its energy on arriving at key decisions and laying plans for the growth of the business. It has made possible more effective centralized control of large, complex corporations. The information resulting from quantitative methods of operations research has helped and will continue to assist management in making sense out of the bewildering number of changes taking place in the real world. Management is now and will continue to do a much better job of sorting out the innumerable courses of action, testing its relative profit potentials, and reducing the resulting risks. As mentioned repeatedly throughout the book, management should utilize the output from OR studies as an additional insight for solving its problems. If there are other important factors bearing on the problem that were not or could not have been included in the OR study or certain basic assumptions were made, the manager must weigh these factors in light of the OR results. To blindly concur with the output from an OR project when other concomitant factors apply is sheer folly on the manager's part. While the function of an operations research group is to advise the manager with their recommendations based on an objective approach to a problem, the manager still must temper these recommendations if certain critical conditions apply. The fact that the manager has the authority and responsibility as well as eventually being held accountable for an important decision is reason enough for seeking the objective assistance of operations research.

Questions

1. What are the emerging directions of operations research now as well as in the future?

2. What are the problems associated with large, complex OR models, such as venture analysis?
3. What effect will computer OR models have on the various levels of management?
4. How can management best utilize operations research in decision making?

Bibliography

R. L. Ackoff and R. Rivett, *A Manager's Guide to Operations Research*, New York: John Wiley & Sons, 1963.

P. E. Green and R. E. Frank, *A Manager's Guide to Marketing Research*, New York: John Wiley & Sons, 1967.

C. McMillan and R. F. Gonzalez, *Systems Analysis*, Homewood, Ill.: Richard D. Irwin, 1968.

D. W. Miller and M. K. Starr, *Executive Decisions and Operations Research*, Englewood Cliffs, N.J.: Prentice-Hall, 1969.

T. H. Williams and C. H. Griffin, *Management Information, A Quantitative Accent*, Homewood, Ill.: Richard D. Irwin, 1967.

Appendixes

Appendixes

Appendix A

Vectors, Matrices, and Determinants

The mathematical methods in this appendix have applications not only in linear programming but also in nonlinear programming, game theory, Markov analysis, queuing theory, and other quantitative techniques. Vectors, matrices, and determinants will be presented with a minimum of mathematical notation. This approach does not reduce the potential value of these methods.

Vectors

A vector is defined as a line with direction and length. All vectors are assumed to start at point zero. Consider vector V_1 consisting of a single number, say 4. This is represented in Figure A-1. Similarly, vector V_2 with a -3 value is represented by a single dimension per Figure A-1. Thus a vector can be seen to have direction ($+$ and $-$) and length (4 units and 3 units).

Vectors, having two elements, can be graphed. They can be expressed either as row vectors $(a_1\ a_2,\ a_3,\ \ldots)$ or column vectors $\begin{pmatrix} a_1 \\ a_2 \\ \vdots \end{pmatrix}$. Consider, for example, vector $V_3 \begin{pmatrix} 3 \\ 3 \end{pmatrix}$ which is graphed in Figure A-2. Whereas one component vector can be graphed in a single dimension, it takes two-dimensional space to graph a two-component vector. Similarly, a three-component vector $V_4 \begin{pmatrix} 1 \\ 2 \\ 3 \end{pmatrix}$ can be represented in three-dimensional space as in Figure A-3. In general, it takes n-dimensional space to represent an n-component vector. Any vector larger than a three-component vector cannot be graphed.

A vector may have one or more negative coordinates as shown in Figure A-4. The vector $V_5 \begin{pmatrix} 3 \\ -3 \end{pmatrix}$ indicates the end of the vector is located by moving 3 units in a positive direction on the x axis and 3 units in a nega-

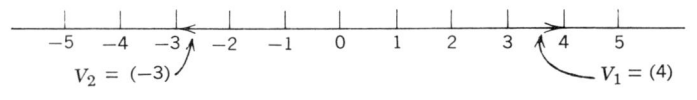

$V_2 = (-3)$ $V_1 = (4)$

Figure A-1

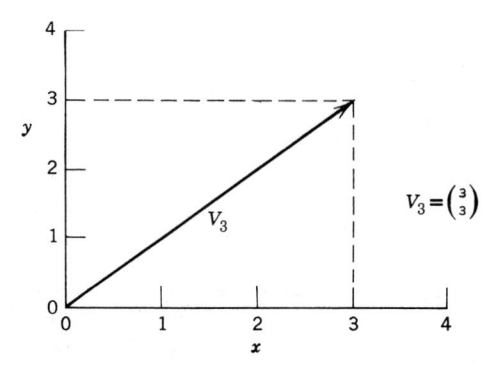

Figure A-2

$$V_3 = \begin{pmatrix} 3 \\ 3 \end{pmatrix}$$

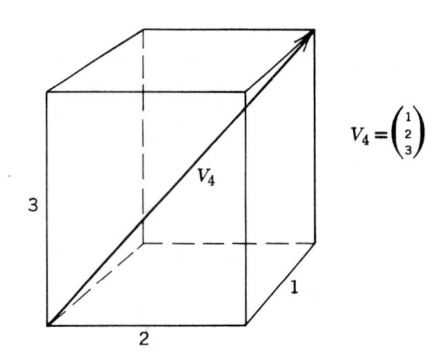

Figure A-3

$$V_4 = \begin{pmatrix} 1 \\ 2 \\ 3 \end{pmatrix}$$

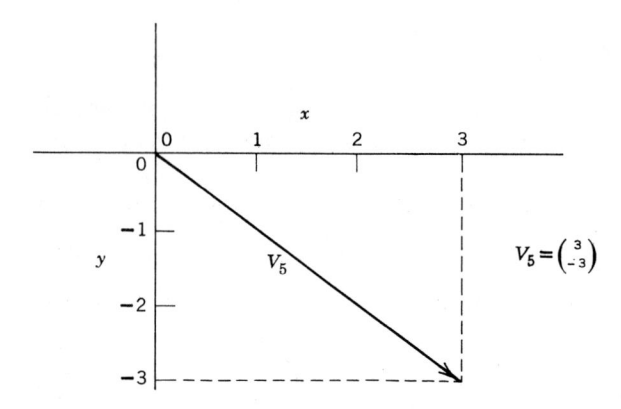

Figure A-4

$$V_5 = \begin{pmatrix} 3 \\ -3 \end{pmatrix}$$

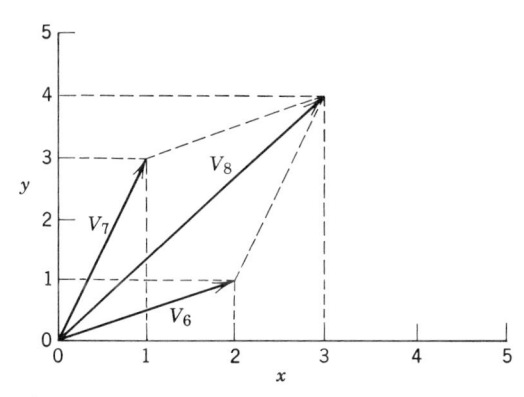

Figure A-5

tive direction on the y axis. The rules for positive and negative signs are taken from geometry.

The length of any vector that does not lie exactly on one of the axes is not known from looking at its vector representation. Referring to geometry, it can be computed in the same manner as the hypotenuse of a right triangle. In Figure A-4, the length of the vector V_5 $\begin{pmatrix} 3 \\ -3 \end{pmatrix}$ is computed as follows:

$$(V_5)^2 = (3^2) + (-3^2)$$
$$= 18$$
$$V_5 = \sqrt{18}$$
$$= 4.3$$

Vectors can be added and subtracted if the two given vectors have the same dimensions, that is, they are the same type of vectors and have the same number of elements. The vector V_6 $\begin{pmatrix} 2 \\ 1 \end{pmatrix}$ can be added to vector V_7 $\begin{pmatrix} 1 \\ 3 \end{pmatrix}$, the sum being V_8 $\begin{pmatrix} 3 \\ 4 \end{pmatrix}$. Both vectors need a two-dimensional space to be represented graphically. The resulting vector V_8 is a diagonal, passing through the origin of the parallelogram formed by the vectors V_6 and V_7. This is shown in Figure A-5.

Just as vectors can be added and subtracted, a vector can be multiplied by any number to form a multiple of the original vector. The multiplier is called a scalar. The process of multiplication is accomplished by multiplying each coordinate of the vector by the scalar. Consider the example in Figure A-6. The vector V_9 $\begin{pmatrix} 2 \\ 3 \end{pmatrix}$ has been multiplied by a scalar, the number 2, with a resulting vector V_{10} $\begin{pmatrix} 4 \\ 6 \end{pmatrix}$. The resultant vector V_{10} is called a scalar multiple of vector V_9.

By using one dimension for a moment, all vectors found are scalar multiples of each other. This concept, shown in Figure A-7 for the x axis, is also applicable to the y axis. This concept can also be applied to two dimen-

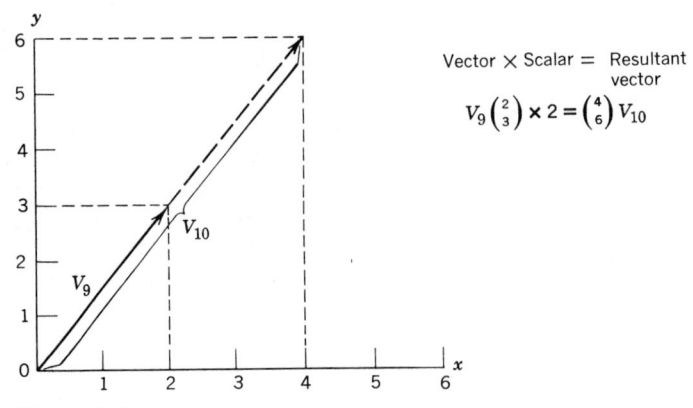

Figure A-6

$$V_9 \begin{pmatrix} 2 \\ 3 \end{pmatrix} \times 2 = \begin{pmatrix} 4 \\ 6 \end{pmatrix} V_{10}$$

Vector × Scalar = Resultant vector

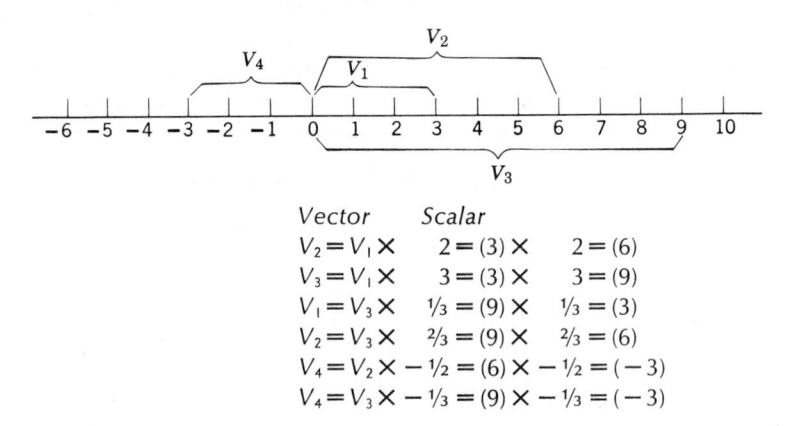

Vector	Scalar		
$V_2 = V_1 \times$	$2 = (3) \times$	$2 = (6)$	
$V_3 = V_1 \times$	$3 = (3) \times$	$3 = (9)$	
$V_1 = V_3 \times$	$1/3 = (9) \times$	$1/3 = (3)$	
$V_2 = V_3 \times$	$2/3 = (9) \times$	$2/3 = (6)$	
$V_4 = V_2 \times$	$-1/2 = (6) \times$	$-1/2 = (-3)$	
$V_4 = V_3 \times$	$-1/3 = (9) \times$	$-1/3 = (-3)$	

Figure A-7 All vectors are scalar multiples of each other.

sions. In Figure A-8, vectors V_5 and V_6 are reference vectors while vector V_7 is a vector in space that can be described as a scalar multiple of the two reference or basis vectors, V_5 and V_6. In three dimensions, three reference vectors would be required, one for each dimension.

Vector V_7 in Figure A-8 can be formed with the basis vectors V_5 and V_6 by finding the appropriate scalars with which to multiply the reference or basis vectors:

Vector $V_7 =$ (some scalar)(V_5) + (some scalar)(V_6)

Letting A equal the appropriate scalar for vector V_5 and B equal the appropriate scalar for vector V_6, the resulting equation is:

$$V_7 = A \begin{pmatrix} 4 \\ 2 \end{pmatrix} + B \begin{pmatrix} 2 \\ 4 \end{pmatrix}$$

Since we know that the resultant vector $V_7 = \begin{pmatrix} 4 \\ 4 \end{pmatrix}$, the preceding equation

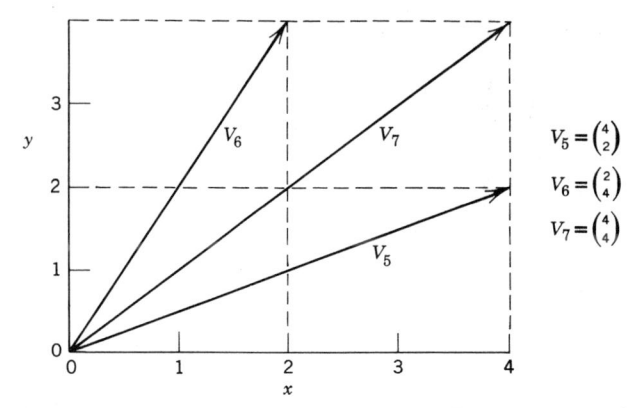

Figure A-8 V_5 and V_6 are reference or basis vectors while V_7 is a scalar multiple of V_5 and V_6.

can be written as:

$$\begin{pmatrix} 4 \\ 4 \end{pmatrix} = \begin{pmatrix} 4A \\ 2A \end{pmatrix} + \begin{pmatrix} 2B \\ 4B \end{pmatrix}$$

$$4 = 4A + 2B$$
$$4 = 2A + 4B$$

Using simultaneous equations, multiply the top equation by 2, subtract, and divide the result by 6:

$$8 = 8A + 4B$$
$$-(4 = 2A + 4B)$$
$$\frac{4}{6} = \frac{6A}{6}$$
$$A = \frac{2}{3}$$

Substituting A into the first equation yields:

$$4 = 4\left(\frac{2}{3}\right) + 2B$$
$$4 = 2\frac{2}{3} + 2B$$
$$4 - 2\frac{2}{3} = 2B$$
$$\frac{1\frac{1}{3}}{2} = \frac{2B}{2}$$
$$B = \frac{2}{3}$$

This may be checked by substituting the scalars (A and B) back into the original equation as follows:

APPENDIXES 607

$$V_7 = A\begin{pmatrix}4\\2\end{pmatrix} + B\begin{pmatrix}2\\4\end{pmatrix}$$

$$= \frac{2}{3}\begin{pmatrix}4\\2\end{pmatrix} + \frac{2}{3}\begin{pmatrix}2\\4\end{pmatrix}$$

$$= \begin{pmatrix}2\frac{2}{3}\\1\frac{1}{3}\end{pmatrix} + \begin{pmatrix}1\frac{1}{3}\\2\frac{2}{3}\end{pmatrix}$$

$$= \begin{pmatrix}4\\4\end{pmatrix}$$

The two-dimensional space in Figure A-9 contains two vectors, V_8 and V_9, and a third vector, V_{10}. It is not possible to find the direction of a third vector using vectors V_8 and V_9 since both have y coordinates of 0. Being scalar multiples of each other, V_8 and V_9 are called dependent vectors. In mathematics, dependent vectors cannot be basis vectors, which is the name given to a pair of vectors that can be used to derive a third vector, such as V_{10}.

Previously, we stated that an n-dimensional vector can be represented as a linear combination of n linearly independent vectors. The problem is to determine the specific combination of given linearly independent vectors with which to form a given vector. Consider the two linearly independent vectors, $V_1 \begin{pmatrix}2\\3\end{pmatrix}$ and $V_2 \begin{pmatrix}1\\2\end{pmatrix}$. The problem is to determine what linear combination of V_1 and V_2 will form the resultant vector $V_3 \begin{pmatrix}40\\50\end{pmatrix}$. In other words, find the scalars (A and B) for the following equation:

$$\begin{pmatrix}40\\50\end{pmatrix} = A\begin{pmatrix}2\\3\end{pmatrix} + B\begin{pmatrix}1\\2\end{pmatrix}$$

$40 = 2A + B$ (multiply by 2) $80 = 4A + 2B$
$50 = 3A + 2B$ $\underline{50 = 3A + 2B}$
                                                                   $A = 30$

$40 = 2(30) + B$
$40 = 60 + B$
$B = -20$

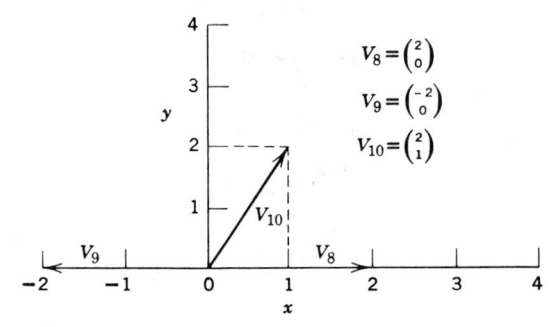

Figure A-9 Vectors V_8 and V_9 are dependent since they are not basis vectors, but they are scalar multiples of each other.

The scalars ($A = 30$ and $B = -20$) can be checked by substituting them back into the original equation as follows:

$$\begin{pmatrix} 40 \\ 50 \end{pmatrix} = (30) \begin{pmatrix} 2 \\ 3 \end{pmatrix} + (-20) \begin{pmatrix} 1 \\ 2 \end{pmatrix}$$

$$= \begin{pmatrix} 60 \\ 90 \end{pmatrix} - \begin{pmatrix} 20 \\ 40 \end{pmatrix}$$

$$= \begin{pmatrix} 40 \\ 50 \end{pmatrix}$$

Note that the specific linear combination above was obtained by transforming vectors into linear equations. Likewise, linear equations can be transformed into vectors. Linear programming, which involves a set of linear equations, can be solved by the vector method. It should be pointed out that most linear programming problems are not this simple. However, the foregoing material should provide a general understanding of vectors.

Matrices

Matrix algebra is extremely useful in solving a set of linear equations. Any linear programming problem can be solved with the help of matrix algebra, in particular, the algorithm (a systematic procedure) of the simplex method is based on the concepts of matrices and inversion of matrices. Therefore it is essential that the individual become familiar with matrices. Matrices also appear in several other chapters.

A matrix is a rectangular array of ordered numbers, arranged into rows and columns. The purpose of a matrix is to convey information in a concise manner and in an acceptable form for mathematical manipulation. Taken as a whole, a matrix has no numeric value. Any matrix in which the number of rows equals the number of columns is called a square matrix. A vector is a special case of a matrix with only one row or one column. Given below are several examples of matrices:

(a)
$$\begin{pmatrix} 2 & 4 \\ 1 & 5 \end{pmatrix}$$
2×2 matrix

(b)
$$\begin{pmatrix} 2 & 1 & 3 \\ 4 & 0 & 1 \end{pmatrix}$$
2×3 matrix

(c)
$$\begin{pmatrix} 4 & 4 & 4 \\ 1 & 8 & 6 \\ 7 & 1 & 2 \end{pmatrix}$$
3×3 matrix

The number of rows and columns in a given matrix determines the dimension or order of the matrix. Matrix (a) is a 2×2 matrix, matrix (b) is a 2×3 matrix, and matrix (c) is a 3×3 matrix. When specifying the order or dimension of a matrix, the first number relates to the row and the second number refers to the column of the matrix. Thus the dimension of a matrix with m rows and n columns is $m \times n$. Rows in the matrix are numbered from top to bottom while columns are numbered from left to right. The values within a matrix are referred to as the "elements" of the matrix.

Referring to the matrix (b) above, we can observe that this matrix consists of two row vectors placed together or three column vectors placed together. This is shown as follows:

$$\begin{pmatrix} 2 & 1 & 3 \\ 4 & 0 & 1 \end{pmatrix} \begin{pmatrix} 2 \\ 4 \end{pmatrix} \begin{pmatrix} 1 \\ 0 \end{pmatrix} \begin{pmatrix} 3 \\ 1 \end{pmatrix}$$

Thus it can be shown that vectors and matrices are interrelated.

Two given matrices can be added only if they have the same dimensions. Once it is established that the number of rows and columns of the two matrices are identical, their respective elements can be added together. Matrix addition is known as *elementwise* addition. The rules for matrix subtraction are the same as those for matrix addition. The subtraction process is an elementwise subtraction. The following are examples of matrix addition and subtraction:

Addition
Matrix A + Matrix B = Matrix C

$$\begin{pmatrix} 2 & 4 & 2 \\ 6 & 2 & 6 \end{pmatrix} + \begin{pmatrix} 1 & 1 & 2 \\ 4 & 4 & 6 \end{pmatrix} = \begin{pmatrix} 3 & 5 & 4 \\ 10 & 6 & 12 \end{pmatrix}$$

$$\begin{pmatrix} 2 & 4 & -2 \\ -6 & 2 & 6 \end{pmatrix} + \begin{pmatrix} 1 & -1 & 2 \\ 4 & -4 & 6 \end{pmatrix} = \begin{pmatrix} 3 & 3 & 0 \\ -2 & -2 & 12 \end{pmatrix}$$

Subtraction
Matrix A − Matrix B = Matrix C

$$\begin{pmatrix} 1 & 3 & 4 \\ 8 & 1 & 2 \end{pmatrix} - \begin{pmatrix} 1 & 9 & 2 \\ 4 & 1 & 1 \end{pmatrix} = \begin{pmatrix} 0 & -6 & 2 \\ 4 & 0 & 1 \end{pmatrix}$$

$$\begin{pmatrix} 1 & -3 & 4 \\ 8 & 1 & -2 \end{pmatrix} - \begin{pmatrix} 1 & -9 & 2 \\ 4 & 1 & -1 \end{pmatrix} = \begin{pmatrix} 0 & 6 & 2 \\ 4 & 0 & -1 \end{pmatrix}$$

The definition for multiplication of a row vector by a column vector can be easily extended to cover matrix multiplication. Two matrices can be multiplied together if the number of columns in the first matrix equals the number of rows in the second matrix. Unless this condition is met, the multiplication is impossible. However, if two matrices placed side by side do not meet the test, swapping positions may qualify them for multiplication but may fail to give the correct solution since matrix multiplication is not commutative. The following are some examples of matrices that can or cannot be multiplied:

First Matrix (*A*)   Second Matrix (*B*)

First Example:

$$\begin{pmatrix} 4 \\ 5 \end{pmatrix} \quad \times \quad (3 \quad 8) \quad \text{can be multiplied}$$

$2 \times ① \longleftarrow = \longrightarrow ① \times 2$

Second Example:

$$\begin{pmatrix} 4 \\ 1 \\ 6 \end{pmatrix} \quad \times \quad \begin{pmatrix} 1 & 4 & 8 \\ 4 & 2 & 6 \end{pmatrix} \quad \begin{array}{l}\text{cannot be multi-}\\\text{plied (consider}\\\text{swapping}\\\text{positions)}\end{array}$$

610   APPENDIXES

$$3\times\textcircled{1}\leftarrow\neq\rightarrow\textcircled{2}\times 3$$

$$\begin{pmatrix} 1 & 4 & 8 \\ 4 & 2 & 6 \end{pmatrix} \qquad \begin{pmatrix} 4 \\ 1 \\ 6 \end{pmatrix}$$

can be multiplied after swapping positions

$$2\times\textcircled{3}\leftarrow=\rightarrow\textcircled{3}\times 1$$

Third Example:

$$\begin{pmatrix} 4 & 1 & 4 \\ 8 & 7 & 3 \\ 2 & 4 & 2 \end{pmatrix} \qquad \begin{pmatrix} 1 \\ 9 \\ 6 \\ 2 \end{pmatrix}$$

cannot be multiplied (consider swapping positions)

$$3\times\textcircled{3}\leftarrow\neq\rightarrow\textcircled{4}\times 1$$

$$\begin{pmatrix} 1 \\ 9 \\ 6 \\ 2 \end{pmatrix} \qquad \begin{pmatrix} 4 & 1 & 4 \\ 8 & 7 & 3 \\ 2 & 4 & 2 \end{pmatrix}$$

still cannot be multiplied

$$4\times\textcircled{1}\leftarrow\neq\rightarrow\textcircled{3}\times 3$$

Using the first example above, we know the two matrices can be multiplied. If we look at the outer numbers (2 for Matrix A and 2 for Matrix B), this indicates the size of the matrix for the answer. If we know the final answer is a 2×2 matrix, four elements must be contained in the matrix. To obtain any element in the final answer, it is necessary first to determine the row and column location of that element in the solution. Using the first example below, we want to know how the element 32 was computed. This element is in the first row and the second column. To compute it, we multiply the first row of matrix A by the second column of matrix B, or 4×8=32.

Matrix A × Matrix B = Matrix C

$$\begin{pmatrix} 4 \\ 5 \end{pmatrix} \times \begin{pmatrix} 3 & 8 \end{pmatrix} = \begin{pmatrix} 12 & 32 \\ 15 & 40 \end{pmatrix}$$

1st row (4) × 1st col. (3) = 1st row, 1st col. (12)
1st row (4) × 2nd col. (8) = 1st row, 2nd col. (32)
2nd row (5) × 1st col. (3) = 2nd row, 1st col. (15)
2nd row (5) × 2nd col. (8) = 2nd row, 2nd col. (40)

A more involved matrix multiplication (3×3 matrix) is shown on the next page.

Finally, note that the multiplication of a matrix by a vector follows the rules of regular matrix multiplication as set forth above. The multiplication of a matrix by a scalar is accomplished by multiplying each term in the matrix by the scalar value.

Associated with every $m \times n$ matrix is another matrix whose rows are the columns of the given matrix, in exactly the same order. To state it another way, the first row of the original matrix becomes the first column in the derived matrix, the second row becomes the second column, and so

$$\begin{array}{ccccc}
\text{Matrix } A & \times & \text{Matrix } B & = & \text{Matrix } C \\
\begin{pmatrix} 4 & -4 & 0 \\ 1 & -2 & 6 \\ 7 & -1 & 2 \end{pmatrix} & \times & \begin{pmatrix} -2 & 6 & -3 \\ 0 & 7 & 0 \\ -4 & 8 & 1 \end{pmatrix} & = & \begin{pmatrix} -8 & -4 & -12 \\ -26 & 40 & 3 \\ -22 & 51 & -19 \end{pmatrix}
\end{array}$$

	Matrix A	Matrix B			Where figure is located in answer
1st row	$(4\ -4\ 0) \times$ 1st col.	$\begin{pmatrix} -2 \\ 0 \\ -4 \end{pmatrix}$	$= -8+0+0$	$= -8$	1st row, 1st col.
1st row	$(4\ -4\ 0) \times$ 2nd col.	$\begin{pmatrix} 6 \\ 7 \\ 8 \end{pmatrix}$	$= 24+(-28)+0$	$= -4$	1st row, 2nd col.
1st row	$(4\ -4\ 0) \times$ 3rd col.	$\begin{pmatrix} -3 \\ 0 \\ 1 \end{pmatrix}$	$= -12+0+0$	$= -12$	1st row, 3rd col.
2nd row	$(1\ -2\ 6) \times$ 1st col.	$\begin{pmatrix} -2 \\ 0 \\ -4 \end{pmatrix}$	$= -2+0+(-24)$	$= -26$	2nd row, 1st col.
2nd row	$(1\ -2\ 6) \times$ 2nd col.	$\begin{pmatrix} 6 \\ 7 \\ 8 \end{pmatrix}$	$= 6+(-14)+48$	$= 40$	2nd row, 2nd col.
2nd row	$(1\ -2\ 6) \times$ 3rd col.	$\begin{pmatrix} -3 \\ 0 \\ 1 \end{pmatrix}$	$= -3+0+6$	$= 3$	2nd row, 3rd col.
3rd row	$(7\ -1\ 2) \times$ 1st col.	$\begin{pmatrix} -2 \\ 0 \\ -4 \end{pmatrix}$	$= -14+0+(-8)$	$= -22$	3rd row, 1st col.
3rd row	$(7\ -1\ 2) \times$ 2nd col.	$\begin{pmatrix} 6 \\ 7 \\ 8 \end{pmatrix}$	$= 42+(-7)+16$	$= 51$	3rd row, 2nd col.
3rd row	$(7\ -1\ 2) \times$ 3rd col.	$\begin{pmatrix} -3 \\ 0 \\ 1 \end{pmatrix}$	$= -21+0+2$	$= -19$	3rd row, 3rd col.

forth. This derived matrix is called the transpose of a matrix. The transpose is a method often used to show data in a different form. The transpose of a matrix is shown as follows:

Original Matrix	Transpose of a Matrix
$\begin{pmatrix} 4 & 4 & 2 \\ 2 & 1 & 7 \\ -8 & 6 & 8 \end{pmatrix}$	$\begin{pmatrix} 4 & 2 & -8 \\ 4 & 1 & 6 \\ 2 & 7 & 8 \end{pmatrix}$

Each element of a squared matrix that is 2×2 and larger has associated with it a cofactor. A cofactor can be defined as that element or group of elements that remains when a row and a column have been removed from the matrix with the appropriate sign. In the matrix below, the cofactor of the circled element ④ has been formed:

Original Matrix − Row and Column Removed = Cofactor

$$\begin{pmatrix} 4 & 1 \\ 3 & 5 \end{pmatrix} \qquad \begin{pmatrix} 4 & 1 \\ 3 & \end{pmatrix} \qquad \begin{pmatrix} & \\ & 5 \end{pmatrix}$$

The same type of procedure is performed for the other three cofactors as follows:

Original Matrix − Row and Column Removed = Cofactor

$$\begin{pmatrix} 4 & 1 \\ 3 & 5 \end{pmatrix} \qquad \begin{pmatrix} 4 & 1 \\ & 5 \end{pmatrix} \qquad \begin{pmatrix} -3 & \\ & \end{pmatrix}$$

$$\begin{pmatrix} 4 & 1 \\ 3 & 5 \end{pmatrix} \qquad \begin{pmatrix} 4 & \\ 3 & 5 \end{pmatrix} \qquad \begin{pmatrix} & -1 \\ & \end{pmatrix}$$

$$\begin{pmatrix} 4 & 1 \\ 3 & 5 \end{pmatrix} \qquad \begin{pmatrix} & 1 \\ 3 & 5 \end{pmatrix} \qquad \begin{pmatrix} & \\ 4 & \end{pmatrix}$$

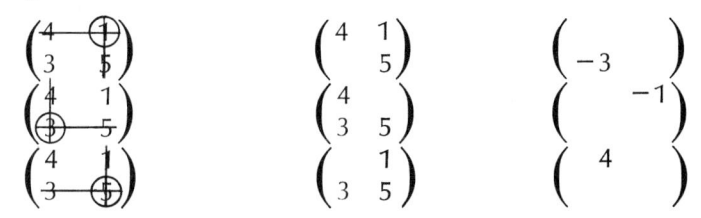

The original matrix has been transformed into its cofactors. Notice that the sign of two cofactors has been changed. In order to determine the sign of the cofactor, it is necessary to add together the location of the row and column which have been removed. If the total is an even number, the sign of the cofactor is unchanged. In the example above, the second cofactor (−3) was formed by deleting the first row and second column (1+2=odd). The odd number means the sign is changed (from +3 to −3).

After finding the cofactors, the matrix of cofactors must be computed in order to form the adjoint of a matrix. If each of the numbers in the original matrix were replaced by its cofactor, we would form the matrix of cofactors. Using the same example, this is shown as follows:

Original Matrix $\begin{pmatrix} 4 & 1 \\ 3 & 5 \end{pmatrix} \qquad \begin{pmatrix} a & b \\ c & d \end{pmatrix}$

Cofactors
$$\overset{a}{\begin{pmatrix} & \\ & 5 \end{pmatrix}} \quad \overset{b}{\begin{pmatrix} & \\ -3 & \end{pmatrix}} \quad \overset{c}{\begin{pmatrix} & -1 \\ & \end{pmatrix}} \quad \overset{d}{\begin{pmatrix} 4 & \\ & \end{pmatrix}}$$

Matrix of Cofactors $\begin{pmatrix} 5 & -3 \\ -1 & 4 \end{pmatrix}$ Original numbers (a, b, c, and d) have been replaced by their cofactors.

In 3×3 matrices and larger, the deletion of a row and a column which intersect each other forms a cofactor of a 2×2 size or larger. Consider the following example:

Original Matrix
$$\begin{pmatrix} 4 & 8 & 4 \\ 1 & 2 & 1 \\ 6 & 4 & 9 \end{pmatrix}$$

Cofactor formed by deleting 1st row and 1st column (even: sign unchanged)
$$\begin{pmatrix} 2 & 1 \\ 4 & 9 \end{pmatrix}$$

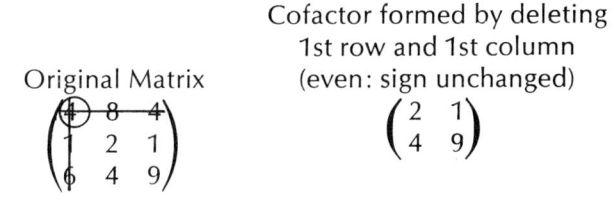

Since determinants can be used in solving for the value of a cofactor, they will be explained in the next section. It is sufficient to say that the numerical value of a 2×2 determinant can be found by multiplying together the ele-

APPENDIXES 613

ments lying on the primary diagonal (p) and subtracting the product of the elements lying on the secondary diagonal (s). In our example,

$$\begin{matrix} p & s \\ 2 & 1 \\ 4 & 9 \end{matrix}$$

the numerical value of the determinant (cofactor) is 14 (18−4). Again, the sign of the cofactor will reflect the location of the row and column removed. Since we have deleted the first row and the first column in the example, the sign remains unchanged.

The adjoint of a matrix is the transpose of the matrix of cofactors; it is useful in the study of games and optimum strategies. The adjoint of a matrix can also be very useful in finding the inverse of a given matrix. Returning to the earlier example, the adjoint of the matrix is as follows:

Original Matrix $\begin{pmatrix} 4 & 1 \\ 3 & 5 \end{pmatrix}$ Matrix of Cofactors $\begin{pmatrix} 5 & -3 \\ -1 & 4 \end{pmatrix}$ Adjoint of Matrix $\begin{pmatrix} 5 & -1 \\ -3 & 4 \end{pmatrix}$

An identity (unit) matrix is a square matrix whose primary diagonal (p) is formed entirely of ones and the remainder of the terms are zeros. Several examples are:

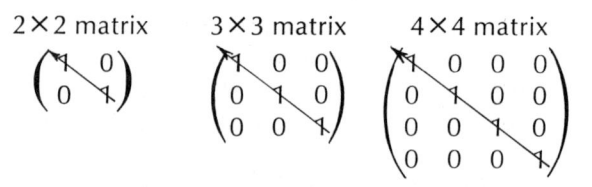

2×2 matrix $\begin{pmatrix} 1 & 0 \\ 0 & 1 \end{pmatrix}$ 3×3 matrix $\begin{pmatrix} 1 & 0 & 0 \\ 0 & 1 & 0 \\ 0 & 0 & 1 \end{pmatrix}$ 4×4 matrix $\begin{pmatrix} 1 & 0 & 0 & 0 \\ 0 & 1 & 0 & 0 \\ 0 & 0 & 1 & 0 \\ 0 & 0 & 0 & 1 \end{pmatrix}$

The initial tableau for the simplex method of linear programming with a squared matrix is a good example. Notice that the identity matrix is a combination of vectors (each of one unit in length) which forms a basis for space. For example, the 3×3 matrix used in three dimensions is graphed in Figure A-10. Because each axis of the space is one unit in length, finding scalar multiples of these bases is relatively easy.

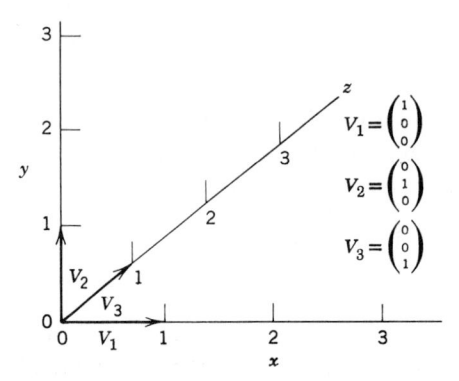

$V_1 = \begin{pmatrix} 1 \\ 0 \\ 0 \end{pmatrix}$ $V_2 = \begin{pmatrix} 0 \\ 1 \\ 0 \end{pmatrix}$ $V_3 = \begin{pmatrix} 0 \\ 0 \\ 1 \end{pmatrix}$

Figure A-10 Three-dimension graph.

The last area of matrix algebra covered is the inversion of a matrix. This is used in the simplex method of linear programming. The following example is used:

$$\begin{array}{ccccc} \text{Original Vector} & & \text{Original Matrix} & & \text{New Vector} \\ (2 \ \ 1) & \times & \begin{pmatrix} 4 & 6 \\ 8 & 10 \end{pmatrix} & = & (16 \ \ 22) \\ 1 \times \textcircled{2} & = & \textcircled{2} \times 2 & & \text{can be multiplied} \end{array}$$

The multiplication of vector (2 1) by the original matrix $\begin{pmatrix} 4 & 6 \\ 8 & 10 \end{pmatrix}$ will change the vector (2 1) to a new vector in two dimensions since the matrix acts as a combination of scalars. Remember that vectors are a special case of a matrix. Multiplying the inverse of a matrix by the new vector (16 22) will return a vector from some point in space to its original location, (2 1) in our problem.

An inverse can be formed for this problem. There are eight procedures, four involving rows and four involving columns that can be used on the original matrix to form an inverse. The method must be limited to rows or columns but not both. The row and column procedures are:

1. One row may be interchanged with another row.
2. A row can be multiplied by a constant.
3. One row can be added to or subtracted from another row.
4. A multiple of a row can be added to or subtracted from another row.
5. One column can be interchanged with another column.
6. A column can be multiplied by a constant.
7. One column can be added to or subtracted from another column.
8. A multiple of a column can be added to or subtracted from another column.

These procedures (rows and columns) have as their objective the conversion of the original matrix into an identity matrix. Row procedures is used in the example.

Original Matrix	Identity Matrix	Steps Performed
$\begin{pmatrix} 4 & 6 \\ 8 & 10 \end{pmatrix}$	$\begin{pmatrix} 1 & 0 \\ 0 & 1 \end{pmatrix}$	1. Set up the original matrix and the identity matrix
$\begin{pmatrix} 1 & 1\frac{1}{2} \\ 8 & 10 \end{pmatrix}$	$\begin{pmatrix} \frac{1}{4} & 0 \\ 0 & 1 \end{pmatrix}$	2. First row multiplied by $\frac{1}{4}$ (rule 2)
$\begin{pmatrix} 1 & 1\frac{1}{2} \\ 0 & -2 \end{pmatrix}$	$\begin{pmatrix} \frac{1}{4} & 0 \\ -2 & 1 \end{pmatrix}$	3. Multiply first row by 8 and subtract it from 2nd row (rule 4)
$\begin{pmatrix} 1 & 1\frac{1}{2} \\ 0 & 1 \end{pmatrix}$	$\begin{pmatrix} \frac{1}{4} & 0 \\ 1 & -\frac{1}{2} \end{pmatrix}$	4. Second row multiplied by $-\frac{1}{2}$ (rule 2)
$\begin{pmatrix} 1 & 0 \\ 0 & 1 \end{pmatrix}$	$\begin{pmatrix} -\frac{5}{4} & \frac{3}{4} \\ 1 & -\frac{1}{2} \end{pmatrix}$	5. Subtract $1\frac{1}{2}$ times row 2 from row 1 (rule 4)

The calculations can be checked by multiplying the inverse times the new

APPENDIXES 615

vector (16 22) to determine if the multiplication will return the vector back to its original point (2 1). This is calculated as follows:

$$\underset{\text{New Vector}}{(16 \quad 22)} \times \underset{\substack{\text{Inverse of} \\ \text{Original Matrix}}}{\begin{pmatrix} -\frac{5}{4} & \frac{3}{4} \\ 1 & -\frac{1}{2} \end{pmatrix}} = \underset{\text{Original Vector}}{(2 \quad 1)}$$

Another way of stating what has occurred is to say that the inverse represents the group of scalars which returns the new vector back to its original point. The inverse of a matrix can be thought of as the reciprocal of a matrix.

An inspection of the example used in Chapter 6 for the simplex method of linear programming might help clarify the use of matrix inversion. The original and identity matrices are shown below:

	Original Matrix	Identity Matrix
First Tableau	$\begin{pmatrix} 2 & 3 \\ 3 & 2 \\ 1 & 1 \end{pmatrix}$	$\begin{pmatrix} 1 & 0 & 0 \\ 0 & 1 & 0 \\ 0 & 0 & 1 \end{pmatrix}$
Third and Final Tableau	$\begin{pmatrix} 0 & 1 \\ 0 & 0 \\ 1 & 0 \end{pmatrix}$	$\begin{pmatrix} 1 & 0 & -2 \\ 1 & 1 & -5 \\ -1 & 0 & 3 \end{pmatrix}$

The original matrix must be square for a complete inversion to occur. Many linear programming problems will reach an optimum solution before a complete inversion takes place. Those square matrices in linear programming problems that fail to reach a complete inversion are tending in that direction. Moreover, the procedural steps in the simplex method of linear programming are somewhat different from the row and column procedures when forming an inverse.

Determinants

The last subject to be discussed as a mathematical background for Chapter 6 and following chapters is determinants. Whereas the matrix does not imply any mathematical operation, a determinant does imply certain operations. When a determinant appears in its regular form, it is said to be unexpanded. To evaluate a determinant, we expand it according to certain rules in order to obtain a single numerical value. Thus a determinant is a square array of numbers arranged into rows and columns and has a numerical value. The number of rows always precedes the number of columns when specifying the size of the determinant. They are extremely useful in solving simultaneous equations. Several examples of determinants are found on the top of the next page.

A 2×2 determinant has one primary diagonal and one secondary diagonal. Determinants larger than 2×2 have multiple primary diagonals and multiple secondary diagonals. As stated in the previous section, the numerical value of a 2×2 determinant is found by multiplying together

$$\begin{vmatrix} 1 & 4 \\ 6 & 2 \end{vmatrix} \quad \text{2×2 determinant}$$

$$\begin{vmatrix} 4 & 6 & 5 \\ 1 & -1 & 6 \\ 8 & 9 & 7 \end{vmatrix} \quad \text{3×3 determinant}$$

$$\begin{vmatrix} 15 & -4 & 8 & 9 \\ 11 & -6 & 7 & 2 \\ 8 & -1 & 6 & 5 \\ 4 & 0 & 4 & 2 \end{vmatrix} \quad \text{4×4 determinant}$$

the elements lying on the primary or main diagonal (p) and subtracting the product of the elements lying on the secondary diagonal (s). The value of the 2×2 determinant above is -22, determined as follows:

$$\text{Value} = (2)(1) - (6)(4)$$
$$= 2 - 24$$
$$= -22$$

The mathematical process for finding the value of a 3×3 determinant is determined with a slight modification of the procedure used on a 2×2 determinant. For the 3×3 determinant above, it is obvious that neither the second and third primary diagonals nor the second and third secondary diagonals pass through all three elements. This can be remedied by repeating the first two columns of the determinant, which appear as follows:

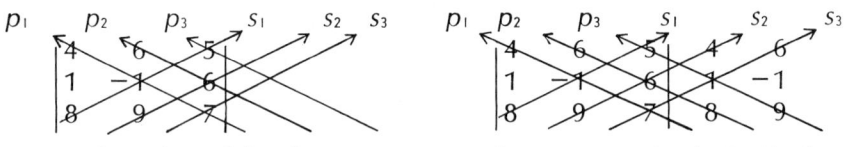

The value of the determinant equals $(p_1 + p_2 + p_3) - (s_1 + s_2 + s_3)$:

$$[\underbrace{(7)(-1)(4)}_{p_1} + \underbrace{(8)(6)(6)}_{p_2} + \underbrace{(9)(1)(5)}_{p_3}] - [\underbrace{(8)(-1)(5)}_{s_1} + \underbrace{(9)(6)(4)}_{s_2} + \underbrace{(7)(1)(6)}_{s_3}]$$

$$(-28 + 288 + 45) - (-40 + 216 + 42) = 305 - 218 = 87$$

The preceding two examples have made use of diagnoals to find the numerical value of a determinant. However, the diagonal method is rather restrictive from the standpoint of the size of the determinant. There is another procedure for finding the numerical value of any size determinant, called expanding a determinant. Any square determinant can be solved for its numerical value by expanding any one of its rows or any one of its columns. If a determinant is expanded by a row, this means selecting a particular row and then eliminating, in turn, each column which intersects that row. Expanding a determinant by a column means choosing a specific column and eliminating each row which intersects that column. Recall that the sign must be changed if the sum of the row and column which are eliminated is an odd number. Otherwise, if the sum of the number of the row and column that are eliminated is an even number, the sign is not changed.

Using the 2×2 determinant set forth previously, we shall expand this determinant by its first row. A line has been drawn through the first row to indicate this.

Step 1 $\begin{vmatrix} ① & 4 \\ 6 & 2 \end{vmatrix}$ Since the first row is being expanded, the first column that intersects the first row needs to have a line drawn through it.

Step 2 $2 \times ① = 2$ Multiply the one element which is not lined out by the circled element 1. The sign is unchanged because we are adding together the number of the row and the column which were eliminated. The value in the first part of the expansion is 2.

Step 3 $\begin{vmatrix} 1 & ④ \\ 6 & 2 \end{vmatrix}$ Expanding on the first row, the second column that intersects the first row is column 2.

Step 4 $6 \times ④ = -24$ Multiply the one element which is not lined out by the circled element 4. The sign is changed because we are adding together the number of the row and the column which were eliminated. The value of the second part of the expansion is -24.

Step 5 $2 - 24 = -22$ Add together the value of the two parts of the expansion for a value of the determinant, or -22. (Same answer as obtained with diagonal method.)

Returning to the previous illustration for a 3×3 determinant, we will expand this determinant by its first column. When a row and a column are eliminated, a 2×2 determinant remains. The value of this 2×2 determinant, in turn, is multiplied by the circled element. The method for changing the sign remains. The original 3×3 determinant is:

3×3 determinant $\begin{vmatrix} 4 & 6 & 5 \\ 1 & -1 & 6 \\ 8 & 9 & 7 \end{vmatrix}$

First part of expansion $\begin{vmatrix} ④ & 6 & 5 \\ 1 & -1 & 6 \\ 8 & 9 & 7 \end{vmatrix} = \begin{vmatrix} -1 & 6 \\ 9 & 7 \end{vmatrix} \times 4 = -61 \times 4 = -244$

Row 1 + col. 1 = even, sign is unchanged

Second part of expansion $\begin{vmatrix} 4 & 6 & 5 \\ ① & -1 & 6 \\ 8 & 9 & 7 \end{vmatrix} = \begin{vmatrix} 6 & 5 \\ 9 & 7 \end{vmatrix} \times 1 = -3 \times 1 = 3$

618 APPENDIXES

Third part of expansion $\begin{vmatrix} 4 & 6 & 5 \\ 1 & -1 & 6 \\ \text{\textcircled{8}} & 9 & 7 \end{vmatrix} = \begin{vmatrix} 6 & 5 \\ -1 & 6 \end{vmatrix} \times 8 = 41 \times 8 = 328$

Row 2 + col. 1 = odd, sign is changed

Row 3 + col. 1 = even, sign is unchanged

The sum for three parts of the expansion
$= -244 + 3 + 328 = 87$ value of determinant
(same value as for diagonal method).

The procedure for expanding a 4×4 determinant is the same as for a 3×3 determinant, except that the deletion of a row and a column would leave a 3×3 determinant to be multiplied by the circled element in each step. As one might suspect, the calculation for the value of a larger determinant becomes quite complex. It is suggested that a digital computer be employed.

Determinants, as noted previously, are quite useful in solving simultaneous equations. The following set of simultaneous equations will be used to illustrate this point:

$$4X + 6Y + 3Z = 18$$
$$3X + 5Y + 6Z = 24$$
$$2X + 8Y + 4Z = 12$$

The value for each of the unknown variables (X, Y, and Z) is determined by solving a particular set of two determinants which form a fraction. The determinant which forms the numerator of each fraction changes with each variable (X, Y, or Z). The determinant which forms the basis for the denominator of each fraction remains the same. The determinants used to solve for X are shown as follows:

$$X = \frac{\begin{vmatrix} 18 & 6 & 3 \\ 24 & 5 & 6 \\ 12 & 8 & 4 \end{vmatrix}}{\begin{vmatrix} 4 & 6 & 3 \\ 3 & 5 & 6 \\ 2 & 8 & 4 \end{vmatrix}} \quad \begin{matrix} \text{numerator} \\ \\ \text{denominator} \end{matrix}$$

Inspection of the determinant for the denominator reveals that this is nothing more than coefficients of the three unknowns arranged in the same form as they appear in the above equations. The same cannot be said for the numerator. The column of coefficients for the unknown variable X has been replaced by the value to the right of the equality sign in the original equations. However, the second and third columns are identical to those found in the denominator. In like manner, the determinant for the numerator of the unknown variable Y is formed by eliminating the coefficients for Y and replacing it with the values to the right of the equality sign in the original equations. The determinant for the last unknown variable Z is formed in a similar fashion. The determinants for X, Y, and Z are shown below with their respective values:

$$X = \frac{\begin{vmatrix} 18 & 6 & 3 \\ 24 & 5 & 6 \\ 12 & 8 & 4 \end{vmatrix}}{\begin{vmatrix} 4 & 6 & 3 \\ 3 & 5 & 6 \\ 2 & 8 & 4 \end{vmatrix}} = \frac{-252}{-70} = 3.6$$

$$Y = \frac{\begin{vmatrix} 4 & 18 & 3 \\ 3 & 24 & 6 \\ 2 & 12 & 4 \end{vmatrix}}{\begin{vmatrix} 4 & 6 & 3 \\ 3 & 5 & 6 \\ 2 & 8 & 4 \end{vmatrix}} = \frac{60}{-70} = 0.8571$$

$$Z = \frac{\begin{vmatrix} 4 & 6 & 18 \\ 3 & 5 & 24 \\ 2 & 8 & 12 \end{vmatrix}}{\begin{vmatrix} 4 & 6 & 3 \\ 3 & 5 & 6 \\ 2 & 8 & 4 \end{vmatrix}} = \frac{-204}{-70} = 2.9143$$

Now we have solved for the unknown variables X, Y, and Z, the values can be verified by substituting them into the original equations. The values (X, Y, and Z) satisfy the equations:

$$4X + 6Y + 3Z = 18$$
$$4(3.6) + 6(-0.8571) + 3(2.9143) = 18$$
$$14.4 - 5.14 + 8.74 = 18$$
$$18 = 18$$

$$3X + 5Y + 6Z = 24$$
$$3(3.6) + 5(-0.8571) + 6(2.9143) = 24$$
$$10.8 - 4.286 + 17.486 = 24$$
$$24 = 24$$

$$2X + 8Y + 4Z = 12$$
$$2(3.6) + 8(-0.8571) + 4(2.9143) = 12$$
$$7.2 - 6.857 + 11.657 = 12$$
$$12 = 12$$

In Chapter 9 on Markov analysis, a 4×4 determinant will be solved. The problem has actually five equations with four unknowns. Due to the structure of Markov analysis, one equation can be dropped, which permits us to utilize a 4×4 determinant.

This concludes a brief discussion of vectors, matrices, and determinants. The simplex method of linear programming is based on the concept of matrices, vectors, and inversion of matrices. Also, this will be apparent in the chapter on nonlinear programming. Some of the material presented in this Appendix will be useful in other chapters. It is important that the reader become familiar with these three areas of mathematics and their basic properties.

Appendix B

Differentiation and Integration

Calculus (differentiation and integration) has wide application not only for classical optimization techniques but also for inventory models, nonlinear programming, queuing theory, dynamic programming, and behavioral models. Similarly, advanced OR models make great use of calculus. In this appendix, differentiation and integration are presented from an overview standpoint along with their formulas.

Differentiation

Differentiation (differential calculus), sometimes called the mathematics of change, is used for determining the slope of a line tangent to a curve at a point on the curve. As will be seen in chapters of the text, this concept can be directed toward the solution of complex business problems.

Let us consider any curve $y = f(x)$ where y is a function of x. Suppose that curve M in Figure B-1a is a graph of the function $y = f(x)$. The slope of the curve at a particular point on the curve is defined as the slope of the tangent to the curve at the given point. A tangent is defined as a straight line intersecting a curved line at only one point.

To determine the slope of curve M at point A, draw a straight line l which passes through point A and intersects M at some point B. The co-

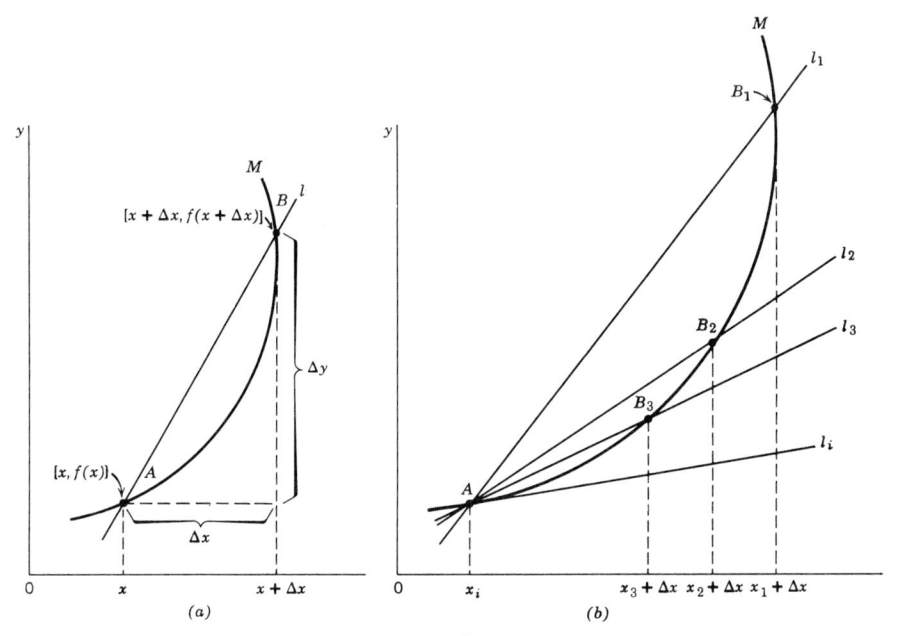

Figure B-1 Geometric interpretation of derivative.

ordinates of point A are [x, f(x)]. Starting at point A on the curve and going to point B, the x and y coordinates change to their values at B from their values at A. The change in x is shown as Δx and the change in the function is shown as Δy. The coordinates of point B become [x+Δx, f(x+Δx)]. In terms of the coordinates of A and B, Δy=f(x+Δx)−f(x) and Δx=(x+Δx)−x. The slope of the line AB is:

$$\frac{\Delta y}{\Delta x} = \frac{f(x+\Delta x) - f(x)}{(x+\Delta x) - x}$$

$$\text{Slope } AB = \frac{f(x+\Delta x) - f(x)}{\Delta x} \qquad \text{(Equation B-1)}$$

Now imagine that several straight lines (l_1, l_2, l_3, l_i) can pivot at a fixed point A, as in Figure B-1b. As the straight lines pivot in a clockwise direction about point A, point B becomes closer to point A on curve M. It should be noted that the closer B is to A, Δx becomes increasingly smaller. As B approaches A, B approaches a position where B and A coincide. At this point (just prior to A and B coinciding) the line between A and B is tangent to the curve. For all practical purposes, A and B are now the same point. We can now state that the ratio Δy/Δx, the slope of the straight line through A and B, approaches the slope of the line tangent to the curve A as Δx approaches zero. This is called the *first derivative* and is the instantaneous change in the dependent variable y(dy) divided by the instantaneous change in the independent variable x(dx). Note that at the limit, the delta (Δ) form of the operator is expressed as a lower-case d. The equational form of this process is called differentiation and is defined by:

$$\frac{dy}{dx} = \lim_{\Delta x \to 0} \frac{\Delta y}{\Delta x} = \lim_{\Delta x \to 0} \frac{f(x+\Delta x) - f(x)}{\Delta x} \qquad \text{(Equation B-2)}$$

where y is a function of x. The geometric counterpart of the derivative, then, is the slope of a line tangent to a curve at a point.

First Derivative and Second Derivative

The slope of a curve at a point is found by evaluating the derivative at the point. Our interest is in finding points where the slope is zero or points where a tangent to the curve is horizontal. Not only is zero slope analysis helpful in plotting curves, but also it is most helpful in the determination of maximum and minimum values of a function, that is, maximum profit, minimum cost, and the like.

The procedure for finding points of zero slope is to set the first derivative equal to zero, then solve the resultant equation. The point of zero slope can be determined by the first derivative test. If the maximum point has been reached, the slope to the left is positive, while the slope to the right is negative. In effect, the slope changes from positive to negative as we traverse a maximum. On the other hand, the slope changes from negative to positive as we traverse a minimum. However, the slope does not change signs as we pass through an inflection point (a point where the curvative changes from concave downward to concave upward or vice versa). In applying the first derivative test, we evaluate the first derivative a little to the right and left of the point of zero slope. The convention is that slope is positive if the curve rises as we go to the right and negative if it descends to the right.

In the second derivative test, a point of zero slope is a maximum if the second derivative at that point is negative, a minimum if the second derivative at the point is positive. If the second derivative is zero for a point of zero slope, the test fails. It is necessary to apply the first derivative test. If the first derivative is zero, we apply the first derivative test by finding the value of the first derivative a little to the left and to the right of the point. The second and subsequent derivatives are found by repeating the process used in determining the previous derivative. The function notation for the higher derivative is:

$$\frac{d}{dx}\left(\frac{d}{dx}\right) = \frac{d^2}{dx^2}, \quad \frac{d}{dx}\left(\frac{d^2}{dx^2}\right) = \frac{d^3}{dx^3}, \quad \ldots, \quad \frac{d}{dx}\left(\frac{d^{n-1}}{dx^{n-1}}\right) = \frac{d^n}{dx^n}$$

Differentiation Formulas

Mathematicians have developed differentiation formulas or rules with which we are able to find the derivative of a given differentiable function. The more commonly used formulas where C is contant and u and v are functions of x are listed on the next page. It should be pointed out that the derivative of an expression may be taken term by term when these terms are added or subtracted per formulas 4 and 5.

Integration

While differentiation is the process of measuring small changes in value, its opposite, the process of summing the intervals under a curve, is called integration. A way of relating integration to differentiation is to evaluate an integral by means of antiderivatives, that is, by procedures which reverse the process of finding derivatives. In this section, a very brief mathematical background will be given for integration just as was done for differentiation.

Indefinite Integral

In reversing the process of differentiation, we have performed the process of indefinite integration. The function found with antidifferentiation is called the indefinite integral. The indefinite integral of function f is defined as:

$$y = \int f(x)dx = F(x) + C \qquad \text{(Equation B-3)}$$

Equation B-3 is read "the integral ($\int$) of f(x)dx is F(x)+C." It is important to note in this equation that y represents the indefinite integral of f(x) while F(x) is an antiderivative of y where C equals zero. Since it not known that C equals 0 (the derivative of any constant equals zero), the constant must appear in every indefinite integration.

We can interpret the mathematical notation of the indefinite integral in two ways. We can think of the symbol $\int \ldots dx$ to mean the "integral

Formulas for Differentiation

1. $\dfrac{d}{dx}(C) = 0$ — The derivative of a constant (C) is zero.

2. $\dfrac{d}{dx}(Cx) = C\dfrac{d}{dx}(x)$ — The derivative of a constant (C) times the variable (x) equals the constant times the derivative of the variable.

3. $\dfrac{d}{dx}(x) = 1$ — The derivative of the variable (x) is 1.

4. $\dfrac{d}{dx}(u+v) = \dfrac{du}{dx} + \dfrac{dv}{dx}$ — If u and v are functions of x, the derivative of the first function is added to the derivative of the second function.

5. $\dfrac{d}{dx}(u-v) = \dfrac{du}{dx} - \dfrac{dv}{dx}$ — If u and v are functions of x, the derivative of the second function is subtracted from the derivative of the first function.

6. $\dfrac{d}{dx}(uv) = \dfrac{u\,dv}{dx} + \dfrac{v\,du}{dx}$ — If u and v are functions of x, the derivative of the product uv with respect to x is the "first" (u) times the derivative of the "second" (v) plus the "second" (v) times the derivative of the "first" (u).

7. $\dfrac{d}{dx}\left(\dfrac{u}{v}\right) = \dfrac{v\dfrac{du}{dx} - u\dfrac{dv}{dx}}{v^2}$ — If u and v are functions of x, the derivative of the quotient u/v is the denominator times the derivative of the numerator minus the numerator times the derivative of the denominator, all over the denominator squared.

8. $\dfrac{d}{dx}(u^n) = nu^{n-1}\dfrac{du}{dx}$ — The derivative of the function (u) to a power is the original power (n) times the function (u) to the original power minus one times the derivative of the function (u) with respect to x.

9. $\dfrac{d}{dx}(\ln u) = \dfrac{1}{u}\dfrac{du}{dx}$ — The derivative of the natural logarithm (u) is one over u times the derivative of the function (u) with respect to x.

10. $\dfrac{d}{dx}(e^u) = e^u\dfrac{du}{dx}$ — The derivative of e to the function (u) is e^u times the derivative of the function (u) with respect to x.

of . . . with respect to x." This symbol can be interpreted as the reverse d/dx . . . , which means "the derivative of . . . with respect to x." The second way is to consider Equation B-3 written as follows (before performing the operation indicated by the integral sign):

$$dy = f(x)\,dx \qquad \text{(Equation B-4)}$$

In this case, f(x) is the derivative of y for every value of x in the closed interval (a,b) where dy is called the differential of y and dx the differential of x.

When the integral sign is introduced in Equation B-4 (integrate both sides of the equation), the new equation is:

$$\int dy = \int f(x)\, dx$$

Applying Equation B-3 gives:

$$y = \int dy = F(x) + C \qquad \text{(Equation B-5)}$$

In this situation, we have integrated the differential of function y to get the antiderivative $F(x)$ plus some constant C. In either of the two mathematical interpretations of Equation B-3, the operation denoted by the integral sign means the inverse of the operation indicated by the symbol d for differentiation.

Definite Integral

Integration is sometimes called the process of summation with respect to the definite integral. There is, in addition to the previous meaning of the term "to integrate," a meaning "to indicate or give the sum of" areas bounded by curves, volumes of solids, and the like. Thus the process of summation will lead to a definition of the definite integral.

It can be shown that areas can be computed by definite integration. Consider Figure B-2, where we want to determine the area bounded by the graph of f, the lines $x = a$ and $x = b$. We will let $f(x)$ be the value of the continuous (non-negative) function f in the interval (a,b). Area A will be a function of the independent variable x. We will let ΔA be the incremental increase in area A as x increases from x_1 to $(x_1 + \Delta x)$.

As Δx approaches zero, $\Delta A / \Delta x$ approaches the instantaneous rate with which A changes with respect to the variable x. The derivative of a function becomes:

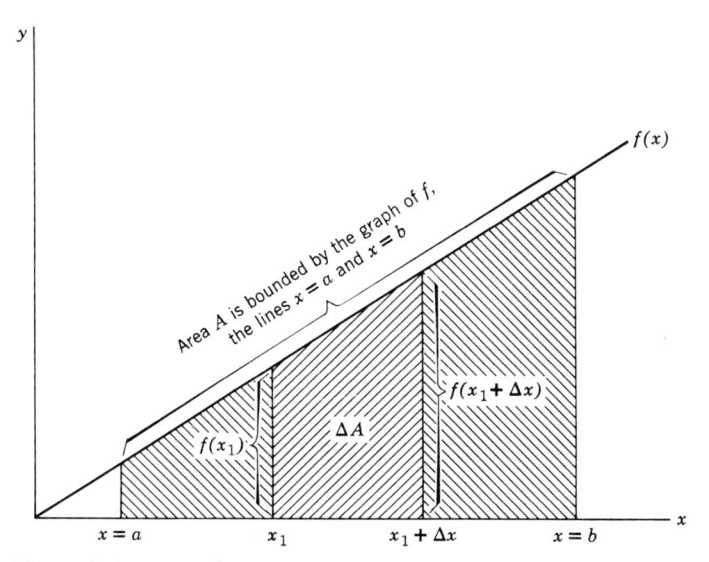

Figure B-2   Areas by integration.

$$\underset{\Delta x \to 0}{\text{limit}} \frac{\Delta A}{\Delta x} = \frac{dA}{dx} = f(x_1) \qquad \text{(Equation B-6)}$$

Since x_1 can be any value of x in the interval (a,b), we can substitute x for x_1, which becomes:

$$\frac{dA}{dx} = f(x) \quad \text{or} \quad dA = f(x)\, dx \qquad \text{(Equation B-7)}$$

The meaning of Equation B-7 is that the rate with which area A is changing is always equal to the coordinate value $y = f(x)$ at any value x in the interval (a,b). Integrating this equation for A results in the following:

$$A = \int dA = \int f(x)\, dx \qquad \text{(Equation B-8)}$$

Finally, letting $F(x)$ be a function such that $(d/dx)F(x) = F'(x) = f(x)$, the new equation for A (the right-hand side is the same as equation B-3) is:

$$A = \int f(x)\, dx = F(x) + C \qquad \text{(Equation B-9)}$$

Referring to Figure B-2, area A is a function of the independent variable x_1, that is, when x_1 decreases, approaching $x = a$, area A decreases; and when $x_1 = a$, area A is zero. Using this as a basis for substituting values in Equation B-9, the new equation (when $A = 0$ and $x = a$) is:

$$0 = F(a) + C$$
$$C = -F(a)$$

Substituting the above term $[-F(a)]$ for C into Equation B-9, the area A equals:

$$A = F(x) + [-F(a)] \qquad \text{(Equation B-10)}$$
$$A = F(x) - F(a)$$

In order to determine the area bounded by $x = a$ and $x = b$, we substitute b for x in Equation B-10, which becomes:

$$A = F(b) - F(a) \qquad \text{(Equation B-11)}$$

Stating Equation B-11 in terms of an integral sign (refer also to Equation B-9), the integrated equation for area A is:

$$A = \int_a^b f(x)\, dx = F(b) - F(a) \qquad \text{(Equation B-12)}$$

When reading Equation B-12, the letter a at the bottom of the integral sign is the lower limit of integration and the letter b is the upper limit of integration or the value of x at which the area ends. This, being a definite integral, can be restated in the following form:

$$A = \int_a^b f(x)\, dx = F(x) \Big|_a^b = F(b) - F(a) \qquad \text{(Equation B-13)}$$

Integration Formulas

Integration formulas or rules which are part of the mathematical system of calculus are stated below. Before giving the formulas, we must remember that an expression such as:

$$\int_a^b x^2$$

which indicates the integral of x^2 over the interval from a to b, should be written:

$$\int_a^b x^2\, dx$$

where the symbol dx is called the differential of x. The value of the integral depends upon the limits (a,b) and not on a particular letter of the integrand. As indicated previously when writing formulas for the indefinite integral (integrals without limits), the constant C, called the constant of integration, must be appended.

1. $\int (0) dx = C$ — Integration of zero is equal to the constant of integration (C).

2. $\int Au\, du = A \int u\, du + C$ — Integral of a constant (A) times a function (u) equals the constant times the integral of the function plus another constant (C).

3. $\int (1)\, dx = x + C$ — Integration of one is x plus some constant of integration (C).

4. $\int (u+v)\, dx = \int u\, dx + \int v\, dx + C$ — Integration of the first term (u) plus integration of the second term (v) plus some constant of integration (C).

5. $\int (u-v)\, dx = \int u\, dx - \int v\, dx + C$ — Integration of the first term (u) less integration of the second term (v) plus some constant of integration (C).

6. $\int u^n\, du = \dfrac{u^{n+1}}{n+1} + C$

where $n \neq -1$

Integration of a function (u) to a power is u^{n+1} for the numerator and $n+1$ for the denominator plus some constant of integration (C) where n does not equal -1.

7. $\int u^n\, du = \ln u + C$

where $n = -1$

Integral of a function (u) to a power is the natural logarithm of u plus some constant of integration (C) where n equals -1.

8. $\int e^u\, du = e^u + C$ — Integration of the function e^u is e^u plus some constant of integration (C).

APPENDIXES 627

Appendix C Areas under the Curve

	.00	.01	.02	.03	.04	.05	.06	.07	.08	.09
0.0	.50000	.50399	.50798	.51197	.51595	.51994	.52392	.52790	.53188	.53586
0.1	.53983	.54380	.54776	.55172	.55567	55692	.56356	.56749	.57142	.57535
0.2	.57926	.58317	.58706	.59095	.59483	.59871	.60257	.60642	.61026	.61409
0.3	.61791	.62172	.62552	.62930	.63307	.63683	.64058	.64431	.64803	.65173
0.4	.65542	.65910	.66276	.66640	.67003	.67364	.67724	.68082	.68439	.68793
0.5	.69146	.69497	.69847	.70194	.70540	.70884	.71226	.71566	.71904	.72240
0.6	.72575	.72907	.73237	.73536	.73891	.74215	.74537	.74857	.75175	.75490
0.7	.75804	.76115	.76424	.76730	.77035	.77337	.77637	.77935	.78230	.78524
0.8	.78814	.79103	.79389	.79673	.79955	.80234	.80511	.80785	.81057	.81327
0.9	.81594	.81859	.82121	.82381	.82639	.82894	.83147	.83398	.83646	.83891
1.0	.84134	.84375	.84614	.84849	.85083	.85314	.85543	.85769	.85993	.86214
1.1	.86433	.86650	.86864	.87076	.87286	.87493	.87698	.87900	.88100	.88298
1.2	.88493	.88686	.88877	.89065	.89251	.89435	.89617	.89796	.89973	.90147
1.3	.90320	.90490	.90658	.90824	.90988	.91149	.91309	.91466	.91621	.91774
1.4	.91924	.92073	.92220	.92364	.92507	.92647	.92785	.92922	.93056	.93189
1.5	.93319	.93448	.93574	.93699	.93822	.93943	.94062	.94179	.94295	.94408
1.6	.94520	.94630	.94738	.94845	.94950	.95053	.95154	.95254	.95352	.95449
1.7	.95543	.95637	.95728	.95818	.95907	.95994	.96080	.96164	.96246	.96327
1.8	.96407	.96485	.96562	.96638	.96712	.96784	.96856	.96926	.96995	.97062
1.9	.97128	.97193	.97257	.97320	.97381	.97441	.97500	.97558	.97615	.97670
2.0	.97725	.97784	.97831	.97882	.97932	.97982	.98030	.98077	.98124	.98169
2.1	.98214	.98257	.98300	.98341	.98382	.98422	.98461	.98500	.98537	.98574
2.2	.98610	.98645	.98679	.98713	.98745	.98778	.98809	.98840	.98870	.98899
2.3	.98928	.98956	.98983	.99010	.99036	.99061	.99086	.99111	.99134	.99158
2.4	.99180	.99202	.99224	.99245	.99266	.99286	.99305	.99324	.99343	.99361
2.5	.99379	.99396	.99413	.99430	.99446	.99461	.99477	.99492	.99506	.99520
2.6	.99534	.99547	.99560	.99573	.99585	.99598	.99609	.99621	.99632	.99643
2.7	.99653	.99664	.99674	.99683	.99693	.99702	.99711	.99720	.99728	.99736
2.8	.99744	.99752	.99760	.99767	.99774	.99781	.99788	.99795	.99801	.99807
2.9	.99813	.99819	.99825	.99831	.99836	.99841	.99846	.99851	.99856	.99861
3.0	.99865	.99869	.99874	.99878	.99882	99886	.99899	.99893	.99896	.99900
3.1	.99903	.99906	.99910	.99913	.99916	.99918	.99921	.99924	.99926	.99929
3.2	.99931	.99934	.99936	.99938	.99940	.99942	.99944	.99946	.99948	.99950
3.3	.99952	.99953	.99955	.99957	.99958	.99960	.99961	.99962	.99964	.99965
3.4	.99966	.99968	.99969	.99970	.99971	.99972	.99973	.99974	.99975	.99976
3.5	.99977	.99978	.99978	.99979	.99980	.99981	.99981	.99982	.99983	.99983
3.6	.99984	.99985	.99985	.99986	.99986	.99987	.99987	.99988	.99988	.99989
3.7	.99989	.99990	.99990	.99990	.99991	.99991	.99992	.99992	.99992	.99992
3.8	.99993	.99993	.99993	.99994	.99994	.99994	.99994	.99995	.99995	.99995
3.9	.99995	.99995	.99996	.99996	.99996	.99996	.99996	.99996	.99997	.99997

Directions: To find the area under the curve between the left-hand end and any point, determine how many standard deviations that point is to the right of the average, then read the area directly from the body of the table. *Example:* The area under the curve from the left-hand end and a point 1.86 standard deviations to the right of the average is .96856 of the total area under the curve.

Appendix D

Values of the Exponential Function

x	e^x	e^{-x}	x	e^x	e^{-x}
.00	1.0000	1.0000	2.05	7.7679	.1287
.05	1.0513	.9512	2.10	8.1662	.1225
.10	1.1052	.9048	2.15	8.5849	.1165
.15	1.1618	.8607	2.20	9.0250	.1108
.20	1.2214	.8187	2.25	9.4877	.1054
.25	1.2840	.7788	2.30	9.9742	.1003
.30	1.3499	.7408	2.35	10.4856	.0954
.35	1.4191	.7047	2.40	11.0232	.0907
.40	1.4918	.6703	2.45	11.5883	.0863
.45	1.5683	.6376	2.50	12.1825	.0821
.50	1.6487	.6065	2.55	12.8071	.0781
.55	1.7333	.5769	2.60	13.4637	.0743
.60	1.8221	.5488	2.65	14.1540	.0707
.65	1.9155	.5220	2.70	14.8797	.0672
.70	2.0138	.4966	2.75	15.6426	.0639
.75	2.1170	.4724	2.80	16.4446	.0608
.80	2.2255	.4493	2.85	17.2878	.0578
.85	2.3396	.4274	2.90	18.1741	.0550
.90	2.4596	.4066	2.95	19.1060	.0523
.95	2.5857	.3867	3.00	20.086	.0498
1.00	2.7183	.3679	3.05	21.115	.0474
1.05	2.8577	.3499	3.10	22.198	.0450
1.10	3.0042	.3329	3.15	23.336	.0429
1.15	3.1582	.3166	3.20	24.553	.0408
1.20	3.3201	.3012	3.25	25.790	.0388
1.25	3.4903	.2865	3.30	27.113	.0369
1.30	3.6693	.2725	3.35	28.503	.0351
1.35	3.8574	.2592	3.40	29.964	.0334
1.40	4.0552	.2466	3.45	31.500	.0317
1.45	4.2631	.2346	3.50	33.115	.0302
1.50	4.4817	.2231	3.55	34.813	.0287
1.55	4.7115	.2122	3.60	36.598	.0273
1.60	4.9530	.2019	3.65	38.475	.0260
1.65	5.2070	.1920	3.70	40.447	.0247
1.70	5.4739	.1827	3.75	42.521	.0235
1.75	5.7546	.1738	3.80	44.701	.0224
1.80	6.0496	.1653	3.85	46.993	.0213
1.85	6.3598	.1572	3.90	49.402	.0202
1.90	6.6859	.1496	3.95	51.935	.0193
1.95	7.0287	.1423	4.00	54.598	.0183
2.00	7.3891	.1353	4.10	60.340	.0166

4.20	66.686	.0150	5.20	181.272	.0055
4.30	73.700	.0136	5.40	221.406	.0045
4.40	81.451	.0123	5.60	270.426	.0037
4.50	90.017	.0111	5.80	330.300	.0030
4.60	99.484	.0101	6.00	403.43	.0025
4.70	109.947	.0091	7.00	1096.63	.0009
4.80	121.510	.0082	8.00	2980.96	.0003
4.90	134.290	.0074	9.00	8103.08	.0001
5.00	148.413	.0067	10.00	22026.48	.00005

Appendix E
Random Numbers Table

1581922396	2068577984	8262130892	8374856049	4637567488
0928105582	7295088579	9586111652	7055508767	6472382934
4112077556	3440672486	1882412963	0684012006	0933147914
7457477468	5435810788	9670852913	1291265730	4890031305
0099520858	3090908872	2039593181	5973470495	9776135501
7245174840	2275698645	8416549348	4676463101	2229367983
6749420382	4832630032	5670984959	5432114610	2966095680
5503161011	7413686599	1198757695	0414294470	0140121598
7164238934	7666127259	5263097712	5133648980	4011966963
3593969525	0272759769	0385998136	9999089966	7544056852
4192054466	0700014629	5169439659	8408705169	1074373131
9697426117	6488888550	4031652526	8123543276	0927534537
2007950579	9564268448	3457416988	1531027886	7016633739
4584768758	2389278610	3859431781	3643768456	4141314518
3840145867	9120831830	7228567652	1267173884	4020651657
0190453442	4800088084	1165628559	5407921254	3768932478
6766554338	5585265145	5089052204	9780623691	2195448096
6315116284	9172824179	5544814339	0016943666	3828538786
3908771938	4035554324	0840126299	4942059208	1475623997
5570024586	9324732596	1186563397	4425143189	3216653251
2999997185	0135968938	7678931194	1351031403	6002561840
7864375912	8383232768	1892857070	2323673751	3188881718
7065492027	6349104233	3382569662	4579426926	1513082455
0654683246	4765104877	8149224168	5468631609	6474393896
7830555058	5255147182	3519287786	2481675649	8907598697
7626984369	4725370390	9641916289	5049082870	7463807244
4785048453	3646121751	8436077768	2928794356	9956043516
4627791048	5765558107	8762592043	6185670830	6363845920
9376470693	0441608934	8749472723	2202271078	5897002653
1227991661	7936797054	9527542791	4711871173	8300978148
5582095589	5535798279	4764439855	6279247618	4446895088
4959397698	1056981450	8416606706	8234013222	6426813469
1824779358	1333750468	9434074212	5273692238	5902177065
7041092295	5726289716	3420847871	1820481234	0318831723
3555104281	0903099163	6827824899	6383872737	5901682626
9717595534	1634107293	8521057472	1471300754	3044151557
5571564123	7344613447	1128117244	3208461091	1699403490
4574262892	2809456764	5806554509	8224980942	5738031833
8461228715	0746980892	9285305274	6331989649	8764467686
1838538678	3049068967	6955157269	5482964330	2161984904
1834182305	6203476893	5937802079	3445280195	3694915658
1884227732	2923727501	8044389132	4611203081	6072112445
6791857341	6696243386	2219599137	3193884236	8224729718

3007929946	4031562749	5570757297	6273785046	1455349704
6085440624	2875556938	5496629750	4841817356	1443167141
7005051056	3496332071	5054070890	7303867953	6255181190
9846413446	8306646692	0661684251	8875127201	6251533454
0625457703	4229164694	7321363715	7051128285	1108468072
5457593922	9751489574	1799906380	1989141062	5595364247
4076486653	8950826528	4934582003	4071187742	1456207629

Dudley J. Cowden and Mercedes S. Cowden, *Practical Problems in Business Statistics*, 2d ed., © 1960, by permission of Prentice-Hall, Inc., Englewood Cliffs, N.J.

Appendix F

Answers to Problems

Chapter 3

3-1 (a) .0625, .0625
(b) .9375
(c) .0256, .4096, .9984
(d) Joint probability under statistical independence

3-2 (a) .667
(b) .25
(c) Conditional probability under statistical dependence

3-3 (a) .1960
(b) .3047
(c) .3236
(d) Joint probability under statistical dependence

3-4 Product X—yields highest expected profits

3-5 Vendor B—lowest expected future cost

3-6 (a) Total expected sales = $2,602,370
(b) Joint probability under statistical dependence

3-7 Accept A and B $6,500 (Original Problem)
Marginal (or joint) probability under statistical independence
Accept A and B $5,000 (Revised Problem)
Joint probability under statistical dependence

3-8 (a) Accept A and B $7,500 (Original Problem)
(b) Joint probability under statistical dependence
(a) Accept A and B $10,000 (Revised Problem)
(b) Marginal (or joint) probability under statistical independence

3-9 Assign .833 probability to recession

3-10 (a) .99 versus .8; continue manufacturing
(b) .007 versus .8; do not continue manufacturing

3-11 (a) $P(\text{correct setup} | 4\ GP) = .999$
$P(\text{correct setup} | 3\ GP, 1BP) = .983$
$P(\text{correct setup} | 2\ GP, 2BP) = .442$
$P(\text{correct setup} | 1\ GP, 3BP) = .0104$
$P(\text{correct setup} | 4\ BP) = .0001$
Compare all values to .9
(b) Marginal, joint, and conditional probabilities

3-12 (a) Highest profit per unit—$0.25 at 200,000 units
(b) Highest profit at 400,000 units, $60,000

3-13 Quote $2.30, use Method A
Marginal probability under statistical independence

3-14 Choose DCA for lowest development cost of $2,267,250

3-15 (a) No. of alternatives = 20
(b) Don't take strike; bid $4.30; invest $2.6 million; highest expected profit is $1,665,000

3-16 Use decision tree to plot alternatives

Chapter 4

4-1 (a) See Tables 4-1 and 4-4 for approach
 (b) Expected profits:
     stock 50—$250.00
     stock 51— 253.50
     stock 52— 251.75
     stock 53— 244.00
     Expected losses:
     stock 50—($8.00)
     stock 51—(4.50)
     stock 52—(6.25)
     stock 53—(14.00)
 (c) EVPI = $4.50

4-2 (a) 1120 units
 (b) $65.80 under uncertainty
 (c) $68.23 under certainty

4-3 (a) 26 dozens
 (b) $23.30 under uncertainty

4-4 Firm should purchase $1100 machine based upon three alternatives

4-5 (a) $MP = \$1.33$, $ML = \$8.00$
 (b) No, carry 81 units

4-6 (a) Manufacture 70,000 pairs
 (b) Total expected profits—$126,000

4-7 (a) Investment appears sound, expected profits of $15,412.50 per year for for five years
 (b) Time value of money, rate of return, comparison with other projects, reliability of data, etc.

4-8 Carry 31 units
4-9 Carry 18 units

Chapter 5

5-1 Rank according to "expected value" estimates—2, 4, 3, 1, and 5
5-2 Critical path: 0–1–2–11–12–13–14
    See text for recommendations
5-3 Critical path: 1–2–3–7–8–9–10–13–14–16
    See text for recommendations
5-4 Sales prices $90,000
    Costs—var. and fixed   83,000
    Profit $ 7,000
5-5 Critical path initially 1–4–6–7; modified cash plan—19⅓ weeks and cost —$235,500; and total cash cost $268,500
5-6 (a) Recommend 13 weeks, profit of $21,000
 (b) 79 percent chance of completing the contract one week after the normal delivery time

Chapter 6

6-1 S—1000 Model = 355½ units
S—2000 Model = 0 units
Contribution, $14,220
Slack time:
    M. F. Dept., 178 hours
    E. W. Dept., 311¼ hours
    A. Dept., 0 hours

6-2 (a) Model Z—1200 = 150 units
    Model Z—1500 = 70 units
  (b) Increase contribution by $4000
  (c) Range for Model Z—1200, 100 to 150 units
    Range for Model Z—1500, 70 to 120 units
    Any combination of the above that totals 220 units
  (d) Model Z—1200 = 55 units
    Model Z−1500 = 0 units
    Model Z—1800 = 150 units
    Contribution, $11,000
  (e) Solution is not unique

6-3 Range for Magazine 1, 20 to 35 runs
Range for Magazine 2, 10 to 16 runs
Any combination of the above that totals $120,000

6-4 Product A = 20,000 units
Product B = 0 units
Product C = 7500 units
Contribution, $9750

6-5 (a) X_1 = 3000 pounds
    X_2 = 5000 pounds
    X_3 = 2000 pounds
  (b) Lowest cost = $96,000
  (c) Slack pounds, X_6 = 3500

6-6 (a) Resin = 40%
    Fiber = 40%
    Glass cloth = 20%
  (b) Lowest cost composition, $48.00 per pound

6-7 (a) Product C = 300 units
    Product D = 600 units
    Product E = 500 units
    Product F = 1100 units
  (b) Contribution, $17,900
  (c) Slack time:
    Planner, 0 hours
    Milling, 0 hours
    Drilling, 950 hours
    Assembly, 200 hours

6-8 (a) Present mix and contribution is not optimum
    Product K = 976.5 units

Product $L = 30$ units
Product $M = 957.5$ units
Product $N = 25$ units
Contribution, $18,433.25
  (b) Basically, eliminate bottlenecks in dept. 1 and dept. 3

6-9 $P_1 = 1000$ units (Method A)
$P_2 = 3000$ units (Method A)
$P_3 = 600$ units (Method A)
$P_3 = 1000$ units (Method B)
$P_4 = 2000$ units (Method B)
Contribution, $153,000

Chapter 7

7-1 Factory 1 to Jacksonville, 600
Factory 2 to Newark, 1000
Factory 3 to Newark, 200
Factory 3 to Jacksonville, 200
Factory 3 to San Diego, 1000
Total cost = $16,400

7-2 (a) Total cost = $7800
  (b) Drop out column C, slack column now totals 550.
  (c) Insert a row for an artificial factory, but using a very high cost (M) so this factory will not enter the final solution

7-3 Total cost = $11,000

7-4 Dalton to Plant C, 800 units
Dalton to Plant D, 1200 units
Doran to Plant A, 800 units
Doran to Plant C, 100 units
Doran to Plant E, 500 units
Riggs to Plant B, 1000 units
Riggs to Plant E, 1000 units
Total cost = $30,300

7-5 Manufacturing schedule:
Plant A, 450 standard
Plant A, 350 deluxe
Plant B, 600 new deluxe
Plant C, 700 deluxe
Total contribution = $21,785

7-6 $J_1 = 5W_3$
$J_2 = 15W_2$
$J_2 = 5W_3$
$J_3 = 10W_1$
Lowest cost/hour, $137.25

7-7 From $A \begin{pmatrix} 2 \\ 5 \\ 1 \end{pmatrix}$ to $\begin{pmatrix} R \\ T \\ U \end{pmatrix}$

From $B \begin{pmatrix} 6 \\ 2 \end{pmatrix}$ to $\begin{pmatrix} S \\ U \end{pmatrix}$

From C (6) to (S)

From D (3) to (U)

7-8 (a) Solution is optimal
(b) Solution is unique

7-9 To press 1:
    Order 3,   6,000
    Order 6, 44,000

To press 2:
    Order 1, 28,000
    Order 3,   2,000
    Order 4, 20,000

To press 3:
    Order 2, 15,000
    Order 3,   7,000
    Order 5, 38,000
               160,000

7-10 Machine 1:
    Product D   1,240

Machine 2:
    Product B   1,240
    Product C   1,800
    Product D   510

Machine 3:
    Product A   1,620
    Product B   760
                 7,170

Chapter 8

8-1 (a) Game value $= -4$
Strategies:
$X = 1, 0, 0$
$Y = 0, 0, 1$

(b) Game value $= \dfrac{25}{7}$

Strategies:
$X = \dfrac{6}{7}, \dfrac{1}{7}, 0$
$Y = 0, \dfrac{4}{7}, \dfrac{3}{7}$

8-2 Game value $= -\dfrac{67}{19}$

Strategies:
$X = \dfrac{2}{19}, \dfrac{17}{19}, 0$

$$Y = \frac{14}{19}, 0, \frac{5}{19}$$

8-3 Game value = 1
Strategies:
$$Y = 0, \frac{1}{2}, 0, \frac{1}{2}, 0$$

8-4 Strategy—Firm A:
$20,000 ($a_2$, b_2), saddle point

8-5 Firm A, spend $\frac{1}{3}$ on medium advertising and $\frac{2}{3}$ on large advertising

8-6 Game value = $-\frac{5}{12}$ %
Strategies:
$$RBM = \frac{7}{12}, \frac{5}{12}$$
$$T.S. = \frac{7}{12}, \frac{5}{12}$$

8-7 Game value = $0.1446 increase in hourly wages
Strategies:
$$Union = \frac{7}{13}, 0, \frac{6}{13}, 0$$
$$Company = 0, \frac{1}{13}, \frac{12}{13}, 0$$

8-8 (a) Game value = $-\frac{5}{6}$ %
(b) Roover Company should consider a major change
(c) Reaction of competitor, profitability of change, cost factors, etc.

8-9 Game value = $\frac{112}{121}$
Strategies for Capco
$A = .471$
$B = .000$
$C = .198$
$D = .331$

Chapter 9

9-1 (a) $A = 0$, $B = .667$, $C = .333$
(b) $A = 1.0$, $B = 0$, $C = 0$

9-2 $K = .40$, $A = .374$, $B = .226$
$K = .43$, $A = .279$, $B = .291$

9-3 (a) Yes
Test areas 1 and 2 = 27.8%
(b) Test area 1 = 25%
Test area 2 = 43.8%
Select campaign for test area 2

9-4 (a) $H = .244$, $A = .268$, $B = .283$, $C = .205$
(b) $H = .25$, $A = .25$, $B = .25$, $C = .25$

9-5 (a) $A = .59$, $B = .16$, $C = .25$
(b) $A = .5820$, $B = .1587$, $C = .2593$
9-6 Neither advertising program is profitable for the firm

Chapter 10

10-1 $p = \dfrac{v}{2} - \dfrac{b}{2e}$

where
p = selling price
v = total var. costs per unit
b = demand intercept
e = demand slope

10-2 (a) Selling price = $237.50
(b) Use second derivative test, minus indicates a maximum selling price
(c) Number of units = 4875 units
(d) First year profits = $692,187.50

10-3 (a) Number of units = 1150
(b) First year profits = $4290

10-4 Expected profits for next year, $9,622.50

10-5 (a) Advertising = $914
(b) $\dfrac{d^2P}{dx^2} = \dfrac{-4{,}000{,}000}{(500 + 914)^3}$
(Minus sign indicates maximum profit)

10-6 (a) Optimal advertising budget = $1,432,000 approx.
(b) Reaction of competition, expected profit from optimal advertising outlay, sales volume, etc.

10-7 Price $75 and $76 in the nontaxing and taxing states, respectively, to maximize profits for the firm

10-8 Forecasted sales = 106,667 units

10-9 Sales in 12th month = $31,767

10-10 Machine will not pay for itself after 5 years—savings of $3000 after 5 years versus cost of $10,000

10-11 First five year sales:
1st = $28,086
2nd = $64,286
3rd = $82,271
4th. = $91,186
5th = $95,629

10-12 3-month advertising program: ratio of additional sales to additional advertising = 3.4 to 1
2-month advertising program: 2.3 to 1
The 3-month advertising program is better

10-13 (a) Selling price = $2.00, profits = $49.9 million; increase in profits = $0.2 million at $2.10 selling price, profits = $50.1 million
(b) See text
(c) Additional profits = $0.16 million
(d) Return on additional inv. = 32%

Chapter 11

11-1 (a) $K_1 \times \sqrt{\dfrac{2R}{CI}}$ where $K_1 = \sqrt{S}$

    (b) $K_2 \times \sqrt{RS}$ where $K_2 = \sqrt{\dfrac{2}{CI}}$

    (c) $K_3 \times \sqrt{\dfrac{R}{C}}$ where $K_3 = \sqrt{\dfrac{2S}{I}}$

    (K is a constant)

11-2 (a) $X = \dfrac{1}{12}\sqrt{\dfrac{AI}{2S}}$

    (b) $X = \dfrac{1}{4}\sqrt{\dfrac{2RS}{CI}}$

11-3 (a) EOQ = 1330 units (approx.)
    (b) 48 days' supply (approx.)
    (c) 7.5 orders per year (approx.)

11-4 Offer should not be accepted. Counteroffer 1.4% or better

11-5 (a) Offer should not be accepted
    (b) Counteroffer 3.05% or better. Purchase amount $13,112.50

11-6 Accept Grabbers, Inc. proposal—lowest cost

11-7 Quantity of 500 should be purchased

11-8 (a) 343 parts (approx.)
    (b) 80 orders per year
    (c) Additonal cost with air freight—$57,337.50

11-9 Best price, $9.15; range: 1001–1500 pallets

11-10 Reorder point = 1375 units

11-11 Reorder point = 525 bags

11-12 (a) EOQ = 1095 units
    (b) Required safety stock, 283; reorder point, 1483 units
    (c) Review period, 9 days; safety stock, 390 units

11-13 (a) 2,000 units; (b) 190 units, 1190 units; (c) 20 days, 330 units

11-14 (a) EOQ = 68,700 units (approx.);
    (b) Reorder point = 12,000 + s.s.
    (c) As usage goes up, the reorder quantity does likewise

11-15 (a) 4.7 cycles (approx.) per year
    (b) B—2000, 16 days; F—1000, 33 days

11-16 8.4 cycle (approx.) per year

11-17 3.2 cycles (approx.) per year; 78 days for each cycle

Chapter 12

12-1 Wood TV sets = 2 units
    Plastic TV sets = 16 units
    Metal TV sets = 182 units

12-2 $N1 = 3, N2 = 3$; or $N1 = 2, N2 = 4$

12-3 Product A = 200 units
    Product B = 40 units
    Contribution = $4520

12-4 Products *D* and *E* = 100 units each
      Contribution = $4050
12-5 Products *F* and *G* = 40 units each
      Daily contribution = $512
12-6 $x = 5\frac{1}{3}$, $y = 6\frac{1}{3}$
      Contribution = $103.32
12-7 $x = 4.5$, $y = 5.5$
      Contribution = $101.25

Chapter 13

13-1 (a) 24 men in line after 4 hours
      (b) Add another attendant
      (c) One attendant for 40/hour service rate
13-2 Hire fast repairman, total cost of $116 per day
13-3 (a) 2 trucks
      (b) ¼ hour
      (c) 1⅓ trucks
      (d) ⅙ hour
      (e) 12.47 trucks per hour
13-4 (a) ⅓ hour
      (b) 1⅓ persons
      (c) ½ hour
      (d) 7.58 persons per hour
13-5 (a) 3½ loads
      (b) 0.36 hour
      (c) 7.1 loads per hour
13-6 Service rate of 0.5 gives a lower total cost
13-7 (a) 4.52 customers
      (b) 9.04 minutes
      (c) 1.52 customers
      (d) 3.04 minutes
      (e) 30 hours per week
      (f) .5076 probability
      (g) One employee idle on the average
13-8 (a) 26.67 hours per week
      (b) 43.32 minutes
13-9 (a) 53.33 minutes
      (b) Approximately 17 machines
13-10 Operates 3 cranes for lowest cost
13-11 Use 2 attendants for lowest cost
13-12 (a) 1.03 minutes
      (b) 48.5 minutes (about half of the time)
      (c) 3.74 minutes (From Appendix E, random number for arrivals: upper right-hand corner, starting with 4637567488, and go downward, let 5 = an arrival; random number for service time: last row starting with 4076486653, go across and use each number)

13-13 (a) .95 customer
(b) 3.04 minutes
(c) 7.59 minutes
(d) Hire 2 attendants (From Appendix E, random numbers for arrival and service times: first 2 columns downward, starting in left-hand corner —15, 09, 41, 74, etc.)

13-14 Use 3 machines for lowest cost

Chapter 14

14-1 See text for approach
14-2 Average delay expected = 3.5 weeks (for random numbers used)
14-3 Do not add an additonal clerk
14-4 Monte Carlo simulation: cost comparison for various number of machines —11 machines with a lowest total cost
14-5 Replace three vacuum tubes at a time; consider preventive maintenance, new equipment, etc.
14-6 Lowest cost with 2 repairmen

Chapter 15

15-1 Production schedule:
　　1st month = 650
　　2nd month = 820
　　3rd month = 950
　　4th month = 920
　　5th month = 800
　　6th month = 500
Total inventory cost = $27,409

15-2 Part 23, 4 units
Part 56, 2 units
Part 42, 1 unit
Total cost = $380 ($\angle$$390)

15-3 Sales Area 1 = 2 salesmen
Sales Area 2 = no salesmen
Sales Area 3 = 7 salesmen
Total profits = $218,000
Note: it is recommended that at least one salesman be in each area. Thus, one salesman from area 3 should be shifted to area 2.

15-4 Districts 1 and 2—1 truck in District 1 and 4 trucks in District 2 or 2 trucks in District 1 and 3 trucks in District 2
Districts 3 and 4—1 truck each

15-5 If return in months 1 or 2 is $800,000, make the $2 million investment, otherwise wait. If return in months 3 or 4 is either $600,000 or $800,000, make the $2 million investment, otherwise wait. If no investment made by month 5, make the investment at the return prevailing in month 5

15-6 One-year basis—dividends:
　　$500,000 beginning of first year
　　$500,000 end of first year

Two-year basis—dividends:
  $500,000 beginning of first year
  $500,000 end of first year
  $500,000 end of second year
Three-year basis—dividends:
  $300,000 beginning of first year
  $500,000 end of first year
  $600,000 end of second year
  $630,000 end of third year

Chapter 16

16-1 Important factors in vendor evaluation—price, delivery, quality, procedural compliance, technical capability, and guarantees

16-2 See text for approach

16-3 See text for approach

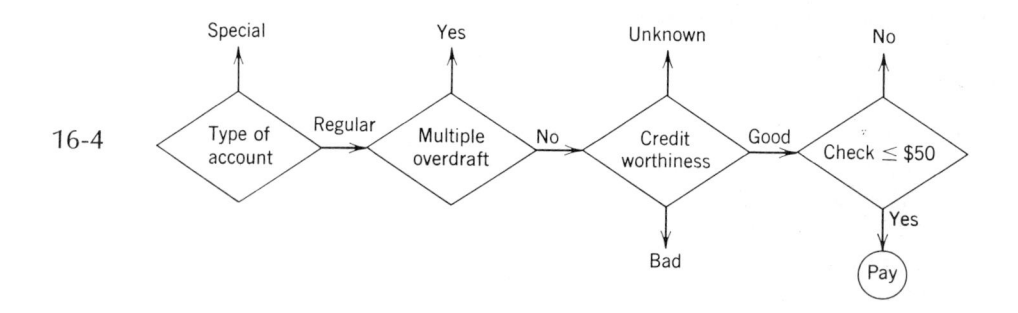

16-4 [Flowchart: Type of account —Regular→ Multiple overdraft —No→ Credit worthiness —Good→ Check ≤ $50 —Yes→ Pay; Type of account →Special; Multiple overdraft →Yes; Credit worthiness →Unknown; Credit worthiness →Bad; Check ≤ $50 →No]

16-5 Minimum time to complete the order is 14 weeks

Chapter 17

17-1 (a) Age, marital status, living facilities (own or rent), years at present address, years at previous address, occupation, listed telephone, savings account balance, etc.
 (b) Discriminant analysis and simulation

17-2 (a) Seek and use ideas from subordinates, support subordinates, share organizational information, emphasize rewards, etc.
 (b) Markov analysis and PERT

17-3 (a) Proposal to promote both products within the same advertisement for a given income group to attain the greatest sales volume is inappropriate
 (b) Same answer as (a) for all products

17-4 Advertising at $25,000 sales level, $141.02
 Advertising at $35,000 sales level, $296.15
 Advertising at $45,000 sales level, $761.54

17-5 (a) Next period—$N_1 = .1025$, $N_2 = .20$, $N_3 = .28$, $N_4 = .285$, $N_5 = .1325$
 (b) Steady state—$N_1 = .0905$, $N_2 = .1797$, $N_3 = .2461$, $N_4 = .3015$, $N_5 = .1822$

Index

Accounting, 49, 480, 587-589
Ackoff, R. L., 7, 14
Activity, 124
ALGOL, 460
Algorithm, simplex, 179
American Institute of Decision Sciences, 8
American Management Association, 451
American Products Corporation, 51-52
  calculus application, 334-335
  decision tree application, 86-87
  dynamic programming application, 512-515
  game theory application, 276-277
  heuristic programming application, 536-537
  inventory application, 373-376
  linear programming application, 204-206
  Markov analysis application, 302-303
  nonlinear programming application, 405-406
  personnel behavioral application, 558-560
  PERT application, 145-147
  queuing (servicing) application, 441-443
  simulation application, 483-485
  transportation application, 245-247
  uncertain demand application, 113-115
Antiderivatives, 321, 623
Approach, conventional, 3
  cookbook, 37
  observational, 3
  systematic, 3
Areas under a curve, 628
Arithmetic mean, 108-113
Arnoff, E. L., 14
Arrow, dummy, 124
Ayer & Sons, N. W., 573

Babbage, C., 3
Babington-Smith, 464-465
Bayes' theorem, 64, 67-68, 71, 73
Behavioral models, definition, 541-542
  designing, 544-546
  employee, 552-558
  marketing, 546-552
  underlying theory, 542-543
Bellman, R., 495
Beta distribution, 125-127
Blackett, P. M. S., 6
Blackett's circus, 6
Bolzano, B., 521
Booz, Allen Applied Research, Inc., 451
Booz, Allen & Hamilton, 121, 451
Boulden, J. B., 589
Bowersox, D. J., 575

British Iron and Steel Research Associates, 7
British Operational Research Society, 8
British Petroleum, 7
Brownian motion, 283
Buffa, E. S., 590
Buffer stock, 361-364
Buridan, J., 80
Burroughs, 586

CALL PLAN, 572
Campbell, H. G., 534
Carr, C. R., 400
Case Institute of Technology, 8
Chung, K. H., 554
Churchman, G. W., 14
Clarkson, G. P., 522, 535
Classical optimization method, 384
COBOL, 460
Coefficient of optimism, 77
Coefficients, 172-174
Communication, ineffective, 42-43
Compiling, input data, 40
Computer, analog, 235, 238-239
  digital, 233-235
  groping, 41
  relationships, 8-9
Conditional, losses, 8-9, 101-103, 107
  profits, 98-101, 107
Connors, M. M., 576
Constraint inequalities, 161-162, 164
Continued fractions, 497
Continuous distribution, 108-109
Controls, establishment of proper, 37
  failure to establish, 43
Coray, C., 576
Corporate planning, 589-595
CORSIM, 593
COSMOS, 574
Cost, incremental, 135
Crash program, 135-139
  modified, 138-139
Criterion, selection of best, 73-81
Critical path, 128-129, 131
Crowther, J. G., 6
Cuccaro, W. K., 576
Curve, bell shaped, 109, 125
Cutting plane technique, 388-391

Dantzig, G. D., 157, 495
Davall, B. M., 587
Davis, R. C., 35

Decision criterion, competitive conditions, 73, 81
   Hurwicz, 77-78, 81
   Laplace, 80-81
   Savage, 79-81
   under certainty, 73-74
   under risk, 73-76
   under uncertainty, 73, 76-81
   Wald, 78, 81
Decision trees, 82-86
Decouple inventories, 343-344
Degeneracy, 179-180, 219, 225-228
Demski, J., 588
Department of Defense, 8
Dependence, statistical, 63-66
Derivative, definition, 420, 621-622
   first, 311-312
   partial, 322-328
   second, 312-313
Descartes, Reńe, 521
Determinants, 296-300, 616-620
Diet problem, 157
Differentiation, 311-314, 621-623
   formulas, 623-624
Discounted cash flow, 86
Distribution, 244-245
Doeblin, W., 283
Doob, J. L., 283
Dudek, R. A., 534
Dynamic programming, characteristics, 385, 495-496
   comparison, 512
   distribution of salesmen, 501-509
   production smoothing problem, 497-501
   purchasing under uncertainty, 509-511
   state variable, 496
   structure, 496-497
DYNAMO, 461, 463-464

Economic ordering quantity, algebraic approach, 349-352
   computer, 353-355
   differentiation approach, 352-353
   graphic approach, 348-349
   nomograph, 376-377
   production for stock, 368
   simultaneous sales and production for one item, 368-370
   simultaneous sales and production for two or more items, 371-373
   tabular approach, 347-348
Edelman, F., 583
Edison, T., 5
Equipment investment problem, 324-327
Erlang, A. K., 5, 413
Estimate, crash time, 134
   normal time, 134
Events, collectively exhaustive, 59
   defined, 124
   mutually exclusive, 59

Event time, earliest expected, 127-128, 131
   latest allowable, 128, 131
Expected profits, under certainty, 102-103
   under uncertainty, 69, 99-101
Expected time, 125-127, 131
Experimentation, 36
Exponential function, 326-327, 629
   smoothing, 374-375

Fabrycky, W. J., 427
Fayol, H., 5
Feller, W., 283
Finance, 49, 480-481, 535-536, 583-587, 589
Financing module, 453
Ford Foundation, 541
FORTRAN, 460, 463-464
Fortune's 500, 8
Foundation for Research on Human Behavior, 541
Frank, R. E., 577
Fry, T. D., 413

Games and strategies, algebraic method, 261-263
   arithmetic method, 261
   dominance, 257-260
   graphic method, 268-270
   joint probability method, 263-264
   limitations, 275-276
   linear programming, 271-275
   mixed strategies, 260-275
   pure strategy, 256-257
   rules for game theory, 256-260, 271
   saddle point, 256-257
   subgames, 264-268
   two-person zero-sum, 255-256
Gantt, 4-5
Gantt chart, 121-123
GASP, 461, 464
General Electric Company, 463
GIGO principle, 24
Gilbreth, F. B., 4-5
Gilbreth, L. E., 4-5
Goal programming, 578-580
Gomory's technique, 388-391
GPSS, 461-463
Gradient method, 385
Green, P. E., 577
Green, W. K., 575
Greensburg, R. W., 533

Haessler, R. W., 533
Haines, G. H., 525
Hamburger, M. J., 524
Harris, F., 347
Harvard University, 541
Heskiaoff, H., 534
Heuristic, 521
Heuristic programming, advantages and limitations, 536

characteristics, 523-524
definition, 521-522
locating warehouses, 524-525
other applications, 531-536
project scheduling, 527-531
traveling salesman problem, 525-527
Hitchcock, F. L., 157, 213
Howe, C. W., 400
Huchfeldt, V. E., 527
Hurwicz, 77-78
Hypotheses, multiple, 35

Implementation, 36-37
Independence, statistical, 60-62
Index values, 229-230
Inflection point, 312
Input-output method, 157
Integer programming, 383-393
 linear, 383, 385-393
 mixed integer, 383
Integral, definite, 625-626
 indefinite, 623-625
Integration, 321-324, 623-626
 formulas, 626-627
Intercept, 315
Interdisciplinary team, 9-11
Inventory, acquisition costs, 344-345
 average, 346-347
 carrying costs, 345-346
 control models, 343-376
 costs, 344-346
 fixed cycle-variable quantity, 366-367
 fixed quantity-variable cycle, 364-367
 future methods, 373
 holding costs, 345-346
 ordering costs, 344-345
 outage costs, 346
 reorder point, 361-364
 safety stock, 361-364
 simulation, 476-480
Investment, capital, 83-84

Jaaskelainen, V., 578
Jethro, 3
Johns, E. C., 533
Jones, C. H., 579

Kaufman, R., 582
Kendall, 464-465
Khoury, E. H., 585
Kimball, G. E., 14
Kiviot, P. J., 464
Kolmagorov, A. N., 283
Koopmans, 157, 213
Kriegsspiel, 450
Kuark, J. Y. T., 586
Kuehn, A. A., 524

Lagrange multiplier, 328-329, 332-334, 384
Lambin, J. J., 570

Laplace, 80-81
Lavidge, 546
Lee, S., 577
Lee, W. B., 593
Leontief, W. W., 157
Levenson, H. C., 5
Levy, P., 283
Linear programming, advantages, 195-202
 algebraic, 165-171
 applications of, 203-204
 cautions of, 202
 defined, 157-158
 dual problem, 192-195
 graphic, 159-165
 maximization, 172-181
 minimization, 181-191
 primal problem, 192
 requirements, 157-159
 simplex method, 171-207
Line of balance, 140-142
Lockheed Aircraft, 121
Lodish, L. M., 533, 572
Los Alamos Scientific Laboratory, 454
Low, D. W., 575

Magee, J. F., 524
Management Steering Committee, 47
Manufacturing, 48-49, 468-480, 533-535, 577-583
Manufacturing module, 453
Marginal, analysis, 104-108
 cost, 318, 320
 loss, 104-108
 profit, 104-108
 revenue, 318, 320
Marketing, 47-48, 465-466, 532-533, 569-574, 576-577
Marketing module, 453
Markov, A. A., 283
Markov analysis, brands as chains, 283-286
 determinants, 296-300
 equilibrium, 292-300
 first-order, 287
 hard core component, 284, 287
 higher order, 287
 management uses, 300-301, 554-558
 matrix of transition probabilities, 283-286
 other uses, 301-302
 second-order, 287
 simultaneous equations, 293-296
 sink or basin of one state or two states, 293
 switching component, 284, 287
 third-order, 287, 291-292
Markowitz, H. M., 575
Maslow's hierarchy of needs, 542-543, 554-560
Matrices, 609-616
Matrix, adjoint of a, 613-614
 body, 173-174
 cofactors, 613-614
 identity, 173-174, 615-616

INDEX 647

payoff, 74
regret, 79
transpose of a, 612
Maximax, 77
Maximin, 78
Maxwell, J. E., 239
Mayo, E., 541
McCloskey, 7
Metropolis, 464
Milestones, 121-123
Miller, D. W., 14
Minimax, 79
M.I.T. Computation Center, 463
Model, analogue, 16-17
  behavioral, 28
  constructing the, 21
  custom-made, 18
  definition, 16
  descriptive, 19
  deterministic, 18-19
  development, 35
  dynamic, 19
  essential aspects, 20-24
  evaluation of, 22-24
  iconic, 16
  mathematical, 17-20
  nonsimulation, 19-20
  optimizing, 19
  probabilistic, 18-19
  qualitative, 18
  quantitative, 18, 24-29
  role of, 21
  simulation, 19-20
  standard, 18
  static, 19
  symbolic, 17
  types of, 16-17
  validation, 35
Molina, 413
Morgenstern, 81, 255
Morse, P. M., 14, 429
Motion study, 4
Murdar, P. J., 525

National Coal Board, 7
Navy Special Projects Office, 121
Nelson, H. W., 585
Newell, A., 521-522
Nodes, 124
Nonlinear programming approximation method, 395, 397
  classical optimization method, 384
  gradient method, 385
  nonlinear objective function, 384, 393-395
  nonlinear objective function and nonlinear constraint, 384, 395-397
  quadratic programming, 384, 397-404
Northwest corner role, 217-219

Objective function, 158, 162-164

Observation, 33-34
Operational analysis, 6
Operational research, 6
Operations research, characteristics, 9-14
  definition, 14-15, 29
  future, 597-599
  guidelines for success, 33-40
  history, 5-8
  organizing for, 43-47
  overview, 595-599
  present, 596-597
  problem areas, 40-43
  successful areas, 47-50
Operations research and operations evaluation, 6
Operations research group, internal, 43-44
Operations research problems, initial, 44-45
Operations Research Society of America, 8, 15
Operations research team, location of, 46-47
  mixture of, 45-46
Optimization, 10
OR Task Force, 47
Organization, lack of, 42
  problem solving, 39-40
Overoptimization, 10

Palda, K. S., 547
Pappus, 521
Payoff matrix, 74
Perfect information expected profits with, 102-103
Personnel, 49-50
PERT, advantages, 132-133
  disadvantages, 133-134
PERT/Cost, 134-140, 560
PERT/LOB, 140-143
PERT/LOB/Cost, 142-143
PERT network, 123-124, 130-131
PERT packages, computer, 132, 139
PERT, probability of a finishing a project, 143-145
PERT/Time, 121-134, 560
Physical distribution, 47-48, 466-468, 574-577
Planned approach, 9, 11-13, 33-38
Planning, overall, 50
PL/1, 460
Poisson distribution, 417-434
Polaris project, 121
Polya, G., 521-522
Porter, L. W., 557
Postoptimality analysis, 193-195
Pricing, 85
Probability, associated, 75
  conditional, 62-65
  formulas, 66
  joint, 60-62, 65-66
  marginal, 58-60, 63
  mathematical relationships, 67-68
  objective, 57-58
  problem, 68-70

revision, 70-73
subjective, 57-58
terms, 57-59
tree, 61-62, 85-86
unconditional, 58-59
Probability distribution, continuous, 108-113
discrete, 97-108
Problem, real, 34-35
solve, 37-38
uncovered, 13-14
Projects, select, 38-39
Purchasing, 48

Quadratic, 313
Quadratic programming, 384
Quantitative models, allocation models, 25-26
assignment models, 26
behavioral models, 28
classical optimization techniques, 26-27
combined OR methods, 28-29
competition models, 26
decision theory, 25
dynamic programming models, 28
heuristic methods, 28
inventory models, 27
queuing models, 27
replacement models, 27
routing models, 28
sequencing models, 25
simulation techniques, 27
Quantity discounts, cost comparison approach, 355-356
price break approach, 359-361
price change approach, 357-359
Queuing, application, 414-415
arrival rates, 413-416
exponential service, 418-419
minimum cost service rate, 426-427
Monte Carlo, 434-441
multichannel, 429-434, 438-441
nonexponential service, 427-429
Poisson arrivals, 417-418, 429
service rates, 413-416
single-channel, 416-429, 434-438

Rand Corporation, 463-464, 521
Random number generator, 464-465
Random numbers, 434-441, 630
Recursion, 497
Remaining row, 177-182
Reorder point, 361-364
Replaced row, 176, 182
Replacing row, 176-177, 182
Research and development, 50
Richard Thomas & Baldwin, 7
Rivett, R., 7
Roethlisberger, F. J., 541
Rollbach, 85

Safety stock, 361-364
Savage, 79-80
Scalar multiple, 605-609
Scientific management, definition, 3
history, 3-5
Scientific method, 3, 9, 11-13, 33-38
Sensitivity analysis, 35, 193-195, 557
Series, converging geometric, 423
converging infinite, 423
Shaw, J. C., 521
Siemens, N., 535
Sigma, 109-113
Simon, H. A., 521-522
SIMPAC, 461
Simplex method, 172-206
SIMSCRIPT, 461-463
SIMULATE, 461
Simulation, advantages, 457-459
computer approach, 459-461
defined, 449-450
general languages, 461-464
limitations, 457-459
Monte Carlo method, 454-455
operational gaming method, 450-454
system simulation method, 455-456
Skinner, B. F., 541
Slack, free, 129
negative, 130
positive, 129
total, 129
Smith, M. L., 534
Smoothing factor, 374-375
Solutions, alternative, 35-36
Stages, 496-497
Standard deviation, 109-113, 143-145, 364-366
Starr, M. K., 14
State of nature, 74
Steiner, 546
Stern, H., 581
Stigler, 157
Strategy, 74
Suboptimization, 10
Svestka, J. A., 527
System, effectiveness, 20-21
function relationship, 9-10
overview, 9-10

Table, conditional losses, 101-102
conditional profits, 98-99
Tableaus, simplex method, 172-206
Taylor, F. W., 3-5
Technique, overemphasis, 41-42
tailor made, 37
Tests, frequency, 465
gap to check, 465
poker, 465
serial, 465
The Institute of Management Service, 8
Torgersen, P. E., 427
Transportation problem, key value method, 213

modified distribution method, 213, 228-233
northwest corner rule and inspection, 217-227
other problems, 243-244
simplex method, 213, 233-239
slack, 217-218
steppingstone method, 213, 217-227
Vogel's approximation method, 213-217
Traveling salesman problem, 525-527
Trefethen, 7
Turner, E. M., 532

Ulam, S., 449
United States Air Force, 157
United States Army's Fort Leavenworth War Games Facility, 451
United Steel Companies, 7
University of Denver, 586
University of Penn., 572

Variable, artificial, 184-185
controllable, 20-21
deviational, 578-580
endogenous, 315
exogenous, 315
slack, 165, 183-185
state, 496
surplus, 165, 205
uncontrolled, 20-21
Vectors, 603-609
basis or reference, 606
Venture analysis, 583-585
Vidale, M. L., 551
Vogel's approximation method, 215-217
Von Neumann, 81, 255, 449, 454, 464
Von Reisswitz, 450

Wald, 78, 255
Wagner, H. M., 15
Watson, H. J., 535
Watson-Watt, Sir R., 6
Weich'i, 450
Weighting factor, 374-375
Western Electric, 541
Wharton School of Finance, University of Penn., 572
Whiddington, R., 6
Wiener, N., 283, 541
Wiest, J. D., 527
Wilkinson, J. W., 587
Wilson, A., 450
Wolfe, H. C., 551
Wood, M., 157